Critical Approach to Sustainability Discourse and Action in International Relations

Şeyda Güdek-Gölçek
https://orcid.org/0000-0001-8753-2998
Niğde Ömer Halisdemir University, Turkey

Günseli Durmaz
https://orcid.org/0000-0003-2146-769X
Niğde Ömer Halisdemir University, Turkey

Aybüke İnan-Şimşek
https://orcid.org/0000-0002-4684-380X
Niğde Ömer Halisdemir University, Turkey

IGI Global
Scientific Publishing
Publishing Tomorrow's Research Today

Published in the United States of America by
IGI Global Scientific Publishing
701 East Chocolate Avenue
Hershey, PA, 17033, USA
Tel: 717-533-8845 | Fax: 717-533-7115
Website: https://www.igi-global.com E-mail: cust@igi-global.com

Library of Congress Cataloging-in-Publication Data

Names: Gudek-Golcek, Seyda, 1990- editor | Durmaz, Günseli, 1988- editor | İnan-Şimşek, Aybüke, 1989- editor
Title: Critical approach to sustainability discourse and action in international relations / edited by Şeyda Güdek-Gölçek, Günseli Durmaz, Aybüke İnan-Şimşek.
Description: Hershey, PA : IGI Global Scientific Publishing, 2026. | Includes bibliographical references and index. | Summary: "This book aims to contribute to critical debates in international relations, environmental policy, development, gender, sustainability and outer space studies by challenging mainstream discourses of sustainability visions. It aims to deepen academic discourse on the gap between global actors' commitments and actual environmental, political, economic and social outcomes"-- Provided by publisher.
Identifiers: LCCN 2025023220 (print) | LCCN 2025023221 (ebook) | ISBN 9798337317076 hardcover | ISBN 9798337317083 paperback | ISBN 9798337317090 ebook
Subjects: LCSH: Sustainability--International cooperation
Classification: LCC JZ1324 .C75 2025 (print) | LCC JZ1324 (ebook)
LC record available at https://lccn.loc.gov/2025023220
LC ebook record available at https://lccn.loc.gov/2025023221

British Cataloguing in Publication Data
A Cataloguing in Publication record for this book is available from the British Library.

Table of Contents

Detailed Table of Contents

This chapter examines the European Green Deal as a response to the EU's ongoing polycrisis and investigates its class dynamics through a Neo-Gramscian and historical materialist lens. By analyzing policy communications from the European Round Table for Industry and the European Trade Union Confederation (2011–2023), the chapter shows how the green transition reflects green capitalism, shaped by structural asymmetries between capital and labor within the EU's evolving political economy. By comparing competing visions of the green transition, the chapter contributes to a critical political economy of European integration and highlights the class dynamics underpinning the EU's climate strategy.

In the context of international processes of addressing climate change where we are increasingly seeing negative social impacts of climate policy, the concept of the 'eco-social' has been seen as critical as it both addresses social and environmental goals. However, it suffers from concept stretching as discussed by Sartori. First, environmental politics, across different waves and ideologies, has incorporated both social and environmental benefits into proposed policies and practices, making all such policies effectively "eco-social" based on the consensus definition. Furthermore, as political domains are increasingly expected to address the environmental question due to the rising salience of climate change, social policies were increasingly asked to incorporate environmental and climate considerations. To address the problem

This chapter examines greenwashing through the lens of World-Systems Analysis, arguing that environmental deception is not a marginal or accidental feature of global capitalism but a structural mechanism that sustains core–periphery inequalities. By connecting concepts such as carbon colonialism and the transboundary waste trade, the chapter shows how sustainability narratives in core countries often mask the outsourcing of environmental harm to semi-peripheral and peripheral zones. Drawing on critical literature, the study contends that greenwashing serves to legitimize ongoing resource extraction, pollution, and ecological injustice. It concludes that meaningful responses require moving beyond superficial reputational fixes and addressing the systemic dynamics that enable the externalization of ecological costs in the world economy.

The ecological and social challenges associated with renewable energy technologies necessitate a critical reassessment of the green transition. Addressing these issues requires stronger policy interventions, ethical supply chain practices, and sustainable material management. A more just and equitable approach to green technology development must incorporate interdisciplinary solutions that balance economic interests with ecological and social well-being.This chapter critically examines the environmental damage and social injustices embedded in the supply chains of rare earth minerals and other critical materials essential for green technology. The analysis extends to trade disputes and waste accumulation, arguing that the current market-driven approach to renewable energy exacerbates global inequalities. The chapter concludes by exploring circular economy models and regulatory frameworks that could mitigate these negative consequences.

This chapter explores the concept of climate justice in the context of the Global South, emphasizing the disproportionate impacts of climate change on historically marginalized nations and communities. It first traces the evolution of climate justice from its roots in environmental justice, highlighting how the movement has expanded to address global power imbalances and historical responsibility for carbon emissions. The theoretical framework of climate justice is analyzed through four key dimensions: distributional, procedural, recognitional, and capacity-related justice. The chapter then examines the practical applications of climate justice by assessing global emissions data, coal-related conflicts, and the concept of "climate debt," which holds historically high-emitting countries accountable for financing mitigation and adaptation efforts. Additionally, it discusses within-country inequalities and the role of redistributive policies, such as wealth taxation.

India's tribal communities, particularly the Gond tribe, possess rich cultural traditions and deep-rooted ecological knowledge integral to environmental sustainability. This chapter critically examines the paradox of symbolic representation versus substantive exclusion of the Gond tribe in India's sustainability governance. The study explores how policies like the Forest Rights Act (FRA) 2006, while progressive in intent, have been undermined by bureaucratic inertia, corporate interests, and colonial legacies. Using a postcolonial and environmental justice lens, the chapter highlights how indigenous knowledge is often appropriated without empowering tribal communities. To address this gap, the chapter proposes a participatory governance model emphasizing legal recognition, community-based resource management, and indigenous knowledge co-production. Strengthening traditional institutions like the Gotul and operationalizing Free, Prior, and Informed Consent (FPIC) are identified as key strategies.

This chapter analyzes how gender equality is represented within the Sustainable Development Goal (SDG) regime and examines the extent to which this representation is reflected in its official indicators, from a feminist critical theory perspective. Gender equality is addressed as both a standalone goal (SDG 5) and a prerequisite for all other goals. Through a comparative analysis of the UN's Gender Snapshot reports (2021–2024), SDG indicators, and the SDG Index, the chapter assesses the alignment between discourse and implementation. Drawing on feminist epistemology and using qualitative content analysis with thematic coding, it identifies key themes and evaluates their translation into measurable outcomes. The findings indicate that although the discourse increasingly reflects intersectional inequalities, the indicator framework lags behind. This gap suggests that gender equality in the SDG agenda is constrained by technical tools. The chapter concludes by urging a revision of global data policies to enable a more inclusive and transformative SDG framework.

This chapter examines how international law, along with sanctions regimes, can interfere with the quest for sustainability by surprisingly stopping progress on global development goals. While the Sustainable Development Goals and the Paris Agreement now make sustainability a main goal, international sanctions are seen as conflicting tools in that field. Using research and case studies from Iran, Russia, North Korea and Venezuela, it focuses on how sanctions prevent effective action in climate, health, energy transition and environmental protection. It looks at how sanctions have evolved, from covering all groups to just specific targets and asks whether these actions still follow basic rules of international law. The chapter ultimately calls for more sustainable thinking about sanctions and suggests innovations including impact assessments, special carve-outs for humanitarian action and ESG standards mechanism. Because we are facing climate, conflict and weakening institutions all at once, the chapter suggests supporting both peace and sustainable development more thoroughly.

The research examines how sustainability functions as a strategic narrative framework for global environmental management, using Canada as a case study. The research establishes the Canadian aporetic condition through the analysis of climate targets and ongoing resource extraction activities, studying three specific areas to demonstrate how narrative coherence enables people to accept conflicting material outcomes. The chapter employs discourse analysis and critical political ecology to evaluate Canadian policy statements by comparing them with Indigenous land governance and just-transition planning, and degrowth frameworks. This chapter presents two counterarguments regarding incremental reform and establishes fundamental definitions for readers unfamiliar with this subject area. The final section outlines specific steps organizations should take to achieve their targets through structural adjustments and enhanced monitoring systems.

This chapter examines how natural resource governance affects peacebuilding in divided societies. While extractive wealth is often viewed as a catalyst for cooperation, in practice it frequently reinforces exclusion, entrenches geopolitical divisions, and marginalizes civic and environmental voices. Drawing on political ecology, critical peacebuilding, and international political economy, the chapter frames extractivism as a political project tied to contested authority and unequal recognition. It identifies four recurring dynamics: exclusionary control over resources, militarization of extractive zones, suppression of community perspectives, and the shifting status of hydrocarbons from assets to liabilities. Rather than offering technical fixes, the chapter advocates for justice-based, post-extractivist approaches centered on sustainability, inclusion, and democratic participation. Examples from Cyprus, Palestine, Western Sahara, and Northern Iraq show how extractive regimes deepen conflict, and how alternative governance models may open pathways toward more sustainable peace.

This paper critically analyzes the sustainability narratives of mega-satellite constellations like Starlink, OneWeb, and Amazon Kuiper. While promising digital inclusion and global internet access, these projects reveal structural contradictions that exacerbate environmental neglect, transparency issues, and social inequalities. Using a Marxist political economy approach and Critical Discourse Analysis, it demonstrates that these initiatives serve as ideological justifications for capital accumulation rather than technical solutions. The findings indicate that they cause both direct and indirect conflicts with sustainable development goals. The study also advocates for binding international regulations, environmental impact assessments, and transparent partnership mechanisms to monitor the social and environmental effects of these projects. Consequently, the sustainability discourse often functions as a marketing tool, acting as a form of ideological dominance that sustains global inequalities.

Preface

As editors, we find it important to situate ourselves within the intellectual and social geographies that shape this book. We are three young female scholars working at Niğde Ömer Halisdemir University, a public institution located in the periphery of Türkiye's academic landscape. Türkiye itself often occupies a peripheral position in the global academy, and within this national context, we are situated at *the periphery of the periphery*.

This position is not only geographic but also deeply experiential. As junior academics, we often encounter the structural exclusions that come with peripherality: limited resources, uneven recognition, and the sense that intellectual contributions from the margins are too easily overlooked. These challenges are compounded by gender. To be women in the academy is often to face additional scrutiny and diminished recognition, and when gender intersects with peripheral location, the difficulties multiply. What might be challenging in well-resourced, male-dominated centers becomes doubly difficult in settings where women's voices are more easily ignored or trivialized. At times, even interactions with more senior female academics reproduce these dynamics, reminding us that hierarchies are not only gendered but also generational.

This layered marginality is not separate from the themes of this book; it is, in fact, part of what we live as we study sustainability discourse in the periphery and the Global South. We are not only analyzing how global hierarchies are reproduced through sustainability narratives, we inhabit these dynamics ourselves. To bring this volume to life under such conditions is both scholarship and resistance: a collective affirmation that voices from the margins matter, and that critical knowledge can emerge precisely from places where recognition is scarce but determination is strong.

We believe this positionality is not a weakness, but a source of strength. It sharpens our sensitivity to exclusion, heightens our awareness of injustice, and grounds our commitment to amplifying diverse and critical voices. It also underscores the necessity of solidarity among scholars working in peripheral contexts. By foregrounding our position, we not only acknowledge the struggles behind the making of this book but also remind readers that knowledge production is never neutral. Just as sustainability discourses must be interrogated for the power relations they mask, so too must academic discourse.

This book, then, is both a contribution to critical scholarship on sustainability and a lived example of how young, female, junior, and peripheral scholars can create, collaborate, and intervene in global debates.

Şeyda Güdek-Gölçek
Niğde Ömer Halisdemir University, Turkey

Günseli Durmaz
Niğde Ömer Halisdemir University, Turkey

Aybüke İnan-Şimşek
Niğde Ömer Halisdemir University, Turkey

Acknowledgment

This book was not produced in comfortable conditions, with abundant resources or institutional privilege. It was built slowly, sometimes against the current, in the margins of academia. As three young women working in the periphery of Türkiye's academic landscape, we know what it means to persist when encouragement is scarce and recognition uneven. In this sense, the making of the book mirrors its content: just as our chapters interrogate the silences and exclusions of sustainability discourse, we too experienced the challenges of speaking from the margins.

From its earliest conception, this project was envisioned as a space where critical voices could come together to rethink sustainability not as a neutral, technical concept, but as a deeply political and contested discourse. Each chapter testifies to that vision. The range of approaches—neo-Gramscian theory, world-systems analysis, feminist critique, postcolonial perspectives, posthumanist ethics, and legal and policy analysis—not only enriches the dialogue but also demonstrates the vitality of critical scholarship across disciplines, geographies, and generations.

We extend our deepest gratitude to all the authors whose contributions form the heart of this volume. Their patience, perseverance, and generosity throughout the editorial process, willingness to revise, engage in dialogue, and refine their work were indispensable in creating a coherent and high-quality collection. Our sincere appreciation also goes to the reviewers, who devoted their expertise with care and rigor. Your constructive feedback not only sharpened individual chapters but also strengthened the intellectual fabric of the book as a whole.

We would also like to thank the IGI Global team for their professional guidance and support throughout the publication process. Their meticulous attention to editorial standards and their commitment to ensuring quality have been essential in bringing this book to fruition.

We would also like to express our sincere gratitude to our colleague Ali Gökhan Gölçek for his continuous support throughout the editorial process. His guidance and encouragement have been invaluable in bringing this project to completion.

What sustained us was not institutional privilege, but solidarity. The generosity of our authors, the patience of our families, and the encouragement of colleagues, students, and friends, near and far, made this work possible. Informal communities of care and exchange—from reading groups to conference panels—became our real intellectual home. We thank each of you for reminding us that scholarship can thrive outside traditional hierarchies, and that critical voices, when they come together, can create something powerful.

Finally, we celebrate the collaborative spirit that animates this endeavor. Bringing together contributors from Canada, India, Austria, Italy, Germany, Türkiye, and Turkish Republic of Northern Cyprus, this book affirms that knowledge is never neutral and that critical scholarship flourishes when voices from the periphery and the Global South are given space. In particular, we celebrate the perspectives from India, Türkiye, and Turkish Republic of Northern Cyprus, which highlight experiences too often marginalized in sustainability debates. Their analyses remind us that global sustainability cannot be understood, or achieved, without attending to histories of inequality, uneven development, and struggles for justice.

This book is, above all, the product of persistence, solidarity, and hope. To everyone who contributed, supported, and inspired us: we thank you deeply.

Şeyda Güdek-Gölçek
Niğde Ömer Halisdemir University, Turkey

Günseli Durmaz
Niğde Ömer Halisdemir University, Turkey

Aybüke İnan-Şimşek
Niğde Ömer Halisdemir University, Turkey

Introduction

In the twenty-first century, *sustainability* is everywhere and settled nowhere. It appears in summit communiqués, corporate ESG reports, national development plans, and university curricula, but its meaning is pulled in different directions by competing interests and unequal power. This book begins from that productive tension. Rather than treating sustainability as a neutral, technical pathway, we approach it as a *political project* and a *contested discourse*. Across diverse sites, global value chains, infrastructure corridors, sanctions regimes, gender metrics, indigenous governance, and even orbital space, we ask what work sustainability does: whom it empowers, what it renders visible or invisible, and how it translates ecological crises into governable problems or, alternatively, into opportunities for contestation and transformation.

Our contributors use critical international relations and political economy lenses, Neo-Gramscian, feminist, postcolonial, posthumanist, and critical legal, alongside empirically grounded analyses. Together, they demonstrate how *green* agendas can stabilize existing hierarchies by absorbing critique (what we call *green trasformismo*), and how counter-hegemonic projects articulate alternatives premised on justice, inclusion, and democratic accountability. The result is neither cynicism nor naïveté. It is a careful mapping of the ways sustainability can reproduce the contradictions of capitalism and the ways it can be reclaimed to widen democratic horizons and material redistribution.

Our editorial standpoint matters. As three young women working in the periphery of Türkiye's academic landscape, a periphery within the global periphery, our everyday experience of limited resources and uneven recognition sharpens our sensitivity to how authority is constituted and whose knowledges count. This volume therefore aims not only to analyze sustainability discourses but also to pluralize them: to center perspectives too often sidelined, and to connect theory with grounded struggles. We see the book as a contribution to a broader scholarly and civic conversation that insists sustainability must be more than a managerial slogan.

It must be a democratic, justice-oriented project capable of confronting planetary limits without reproducing old exclusions.

The urgency of this project could not be more evident. Everywhere, net-zero pledges proliferate, filling speeches, strategies, and press releases, yet fossil fuel subsidies endure, pipelines expand, and extractive frontiers push deeper into fragile territories. Borders harden in the name of security, while the atmosphere remains open for exploitation. Digital dashboards and glossy indicators promise transparency and progress, but they often strip away politics, recoding fierce struggles over distribution and justice into neutral technical checklists. This depoliticization does not resolve conflict—it conceals it, narrowing democratic debate and silencing those most affected. At the same time, entirely new domains are being rapidly drawn into the orbit of *sustainability*: critical minerals needed for the green transition, renewable technologies embedded in precarious supply chains, AI-enabled monitoring systems, mega-satellite constellations that alter the very infrastructure of communication, even ambitions extending into cislunar space. Each of these frontiers arrives draped in the language of sustainability, yet behind the rhetoric, regulation and law trail far behind. It is in these gaps—between promise and practice, ambition and accountability—that inequalities are not only reproduced but reinscribed into new infrastructures and standards that will shape the coming decades. To take sustainability seriously, then, is not to accept its surface optimism but to scrutinize these contradictions, to expose the continuities of power beneath the banners of transformation, and to insist on justice where others would settle for technocratic compliance.

These contradictions are not incidental; they are constitutive. They reveal sustainability's double life as both a language of legitimation and a repertoire for resistance. They play out across scales, from indigenous land governance to multilateral forums and from supply-chain audits to sanctions regimes. They shape how climate justice claims are made legible (or not) in metrics, markets, and law. Addressing them requires tools that are theoretically sharp and empirically grounded—tools that this volume assembles and applies across thirteen chapters spanning five sections. In bringing together scholars from Canada, India, Austria, Italy, Germany, Türkiye, Cyprus, and Iran, the book also performs the plural conversation it advocates.

This collection is designed for a diverse audience that spans both academic and policy communities. For scholars and researchers, it provides cutting-edge theoretical insights and empirical case studies that speak directly to key debates in international relations, global political economy, environmental politics, development studies, feminist and postcolonial theory, indigenous studies, peace and conflict studies, and international law. By drawing on critical traditions such as Neo-Gramscian political economy, feminist critique, posthumanist ethics, and postcolonial approaches, the book positions itself as a valuable contribution for those seeking to understand how sustainability functions not only as a policy goal but also as a contested discourse and practice. For graduate and advanced undergraduate students, the chapters offer accessible yet sophisticated analyses that connect theory to practice across multiple global contexts. They provide concrete cases—from the Belt and Road Initiative to mega satellite constellations—that can be used in classrooms to illustrate abstract concepts and stimulate comparative, critical discussions. For policy practitioners and analysts in governments, international organizations, and think tanks, the book offers a critical mirror to mainstream approaches, unpacking how sustainability agendas interact with sanctions regimes, trade disputes, indigenous governance, and security logics. The recommendations embedded in several chapters—such as circular economy reforms, safeguards in sanctions design, or participatory governance models—translate theoretical critique into practical guidance for decision-making. Finally, the book speaks directly to civil society and advocacy groups including climate justice networks, indigenous organizations, labor and community coalitions, and watchdog NGOs. For these actors, the volume offers analytical frames that illuminate lived struggles, sharpen advocacy strategies, and highlight leverage points where dominant sustainability narratives can be challenged and reimagined. By pairing conceptual innovation with empirically rich chapters, the volume supports both rigorous teaching and policy dialogue, bridging the worlds of scholarship, policymaking, and activism, and creating a common ground for more democratic and justice-oriented approaches to sustainability.

ORGANIZATION OF THE BOOK

We begin with conceptual ground-clearing. Sustainability gains power through vagueness; these chapters insist on precision, theory, and alternative ethics.

Section 1: Theoretical and Critical Frameworks

The Political Economy of Green Trasformismo: Green Capitalism Discourses in the Age of Climate Crisis: This chapter introduces *green trasformismo* to explain how ecological critique is absorbed and reorganized into a hegemonic *green capitalism*. It stitches together arenas such as the Paris Agreement, the SDGs, the European Green Deal, energy transitions, and carbon-neutral innovations to show how greening has become raison d'état for contemporary political economy. By reading these developments through a Neo-Gramscian lens, Durmaz identifies the emergent historic bloc that stabilizes green growth while constraining transformative alternatives. The chapter's importance lies in naming the mechanism through which power metabolizes critique and in mapping the institutional and technological assemblages that make it durable. It equips readers with a vocabulary for distinguishing between systemic reorganization and systemic transformation. It also frames the book's central dilemma: can green capitalism resolve the crises it inherits, or does it merely repackage them? In doing so, it offers an anchor for subsequent empirical chapters.

Eco-Social Policy and the Risk of Concept Stretching: Nulman tackles a core methodological problem: as *eco-social* becomes a catch-all descriptor, it risks losing analytical traction. Using Sartori's ladder of abstraction, the chapter demonstrates how concept stretching occurs when ambition outruns precision. It proposes a path of *rung descension*—making the term *more specific*—to recover clarity in research and policy design. This intervention matters because imprecise categories enable performative compliance: actors can claim eco-social credentials without changing material relations. The chapter provides diagnostic criteria for scholars and policymakers to evaluate whether policies genuinely integrate social and environmental aims or merely badge-engineer them. By closing with concrete operational guidance, it serves as a bridge between theory, measurement, and implementation across the volume.

Critical-Posthumanist Sustainability of Future Media Ecologies: Kronberger critiques the anthropocentrism of media ecology and advances a posthumanist ethics grounded in entanglement, care, and relationality. The chapter connects extractive infrastructures of data and devices to climate justice debates, showing how *natural resources* and *culture/technology* dualisms obscure responsibility. Its contribution is twofold: it reorients sustainability from managerial optimization toward ethical responsibility, and it offers an actionable vocabulary—alter-biopolitics, relational ecologies—for designers, regulators, and scholars. By foregrounding the shared vulnerability of humans and non-humans within techno-ecological systems, the chapter widens the field's normative horizon. It encourages policy makers to consider life-cycle impacts, repairability, and e-waste justice alongside speech, privacy, and access. In short, it equips readers to think sustainability *with* technology rather than *about* it in isolation.

Section 2: Global Political Economy and Development Contradictions

Unveiling the Ecological and Geopolitical Contradictions of Large-Scale Development Initiatives: A Critical Analysis of the Belt and Road Initiative: Focusing on Southeast Asia and Africa, the authors deconstruct *Green BRI*, *ecological civilization*, and *win-win cooperation* narratives that accompany China's flagship infrastructure program. Through political economy, post-development, and discourse analysis, they reveal how sustainability language legitimizes extractive projects, suppresses dissent, and deepens debt dependencies. The chapter's importance lies in showing that contradictions are baked into the model rather than arising from implementation failures. It provides a typology of harms—ecological degradation, displacement, and fiscal entanglement—and links them to institutional logics and geopolitical strategies. Importantly, the authors propose accountability and participation mechanisms for future infrastructure planning, making the critique constructive. The chapter becomes a touchstone for evaluating other mega-projects claiming sustainability credentials.

Reading Greenwashing Practices from a World-Systems Analysis Perspective: Moving beyond firm-level deception, this chapter treats greenwashing as a structural feature of the world-economy. By connecting carbon colonialism, transboundary waste trade, and reputational strategies, it illustrates how ecological burdens are externalized to semi-peripheral and peripheral zones while green value is retained in the core. The importance of this contribution is theoretical and practical: it reframes greenwashing as a system-maintenance mechanism and identifies where regulation must target supply-chain relations rather than marketing claims alone. The authors synthesize critical literature into a clear analytical framework that is teachable and deployable by watchdogs. Their account helps explain why disclosure regimes, absent structural change, struggle to curb harm. It also equips practitioners with indicators for distinguishing substantive transitions from PR-driven optics.

Green, but at What Cost? Ecological and Social Realities of Renewable Energy: Narang and Ahuja examine the full material footprint of *clean* technologies, from rare-earth mining and cobalt extraction to manufacturing waste and end-of-life hazards. They show how market-driven approaches distribute risks along racialized and classed lines and trigger trade disputes over critical materials. The chapter's significance is its insistence that renewable transitions must be evaluated not only by carbon metrics but also by justice metrics—worker safety, community consent, and ecological integrity. It offers concrete policy levers: circular economy design, producer responsibility, ethical procurement, and trade rules aligned with social-ecological goals. By bridging critical diagnosis with implementable reforms, it is immediately useful for governments, multilaterals, and civil society. The chapter thus inoculates against *solutionism* while preserving the urgency of decarbonization.

Section 3: Justice, Agency, and Social Struggles

Climate Justice in the Global South: Gönenç traces the evolution of climate justice from environmental justice roots to global debates on climate debt and responsibility. Organizing the discussion around distributional, procedural, recognitional, and capacity-related dimensions, the chapter links macro emissions histories to micro level vulnerabilities. Its importance is to assemble a rigorous, balanced framework for evaluating policies—carbon pricing, adaptation finance, loss-and-damage—against justice criteria. The chapter also probes within-country inequalities and fiscal tools (such as progressive wealth taxation) that can align domestic policy with transnational justice claims. It is richly suited for teaching and for policy evaluation because it integrates theory with comparative evidence. Ultimately, it shifts the question from how much is emitted to who bears costs and who gains power in transition pathways.

Beyond Representation: Reclaiming Indigenous Agency in Sustainability Governance – A Case of Indian Tribes: This chapter interrogates the paradox of symbolic inclusion and substantive exclusion in Indian sustainability governance, with a focus on the Gond tribe. It shows how the Forest Rights Act (2006) and related policies, though progressive on paper, are undermined by bureaucratic inertia, corporate capture, and colonial legacies. The contribution is methodological and normative: it demonstrates how participatory models grounded in Free, Prior, and Informed Consent (FPIC), community resource management, and traditional institutions like the Gotul can re-center indigenous knowledge. By articulating pathways for knowledge co-production and legal empowerment, the chapter moves beyond critique to institutional design. It is especially valuable for practitioners designing safeguards and community benefit agreements. In reframing *agency* as governance practice rather than representational tokenism, it resonates across cases globally.

Transformative Discourse vs. Limited Measurement: The Politics of Gender Data in the SDGs: Güdek-Gölçek assesses how gender equality is articulated across SDG discourse and how far it travels into indicators and indices. Through analysis of UN Gender Snapshot reports (2021–2024) and the SDG Index, the chapter reveals significant misalignment: intersectional realities are acknowledged rhetorically but remain under-measured in practice. The importance of this argument is that measurement is politics; inadequate indicators depoliticize feminist claims and constrain policy ambition. The chapter offers criteria for intersectional data governance and suggests reforms that would better capture care economies, unpaid labor, and structural violence. It is actionable for national statistical offices and international bodies seeking to upgrade their gender metrics. By anchoring a broader debate about datafication and depoliticization, it strengthens the book's through-line.

Section 4: Law, Governance, and International Contradictions

Analyzing the Impact of International Law and Sanctions Mechanisms Towards Sustainable Outcomes: Shekhawat and Khare confront an under-examined contradiction: sanctions regimes and sustainability commitments frequently collide. Using cases from Iran, Russia, North Korea, and Venezuela, they show how sanctions impede climate cooperation, clean-energy transitions, and public health, even when formally targeted. The chapter's importance is to connect legal analysis with material consequences and to propose reforms—humanitarian carve-outs, ESG-style safeguards, and ex-ante impact assessments—that align coercive instruments with global sustainability obligations. It equips diplomats, lawyers, and policymakers with a vocabulary and toolkit for mitigating unintended harms. By reframing compliance and exceptions around sustainability metrics, the authors open a path to more coherent foreign policy. The chapter also supplies a replicable assessment template for future sanctions design.

Sustainability as Strategic Narrative: The Canadian Aporetic Condition and Global Environmental Governance: Bessai examines how Canada sustains a narrative of climate leadership while expanding extractive activities, producing what he terms an *aporetic condition*. Combining discourse analysis with critical political ecology, the chapter juxtaposes federal targets and just-transition rhetoric with indigenous land governance and degrowth proposals. Its importance lies in showing how narrative coherence is constructed amidst material contradiction—and why incremental reforms often stall. The chapter provides conceptual tools to analyze narrative governance in other jurisdictions and outlines structural steps organizations can take to align targets with practice, including institutional redesign and monitoring. By clarifying the politics of *strategic narrative*, it becomes a portable lens for scholars and practitioners confronting similar policy paradoxes elsewhere.

Section 5: Security, Militarization, and Planetary Frontiers

Natural Resources as Strategic Liabilities: Extractivism and Conflict Persistence in Divided Societies: Ersözer challenges the assumption that resource extraction reliably fosters peace in post-conflict or divided societies. Drawing on cases from Cyprus, Palestine, Western Sahara, and Northern Iraq, he shows how hydrocarbons act as liabilities: they entrench exclusionary sovereignties, militarize territories, marginalize environmental and civic voices, and lock in geopolitical rivalries. The chapter's importance is its reframing of peacebuilding debates away from technocratic revenue-sharing toward political ecology and recognition. It offers a four-part framework—sovereignty claims, securitization, marginalization, and shifting asset/liability perceptions—that practitioners can use to diagnose risks. The argument advances a post-extractivist, justice-oriented agenda that foregrounds inclusion and ecological sustainability. It provides scholars and policymakers with clear cautionary lessons for *resource-led peace* projects.

The Sustainability Discourse of Mega Satellite Constellations: İnan-Şimşek takes sustainability debates literally to new heights by interrogating mega satellite constellations like Starlink. Through a Marxist and critical discourse analysis, she shows how corporate claims about advancing the SDGs obscure environmental risks (space debris, orbital carrying capacity, energy use), social risks (data monopolies, surveillance), and geopolitical asymmetries (Global South dependence on Northern infrastructures). The importance of this chapter is twofold: it demonstrates how sustainability rhetoric travels into frontier domains, and it proposes justice-oriented alternatives for space governance—public interest obligations, debris liability, open data standards, and inclusive rule-making. By extending critical political economy into the orbital commons, the chapter expands the scope of sustainability scholarship and policy design. It is indispensable reading for regulators and multilateral forums now racing to write the rules of the near-Earth environment.

The chapters collected in this volume speak with different voices, but together they insist on one central truth: sustainability is not a neutral path to be managed, but a terrain of struggle where the future is being contested. What emerges across these pages is a vivid map of contradictions. We see how sustainability becomes a shield for extractive projects, a narrative to justify surveillance and militarization, or a banner under which corporations extend control into new technological and territorial frontiers. Yet we also see how sustainability can be reclaimed: as a demand for justice in the Global South, as a claim for indigenous agency, as a feminist critique of data regimes, as a call for posthumanist ethics that take seriously the entanglement of humans, technologies, and ecologies. It is in this friction—between co-optation and resistance, reproduction and transformation—that the meaning of sustainability is being decided.

The impact of this book lies not only in its theoretical interventions or its empirical range, but in its insistence that the stakes are democratic and ethical. To read sustainability only as a technical fix is to miss the deeper story: that it is about who gets to decide, whose voices are heard, whose lives are protected, and whose futures are imagined as expendable. By bringing together contributors from across disciplines and geographies—scholars working in and with the peripheries of the world system—we aim to pluralize the debate and to provide readers with sharper tools of critique and resistance. Our hope is that the book will travel across classrooms, conferences, and activist networks, equipping students, researchers, practitioners, and advocates with ways to see through the gloss and to insist on accountability, justice, and solidarity. Sustainability will remain a contested field for decades to come. This volume does not resolve that contestation—it deepens it, clarifies it, and aligns it with the struggle for more democratic, inclusive, and livable futures.

Şeyda Güdek-Gölçek
Niğde Ömer Halisdemir University, Turkey

Günseli Durmaz
Niğde Ömer Halisdemir University, Turkey

Aybüke İnan-Şimşek
Niğde Ömer Halisdemir University, Turkey

Section 1

Theoretical and Critical Frameworks

Chapter 1
The Political Economy of Green Trasformismo:
Green Capitalism Discourses in the Age of Climate Crisis

Günseli Durmaz
https://orcid.org/0000-0003-2146-769X
Niğde Ömer Halisdemir University, Turkey

ABSTRACT

This chapter examines the European Green Deal as a response to the EU's ongoing polycrisis and investigates its class dynamics through a Neo-Gramscian and historical materialist lens. By analyzing policy communications from the European Round Table for Industry and the European Trade Union Confederation (2011–2023), the chapter shows how the green transition reflects green capitalism, shaped by structural asymmetries between capital and labor within the EU's evolving political economy. By comparing competing visions of the green transition, the chapter contributes to a critical political economy of European integration and highlights the class dynamics underpinning the EU's climate strategy.

INTRODUCTION

> *"We have a finite environment – the planet. Anyone who thinks that you can have infinite growth in a finite environment is either a madman or an economist."*
> — David Attenborough, in Carrington, *The Guardian* (2013)

Climate change stands today not merely as a technical challenge but as the defining contradiction of twenty-first-century politics and the central fault line of global economic governance. This chapter exposes the historical conditions that enabled

DOI: 10.4018/979-8-3373-1707-6.ch001

green capitalism to claim center stage as the dominant framework for confronting the climate crisis. Capitalism, understood as a system of social and political power rooted in the imperative of infinite accumulation on a finite planet, is itself the engine of ecological destruction. The discourse of green capitalism, which reduces climate change to a market failure, deliberately obscures this reality. It recasts the crisis as a solvable malfunction rather than a systemic outcome of industrial expansion, extractivism, deforestation, pollution, and biodiversity collapse. By doing so, it presents itself as corrective rather than culprit. Yet what is offered is not transformation, but repair: green capitalism preserves existing relations of production and entrenched North–South hierarchies, while marketing green reforms and technological quick fixes as the only viable horizon of action.

Drawing on a neo-Gramscian lens, the chapter argues that green growth has become the raison d'état of contemporary capitalism: its hegemonic solution to the insoluble contradiction of reconciling endless accumulation with planetary limits. This project is not driven by climate movements, Green parties, or radical demands for justice, but by multinational capital and ruling elites. The promise that growth can be decoupled from ecological limits through technological innovation and research legitimizes the very groups most responsible for crisis and secures their reproduction. Green growth, in this sense, is less a pathway to sustainability than an ideological maneuver that deflects attention from structural drivers of catastrophe while consolidating a new hegemony. Through the promotion of green commodities, sustainable consumption, and renewable substitution, it transforms ecological collapse into yet another frontier for accumulation. Far from challenging capitalism, it offers capitalism a second life. As such, green growth operates as the hegemonic common sense of our era, anchoring a new historical bloc in which diverse actors converge around a green capitalist order.

The chapter unfolds in four stages. Section 2 lays out why a neo-Gramscian framework is indispensable for analyzing the green trasformismo of capitalism and introduces the theoretical tools mobilized in this study. Section 3 explains how climate change has come to embody the spirit of the age, tracing the fragmented, contested structure of international climate governance alongside the rise of climate justice movements, transnational activism, and the growing force of Green parties. Section 4 situates the global politics of green capitalism, examining the European Union's ambitions to lead the green transition in the wake of U.S. retreat from the Paris Agreement and the ways Russia's war on Ukraine has laid bare Europe's energy vulnerabilities. It then contrasts the competing green projects of the United States, the EU, and China, showing how each seeks to institutionalize its own variant of green capitalism. The chapter concludes by arguing that this so-called green race is best understood as a hegemonic struggle within an emerging green capitalist order, one that is actively consolidating a new historical bloc and scripting the parameters of the future world order.

NEO-GRAMSCIAN APPROACH TO THE GREEN TRANSFORMATION OF CAPITALIST RELATIONS

To understand why neo-Gramscian approach is better equipped with necessary theoretical dept to analyze current green transformation of capitalist relations, this section first starts with revisiting Antonio Gramsci's original insights. Gramsci's concepts of critical economy, integral state, hegemony, common sense, and historical bloc provide the theoretical foundations upon which neo-Gramscian scholars have built their analyses of international political economy. Although his work was mainly focused on the national context of early 20th-century Italy, its theoretical and methodological dept provide scholars with necessary tools to analyze structures of power, seeds of consent and conflict among actors laying the foundation for future changes. Thus, the following section briefly outlines these key concepts in order to establish the analytical basis for subsequent discussions on neo-Gramscian interpretations of state, globalization, and the evolving forms of capitalist relations.

Gramsci's Critical Economy and the Foundations of Integral State, Common Sense, Hegemony, and Historical Bloc

The neo-Gramscian approach in International Political Economy (IPE) is deeply rooted in the theoretical contributions of Antonio Gramsci, whose *Prison Notebooks*, written between 1929 and 1935 while imprisoned under Mussolini's regime, provide a fertile ground for critical analysis of capitalist relations (Gramsci, 1971). Gramsci's intellectual legacy was revitalized in the 1980s by Robert Cox, who applied his perceptions to the study of world politics, so opening novel analytical ways for understanding the interplay of power, ideology, and social relations in the international arena (Cox, 1981, 1983). While the term *neo-Gramscian* indicates continuity, the *neo* underscores the reinterpretation and adaptation of Gramsci's ideas to new historical circumstances rather than a simple reproduction of his early 20th-century concerns (Morton, 2007).

Gramsci set apart what he called *Critical Economy* from the *Classical Economy* associated with Adam Smith and David Ricardo. Rather than constructing abstract models based on timeless assumptions about a generic "economic man," Critical Economy insisted on embedding analytical categories in their historical setting and interpreting them in light of the specific circumstances that produced them (Gramsci, 1995). Building on this approach, Gramsci developed an understanding of political and civil society as interconnected spheres that together compose the "integral state," and advanced the concept of common sense as a key element in the organization of hegemony. These ideas have since been taken up, debated, and reworked across a wide range of contexts and disciplines.

Integral State

For Gramsci, the state signified the ensemble of practical and theoretical activities through which a dominant class not only preserves its rule but also secures the active consent of subordinate groups (Gramsci, 1971). The state, in this sense, exceeded the boundaries of formal political institutions or the authority of governmental leaders. Rather, it encompassed both the coercive apparatuses of the public sphere—such as government, political parties, and the military—and the institutions of civil society—including the church, media, and education—through which hegemonic leadership is organized and reproduced (Gramsci, 1971). From this vantage point, the state is not reducible to a fixed institution or autonomous entity; it is more accurately understood as a complex web of social relations that both shape and are shaped by the dynamics of capitalism and hegemony (Poulantzas, 1978). This expanded conception moves beyond a reductive interpretation of the state as a mere instrument of repression, emphasizing instead its character as a relational configuration in which power operates through a shifting balance of coercion and consent (Thomas, 2009).

Political society, involving government, parties, military, and the legal apparatus, functions through coercive means, whereas civil society, encompassing institutions such as schools, churches, the media, and cultural organizations, became the field where consent is manufactured (Buci-Glucksmann, 1980). Gramsci's persistence on the unity of political and civil society within the integral state was a methodological innovation that enabled later scholars to analyze not only how states exercise power domestically, but also how ideological hegemony operates across borders.

Hegemony

Gramsci's conception of the state is closely tied to his theory of hegemony. He viewed the state as encompassing both the realm of coercive power, where different classes compete for control, and civil society, where these same actors struggle to win consent for their vision of a "good society," that is, their ideology. Together, these constitute what he termed the integral state (D'Alisa & Kallis, 2016). For Gramsci, hegemony cannot be equated with coercion alone; it is the capacity of a dominant class to present its own particular interests as the universal interests of society, thereby securing the consent of subordinate groups (Gramsci, 1971). The strength of a hegemonic order, then, depends on how effectively a ruling class succeeds in framing its interests as common to all, and on the degree to which other groups accept and endorse this framing. Importantly, hegemony is not embodied by actors themselves but by elements of common sense—shared worldviews, social relations, or specific discursive formations situated in time and space—that acquire hegemonic status (Wullweber, 2019).

As Gramsci emphasized, no ruling class can survive indefinitely by relying exclusively on force; it must establish ideological leadership that secures a broad base of consent (Gramsci, 1971; Simon, 1982). This insight allows us to understand hegemony not as a fixed achievement but as a constantly contested process. Dominant ideologies must continuously adapt to everchanging social conditions, selectively incorporating elements of opposition in order to neutralize resistance, a mechanism Gramsci termed *trasformismo* (Gramsci, 1971).

Common Sense

The concept of common sense provides a critical connection between hegemony and everyday life.

> *every social stratum has its own commonsense and its good sense, which are basically the most widespread conception of life and of human being. Every philosophical current leaves behind a sedimentation of commonsenses: this is the document evidence of its historical effectiveness. Commonsense is not something rigid and immobile, but is continually transforming itself, enriching itself with scientific ideas and with philosophical opinions, which have entered ordinary life. Commonsense is the folklore of philosophy, and is always half-way between folklore properly speaking . . . and the philosophy, science, the economics of the specialists. Commonsense creates the folklore of the future, that is as a relatively rigid phase of popular knowledge in a given place and time. (Gramsci, Hoare & Nowell-Smith, 1971)*

Gramsci treats common sense as a concept that must be historicized, contextualized, and put into practice. For him, common sense is never singular but inherently plural: within any society, multiple *sensi comuni* coexist. Hegemonic discourse works by elevating and organizing certain strands of common sense while marginalizing others, yet in doing so it also leaves space for alternative interpretations to emerge and challenge the dominant order (D'Alisa & Kallis, 2016). Each social group carries its own version of common sense, which is continuously reshaped through historical experiences and ongoing ideological struggles.

Common sense, in this view, is the terrain upon which hegemonic projects are constructed. Dominant classes succeed in establishing hegemony depending on how successful they articulate their interests as natural and self-evident within the frameworks of popular common sense (Crehan, 2016). At the same time, common sense retains a contradictory character: it contains within it the seeds of alternative good sense, which can be mobilized to challenge dominant ideologies (Gramsci, 1971; Hall, 1986). This dialectical potential makes common sense a dynamic site of both preservation of current dominant structures and emergence of any other alternative which is able to resist, challenge and ultimately change the existing hegemonic relations.

Historical Bloc

Gramsci's concept of the historical bloc emerges directly from his reflections on hegemony and common sense. As he explains, it is only when an "organic cohesion" binds intellectuals and the people-nation—leaders and the led, rulers and the ruled—that the mutual exchange between these groups can generate a shared life, which in turn becomes a genuine social force. This organic unity constitutes the foundation of what Gramsci terms the "historic bloc" (Gramsci, 1971).

The historical bloc, therefore, signifies the institutionalization of a constellation of ideas, practices, and social relations that consolidate and reproduce a particular structure of domination. Yet its hegemony is never uncontested or permanent: it requires constant rearticulation, reinforcement, and defense against rival social forces (van Apeldoorn & Horn, 2018). In this framework, ideologies are not abstract or arbitrary; they are historically situated and function as instruments of domination. As such, unveiling and contesting them becomes essential for fostering the intellectual independence of subaltern groups and enabling the disintegration of one hegemonic formation in favor of another, a precondition for transformative praxis (Stephen, 2011). Gramsci (1996) further observed that ideology is the sphere in which individuals become conscious of the conflicts embedded within the economic structure. Consequently, the cultivation of an alternative ideological culture that challenges the prevailing worldview disrupts the very foundations of hegemony by encouraging new ways of thinking and acting.

The apparent coherence of any historical bloc is thus inherently fragile, continually threatened by counter-hegemonic projects that seek to displace dominant common sense and advance alternative visions of social order (Morton, 2007; Gill, 1993). Historical blocs should, therefore, be conceived as dynamic and unstable configurations, perpetually reshaped in response to crises of legitimacy, shifts in economic conditions, and struggles over social transformation.

National and International Dimensions

Gramsci approached the problem of hegemony by examining the interplay between national and international dimensions. While he regarded the national terrain as the primary site for confronting class exploitation and the defense of private property, he simultaneously emphasized that capitalism is a world-historical system shaped by patterns of uneven development (Gramsci, 1977). In his view, no historical process could be meaningfully confined within narrowly bounded national frameworks, since "history is always world history and ... particular histories exist only within the frame of world history" (Gramsci, 1985). On this basis, Gramsci analyzed both the "relations within society"—such as the development of productive forces, the deployment of coercion, and the dynamics of political parties that constitute hegemonic formations at the state level—and the "relations between international forces," including power balances, sovereignty, and inter-state alliances, that together produce and reproduce hegemonic orders on a global scale (Gramsci, 1971).

This recognition of the interconnection between domestic and international arenas was subsequently extended by Neo-Gramscian scholars. They conceptualized neoliberalism as a global hegemonic project, reproduced not only through the agency of states but also through the activities of transnational actors and social forces. While rooted in distinct national contexts, these actors coalesce to advance shared class interests and sustain a transnational order. Gramsci's insistence on locating capitalism within a world-historical framework of uneven development thus provides a crucial lens for understanding how local class struggles are embedded in, and shaped by, broader global power relations. This relational perspective proved foundational for the field of critical international political economy, most notably in the work of Robert Cox, who reinterpreted Gramsci's concepts to analyze world orders and the historical transformations of global capitalism.

Having outlined the key theoretical notions from Gramsci, that are used in this chapter, the next sub-section will analyze his ideas have been revisited by scholars of International Political Economy. The move from Gramsci to a neo-Gramscian framework reflects both continuity and innovation: continuity in applying his relational concepts of hegemony, integral state, and historical bloc, and innovation in extending these ideas to the analysis of transnational structures, global capitalism, and world orders. This transition was initiated most notably by Robert Cox, whose work in the 1980s presented a critical theoretical agenda that challenged mainstream international relations and emphasized the historical and contested nature of global order.

From Gramsci to Neo-Gramscian International Political Economy

The revival of Gramscian thought within International Relations (IR) is closely associated with the pioneering interventions of Robert W. Cox in the early 1980s. Dissatisfied with the limitations of positivist approaches, Cox advanced a critical perspective that integrated Gramsci's relational understanding of power, ideology, and production into the analysis of global order (Cox, 1981, 1983). His well-known assertion that "theory is always for someone and for some purpose" (Cox, 1981) marked a decisive departure from problem-solving theories—which accept prevailing social structures as given—toward a critical theory committed to exposing their historical contingency and opening possibilities for transformation.

Central to Cox's framework was the claim that transformations in relations of production give rise to distinct social forces that function as sources of power both within states and across the international order (Cox, 1987). By embedding hegemony in broader historical structures composed of interrelated material, institutional, and ideological dimensions, he expanded the concept beyond its conventional focus (Cox, 1981). For Cox, hegemony was not reducible to interstate dominance; it also entailed the diffusion of a prevailing mode of development into national contexts, mediated through ruling classes. Global hegemony thus materializes in the universalization of values and norms institutionalized through international organizations and regulatory regimes, which structure the behavior of states and transnational social forces alike (Cox, 1983).

Within this framework, the form the state assumes is shaped by the historical bloc or class configuration that defines its raison d'état (Cox, 1989). From this perspective, processes of globalization and the ascendancy of new transnational forces of capital and labor do not necessarily herald the decline of the state. Rather, they engender novel forms of statehood, as states internalize these shifting social relations and reflect the struggles between national and transnational fractions of capital and labor (Bieler & Morton, 2003). This approach provides a powerful analytical lens for uncovering the social foundations of state forms and for conceptualizing the historically specific configurations underpinning different expressions of state power.

Neo-Gramscian Hegemony, Common Sense and Globalization

Unlike mainstream IR theories, which often equate hegemony with the material dominance of powerful states, the neo-Gramscian approach conceptualizes hegemony as a multidimensional phenomenon encompassing material, institutional, and ideational power (Bieler & Morton, 2004). For Cox and following neo-Gramscians, global hegemony is sustained through the diffusion of universalized norms and values, often institutionalized in international organizations such as the International Monetary Fund, the World Bank, and the World Trade Organization (Gill, 1993; van Apeldoorn, 2002). These institutions not only regulate state behavior but also insert and reproduce the dominant relations of production and the ideological assumptions that support them.

Globalization, in this perspective, is not a neutral or inevitable process but a hegemonic project reflecting the interests of transnational sections of capital. The rise of neoliberal globalization in the late 20th century can be understood as the consolidation of a new historical bloc in which global finance, multinational corporations, and supportive states aligned to institutionalize a regime of market liberalization, deregulation, and austerity (Gill, 1995; Bieler & Morton, 2004). By naturalizing neoliberal *common sense*, this bloc reconfigured both domestic state forms and international institutions to secure its dominance.

Neo-Gramscians emphasize that globalization involves not the retreat of the state, but its reconfiguration. States internalize the essentials of global capital by restructuring policies, institutions, and regulations in ways that align with transnational class interests (Cox, 1987; Morton, 2007). The *relative autonomy* of the state enables it to regulate competing class divisions, but this autonomy is applied within the constraints of global capitalist essentials. Thus, rather than vanishing, states become active mediators of transnational hegemony.

Building on Gramsci's notion of common sense, neo-Gramscians argue that globalization is legitimated through the production of new common senses that naturalize neoliberal values such as competitiveness, flexibility, and individual responsibility (Gill, 1995). Global civil society, consists of NGOs, think tanks, media, and educational institutions, plays a central role in disseminating these ideas, often framing them as universal solutions to global problems. Yet, as Gramsci noted, common sense is never uniform; it is internally contradictory and open to contestation. This vision allows neo-Gramscians to analyze the emergence of counter-hegemonic movements, from global justice campaigns to climate activism, which articulate alternative common senses challenging neoliberal orthodoxy (Bieler & Morton, 2004; Ayers, 2008).

Neo-Gramscian State as a Terrain of Struggle between Different Social Forces

For neo-Gramscians, the state must be analyzed in terms of its relationship to global production relations and social forces. Different forms of state link to different historical blocs, each defined by a particular alignment of class forces (Cox, 1987). The state does not simply reflect the interests of a dominant class; rather, it functions as a site of struggle in which competing fractions of capital and labor negotiate the terms of hegemony.

In the context of globalization, states have increasingly internalized the requirements of transnational capital, aligning domestic policies with global neoliberal norms. Yet this process is uneven and contested, shaped by national histories, institutional legacies, and popular resistance (Morton, 2007). The European Union, for example, has been analyzed by neo-Gramscians as a regional project of capitalist integration that reflects the interests of transnational capital while simultaneously embodying the contradictions of uneven development within Europe (van Apeldoorn, 2002; Bieler & Morton, 2004).

The analytical power of the neo-Gramscian approach lies in its ability to historicize contemporary social relations, revealing how current configurations of global capitalism emerged, how they are sustained, and how they might be contested. By foregrounding the interplay of ideas, institutions, and material capabilities, this framework transcends the reductionist accounts of power that prioritize either structure or agency. Instead, it provides a relational and dynamic understanding of global order.

Passive Revolution and Trasformismo

Gramsci's concepts of passive revolution and trasformismo have become central to Neo-Gramscian analyses of hegemony, the historical bloc, and the dynamics of revolution and counter-revolution. As noted earlier, hegemony cannot be secured by advancing only the dominant class's interests. It requires compromise, which may take the form of either expansive hegemony or passive revolution. Expansive hegemony—what Gramsci called a Jacobin-style political revolution—arises when active and broad consensus is built by incorporating other classes' demands into a collective national-popular project (Mouffe, 1979). Passive revolution, by contrast, is closely tied to the consolidation and extension of capitalism, but along narrower hegemonic lines (Morton, 2010). Historically, Gramsci contrasted the radical Jacobin strategy with the Italian Moderates' reliance on a limited class alliance between landowning elites and co-opted opposition leaders, a strategy he identified as trasformismo (Forgacs, 1988).

Trasformismo represents a distinct mechanism of passive revolution. It describes the limited incorporation of alter- or counter-hegemonic forces through reforms that appear to accommodate dissent while actually reinforcing existing power structures (Ramos, 2006). Whereas passive revolution emphasizes the lack of mass participation, trasformismo highlights the deliberate strategies used to block popular mobilization and systemic change, often through ideological dilution and institutional manipulation (Paterson, 2009). By absorbing and neutralizing oppositional ideas, trasformismo obstructs the formation of organized class-based resistance (Cox, 1983).

In this sense, it functions as a politics of assimilation: movements and actors who challenge dominant power are drawn into the prevailing framework, their discourse reshaped to fit established rhetoric and policies (Paterson, 2006; Moore, 2007). Passive revolution therefore sustains the status quo by relying on co-optation and trasformismo—both of which preserve the civil-political order through incremental reforms and symbolic gestures.

Paterson (2006) points out that alternative visions promoted by subordinate groups—such as sustainable development, the right to life, or ecological protection—may be acknowledged in official discourse, yet the underlying neoliberal accumulation model remains unchanged. Under such conditions, trasformismo predominates, operating not as genuine transformation but as a gradual absorption of class contradictions. Gramsci described this process as "molecular" change: incremental adjustments that modify the existing balance of forces without fundamentally overturning them (Hesketh & Morton, 2014; Gramsci, 1971). In contemporary contexts, trasformismo thus signifies the ruling bloc's ability to accommodate disruptive pressures while deploying material, institutional, and discursive resources to ensure that any shifts in socio-technical arrangements do not destabilize entrenched social hierarchies or political power relations (Newell, 2019).

This section has reexamined Gramsci's critical economy and his key notions, integral state, hegemony, common sense, and historical bloc, in order to show why a neo-Gramscian approach has the necessary theoretical depth to analyze the current green transformation of capitalist relations. Taking the state as a social relation that unites political and civil society highlights how coercion and consent operate together; conceiving hegemony as the universalization of particular interests reveals the seeds of consent and conflict among actors; treating common sense as plural and contested identifies the everyday terrain on which ideologies are made and unmade; and understanding historical blocs as unstable configurations clarifies how alliances are assembled and rearticulated across national and international scales. Neo-Gramscian reinterpretations extend these insights to globalization, specifying how ideas, institutions, and material capabilities co-produce world orders. Finally, the paired concepts of passive revolution and *trasformismo* explain how dominant actors selectively incorporate ecological critique to stabilize leadership while narrowing alternatives. With this analytical basis in place, Section 3 examines how climate change becomes the zeitgeist of the 21st century and the primary arena in which green *trasformismo* is enacted and resisted.

CLIMATE POLITICS AS THE ZEITGEIST OF THE 21ST CENTURY

Climate change has become the defining political, social, and economic issue of the 21st century, shaping both global governance structures and grassroots mobilizations. The institutional architecture of climate governance has evolved from legally binding treaties to flexible systems, embedding carbon markets at its core. Parallel to this approach, the climate justice movement has articulated a counter-hegemonic critique, exposing the inequities of North–South relations and insisting on the recognition of ecological debt. At the same time, rising climate activism, driven especially by youth, has expanded public engagement and increased the visibility and influence of Green parties across regions, most prominently in Europe. Taken together, these dynamics illustrate how climate change has emerged as the *zeitgeist* of our era: not only an environmental challenge but also a site of political contestation, ideological struggle, and opportunities for reimagining global futures.

International Governance of Climate Change

Global environmental governance today is marked by a shift away from exclusively nation-state–driven approaches toward increasingly multi-level and multi-actor frameworks. These now encompass not only states but also international organizations, transnational networks of experts, environmental NGOs, and multinational corporations (Biermann & Pattberg, 2008). The scope of governance extends well beyond environmental protection to include broader goals of sustainable development and biodiversity preservation, aiming to safeguard the planet for future generations. Within this architecture, powerful actors—such as states, regions, corporations, and international organizations—interact with weaker ones, creating tensions between continuity and disruption in global efforts to address climate change.

A brief genealogy illuminates how today's regime took shape. The United Nations Framework Convention on Climate Change (UNFCCC) was adopted in 1992 and entered into force in 1994, establishing the structure of global action: common commitments to inventory and report anthropogenic greenhouse gases (GHGs), cooperate on adaptation, and periodically review implementation through the Conference of the Parties (COP) (UNFCCC, 1992). The Convention also institutionalized differentiation between Annex I Parties (industrialized economies) and non-Annex I Parties (developing countries), with additional expectations for the former, more frequent reporting, finance, and technology transfer (Bodansky, 2016). This differentiation has later become the main point of contention between the developed and developing countries.

The Kyoto Protocol (adopted 1997; in force 2005) translated collective concern into binding targets for a subset of industrialized countries and, crucially, financialized emissions. Its flexibility mechanisms, international emissions trading (Art. 17), the Clean Development Mechanism (CDM), and Joint Implementation (JI)—enabled the emergence of carbon markets, treating units of GHG reduction as exchangeable commodities (UNFCCC, 1997). Advocates argued that pricing carbon would deliver cost-effective mitigation and spur innovation (Keohane & Raustiala, 2010). However, these arguments were heavily criticized by other scholars since that commodifying pollution actually misplaces responsibility, produces dubious offsets, and inserts neoliberal logics that prioritize market solutions over structural change (Böhm, Misoczky, & Moog, 2012).

The Copenhagen summit (COP15, 2009) marked a critical turn toward pledge-and-review, affirming sovereignty and voluntary nationally determined approaches (Falkner, 2016). The Paris Agreement (COP21, 2015) then generalized this architecture by requiring all Parties to submit Nationally Determined Contributions (NDCs), embedding iterative global stock takes, transparency rules, and a *ratchet* mechanism intended to raise ambition over time (UNFCCC, 2015). The Glasgow Climate Pact (COP26, 2021) advanced these mechanisms and renewed technical questions around Article 6 carbon markets, while again exposing the core bargain between historical and emerging emitters: time and flexibility for transition on one side, and constrained public finance on the other (Hermwille, 2022).

Change, 2025), a "right to pollute" has effectively been institutionalized, allowing states to buy and sell emission units in global markets. Beyond governments, corporations and even individuals can now participate in carbon trading schemes, offsetting their emissions by purchasing credits from actors that remove or reduce greenhouse gases (UNDP, 2022). The Copenhagen Conference of 2009 (UNFCCC COP15) reinforced this trajectory by preserving state sovereignty, loosening constraints on emission reductions and financing, and prioritizing voluntary contributions (Aykut & Dahan, 2022). Later, the Glasgow Conference of 2021 (UNFCCC COP26) consolidated this approach, securing a compromise among the world's largest emitters—past and future—by enabling some to delay their transitions and others to evade financing commitments, a compromise that continues to fuel tensions in global climate politics (Aykut & Maertens, 2022; Aykut et al., 2022a). From a liberal perspective, carbon markets create opportunities for developing countries to pursue socio-economic growth while transitioning to low-carbon economies, pricing carbon, encouraging trading, and opening new avenues for corporate profit (UNDP, 2025). In this way, carbon markets designed and overseen by international organizations and shaped by powerful state and corporate actors—have come to embody the liberal international governance of climate change.

Over time, the institutional architecture of climate governance has shifted away from binding emission-reduction targets toward voluntary pledges, embedding neoliberal tools such as carbon markets at its very center. These frameworks have succeeded in expanding participation, but they do so by dispersing accountability and privileging market mechanisms over deep structural change. As a result, the global system of climate governance is fragile: it maintains cooperation while simultaneously reinforcing inequalities, leaving ample room for counter-mobilizations that challenge the legitimacy and effectiveness of existing arrangements.

The Climate Justice Movement

The consolidation of global climate governance has accentuated long-standing divisions between developed and developing countries. Industrialized states—whose historical trajectories of industrialization are primarily responsible for the present ecological crisis—have positioned themselves as leaders of global climate action. Yet developing countries contend that these same powers evade accountability for past emissions while simultaneously curtailing the Global South's right to pursue its own development. The adoption of carbon trading mechanisms deepened these conflicts, complicating governance arrangements and widening fractures around climate justice.

Initially, the climate justice movement sought above all to secure recognition of climate change as a political priority, drawing on scientific evidence to counter entrenched denialism (Hadden, 2015). Over time—especially during the Kyoto Protocol negotiations—its agenda became increasingly politicized, centering on disputes over carbon markets, North–South equity, and the legitimacy of disruptive protest tactics (Martínez-Alier, 2012). In this period, activist networks such as Friends of the Earth International, Carbon Trade Watch, and ActionAid Asia coalesced with the newly founded Climate Justice Now! (CJN) coalition, launched in Bali in 2007. CJN rooted its mobilization in critiques of global inequality, framing climate change as a justice issue and organizing mass protests (Cassegård & Thörn, 2017). These actions frequently provoked repression: during COP20 in Lima in 2014, thousands marched under slogans such as "Keep the oil in the soil" and "Change the system, not the climate," while in Ecuador, an Indigenous leader opposing mining was tortured and killed (Goldenberg, 2014).

The contestation also crystallized around the concept of ecological debt. Developing countries argued that industrialized nations bore disproportionate responsibility for the climate crisis and should repay this debt (Martínez-Alier, 2012). At the 2009 Copenhagen Summit, Bolivia's UN ambassador Pablo Solón denounced the Global North's inaction, likening it to "burning your house and then refusing to pay for it." He insisted that those most responsible must bear the costs, rather than shifting the burden onto vulnerable populations. While the United States, the EU, and Japan rejected this demand, more than 20 heads of state or ministers explicitly invoked ecological or climate debt, with some even employing the language of reparations.

From these struggles, two central fault lines emerged in climate governance. First, developing states resent industrialized nations for the environmental destruction—industrial pollution, deforestation, biodiversity loss—generated by their growth trajectories. Second, they perceive climate protection measures as unjust constraints on their own development opportunities. The climate justice movement arose from these structural divisions and quickly diffused globally, shaping transnational social movements and pressuring elites within the global political economy to respond (Martínez-Alier, 2012, p. 59; Svensson & Wahlström, 2023).

In this sense, the climate justice movement—grounded in Global South demands for recognition of ecological debt and politicized through resistance to carbon markets—converged with the degrowth critique of capitalism, forming what Martínez-Alier (2012, pp. 58–59) describes as an alliance between environmental justice and degrowth movements. Its central aim has been to re-politicize climate change as a structural injustice, foregrounding responsibility, capacity, and need as the normative basis of climate negotiations. This is reflected in the growing salience of equity concerns within debates on climate finance, technology transfer, and loss-and-damage agendas since the Paris Agreement (Bodansky, 2016; UNFCCC, 2015).

Global environmental politics have thus evolved from initial phases of indifference and denial to widespread acknowledgment of climate science, driven by a succession of crises: rising sea levels threatening coastal and island populations, intensifying floods and wildfires, and accelerating biodiversity loss with cascading ecological consequences. Alongside these material pressures, climate activism has gained unprecedented visibility. While the climate justice movement emphasizes the rights and struggles of the Global South, it has been joined by broader transnational mobilizations that channel growing public concern as climate impacts intensify worldwide.

In this context, the climate justice movement has emerged as a powerful counter-hegemonic force. By advancing notions of ecological debt, loss and damage, and reparations, activists have challenged the commodification of emissions and redefined climate change as a matter of responsibility, equity, and redistribution. In doing so, they have pushed climate politics beyond technocratic governance toward a confrontation with the structural inequalities of global capitalism, directly contesting the terms under which climate action is conceived and pursued.

Rising Climate Activism and the Increasing Appeal of Green Parties

The shortcomings of global climate governance have fueled frustration among younger generations, many of whom feel compelled to intervene directly in political decision-making. Youth climate activism—particularly among those aged twelve to eighteen in secondary schools—has expanded rapidly in recent years (Rousell & Cutter-Mackenzie-Knowles, 2020). For these young people, the failure of political leaders to avert ecological breakdown has created a profound sense of urgency. They view themselves as responsible not only for protecting their own futures but also for defending the planet. In this context, experiences of climate concern, despair, and eco-anxiety are widespread, with many struggling to cope with feelings of helplessness in the face of accelerating environmental crises (Han & Ahn, 2020). Refusing to remain passive spectators of planetary decline, they have instead mobilized collectively on a global scale.

In 2018, Swedish teenager Greta Thunberg began staging Friday school strikes outside the Swedish parliament to demand stronger action on climate change (Watts, 2019). Her initiative quickly inspired a wave of climate strikes that evolved into a transnational youth movement calling for transformative climate policies. At Davos in 2019, Thunberg delivered a forceful address to political and economic elites, challenging them to act decisively. Her activism sparked what came to be known as "The Greta Thunberg Effect," a term capturing her role in energizing young people around the world to pressure governments into meaningful action (Chung, 2019). By spearheading the Fridays for Future movement, she not only gave her peers a sense of agency but also confronted older generations with their failure to respond adequately to the climate emergency.

Youth climate activism predates Greta Thunberg, most notably when 12-year-old Severn Cullis-Suzuki addressed the 1992 Earth Summit in Rio, urging leaders to take responsibility for future generations and helping to frame climate change as a justice issue (Cullis-Suzuki, 1992; Stevenson & Peterson, 2015). Since then, new waves of activists such as Xiuhtezcatl Martinez and Isra Hirsi in the United States, John Paul Jose in India, and Luisa Neubauer in Germany have showed how climate struggles are both transnational and locally rooted, challenging political elites and experimenting with new strategies (Trihartono, Viartasiwi, & Nisya, 2020; Han & Ahn, 2020, p. 1). At the U.N. Youth Climate Summit, Thunberg and 14 other children filed a complaint under the Convention on the Rights of the Child, claiming that governmental inaction violated international obligations, while in Europe youth mobilized through the European Citizens' Initiative to demand greater emission cuts, border carbon adjustments, trade restrictions for non-compliant states, and climate education (Han & Ahn, 2020, p. 7; UNFCCC, 2015). Thunberg's crucial moment came at the 2019 U.N. Climate Action Summit, where her passionate speech condemning world leaders for inaction underlined the moral urgency of the crisis and stimulated millions of young people worldwide to demand stronger commitments (Milman, 2019).

In recent decades, organized climate activism has consistently pressed political leaders to adopt measures far more ambitious than those agreed upon at successive UNFCCC summits. Such mobilizations have not only played a decisive role in securing broad public recognition of the climate crisis but have also constrained political and economic elites, forcing them to engage with the issue. As climate change became increasingly politicized within the public sphere, conditions emerged for the growth of green parties across different regions. Today, green parties are present in nearly 80 percent of European countries, about half of the states in the Americas and Africa, and roughly one-fifth of Asia-Pacific nations (Burchell, 2002; van Haute, 2016). Their electoral strength, however, remains uneven, shaped by variations in institutional arrangements, the salience of environmental issues, and the strength of links between movements and parties.

In majoritarian systems like the United States, structural barriers, including first-past-the-post rules, high campaign finance thresholds, and restrictive ballot access, have limited parliamentary representation (Rosenstone, Behr, & Lazarus, 2018). Still, green actors have shaped agenda-setting through local ballot initiatives, climate litigation support, and city-level policy diffusion. In the Asia-Pacific, the earliest green party, the New Zealand Values Party (1972), created stronger representation in New Zealand and Australia, where Greens are regular parliamentary actors and occasional coalition partners (Blühdorn, 2009). Elsewhere in the region, representation is irregular or localized due to party-system constraints and varied salience of environmental issues.

Without question, Europe remains the terrain where Green parties have exercised the greatest political leverage, shaping both electoral outcomes and policy debates in ways unmatched elsewhere. Since the 1990s, cross-border coordination—first via the European Federation of Green Parties and later the European Green Party, has enabled organizational learning, shared platforms, and coalition strategies. Greens have served in governments or confidence-and-supply arrangements in Germany, Austria, Finland, Ireland, Luxembourg, and France, among others, while remaining marginal in countries such as Spain, Poland, and Norway (Müller-Rommel, 2022; van Haute, 2016). This irregularity reflects national political economies, energy mixes, and the strength of incumbent parties. Essentially, greens emerged from the student, peace, and anti-nuclear movements of the 1960s–1980s. Their core values typically include ecology, social justice, grassroots democracy, non-violence, gender equality, diversity, and future-oriented sustainability (Poguntke, 2002). Sociologically, their supporters skew younger, urban, more educated, and less religious, although this profile has broadened as climate concern mainstreamed (van Haute, 2016).

Youth climate activism and the growing prominence of green parties further underline the extent to which climate change now defines political imagination. What began as fragmented acts of protest has become a global wave of mobilization that pressures governments, reshapes party systems, and reframes ecological survival as a moral imperative. The institutional successes of green parties and the mass legitimacy of youth movements demonstrate how climate politics has penetrated both the streets and the ballot box. Together, they testify that climate change is no longer a niche concern but the defining issue through which power, justice, and legitimacy are contested in the 21st century.

Considered together, the evolution of international climate governance, the emergence of the climate justice movement, and the surge of climate activism underscore why climate change has become the defining zeitgeist of the twenty-first century. Global governance frameworks have institutionalized climate action, but largely through market-based instruments and the reaffirmation of state sovereignty, thereby marginalizing deeper questions of equity and redistribution. Counter-movements have challenged these exclusions, mobilizing under the banner of climate justice to demand repair, redistribution, and democratic control. Simultaneously, mass mobilizations—most visibly among youth—as well as the consolidation of green parties have transformed climate change into a durable political cleavage, reshaping electoral dynamics and collective imaginaries. The result is a contested historical bloc in which ecological critique is at once absorbed and resisted: climate change is normalized as an arena of policy and markets, yet continues to serve as a focal point for counter-hegemonic struggle. This tension sets the stage for the following section, which examines how these dynamics play out within the global political economy of green capitalism, where competing powers seek to harness ecological imperatives as strategies of accumulation, legitimacy, and geopolitical influence.

MAKING A GREEN WORLD ORDER: HEGEMONY, CONTESTATION, AND THE POLITICAL ECONOMY OF THE TRANSITION

This section examines how a *green* world order is being constructed and contested. It first traces the geopolitical struggle over the transition, across the United States, the European Union, China, and the shock of Russia's war on Ukraine, to show how climate policy has become a terrain of state strategy, industrial policy, and energy security. It then positions these rival projects within a broader race to institutionalize green capitalism: the spread of green-growth discourse through international organizations; the infrastructures of finance, standards, and entrepreneurship that channel investment; and the risks of greenwashing that follow from market-led decarbonization. Bringing these strands together, the section analyzes contemporary climate politics through a neo-Gramscian lens of green trasformismo: ecological critique is selectively incorporated to build an emergent historic bloc that promises prosperity and planetary repair, even as distributional conflicts, North–South asymmetries, and democratic deficits persist. The transition is real and material, laws, funds, supply chains, but also deeply political, organized by struggles over rule-making power, value capture, and social protection. Whether this combines into a just green order or a greener stabilization of the status quo remains an open question.

Geopolitics of Green Hegemony: Contesting Power in the Green Transition

This subsection maps the geopolitical contest over the green transition across four interconnected cases. It begins in the United States, where post-truth polarization and the stalled Green New Deal constrained federal climate legislation even as clean-industry narratives gained traction. It then turns to Europe's "man on the moon" moment, reading the European Green Deal as an attempt to convert decarbonization into a growth strategy while navigating distributional conflicts and just-transition politics. The third subsection examines China's *ecological civilization*, tracing how a state-coordinated industrial strategy and elements of a *green* Belt and Road have positioned China across critical low-carbon value chains amid enduring externalization risks. The section closes with Russia's war on Ukraine as a stress test of Europe's energy order, exposing gas dependence, accelerating renewables and grid investment, and reshaping regional energy geopolitics. Taken together, these cases show how ecological critique is incorporated into rival projects of green capitalism, what this chapter terms *green trasformismo*, and how rule-making power, industrial capacity, and energy security now structure the struggle for hegemony in a warming world.

U.S. Polarization and the Stalled Green New Deal

Although Greta Thunberg has received widespread international recognition, she has also faced ridicule, most notably from former U.S. President Donald J. Trump. Rejecting the urgency of the climate crisis, Trump employed rhetoric characteristic of a post-truth political climate. In a speech, he dismissed climate activists as "prophets of doom" who had consistently exaggerated threats, citing past alarms about overpopulation in the 1960s, mass starvation in the 1970s, and the depletion of oil in the 1990s. According to Trump, such "alarmists" sought unchecked authority to reshape society, while he pledged to resist what he framed as attempts by "radical socialists" to undermine the economy, national prosperity, and individual liberty (Elliott & Wearden, 2020). His remarks reflected a broader undercurrent of denialism: surveys indicate that roughly one in three Americans reject the idea of anthropogenic climate change (Marlon et al., 2018). A prominent example of such skepticism can be found in Senator James Inhofe's book *The Greatest Hoax: How the Global Warming Conspiracy Threatens Your Future* (2012). Despite overwhelming scientific evidence demonstrating the catastrophic consequences of human-driven global warming, public debates persist over its very existence, its anthropogenic origins, and the scale of its threat (Brüggemann et al., 2020).

Despite its evident shortcomings, the Paris Agreement has generally been interpreted as a constructive step toward collective international engagement on climate change. Yet only two years after its adoption, President Trump announced the withdrawal of the United States in 2017, creating significant challenges for global climate governance. Given the country's historical responsibility for greenhouse gas emissions and its political weight in international affairs, this decision weakened the UNFCCC's role as the principal arena of multilateral cooperation (Aykut et al., 2022b, p. 532). The U.S. retreat from environmental leadership simultaneously created space for the European Union to position itself as a central actor in global climate politics.

At the same time, progressive actors within the United States sought to redirect national politics toward a post-carbon order. However, the U.S. faced declining legitimacy: decades of military intervention in the Middle East had eroded its moral authority, while China emerged as a formidable competitor by investing heavily in renewable energy and green industrial production. Within this shifting context, the Democratic Party advanced the proposal of a "Green New Deal" (GND), championed most prominently by figures such as Alexandria Ocasio-Cortez and Bernie Sanders, as an ambitious framework for linking climate action with social and economic transformation.

The Green New Deal (GND) called for reducing reliance on fossil fuels in order to achieve net-zero greenhouse gas emissions within a decade, while also promising Americans well-paid jobs and access to quality health care. Yet, the proposal collapsed in the Senate, failing 57–0 in a procedural vote as every Republican and four Democrats opposed it (Gradoni & Sonmez, 2019). What followed quickly turned into a political spectacle: President Trump and Republican leaders openly mocked the initiative, while prominent Democrats also distanced themselves. Ernest Moniz, President Obama's former energy secretary, deemed the prospect of a fully renewable economy by 2030 "unrealistic," and former Colorado Governor John Hickenlooper described the resolution as having "laudable aims" but little chance of success given technological limits (Gradoni & Sonmez, 2019).

At its core, the GND envisioned a strong state role in reshaping the economy—tightening regulations on carbon-intensive sectors such as energy, manufacturing, and transportation, while channeling major public investments into renewable energy and the creation of "green jobs" (U.S. House of Representatives, 2019). Although it passed in the Democrat-controlled House, the resolution failed in the Republican-controlled Senate, reflecting the entrenched polarization of U.S. climate politics in the late 2010s. In this climate of post-truth polarization, climate activism was derided as alarmist, and climate science itself was reframed as ideology. Surveys revealed that roughly one-third of Americans continued to reject the scientific consensus on anthropogenic climate change (Marlon et al., 2018), while denialist texts such as Inhofe's *The Greatest Hoax* (2012) circulated widely. This contentious discursive environment severely constrained federal climate policy, even as evidence of climate disruption mounted and social mobilization intensified.

The Trump administration's withdrawal from the Paris Agreement weakened the UNFCCC's moral authority and signaled a retreat from multilateral climate leadership (UNFCCC, 2015). In response, progressives advanced the GND, a resolution that combined ambitious decarbonization targets with redistributive social policy. Substantively, the GND reflected two *common senses*: (1) climate change constitutes an urgent threat requiring immediate action, and (2) economic growth remains possible if decoupled from carbon and equitably redistributed. Much like the European Green Deal, the GND's underlying political economy depended on faith in technological innovation and industrial policy to reconcile decarbonization with prosperity, an approach aligned with green growth rather than radical transformation. The Biden administration later pivoted to climate-related industrial policy (e.g., clean-energy incentives), partly realigning the U.S. with its Western partners, but this momentum was disrupted by the COVID-19 pandemic and the geopolitical consequences of the war in Ukraine. In short, U.S. climate leadership in the late 2010s was fragmented, contested, and inconsistent, creating opportunities for other actors to assert global leadership.

Europe's "Man on the Moon" Moment: The European Green Deal

In the apparent absence of U.S. leadership in shaping and implementing international climate policies, the European Union (EU) has assumed a more prominent role. On the day the European Commission adopted the European Green Deal (EGD), Commission President Ursula von der Leyen described it as *"Europe's man on the moon moment"* (European Commission, 2019b). The following day, after the European Council meeting on 12 December 2019 in Brussels, she further emphasized the EU's leadership role, stating: *"If we want to convince others like India or China to join, we have to be a role model. We have to be united and bold, step forward and prove that change is possible, and that it is of benefit for the people and for the economy"* (European Commission, 2019c).

The EU's self-proclaimed role as a global pioneer in transitioning toward a green and sustainable economy can be interpreted as a response to growing public demands for stronger climate action. Electoral outcomes reinforced this trend, as Green parties achieved unprecedented success in the 2019 European elections, particularly in large Western member states (Grant & Tilley, 2019). This leadership also represented a counterbalance to the rise of climate change denial in countries such as the United States under Donald Trump and Brazil under Jair Bolsonaro, which threatened the cooperative framework of the Paris Agreement (Fraune & Knodt, 2018).

Despite its ambition, the EGD has generated significant controversy. The Commission's target of making Europe the first carbon-neutral continent by 2050 was perceived by some less-developed member states as an unfair economic burden, while labor groups criticized it as a form of unjust taxation. This reflects what Gramsci would call "restrictive hegemony," whereby participation is limited and concessions are selectively offered. For example, European labor unions were excluded from legislative processes, while capital interests engaged in frequent consultations with policymakers. Meanwhile, reluctant member states were granted longer timelines to achieve neutrality, as well as financial aid through the Just Transition Fund (JTF).

The COVID-19 pandemic further strained consensus. On March 16, 2020, Czech Prime Minister Andrej Babiš declared, *"Europe should forget about the Green Deal now and focus on the coronavirus instead"* (Gotev, 2020a). Similarly, Polish officials argued that pandemic recovery should take priority over climate policies, with Deputy Minister Janusz Kowalski suggesting that the EU Emissions Trading System (ETS) should be suspended or that Poland should be excluded (Gotev, 2020b). Romanian MEP Traian Băsescu echoed these concerns, claiming that the €10 billion allocated for Romania's transition was "ridiculous" and warning that the Green Deal could push countries toward leaving the EU (Simon, 2020). It is important to note that these criticisms preceded the pandemic. Leaders from Poland, Hungary, and the Czech Republic had already argued that the transition placed disproportionate burdens on developing members. As Polish Prime Minister Mateusz Morawiecki insisted, *"Poland must take a longer road to neutrality of carbon dioxide emissions than many other EU countries"* (McKinsey & Company, 2020). Hungarian Prime Minister Viktor Orbán opposed reallocating cohesion funds to climate goals, while Babiš maintained that only the most-affected states should benefit from the JTF (Bayer & Tamma, 2020).

The economic structures of these member states provide the basis for their resistance. Poland, for example, still derives one-third of its energy from coal, requiring investments of up to 2% of its GDP annually to achieve neutrality by 2050 (McKinsey & Company, 2020). To address these inequalities, the EU established the Just Transition Mechanism (JTM), of which the JTF is the first pillar, to support territories most affected by decarbonization (European Commission, 2025). The JTM funds projects ranging from clean energy and environmental rehabilitation to reskilling programs for displaced workers. This approach has already facilitated commitments from Greece, Spain, and Italy. Greece pledged to end coal-fired power by 2028, Italy is transforming its steelworks in Taranto, and Spain—after shutting down 26 coal mines in 2018—argued that JTF resources should reward proactive transition efforts, not only laggards (Bayer & Tamma, 2020). Nevertheless, the EGD has reignited class antagonisms across the EU. France's "Yellow Vests" (*Gilets Jaunes*) uprising, initially a protest against fuel taxes, evolved into a broader critique of inequality. Their slogan, *"Fin du monde, fins de mois / mêmes coupables, même combat"* ("end of the world, end of the month / same culprits, same fight"), underscored the perceived link between ecological and social struggles (Martin & Islar, 2020). EU officials, however, attempted to downplay the protests' implications for the EGD. Frans Timmermans, the Commission's Executive Vice-President, argued that the protests reflected poor political framing rather than opposition to climate targets (P., 2020).

Although the pandemic temporarily shifted attention away from climate policy, climate change remains an enduring challenge. With wage labor increasingly precarious after four decades of neoliberal reforms, skepticism toward the EGD persists among vulnerable social groups who fear bearing disproportionate costs. If the EU is serious about its climate ambitions, the Just Transition Mechanism must function not only as a structural adjustment tool but also as a mechanism for redressing long-standing socio-economic inequalities (Elkerbout et al., 2020).

China and Its Ecological Civilization Through "Going Green"

China's role within global capitalism is shaped by the distinctive manner in which it has been integrated into the international political economy. McNally (2012) characterizes this model as "Sino-capitalism," a system that is global in scope yet structurally different from Anglo-American capitalism. Whereas the latter is rooted in codified legal frameworks and transparent market rules, Sino-capitalism relies heavily on informal business networks and places the state at the center of directing and facilitating capital accumulation. Competing interpretations of China's rise reflect contrasting perspectives in political economy. For Bremmer (2010), Chinese state capitalism constitutes a challenge to the liberal free-market order, as its state-owned and state-backed corporations undermine global market norms and may inspire developing countries to turn away from neoliberal orthodoxy. Steinfeld (2010), by contrast, contends that China has not sought to overturn the Western-led order but has instead been absorbed into it through domestic market reforms and deep participation in transnational production networks.

Over the past decade, China's growth model has undergone profound structural pressures for change. These demands have stemmed not only from external actors, such as international organizations and foreign governments, but also from domestic business elites and political stakeholders. According to the World Bank (2023a, 2023b), China's investment-driven, export-led, low-cost manufacturing model has reached its limits, producing severe economic, social, and environmental strains. Moving forward, the country faces the need to rebalance toward services over manufacturing, consumption over investment, and low-carbon development over resource-intensive growth. This transformation requires strengthening regulatory institutions, reinforcing the rule of law, and expanding equitable access to public goods. At the same time, international pressures within the liberal order have pushed China to adopt more sustainable practices, including reducing pollution, managing natural resources responsibly, and transitioning to cleaner energy and transport systems. Domestically, localized environmental protests—though often framed as "not in my backyard" mobilizations—have since the early 2000s compelled the state to address escalating environmental concerns (Hoffmann & Ergenc, 2022).

Within this shifting context, President Xi Jinping launched two flagship initiatives in 2013: the "Silk Road Economic Belt" and the "21st Century Maritime Silk Road," collectively known as the Belt and Road Initiative (BRI), designed to connect 65 countries and 4.4 billion people across Asia, the Middle East, Russia, and Europe (Du, 2016). In 2014, Xi introduced the notion of the "new normal," which emphasized mid-to-high-speed growth that was more sustainable, efficient, and cost-effective (Xi, 2014). Embedded within this discourse, green and low-carbon development became central both to China's domestic modernization strategy and to the international orientation of the BRI. This was framed under the policy paradigm of "ecological civilization," aimed at tightening environmental regulation, reducing pollution, and fostering green innovation. Nonetheless, this discourse has been criticized for externalizing ecological costs by relocating polluting industries to less developed countries—for instance, the transfer of overcapacity from China's highly polluting cement sector to Tajikistan (Tracy, Shvarts, Simonov, & Babenko, 2017). In response, the Ministry of Commerce (MOFCOM) and the Ministry of Ecology and Environment (MEE) issued the 2021 Green Development Guidelines for Overseas Investment and Cooperation, urging Chinese firms to comply with international environmental standards in contexts where host-country regulations remain weak (Nedopil, De Boer, Danting, & Tang, 2021). This policy shift signaled a significant step toward aligning the BRI with global sustainability norms and underscored an evolving commitment to ecological governance in China's international engagement.

Importantly, China's embrace of green development is not purely ecological but also strategic. Green capitalism has provided new avenues for China to expand its global economic influence. The country has become the world's leading producer of renewable technologies, including wind power, electric vehicles, and waste recycling systems, surpassing the combined output of the United States and the European Union (Lan, Tang, & Hu, 2022). By adopting green capitalism's rules, China has secured first-mover advantages in emerging markets, positioning itself not only as a rule-taker but as a potential rule-maker in the evolving global order (Froggatt & Quiggin, 2021). Thus, while China's ecological civilization policy has contradictions, it represents perhaps the first historical moment in which China has the opportunity to reshape global capitalism on its own terms, rather than simply adapting to rules imposed by Western economies.

Russian Gas and the War on Ukraine: Geopolitics of Europe's Green Transition

The European Green Deal (EGD) extends far beyond a climate strategy confined to the EU level. Its scope demands coherence across multiple domains—including energy, trade, and social policy—while simultaneously shaping the Union's external political and economic relations. Among the most consequential events to affect the trajectory of the EGD was Russia's full-scale invasion of Ukraine. The war exposed the EU's deep structural vulnerability tied to its dependence on Russian natural gas, underscored Moscow's territorial ambitions in Ukraine, and intersected with Kyiv's longstanding aspiration for EU membership (Zaniewicz & Bieliszczuk, 2021).

This crisis reignited long-standing European debates over phasing out nuclear power, replacing coal with natural gas, and managing the geopolitical risks of reliance on Russian energy. These dynamics were particularly visible in the contentious negotiations surrounding the Nord Stream 2 (NS2) pipeline. For instance, Germany and the United States agreed to allocate $1 billion to support Ukraine's energy transition, yet Ukraine itself was excluded from the decision-making process. Critics warned that deepening Russian–German energy cooperation risked weakening Europe's capacity to resist Russian aggression, thereby emboldening Moscow's actions in the Donbas (Laffitte, 2021). By late 2021, analysts cautioned that NS2's completion enhanced Russia's leverage by enabling it to bypass Ukraine and secure direct access to European markets, despite Berlin's reassurances of support and the establishment of a green fund for Ukraine. Ukraine's concerns were ultimately validated when Russia launched its invasion in February 2022.

Despite Europe's reliance on Russian energy, EU leaders supported Ukraine and imposed wide-ranging sanctions on Russia (European Council, 2025). In the autumn of 2022, suspected sabotage of the Nord Stream 1 and 2 pipelines further destabilized the situation. On September 26, a leak was reported on NS2, followed the next day by two leaks on NS1. These incidents ended any remaining hope that Europe could receive Russian gas through the pipelines before winter (Carrel & Jacobsen, 2022). Kremlin spokesperson Dmitry Peskov described the explosions as "an act of terrorism, possibly on a state level" (Reuters, 2022). In response, President Vladimir Putin proposed redirecting supplies to Turkey to establish a regional gas hub (Soldatkin & Kobzeva, 2022). President Recep Tayyip Erdoğan welcomed the idea, viewing it as an opportunity to secure discounts and partial payments in Turkish lira. Reports indicated that Ankara requested a three-year deferral on 25% of its gas payments to Gazprom, while Moscow sought state guarantees and interest equal to Russia's key rate (Akman & Kozok, 2022). For Erdoğan, the proposal served not only economic goals but also his domestic political strategy, providing leverage ahead of the 2023 presidential elections.

The war thus functioned as both a stress test and a catalyst for the EGD. Short-term, European governments scrambled to secure alternative LNG supplies, reopen coal plants, and cushion households from soaring energy prices. Medium-term, the crisis accelerated electrification, renewables investment, and grid integration, while reopening debates about the role of gas and nuclear power in Europe's transition taxonomy. Regionally, Turkey's pursuit of hub status illustrated the shifting geopolitics of energy.

The New Hegemonic Race over Green Capitalist Transformation

This section situates *green trasformismo* within a wider hegemonic race over green capitalism. It first compares the strategic narratives of the United States, China, and the European Union (EU). It then examines green growth as the formal strategy of leading international organizations, before clarifying what green capitalism both encompasses and obscures. Finally, it surveys the financial and entrepreneurial infrastructures—green finance, green bonds, and green entrepreneurship—that are materializing this new regime, while noting the ever-present risk of greenwashing.

Green Race

In 2009, U.S. President Barack Obama cast climate policy squarely as industrial policy and national strategy. He declared that the nation leading in clean-energy innovation would dominate the twenty-first-century global economy, insisting that clean energy must become profitable, that its industries would generate secure, high-wage employment, and that the United States must seize this opportunity rather than yield it to others (Obama, 2009). This framing crystallized a distinctly

American narrative: climate action as a vehicle for economic renewal, a foundation for "non-offshorable" jobs, and a shield against the volatility of speculative growth. Although partisan polarization later constrained legislative follow-through, the strategic orientation endured. Clean energy was consistently promoted as profitable, innovation as the engine of prosperity, and industrial policy as the guarantor of re-shoring and supply-chain security—a distinctly American articulation of the broader doctrine of green growth.

In 2011, Chinese policymakers advanced a strikingly similar yet distinctly national narrative. The China Council for International Cooperation on Environment and Development (CCICED) urged Beijing to enter what it explicitly called a global "Green Race." Its report on the "Green Transformation of Economic Development Pattern" argued that rising populations, higher living standards, and rapid urbanization would intensify competition over resources and make green innovation indispensable. The 12th Five-Year Plan was identified as the launching pad for China's competitive positioning. Rejecting dependence on external pressures, the report asserted that China's course would be determined by its own leaders and citizens (CCICED, 2011). This vision aligned with a sweeping reorientation of industrial policy already underway: expansion into low-emission technologies, investment in renewables and battery production, and the development of exportable green solutions. By accelerating leadership in solar, wind, batteries, and electric vehicles, China positioned itself not only to mitigate climate risks but to claim the commanding heights of future industries.

The European Union, likewise, embedded climate policy within a framework of competitiveness and security well before the adoption of the European Green Deal. The 2006 Green Paper A European Strategy for Sustainable, Competitive and Secure Energy argued that the EU's institutional capacity, market scale, and regulatory expertise enabled it to lead the global search for sustainable energy solutions. It directly linked climate action to industrial competitiveness, regulatory predictability, and employment, while mandating a high-level group to explore ways to balance decarbonization with competitiveness (European Commission, 2006). This orientation flowed into the Europe 2020 strategy, which emphasized "smart, sustainable, and inclusive growth" (European Commission, 2010), and culminated in the European Green Deal, explicitly branded as "the EU's new growth strategy," with climate neutrality by mid-century as its central target (European Commission, 2019d). In this vision, climate action was less about sacrifice than about consolidating industrial advantage, projecting leadership, and safeguarding European energy security.

Taken together, these trajectories reveal how the United States, China, and the European Union each sought to harness the climate crisis as an opportunity to re-legitimize capitalism and reposition themselves within the global political economy. Each framed ecological transformation not as rupture but as industrial strategy: a means of seizing competitive advantage, securing geopolitical leverage, and setting the rules of transition. From a neo-Gramscian perspective, this "green race" should be understood as a struggle for hegemony within an emerging green capitalist order—an effort by competing powers to assemble alliances, institutionalize authority, and inscribe ecological modernization as the dominant common sense of the twenty-first century.

Competing Projects: United States, China, and the European Union

United States

A decade before the EGD, President Obama stated that *"the nation that leads in the creation of a clean-energy economy will lead the 21st-century global economy,"* thereby articulating a growth-through-decarbonization vision that hinged on innovation, manufacturing, and employment (Obama, 2009). Although partisan polarization slowed legislative follow-through, the underlying orientation remained intact. In recent years, industrial policy instruments have been redeployed to prioritize domestic supply chains, stimulate clean-manufacturing capacity, and safeguard strategic sectors. This techno-industrial approach reflects green-growth premises: align market incentives, mobilize private investment through public risk-sharing, and rely on innovation to drive efficiency, competitiveness, and emissions reductions.

European Union

Long before adopting the EGD, the EU's energy strategy linked climate action to competitiveness and security (European Commission, 2006). Europe 2020 translated these aims into policy—in particular, "smart" (innovation-led), "sustainable" (resource-efficient), and "inclusive" (high-employment and cohesive) growth (European Commission, 2010). The EGD then wove these strands together as a comprehensive growth strategy for the single market, committing to climate neutrality by mid-century while upgrading the industrial base and technologies. The European narrative, therefore, combines leadership by example (regulatory standards, carbon pricing, and diplomacy) with a project of internal market-making and innovation support.

China

China's experience with green transition is central to the hegemonic race over green capitalism. McNally (2012) terms this "Sino-capitalism", state-coordinated, networked accumulation, seen by some as a challenge to liberal globalization (Bremmer, 2010) and by others as incorporation into it (Steinfeld, 2010). In practice, Beijing has pivoted to strategic low-carbon sectors, solar, batteries, and electric vehicles, to advance industry and extend external leverage. This *green* turn is driven by external conditionality from financiers and trade partners and internal pressures from pollution, public-health concerns, and localized environmental protest (Hoffmann & Ergenç, 2022). In this perspective, China relied on the discourses of ecological civilization, a "green" Belt and Road narrative (Du, 2016), the 2014 "new normal" emphasizing quality over speed (Xi, 2014), and promoted 2021 guidelines steering overseas investment toward international standards (Nedopil, De Boer, Danting, & Tang, 2021). Industrial policy has yielded first-mover gains across clean-tech value chains (Lan, Tang, & Hu, 2022) and growing influence over upstream materials and midstream manufacturing. Yet contradictions persist, coal dependence, offshored pollution, and uneven overseas practices. In Gramscian terms, China is building a historic bloc in which green industrial leadership supports domestic legitimacy and projects rule-setting power, selectively incorporating ecological critique within a strategy of continued accumulation.

Green Growth as the Formal Strategy of Neoliberal Institutions

Well before the European Union embraced the concept, green growth had already been institutionalized by the world's major neoliberal organizations. The United Nations Environment Programme launched its Green Economy Initiative in 2008, followed by an OECD declaration in 2009 that commissioned the organization to craft an implementation strategy—culminating in Towards Green Growth (OECD 2011a). UNEP quickly reframed the "greening of economies" as a new driver of expansion (UNEP 2011), while the OECD depicted green growth as a seamless continuation of established economic orthodoxy—"with the added realization" that environmental and economic goals could be made mutually reinforcing (OECD 2011a). In the years that followed, green growth became the dominant vocabulary of green capitalism, buttressed by related discourses of the "green economy" and the "green transition." Collectively, these frameworks promised solutions to converging crises of resource scarcity, energy costs, food insecurity, water shortages, climate instability, and ecological degradation (Jänicke 2012; OECD 2011b; World Bank 2018).

By 2011, the OECD was defining green growth as a model of expansion that safeguards natural assets while ensuring their continued provision of resources and ecosystem services (OECD 2011a). The World Bank echoed this definition, portraying green growth as efficient in resource use, clean in reducing ecological impacts, and resilient in the face of natural hazards through integration of environmental management into disaster prevention (World Bank 2018). In Asia, a joint ESCAP–ADB–UNEP report advanced a similar vision, presenting green growth as low-carbon, resource-efficient, and socially inclusive development. It argued that "greening" growth could absorb mounting demands for food, housing, mobility, energy, and construction with fewer resources and lower emissions (ESCAP/ADB/UNEP 2021). Significantly, the report was categorical: "Green growth is a prerequisite for building a green economy," and the green economy itself was defined in terms of large-scale investment in renewables, low-carbon transport, sustainable agriculture and forestry, water-efficient infrastructure, fisheries management, and ecosystem restoration.

The institutional consolidation of green growth deepened with the founding of the Global Green Growth Institute (GGGI) in 2012, a treaty-based intergovernmental body designed to mainstream the agenda globally. Through platforms on green policy, green industry, and green finance, GGGI has sought to expand access to climate finance and mobilize multibillion-dollar investment commitments by 2030 (GGGI 2025). Within this global architecture of sustainability governance, the EU's European Green Deal appears less as an exception than as a regional expression of a broader consensus already shaped by neoliberal institutions. The orientation first took form with the Europe 2020 strategy (European Commission 2010) and was consolidated in the EGD, framed as "the EU's new growth strategy, aiming to transform the EU into a fairer and more prosperous society… with no net emissions of greenhouse gases by mid-century" (European Commission 2019d).

At its core, green growth denotes the restructuring of production toward resource- and energy-efficient systems (Jänicke 2012). As a constitutive element of the "green economy" or "low-carbon economy," it rests on the assumption that technological innovation, sustained R&D, and market-based instruments can deliver the decoupling of growth from both resource depletion and carbon emissions. The EU's Green Deal operationalizes this logic by privileging "green technologies"—those that improve efficiency, expand renewables, and reduce emissions—while simultaneously preserving Europe's industrial competitiveness (Ossewaarde & Ossewaarde-Lowtoo 2020). In this sense, green growth is not merely a policy framework but a hegemonic strategy: it stabilizes neoliberal capitalism under ecological crisis by rebranding accumulation as sustainability.

What Green Capitalism Contains and Conceals

At its heart, green capitalism rests on two propositions. First, climate change is treated as a *market failure*: carbon is mispriced, ecosystems are externalities, and innovation will correct these distortions if given the right price signals and regulatory certainty (Stern, 2007). Second, technological solutionism promises to *decouple* growth from resource use through efficiency gains, clean energy, and circularity (Jänicke, 2012). Both propositions legitimize "fixing" capitalism via greener rules and instruments rather than questioning the production and consumption imperatives that structure accumulation. In this vision, the problem is not capitalism per se, but an outdated rulebook.

Critical political economy scholarship raises doubts on several fronts. Carbon markets can displace responsibility, create speculative rents, and generate dubious offsets; they can also entrench corporate power by translating ecological obligations into tradable assets (Böhm, Misoczky, & Moog, 2012). Historical experience warns that deep *absolute* decoupling at the speed and scale required is rare, especially when globalized production networks distribute environmental costs unevenly and induce rebound effects. Sustainable development—what some term a "liberal environmentalist compromise"—often predicates environmental protection on preserving liberal market order, thereby narrowing the policy imagination (Falkner, 2012; Bernstein, 2001). From a neo-Gramscian standpoint, green capitalism can function as *trasformismo*: selectively incorporating ecological critiques (e.g., pollution control, efficiency, circularity) to renew hegemony while leaving core accumulation dynamics intact. Meanwhile, climate science underscores the anthropogenic nature of warming and the biophysical limits to growth (NASA, 2025).

Infrastructures of Green Capitalism: Entrepreneurship, Finance, and Greenwashing

Green Entrepreneurship

Green entrepreneurship is generally understood as business activity aimed at reducing environmental harm, ranging from conventional pollution control and resource efficiency to the adoption of low-carbon technologies and biodiversity conservation. It encompasses both the creation of entirely new "green products and services" and the greening of production methods for existing goods (Demirel, Li, Rentocchini, & Tamvada, 2019). The International Labour Organization (ILO) has endorsed this approach as vital for sustaining a green economy, highlighting its potential to generate green jobs and facilitate a just transition (ILO, 2020). While OECD countries continue to lead in many areas of green technology, emerging economies such as China and India are rapidly scaling up their capacities. Backed by international organizations and national policy frameworks, green entrepreneurship is gaining traction worldwide, embedding ecological objectives within start-up ecosystems and corporate innovation. Critics, however, caution that it may also be co-opted into established value chains—delivering incremental decarbonization at the margins while leaving growth-driven business models fundamentally unchallenged.

Green Finance

Closely tied to the agendas of green economy and green growth, green finance is promoted as the financial infrastructure enabling the transition. The European Investment Bank pioneered this field by issuing the first green bond in 2007, followed by the World Bank in 2008. Since then, heightened awareness of climate risk has spurred the rapid expansion of green debt markets, sustainability-linked loans, and transition instruments. Broadly defined, green finance refers to environmentally sustainable financing and investment, centered on two fundamental questions: (a) which sectors and activities qualify as "green" and therefore eligible for funding, and (b) how securities, products, and services are labeled, disclosed, and verified as such (Berrou, Dessertine, & Migliorelli, 2019; Berrou, Ciampoli, & Marini, 2019). Scholars further note distinctions across funding sources—ranging from bank lending and philanthropic or conventional venture capital to public funds—each carrying different expectations of risk, return, and time horizons (Migendt et al., 2017).

Illustrations of these dynamics abound. In the United States, the Californian "Green Wave" initiative mobilized major public pension funds (CalPERS and CalSTRS) toward clean-tech investments. In Germany, substantial capital flowed into solar and wind projects through policy-mediated financing mechanisms. At the EU level, the Sustainable Finance agenda—including the Taxonomy Regulation and new corporate disclosure standards—seeks to harness private capital while curbing "greenwashing" through standardized definitions, reporting, and oversight (European Commission, 2019a; Alves, 2023; Kavvadia, 2022). Reflecting this shift, in 2019 the European Investment Bank rebranded itself as the EU Climate Bank, pledging to phase out fossil-fuel lending after 2021 and to align its portfolio fully with the Paris Agreement's objectives.

Greenwashing Risks

As *green* labels boom, so do credibility problems. Without robust criteria and third-party verification, firms can overstate environmental benefits or misclassify activities, thereby legitimizing business-as-usual under a greener veneer. Studies of environmental claims in advertising show the frequency of vague or misleading assertions (Baum, 2012), while management research traces organizational drivers of greenwashing, including symbolic compliance and decoupling (Delmas & Burbano, 2011). This risk is inherent in market-mediated decarbonization: if environmental value is commodified without strong rules, enforcement, and sanctions, the appearance of transition can outrun the substance. Hence, effective public regulation, independent auditing, and penalties for misrepresentation are essential complements to market-based instruments.

Re-Centering Green Trasformismo

Bringing these strands together, *green trasformismo* names a specific dynamic within green capitalism's hegemonic race. Leading actors—the United States, China, and the EU—seek to consolidate domestic coalitions, forge international alignments, and define the *common sense* of ecological modernization. International organizations have furnished the shared vocabulary *green growth, green economy, just transition*) and the tools (taxonomies, disclosure regimes, financial standards) through which states and firms can coordinate. The result is not a linear convergence but a contested historical bloc, in which green industrial strategies are used to legitimate accumulation, secure consent, and extend geopolitical influence.

From this vantage, the promise of green capitalism rests on a bet: that technological innovation, guided by smart regulation and financed at scale, can deliver absolute decoupling fast enough to remain within planetary boundaries while preserving competitiveness, employment, and social cohesion. The critique, equally visible in the European debates around the EGD, the U.S. polarization over climate policy, and China's externalization tensions, is that such a project risk reproducing uneven development and class asymmetries unless it is coupled with robust redistribution, worker-protective transition policies, and meaningful democratic participation in agenda-setting.

In short, the *new hegemonic race* is not merely rhetorical competition over who gets to brand the green transition. It is a struggle over the institutions, standards, and investments that will organize the next phase of global capitalism; over who bears the costs of adjustment and who reaps the rents from new technological monopolies; and over whether ecological limits are addressed through transformative social change or managed through incremental efficiency within existing hierarchies. The European Green Deal, U.S. industrial climate policy, and China's ecological-civilization package each exemplify an attempt to construct hegemony by selectively incorporating ecological critique into projects of growth and state leadership. Whether this constitutes a pathway beyond crisis or a stabilization of business-as-usual in greener hues remains, decisively, a political question.

CONCLUSION: GREEN TRASFORMISMO AND THE HEGEMONIC CONTEST

This chapter has argued that a neo-Gramscian lens is indispensable for making sense of climate politics in the present conjuncture. Far from signaling a rupture with capitalist social relations, *green capitalism* operates as a hegemonic project that seeks to reconcile the doctrine of infinite growth with ecological limits. Its central promise, *decoupling* prosperity from emissions via innovation, efficiency, and market instruments, has been universalized through the discourse of *green growth*, promoted by multinational firms, international organizations, and supportive states (European Commission, 2019a). Naturalized as *common sense*, this discourse captures consent for a reorganization of capitalism while marginalizing more transformative programs associated with climate justice or degrowth (Brand & Wissen, 2021).

From this perspective, the European Green Deal (EGD) functions as a state-forming and bloc-building initiative. It couples an expansive legislative complex (climate law, ETS reform, CBAM, sustainable-finance standards, and a Just Transition architecture) with a narrative of shared destiny, President von der Leyen's "*man on the moon moment*", that aims to make growth-through-decarbonization appear both desirable and inevitable (European Commission, 2019b). In Gramsci's terms, the EGD is an effort to build a *historic bloc*: aligning segments of capital, finance, parts of organized labor, expert networks, and civil society behind a green accumulation strategy while projecting EU rule-making beyond its borders.

Yet hegemony is never uncontested. Environmental movements, critical intellectuals, and actors in the Global South articulate alternative common senses that expose the exclusions and externalizations embedded in green capitalism (Nulman, 2015; Swyngedouw, 2010). These counter-hegemonic arguments maintain that decarbonization without redistribution entrenches uneven development, and that market-centric fixes reproduce the very hierarchies that produced the crisis.

Situating Europe within the wider geopolitical economy explains the scale of hegemonic struggle over global green transition. The United States is reassembling a techno-industrial approach under diverged conditions, re-shoring supply chains, subsidizing clean manufacturing, and translating climate policy into a jobs-and-competitiveness narrative. China is consolidating leadership across strategic green value chains while projecting a doctrine of *ecological civilization*, supported by state coordination and industrial policy. The EU pulls regulatory power, standards, taxonomies, border adjustments, to discipline markets in a greener way and to anchor decarbonization to the single market. Meanwhile, multilateral organizations normalize *green growth* through metrics, indicators, and *best practices*, while green finance provides channels for capital mobilization, alongside the hazards of *greenwashing*. Together, these dynamics amount to a hegemonic race over green capitalism: a contest to define standards, infrastructures, and value chains that coordinate investment and legitimate accumulation.

From a neo-Gramscian perspective, this conjuncture is best analyzed by the notion of green trasformismo. As Gramsci used *trasformismo* to describe how ruling groups incorporate and neutralize elements of opposition, here dominant actors absorb ecological critiques—sustainability, resilience, circularity, and modify them as instruments of renewed leadership. The result is a *passive revolution* where significant policy change occurs without a transformation of ownership structures or growth imperatives. Green jobs and just-transition funds are meaningful developments; disclosure rules and taxonomies improve transparency; innovation policy accelerates organization. But without deep democratization of decision-making, binding equity mechanisms, and public provisioning in the foundational economy, these advances can only stabilize a greener version of the status quo (Brand & Wissen, 2021; Swyngedouw, 2010).

What follows from this analysis for climate mitigation and for the future of capitalist relations is that the consolidation of a green-growth common sense will indeed accelerate the deployment of low-carbon technologies and policies. Yet the durability of this transition depends on real transformations in energy, industry, mobility, and housing, rather than the financial *greening* of portfolios or symbolic market adjustments. Integrity in mitigation requires not only subsidizing renewables but also phasing down fossil fuels, investing in infrastructures such as grids and storage, and actively governing demand. Without these material shifts, acceleration risks becoming superficial, leaving intact the structural drivers of ecological crisis.

Equally important is the question of social embedding. Decarbonization cannot be pursued as a technocratic project alone, but must be tied to wages, prices, and the everyday lives of workers and communities. If carbon pricing, industrial policies, or trade mechanisms impose disproportionate burdens without corresponding protections, such as wage supports, targeted transfers, labor standards, and public ownership arrangements, the legitimacy of climate policy will fade over time. The experience of the Gilets Jaunes protests illustrates that distributive conflicts can derail ambitious environmental measures if justice is treated as an add-on rather than as a constitutive element of the transition. Climate policies must therefore be designed as social policies as much as environmental ones.

Finally, the struggle over green capitalism is geopolitical as well as social. Mitigation will falter if it is achieved by externalizing costs to the Global South, where concessional finance, technology access, and loss-and-damage arrangements are not optional but necessary for legitimacy. At the same time, the capacity to *write the rules* of green capitalism, setting taxonomies, border adjustment mechanisms, and standards, will determine who captures value in global supply chains. Here the EU's regulatory power, the United States' techno-industrial scaling, and China's manufacturing and state coordination model collide in shaping the terms of the new economy. From a neo-Gramscian perspective, this hegemonic contest narrows the horizon of possibilities to market-mediated solutions, while counter-hegemonic project, centered on climate justice, public provisioning, and democratic ownership, remain marginalized. The European Green Deal exemplifies both the strengths and contradictions of green trasformismo: it has already begun to reorder investment and legislation, yet its future hinges on the pace and depth of emissions decline, the distribution of costs and benefits, and the degree of democratization in decision-making. Whether this moment becomes one of passive renewal or genuine transformation will depend on whether counter-hegemonic openings can be widened into viable alternatives beyond green capitalism.

ACKNOWLEDGEMENT

The author acknowledges that this chapter draws on and extends material from her doctoral dissertation, *European Green Deal from a Neo-Gramscian Perspective: A Case of Green Trasformismo* (Durmaz, 2024), submitted to the Graduate School of Social Sciences, Middle East Technical University (Ankara, Türkiye).

REFERENCES

Akman, B., & Kozok, F. (2022, October 14). Erdogan welcomes Putin's idea to make Turkey a gas hub. *Bloomberg*. https://www.bloomberg.com/news/articles/2022-10-14/erdogan-welcomes-putin-s-idea-to-make-turkey-a-natural-gas-hub

Ayers, A. J. (2008). *Gramsci, political economy, and international relations theory: Modern princes and naked emperors*. Palgrave Macmillan.

Aykut, S. C., & Dahan, A. (2022). Geopolitical boomerang: Can we still hope to meet the climate challenge? *GREEN*, *2*(1), 31–38. DOI: 10.1016/j.green.2022.100031

Aykut, S. C., & Maertens, L. (2022). The climatization of global politics: Introduction to the special issue. In Aykut, S. C., Morena, E., & Foyer, J. (Eds.), *The climatization of global politics* (pp. 1–18). Springer., DOI: 10.1007/978-3-030-88551-9_1

Aykut, S. C., Morena, E., & Foyer, J. (Eds.). (2022a). *The climatization of global politics*. Springer., DOI: 10.1007/978-3-030-88551-9

Aykut, S. C., Pavenstädt, C. N., Datchoua-Tirvaudey, A., D'Amico, E., Braun, M., Hinks, E. K., . . . Rödder, S. (2022b). *Circles of global climate governance* (CSSR Working Paper No. 2). University of Hamburg, Center for Sustainable Science Research. https://www.cen.uni-hamburg.de/en/cen-forschung/working-papers/working-paper-2.pdf

Baum, L. M. (2012). It's not easy being green. Or is it? A content analysis of environmental claims in magazine advertisements from the United States and United Kingdom. *Environmental Communication*, *6*(4), 423–440. DOI: 10.1080/17524032.2012.724022

Bayer, L., & Tamma, P. (2020, July 9). EU countries scrap for cash from new green scheme. *Politico*. https://www.politico.eu/article/eu-countries-scrap-for-just-transition-cash/

Bernstein, S. (2001). *The compromise of liberal environmentalism*. Columbia University Press.

Bieler, A., & Morton, A. D. (2003). Globalisation, the state and class struggle: A 'Critical Economy' engagement with Open Marxism. *British Journal of Politics and International Relations*, *5*(4), 467–499. DOI: 10.1111/1467-856X.00114

Bieler, A., & Morton, A. D. (2004). A critical theory route to hegemony, world order and historical change: Neo-Gramscian perspectives in international relations. *Capital and Class*, *28*(1), 85–113. DOI: 10.1177/030981680408200106

Biermann, F., & Pattberg, P. (2008). Global environmental governance: Taking stock, moving forward. *Annual Review of Environment and Resources*, *33*, 277–294. DOI: 10.1146/annurev.environ.33.050707.085733

Blühdorn, I. (2009). *Reinventing green politics: Environmentalism and the pursuit of sustainability*. Routledge.

Bodansky, D. (2016). The Paris climate change agreement: A new hope? *The American Journal of International Law*, *110*(2), 288–319. DOI: 10.5305/amerjintelaw.110.2.0288

Böhm, S., Misoczky, M. C., & Moog, S. (2012). Greening capitalism? A Marxist critique of carbon markets. *Organization Studies*, *33*(11), 1617–1638. DOI: 10.1177/0170840612463326

Brand, U., & Wissen, M. (2021). *The imperial mode of living: Everyday life and the ecological crisis of capitalism*. Verso.

Bremmer, I. (2010). The end of the free market: Who wins the war between states and corporations? *European View*, *9*(2), 249–252. DOI: 10.1007/s12290-010-0124-y

Brüggemann, M., Elgesem, D., Bienzeisler, N., Gertz, H. D., & Walter, S. (2020). Mutual group polarization in the blogosphere: Tracking the hoax discourse on climate change. *International Journal of Communication*, *14*, 1026–1052.

Buci-Glucksmann, C. (1980). *Gramsci and the state*. Lawrence & Wishart.

Burchell, J. (2002). *The evolution of green politics*. Earthscan.

Carrington, D. (2013, October 16). David Attenborough: Anyone who thinks you can have infinite growth on a finite planet is either a madman or an economist. *The Guardian*. https://www.theguardian.com/environment/2013/oct/16/attenborough-poorer-countries-concerned-environment

CCICED (China Council for International Cooperation on Environment and Development). (2011). *Development mechanism and policy innovation of China's green economy*. CCICED.

Chung, F. (2019, September 24). Nearly 30 years before Greta Thunberg, a 12-year-old girl shamed world leaders at the United Nations. *News.com.au.* https://www.news.com.au/technology/environment/climate-change/nearly-30-years-before-greta-thunberg-a-12yearold-girl-shamed-world-leaders-at-the-united-nations/news-story/7ccf24544d7f47e4d6cb0da1ea8a0f51

Cox, R. W. (1981). Social forces, states and world orders: Beyond international relations theory. *Millennium, 10*(2), 126–155. DOI: 10.1177/03058298810100020501

Cox, R. W. (1983). Gramsci, hegemony and international relations: An essay in method. *Millennium, 12*(2), 162–175. DOI: 10.1177/03058298830120020701

Cox, R. W. (1987). *Production, power and world order: Social forces in the making of history.* Columbia University Press.

Crehan, K. (2016). *Gramsci's common sense: Inequality and its narratives.* Duke University Press.

D'Alisa, G., & Kallis, G. (2016). A political ecology of maladaptation: Insights from a Gramscian theory of the state. *Global Environmental Change, 38*, 230–242. DOI: 10.1016/j.gloenvcha.2016.03.006

Delmas, M. A., & Burbano, V. C. (2011). The drivers of greenwashing. *California Management Review, 54*(1), 64–87. DOI: 10.1525/cmr.2011.54.1.64

Demirel, P., Li, Q. C., Rentocchini, F., & Tamvada, J. P. (2019). Born to be green: New insights into the economics and management of green entrepreneurship. *Small Business Economics, 52*(4), 759–771. DOI: 10.1007/s11187-017-9933-z

Du, M. M. (2016). China's "One Belt, One Road" initiative: Context, focus, institutions, and implications. *The Chinese Journal of Global Governance, 2*(1), 30–43. DOI: 10.1163/23525207-12340009

Durmaz, G. (2024). *European Green Deal from a Neo-Gramscian perspective: A case of green trasformismo* (Doctoral dissertation, Middle East Technical University). Middle East Technical University Open Access Repository. https://open.metu.edu.tr/handle/11511/109116

Elkerbout, M., Egenhofer, C., Núñez Ferrer, J., Catuti, M., Kustova, I., & Rizos, V. (2020). *The European Green Deal after Corona: Implications for EU climate policy* (CEPS Policy Insights 2020-06). CEPS. https://www.ceps.eu/ceps-publications/the-european-green-deal-after-corona/ ESCAP/ADB/UNEP. (2012). *Green growth, resources and resilience: Environmental sustainability in Asia and the Pacific.* United Nations ESCAP & Asian Development Bank.

ESCAP/ADB/UNEP. (2021). *Green growth, resources and resilience: Environmental sustainability in Asia and the Pacific*. United Nations ESCAP & Asian Development Bank. https://www.unescap.org/sites/default/files/Full-report.pdf

European Commission. (2006). *Green paper: A European strategy for sustainable, competitive and secure energy* (COM(2006) 105 final). Author. https://europa.eu/documents/comm/green_papers/pdf/com2006_105_en.pdf

European Commission. (2010). *Europe 2020: A strategy for smart, sustainable and inclusive growth* (COM(2010) 2020). Author.

European Commission. (2019a). *The European Green Deal* (COM/2019/640 final). Author.

European Commission. (2019b). Press remarks by President von der Leyen on the occasion of the adoption of the European Green Deal Communication. *Press corner*. European Commission. https://ec.europa.eu/commission/presscorner/detail/en/speech_19_6749

European Commission. (2019c). Turning challenge into opportunity on the course to becoming the first climate-neutral continent [Press remarks]. *Press corner*. European Commission. https://ec.europa.eu/commission/presscorner/detail/en/ac_19_6778

European Commission. (2019d). *Industry and the Green Deal*. Author. https://commission.europa.eu/strategy-and-policy/priorities-2019-2024/european-green-deal/industry-and-green-deal_en

European Commission. (2025). *Just transition funding sources*. Author. https://commission.europa.eu/strategy-and-policy/priorities-2019-2024/european-green-deal/finance-and-green-deal/just-transition-mechanism/just-transition-funding-sources_en

European Council. (2025). *EU sanctions against Russia explained*. https://www.consilium.europa.eu/en/policies/sanctions/restrictive-measures-against-russia-over-ukraine/sanctions-against-russia-explained/#sanctions

Falkner, R. (2012). Global environmentalism and the greening of international society. *International Affairs*, *88*(3), 503–522. DOI: 10.1111/j.1468-2346.2012.01085.x

Falkner, R. (2016). The Paris Agreement and the new logic of international climate politics. *International Affairs*, *92*(5), 1107–1125. DOI: 10.1111/1468-2346.12708

Forgacs, D. (Ed.). (1988). *A Gramsci reader*. Lawrence & Wishart.

Froggatt, A., & Quiggin, D. (2021). *China, EU and US cooperation on climate and energy*. Chatham House. https://www.chathamhouse.org/sites/default/files/2021-03/2021-03-26-china-eu-uscooperation-froggatt.pdf

Gill, S. (1993). Epistemology, ontology and the 'Italian School. In Gill, S. (Ed.), *Gramsci, historical materialism and international relations* (pp. 21–48). Cambridge University Press.

Gill, S. (1995). Globalisation, market civilisation, and disciplinary neoliberalism. *Millennium, 24*(3), 399–423. DOI: 10.1177/03058298950240030801

Gotev, G. (2020a, March 17). Czech PM urges EU to ditch Green Deal amid virus. *Euractiv*. https://www.euractiv.com/section/energy-environment/news/czech-pm-urges-eu-to-ditch-green-deal-amid-virus/

Gotev, G. (2020b, March 17). EU should scrap emissions trading scheme, Polish official says. *Euractiv*. https://www.euractiv.com/section/emissions-trading-scheme/news/eu-should-scrap-emissions-trading-scheme-polish-official-says/

Gramsci, A. (1971). *Selections from the prison notebooks* (Hoare, Q., & Smith, G. N., Eds. & Trans.). International Publishers.

Gramsci, A. (1977). *Selections from political writings, 1910–1920 (Q. Hoare* (Matthews, J. Ed. & Trans.). Lawrence & Wishart.

Gramsci, A. (1985). *Selections from cultural writings* (D. Forgacs & G. Nowell-Smith, Eds.; W. Boelhower, Trans.). Lawrence & Wishart.

Gramsci, A. (1995). *Further selections from the prison notebooks* (Boothman, D., Ed. & Trans.). Lawrence & Wishart.

Gramsci, A. (1996). *Prison notebooks* (Vol. 2; Buttigieg, J. A., Ed. & Trans.). Columbia University Press.

Gramsci, A., Hoare, Q., & Nowell-Smith, G. (1971). *Selections from the Prison Notebooks of Antonio Gramsci*. International Publishers.

Hadden, J. (2015). *Networks in contention: The divisive politics of climate change*. Cambridge University Press.

Hall, S. (1986). Gramsci's relevance for the study of race and ethnicity. *The Journal of Communication Inquiry, 10*(2), 5–27. DOI: 10.1177/019685998601000202

Han, H., & Ahn, S. W. (2020). Youth mobilization to stop global climate change: Narratives and impact. *Sustainability, 12*(10), 4127. DOI: 10.3390/su12104127

Hermwille, L. (2022). The 2021 Glasgow Climate Pact—A fragile victory for multilateralism. *Climate Policy*, *22*(2), 147–152. DOI: 10.1080/14693062.2022.2036952

Hesketh, C., & Morton, A. D. (2014). Spaces of uneven development and class struggle in Bolivia: Transformation or trasformismo? *Antipode*, *46*(1), 149–169. DOI: 10.1111/anti.12033

Hoffmann, C., & Ergenc, C. (2022). A greening dragon in the desert? China's role in the geopolitical ecology of decarbonisation in the Eastern Mediterranean. *Journal of Balkan & Near Eastern Studies*, *24*(5), 1–20. DOI: 10.1080/19448953.2022.2067424

ILO (International Labour Organization). (2020). *Green entrepreneurship: Creating green jobs through sustainable enterprise development*. ILO. https://www.ilo.org/wcmsp5/groups/public/---ed_emp/---emp_ent/documents/publication/wcms_250688.pdf

Inhofe, J. (2012). *The greatest hoax: How the global warming conspiracy threatens your future*. WND Books.

Jänicke, M. (2012). "Green growth": From a growing eco-industry to economic sustainability. *Energy Policy*, *48*, 13–21. DOI: 10.1016/j.enpol.2012.04.045

Keohane, R. O., & Raustiala, K. (2010). Toward a post-Kyoto climate change architecture: A political analysis. In Dryzek, J. S., Norgaard, R. B., & Schlosberg, D. (Eds.), *The Oxford handbook of climate change and society* (pp. 103–122). Oxford University Press.

Laffitte, T. (2021, November 29). Europe's energy transition: Ukraine's salvation? *Green European Journal*. https://www.greeneuropeanjournal.eu/europes-energy-transition-ukraines-salvation/

Lan, Q., Tang, W., & Hu, Q. (2022). Estimation of China's green investment efficiency in Belt and Road countries based on SBM-Undesirable Model and Malmquist Index Model. *Frontiers in Energy Research*, *9*, 907. DOI: 10.3389/fenrg.2021.778907

Marlon, J. R., Howe, P. D., Mildenberger, M., Leiserowitz, A., & Wang, X. (2018). Yale Climate Opinion Maps 2018. *Yale Program on Climate Change Communication*. https://climatecommunication.yale.edu/visualizations-data/ycom-us-2018/

Martin, M., & Islar, M. (2020). The "end of the world" vs. the "end of the month": Understanding social resistance to sustainability transition agendas, a lesson from the Yellow Vests in France. *Sustainability Science*, *16*(3), 601–614. DOI: 10.1007/s11625-020-00844-0

McKinsey & Company. (2020). *Carbon-neutral Poland 2050: Turning a challenge into an opportunity*. McKinsey & Company. https://www.mckinsey.com/~/media/McKinsey/Industries/Electric%20Power%20and%20Natural%20Gas/Our%20Insights/Carbon%20neutral%20Poland%202050%20Turning%20a%20challenge%20into%20an%20opportunity/Carbon-neutral-Poland-2050.pdf

McNally, C. A. (2012). Sino-capitalism: China's reemergence and the international political economy. *World Politics*, *64*(4), 741–776. DOI: 10.1017/S0043887112000146

Migendt, M., Polzin, F., Schock, F., Täube, F. A., & von Flotow, P. (2017). Beyond venture capital: The finance-innovation-policy nexus in cleantech. *Industrial and Corporate Change*, *26*(6), 973–996. DOI: 10.1093/icc/dtx018

Milman, O. (2019, September 23). Greta Thunberg condemns world leaders in emotional speech at UN. *The Guardian*. https://www.theguardian.com/environment/2019/sep/23/greta-thunberg-speech-un-2019-address

Moore, P. (2007). *Globalisation and labour struggle in Asia: A neo-Gramscian critique of South Korea's political economy*. Bloomsbury.

Morton, A. D. (2007). *Unravelling Gramsci: Hegemony and passive revolution in the global economy*. Pluto Press.

Morton, A. D. (2010). The continuum of passive revolution. *Capital and Class*, *34*(3), 315–342. DOI: 10.1177/0309816810378294

Mouffe, C. (1979). Hegemony and ideology in Gramsci. In Mouffe, C. (Ed.), *Gramsci and Marxist theory* (pp. 168–204). Routledge & Kegan Paul.

Müller-Rommel, F. (2022). The "lifespan" of Green parties in Western Europe: An evaluation. In *Parties, institutions and preferences: The shape and impact of partisan politics* (pp. 123–148). Springer Fachmedien Wiesbaden., DOI: 10.1007/978-3-658-34553-8_7

NASA. (2025). *What is climate change?* NASA. https://climate.nasa.gov/global-warming-vs-climate-change/

Nedopil, C., De Boer, D., Danting, F., & Tang, Y. (2021, August 18). What China's new guidelines on "green development" mean for the Belt and Road. *China Dialogue*. https://chinadialogue.net/en/business/what-chinas-new-guidelines-on-green-development-mean-for-the-belt-and-road/

Newell, P. (2019). Trasformismo or transformation? The global political economy of energy transitions. *Review of International Political Economy*, *26*(1), 25–48. DOI: 10.1080/09692290.2018.1511448

Nulman, E. (2015). *Climate change and social movements: Civil society and the development of national climate change policy*. Palgrave Macmillan.

Obama, B. H. (2009, June 27). Weekly presidential address [Video]. *C-SPAN*. https://www.c-span.org/video/?287322-101/weekly-presidential-address

OECD. (2011a). *Towards green growth: A summary for policymakers*. OECD.

OECD. (2011b). *Towards green growth: Monitoring progress—OECD indicators*. OECD.

Ossewaarde, M., & Ossewaarde-Lowtoo, R. (2020). The EU's Green Deal: A third alternative to green growth and degrowth? *Sustainability*, *12*(23), 9825. DOI: 10.3390/su12239825

Paterson, B. (2009). Trasformismo at the World Trade Organization. In Bieler, A., & Morton, A. D. (Eds.), *Gramsci and global politics* (pp. 56–71). Routledge.

Poguntke, T. (2002). Green parties in national governments: From protest to acquiescence? *Environmental Politics*, *11*(1), 133–145. DOI: 10.1080/714000579

Poulantzas, N. (1978). *State, power, socialism* (Camiller, P., Trans.). Verso.

Reuters. (2022, September 29). Kremlin says Nord Stream incidents look like state-sponsored "terrorism." *Reuters*. https://www.reuters.com/business/energy/kremlin-says-nord-stream-gas-leaks-look-like-act-terrorism-2022-09-29/

Rosenstone, S. J., Behr, R. L., & Lazarus, E. H. (2018). *Third parties in America: Citizen response to major party failure* (2nd ed.). Princeton University Press.

Rousell, D., & Cutter-Mackenzie-Knowles, A. (2020). A systematic review of climate change education: Giving children and young people a 'voice' and a 'hand' in redressing climate change. *Children's Geographies*, *18*(2), 191–208. DOI: 10.1080/14733285.2019.1705010

Simon, F. (2020, March 17). Basescu: European Green Deal risks pushing "two or three countries" towards EU exit. *Euractiv*. https://www.euractiv.com/section/energy-environment/interview/basescu-european-green-deal-risks-pushing-two-or-three-countries-towards-eu-exit/

Simon, R. (1982). *Gramsci's political thought: An introduction*. Lawrence & Wishart.

Soldatkin, V., & Kobzeva, O. (2022, October 12). Putin moots gas hub in Turkey with Nord Stream supplies. *Reuters*. https://www.reuters.com/world/europe/putin-moots-major-gas-hub-turkey-with-nord-stream-supplies-2022-10-12/

Steinfeld, E. S. (2010). *Playing our game: Why China's rise doesn't threaten the West*. Oxford University Press.

Stephen, M. (2011). Globalisation and resistance: Struggles over commonsense in the global political economy. *Review of International Studies, 37*(1), 209–228. DOI: 10.1017/S0260210510000530

Stern, N. (2007). *The economics of climate change: The Stern review*. Cambridge University Press.

Stevenson, K., & Peterson, N. (2015). Motivating action through fostering climate change hope and concern and avoiding despair among adolescents. *Sustainability, 8*(1), 6. DOI: 10.3390/su8010006

Svensson, A., & Wahlström, M. (2023). Climate change or what? Prognostic framing by Fridays for Future protesters. *Social Movement Studies, 22*(1), 1–22. DOI: 10.1080/14742837.2022.2107954

Swyngedouw, E. (2010). Apocalypse forever? Post-political populism and the spectre of climate change. *Theory, Culture & Society, 27*(2–3), 213–232. DOI: 10.1177/0263276409358728

Thomas, P. (2009). *The Gramscian moment: Philosophy, hegemony and Marxism*. Brill.

Trihartono, A., Viartasiwi, N., & Nisya, C. (2020). The giant step of tiny toes: Youth impact on the securitization of climate change. *IOP Conference Series: Earth and Environmental Science, 485*(1), 012007. IOP Publishing. https://doi.org/DOI: 10.1088/1755-1315/485/1/012007

UNEP (United Nations Environment Programme). (2011). *Towards a green economy: Pathways to sustainable development and poverty eradication*. UNEP.

UNFCCC. (1992). *United Nations Framework Convention on Climate Change*. United Nations.

UNFCCC. (1997). *Kyoto Protocol to the United Nations Framework Convention on Climate Change*. United Nations.

UNFCCC. (2015). *Paris Agreement*. United Nations. https://unfccc.int/sites/default/files/english_paris_agreement.pdf

United Nations. Climate Change. (2025). *Emissions trading*. https://unfccc.int/process/the-kyoto-protocol/mechanisms/emissions-trading

United Nations Development Programme. (2022). What are carbon markets and why are they important? *UNDP Climate Promise*. https://climatepromise.undp.org/news-and-stories/what-are-carbon-markets-and-why-are-they-important

United Nations Development Programme. (2025). *Carbon justice for all: How carbon markets can advance equitable climate action globally*. UNDP Climate Promise. https://climatepromise.undp.org/news-and-stories/carbon-justice-all-how-carbon-markets-can-advance-equitable-climate-action

van Apeldoorn, B. (2002). *Transnational capitalism and the struggle over European integration*. Routledge.

van Apeldoorn, B., & Horn, L. (2018). *Critical political economy*. Freie Universität Berlin.

van Haute, E. (2016). Green parties in Europe. In van Haute, E. (Ed.), *Green parties in Europe* (pp. 1–14). Routledge.

Watts, J. (2019, April 23). The Greta Thunberg effect: At last, MPs focus on climate change. *The Guardian*. https://www.theguardian.com/environment/2019/apr/23/greta-thunberg

World Bank. (2018, May 9). *Green growth for sustainable development* [Video]. World Bank. https://www.worldbank.org/en/news/video/2018/05/09/green-growth-for-sustainable-development

World Bank. (2023a, April 20). *China: Overview – Context*. World Bank. https://www.worldbank.org/en/country/china/overview

World Bank. (2023b, April 20). *China: Overview – Strategy*. World Bank. https://www.worldbank.org/en/country/china/overview#2

Wullweber, J. (2019). Constructing hegemony in global politics: A discourse-theoretical approach to policy analysis. *Administrative Theory & Praxis*, *41*(2), 148–167. DOI: 10.1080/10841806.2019.1593544

Xi's. "new normal" theory. (2014, November 10). *China.org.cn*. http://www.china.org.cn/world/2014-11/10/content_34012582.htm

Zaniewicz, M., & Bieliszczuk, B. (2021). *Implications of Nord Stream 2's completion for Ukraine*. Polish Institute of International Affairs. https://pism.pl/publications/implications-of-nord-stream-2s-completion-for-ukraine

KEY TERMS AND DEFINITIONS

Common Sense: For Gramsci, is the everyday worldview sedimented through history, shaped by philosophy, science, and social struggle. It is plural and contradictory, functioning both as a site of hegemonic domination and as a source of alternative "good sense" that can resist it.

Green Capitalism: Frames climate change as a market failure to be corrected through proper carbon pricing, regulatory certainty, and technological innovation. It seeks to "fix" capitalism by greening its rules and instruments, without questioning the deeper imperatives of growth and accumulation.

Green Growth: Is the policy agenda that aims to reconcile economic expansion with ecological sustainability by decoupling output from resource use and emissions. It emphasizes efficiency, clean technologies, and resilience, promising prosperity through ecological modernization while retaining the growth paradigm.

Hegemony: Is the process by which a dominant class secures legitimacy by presenting its own interests as the common good. It is not fixed but continuously reshaped through consent, ideological leadership, and the neutralization of opposition.

Passive Revolution: Describes significant reforms that stabilize the existing order without transforming ownership structures or growth imperatives.

Trasformismo: As its mechanism, incorporates and neutralizes oppositional ideas and actors, converting them into supports for renewed hegemonic leadership.

Chapter 2
Eco-Social Policy and the Risk of Concept Stretching

Eugene Nulman
https://orcid.org/0000-0002-3358-9144
University of Florence, Italy

ABSTRACT

In the context of international processes of addressing climate change where we are increasingly seeing negative social impacts of climate policy, the concept of the 'eco-social' has been seen as critical as it both addresses social and environmental goals. However, it suffers from concept stretching as discussed by Sartori. First, environmental politics, across different waves and ideologies, has incorporated both social and environmental benefits into proposed policies and practices, making all such policies effectively "eco-social" based on the consensus definition. Furthermore, as political domains are increasingly expected to address the environmental question due to the rising salience of climate change, social policies were increasingly asked to incorporate environmental and climate considerations. To address the problem of concept stretching, we turn to Sartori's ladder of abstraction (1970) and present two solutions: intension increase and rung descension. This chapter argues that the latter is the best way to avoid concept stretching for eco-social policy.

INTRODUCTION

In the context of the international system of addressing climate change, various actors have noted that focusing on short-term social wellbeing in the form of economic growth undermines policy goals for addressing climate change (Hickel, 2019)

DOI: 10.4018/979-8-3373-1707-6.ch002

while some climate policies are challenged for undermining social conditions, such as through what is increasingly becoming referred to as climate colonialism. Considering the need to address both environmental and social challenges at the same time, the growth of the concept of the eco-social and eco-social policy is important and encouraging as its consensus definition entails the addressing of both challenges.

Like many concepts, eco-social has been modified and adapted within and across disciplines to mean different things in different contexts. Whether it is radical shifts in policy change that conflicts with capitalism's drive for economic growth (e.g., Hancock, 2015) and radical shifts in perspectives concerning ecological, social, and material embodiment (Merz et al., 2021), or simply a mix of environmental and social concerns (e.g., Matthies et al., 2000) and small-scale reforms (e.g., Gough et al., 2012). It is also used to critically challenge existing views on dealing with environmental and social issues and is sometimes a concept used within critical approaches. I want to caution against its use primarily because I believe that the term 'eco-social' risks being conceptually stretched to be not so meaningful and has the potential to be coopted.

Defining 'eco-social' has proven to be a difficult challenge, even when focusing solely on the domains of politics, broadly defined, or policy, more specifically. Previously, some have noted the lack of a standard or precise definition (Bell, 2016, p. 72; Gugushvili & Otto, 2023) and, as Plumhans notes, "authors generally fail to describe in greater detail what is meant by eco-social policies and what differentiates them from other types of policies" (Plumhans, 2021). In addition, sometimes the use of the term appears to differ even within the same text (e.g., UNRISD, 2016).

In general, concepts are foundational for research (Collier & Mahon, 1993) but they are only useful so long as they don't suffer from Sartori's cat-dog problem (Sartori, 1991). To facilitate a discussion on problematic conceptualization, Sartori came up with the story of a young researcher hypothesizing that cat-dogs would bark. The researcher's findings proved that while some barked others meowed. In Sartori's story it took the oracle of Delphi to point out that cat-dogs don't exist. Sartori's point is that academics continue to utilize concepts in ways that are analytically problematic. Such a problem in the academic and policy fields for the case of 'eco-social' may not only lead to confusion but also to greenwashing.

Sartori argues that various factors explain the existence of such cat-dog concepts. First, is 'parochialism' or essentially misnaming something that does not traditionally fit into the category of the concept. Sartori (1991, pp. 247-8) uses the example of a study looking at the "coalition government in the United States" in which the use of the standard definition of 'coalition government' could not be used to describe the political system of the United States. Second, there is the problem of misclassification or the creation of a pseudo-class in which "orderings derived from a single criterion" (Sartori,1991, p. 248) are derived from different criteria such as the example of labelling both Japan and China one-party states. Sartori also pointed to the issue of concept stretching which means expanding the definition of a concept so much that it includes all subjects of study. For example, if by 'constitutions' we meant any state form, or if the concept of ideology is applied to every conceivable thing, then we have a problem of concept stretching.

I argue that the concept of 'eco-social', unfortunately, suffers from all three of these problems. Although it seems the concept was first used in the late 1960s, its use began to flourish (and diversify) in the 1990s, somewhat stabilizing in meaning much more recently. Given its relative immaturity as a concept, a struggle of its meaning was expected. Both parochialism and misclassification could be applied to understanding this early period. Currently, while now much more settled in its meaning, the concept continues to struggle from the third issue: concept stretching. This is what I will attempt to explore in this chapter. For reasons I will explain in the chapter, concept of eco-social - broadly used to describe politics that blend both social and environmental concerns - can be increasingly applied to a wide range of policies and practices as to make the concept lose much of its meaning.

This chapter looks at a brief history of the term as well as its current usage to explain and address these cat-dog problems, acknowledging that some, such as Mandelli (2022a), have made significant progress in attempting to formalize the concept and address some of these concerns as it applies to eco-social policy in particular. However, the problem of concept stretching pertaining to the eco-social (and eco-social policy) persists. As I see it, there are two options for dealing with these problems, which relate to the concept's placement on Sartori's (1970) 'ladder of abstraction'. The first is adding criteria to the definition of eco-social – which I call *intension increase* – and the second is moving away from the labels eco-social and eco-social policies to more specific but divergent concepts - what I refer to as *rung descension.* I argue that the academic community should employ rung descension when discussing 'eco-social' in order to create a clearer concept, avoid the problem of concept stretching, and prevent the cooption of the concept.

EARLY CONCEPTUALIZATIONS OF THE ECO-SOCIAL

To understand the growth and use of the concept of 'eco-social', I wanted to trace its origins and its early uses. It is in this period, between the 1980s and the early 2000s, that the current meaning of the concept and how it is widely used became established, developing from four starting points that have influenced the current conception to different extents.

It is worth pointing out, however, that the concept had earlier origins. To my knowledge, the label "eco-social" was first used in the academic literature within the field of anthropology with the intention of discussing human ecology. Edwin A Cook, an anthropologist specializing in Manga culture in Papua New Guinea, wrote in 1969 about trends in the anthropological research in Melanesia, identifying two projects as sharing "a common interest in variant responses of population units in variant eco-social environments" (Cook, 1969). Its anthropological usage continued as demonstrated in a 1975 article in *Reviews in Anthropology, which discussed* the book *Women and Men*'s "eco-social" approach (Leibowitz, 1975). Later, "eco-social" began to be used in some literatures to discuss the interactive effects of the environment and the social world as coming together in one "environment" or variable, especially but not exclusively in agricultural research during the 1980s (see e.g., Knox, 1981; Xi-Ji, 1986). This includes the first English language use of "eco-social policy", as far as I am aware, which dates to 1998 (Erjavec & Turk, 1998 p. 28).

It was the 1990s that really brought "eco-social" to life through a variety of somewhat divergent ways. Four ways are particularly important for our purposes, with one serving as the central precursor to its contemporary use.

Eco-social entanglement

Although this use was already in its nascent stages in the mid-1980s (e.g., Adams et al., 1985), the 1990s saw a sharp increase in the use of "eco-social" by academics to mean the entanglement of the social world and the environment that led to the rise of ecological issues (Beck et al., 1994; e.g., Bryant, 1995). For example, Hayward (1990, pp. 4-5) describes externalities as "ecological and social costs of production" or "'eco-social' costs". This use persists to some extent (see e.g. Jones et al., 2011, p. ix) and such ideas of entanglement were often developed from deep or social ecology, which are covered in more detail below.

Eco-social movements

Scholars (and activists) used the hyphenated term to discuss social movements that are concerned with both social and ecological issues (e.g., Martinez-Alier, 1993; Spretnak, 1994; Legge, 1999). As one article in the *Journal of Latin American Studies* put it,

> *"If poverty is a cause of environmental degradation, and if poverty is rooted in unequal class relations based on institutions of power and ownership, then social movements opposed to political domination and to existing patterns of distribution of assets will sometimes also be ecological movements. The complaints and actions of such eco-social movements (tribal, peasant, or urban) increase the costs that firms or governments have to pay for natural resources" (Martinez-Alier 1991, 622).*

This relates closely to Martinez-Alier's conception of the environmentalism of the poor.

Eco-social market economies

Though developed in the 1970s and 1980s by Hans Christoph Binswanger (Fathi, 2022), the eco-social was used in economics particularly in the 1990s to discuss market economies trying to ensure fair and sustainable natural resource use. The eco-social market economy was described as a means of environmental protection not through regulations of what businesses should not do, but incentivizing what market actors should do, as, for example, was the case of Austria's neoliberal Austrian People's Party (Muller & Steininger, 1996, p. 95); a system in which to maintain or foster a role for cooperatives, such as in some post-communist countries (Turnock, 1995); and a general political consensus of modernizing the state in order to have positive market economic and environmental outcomes, as in Germany (Weidner, 1993).

Eco-social politics

Perhaps unsurprisingly, eco-social politics can be seen as the most direct antecedent to eco-social policy as discussed today. The 'eco-social' became a political concept in its own number of ways, failing to get a stranglehold on any one interpretation until its later adaptation.

In 1989, Murray Bookchin discussed a 'new eco-social history' sparked by his proposed confederalist model of governance which is "marked by a participatory evolution within society and between society and the natural world" (Bookchin, 1989). This draws on this joint environmental and social perspective but applied to a particular political vision. In 1991 and 1993, John Ely, discussed "eco-social" in terms of a difficult but desirable project to reconcile the "systemic contradiction" of economic growth and ecological breakdown, without necessarily attaching the label to a particular economic plan (Ely, 1991, pp. 122-123); in this way, eco-social works as a set of principles by which the German Green Party in particular, and others borrowing from their policy positions, would institute an "ecologically restructuring of industrial society" via neo-Keynesian methods (Ely, 1993). Also in 1993, Andre Gorz wrote of eco-social politics as a position among German and French Greens and environmentalists who argued for what we would now refer to as a universal basic income that would facilitate a reduction in working hours and thus, in effect – or so it is argued - reducing production (Gorz, 1993). This was one response to what Gorz called the eco-social rationality in which capitalist logic should be subordinated to ecological concerns (Gorz, 2012, 1991). It was later described as the "eco-social compromise" (Sanne, 2002). These two types of models were sometimes referred to as eco-socialism (see e.g., Dean, 2012).

These four somewhat interconnected meanings and developing discourses helped to shape what the current literature is referring to as the "eco-social". The entanglement of the environmental and the social reinforces the need for tackling either side of the equation, if the desire is to positively influence the other side. Such perspectives were also occasionally included in policy considerations (e.g., Jones et al., 2011). To some extent, the entanglement and interconnection were infused into popular culture through new social movements of the New Left.

As argued by Eyerman and Jamison, environmentalism was "inconceivable without the student movements of the 1960s. The student movements represented "an international revolt...against the modern scientific-technological state" (Eyerman & Jamison, 1991, p. 89) that had been the paradigm of the post-war period. The opposition to such techno-managerialism connected the anti-war sentiments of the student movement with universities' complicity with the war project through science. The connection between environmental destruction caused by war became more apparent and the connection between nuclear weapons and nuclear power was exposed. The student movement produced a liberation cosmology centered around the idea of freedom and environmentalists took that to reconceptualize nature. Thus, eco-social movements helped to bring about, popularize, and activate the 'eco-social' interconnection.

These eco-social movements stretched in a variety of ways within the radical-progressive range. The visions of some of these movements incorporated radical restructuring of the politics of society, as is the case for Bookchin's social ecology and use of the "eco-social", to more moderate but nevertheless transformative proposals such as Gorz's plan for a reduction in time spent working. John Ely's more general 'eco-social' position represented the more institutionalized response and proposals such movements produced in the form of politically competitive Green Parties. While the term's use really began in the early 1990s, theories premised on similar ideas had been developing within radical traditions since the 1970s with the development of deep ecology and social ecology theories (e.g., Naess, 1973; Bookchin 1971, 1986). From a more Marxist background, Ian Gough worked in this area starting in the 1980s with the development of a theory of human need (e.g., Doyal & Gough, 1984, 1986; Gough & Doyal, 1986) which would be published as a book in 1991 (Doyal & Gough, 1991) and covers ideas of welfare within human limits. Indeed, Gough sometimes continues to be cited as the original developer of the term 'eco-social policies' (Stamm, 2023, p. 135).

As environmental discourse, and especially the concern over the environment, became more widely diffused, the issue and language became taken up by centrist and even right political parties. Eco-social market economics became the way of speaking to capitalist moderation without using a term, "socialism", that had lost its appeal with the fall of the Eastern Bloc. At the same time, its emphasis could be pushed closer to the "market" side for parties interested in both maintaining a liberal economic policy position while addressing citizens' concerns regarding environmental harms. As I will demonstrate, these interconnected meanings shape the current use of the term eco-social, almost entirely stripped of its connection with environmental movements and instead speaking to the general political consensus around the integration of the environment, especially climate change, and social justice in the policy-making process.

The interconnections of meaning, however, should not blind us from the vast differences across these original uses. For example, a radical eco-social entanglement would in some ways make any distinctions of the ecological and the social in the other definitions meaningless. This entanglement, often a cultural distinction between the West and many others (Parks & Tsioumani, 2023), requires us to see the ecological and the social in entirely new ways that can no longer be observed separately. Thus, thinking about movements that are both environmental and social or politics that solve both social and environmental problems become meaningless since the very term is supposed to point to their singular existence. Here, Sartori's *misclassification problem* seems to be at play.

The term eco-social as applied in the ways discussed here does not stem from a single criterion. While there's a relationship between them, it is perhaps in part due to a misreading. Furthermore, this early literature (and some more contemporary literature) includes the term 'eco-social' without giving it any real explanation as to how it is being used. Some uses are perhaps subdiscipline specific, but which does not relate to the more frequent uses discussed above (e.g., Heryford, 2020; Hofmeister, 2002). These can be seen as examples of the *parochialism problem*.

As I will demonstrate below, the growth of eco-social within the policy sphere more or less solves these other problems by creating a closer consensus of the meaning of 'eco-social'. However, the problem that remains, even with the area limited to eco-social policy, is *concept stretching*. Let us first look at the concept of eco-social policy and its growth, noting its close connection to eco-social politics.

THE GROWTH OF ECO-SOCIAL POLICY

The eco-social concept is currently experiencing a growth in interest within the context of an increased sense of necessity to tackle ecological problems, especially climate change, and doing so in a socially just way. It paralleled the growth of notions of a just transition and climate justice among trade union and climate movement actors. Eco-social policy was described as still being in its infancy in 2016 (Carmi,

2016, p. 3), as an "emerging discipline[ ]" in 2017 (Helne & Kirvilammi, 2017, p. 48), and a "newly emerging field" in 2019 (Kaasch et al., 2019). However, the idea of eco-social policy grew out of the more general eco-social politics literature discussed above with the first relevant reference to "eco-social policy" or "policies" appearing in the early 2000s.

There has been a steady increase in the use of this terminology starting in the early 2010s and increasing with a greater velocity from 2019 to 2022. There's a clear upward trajectory in the use of the concept (see Figures 1 and 2[1]) and in many cases (particularly in the latter years), the term's meaning becomes assumed within the text. However, it is worth exploring the early uses of the concept of eco-social policy in more detail.

Figure 1. 'Eco-social policy' or 'eco-social policies' using Google Scholar by year (see endnote 2)

Figure 2. 'Eco-social policy' or 'eco-social policies' in titles using Google Scholar by year (see endnote 2)

Early and Expanded Uses of Eco-Social Policy

Based on Google Scholar searches (see endnote 2), the first relevant reference to eco-social policy came in 2000 with Matthies et al's paper discussing eco-social policy in relation to social exclusion in Europe and a broader 'eco-social' approach within social work. Like most of the other early references to eco-social, these were somewhat vague and general, drawing on different traditions of the use – including the entangled and movement uses (Matthies et al., 2000, p. 43). In this case, the term was used to describe 'practical solutions' discussed by environmental activists in Germany. The following year, Frankel's *When the Boat Comes in* provided an analysis of Australian politics with a chapter entitled "After criticism: developing feasible eco-social policies" which discusses normative policy of a vague "eco-social reform agenda" (Frankel, 2001, p. 176). The reforms deprioritize market paths with emphasis on strengthening the public sector which would spur new employment and anti-poverty schemes and income redistribution along with removing tax subsidies for motor vehicles which would encourage public transport.

The use of the term that is more directly focused and rooted in policy came ten years later in the volume *Understanding the Environment and Social Policy*, edited by Tony Fitzpatrick (2011a). While Matthies et al used eco-social policy to discuss vague practical solutions and Frankel discussed eco-social policies to discuss modest reforms, Fitzpatrick viewed eco-social policies as a normative conclusion toward "zero growth" (Fitzpatrick, 2011b), with Nordic countries serving as a model, although conversion to their style of social democracy was described as unrealistic. This means that eco-social policies need to be adjusted to local settings. One suggested eco-social policy was creating cap-and-trade systems that work at small levels (also see Gough 2013a, although others such as Bond (2010) oppose such plans for other social reasons). Lastly, Fitzpatrick is interested in eco-social policies bringing about a political economy of care, a redistribution of political power, a growth of community values, a reworked labour market which may include a substantial reduction of working hours, a responsible social insurance system, and the promotion of global justice.

As we can see, there was no early consensus position on what was meant by eco-social policies. Although Gough's work seems to fit the criteria presented above in relation to Fitzpatrick's use of the term, Gough begins to use the term "eco-social" in relation to "policy" specifically in 2012 when he applies it to policies such as house retrofitting for energy efficiency or 'social' tariffs for domestic energy that would see initial units of energy sold cheaply, with additional uses increased by price, which were meant to replace compensating fuel poor families (Gough et al., 2012)[2]. These discussions are much more green growth-oriented and less about large-scale social transformations.

Sometimes eco-social refers to amending social policy in light of *environmental* policy in order to achieve environmental objectives without creating additional social injustices or while alleviating social injustices. This became increasingly the predominant usage of "eco-social" (see e.g., Gough, 2012; Cook et al., 2012; Utting, 2013; Gough, 2013b). While some of Gough's eco-social policy proposals could be seen as reforms within the present system, elsewhere he discussed eco-social policy in a more radical framework, taking seriously concerns of the world's finite resources and discussing such policies as personal carbon allowances (also see Hildingsson & Koch, 2016), universal basic need provision, and a progressive work-hour reduction policy to facilitate degrowth (Gough, 2013a). Elsewhere he also promotes taxes on high-energy consumption luxuries and the nationalization of energy systems (Gough, 2015).

The same year that Gough began publishing research using this terminology, Cook et al (2012) used it for growth-specific strategies that added ecological thinking to *social* policy. They discussed the concept in terms of justice and equality by highlighting the uncertainties raised by climate change into social policy analysis, fairly compensating those who are disadvantaged by transition policies, facilitating women's participation, and minimizing inequalities and disadvantages (Cook et al.,

2012, p. 13; also see Clarke et al., 2006 regarding race and gender justice in the context of green growth following hurricane Katrina).

We can see that even early on, the eco-social label was beginning to be applied to policies that range from big societal shifts such as work-hour reductions (also see Koch, 2022), which were already being discussed in this context by Gorz in the 1990s, to progressive incentives for reducing energy consumption or house retrofitting. These policies seem to be on a different level of proposed change, even if the latter more modest proposals were described by the authors as "radical" at the time (Gough et al., 2012, p. iii). Other proposals labelled as 'eco-social policies' at this time were discussed in the context of 'eco-socialism' (with a degrowth framework) but also applied the term to existing rather than normative policies such as increased paid paternity leave to balance gender care roles (Murphy, 2013, p. 86).

The scale differences across policies for which the label applied to only grew over time. For example, Coote (2015) discusses eco-social policies in similar terms (as "achieving multiple and mutually reinforcing benefits") but discussed policies that promote more walking and cycling; increased access to green spaces, local food production and consumption; and community schemes such as car-sharing programs, repair centres and childcare cooperatives (Coote, 2015).

Eco-social policy moved away from being merely a policy suggestion that sought to provide benefits to both the ecological and social domains, to also being a marker for existing policies that managed to do both. A few years later, Bell (2016) and Carmi (2016) independently applied the concept of 'eco-social' policies[3] to an analysis of policy proposals whose objectives were both social and environmental. Bell's research looked at the cases of South Korea's 'Green Economy' project, Bolivia's Living Well concept (Bell, 2016), Costa Rica Payment for Ecosystem Services scheme and Ecuador's attempt to receive international payments to prevent fossil fuel extraction as a means of mitigating climate change (Carmi, 2016; for a similar case see Hujo & Carter, 2019, p. 28).

In this section we can see how an eco-social policy was addressed in a variety of ways. As one scholar noted, eco-social policy is "broad and encompasses a range of different approaches and initiatives that can vary quite significantly in terms of their underlying worldviews, main objectives and ambition for change" (e.g., Krause, 2021, p. 332). Over time, the concept of eco-social policy was attributed to an even wider range of policies. While in no way exhaustive, an array of additional existing or normative policy measures which have obtained the label of 'eco-social policy' can be found in Table 1, showing the diversity in both the content and the central policy field that is being discussed.

Table 1. Eco-social policy examples

Social policies with environmental benefits	Environmental policies with additional social benefits	Broad policy strategies
wealth caps (Koch and Buch-Hansen 2020; Buch-Hansen and Nesterova 2023)	taxes on meat (Koch 2022; Khan et al 2022)	Europe 2020 Strategy (Sabato et al 2022)
fair pay ratio policies (Gough 2021a)	train travel subsidisation (Buch-Hansen and Nesterova 2023)	2030 Sustainable Development Agenda (Sabato et al 2022)
recognition of unpaid labour (Gough 2021a)	sustainable pesticide management (Isah et al. 2020, 48)	Green New Deal plans (Gough 2021a)
participation income (Laruffa et al 2022)	organic food production (Buch-Hansen and Nesterova 2023)	European Green Deal (Mandelli 2022b)
work sharing (Buch-Hansen and Koch 2019)		
time-banks (Buch-Hansen and Koch 2019)		
job guarantees (Buch-Hansen and Koch 2019)		
debt auditing (Buch-Hansen and Koch 2019)		
need vouchers (Bohnenberger 2020)		
alternative housing (Koch 2019)		
the creation and promotion of local currencies (Koch 2019)		
maximum and basic incomes (Koch 2022)		
taxes on wealth (Koch 2022)		

As we can see, some policies create prohibitions – such as a wealth cap - while others create incentives – such as train subsidies. Some policies target institutions – such as job guarantees or creating local currencies – while others target individuals – such as taxes on meat or need vouchers. These distinctions can make up the very definitions of how eco-social policies are viewed (e.g., Isah et al., 2020, p. 48; Raimi et al., 2021). This also applied to the scale of the policy change being discussed, which already varied widely in the early days of the concept. For an example of how scale was attributed to the meaning of 'eco-social', one paper defined it as a "transformative change" through "a process that attacks the root causes of poverty, inequality and unsustainable practices through integrated and synergistic policies and reforms… which can transform economic, social, ecological and political structures with the aim of achieving sustainable development" (Hujo & Carter, 2019, p. 8). For most, however, different types of policies can fit into the definition. As we have seen, policies such as taxing meat are not likely to transform structures but are still labelled as eco-social policies.

ENVIRONMENTAL POLITICS, SOCIETY AND CONCEPT STRETCHING

The problem of the concept of eco-social policy is a problem of concept stretching. Since eco-social policies do not have a precise definition and are used to describe a range of policies with some kind of mixture of positive benefits to the environment and society, I will argue that almost all environmental policies can fall under this label. This is because, 1) given the relatively low issue salience of environmental issues they often required a social as well as environmental justification, and 2) environmental policies were often connected to social problems or concerns. Another reason the eco-social is experiencing concept stretching is because climate change has become a master frame and thus many policies seeking to improve people's welfare may contain some kind of environmental objective if only to be seen to be doing something positive (or even just being environmentally neutral). This can be demonstrated throughout the history of environmental politics which can be understood as the political theory, practice, and protest concerning the environment. Throughout this history, environmental concerns were closely tied to social concerns, thus arguably making them all eco-social policies if we use the consensus definition – this is true even across a wide range of environmentalist ideas, which is why such a brief overview is important to present.

Environmental Politics

The history of environmentalism (as drawn on by the West) can be said to have roots as far back as ancient Greece (Grove, 1995, p. 1). At a very general level, environmental policy stretches back to the Achaemenid Empire's restrictions on cutting cedars of Lebanon in 450 B.C. (Grove, 1995, 6). With any development it seemed that people were able to notice the negative impact this had on the environment, even if it took a long time to attempt to address this concern in any serious way. The problem affected the whole of the developing world. In China, writing from as late as the 11th century already identified the concerns of deforestation due to ship building enterprises (Deng, 1997, p. 83). Deforestation caused by shipbuilding led to early tree conservation laws such as in the Canary Islands in the late 1400s (Parsons, 1981, pp. 260-261) and led to one of the first full-fledged scientific inquiries into the issue: John Evelyn's *Sylva* in 1662. The book came out of the Royal Society's discussion on the timber shortage of the time and plans to deal with it (Campbell-

Culver, 2006, p. 59). It called for a tree planting initiative (Grober, 2007), although this plan was never implemented properly due to property rights concerns (Grove, 1995, pp. 56-57). Some have heralded *Sylva* as the origin of modern environmentalism and sustainable development (Campbell-Culver, 2006; Grober, 2007). We can see how these early environmental policies were highly linked to having additional social benefits.

If we look at modern conservationism in the US, which arose in the mid and late 1800s, we find similar 'eco-social' elements. Forest conservation as a movement in the US arguably started in 1872 with the first Arbor Day celebrations. Policies around timber conservation and planting were already being passed when, in 1875, the American Forestry Association was established (Sparhawk, 1949). The American Forestry Association was concerned with the destruction of forests, particularly by those with short term economic interests and who "have no interest in obtaining a future crop of trees" (Newell, 1895, p. 386). They arguably helped to develop the idea of the national forest system (Moore, 1952).

In the US, the movement to conserve forests began decades after the movement to conserve wild animals which was largely for the preservation of big game hunting animals for their future use (see Krausman & Mahoney, 2015). Conservationists want to ensure that nature is maintained for future human use (Carter, 2001, p. 3). They view future generations as being worthy of or entitled to (at least some of) the nature of the present day as it ties into their livelihoods (regarding timber, for example) and their hobbies and interests (regarding big game hunting).

This is somewhat different than another early environmental concern which often found itself with shared interests of, and sharing organizational membership with, the conservationists. These other environmentalists *were* concerned with the beauty of nature, perhaps as their primary motive. These preservationists wanted to prevent humans from harming natural environments. Preservationists wish to remove or prevent human spoiling of natural places, but not necessarily for the wilderness's intrinsic value (see Manning, 1984). Forms of preservation, such as the creation of national parks and protected areas and the preservation of animal species can also be seen as having social benefits – namely their importance for supporting our spiritual lives, as noted in Thoreau's *Walden*, in 1854. Nature thus has a beauty that can be admired and inspire us, but that we should not damage. The discourse used by preservationists often includes some level of human appreciation that goes beyond nature's intrinsic value.

The second wave of environmentalism in the Global North emerged in the late 1960s and became known as "modern environmentalism" (Carter, 2001). Modern environmentalism of the 1960s was fearful for humanity as a whole due to ecological problems. One scholar describes modern environmentalism as a desire for "beauty, health, and permanence", incorporating both concerns for the intrinsic value of nature but also "providing benefits to humans beyond economic need" (Tyrrell, 2002, p. 329), in contrast to the conservationists.

Some people began to observe that the negative impacts of environmental harms were not equally shared across all of society. Poor communities and communities of color were often experiencing the worst kinds of environmental harms. Rather than seeing the environment as a universal issue, the environmental justice movement sprang from these concerns around often more local and more politicized concerns. Oppressed people were not simply political or economically oppressed, but they also had to deal with environmental harms in a different way from other more affluent and privileged communities. Environmental justice was originally developed from a concern specifically focused on environmental racism and is often said to have arisen following protests against the creation of a landfill that was to be used for dumping soil contaminated by illegal and carcinogenic polychlorinated biphenyls (PCBs) (see Geiser & Waneck, 1983).

Even environmental political theories that are referred to as deep green because of their opposition to anthropocentrism have a social element still embedded in many of their normative ideas, meaning their political proposals could fall under the eco-social label. For example, a variety of primitivists argue for a complete return to nature and destruction of most technologies as a way to ensure the primacy of nature and its sustainability as well as creating greater levels of equality and freedom. Some of the key ideas of primitivists root most of the problems of society to the development of technology and thus believe the only way to reach equality and remove coercion is through a massive downscaling (Moore, 2009). Thus, they argue for the environmental and social benefits of their ideas.

Above we explored a wide range of environmental theories and perspectives but all, although they have been focused on issues of nature and the environment, make a claim to also be improving *society* in one way or another. We can thus argue that all forms of environmentalism fit the basic consensus definition of eco-social in their demands. They are seeking objectives that improve both society and the environment. From this standpoint, every environmental movement, organization, and – arguably – policy can be seen as inherently eco-social if we apply the basic definition to it. This is particularly the case if we adopt a definition of eco-social which, as suggested by Mandelli (2022a), is output based, or having eco-social *objectives* (see below). That is, if we take eco-social policy to mean policies *promising* to positively impact both society and the environment, then – it seems – it will include any environmental policy. As I have attempted to demonstrate, policymakers also incorporated the basic ideals and philosophies of the movements and thus often used the same kind of eco-social framing that can be described as win-win. Of course, Mandelli's suggestion is to use this to gauge to what extent policies achieve these stated aims. Nevertheless, when considering if a label is too broad or narrow, including virtually all environmental policies suggests this definition is at the former end of the spectrum.

Social Policy and the Climate Change Master Frame

Since it seems as though all environmental policies could be argued as providing some kind of social benefit, the only question that remains is which social policies also have stated environmental goals. If these are relatively limited then we could consider the idea of 'eco-social' policy as involving all environmental policies but few social policies that fit narrow criteria. While this was often the case in the past, I argue that the increased importance of climate change is beginning to shift this perspective, creating further stretching of the eco-social concept.

The increased issue salience on environmental issues, particularly climate change, is likely to bolster a number of policies with such aims towards dealing with these issues. Given the Global North's separation of the concept of social and environmental goods, we can assume not all policies need to incorporate both elements to satisfy any one. However, broad policies like the European Green Deal can effectively incorporate environmentalism throughout the policymaking process, thus leading to virtually every policy being, to some extent, both ecological and social. Therefore, both social and environmental policies (and some policy areas beyond these which also incorporate these goals) are increasingly policy areas that are almost always eco-social in their objectives.

Arguably, as the effects of climate change become increasingly apparent, it is likely that more and more policies will consider their environmental harms, for example in terms of greenhouse gas emissions. As such policies would also fit the consensus definition of eco-social, we are left with very few policies that do not promise to provide both social and environmental benefits. In that case, what good would the term 'eco-social policy' be? This is Sartori's concept stretching problem. 'Eco-social policy' faces a dilemma. Given that environmental policy has included social logics and benefits, and that increasingly all policy areas are incorporating environmental logics and benefits, 'eco-social' as currently conceived seems to incorporate nearly everything.

While this was not the intention of those using the concept, the nature of politics has shifted in a way in which increasingly more and more policies will fall into the category, at least as things stand currently. This is particularly the case, again, if we adopt the idea of considering the stated aims of policies. That is, we can suspect that the growing importance of climate change politically can lead to more policymakers using climate change as a rhetorical tool for promoting policies that only minimally address the issue.

THE LADDER OF ABSTRACTION, INTENSION INCREASE, AND RUNG DESCENSION

Despite the concerns raised above, it must be stated that just because the concept is universalising does not mean this is a fundamental problem with the concept. While empirically eco-social policy may be closer to the concept of policy more generally in terms of its extension, it still is an empirical (near-)universal rather than a philosophical one. That is, it is still empirically verifiable (Sartori, 1970, p. 1035). The problem is connected to where we place eco-social policy on what Sartori refers to as the ladder of abstraction.

The ladder of abstraction posits that at the top of the ladder we have a lower intension and high extension, and the further down the ladder we go, the more the intension increases, and the extension decreases. Sartori (1970) refers to *intension* (or connotation) as the properties required of an object to fit into a concept. The number of objects that fit the concept based on the intension corresponds to the concept's extension (or denotation) whereby a concept is restricted by fewer properties that are required and thus contains more objects (see Figure 3). For example, at a higher level of abstraction we may have 'social movement' which is defined as "a loose, noninstitutionalized network of informal interactions that may include, as well as individuals and groups who have no organizational affiliation, organizations of varying degrees of formality, that are engaged in collective action motivated by shared identity or concern" (Rootes, 2004). We have a number of properties (intension) that include 1) being a loose, noninstitutionalized network, 2) being engaged in collective action, and 3) being motivated by shared identity or concern. Of course, above this we have other rungs for which 'social movement' itself is only one of many, such as the concept 'network' in which there are other forms besides social movements. For 'network' the intension is smaller because we can remove at least the last two properties required of 'social movement'. However, the extension is greater as not only are all social movements included but so are many other forms of networks. 'Social movement' also has rungs below it on the ladder of abstraction. Environmental movements are social movements, but they add another property to the intension (i.e., being concerned with the environment) which reduces its extension (e.g., the #MeToo movement fits the category of 'social movement' but not 'environmental movement').

Studies on eco-social policy appear to be interested in presenting something that is relatively novel within the policy sphere either through normative policy proposals or through the examination of specific existing policies. As I have tried to argue, the definition used to discuss this appears to cover a much wider range of policies that may be desired. Eco-social policy finds itself at an impasse in which there is conceptual stretching whereby the current intension of the concept aligns with a particular political climate in which the extension becomes very high. As I see it, there are two options to resolve this problem: increase intension and descend the rungs.

Figure 3. The Ladder of Abstraction as described by Sartori (1970)

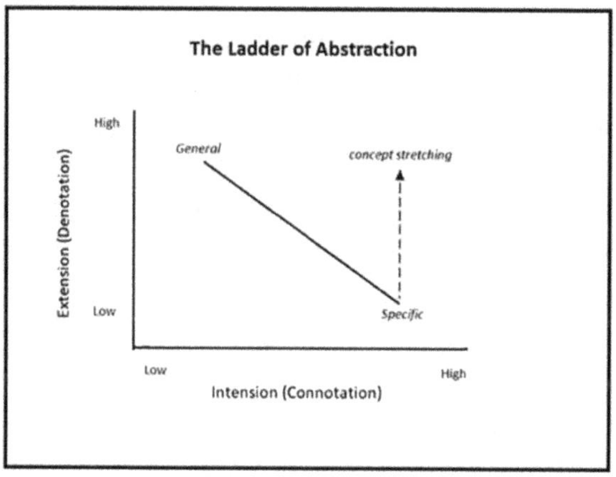

Intension Increase and Eco-Social Policy Conceptualizations

First, if our problem is that eco-social policies account for far more policies than intended, we can reduce the extension by increasing the intension. That is, if we add additional attributes to qualify to be labelled 'eco-social' we can reduce the number of cases. Given the different forms of conceptualization found in the eco-social literature, we can use these to make demarcations as to what does or does not qualify as eco-social policy. These differences, to be discussed in detail below, include outcomes or objective, growth, degrowth or a-growth; additive and integrative; and ecologically or socially focused eco-social policies.

Objective Outcomes vs. Outcome Objectives

Mandelli (2022a) makes a distinction between normative, outcome-based policies and empirically testable objective-based policies. The former conceptualization means a policy can only clearly be labelled as eco-social if it manages to prove successful at improving both ecological and social conditions; the latter is where the stated goals of the policies are to improve both ecological and social conditions, even if they do not succeed in doing so.

Outcome-based conceptualizations can be found in Buch-Hansen and Nesterova's work (2023, p. 5) where, for example, they define eco-social policies as "policies that simultaneously advance the goals of improving human transactions with nature and social equity" (also see Plumhans, 2021; Schoyen et al., 2022). Alternatively, scholars such as Plagerson (2012, 8) argue that eco-social policies can be defined as "combin[ing] social and environmental objectives" (also see Craig, 2017; Gough, 2017b). With policies described as seeking both ecological and social objectives, there is often an expectation that in order to fit the definition, those objectives need to be made clearly. Thus, we find reference to the explicit nature of the policy's objectives, which can also be found in work by Mandelli (2022a) and Gugushvili and Otto (2023).

There are pros and cons to either conception. Looking at outcome means you can only consider a policy to be eco-social after it has demonstrated some level of success. However, it means that the label of eco-social policy is earned based on effect and not on (stated) intention. This means testing a policy for its "eco-social" credentials includes an empirical component. Mandelli (2022a) argues that this prevents us from using the concept of eco-social policies to consider contemporary policies that have yet to make an impact. In addition, this means that we cannot consider which eco-social policies work, in terms of outcome, and which do not. Instead, outcome becomes a basis for inclusion. Furthermore, a criterion for impact is not set. Which ecological and which social dimensions should be advanced, what level of change counts as a benefit, and who would determine what those are? This approach can create more problems than solutions because each scholar using the 'eco-social' label may propose their particular criteria.

However, by not focusing on outcomes we miss policies that largely unintentionally managed to succeed both in providing social goods and environmental goods. They were not eco-social in their promise, but they could be eco-social in their outcomes. If these are side-lined, then we fail to acknowledge policies that actually achieved desirable results.

Here, for example, we may take the UK's furlough policy during COVID which had an economic and social outcome explicitly in the policy but was unrelated to environmental outcomes. Nevertheless, the policy, which saw the government pay up to 80% of the wages for furloughed employees, meant that business could continue to employ people even as they were forced to shut due to pandemic restrictions. It also meant that lockdowns could continue for longer with less negative economic and social impacts due to what otherwise would mean large-scale unemployment. Maintaining the lockdowns reduced emissions as throughput decreased, thus benefiting the environment. The COVID pandemic is often referred to by proponents of degrowth as a lesson in degrowth and a reason for degrowth (e.g., Barlow et al., 2020).

Thus, if we take the outcome approach, we could consider policies as eco-social even if one aspect was not an intended outcome. We do not have to claim that these policies were perfect to include them as 'eco-social', but there is an argument to not exclude them. Likewise, policies that are primarily used for other purposes may include stated ecological objectives without any real desire to improve the environment, a form of greenwashing (de Freitas Netto et al., 2020). In such cases, explicit goals of both environmental and social benefits do not necessarily equate to effective policy instruments. Indeed, some policies that claim environmental benefits while causing environmental harms, such as incentives for hydropower, biomass, electric vehicles and biofuels. In some case, the stated goals are merely cover for building consensus around the policy be appealing to all interested parties, including those who are concerned about the environment. For example, one argument for a policy to continue the use of coking coal, which has high greenhouse gas emissions, was that it was needed to create wind turbines and thus was beneficial for combatting climate change. However, few environmental organizations actually believed this was a legitimate argument for the use of a dirty form of energy. However, finding true motivations is nearly impossible. How can we claim that someone's stated objective is not true? Thus, there is not a good basis of distinguishing 'true' eco-social policies from 'faux' ones. Perhaps instead, we could say a policy is eco-social if there is a relatively equal mix of ecological and social benefits. However, such benefits are incommensurable. Are the social benefits of a 15-minute city (Moreno, 2021), say, greater than or less than its environmental benefits? This would also not solve the definitional problem.

Another basis for avoiding the problem of greenwashing can be taken from Mandelli (2022a) definition of eco-social policies which includes an integration of environmental and social policy. Even though Mandelli notes that this already involves two sets of policy goals, this integration is also about a "convergence of policy…instruments" that are mutually supportive (2022, p. 340). While this provides a more objective basis for categorization, it perhaps crucially misses out not only policies that do not aim to have ecological and social benefits though nevertheless provide those benefits (as discussed above), but also policies that aim to tackle both environmental and social problems but just through the advancement of one policy area. That is, by this definition a policy would not be eco-social if it seeks to benefit the environment and society but only by using environmental or social policy instruments exclusively. Quite a few of the policies that have been labelled eco-social would be excluded, such as working hour reductions and universal basic income or provision. These are social policies with additional environmental objectives but no clear environmental policy instruments at play.

Growth-dependent and degrowth-dependent eco-social policy

In general, the eco-social policy literature has included growth-dependent, degrowth-dependent, and growth-independent policies. Growth-dependent eco-social politics refers to a perception in which all three components of the eco-social-economic trilemma need to be positively resolved across all three areas. Mandelli (2022a) describes this trilemma as developing from the notion of sustainable development which was defined by the Brundtland Commission as "development that meets the needs of the present without compromising the ability of future generations to meet their own needs" (Brundtland, 1987). At the time, the development approach was seen as a means of resolving all three areas but it became increasingly clear that they are often in conflict with one another.

However, for growth-dependent eco-social politics, the objectives are to ensure growth is maintained while also promoting the other aspects. This does not necessitate growth to hold greater importance than the ecological or social, but that their importance should be fairly equal, requiring win-win-win solutions. A win regarding the ecological consists of the reduction of environmental harms and/or improvements to the environment; a win regarding the social would mean social goods are provided, social harms are reduced, and/or either/both are (more) fairly distributed; and an economic win would mean economic growth and development. While all forms of eco-social politics as discussed in the literature are, in one way or another, concerned with the first two wins, growth-dependent eco-social policies are also wedded to the economic growth model, often within the context of present capitalism arrangements with state interventions to improve welfare and the environment.

For example, Cook et al (2012, 5) describes 'eco-social' as "a conceptual framework, analytic tools and policy instruments that overcome the deeply entrenched separation between the social, economic and environmental domains beneath the umbrella of sustainable development." They specifically call for "minimizing contradictions and enhancing complementarities" across the three domains (Cook et al., 2012; also see Carmi, 2016, p. 3; Sabato & Mandelli, 2018; Marston, 2019, p. 38; Sabato et al., 2022). For these scholars the eco-social can be read as eco-social-*economic* politics.

Those that advocate degrowth-dependent eco-social policies (e.g., Vanhercke et al., 2018; also see Brandl & Zielinska, 2020; Mehra et al., 2021) are essentially not concerned with the economic component of the trilemma discussed above and are instead seeking to advance the causes of the environmental and the social through policies and practices which, they argue, can only be achieved if some form of economic degrowth is pursued (see Hickel, 2019)[4]. Essentially, proponents of such positions advocate for policies that promote economic reductions rather than growth because either the ecological or the social goals (though typically the former) cannot be achieved while economies continue to grow. Thus, such proponents seek win-win-lose solutions to the trilemma, viewing it as fundamentally impossible to reconcile the demands of all three fields. This is perhaps a kind of inversion of mainstream contemporary politics in which economic growth is far more fundamental than ecological or social goals, often playing itself out as a game of lose-lose-win. In this view, even if wins may be desired for all areas, the emphasis may still be heavily on growth. When examining the eco-social policy agenda of the EU, Sabato and Mandelli (2018) found that while the EU endorsed a combination of tackling ecological, social, and economic problems, the environmental component was largely just tacked on to its largely growth-oriented strategy of Europe 2020 (also see Koch, 2018, p. 41 regarding EU carbon markets).

Eco-social degrowth advocates believe that growth is incompatible with desirable ecological and social goals and thus the goal of growth, in its strict economic form, should be abandoned in favor of ecological and social benefits. For these advocates, the eco-social approach should be the dominance of the ecological and social over the economic (Brand & Missaoui, 2014; also see Köhler, 2016; Faul, 2016; UNRISD, 2016), or of the 're-fettering' of capitalism (Köhler, 2018). Some of those who fit into this camp have defined eco-social policy as "sustainable welfare without growth" (Dukelow, 2022). Such degrowth eco-social policy perspectives included some of the first publications to use the term (Sanne, 2002).[5]

(Eco-)Social Policy and (Social-)Eco Policy

As Mandelli (2022a, p. 342) notes, underlying eco-social policies may be a "core rationale" of a policy. They can either be trying to reduce the negative social impacts of (or adding a positive social effect onto) environmental policies, or by reducing the ecological impacts of (or adding a positive ecological effect onto) social policy. Mandelli refers to these as socializing the eco state or greening the welfare state, respectively.

We can see this play out in the literature not only through the examples of policies that obtain the label eco-social as analyzed by Mandelli, but through the very conceptualization of eco-social policy. For example, Bell (2016, p. 72) looks at eco-social policies "in the context of considering how to transition to an ecological society whilst achieving greater equity in processes and outcomes" (also see McGann & Murphy, 2023, p. 18; Hirvilammi & Koch, 2020; Cook et al., 2012). This fits the 'socializing the eco state' side of the spectrum as the central policy aim is assumed to be *environmental* sustainability but needing social policy to improve the welfare and equality of the population. Alternatively, Drolet (2016, p. 13) describes eco-social policies as "designing social policy initiatives that also incorporate environmental concerns" (also see UNRISD, 2016, p. 10). Such conceptualizations want to introduce some environmentally friendly policies within policies primarily geared toward improving welfare. Heavily emphasizing the "social" in their work, these look to green social policy because that is where their policy research is rooted. That being said, while examples of conceptualization leaning in one direction or another have been presented, the vast majority of definitions and descriptions of what eco-social policies are either do not make a clear distinction or necessitate a kind of balanced approach.

Rather than thinking about equality across environmental and social benefits of a policy, which may be difficult to gauge, some scholars have used the idea of simultaneity as the basis for which a policy can be designated as eco-social. That is, the policy improves ecological and social conditions at the same time. In fact, Carmi also discusses eco-social in this way: "[eco-social policy] simultaneously addresses social and environmental goals and brings about benefits in both dimensions" (also see Gough, 2013c, p. 6; Gough, 2017a, p. 161; Gugushvili & Otto, 2023; Hasanaj, 2023; Buch-Hansen & Nesterova, 2023; Schoyen et al., 2022; Singh, 2021). Others use the notions of integration (Singh, 2023; Mandelli, 2022a, p. 340; Alcidi et al., 2022; Bell, 2016, p. 72), synergy (Gough, 2021; Hujo & Carter, 2019) complementarity, and combination (Schoyen & Hvinden, 2017; Krause, 2021) for similar purposes.

The distinction between the additive approach by which the eco- or social-component supplements the other policy field compared to a conceptualization in which there is fairly equal integration of the ecological and social is addressed by Alcidi et al (2022). They discuss this bifurcation as the compensatory logic versus the integrated logic. According to them, the compensatory logic only links social and environmental objectives "to the extent to which the latter produce negative externalities" (also see Hasanaj, 2023, 3). As an example, they discuss workers losing their job in carbon intensive sectors being re-trained and re-skilled to move into a new occupation. Here social policy plays a role in creating social justice following an environmental policy which, without this social intervention, would create a social problem. We can imagine a situation where the reverse is true without changing the example very much. Industrial policy is used to bolster employment but is applied to a carbon-intensive sector and thus environmental policy should be added to ensure the process is environmentally sustainable, such as through carbon capture and storage policies or carbon offsetting (both of which are likely to be insufficient when the climate is concerned but serve as hypothetical examples of what may fall under eco-social policy).

Some have argued that simply taking on an environmental or social component to a social or environmental policy, respectively, should not satisfy the criteria of being 'eco-social' because the question of relative equality is important (Plumhans, 2021). This view is shared by the second, integrated logic. The integrated logic as discussed by Alcidi et al. (2022) is one in which "social policies and goals are designed together with ecological objectives and goals". Thus, social policies are not simply there to alleviate social problems caused by environmental concerns, or vice versa, but "welfare policies… are also conceived as a necessary pre-condition to facilitate the ecological transition". Here is where we might think about producing green jobs as a way of fostering, for example, the development of green energy technologies such as photovoltaic panels or wind turbines. This actually can help accelerate a quicker transition to a fossil free economy while also providing relatively well-paid employment opportunities. This could also be mixed in with, say, racial, gender, and other kinds of quotas to ensure greater equality or can be positioned geographically in places where employment is needed most or helps offset unemployment from the decline of carbon-intensive industries. Rather than additive, such a policy would facilitate gains in both ecological and social domains (even if clearly siding on the growth side of another divide). Another example that fits this definition - but can be questionable regarding its impact – was the policy of Brazil's federal government to promote biodiesel through the growing of biomass plantations and using the plantations and the processing of the vegetables to employ people and ease issues of urban labor migration (Eyer do Valle, 2009, p. 211).

These two logics can be conceptualized as a continuum or spectrum from ecologically-centered with added social policy to welfare-centered with added environmental policy and in between the conjunction of the two, where both are approached more or less equally and/or simultaneously (see Figure 4). Adding policies that increase wellbeing and equality onto environmental policies can be illustrated through the idea of a poppy field where we add 'red' components to a 'green' terrain (poppy field policies). Adding policies that increase environmental sustainability onto welfare policies can be thought of as terraforming where we add 'green' policies to a 'red' terrain (terraform policies). Blending green and red light gives us yellow so we can refer to the integrated logic as 'canola policies'.

Figure 4. A spectrum of (eco-) social to (social-)eco policies

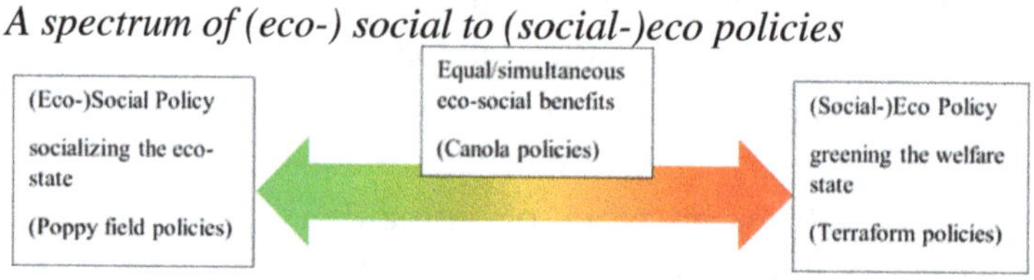

Alternatively, they can be conceptualized as a continuum between additive approaches and integrated approaches (in either direction). As discussed above, additive eco-social policies would consist of policy proposals that offset the negative impacts of environmental policies on society or equality or the negative impacts of social policy on the environment. Integrated eco-social policies are policy proposals that provide win-win solutions for both environmental and social progress.

As discussed above, some have drawn lines in the sand as to what eco-social refers to. For others it is less clearly demarcated. If we redefine eco-social to mean one of these specific versions, then we will be able to arrive at the level of intension and extension desired and avoid concept stretching. Making a demarcation, however, seems to be somewhat arbitrary. Which version would we select, and would the exclusion of the others be an injustice to the concept? Intension increase would certainly cut down on the number of policies that fit the category if they needed to be degrowth policies, for example. But would a consensus form around such a proposal? Would the proposal be justifiable?

There are also additional difficulties. If we decide, as some have suggested, to increase the intension by focusing on policies with relatively equal ecological and social outcomes or objectives, we face the problem of incommensurability. There is also difficulty in thinking about relative equality between social and environmental benefits because the types of benefits they provide may not be comparable. E.g., Is designating a piece of land a national park and working to preserve it of greater environmental importance than the pleasure people today or in the future would have from visiting it?

This is further complicated by policies which create clashes *within* competing social or ecological interests. For example, Italy's Decreto Semplificazioni Bis was a policy implemented to ease the approval of renewable energy production as part of the Recovery Plan for Energy Transition and the National Integrated Energy and Climate Plan. This would mean both helping to mitigate climate change (which has its own social benefits) as well as to bolster jobs in the renewable energy sector. However, such a policy fast-tracks such ventures by limiting the applicability of Environmental Impact Assessment (Sposato, 2021). This means that while the policy may help to mitigate climate change, it may also cause other environmental problems such as threatening species living where new solar or wind energy generation will take place, or, in the case of wind turbines, threatening bird populations. Likewise, while providing jobs or social benefits from climate change mitigation, the policy can also undermine democratic processes and negatively impact communities who oppose the building of renewable energy plants where they are proposed (see e.g. Jeffery et al., 2013; Ogilvie & Rootes, 2015).

Increasing intension by effectively mandating that eco-social policies must be X (see Table 2) or any combination of these would arguably solve the problem of concept stretching. Such a step would certainly decrease extension and, in most cases, do so to a degree in keeping with the aims of the concept. However, deciding on which conceptualization stays and which goes is unlikely to be decided without the continued diverse use of the concept of eco-social, which each scholar using it in their own precise way but unlikely to reach a consensus. This solution produces its own problems.

Table 2. List of Ways to Increase Intension

determined by outcome	determined by stated objectives	
growth dependent	degrowth dependent	growth independent
poppy field policies	terraform policies	canola policies
additive social to environmental	additive environmental to social	integrated

Rung Descension and Conceptual Furcation

We can avoid the problem of concept stretching and the problem of dropping some useful cases when increasing the intension by instead engaging in rung descension. If the 'eco-social policy' concept cannot justifiably decrease extension through intension increase, then perhaps we simply need to work with concepts at the lower rungs of the ladder of abstraction. This would be the equivalent of looking at environmental movements rather than social movements more generally but in this case use the various divisions discussed above to serve as the conceptual distinction. Instead of discussing the more abstract 'eco-social policy' we may start discussing 'growth-dependent eco-social policies', 'poppy field policies', 'additive eco-social policies', etc.

The risk of rung descension is that eco-social may lose any shared meaning – conceptual furcation. Each subcategory has reduced extension to a satisfactory level, but it is hard to imagine how well each of these subcategories would engage with others. To some extent, that fate is already shared by the broader, more abstract, 'eco-social' concept. Whereas eco-social policies, I argue, are closely aligned to 'policies' in their extension, other aspects of eco-social (such as eco-social movements) are not often discussed together with eco-social policies despite sharing much more in common than the networks above. It often feels that eco-social policy is one literature, and things such as eco-social states and eco-social movements are discussed separately.

In fact, there are a whole host of terms that have occurred as part of an existing furcation process, some with greater connection to eco-social policies than others. Terms such as eco-social contract (Gough 2022), eco-social transformative action (Bärnthaler, 2023), eco-social citizenship (e.g., Hirvilammi et al 2023), eco-welfare state interventions (Gough, 2021a, p. 27), eco-social well-being, eco-social commons (Steele, 2022), eco-social policy orientation (e.g., Hirvilammi et al 2023), "global eco-social policy" (Lakeman, 2021, p. 263) have all been utilized[6]. As discussed, even 'eco-social policy' grew from other 'eco-social' terminology including eco-social political parties (e.g., Dabis, 2014; Fink-Hafner & Knep, 2015; Fink-Hafner et al., 2015), eco-social movements (e.g., Steele, 2022; Peters, 2017; Cattaneo & Engel-Di Mauro, 2015; Meyer-Renschhausen, 2014; Jessoula & Mandelli, 2019), eco-social values/publics in some form (Otto & Gugushvili, 2020; Sacchi, 2019; Gunn et al., 2021; Vastola et al., 2020; Steele, 2022), and eco-social state (Koch & Fritz, 2014; Jakobsson et al., 2018; Schoyen & Hvinden, 2017).

The problems of conceptual furcation are not so grave if the concept is otherwise likely to be too broad to be useful. If we focus on using concepts at a lower rung we can help solve the problem of concept stretching. If we are more specific with how we label eco-social policies, we can avoid the concept altogether and instead focus on more specific forms.

CONCLUSION

Given its current broad conceptualization and a shifting political climate, eco-social suffers from the problem of concept stretching as described by Sartori (1991). The consensus definition of eco-social is the combination of a positive orientation toward both ecological and social aims or outcomes. As demonstrated in this paper, environmental politics – which has an inherent attachment to the ecological side of the equation – has always incorporated a social element as well. Thus, every element of environmental politics could be seen as being eco-social. Given the growing importance of climate change politics in many countries, policy arenas outside of those focused on the environment are increasingly having to address the question of the environment and their own impacts. If the trend continues, we can imagine that nearly all politics, and policies in particular, would fit this general definition of eco-social. This is particularly true if we take a perspective that the eco-social is defined based on its mutual ecological and social *stated objectives*. In this case, even policies with no real intention of achieving environmental (or, for that matter, social) benefits may be included. The notion of greenwashing speaks to this risk. More generally, if everything fits the definition, the concept loses much of its purpose. Sartori notes that this problem of concept stretching exists when the extension of the concept is too great.

I have argued that there are two straightforward ways to address this problem. One is to decrease extension by increasing intension. That is, by increasing the number of conditions to satisfy the definition of eco-social, we can reduce the number of cases that fit the definition. Many who have written about eco-social policies have proposed a variety of ways in which this could be done, e.g. distinguishing by orientation toward economic growth, whether they are additive or integrative,

REFERENCES

Adams, C. E., Charles, C., Green, J., & Swan, M. (1985). New Designs in Conservation/Ecology Education. *The American Biology Teacher, 47*(8), 463–469.

Alcidi, C., Corti, F., Gros, D., & Liscai, A. (2022). Towards a Socially Just Green Transition: The Role of Welfare States and Public Finances. In Cerniglia, F., & Saraceno, F. (Eds.), *Greening Europe: 2022 European Public Investment Outlook.* Open Books.

Barlow, N., Hepp, C., Herbert, J., Rilović, A., Saey-Volckrick, J., Smessaert, J., & von Andrian, N. (2020). A degrowth perspective on the coronavirus crisis. *Visions for Sustainability*, 14. https://doi.org/DOI: 10.13135/2384-8677/5280

Bärnthaler, R. (2023). Towards eco-social politics: A case study of transformative strategies to overcome forms-of-life crises. *Environmental Politics*. Advance online publication. DOI: 10.1080/09644016.2023.2180910

Beck, U., Giddens, A., & Lash, S. (1994). *Reflexive Modernization: Politics, Tradition and Aesthetics in the Modern Social Order*. Stanford University Press.

Bell, K. (2016). Green Economy or Living Well? Assessing divergent paradigms for equitable eco-social transition in South Korea and Bolivia. *Journal of Political Ecology, 23*, 71–92.

Bohnenberger, K. (2020). Money, Vouchers, Public Infrastructures? A Framework for Sustainable Welfare Benefits. *Sustainability, 12*(2), 596. DOI: 10.3390/su12020596

Bond, P. (2010, January 19). The carbon market ship is sinking fast, *ZNet*. https://ccs.ukzn.ac.za/files/bond%20climate%20justice%20articles%20Sept%2009%20through%20may%2010.pdf

Bookchin, M. (1971[1986]). *Post-Scarcity Anarchism*, Oakland: AK Press.

Bookchin, M. (1989). The Meaning of Confederalism, *Green Perspectives* 20. http://dwardmac.pitzer.edu/anarchist_archives/bookchin/gp/perspectives20.html

Brand, B., & Missaoui, R. (2014). Multi-criteria analysis of electricity generation mix scenarios in Tunisia. *Renewable & Sustainable Energy Reviews, 39*, 251–261. DOI: 10.1016/j.rser.2014.07.069

Brandl, J., & Zielinska, I. (2020). Reviewing the Smart City Vienna Framework Strategy's Potential as an Eco-Social Policy in the Context of Quality of Work and Socio-Ecological Transformation. *Sustainability, 12*, 859.

Brundtland, G. H., & WCED. (1987). Report of the world commission on environment and development: "Our common future." United Nations.

Bryant, L. (1995). Book reviews: THE ENVIRONMENTAL IMPERATIVE: ECO-SOCIAL CONCERNS FOR AUSTRALIAN AGRICULTURE Frank Vanclay and Geoffrey Lawrence. *Journal of Sociology (Melbourne, Vic.)*, *34*(1), 96–97.

Buch-Hansen, H. & Koch, M. (2019). Degrowth through income and wealth caps? *Ecological Economics*, *160*, 264–271.

Buch-Hansen, H., & Nesterova, I. (2023). Less and more: Conceptualising degrowth transformations. *Ecological Economics*, *205*. Advance online publication. DOI: 10.1016/j.ecolecon.2022.107731

Campbell-Culver, M. (2006). *A Passion For Trees: The Legacy Of John Evelyn*. Transworld Publishers.

Carmi, D. (2016). Implementing eco-social policies: Barriers and opportunities. A preliminary comparative analysis, UNRISD Working Paper, No. 2016-12, United Nations Research Institute for Social Development (UNRISD), Geneva

Carter, N. (2001). *The Politics of the Environment: Ideas, Activism, Policy*. Cambridge University Press.

Cattaneo, C., & Engel-Di Mauro, S. (2015). Urban Squats as Eco-Social Resistance to and Resilience in the Face of Capitalist Relations. *PArtecipazione e COnflitto*, *8*(2), 343–366.

Clarke, B. J., Ellis, J., Bullard, R., Chen, D., Epstein, P., Gelobter, M., Pastor, M., Pastor, P., Talberth, J., & Wolf, L. (2006). Equity and the Environment: Rebuilding Green—Rebuilding Black. *Race, Poverty & the Environment*, 13(1), 27–32. http://www.jstor.org/stable/41495681

Collier, D., & Mahon, J. E.Jr. (1993). Conceptual "Stretching" Revisited: Adapting Categories in Comparative Analysis. *The American Political Science Review*, *67*(4), 845–855.

Cook, E. A. (1969). Some Recent Anthropological Research Trends in Melanesia. *Anthropologica*, *11*(1), 117–150.

Cook, S., Smith, K., & Utting, P. (2012). Green economy or green society? Contestation and policies for a fair transition, UNRISD Occasional Paper: Social Dimensions of Green Economy and Sustainable Development, No. 10, ISBN 978-92-9085-091-5, United Nations Research Institute for Social Development (UNRISD), Geneva

Coote, A. (2015). People, Planet, Power: Toward a New Social Settlement. *International Journal of Social Quality*, *5*(1), 8–34.

Cotta, B. (2024). Unpacking the eco-social perspective in European policy, politics, and polity dimensions. *European Political Science*, *23*(1), 1–13.

Craig, M. P. A. (2017). *Ecological Political Economy and the Socio-Ecological Crisis*. Palgrave Macmillan.

Dabis, A. (2014). The South Tyrolean Party System. *Minority Research*, *17*, 33–52.

de Freitas Netto, S. V., Sobral, M. F. F., Ribeiro, A. R. B., & da Luz Soares, G. (2020). Concepts and forms of greenwashing: A systematic review. *Environmental Sciences Europe*, *32*(19). Advance online publication. DOI: 10.1186/s12302-020-0300-3

Dean, H. (2012). *Social Policy*. Polity Press.

Deng, G. (1997). Chinese Maritime Activities and Socioeconomic Development, c. 2100 B.C. – 1900 A.D., Westport: Greenwood Press.

Doyal, L., & Gough, I. (1984). A theory of human needs. *Critical Social Policy*, *4*(10), 6–38. DOI: 10.1177/026101838400401002

Doyal, L., & Gough, I. (1986). Human Need and Strategies for Social Change. In Ekins, P. (Ed.), *The Living Economy: A New Economics in the Making* (pp. 68–79). Routledge.

Doyal, L., & Gough, I. (1991). *A Theory of Human Need*. Macmillan Press.

Drolet, J. (2016). Introduction. In Drolet, J. (Ed.), *Social Development and Social Work Perspectives on Social Protection* (pp. 1–16). Routledge.

Dukelow, F. (2022). What Role for Activation in Eco-Social Policy? *Social Policy and Society*, *21*(3), 496–507.

Ely, J. (1991). Review essay. *Capitalism, Nature, Socialism*, *2*(3), 111–126. DOI: 10.1080/10455759109358464

Ely, J. (1993). Post-Fordist restructuring in Germany: What role for the new social movements? *New Political Science*, *12*(1-2), 145–173. DOI: 10.1080/07393149308429682

Erjavec, E., & Turk, J. (1998). Agricultural reform, markets and prices in Slovenia. In Mergos, G. (Ed.), *Agricultural price reform under transition in Bulgaria, Romania, and Slovenia* (pp. 19–35). CIHEAM.

Eyer do Valle, C. (2009). Innovative Actions That contributed Toward Protecting the Environment in Brazil. In *Science Without Borders: Transactions of the International Academy of Science H&E, 2007/2008*, 3, 209-2016.

Eyerman, R., & Jamison, A. (1991). *Social Movements: A Cognitive Approach*. The Pennsylvania State University Press.

Fathi, K. (2022). *Multi-Resilience - Development – Sustainability: Requirements for securing the future of societies in the 21st century*. Springer.

Faul, M. V. (2016). *Multi-Sectoral Partnerships and Power: Background paper prepared for the UNRISD Flagship Report 2016 Policy Innovations for Transformative Change*. UNRISD.

Fink-Hafner, D., & Knep, M. (2015). Factors affecting green party development: Explaining the decline of green parties in Slovenia. *Romanian Journal of Political Science, 15*(1), 129–158.

Fink-Hafner, D., Knep, M., & Novak, M. (2015). *The Slovenian Greens: From Early Success to Long-Term Failure*. FDV.

Fitzpatrick, T. (2011a). Introduction. In Fitzpatrick, T. (Ed.), *Understanding the Environment and Social Policy* (pp. 1–16). The Policy Press.

Fitzpatrick, T. (2011b). Challenges for social policy. In Fitzpatrick, T. (Ed.), *Understanding the Environment and Social Policy* (pp. 61–90). The Policy Press.

Frankel, B. (2001). *When the Boat Comes in: Transforming Australia in the Age of Globalisation*. Pluto Press.

Geiser, K., & Waneck, G. (1983). PCBs and Warren County. *Science for the People*, (July), 13–17.

Gorz, A. (1993). Political ecology: Expertocracy versus self-limitation. *New Left Review*, •••, 55–55.

Gorz, A. (2012). *Capitalism, Socialism, Ecology*. Verso. (Original work published 1991)

Gough, I. (2011). Climate change, double injustice and social policy: A case study of the United Kingdom, UNRISD Occasional Paper: Social Dimensions of Green Economy and Sustainable Development, No. 1, ISBN 978-92-9085-083-0, United Nations Research Institute for Social Development (UNRISD), Geneva

Gough, I. (2012). *New policies are needed to reconcile climate mitigation and social equity in the UK. Debating Environmental Policy.* British Politics and Policy Blog. August.

Gough, I. (2013a). Climate change, social policy, and global governance. *Journal of International and Comparative Social Policy*, 29(3), 185-203. ISSN 2169-9763 DOI: DOI: 10.1080/21699763.2013.852128

Gough, I. (2013b). Carbon Mitigation Policies, Distributional Dilemmas and Social Policies. *Journal of Social Policy*, *42*(2), 191–213.

Gough, I. (2013c). The challenge of climate change for social policy. In *Social Policy Association Annual Conference*,8-10 July, 2013, Sheffield, UK.

Gough, I. (2015). Macroeconomics, climate change and 'recomposition' of consumption. *PRIME*, 1-17.

Gough, I. (2017a). *Heat, Greed and Human Need: Climate Change, Capitalism and Sustainable Wellbeing*. Edward Elgar.

Gough, I. (2017b). Recomposing consumption: Defining necessities for sustainable and equitable well-being. *Phil. Trans. R. Soc. A., 3752016037920160379*. Advance online publication. DOI: 10.1098/rsta.2016.0379

Gough, I. (2021a). Climate change: the key challenge the key challenge A framework for an eco-social A framework for an eco-social contract contract', ETUI – Conference Report.

Gough, I. (2021b). Two scenarios for sustainable welfare: New Ideas for an eco-social contract, *etui*, working paper.

Gough, I. (2022). Two scenarios for sustainable welfare: A framework for an eco-social contract. *Social Policy and Society*, *21*(3), 460–472.

Gough, I., Abdallah, S., Johnson, V., Ryan-Collins, J., & Smith, C. (2012). The distribution of total greenhouse gas emissions by households in the UK, and some implications for social policy. *Centre for Analysis of Social Exclusion. CASE (Philadelphia, Pa.)*, •••, 152.

Gough, I., & Doyal, L. (1986). Human Needs and Socialist Welfare. *PRAXIS International*, *1*, 43–69.

Grober, U. (2007). *Deep roots - a conceptual history of 'sustainable development'* (Nachhaltigkeit). (Discussion Papers / Wissenschaftszentrum Berlin für Sozialforschung, 2007-002). Berlin: Wissenschaftszentrum Berlin für Sozialforschung gGmbH. https://nbn-resolving.org/urn:nbn:de:0168-ssoar-110771

Grove, R. H. (1995). *Green imperialism: Colonial expansion, tropical island Edens and the origins of environmentalism, 1600-1860*. Cambridge University Press.

Gugushvili, D., & Otto, A. (2023). Determinants of Public Support for Eco-Social Policies: A Comparative Theoretical Framework. *Social Policy and Society*, *22*(1), 1–15.

Gunn, E. L., Rica, M., Zorrilla-Miras, P., Vay, L., Mayor, B., Pagano, A., Altamirano, M., & Giordano, R. (2021). The natural assurance value of nature-based solutions: A layered institutional analysis of socio ecological systems for long term climate resilient transformation. *Ecological Economics*, *186*, 107053.

Hancock, T. (2015). Population health promotion 2.0: An eco-social approach to public health in the Anthropocene, *Canadian. Public Health*, *106*(4), e252–e255.

Hasanaj, V. (2023). The shift towards an eco-welfare state: Growing stronger together. *Journal of International and Comparative Social Policy*, ●●●, 1–22. DOI: 10.1017/ics.2023.2

Hayward, T. (1990). Ecosocialism – Utopian and Scientific. *Radical Philosophy*, *56*, 2–14.

Helne, T., & Hirvilammi, T. (2017). The relational conception of wellbeing as a catalyst for the ecosocial transition. In Matthies, A.-L., & Närhi, K. (Eds.), *The Ecosocial Transition of Societies: The contribution of social work and social policy* (pp. 36–53). Routledge.

Heryford, R. (2020). "The Mold-life": Dickinson's Poetics of Decay. *The Emily Dickinson Journal*, *29*(1), 27–47.

Hickel, J. (2019). Degrowth: A theory of radical abundance. *Real-World Economics Review*, *87*(19), 54–68.

Hildingsson, R., & Koch, M. (2016). Market solutions to climate change: examples of personal carbon-trading and carbon-rationing. In Koch, M., & Mont, O. (Eds.), *Sustainability and the Political Economy of Welfare* (pp. 109–124). Routledge.

Hirvilammi, T., Häikiö, L., Johansson, H., Koch, M., & Perkiö, J. (2023). Social Policy in a Climate Emergency Context: Towards an Ecosocial Research Agenda. *Journal of Social Policy*, *52*(1), 1–23. DOI: 10.1017/S0047279422000721

Hirvilammi, T., & Koch, M. (2020). Sustainable Welfare beyond Growth. *Sustainability*, *12*(5), 1824. DOI: 10.3390/su12051824

Hofmeister, S. (2002). Intermediate 'Time-spaces': The Rediscovery of Transition in Spatial Planning and Environmental Planning. *Time & Society, 11*(1), 105–130. DOI: 10.1177/0961463X02011001007

Hujo, K., & Carter, M. (2019). *Transformative Change for Children and Youth in the Context of the 2030 Agenda for Sustainable Development.* UNRISD, Innocenti Working Paper WP-2019-02.

Isah, H. M., Sawyerr, H. O., Raimi, M. O., Bashir, B. G., Haladu, S., & Odipe, O. E. (2020). Assessment of Commonly Used Pesticides and Frequency of Self-Reported Symptoms on Farmers Health in Kura, Kano State, Nigeria. *Journal of Education and Learning Management, 1*(1), 31–54.

Jakobsson, N., Muttarak, R., & Schoyen, M. A. (2018). Dividing the pie in the eco-social state: Exploring the relationship between public support for environmental and welfare policies. *Environment and Planning C. Politics and Space, 36*(2), 313–339.

Jeffery, R. D., Krogh, C., & Horner, B. (2013). Adverse health effects of industrial wind turbines. *Canadian Family Physician Médecin de Famille Canadien, 59*(5), 473–475.

Jessoula, M., & Mandelli, M. (2019). *The Right to Energy for All Europeans Coalition: A Case of Green-Red Mobilization?* Laboratorio di Politica Comparata e filosofia Pubblica, working paper. Torino: LEPF Centro Einaudi.

Jones, P., Miles, D., Francis, A., & Rajeev, S. P. (2011). Preface. In Jones, P., Miles, D., Francis, A., & Rajeev, S. P. (Eds.), *Eco-social Justice: Issues, Challenges and Ways Forward, Voices from De Novo'11.* Books for Change.

Kaasch, A., Koch, M., & Martens, K. (2019). Exploring theoretical approaches to global social policy research: Learning from international relations and inter-organisational theory. *Global Social Policy, 19*(1-2), 87–104.

Khan, J., Emilsson, K., & Fritz, M.. (2022). Ecological ceiling and social floor: Public support for eco-social policies in Sweden. *Sustainability Science.* Advance online publication. DOI: 10.1007/s11625-022-01221-z

Knox, P. L. (1981). Convergence and Divergence in Regional Patterns of Infant Mortality in the United Kingdom from 1949-51 to 1970-72. *Social Science & Medicine, 5*(4), 537–539.

Koch, M. (2018). Sustainable welfare, degrowth and eco-social policies in Europe. In Banhercke, B., Ghailani, D., & Sabato, S. (Eds.), *Social policy in the European Union: state of play 2018* (pp. 35–50). ETUI.

Koch, M. (2019). Elements of a political economy of the postgrowth era, *Real-world economics review*, 87.

Koch, M. (2020). The state in the transformation to a sustainable postgrowth economy. *Environmental Politics*, *29*(1), 115–133. DOI: 10.1080/09644016.2019.1684738

Koch, M. (2022). State of the Art Social Policy Without Growth: Moving Towards Sustainable Welfare States. *Social Policy and Society*, *21*(3), 447–459.

Koch, M., & Buch-Hansen, H. (2020). The IPE of degrowth and sustainable welfare. In Vivares, E. (Ed.), *The Routledge Handbook to Global Political Economy: Conversations and Inquiries* (pp. 375–390). Routledge.

Koch, M., & Fritz, M. (2014). Building the Eco-social State: Do Welfare Regimes Matter?'. *Journal of Social Policy*, *43*(4), 679–703.

Köhler, G. (2016). Tapping the Sustainable Development Goals for progressive gender equity and equality policy? *Gender and Development*. Advance online publication. DOI: 10.1080/13552074.2016.1142217

Köhler, G. (2018). *Creative Coalitions in a Fractured World An Opportunity for Transformative Change?* Draft paper prepared for the UNRISD Conference Overcoming Inequalities in a Fractured World: Between Elite Power and Social Mobilization 8–9 November 2018, Geneva, Switzerland.

Krause, D. (2021). Uncovering different degrees of eco-social policy. *Global Social Policy*, *21*(2), 332–334.

Krausman, P., & Mahoney, S. P. (2015). How the Boone and Crockett Club (B&C) shaped North American conservation. *The International Journal of Environmental Studies*, *72*(5), 746–755. DOI: 10.1080/00207233.2015.1073474

Lakeman, S. (2021). IOs and Climate Change: Toward Global Eco-Social Policy. In Martens, K., Niemann, D., & Kaasch, A. (Eds.), *International Organizations in Global Social Governance* (pp. 255–273). Palgrave Macmillan.

Laruffa, F. (2022). The dilemma of "sustainable welfare" and the problem of the future in capacitating social policy. *Sustainability: Science. Practice and Policy*, *18*(1), 822–836. DOI: 10.1080/15487733.2022.2143206

Laruffa, F., McGann, M., & Murphy, M. P. (2022). Enabling Participation Income for an Eco-Social State. *Social Policy and Society*, *21*(3), 508–519.

Legge, M. (1999). Wild geese and solidarity: Conjunctural praxis for a spirit-filled ethics. *Union Seminary Quarterly Review*, *53*(3/4), 165–185.

Leibowitz, L. (1975). Changing views of women in society, 1975. *Revista de Antropologia*, *2*(4), 532–538. DOI: 10.1080/00988157.1975.9977205

Mandelli, M. (2022a). Understanding eco-social policies: A proposed definition and typology. *Transfer: European Review of Labour and Research*, *28*(3), 333–348.

Mandelli, M. (2022b). *Mapping eco-social policy mixes for a just transition in Europe*. ETUI, working paper.

Manning, R. E. (1984). Men and Mountains Meet: Journal of the Appalachian Mountain Club, 1876-1984. *Journal of Forest History*, *28*(1), 24–33.

Marden, S., & Gough, I. (2011). Fiscal costs of climate mitigation programmes in the UK: A challenge for social policy? Centre for Analysis of Social Exclusion. *CASE (Philadelphia, Pa.)*, •••, 145.

Marston, G. (2019). Basic Income in Australia: Implementation Challenges. In Klein, E., Mays, J., & Dunlop, T. (Eds.), *Implementing a Basic Income in Australia: Pathways Forward*. Palgrave Macmillan.

Martinez-Alier, J. (1991). Ecology and the Poor: A Neglected Dimension of Latin American History. *Journal of Latin American Studies*, *23*(3), 621–639.

Martinez-Alier, J. (1993). Distributional Obstacles to International Environmental Policy: The Failures at Rio and Prospects after Rio. *Environmental Values*, *2*(2), 97–124.

Matthies, A.-L., Turunen, P., Albers, S., Boeck, T., & Närhi, K. (2000). An eco-social approach to tackling social exclusion in European cities: A new comparative research project in progress. *European Journal of Social Work*, *3*(1), 43–52. DOI: 10.1080/714052811

McGann, M., & Murphy, M. P. (2023). Income Support in an Eco-Social State: The Case for Participation Income. *Social Policy and Society*, *22*(1), 16–30.

Mehra, P., Babita, K., & Gangandeep, B. (2021). The Degrowth Alternative: Need Of The Hour. In Thakur, D. J., Verma, P., & Sharma, D. (Eds.), *Management Practices Amidst COVID-19*. Weser Books.

Merz, S., Jaehn, P., Mena, E., Pöge, K., Strasser, S., & Saß, A.-C. Rommel, A., Bolte, G. & Holmberg, C. (2021). Intersectionality and eco-social theory: A review of potentials for public health knowledge and social justice. *Critical Public Health*. Advance online publication. DOI: 10.1080/09581596.2021.1951668

Meyer-Renschhausen, E. (2014). Community gardening in Berlin and New York: A new eco-social movement. In A. Viljoen & K. Bohn (Eds.) *Second Nature Urban Agriculture: Designing Productive Cities* (pp. 146-153), London: Routledge. 146-153.

Moore, B. (1952). Review: *Bernhard Eduard Fernow* by Andrew Denny Rodgers. *Empire Forestry Review, 31*(1), 57–59.

Moore, J. (2009). *A Primitivist Primer*, Library.Anarhija.Net.

Moreno, C., Allam, Z., Chabaud, D., Gall, C., & Pratlong, F. (2021). Introducing the "15-Minute City": Sustainability, Resilience and Place Identity in Future Post-Pandemic Cities. *Smart Cities, 4*, 93–111.

Muller, W. C., & Steininger, B. (1996). Christian Democracy in Austria: The Austrian People's Party. In Hanley, D. (Ed.), *Christian Democracy in Europe: A Comparative Perspective* (pp. 87–100). Pinter.

Murphy, M. P. (2013). Translating degrowth into contemporary policy challenges: A symbiotic social transformation strategy. *Irish Journal of Sociology, 21*(2), 76–89.

Naess, A. (1973). The shallow and the deep, long-range ecology movement: A summary. *Inquiry: An Interdisciplinary Journal of Philosophy, 16*(1–4), 95–100. DOI: 10.1080/00201747308601682

Newell, F. H. (1895). The American Forestry Association. *Science, 2*(39), 385–390.

Ogilvie, M., & Rootes, C. (2015). The impact of local campaigns against wind energy developments. *Environmental Politics, 24*(6), 874–893.

Otto, A., & Gugushvili, D. (2020). Eco-Social Divides in Europe: Public Attitudes towards Welfare and Climate Change Policies. *Sustainability, 12*, 404. DOI: 10.3390/su12010404

Parks, L., & Tsioumani, E. (2023). Transforming biodiversity governance? Indigenous peoples' contributions to the Convention on Biological Diversity. *Biological Conservation, 280*, 109933.

Parsons, J. J. (1981). Human Influences on the Pine and Laurel Forests of the Canary Islands. *Geographical Review, 71*(3), 253–271.

Peters, M. A. (2017). Oil geopolitics and eco-nightmares. *Educational Philosophy and Theory, 49*(5), 435–438. DOI: 10.1080/00131857.2017.1286135

Plagerson, S. (2012). *'Human Well-Being and Capabilities', From Science to Practice: Research and Knowledge to Achieve the SDGs*. Consultation Document.

Plumhans, L.-A. (2021). *Operationalizing eco-social policies: a mapping of energy poverty measures in EU member states.* Working Paper Reihe der AK Wien - Materialien zu Wirtschaft und Gesellschaft 212, Kammer für Arbeiter und Angestellte für Wien, Abteilung Wirtschaftswissenschaft und Statistik.

Raimi, M. O., Vivien, O. T., Alima, O., Akpojubaro, E. H., & Williams, E. A. (2021). Articulating the Effect of Pesticides Use and Sustainable Development Goals (SDGs): The Science of Improving Lives through Decision Impacts. https://ssrn.com/abstract=3838210

Raworth, K., Wykes, S. & Bass, S. (2014). *Securing social justice in green economies: A review and ten considerations for policymakers.* International Institute for Environment and Development, Issue Paper, October.

Rootes, C. (2004). Environmental Movements. In Snow, D., Sarah, A. S., & Hanspeter, K. (Eds.), *The Blackwell Companion to Social Movements* (pp. 608–640). Blackwell.

Sabato, S., & Mandelli, M. (2018). The EU's potential for promoting an ecosocial agenda. Report prepared for the project "Sustainable welfare societies: Assessing linkages between social and environmental policies", NOVA Norwegian Social Research. Brussels: European Social Observatory, December, 35p.

Sabato, S., Mandelli, M., & Jessoula, M. (2022). Towards an EU eco-social agenda? From Europe 2020 to the European Green Deal. In M. A. Schoen, B. Hvinden & M. D. Leiren (Eds.), *Towards Sustainable Welfare States in Europe: Social Policy and Climate Change* (pp. 199-219), Cheltham, Edward Elgar.

Sacchi, G. (2019). Social innovation matters: The adoption of participatory guarantee systems within Italian alternative agri-food networks. *Strategic Change, 28,* 241–248.

Sanne, C. (2002). Willing costumers – or locked-in? Policies for a sustainable consumption. *Ecological Economics, 42*(1-2), 273–287.

Sartori, G. (1970). Concept Misformation in Comparative Politics. *The American Political Science Review, 64*(4), 1033–1053.

Sartori, G. (1991). Comparing and Miscomparing. *Journal of Theoretical Politics, 3.* Advance online publication. DOI: 10.1177/0951692891003003001

Schoyen, M. A., & Hvinden, B. (2017). Climate change as a challenge for European welfare states. In Kennett, P., & Lendvai-Bainton, N. (Eds.), *Handbook of European Social Policy* (pp. 371–385). Edward Elgar.

Schoyen, M. A., Hvinden, B., & Leiren, M. D. (2022). Welfare state sustainability in the 21st century. In M. A. Schoen, B. Hvinden & M. D. Leiren (Eds.), *Towards Sustainable Welfare States in Europe: Social Policy and Climate Change* (pp. 2-27), Cheltham, Edward Elgar.

Singh, S. (2021). Socio-Economic Dimensions of Sustainable Development. In D. K. Singh & P. S. Khare (Eds.), *Earth-II [Environmental Sustainability and Conservation]*. Prayagraj: Krishna Computer Sansthan.

Sparhawk, W. N. (1949). The History of Forestry in America. In Stefferud, A. (Ed.), *Trees: the yearbook of agriculture, 1949*. D.C., US Government Printing Office.

Sposato, G. (2021). Italy: Approval and EIA process for RE power plants simplified. Rödl & Partner, 17 November. https://www.roedl.com/insights/renewable-energy/2021/november/italien-approval-eia-process-simplified

Spretnak, C. (1994). A Living Memorial. In Kelly, P. K. (Ed.), *Thinking Green! Essays on Environmentalism, Feminism, and Nonviolence* (pp. 151–154). Parallax Press.

Stamm, I. (2023). Ecosocial work and services for unemployed people: The challenge to integrate environmental and social sustainability. *Nordic Social Work Research, 13*(1), 134–147. DOI: 10.1080/2156857X.2021.1975154

Steele, W. (2022). Wild infrastructure. *Current Opinion in Environmental Sustainability, 55*, 101171.

Turnock, D. (1995). The Rural Transition in Eastern Europe. *GeoJournal, 36*(4), 420–426.

Tyrrell, I. (2002). Modern Environmentalism. In Agnew, J.-C., & Rosenzweig, R. (Eds.), *A Companion to Post-1945 America* (pp. 328–342). Blackwell Publishing.

UNRISD. (2016). *Policy Innovations for Transformative Change: Implementing the 2030 Agenda for Sustainable Development*. United Nations Research Institute for Social Development.

Utting, P. (2013). Pathways to sustainability in a crisis-ridden world. In Genevey, R., Pachauri, R., & Tubiana, L. (Eds.), *Reducing inequalities: A Sustainable Development Challenge* (pp. 175–190). TERI Press.

van den Bergh, J. C. J. M., & Kallis, G. (2012). Growth, A-Growth or Degrowth to Stay within Planetary Boundaries? *Journal of Economic Issues, 46*(4), 909 919.

Vanhercke, B., Sabato, S., & Ghailani, D. (2018). Conclusions: The European Pillar of Social Rights as a game changer. In Vanhercke, B., Ghailani, D., & Sabato, S. (Eds.), *Social Policy in the European Union: state of play 2018*. ETUI.

Vastola, A., Cozzi, M., Viccaro, M., Grippo, V., Romano, S., Kawakami, J., & Shimpo, N. (2020). Exploring Urban Gardening Experiences in Europe and Asia: Rome vs. Tokyo. In *Green Metamorphoses: Agriculture, Food, Ecology, Proceedings of the LV Conference of SIDEA Studies* (pp. 289-294), Wageningen Academic Publishers: Wageningen, The Netherlands.

Weidner, H. (1993). Mediation as a policy instrument for resolving environmental disputes: With special reference to Germany, WZB Discussion Paper, No. FS II 93-301, Wissenschaftszentrum Berlin für Sozialforschung (WZB), Berlin.

Xi-Ji. (1986). Pricing System Reform for Agricultural Products and Price Policy Adjustment in China (1979-1984). In A. Maunder & U. Renborg (Eds.), *Agriculture in a Turbulent World Economy: Proceedings of the Nineteenth International Conference of Agricultural Economists* (pp. 449-465), Gower.

KEY TERMS AND DEFINITIONS

Concept Stretching: A concept whose definition is expanded to include all subjects of study

Conceptual Furcation: Breaking up abstract concepts into more specific concepts that avoid concept stretching.

Eco-Social: Although the nature of this paper is to examine and problematize this concept, one definition particularly addressing eco-social policy is that it "addresses social and environmental goals and brings about benefits in both dimensions" (Carmi 2016)

Extension: The range of real-world examples.

Intension: The internal meaning or set of characteristics that define what a word or concept is.

Ladder of Abstraction: A concept developed by Sartori (1970) that describes how language can move from very concrete, specific ideas to more abstract, general ones using the concept of extension and intension

Rung Descension: Moving down the ladder of abstraction by focusing on more precise concepts with fewer real-world examples, and at some level, abandoning the more abstract concept.

ENDNOTES

1 To understand the growth of the concept I used a Google Scholar search for the terms "eco-social policy" and, independently, "eco-social policies". I first looked at any references from 1900-1989 and then for each following year separately, through 2022. As many will be aware, Google Scholar searches are not highly accurate. For example, one article containing 'eco-social policy' is attributed to J Sutton and dated to 1947 but is actually a report by Button and Coote from 2016 (and the only mention of 'eco-social' is in a short biography of one of the authors. Issues arose across misattributed dates, "eco-social" only showing up in the bibliographies of texts, "eco-social" being identified as a search term erroneously due to the formatting of the document, etc. I was therefore required to manually investigate the results, which ensured both the accuracy of the date and the presence of the term in the right context. This search was also used to exclude texts that not of sufficient academic standards - undergraduate or master's dissertations, and conference PowerPoint presentations or abstracts. Only English-language sources were used. The data captured using this method shows us how the concept grew over time across two dimensions – their use within texts (Figure 1) and their use in text titles (Figure 2). The former includes a line indicating texts with either eco-social policies or policy. This does not represent the sum total of the two sets of bars because many texts used both 'eco-social policy' and 'eco-social policies' and thus were only counted once. The latter can help show the prominence of the concept, although it does not always align with the rate of usage within any given text. Such relative rates would be difficult to calculate given the varied sizes of texts (from short special issue introductions to books). Thus, the inclusion of 'eco-social policy' or 'eco-social policies' in titles were used as an indicator of prominence.

2 Such policies were already described by Gough as 'eco-social investments' in papers published in 2011 (Gough 2011; Marden and Gough 2011).

3 Eco-social transition policies in the case of Bell.

4 Others have discussed eco-social policies in relation postgrowth or steady state economics (Büchs and Koch; Koch 2018; Koch 2020). Here we are using degrowth in ways that include these other conceptualizations.

5 Of course, some conceptualizations of eco-social policies do not incorporate growth in any way and are thus flexible when it comes to the issue of the economy (e.g., Laruffa 2022). For these definitions, policies that incorporate degrowth or growth strategies may be considered equally as eco-social. Some

have referred to this perspective as a-growth (see van den Bergh and Kallis 2012). That does not mean the economic question does not get raised. For example, some have discussed the 'eco-social' as integrating priorities concerning social justice and sustainability within the context of economic opportunities and constraints, to produce a new green and just *economy*, where economic change is central but in order to achieve eco-social goals (Raworth et al 2014). In any case, where growth and degrowth are not conceptual distinctions, other differentiation may arise in these conceptualizations. One such distinction may not necessarily be found within the definitions of eco-social, but in their operationalization: the direction of integration.

6 In addition, concepts like "socio-ecological policies" have been used interchangeably with "eco-social policies" by a number of authors (Cotta 2024, 3n1).

Chapter 3
Critical Posthumanist Sustainability of Future Media Ecologies

Alisa Kronberger
https://orcid.org/0009-0000-0410-4112
Ruhr-University Bochum, Germany

ABSTRACT

This paper critically interrogates the anthropocentric foundations of media ecology, proposing a shift from sustainable media practices toward an understanding of humans as entangled with their technological environments. Grounded in critical posthumanist ethics, it addresses ecological crises shaped by extractive, (neo)colonial forces of global capitalism, foregrounding questions of climate justice, care, and responsibility. Emphasizing relational constellations between humans, technologies, and environments, the paper rethinks "natural resources" and challenges nature–culture dualisms. It advocates for a posthumanist ethics of sustainability based on relationality, envisioning ecologies not as systems to manage, but as interwoven networks requiring ethical, alterbiopolitical engagement.

INTRODUCTION

In both communication studies and educational theory, the concept of media ecology has long served as a valuable framework for stimulating discussions about the sustainable and ethical use of media. Traditionally, this approach has focused on questions related to regulating media consumption and cultivating media literacy, aiming to foster a more responsible and mindful engagement with technological tools. However, the field of media cultural studies takes this ecological mode of

DOI: 10.4018/979-8-3373-1707-6.ch003

thinking a step further, expanding its scope beyond the confines of media regulation and individual usage practices. Rather than merely addressing the sustainable use of media from a practical standpoint (Kannengießer, 2022; 2023), cultural media studies employs media ecology as a critical tool to interrogate the deeply ingrained, apparatus- and instrument-centric understandings of media. This approach challenges the prevailing assumptions that have often dominated media discourse, redirecting attention toward the broader, more complex interconnections between technology, culture, and society.

Central to this expanded conceptualization is the shift towards a non-anthropocentric perspective that prioritizes the intricate and often overlooked technoecological relationships that define the media environments we inhabit (Rothe, 2016, p. 46). In this framework, the focus moves away from simply limiting media exposure or acquiring the skills necessary for effective media use, and instead, centers on examining the processes of mediation. These processes, in turn, reveal the ways in which human existence is intricately woven into—and inseparable from—the technological and material environments that we constantly interact with. Media ecology, thus, emerges not as a singular, unified field but rather as a dynamic and contested arena, wherein diverse, often contradictory theoretical perspectives come into play. This multidimensionality complicates any attempts to arrive at a single, authoritative account of the media-ecological condition, prompting ongoing debates about how best to understand and respond to the challenges posed by technological advancements.

Rather than seeking to reconcile these tensions or reduce them to a single theoretical framework, this chapter proposes instead a productive dialogue, one that opens up new pathways for rethinking sustainability within the context of media-cultural theory and its broader implications. At the heart of this inquiry is a re-examination of media ecology through a media-cultural lens, which emphasizes a shared understanding across both communication and media studies: the collective, ethical, and sustainable shaping of media environments. Building upon this common foundation, the paper explores the critical potential of posthumanist ethics, particularly its capacity to illuminate the contemporary media-ecological landscape. Posthumanist thought offers a crucial perspective on the entangled techno-material realities that increasingly define our everyday lives, revealing how deeply our existence is intertwined with both human and non-human entities. This chapter addresses the following research question: How can a critical posthumanist media theory redefine the discourse and practice of sustainability within the field of International Relations?

Before turning to the dominant and often reductive conceptualizations of sustainability in contemporary media discourse—particularly those anchored in Western, Eurocentric, and hegemonic semantic frameworks—I begin by examining the temporal dimensions of climate justice. In doing so, I frame climate justice as a *matter of care* (Bellacasa, 2017), foregrounding its ethical and relational implications. The prevailing frameworks tend to reinforce the objectification of "natural resources" and the passivization of the environment by representing non-human entities merely as resources to be exploited for human benefit. Such thinking not only perpetuates the subjugation of non-human life but also subsumes human existence itself into the extractivist logic of global capitalism. Within this context, sustainability is frequently stripped of its ethical significance and reduced to a set of pragmatic, technocratic solutions. These solutions, while seemingly efficient, fail to address the deeper relational and ethical concerns foregrounded by media ecology—concerns that challenge us to rethink our entanglements with the more-than-human world.

This critique ultimately leads to a central imperative within media-ecological discourse: the need to address the relational configurations and materializations of practices and discourses that link humans, objects, and environments in complex, entangled ways. These configurations are not merely technical or functional; they raise crucial ethical questions regarding responsibility (Kronberger, 2024) and care—questions that are essential to any meaningful conception of sustainability. As such, sustainability must be reconceptualized not merely as an environmental or technological goal but as a deeply ethical principle, one that is better understood through the lens of critical posthumanist thought. To illustrate this argument, the paper engages critically with the concept of "natural resources" as a case study, demonstrating how the entangled economies of life and matter reveal the underlying ethical dilemmas of sustainability.

Against the backdrop of dominant, neoliberal and neocolonial models of care and sustainability—often shaped by optimization, efficiency, and anthropocentric utility—a critical posthumanist ethics foregrounds *matters of care* as an alternative mode of ethical engagement. Drawing on Astrid Schrader's non-anthropocentric and Maria Puig de la Bellacasa's *alterbiopolitical* conception of *caring about*, this framework shifts the focus from instrumentalized forms of "caring for" to relational practices of attention, responsibility, and justice. Such an approach challenges institutionalized exclusions and reorients care as an open-ended, affective, and political act—attuned to the vulnerability and alterity of both human and non-human life. Within this horizon, *future ecologies* emerge as a speculative and ethical framework that resists hegemonic sustainability discourse and reimagines ecological entanglements through the lens of care as alterbiopolitical "caring about". This perspective calls for media ethics that not only acknowledge but actively participate in shaping more just, inclusive, and ecologically responsive futures.

This chapter is structured as follows: I first elaborate on media-ecological thinking and its central concepts. Subsequently, I introduce climate justice as a key framework in International Relations and explore its connection to a posthumanist ethic of care. The third section provides a concrete, empirically grounded case study of media-geological entanglements to illustrate the arguments. Finally, I conclude by summarizing the key contributions and outlining future research directions for a posthumanist approach to sustainability in International Relations.

(FUTURE) MEDIA ECOLOGIES

A distinctive feature of contemporary media landscapes is the emergence of a new class of technologies, often collectively referred to as ambient technologies. This category encompasses concepts such as the "Internet of Things," (Friess, 2022) "ambient intelligence," (Novais et al., 2023) and "ubiquitous computing," (Dourish & Bell, 2011) (which are used to describe digital technologies characterized by their pervasive and networked presence in daily life. These technologies are not confined to the traditional realm of personal devices; instead, they permeate a wide array of spaces, including mobile communications, automated traffic systems, and drone applications. Such technologies transform the very environments in which they exist, which has led to their early descriptions using the term "environment" itself (Sprenger, 2019, p. 18). This transformation reflects a shift towards an increasingly interwoven relationship between technological systems and the physical world, where the boundaries between the two are progressively blurred.

In addressing this phenomenon, Erich Hörl proposes a compelling thesis: the rise of ecological descriptions in the context of technological media should be understood as a form of self-interpretation by Western societies under "technological conditions" (Hörl, 2011, p. 11, transl. by the author). Hörl's perspective suggests that the ecological turn in media studies is not merely a response to environmental concerns but also a reflection of how technological systems are increasingly embedded in and shape our everyday realities (see also Rieger, 2025). Building on this notion, Florian Sprenger has argued that, since the early 21st century, environments have become sites where traditional boundaries—such as those between nature and technology, active subjects and passive artifacts—must and inevitably do intersect and blur (Sprenger, 2019, p. 19). This shift is emblematic of a broader process of environmentalization, where technology and technological sciences themselves are contributing to the redefinition of environmental categories (Hörl, 2013, p. 128). Within this context, the flourishing of ecological terms is not merely an academic exercise, but part of a larger rethinking of the relationship between media, technology, and the environment. The ecological turn thus extends beyond environmentalism to encompass diverse forms of media ecology, which consider the intricate interrelations between technology and ecological systems.

According to Hörl, under media-ecological conditions, there is a pressing need to reformulate the concepts of ecology and technology, thereby positioning both within a continuous and interconnected framework. This reformulation challenges conventional, teleological, and anthropocentric understandings of technology, advocating for a way of thinking that does not merely view technology as a tool serving human ends but as a dynamic, purposeless, and non-anthropocentric entity in its own right (Sprenger, 2019, p. 20; see also Postman, 2006 & McLuhan, 1996). The task, then, is to reconsider the role of technology in our lives without attributing to it a fixed, human-centered purpose, instead allowing for a more nuanced understanding of its relations with the natural and social world.

In this context, the concept of media ecology becomes crucial, as it is uniquely positioned to address the complex ecological interactions that occur within technological media environments. Media ecology, as Florian Sprenger demonstrates, draws upon ecological history to describe technological media as ecologically relational, exploring their interconnections and entanglements (2019, p. 21). Through a media-ecological lens, it becomes possible to move beyond the traditional focus on individual media technologies and their instrumental characteristics, and instead examine the generative interrelations between human and non-human actors, technical apparatuses, media infrastructures, and institutions. This approach allows for a more holistic understanding of how various elements within media environments interact, shaping not only technological developments but also social, cultural, and ecological dynamics and inequalities. Furthermore, media ecology disrupts dualistic thinking—such as the separation between nature and culture, subject and object, or human and non-human—by promoting an understanding of all actors as interconnected and interdependent. From this perspective, the interactions between human and technical agents are not separate or hierarchical, but emerge through their entanglement in dynamic, processual relationships. These actors, whether human or non-human, can enable, promote, or obstruct connections in various ways, thereby shaping the media-ecological system as a whole.

A central question in media-ecological theory, particularly with regard to sustainability, is the need to engage more deeply with the ecological aspects of media technologies. This includes considering the production conditions of media, the resource consumption associated with their creation and use, and the materials from which they are made. To evaluate the sustainability of media ecologies, Evi Zemanek proposes four distinct approaches, each examining different facets of the reciprocal relationship between humans, media, and nature: 1) the dependency of media on natural (and human) resources, from extraction to disposal, including their integration into material and recycling cycles; 2) the durability and effectiveness of the knowledge storage media provide within the cultural and collective household; 3) the consumption behavior associated with media, viewed from social, legal, economic, and media-ethical perspectives; and 4) the discursive, opinion-forming, and action-guiding potential of media content (Zemanek, 2019, p. 397, transl. by the author). These categories offer a multifaceted approach to assessing the sustainability of media environments, highlighting the complex interplay between technology, society, and the environment.

While Zemanek's framework for assessing sustainability in media ecologies does not explicitly delve into ethical concerns, these are nonetheless embedded within her approach. Media sustainability, after all, is not only about efficiency or resource conservation but also about the ethical dimensions of our interactions with technology and the environment. Katja Rothe, in contrast, makes a more explicit connection between media ecology and ethics, arguing that the concept of media ecology is fundamentally ethical in nature (2016, p. 47). This ethical dimension raises a crucial, unresolved question: How can we, in collaboration with both human and non-human actors, design media environments—environments in which we are continuously embedded and embodied—in ways that are just, livable, and sustainable? Rather than attempting to provide a singular or definitive answer to this profound question, this paper seeks to explore the ethical framework of critical posthumanism. This framework not only complements media-ecological thinking but also offers a conceptual lens for developing possible responses to the ethical challenges posed by the entangled relationships between humans, technology, and the environment. Through this exploration, the paper aims to contribute to ongoing discussions about how we can better understand and shape the future of media environments in ways that are not only sustainable but also ethically responsible and just.

Before engaging with the question of what a critical posthumanist ethics might offer for the configuration of future media ecologies, I will first sharpen the conceptual contours of climate justice. This notion foregrounds an ethical obligation to resist relegating the climate crisis to an externalized sphere of "nature," and instead compels us to confront it as a thoroughly social and political phenomenon (Bee, 2025). Crucially, I contend that the discourse of climate justice, almost necessarily, gestures toward a feminist-inflected ethics of *caring about* (Schrader, 2015) the climate—an orientation that reconfigures responsibility not as abstract obligation, but as situated, relational responsiveness (Haraway, 2016).

CLIMATE JUSTICE AS A MATTER OF CARE: LINKING MEDIA THEORY TO INTERNATIONAL RELATIONS

This section explicitly links the discussion to the core themes of the book on International Relations (IR) by positioning media-ecological and posthumanist thought as a critical lens for understanding global sustainability governance. By engaging with posthumanist theory, we can challenge the dominant approaches in IR—such as those centered on state-based policy frameworks like the Sustainable

Development Goals (SDGs) or the Paris Agreement—which often rely on anthropocentric, technocratic, and state-centric assumptions. This chapter argues that a posthumanist perspective challenges these frameworks by introducing a relational and non-human-centric understanding of sustainability.

Drawing on the work of Julia Bee, I conceptualize climate justice as a broadened critical framework—one that, akin to the categories of gender and race, can be operationalized both methodologically and epistemologically. In IR, this approach shifts the focus beyond high-level policy targets like the 1.5-degree Celsius threshold and reframes climate justice as a diagnostic tool for interrogating the structural conditions that produce and perpetuate global hierarchies of vulnerability and worth. In this context, climate justice becomes not merely an environmental concern, but a critical mode of inquiry into the intersecting forms of inequality embedded in climate discourses and policies (see also Blättel-Mink et al., 2021). Physicist and philosopher Friederike Otto (2023), co-founder of the *World Weather Attribution*, advances this argument by introducing the notion of climate injustice, emphasizing that race, gender, and other axes of social differentiation are not external modifiers but foundational to the very production of climate-related risk and harm. From this vantage point, climate must be understood not as a neutral or universal condition, but as a materially and discursively stratified terrain—shaped by historical and ongoing processes of racialization, gendering, ableism, and socio-economic marginalization. In short, climate emerges as a contested and uneven field of power, in which environmental precarity is both distributed and experienced differentially.

Within this framework, both climate justice and extractivism can be understood as historically and epistemically entangled with colonial modernity. (Bee, 2025) Yet despite their frequent juxtaposition, they refer to distinct modalities of racialized violence—climate justice pointing toward struggles over equitable futures, while extractivism names the logics of accumulation, dispossession, and environmental degradation underpinning those violences. Their respective genealogies yield divergent media-theoretical implications: each invites a different reading of how violence becomes sensible—how it is rendered visible, affective, or invisible through media technologies, aesthetic regimes, and representational politics (Bee, 2025).

Not only is the distinction between the terms "extractivism" and "climate justice" fundamentally grounded in a differentiation of their implicit temporal vectors—extractivism being situated in the past and present, while climate justice focuses on the present and future—but the question of matters of concern and matters of care can also be understood along these temporal axes. Bruno Latour has notably introduced the distinction between "matters of fact" and "matters of concern," where "matters of fact" refer to the climate crisis as something that can be apprehended as a set of objective, isolated facts—something that can be referenced, pointed to, and discussed as a fixed entity (Latour, 2004). In contrast, the climate crisis, when understood as a matter of concern, becomes a dynamic "gathering" of ideas, powers, actors, practices, and sites that emerge and evolve through engagement and care. A matter of concern is something that one takes seriously, something that compels attention, care, and worry.

Latour's conceptual shift—from matters of fact to matters of concern—addresses the ethical and political dimensions of constructivist approaches within the field of Science and Technology Studies (STS), particularly in how meaning is assigned to things through their representation. His epistemic shift challenges the notion that facts are neutral and independent, instead suggesting that what we regard as facts are always entangled with interpretive practices and power relations. Within this framework, matters of concern invite us to reconsider the climate crisis not as a set of detached facts, but as a constellation of interconnected issues that demand our ethical and political engagement. In this sense, an attentive approach, one that involves careful observation and nuanced intervention (as is typical in environmental ethics), finds its roots in Latour's epistemological reorientation from "facts" to "concerns." According to social constructivism, facts are easily debunked because opposing parties—scientists, government officials, and activists alike—can dismiss unacknowledged claims from others by labeling them as fiction rather than fact. However, when it comes to concerns, such distancing and essentializing positions are not possible. It becomes much more difficult to make definitive oppositional statements when one sees oneself as part of the material, the people, or the ideas being examined. In this way, claims about matters of concern are far more resistant to refutation, as they are inherently bound to the entanglement of the observer with the observed. "Concern brings us closer to a notion of care," writes Maria Puig de la Bellacasa in her seminal work *Matters of Care*, drawing on Latour (2022, p. 18), thereby addressing the question of caregiving in the context of specific circumstances. Bellacasa argues:

> *"Ways of knowing/caring reaffect objectified worlds, restage things in ways that generate possibility for other ways of relating and living, connect things that were not supposed to be connecting across the bifurcation of consciousness, and ultimately transform the ethico-political and affective perception of things by involvement in the mattering of worlds." (2017, p. 65)*

As Bellacasa argues, *matters of care* differ from the teleological assemblage of *matters of concern*; they are always entangled with an investment that retains a connection to justice. Like justice, care articulates a relationship to the *Other* and a mode of attention (see also Schrader, 2015, p. 668). This distinction between *matters of concern* and *matters of care* carries profound implications for understanding the temporal dynamics at play in the discourse of climate justice. While matters of concern are often framed as open-ended, ongoing issues—dynamic yet somewhat detached from immediate ethical engagement—*matters of care* are inherently ethical and more time-sensitive. They demand an embodied, relational response that is rooted in the present, yet oriented toward a future that is shaped by justice, care, and mutual responsibility. The temporal axis of *matters of concern* thus points to a long-term, perhaps even indefinite, struggle for awareness and accountability, whereas *matters of care* position us within a more immediate, pressing moment, where the actions we take today are entwined with a vision of a just future. "Stay where the trouble is", as Haraway appeals to us human species in an interview (Despret et al., 2011, p. 100). And she continues in another text:

> *"The past, present and future are all very much knotted into each other, full of what we need for the work and play of naturalcultural restoration: less deadly curiosity, materially entangled ethics and politics, and technical and organic well being." (Haraway, 2011, p. 17)*

The concept of climate justice emerges as a critical site where these two temporalities converge. Climate justice, in its full ethical and political weight, does not merely acknowledge the ongoing crisis (as a matter of concern), but insists on an immediate, relational mode of intervention—one that considers past (colonial) injustices as unfinished and speculates about livable futures on a "damaged planet" (Tsing et al., 2017), while actively engaging with issues of present conditions and unequally distributed vulnerability. This movement from concern to *care* in the climate justice framework encapsulates the ethical urgency of responding to the climate crisis not just as an issue of fact, but as a ethical and political responsibility that calls us into its obligation to respond, and that requires collective action in the here and now, to *stay with the trouble* (Haraway, 2026). Thus, care within this context is not simply an abstract or distant notion, but a critical, time-sensitive engagement with the interrelated crises of environment, justice, and human-non-human flourishing.

Building on this relational and time-sensitive framework of climate justice, a critically posthumanist ethics provides a necessary expansion of ethical inquiry. Rather than centering ethical subjects, it is an ethics grounded in the interconnections between human and non-human entities, emphasizing kinship and entanglement. In this context, the relational imperative of care extends beyond human concerns, inviting us to reconsider the nature of responsibility and justice in a world shaped by multiple, intersecting agencies. By connecting this to International Relations, we can see how a posthumanist ethic compels us to move beyond state-centric solutions and consider the well-being of non-human entities and the planet itself as integral to global policy. It raises a crucial question for the discipline: How can we think of a climate-just ethics of sustainability that is as prosperous as possible for all, human and non-human alike?

CRITICAL POSTHUMANISM AND ITS ETHICS

This section provides an ethical framework that allows for a new understanding of sustainability in the context of International Relations. It critiques the traditional, anthropocentric approach to sustainability, which often dominates IR discourse, and introduces a more inclusive, relational ethics. By integrating concepts from feminist philosophy and STS, this section provides the theoretical tools necessary to challenge hegemonic sustainability narratives and to understand sustainability not just as a matter of policy, but as a deeply ethical and political project.

Critical posthumanist ethics, grounded in feminist philosophy and Science and Technology Studies (STS), represents a profound departure from traditional ethical frameworks. Feminist technophilosopher and robot ethicist Toni (formerly Janina) Loh offers a compelling characterization of posthumanist ethics as inherently inclusive, emphasizing a radical shift away from individual moral agents, subjects, and objects toward a focus on the relationships that bind them (Loh, 2022, p. 1073). This approach marks a fundamental inversion of perspective, wherein the focus moves from the relata—the moral agents or entities—to the relational dynamics that emerge between them. In contrast to exclusive ethical systems, which place moral agents at the center of ethical considerations and view them as autonomous individuals acting within a predefined moral framework, critical posthumanist ethics places primary importance on the relational context within which these agents emerge and act.

Exclusive ethical systems, traditionally grounded in Western philosophy (e.g., Aristotle), typically prioritize human beings as the ultimate measure of moral significance, founded on anthropocentric premises. This leads to the construction of a moral hierarchy where humans are positioned as the ideal members of the moral community, while non-human entities are relegated to subordinate positions, often assigned only instrumental value. In stark contrast, critical posthumanist ethics challenges this human-centered view by focusing on the relational web that gives rise to moral agents, effectively dismantling the notion of human exceptionalism and rejecting the moral hierarchy that places human beings above non-human entities. By highlighting these relational dynamics, posthumanism redefines moral consideration as a practice not solely determined by an agent's intrinsic attributes, but by the complex interconnections and interactions that shape their existence.

As Loh explains, exclusive ethical systems—such as those influenced by Kantian philosophy (see especially Kant, 2017 in this context)—tend to define a closed circle of moral agents endowed with intrinsic value. This definition often leads to the exclusion of other beings, who are assigned either instrumental value or, in some extreme cases, no value at all. These excluded entities are frequently subjected to structural discrimination, relegated to positions of moral irrelevance or inferiority. Loh critically examines the underlying assumption that not all entities can possess intrinsic value, arguing that this assumption facilitates the exclusion of certain beings from the moral community. This exclusion, though often accepted intuitively, represents a moral system in which complexity and practical navigation of moral actions can become untenable. Loh provocatively questions: on what criteria are certain beings or entities granted intrinsic or instrumental value, and why are some excluded altogether from the moral community?

While exclusive ethical systems may only address moral exclusion as a problem when it is overt or discriminatory, Loh contends that such systems are inherently discriminatory in structure. These systems fail to recognize the interconnectedness of all entities within the moral landscape, often perpetuating exclusion through an artificial demarcation of what constitutes a "moral agent." Loh's work further distinguishes between rejecting anthropological essentialism—the belief in fixed, human-centered categories—and rejecting essentialism altogether. Drawing on everyday examples, she illustrates how essentialist judgments are often made in routine decisions, such as when crossing a street, where we assess the essential characteristics of cars, traffic lights, bicycles, and potential obstacles like potholes. These judgments may hold ethical implications, yet they do not require assigning moral value to every entity involved, underscoring the nuanced and context-dependent nature of ethical decision-making. In the context of International Relations, this distinction is particularly crucial, as it challenges the essentialist thinking that often underpins the way technological systems, non-human entities, and environmental actors are treated in global sustainability policy.

The inclusive nature of critical posthumanist ethics, as articulated by Loh, stems from its foundational shift in perspective from focusing on moral agents (relata) to focusing on the relationships (relations) themselves. This approach does not require that any specific being prove its moral worth to belong to the moral community. Instead, it centers on the evaluation of relationships, irrespective of the specific identities of the beings involved. From this perspective, ethical considerations emerge not from individual qualities or predefined characteristics, but from the dynamic and interconnected interactions between entities. Critical posthumanists, such as feminist science theorist and biologist Donna Haraway, advocate for relational models, particularly through her concept of the "ethics of kinship." (2003; 2016) Haraway provides a relational-ontological framework for understanding the ecological and technological challenges we face today, emphasizing the ethical dimensions of co-existence. In her view, every ethical relationship—whether with human or non-human entities, organic or technological—forms the basis of subjectivation.

Haraway's ethics of kinship, along with her concept of companion species (2003), is rooted in two core principles: first, that responsibility and ethics cannot be rigidly fixed into predefined normative systems; and second, that we must avoid assuming that any entity is an autonomous, pre-existing subject acting independently of its relational context. These principles echo Emmanuel Levinas's ideas on ethics, though Haraway's posthumanist framework should not be misunderstood as suggesting an equal moral responsibility between humans and non-humans. Rather, her relational-ontological view of companion species emphasizes the relational dynamics between human and non-human entities, but crucially avoids a simplistic, binary distinction between the two. For Haraway, responsibility remains a uniquely human task, one that is deeply embedded in relationality and dependent on the context of these relationships. Katharina Hoppe further explores this notion of "strategic anthropocentrism" in Haraway's thinking, arguing that it is a central feature of her post-anthropocentric political ethics, which seeks to balance human responsibility without reverting to normative, human-centered ethical frameworks (Hoppe, 2021, p. 248, transl. by the author).

Both Haraway and Loh advocate for relational and inclusive ethics that challenge the passive treatment of matter and instead position humans as responsible stewards within the relational dynamics between human and non-human entities. These ethics are not simply a rejection of hierarchical frameworks but a call for a deeper understanding of the interconnectedness of all actors—human and non-human alike—within ethical and ecological systems. This is particularly relevant for International Relations scholars, who often focus on state-level actions and international treaties, which can inadvertently obscure the deep, material entanglements that define global sustainability issues (McDonald & Mitchell, 2017; Dalby, 2013). The intricate entanglement of digital technologies with everyday life creates a dynamic wherein media itself undergoes a transformation, becoming an integral part of the environment. This shift in perception gives rise to the concept of *media ecology* as an essential analytical framework for understanding our interconnected world. In this context, media ecology forces us to reconsider sustainability, not merely as an isolated ecological issue, but as a deeply mediated concern (see Latour, 2004) that is inextricably linked to broader questions of climate justice and the exploitative logics of extractive capitalism. This framework encourages us to recognize that the environmental challenges we face are not simply external phenomena but are shaped by and through media, demanding a critical, relational approach to the ways in which both human and non-human actors are implicated in these global crises. The relational approach championed by critical posthumanist ethics offers a novel and more inclusive way of thinking about responsibility and ethics, one that can help guide our interactions with technology, the environment, and each other, and ultimately provide a framework for more sustainable and ethical practices in media, technology, and beyond.

THE IDEA OF "NATURAL RESOURCE" IN EXTRACTIVE CAPITALISM

Extractive Logics and The Passivization of Matter

This section operationalizes the abstract theoretical concepts introduced earlier by applying them to a concrete case study, thereby linking posthumanist media theory directly to the political realities of international resource management and sustainability

Critical posthumanism (Braidotti, 2013) often associated with the broader movement of New Materialism (Coole & Frost, 2010; Dolphijn & van der Tuin, 2012; Alaimo & Hekman, 2008), has recently made a significant impact on international media studies, particularly through the concept of media ecology. This theoretical framework shifts the focus beyond the materiality of digital cultures to emphasize the agency of materialities within the intricate and multifaceted relationships between humans, technology, and the environment. These shifts are crucial for counteracting the passive and objectifying treatment of matter, which is a central concern within the framework. In the context of posthumanist sustainability, the work of Jussi Parikka offers a compelling starting point for further exploration. When Parikka asserts that "the earth had become a resource" (2015, p. 33), he draws attention to the profound interconnections between media technologies and geological materials such as aluminum, copper, gold, silver, and zinc. These materials became integral to the development of media technologies, especially during the late 19th century, coinciding with the height of European colonization of Africa. Through technological processes of surveillance, mapping, and the exploitation of the earth, these extracted materials gave rise to the 'new' media era, which played a pivotal role in the onset of digitalization.

Today, as discussed in the introduction to this paper, we find ourselves entrenched in a media landscape increasingly defined by a networked environment of technologies that often present the illusion of growing immateriality. However, this so-called environmentalization of media, alongside the rise of smart and mobile digital technologies, demands critical inquiry into the interactions between 'material resources' and the legacies of colonial extraction. This inquiry requires acknowledging the non-passive, agency-laden nature of digital materials, alongside their geopolitical entanglements. Consider, for instance, the batteries that power modern digital devices—composed of materials such as lithium, nickel, cobalt, manganese, aluminum, titanium, and especially copper. These batteries serve as essential media of digitality, yet their increasing wastefulness signals an intensification of the long-standing history of extractive violence and colonial exploitation. A veil of normalization, denial, and repression seems to shield this reality from the growing scrutiny of Western consumerism's escalating demands, masking the true ecological and geopolitical costs (see also Bee, 2025).

Jussi Parikka's work highlights the material dependence of media on 'natural resources,' emphasizing that "[m]edia are of nature, and return to nature" (Parikka 2015, Intro, n.p.). Through his concept of medianatures, he underscores the interconnectedness of media and nature, drawing inspiration from Donna Haraway's concept of "naturecultures," which emphasizes the inseparable bond between nature and culture—two traditionally seen as opposing forces. This connection is especially relevant in current critical posthumanist discussions within media ecology, where there is an increasing integration of postcolonial and decolonial frameworks. A central issue in these debates concerns the materiality of media and its agency—how can we describe and evaluate the relationships between media and matter from a power-critical and ethical perspective? One important insight here is that the passivization of matter, which affects both 'natural resources' and human life, leads to profound objectifications (Mareis & Held, 2023). According to critical posthumanist and New Materialist theorists, when matter is passivized, it is reduced to mere objects—lifeless and passive. This process of passivization forms a cornerstone of what Raj Patel and Jason Moore describe as the capitalist system of "cheap things" (2018), wherein extractive capitalism thrives on the artificially cheapened resources like labor, money, food, nature, energy, and life (Mareis & Held, 2023, p. 12).

However, passivization does not only concern 'natural resources.' Kathryn Yusoff, a human geographer, extends this analysis from a postcolonial perspective, arguing that such passivization also impacts human life. Yusoff critiques the Western epistemologies rooted in racist ideologies and exploitative systems that historically divided life into human and non-human, active and passive categories. She asserts that both 'natural resources' and enslaved people of color—particularly from the global South—have been viewed as passive material, with racialization playing a key role in the physical and mineral division of matter into what is considered active and inert (Yusoff, 2018, pp. 2-3).

Considering Loh's proposed inclusive ethics and the dichotomous distinctions between active and passive, human and non-human, which are closely tied to extractive and (neo)colonial violence, the development of a critical posthumanist concept of sustainability must, first and foremost, address how we evaluate relationships between human and non-human entities—particularly those categorized as active or inert. Put differently, contemporary global sustainability debates must avoid neglecting both the extractive and neocolonial mechanisms on the one hand and the agency of matter on the other, as this could inadvertently reinforce a Western-Eurocentric, hegemonic understanding of sustainability.

From Abstract Concepts to Concrete Praxis: The Case of Global Media Infrastructures

This is where the theoretical lens of posthumanism becomes a crucial tool for analyzing the political realities of international relations. The focus on state-level policy often overlooks the material and social inequalities produced by media infrastructure. For example, the supply chains for rare earth minerals used in smartphones and other digital devices are deeply intertwined with geopolitical dynamics, labor exploitation, and environmental degradation in countries of the Global South. A posthumanist approach to sustainability in International Relations would therefore not only analyze these issues from a policy-making perspective, but also by centering the ethical responsibilities that emerge from these material entanglements.

A prime example of this entanglement is the extraction of cobalt and coltan in the Democratic Republic of Congo (DRC). These "conflict minerals" are essential for the batteries and capacitors in virtually all modern electronic devices, including smartphones. The geopolitical and ethical dimensions of this supply chain are staggering: the mining operations are often linked to armed groups, and the labor conditions, particularly in artisanal mines, are characterized by extreme exploitation, including child labor. The posthumanist perspective, however, encourages us to see beyond the human-centric narrative of exploitation. It asks us to also consider the agency of matter itself—how the cobalt and coltan, as non-human entities, are active participants in this global system. Their material properties make them indispensable, but their presence in certain geological locations (the DRC has over 60% of the world's known cobalt reserves) also makes them central to geopolitical power struggles and a source of immense suffering. This framework allows us to analyze how the materialities of technology are not passive resources but active agents shaping human politics and ecological systems.

Critical posthumanist and postcolonial perspectives offer invaluable theoretical frameworks for evaluating relationships—between humans and non-humans, active and passive entities—in the context of sustainability discourses and their material aspects. This approach is vital for shaping future ecologies, where sustainability involves not just managing current relationships but also anticipating and shaping the long-term interconnectedness of all entities.

This rethinking underscores the critical importance of questioning responsibility and care—concepts that are central to any meaningful discussion of sustainability. In a posthumanist-feminist and postcolonial context, responsibility and care are framed as relational practices and discourses that engage not just humans, but also environments and objects. These concepts are vital, not only for understanding our current role within the world, but also for shaping future ecologies that foster more equitable, inclusive, and sustainable engagements with the world around us.

In this context, I will examine Noam Gramlich's concept of "media-geological care" (2021, p. 65, transl. by the author) as a critical approach to sustainability, particularly within the framework of posthumanist and media-ecological thinking. By critically reflecting on the notion of 'natural resources,' this exploration seeks to illuminate the material and relational interconnectedness of all things, offering a more ethically grounded approach to sustainability. This reflection is crucial for ensuring that the future ecologies we cultivate—whether through technological advancements, social structures, or environmental policies—are not only sustainable but also ethical, informed by an awareness of the material realities that shape our world.

CHALLENGING THE CONCEPT OF "NATURAL RESOURCES"

I would like to begin by offering a succinct, foundational definition of the term "sustainability" as provided by the German Federal Ministry for Economic Cooperation and Development (BMZ):

> *"Sustainability or sustainable development means satisfying the needs of the present in such a way that the opportunities of future generations are not restricted. It is important to consider the three dimensions of sustainability—economically efficient, socially just, and ecologically viable—on an equal footing. In order to preserve global resources in the long term, sustainability should be the basis of all political decisions." (BMZ 2025, transl. by the author)*

While this definition provides a basic understanding, it is essential to delve deeper into its implications, particularly when considering the complex and multifaceted nature of the term "global resources." In this context, I wish to concentrate specifically on the conceptual framework surrounding the term "global resources," a notion that encompasses a wide range of natural materials, both renewable and non-renewable, including vital substances such as oil, coal, and rare earth minerals.

For posthumanist-feminist and decolonial theorists, however, the very conception of "natural resources" obscures an underlying logic. This logic is rooted in a deeply entrenched view of nature as something external to human existence and culture (Haraway, 2003; Latour, [1991] 1998). This dichotomy of nature versus culture, which forms the basis of the dominant Western-modern understanding of sustainability, is inextricably intertwined with historical processes of domination, appropriation, and extraction. These processes, which have been fundamental to capitalist and colonial expansion, continue to shape our environmental and economic practices today. The framing of natural resources as something "outside" of human culture not only reinforces a separation between the natural world and human societies but also perpetuates practices of exploitation and control. However, when examined through the lens of future ecologies, this dichotomy becomes increasingly problematic. Future ecologies, which challenge us to reconsider our relationships with both human and non-human entities, highlight the unsustainability of the traditional nature-culture divide. This divide must be critically reassessed if we are to build more sustainable, equitable ecological futures.

In this regard, sustainability cannot merely be reduced to the management of resource extraction; it must also involve a fundamental rethinking of cultural and economic systems that have historically justified and perpetuated such practices. The concept of "global resources," therefore, is not a neutral descriptor of raw materials; it is deeply entangled with a colonial and capitalist history that has profoundly influenced how we conceptualize, use, and exploit the planet's materials. To forge more just and sustainable future ecologies, it is imperative that we challenge these underlying assumptions and shift towards relational frameworks that do not partition nature from culture, or human from non-human. This requires a profound reimagining of how we define and use resources in the present to shape the future.

A critical point made by Anna L. Tsing in this regard is that the category of "resources" is neither a natural nor an ahistorical category. Rather, it is a construct that emerges through cultural and discursive processes. The term "resource" is intrinsically linked to the modern, capitalist idea of progress—progress that is often defined by scalability, the assumption that certain resources are inexhaustible and interchangeable, and that their exploitation can be expanded indefinitely (Tsing, 2015, pp. 38-39). Expanding on Tsing's argument, Noam Gramlich further contends that scalability functions as a technology that enables the transformation of land into a productive unit within "mediatized environments of plantations and mines." Here, raw materials are extracted through forced or coerced labor, and these materials become units of multiplication, accumulation, mobility, and power (Gramlich, 2021, p. 68, transl. by the author). This process of extractive accumulation leads to the erasure of local relationships and unique particularities, resulting in the transcendence of local contexts and their dissolution into the abstraction of global markets (ibid.).

Tsing effectively argues that behind the concept of "resource" lies a historically contingent, material-discursive form of alienation and disentanglement. This separation between the material and its context is not natural, but rather a key mechanism of capitalist accumulation (Tsing, 2005, p. 133). In a similar vein, Gramlich refers to this as a "technical act of separation" (Gramlich, 2021, p. 69, transl. by the author), wherein raw materials extracted from localities such as African mines are processed and transformed into globally standardized products like pipes, sheets, and wires in European countries. The specificity of locality is thus dissolved, and in its place emerges a newly constructed globality, one that is continuously reproduced through the practices of extraction, trade, and industrial transformation.

From a critical-posthumanist sustainability perspective, it is critical to recognize that the category of "raw material" as a natural unit is not only a discursive fabrication, but one that is deeply implicated in processes of separation, transformation, and transcendence. These processes are central to the operations of extractive capitalism, and they mask the human and environmental costs embedded in their operations. Given this, a crucial question arises when we consider the widely accepted definition of sustainability, which emphasizes the "satisfaction of the needs of the present." Whose needs are we truly addressing when we speak of sustainability in such terms? When we take into account the extractive capitalist system, it becomes apparent that the "needs" in question largely correspond to the demands of the Global North, whose consumption patterns are inextricably linked to media technologies and the functioning of global media infrastructures. In contrast to the homogeneous unification of "raw material" as a standardized, global category—an idea discussed by Gramlich—I propose that a critical posthumanist conceptualization of sustainability necessitates an emphasis on relational modes such as responsibility and care. This shift would guide both theoretical and empirical approaches to sustainability within the context of media communication. Such an approach would not only demand accountability for the neo-colonial extractive powers of the Global North, perpetuated through its insatiable consumerism, but it would also call for an epistemic responsibility in how we define sustainability. To do so, we must first acknowledge the glaring fact that the current media economy in industrialized countries is far from sustainable. From a media ethics perspective, the focus must shift towards scrutinizing media usage, production, and disposal practices, as well as promoting education on resource and energy consumption (Zemanek, 2019, p. 415). However, this shift alone is insufficient.

Despite the widespread knowledge of scientific facts regarding extractive capitalism, neo-colonialism, and anthropogenic climate change, these facts have had little discernible impact on individual media consumption patterns or on fostering broader societal mobilization. We are acutely aware of the environmental destruction caused by these systems, yet we have become desensitized to these facts. We know them, but as a society, we simply do not act upon them—"but we don't *care*." In response to this, my argument points to the urgent need for a critical posthumanist understanding of care. Care, in this context, must not be perceived in a paternalistic sense—such as caring for workers in African mines—nor as an altruistic gesture. Rather, care must be understood as a practice that establishing and sensitizes deep, meaningful connections mindfully cultivating relationships with both human and non-human beings.

This call for a rethinking of care necessitates a shift toward a critical posthumanist conception of caring about (Schrader, 2015)—one that refuses paternalism and moves beyond individualized, altruistic ethics (see also Tronto 2020). Instead, it foregrounds care as a distributed, situated practice of responsibility that is relational at its core, embedding questions of justice and accountability within networks of human and more-than-human entanglements.

FUTURE ECOLOGIES OF CARE, RESPONSIBILITY AND JUSTICE

Astrid Schrader explains her concept of *caring about* by first distinguishing between two broad meanings of care, drawing on Annemarie Mol and Daniel López. One form of care involves the often gendered labor of tending to someone in need, while the other refers to an affective connection, the act of *caring about* something or someone. Caring *for* someone is typically goal-directed, as it entails an effort to "improve the situation of a patient" (Mol, 2011, p. 23). Modeled on health care practices, and even extended to nonhuman animals (Mol et al., 2010), this type of care often defines its recipient by their perceived lack of capacity or autonomy. As Daniel López et al. (2010, p. 82) suggest, "to care for something means being concerned about what threatens or might transform the limits that define it." Following Schrader, to begin *caring about* involves a shift in perspective, one that entails the transformation of the boundary that previously excluded them from our socially recognized sphere of care. In institutionalized forms of care, it is entirely possible to care for someone in need without actually *caring about* them. In other words, the act of caring does not inherently require affection, sympathy, or compassion. To *care about* someone is not necessarily tied to a specific 'need,' nor must it always manifest in a particular action (Schrader, 2015, p. 668). Based on these considerations, Schrader asks herself the following questions:

> *"Would it be possible to begin to care without an a priori identification or categorization of an object of care? Can we conceive of a less anthropocentric notion of care that is attentive to indeterminacies in its practices? As Maria Puig de la Bellacasa (2011) argues, 'matters of care' are different from the (teleological) gathering of 'matters of concerns' (Latour 2004); they come with stakes and retain a link to justice. Like justice, care articulates a relation to the other and a mode of attention [...]." (Schrader, 2015, p. 668, emphasized by author)*

Schrader makes clear that her pursuit of a non-anthropocentric conception of care is, at its core, an *alterbiopolitical* one—a conception that opens up new perspectives on the notion of sustainability and aligns closely with questions of climate justice. Her critically posthumanist notion of care thus enters into direct proximity with an ethics of alterity, as evoked by thinkers such as Donna Haraway (2010; 2012) and Karen Barad (2006), both of whom draw on the work of Emmanuel Levinas. In this context, Stephan Trinkaus emphasizes that alterity is not about the violent projection of our fears onto an imagined outside, but rather about the concrete dependency and vulnerability of life on this planet, and the responsibility toward that which is not like us, that which is radically other (2020, p. 228, transl. by the author).

The concept of *alterbiopolitics* (which highlights the *alter* not the ego) is introduced in Bellacasas monograph *Matters of Care* to describe the ethics of collective empowerment that underpins permaculture movement (2017, p. 125). Alterbiopolitics refers to a collective ethics grounded in the reciprocal relationships between humans and non-human entities. In this framework, care is understood as a practice that encompasses various material forces and vitalities, which interact and coalesce. The concept of alterbiopolitics extends beyond traditional biopolitical frameworks by emphasizing the interconnectedness of all life forms and recognizing the role of non-human entities as active participants in the (world wide) web of life. It challenges anthropocentric perspectives by asserting that care, responsibility and, justice are not limited to human-centered concerns but must be expanded to include the well-being and agency of non-human actors. Thus, alterbiopolitics fosters the relation to the other (Schader, 2015, p. 668) an inclusive, relational understanding of ethics (Loh, 2022; Haraway, 2003) that encourages a more holistic approach to sustainability, one that recognizes the dynamic interdependencies between human and non-human worldings.

Astrid Schraders non-anthropocentric, alterbiopolitical conception of *caring about* directly challenges neoliberal understandings of care and sustainability, which often prioritize functionality, optimization, and efficiency. In contrast, a critical-posthumanist ethics of caring about, responsibility and justice calls for an alternative framework that resists these neoliberal imperatives. Media ethics, therefore, must not merely reflect or perpetuate these hegemonic, Western-Eurocentric sustainability discourses, but must actively work to deconstruct them. Instead, it must strive to foster a more inclusive, relational ethics—one that aligns with the principles of future ecologies. These principles emphasize a relational, just and responsible ethics that not only pertains to ecological concerns but also acknowledges the socio-political and cultural dynamics shaping global interactions. In this context, the concept of future ecologies offers us a compelling invitation to reconsider media sustainability through the lens of care, responsibility, and justice. To build truly sustainable media futures, we must engage with all forms of life—both human and non-human—by integrating care and responsibility into a comprehensive framework of ethical engagement and action, thus ensuring a more just, equitable, and sustainable future for all.

CONCLUSION

In the context of a critical examination of the concept of "resources"—including non-renewable raw materials—within the framework of sustainability, as outlined in the definition previously provided, my objective is not to dismiss the concept of sustainability itself. Rather, my goal is to explore how sustainability can be reimagined and critically reconsidered through the lenses of posthumanist, inclusive ethics, and postcolonial theory. I seek to illuminate the potential that these perspectives hold for enriching and transforming the ongoing debate on sustainability within the field of media and communication studies. To this end, my argument involves critically interrogating the concept of "resources" or "raw materials" from both a posthumanist-feminist and a posthumanist-decolonial standpoint. In particular, the finitude of resources, such as non-renewable raw materials—rare earth elements, for example—should not propel us into a purely techno-solutionist approach, one that remains anchored in the capitalist and neocolonial logics of resource extraction. This techno-solutionism, often framed as the answer to the depletion of finite resources, perpetuates the very structures of exploitation that have historically underpinned global inequalities.

Furthermore, when the term "sustainability" is co-opted by environmental protection rhetoric or used to further the interests of wealth preservation in the Global North, it often becomes a greenwashed label that obscures and displaces the underlying socio-political and economic issues. Sustainability, in this sense, risks becoming a superficial solution—one that masks the deep-seated contradictions of the current global economic order. This transformation must be met with heightened vigilance, as it represents not just a semantic shift, but a potentially dangerous recalibration of priorities that avoids confronting the systemic injustices at play. Although it may not be feasible to entirely extricate ourselves from the pervasive forces of digitalization, extraction, and waste associated with contemporary global capitalism, we can—and must—resist and challenge these processes in their current forms. Such resistance requires us to grapple with the centuries-old histories of oppression, exploitation, and dispossession that are inextricably tied to capitalist domination. A key avenue through which we can confront these histories is through practices of care, but care in a posthumanist sense—one that recognizes the entangled, relational nature of all life forms and resists reductive, anthropocentric approaches.

In the early part of this paper, I referenced the media-ecological thought of scholars such as Eric Hörl and Jussi Parikka, as well as critically posthumanist theories advanced by Donna Haraway and Anna L. Tsing. These frameworks place less emphasis on individual entities, such as specific media technologies, and instead focus on the relationships and interconnections between various actors and systems. As articulated by Janina Loh, these relations are ethically evaluated, foregrounding the importance of relational ethics in understanding sustainability. This perspective advocates for a practice of care that attends to the material and discursive entanglements in which media and communication systems are embedded. This approach requires both theoretical and empirical research into the notions of responsibility and care, as these concepts are essential for further developing sustainable media ecologies. Indeed, the integration of critical posthumanist perspectives into the sustainability discourse within media studies would introduce a much-needed ethical dimension. It would offer an approach that is both posthumanist and postcolonial, addressing the colonial legacy and ongoing responsibility of the Global North in perpetuating extractive practices and unequal power dynamics. Such a shift in perspective calls for a reevaluation of how we engage with resources—whether they are physical "natural resources" or the media infrastructures that depend on them. By adopting an ethical framework that acknowledges the colonial histories of resource extraction and its ongoing effects, we can begin to formulate a more inclusive (Loh, 2022), responsible, and just model of sustainability. This model would challenge not only the material exploitation of the planet but also the epistemic violence (Spivak, 1988) embedded in the ways we understand and conceptualize sustainability in the first place.

In sum, by drawing on critical posthumanist, inclusive ethics, and postcolonial theory, we can reimagine sustainability not as a static or one-dimensional goal, but as an ongoing process that must be deeply attuned to the interdependent, relational nature of the world. Through this approach, sustainability can become a practice of care—one that is grounded in responsibility and justice, and that confronts the global, historical, and ecological entanglements that shape the present and future of media systems and beyond.

REFERENCES

Alaimo, S., & Hekman, S. (Eds.). (2008). *Material feminisms*. Indiana University Press.

Barad, K. (2006). *Meeting the Universe Halfway: Quantum Physics and the Entanglement of Matter and Meaning*. Duke University Press.

Bee, J. (2025 forthcoming). Klimarassismus, Umweltgewalt und Extraktivismus – Medienklimagerechtigkeit aus rassismuskritischer Perspektive. In Alkin, Ö., Amirpur, D., Ha, K. N., & Mustafa, I. (Eds.), *Rassismus. Ein transdisziplinäres Kompendium*. Springer.

Blättel-Mink, B. (Ed.). (2021). *Nachhaltige Entwicklung in einer Gesellschaft des Umbruchs*. Springer VS.

BMZ. Bundeszentrale für wirtschaftliche Zusammenarbeit und Entwicklung (2025). Nachhaltigkeit aus dem Lexikon für Entwicklungspolitik. Online: https://www.bmz.de/de/service/lexikon/nachhaltigkeit-nachhaltige-entwicklung-14700 (12.04.2025).

Braidotti, R. (2013). *The posthuman*. Polity Press.

Coole, D. H., & Frost, S. (2010). *New materialisms: Ontology, agency, and politics*. Duke University Press.

Dalby, S. (2013). Biopolitics and the Anthropocene. *Geoforum*, *48*, 14–19.

Despret, V., Haraway, D., Harrasser, K., & Solhdju, K. (2011). Stay where the trouble is. *Zeitschrift für Medienwissenschaft*, *3*(1), 92–102.

Dolphijn, R., & van der Tuin, I. (2012). *New materialism: Interviews & cartographies*. Open humanities press.

Dourish, P., & Bell, G. (2011). *Divining a Digital Future: Mess and Mythology in Ubiquitous Computing*. MIT Press.

Friess, P. (2022). *Internet of Things*. CRC Press.

Gramlich, N. (2021). *Mediengeologisches Sorgen*. Mit Otobong Nkanga gegen Ökolonialität.

Haraway, D. (2010). When Species Meet: Staying with the Trouble. *Environment and Planning. D, Society & Space*, *28*(1), 53–55.

Haraway, D. (2011). Speculative fabulations for technoculture's generations: Taking care of unexpected country. *Australian Humanities Review*, *50*, 95–118.

Haraway, D. (2012a). Species Matters, Humane Advocacy. In M. DeKoven & M. Lundblad (Eds.), *Species Matters* (pp. 17–26). Columbia University Press; JSTOR.

Haraway, D. (2012b). *The companion species manifesto: Dogs, people, and significant otherness (6th print).* Prickly Paradigm Press.

Haraway, D. (2016). *Staying with the trouble: Making kin in the Chthulucene.* Duke University Press.

Hoppe, K. (2021). *Die Kraft der Revision: Epistemologie, Politik und Ethik bei Donna Haraway.* Campus Verlag.

Hörl, E. (Ed.). (2011). *Die technologische Bedingung: Beiträge zur Beschreibung der technischen Welt* (1. Aufl). Suhrkamp.

Hörl, E. (2013). Tausend Ökologien. Der Prozeß der Kybernetisierung und die allgemeine Ökologie. In D. Diederichsen, A. Franke, & Haus der Kulturen der Welt Berlin (Eds.), *The Whole Earth: Kalifornien und das Verschwinden des Außen (Dritte Auflage).* Sternberg Press.

Kannengießer, S. (2022). *Digitale Medien und Nachhaltigkeit: Medienpraktiken für ein gutes Leben.* Springer Fachmedien Wiesbaden.

Kannengießer, S. (2023). From Millennium Development Goals to Sustainable Development Goals: Transforming development communication to sustainability communication. *Studies in Communication Sciences, 23*(1).

Kant, I. (2017). *The metaphysics of morals.* Cambridge University Press.

Kronberger, A. (2024). Respons-Able Trees. On Permaculture Ethics of Responsibility in the Films of the Exhibition „Cambio“ (2020). Ecozon@: European Journal of Literature. *Culture and Environment, 15*(2), 126–140.

Latour, B. (2004). Why Has Critique Run out of Steam? From Matters of Fact to Matters of Concern. *Critical Inquiry, 30*(2), 225–248.

Latour, B. (2022). *Wir sind nie modern gewesen: Versuch einer symmetrischen Anthropologie* (8th ed.). (Roßler, G., Trans.). Suhrkamp.

Loh, J. (2022). Posthumanism and Ethics. In Herbrechter, S., Callus, I., Rossini, M., Grech, M., de Bruin-Molé, M., & Müller, C. J. (Eds.), *Palgrave handbook of critical posthumanism.* Palgrave Macmillan.

López, D., Callén, B., Tirado, F., & Domènech, M. (2010). How to become a guardian angel Providing safety in a home telecare service. In A. Mol, I. Moser, & J. Pols (Eds.*), Care in Practice* (pp. 73–92). transcript Verlag.

Mareis, C., & Held, M. (2023). Preface. In L. Perraudin, C. Winkler, C. Mareis, & M. Held (Eds.), *Material Trajectories: Designing With Care*? meson press.

McDonald, M., & Mitchell, A. (2017). *Posthuman International Relations*. Cambridge University Press.

McLuhan, M., Fiore, Q., & Agel, J. (1996). *The medium is the massage: An inventory of effects*. HardWired.

Mol, A. (2011). *The logic of care: Health and the problem of patient choice* (Transferred to digital printing 2010). Routledge.

Mol, A., Moser, I., & Pols, J. (Eds.). (2010). *Care in Practice: On Tinkering in Clinics, Homes and Farms*. transcript.

Novais, P., ... (2023). *Ambient Intelligence – Software and Applications* – 14th International Symposium on Ambient Intelligence. 1st ed. 2023. Cham: Springer Nature Switzerland.

Otto, F. (2023). *Klimaungerechtigkeit: Was die Klimakatastrophe mit Kapitalismus, Rassismus und Sexismus zu tun hat*. Ullstein Taschenbuch Verlag.

Parikka, J. (2015). *A geology of media*. University of Minnesota Press.

Patel, R., & Moore, J. W. (2018). *A history of the world in seven cheap things: A guide to capitalism, nature, and the future of the planet*. University of California Press.

Postman, N. (2006). Media Ecology Education. *Explorations in Media Ecology*, *5*(1), 5–14.

Puig de La Bellacasa, M. (2017). *Matters of care: Speculative ethics in more than human worlds*. University of Minnesota press.

Rieger, S. (2025). Bio(techno)logie und Medientheorie. In Ernst, C., Krtilova, K., Schröter, J., & Sudmann, A. (Eds.), *Handbuch Medientheorien im 21. Jahrhundert* (pp. 1–15). Springer Fachmedien Wiesbaden.

Rothe, K. (2016). Medienökologie – Zu einer Ethik des Mediengebrauchs.

Schrader, A. (2015). Abyssal intimacies and temporalities of care: How (not) to care about deformed leaf bugs in the aftermath of Chernobyl. *Social Studies of Science*, *45*(5), 665–690. PMID: 26630816

Spivak, G. C. (1988). Can the Subaltern Speak? In C. Nelson & L. Grossberg (Eds.), *Marxism and the Interpretation of Culture* (pp. 271–313). University of Illinois Press.

Sprenger, F. (2019). Epistemologien des Umgebens: Zur Geschichte, Ökologie und Biopolitik künstlicher environments.

Trinkaus, S. (2020). The Green Sticky Spawn of the Stars' – Trump, Affekt, Fernsehen im Chthulucene. In Maeder, D. (Ed.), *Trump und das Fernsehen: Medien, Realität, Affekt, Politik*. Herbert von Halem Verlag.

Tronto, J. C. (2020). *Moral boundaries: A political argument for an ethic of care* (1st ed.). Routledge.

Tsing, A. L., Bubandt, N., Gran, E., & Swanson, H. A. (Eds.). (2017). *Arts of Living on a Damaged Planet*. University of Minnesota Press.

Yusoff, K. (2018). *A billion black Anthropocenes or none*. University of Minnesota Press.

Zemanek, E. (2019). Medienwissenschaft. In Kluwick, U., & Zemanek, E. (Eds.), *Nachhaltigkeit interdisziplinär: Konzepte, Diskurse, Praktiken: ein Kompendium*. Böhlau Verlag.

KEY TERMS AND DEFINITIONS

Alterbiopolitics: Alterbiopolitics refers to a framework that challenges traditional biopolitical control over life and death by emphasizing care, mutuality, and ethical responsibility in the regulation of life processes. Drawing from feminist and posthumanist thought, it reimagines the relationship between human and non-human life forms, advocating for an ethics that goes beyond mere survival to address the well-being of all interconnected beings. This concept, as explored by theorists like Maria Puig de la Bellacasa and others, critiques the biopolitical management of life by promoting a more inclusive, ethical politics of care that recognizes the agency of diverse life forms and encourages responsible, collective stewardship of life.

Climate Justice: Climate Justice is an ethical framework that links climate change with social justice, emphasizing the disproportionate impact of environmental degradation on marginalized communities. It advocates for equitable solutions that address both environmental harm and systemic inequalities. Drawing on thinkers like Naomi Klein and others, it calls for global responsibility, intersectional action, and the recognition that climate change is not only an ecological issue but also one of human rights and social fairness. Climate Justice seeks to empower vulnerable populations and ensure that future policies are rooted in fairness, solidarity, and reparation

Critical Posthumanist Ethics: Critical Posthumanist Ethics challenges traditional human-centered ethical frameworks by questioning the boundaries between human and non-human entities and emphasizing the interconnectedness of all life forms. Drawing on the works of Janina Loh, Donna Haraway, and Karen Barad, this approach advocates for a more inclusive and relational understanding of ethics. Loh critiques anthropocentric perspectives and argues for an ethics that embraces the entanglement of humans with other beings and the environment. Haraway's "companion species" concept emphasizes co-evolution and mutual responsibility, while Barad's theory of agential realism underscores the material-discursive entanglement of humans and non-humans, urging a reconsideration of ethics based on relationality and intra-action. Together, these scholars advocate for an ethics that moves beyond human exceptionalism, recognizing the agency of non-human actors and fostering responsibility for the collective well-being of all entities in a shared, dynamic world

Extractivism: Extractivism refers to the practice of large-scale extraction of natural resources—such as minerals, oil, and timber—primarily for export and profit, often at the expense of local communities and ecosystems. It is critiqued for its exploitation of both human and non-human resources, reinforcing colonial legacies and environmental degradation. Scholars like Arturo Escobar and Silvia Rivera Cusicanqui highlight the harm it causes to Indigenous territories and local populations, advocating for alternative, more sustainable and equitable models of resource use that prioritize local needs and environmental integrity over profit.

Future Ecologies: "Future ecologies" represents a speculative and ethical framework that critiques traditional sustainability discourses and envisions ecological relationships through a lens of care as alterbiopolitical "caring about." This concept extends beyond the mere management of current environmental interactions, proposing instead a forward-thinking approach that anticipates and actively shapes the interconnectedness between human and non-human entities. It seeks to cultivate more equitable, inclusive, and sustainable engagements with the world, focusing on the long-term well-being of both human and non-human life. Future ecologies incorporate ethical considerations, ensuring that advancements in technology, social structures, and environmental policies are not only sustainable but also responsive to the material realities that underpin global ecological systems, striving for a more just and thoughtful future for generations to come

Section 2
Global Political Economy and Development Contradictions

Chapter 4
Unveiling the Ecological and Geopolitical Contradictions of Large-Scale Development Initiatives:
A Critical Analysis of the Belt and Road Initiative

Shruti Rathore
https://orcid.org/0000-0002-9132-3977
Christ University, India

Judith Anne Lal
https://orcid.org/0009-0003-7198-8685
Christ University, India

ABSTRACT

This chapter critically examines the ecological and geopolitical contradictions within large-scale development initiatives, focusing on China's Belt and Road Initiative (BRI) as a paradigmatic case. While framed as a vehicle for sustainable growth, the BRI often instrumentalizes sustainability discourse to legitimize extractive development, suppress dissent, and extend geopolitical influence. Using interdisciplinary approaches from political economy, post-development theory, and critical discourse analysis, the chapter deconstructs narratives such as 'Green BRI,' ecological civilization, and win-win cooperation. Case studies from Southeast Asia and Africa expose a stark contrast between rhetorical commitments and realities

DOI: 10.4018/979-8-3373-1707-6.ch004

of environmental degradation, displacement, and debt dependency. The chapter advocates for an eco-centric, justice-oriented development paradigm and offers policy recommendations that emphasize accountability, participation, and ecological integrity in future infrastructure planning.

INTRODUCTION

Globalisation in the 21st century is marked by large-scale development initiatives, which form the basis for transnational cooperation, economic modernization, and sustainable development. In this context, China's Belt and Road Initiative (BRI) was launched in 2013 as a global development initiative, spanning across four continents and with projects in over one hundred and fifty countries in sectors of transportation, energy telecommunication and industrial infrastructure. The project's global scope elevated the status of China, making the BRI a paradigmatic case of contemporary development practice.

Though BRI promises development across nations, what poses a major concern is the inability to strike a balance between its commitment to stability and observed ecological and social outcomes. Recent surveys and research also substantiate this point. The partner countries of the BRI are becoming subject to increased environmental pressure in their respective states. A survey was conducted by an organization, AidData, on the leaders of 129 countries across the world to get their insights and impressions on the financial projects of BRI. The report revealed that 45% of the respondents expressed concerns that BRI projects are worsening the levels of air and water pollution (Custer, Horigoshi & Marshall, 2024).

The terms "Green BRI, ecological civilization and win-win cooperation" are used in promoting the initiative and showcasing its alignment with global initiatives for sustainable development (2030 Agenda) and climate control (Paris Climate Agreement). However, the world project sites have witnessed extensive deforestation, loss of biodiversity and community displacement, which is contrary to the BRI claims, inviting critical scrutiny within global development regimes.

This chapter analyses the sustainability rhetoric used by China to advance its BRI projects, concealing the ecological harms emanating from the projects worldwide. It addresses the question: How does BRI's sustainability agenda pan out in advocating the large-scale developments that deteriorate the ecological integrity and social justice? By engaging this central question, the chapter elaborates how the sustainability agenda is being utilized as an instrument to push large-scale development initiatives, which showcases the expansionist mindset of China.

This question broadly addresses rapid climate change, global inequalities and moulding the international development norms by China. The urgency of addressing the ecological consequences of development has never been greater, yet dominant responses remain constrained by growth-oriented paradigms that prioritize economic metrics over environmental limits and socio-political inclusion. As China emerges as a key architect of global development trajectories, understanding how its flagship initiative mobilizes sustainability narratives becomes a matter of critical importance. The BRI offers a salient example of what scholars have termed "developmentality"—a mode of governance that frames development as a technical and apolitical process, thereby obscuring its power-laden and ecologically destructive dimensions (Li, 2007).

The chapter also engages with the concept of geopolitical ecology, which foregrounds the entanglement of environmental governance with strategic statecraft, capital flows, and territorial influence. The BRI operates not only as an economic corridor but also as a geopolitical infrastructure, enabling China to project influence through debt diplomacy, resource access, and infrastructural entanglement. In this context, environmental sustainability becomes a legitimizing discourse that softens the political edges of what is, in many respects, an exercise in infrastructural imperialism, the strategic deployment of infrastructure as a means of securing geopolitical advantage and economic dependency (Easterling, 2014). This process is particularly pronounced in the Global South, where weaker regulatory institutions, socio-political vulnerabilities, and economic precarity render communities disproportionately exposed to the negative externalities of large-scale development.

The chapter adopts a critical interdisciplinary framework that integrates political economy, environmental politics, and international relations. Methodologically, it draws on three key approaches: (1) discourse analysis of BRI policy documents, promotional materials, and official statements to uncover how sustainability is framed and mobilized; (2) political economy analysis to examine the structural imperatives, such as capital accumulation, global market access, and strategic territorialism, that drive the BRI; and (3) case study methodology, with particular focus on selected infrastructure projects in Southeast Asia and Africa that exemplify the ecological and social contradictions embedded within the initiative. These are complemented by both quantitative data and qualitative accounts to ensure an empirically grounded and theoretically informed analysis.

The structure of the chapter is as follows. Section One introduces the BRI's scope, objectives, and its discursive positioning as a sustainability framework. Section Two highlights the contradictions between the rhetoric as claimed by China with respect to the BRI projects and environmental degradation and sustainability discourse. Section Three deals with specific case studies, which present an insight into how BRI projects are impacting the ecological and social aspects. Section Four corroborates the findings through a theoretical lens, particularly discourse, power, and global governance. The last section seeks to find the alternatives for global development that prioritizes ecological balance, social equity, and participatory governance. It also offers policy recommendations for better development models working towards sustainable development.

This chapter, while elaborating on the discourse functionary of BRI on sustainability, contributes to scholarly debates in critical development studies, international political ecology, and post-Western international relations theory. It challenges the deception of narratives which view large-scale development as beneficial and calls for a more comprehensive plan to shape global developments. It exposes the BRI's contradictions in ecological and geopolitical domains and justifies the need for reforms which are more ecological.

PROBLEMATIZING SUSTAINABILITY: A CRITICAL LITERATURE REVIEW

It has become a prevalent practice by states, institutions, and development corporations to use sustainability as a shadow agenda to counter the interventions for their large infrastructure projects. From the 1987 Brundtland Commission's call for "development that meets the needs of the present without compromising the ability of future generations" to the 2030 Agenda for Sustainable Development, the term has gained immense normative appeal (Jarvie, 2016). Yet, this apparent consensus conceals a multitude of theoretical contestations, ideological contradictions, and practical shortcomings, particularly when sustainability is instrumentalized by actors with competing political and economic interests.

This literature review unpacks these contradictions by drawing from three intersecting bodies of scholarship: (a) critical approaches to sustainable development and its post-development alternatives, (b) geopolitical critiques of infrastructure-driven development initiatives such as the BRI, and (c) empirical studies documenting the ecological and social impacts of BRI projects. In doing so, it identifies the conceptual and empirical gap this chapter addresses: the tendency of existing literature to analyze ecological consequences and geopolitical strategies in isolation, thereby obscuring how sustainability functions as a hegemonic narrative that interlaces both.

Development and Sustainability Discourse

The dominant conception of sustainable development has long been critiqued for its embeddedness in a modernization paradigm that privileges economic growth and technological progress. Scholars like Robert Chambers and Amartya Sen have expanded this understanding to include human capabilities and participatory governance, yet the fundamental tension remains: can economic growth be reconciled with environmental protection? (Opaluwah, 2016).

Post-development thinkers, such as Arturo Escobar (1995) and Wolfgang Sachs (1992), reject this reconciliation outright. For Escobar, development is not a neutral process but a discursive regime rooted in colonial and neoliberal power structures that constructs the Global South as deficient and in need of intervention. Sustainability, in this view, becomes a discursive extension of the development project, an ideological tool that obscures ecological extraction behind the veil of green progress (Naz, 2006). Sachs similarly describes sustainable development as a rhetorical compromise that allows for continued capitalist expansion under a greener label, arguing that it has become a "Trojan horse" of conventional growth-driven paradigms (Sachs, 2017).

More recent critiques come from the degrowth movement, which interrogates the ecological limits of capitalism. Giorgos Kallis (2011) and others argue that decoupling economic growth from environmental harm is a myth. Rather than pursuing green growth, degrowth scholars advocate for downscaling production and consumption, relocalization, and a redefinition of prosperity based on well-being rather than GDP. From this standpoint, large-scale infrastructure investments like the BRI, regardless of their sustainability rhetoric, are inherently ecologically unsustainable, as they rely on material throughput, energy extraction, and territorial expansion (Schneider et al., 2010).

This view is supported by the Eco-Marxist perspective with respect to environmental degradation within the structural contradictions of capitalism. John Bellamy Foster's theory of the metabolic rift states how capitalist development disrupts the societal and ecological systems (Clark et al., 2019). James O'Connor's "second contradiction of capitalism" seconds the fact that the system inherently undermines its own ecological foundations. Contextually, sustainability acts as a deceiving instrument which paves the way for the indiscriminate growth within the system (Ramírez, 2021). Altogether, these critiques bring out the fact that sustainability, rather than containing the indiscriminate development, acts as an overcover for ecological disruption, managing dissent and backing up infrastructure that only serves to elites and capitalists.

This critique is also voiced by other scholars from the Global South. Nigerian economists assessed that the environmental reviews of Chinese rail projects were conducted in a superficial manner. Field studies from Malaysia showed that Chinese-backed rail and port projects generated jobs for the Chinese workers only, not giving employment opportunities to the locals in their own country (Merdeka Center for Opinion Research, 2022).

Geopolitics of Development Initiatives

In the second chain of ideologies, there is an addressal of the geopolitical implications of the development initiatives, particularly the BRI. This initiative is a strategic effort by China to introduce reforms in global development norms and expand its footprint in terms of alternative trade routes and infrastructure. However, deeper analysis diverges sharply from its consequential motives.

Some scholars support BRI as a model for South-South cooperation, which aims to fill the void of critical infrastructure in the Global South which were neglected by the developed economies in the West. In 2017, during the "Symposium on International Developments and China's Diplomacy", Foreign Minister Wang Yi emphasized China's commitment to inclusive globalization, depicting BRI as an accessible initiative to all rather than a self-centric enterprise. He also brought out the initiative's role in providing alternatives to institutions such as the IMF and World Bank, which impose conditions on the developing nations. Due to this, BRI overall offered a lucrative avenue for developing nations for partnerships. The claims put BRI as a norm for projects aimed at restructuring global development governance along multifaceted avenues (Ministry of Foreign Affairs: The People's Republic of China, 2017).

But other scholars analyse the initiative with a more stringent approach. Drawing from dependency theory (e.g., Andre Gunder Frank, Samir Amin), analysts state that BRI, when implemented in some nations, locks them into a debt trap, initiates unilateral trade agreements and dependence on technology (Weitzman, 2022). The work of Brautigam (2020) on "debt-trap diplomacy" shows how interest-free or concessional loans offered by China lead to long-term dependency, which works in favour of China, as is the case with Sri Lanka's Hambantota Port and Gwadar port of Pakistan (Imanche et al., 2021).

The concept of "infrastructural imperialism" is also gaining prominence these days, which analyzes how infrastructure (ports, roads, energy corridors) functions not just to influence the economy but also as a tool to exert territorial influence and control (Cowen, 2017).

While studies provide an insight into understanding BRI as a geopolitical tool but they often ignore the ecological aspects of these projects, which is the central point of analysis in this chapter.

Ecological and Social Critiques of the BRI

A growing body of empirical research documents the ecological degradation and social injustice linked to BRI projects, even as they are framed as sustainable.

Hydropower projects in Myanmar and Laos funded by Chinese banks led to massive deforestation, ecological imbalance, as fisheries collapsed, and displacement of indigenous communities (Busbarat et al., 2023). Similarly, the Laos-China railway project, though passed as a green alternative to road transport, has been linked to wildlife habitat disruptions.

The coal power projects of the China-Pakistan Economic Corridor have invited criticisms over increased carbon emissions in vulnerable parts of the South Asian region. Though policy reforms state a shift from coal as a source, green alternatives are not so readily available (Kouser et al., 2020).

The construction of Mombasa–Nairobi Standard Gauge Railway (SGR) in the African continent has also violated environmental regulations, cutting through ecologically sensitive areas and leading to community displacement (Nyumba, 2021). Reports also support the fact that Chinese contractors leveraged political influence to even bypass environmental impact screening to expedite the project clearance.

These empirical studies are crucial in grounding critiques of BRI sustainability rhetoric, but they are often siloed, focusing either on environmental or geopolitical outcomes, without examining how discourses of sustainability operate to connect and obscure both.

Research Gap and Contribution

This chapter addresses a critical gap in the literature: the tendency of existing studies to treat ecological, social, and geopolitical critiques of the BRI in separate analytical silos. While post-development and eco-Marxist scholars expose the ideological functions of sustainability, they often do not engage with the geopolitical realities of state-led infrastructure. Conversely, geopolitical critiques of China's development model frequently overlook the discursive power of sustainability to manufacture consent and marginalize opposition.

By bringing together discourse analysis, political economy, and empirical environmental evidence, this chapter offers an integrated critique of how sustainability is mobilized within the BRI as a hegemonic apparatus. It highlights how sustainability functions not only to legitimize development, but also to extend geopolitical influence, normalize ecological harm, and discipline alternative imaginaries of progress.

In doing so, the chapter contributes to a growing but still nascent field of research that links critical sustainability studies, global political ecology, and post-Western international relations theory. It offers a conceptual bridge between theoretical critique and practical impact, between discourse and materiality, and between geopolitical ambition and ecological consequence.

METHODOLOGY AND ANALYTICAL FRAMEWORK

This chapter adopts an interdisciplinary and critical methodological approach that draws on the traditions of political economy, discourse analysis, and political ecology. These approaches are further substantiated by a case study methodology, informed by both quantitative and qualitative data, to examine the ecological and geopolitical contradictions embedded in the BRI. The methodological choices reflect the chapter's core concern: to interrogate how sustainability is mobilized as a discursive and operational tool in the BRI, legitimizing development practices that often produce ecological degradation, socio-spatial inequalities, and geopolitical asymmetries.

The research design follows a qualitative-dominant mixed-methods strategy, allowing for contextual depth, theoretical reflection, and empirical substantiation. By triangulating textual, spatial, and narrative sources, the chapter situates BRI projects within broader patterns of power and material transformation, while attending to the symbolic language through which sustainability is framed and circulated.

Political Economy as an Analytical Lens

At the core of this chapter's analytical framework is a critical political economy perspective, which conceptualizes infrastructure not merely as a technical or neutral intervention, but as a deeply political act embedded in capitalist accumulation logics and state geopolitical strategies. Following scholars such as David Harvey, Saskia Sassen, and Deborah Cowen, infrastructure is treated as a form of territorialized capital that serves to facilitate flows of goods, finance, and labour, while simultaneously reorganizing space, environment, and social relations.

Applied to the BRI, this perspective enables the analysis of:

- The economic imperatives that underpin infrastructure investments, including market access, energy security, and supply chain integration.
- The ways in which infrastructure serves as a material manifestation of China's geopolitical ambitions, particularly in strategically sensitive regions like Southeast Asia and East Africa.
- The distribution of costs and benefits across global North/South divides and among different socio-ecological groups within recipient states.

Rather than viewing BRI projects as isolated interventions, political economy allows for their systemic interrogation, locating them within a global matrix of debt dependency, uneven development, and ecological externalization (Demiryol, 2019).

Discourse Analysis of BRI Narratives

Complementing the political economy perspective, the chapter employs critical discourse analysis (CDA) to examine the symbolic and rhetorical dimensions of sustainability as deployed in BRI-related texts and practices. Following the work of Michel Foucault, Norman Fairclough, and Maarten Hajer, discourse is conceptualized as a system of meaning-making that constructs what is considered possible, desirable, and legitimate within a given political-economic order (Emerald Publishing, n.d.).

The BRI is rich in discursive formations, terms like Green BRI, ecological civilization, win-win cooperation, and community of shared future function not simply as communicative devices, but as instruments of governance (Cheingkul, 2025). By analyzing the language, imagery, and institutional narratives surrounding BRI projects, this chapter investigates:

- How sustainability is defined, operationalized, and legitimized in official Chinese state discourse and policy documents (e.g., "BRI Vision and Action" white papers, speeches by President Xi Jinping).
- The semantic framing of green finance and environmental responsibility in project branding and promotional materials.
- The absence or marginalization of alternative vocabularies, such as indigenous knowledge systems, environmental justice, or participatory governance.

Texts and visual materials are analyzed for their recurrent themes, framing strategies, and silences, which collectively help to reveal how sustainability becomes a performative and ideological resource within China's global development diplomacy.

Case Study Approach

The empirical core of the chapter rests on an in-depth case study approach, focusing on selected BRI projects in Southeast Asia and Africa. Case selection is based on theoretical sampling; each project exemplifies a key dimension of the sustainability–development–geopolitics nexus.

The selected cases include the Laos–China Railway project, Hambantota Port (Sri Lanka), hydropower projects of Myanmar, and Kenya's Standard Gauge Railway and Lamu Coal Plant project. These case studies are explored not as isolated examples, but as symptomatic expressions of broader patterns. Each is analyzed across three dimensions:

- Discursive (how is sustainability framed?),
- Ecological (what are the material environmental impacts?),
- Political-economic (what forms of power and dependency are produced?).

Mixed Methods: Quantitative and Qualitative Integration

To ground the analysis in empirical evidence, the chapter utilizes a mixed-methods strategy that incorporates both quantitative environmental data and qualitative social research. This enhances the validity and multi-dimensionality of the critique. Together, these data sources support a triangulated analysis that links macro-level dynamics to micro-level impacts, bridging theory and grounded realities.

FRAMING SUSTAINABILITY: BRI'S RHETORIC AND REALITY

China's BRI is one of the most ambitious global development frameworks in contemporary times. Encompassing over one hundred and fifty countries and spanning continents, it is marketed as a new model for inclusive, green, and sustainable development (Green Finance & Development Center, n.d.). The initiative's core rhetoric revolves around narratives of "win-win cooperation", "ecological civilization", and "green infrastructure", aimed at signalling China's commitment to global environmental governance and its role as a responsible global actor. However, collective evidence suggests these discourses are at odds with the ecological and societal outcomes of BRI projects. This section critically elaborates on the BRI's so-called sustainability claims, which are being used as narratives to expand infrastructure while covering the environmental degradations and global dissent.

The "Green BRI" and the Myth of Ecological Civilization

To align its BRI overseas project investments with environmental standards, the term "Green BRI" was formally introduced by China in 2019. Documents such as "Belt and Road Ecological and Environmental Cooperation Plan" and "Guidance on Promoting Green Belt and Road," outline commitments to green finance, renewable energy, biodiversity protection, and sustainable resource management (Ministry of Ecology and Environment: The People's Republic of China, 2017) which are complemented by diplomats at global forums. For instance, President Xi Jinping, in his 2019 keynote speech at the Second Belt and Road Forum, declared:

"We need to pursue open, green and clean cooperation. The Belt and Road is not an exclusive club; it aims to promote green development. We may launch green infrastructure projects, make green investments, and provide green financing to protect the Earth, which we all call home. In pursuing Belt and Road cooperation, everything should be done in a transparent way, and we should have zero tolerance for corruption" (PR Newswire, 2023).

Such statements invoke China's philosophical commitment to ecological civilization, a normative framework rooted in Confucian and Daoist traditions that emphasize harmony between human activity and nature. In official narratives, the Green BRI is thus framed as a natural extension of China's domestic environmental agenda and its aspiration to be a leader in global ecological governance.

However, CDA reveals that the concept of ecological civilization, while seemingly progressive, operates as a discursive strategy to de-politicize and de-materialize environmental concerns. By framing sustainability as a question of moral virtue and cultural tradition, the Chinese state repositions environmental governance away from structural critique, particularly of extractivist development, and toward a technocratic and ideological framework that privileges state authority. The BRI's ecological framing, therefore, becomes an exercise in environmental legitimation, not transformation (Weatherley & Bauer, 2021).

Empirical contradictions abound. For instance, the China–Laos railway, promoted as a green alternative to road transport, resulted in the clearance of vast swathes of forest, threatening biodiversity hotspots and displacing communities. In Pakistan, BRI investments in coal-fired power plants under the China–Pakistan Economic Corridor contradict commitments to decarbonization. These examples illustrate the chasm between rhetorical commitments and operational realities, suggesting that "green" is more often a branding mechanism than a guiding principle.

Win-Win Development and the Politics of Harmony

A recurring motif in BRI discourse is "win-win cooperation"—a phrase that conveys mutual benefit, shared prosperity, and geopolitical benevolence. This narrative is embedded in official white papers such as "Vision and Actions on Jointly Building the Silk Road Economic Belt and 21st-Century Maritime Silk Road (2015)", which emphasizes partnership, inclusivity, and respect for local conditions. The BRI is presented as a horizontal, non-coercive model of development, distinct from Western aid conditionalities and neoliberal reforms (Belt and Road Forum for International Cooperation, 2017).

However, from a CDA perspective, "win-win" functions as a rhetorical trope of strategic ambiguity, deliberately vague and ideologically disarming. It serves multiple purposes: it legitimizes China's presence in foreign territories, deflects accusations of neocolonialism, and reinforces the idea that development is apolitical and consensual. The narrative of "win-win" obscures asymmetric power relations between China and recipient states, many of which are highly indebted, economically dependent, and politically constrained.

Consider the Mombasa–Nairobi Standard Gauge Railway (SGR) in Kenya, often touted as a symbol of Sino-African cooperation. While the project created short-term employment and improved connectivity, it also saddled Kenya with substantial debt, incurred ecological costs (notably the disruption of wildlife corridors), and generated public backlash due to lack of transparency (Africa Defense Forum, 2023). Yet in official Chinese documents, the project is consistently presented as a success story of harmonious cooperation, reinforcing the performative function of "win-win" language in silencing contestation.

Furthermore, the notion of harmony, a deeply embedded value in Chinese political thought, is strategically invoked to naturalize top-down governance and suppress dissent. In the context of the BRI, harmony operates discursively to erase conflict, depoliticize development, and marginalize critical voices. Environmental protests, indigenous resistance, and civil society concerns are either omitted or reframed as "misunderstandings" to be resolved through dialogue and partnership.

Sustainable Infrastructure and the Technocratic Turn

Another central element of BRI sustainability discourse is the promotion of "sustainable infrastructure." Chinese ministries, development banks, and project contractors frequently cite the use of green technologies, climate-resilient designs, and environmental impact assessments (EIAs) as evidence of responsible development. The Asian Infrastructure Investment Bank (AIIB), a multilateral financial institution aligned with BRI objectives, has produced numerous reports touting sustainability metrics, climate screening tools, and ESG (environmental, social, and governance) integration (Global Times, 2019).

Yet, CDA uncovers that the emphasis on technical solutions and managerial metrics reflects a broader technocratic turn in environmental governance, one that prioritizes efficiency, cost-benefit analysis, and engineering over democratic participation and ecological justice. Terms like "ecological modernization" and "green finance" become buzzwords that signal progress while concealing extractivist logics. Infrastructure, under this paradigm, is not interrogated for *why* or *for whom* it is built, but rather *how* it can be made less harmful (Ecologic Institute, 2015-2018).

This technocratic rationality is evident in projects like the Myitsone Dam in Myanmar, a Chinese-funded hydropower project that promises renewable energy but threatens indigenous livelihoods, sacred sites, and biodiversity. Environmental impact assessments are often either absent or superficial, and mitigation strategies are developed without local consultation. Despite this, the project is framed in BRI literature as part of a green energy transition, thus normalizing environmental violence as necessary trade-offs for development.

The problem with ecological modernization, as scholars like Maarten Hajer and Arthur Mol argue, is that it reproduces the logic of capitalist expansion, merely "greening" it rather than transforming its structural foundations. By emphasizing carbon neutrality, efficiency, and innovation, the BRI's sustainability narrative redefines environmental responsibility as a managerial challenge—disconnected from the socio-political contexts in which infrastructure is embedded (Foster, 2012).

The Hegemonic Function of Sustainability Discourse

Taken together, the themes of "Green BRI," "win-win development," and "sustainable infrastructure" constitute a hegemonic sustainability discourse, a system of meaning-making that frames China's global development ambitions as morally legitimate, environmentally conscious, and politically benign. Drawing on Gramscian theory, this discourse functions hegemonically not through coercion but through consent-building, normalization, and the production of common sense (Ashok et al., 2023).

The BRI's sustainability narrative operates as what James Ferguson might call an "anti-politics machine," a mechanism that recasts political interventions as technical solutions, thereby obscuring questions of power, inequality, and resistance. Infrastructure becomes not a contested terrain but a pathway to shared prosperity. Environmental harm is reframed as a problem to be managed, not prevented. Displacement and dispossession are rendered invisible in the glossy images of ports, railways, and power plants (Ferguson, 1990).

Importantly, this discourse does not emerge in a vacuum. It is supported by an international ecosystem of think tanks, consultancies, development agencies, and multilateral institutions that reinforce the legitimacy of BRI narratives. Even global actors critical of China often adopt similar vocabularies of green growth, smart cities, and resilient infrastructure, contributing to the discursive hegemony of sustainability.

EMPIRICAL CASE STUDIES: CONTRADICTIONS IN PRACTICE

This section grounds the preceding theoretical and discursive analysis in empirical evidence from select Belt and Road Initiative infrastructure projects across Asia and Africa. It critically examines how environmental degradation and social displacement occur in practice, despite China's consistent invocation of sustainability, green finance, and ecological civilization in official narratives.

Environmental Impacts

Laos–China Railway: Deforestation and Biodiversity Loss

The Laos–China Railway, a central component of China's Belt and Road Initiative, spans approximately 422 kilometers from Boten on the Chinese border to the capital city Vientiane. While hailed by the Lao government as a transformative infrastructure project promising economic integration and regional connectivity, its environmental and social costs have raised significant concerns.

Between 2017 and 2020, Laos experienced widespread environmental degradation linked to the construction of the railway and associated infrastructure. According to Global Forest Watch, Laos lost over 318,000 hectares of natural forest in 2021 alone, with substantial tree cover reduction occurring in the northern provinces of Luang Prabang, Oudomxay, and Luang Namtha, precisely the regions through which the railway passes. Since 2000, nearly 4 million hectares of forest have been cleared in Laos, much of it biodiverse primary forest crucial for carbon sequestration (Jones, 2022).

These impacts were compounded by weak environmental safeguards. Environmental Impact Assessments submitted for approval often failed to consider cumulative impacts and lacked meaningful community engagement. Interviews conducted by EarthRights International revealed that many local communities were not adequately consulted, received no formal compensation, and suffered displacement without clear legal recourse.

The railway has also contributed to habitat fragmentation, affecting endangered species such as the Indochinese tiger and Asian elephants, whose migratory corridors now intersect with rail infrastructure and access roads. Additionally, the influx of investment into "special economic zones" and commercial plantations along the railway route has intensified pressure on forests, including through illegal logging and agricultural encroachment.

While the Lao government has pledged to achieve 70% forest cover by 2035 and passed a 2019 Forestry Law banning the export of rare woods, enforcement remains inconsistent (RECOFTC, 2023). Timber brokers report continued trade in endangered hardwoods, fuelled by Chinese demand, with stockpiles often hidden and awaiting informal sale.

Though proponents highlight the railway's potential to increase national income, by up to 21% according to the World Bank, and promote low-carbon mobility, its real cost is borne by displaced communities and degraded ecosystems. As one displaced villager in Oudomxay noted, "This is China already. We don't have anything left for us—it's all for them" (Jones, 2022).

Hambantota Port, Sri Lanka: Coastal Erosion and Marine Disruption

Sri Lanka's Hambantota Port, built with substantial Chinese financing and later leased to China Merchants Port Holdings for 99 years, is another emblematic case of ecological disruption under the guise of development. Billed as a component of the "Maritime Silk Road," the port was intended to stimulate regional trade and bolster blue economy initiatives. One of the most prominent concerns relates to the port's location, which was developed despite prior expert warnings about its proximity to ecologically sensitive coastal areas, including marine biodiversity zones and sea turtle nesting grounds. This oversight reflects a broader pattern of sidelining ecological considerations in favour of geopolitical and economic expediencies (Gamage, 2024).

The Hambantota Port project has led to environmental degradation attributed to multiple activities. Disruption of marine and coastal ecosystems by dredging during infrastructure expansion has led to fragmented habitats. This project has also led to loss of vegetation and vital ecosystems such as mangroves and coral reefs, which act as buffer agents and reservoirs. Local fishing communities have now reported declining fish stocks and conflicts over access to marine spaces, threatening food and life security. These large-scale development initiatives undermine the ecological imbalance undertaken in a fragile environmental setting (Gamage, 2024).

Moreover, the construction of the port led to the displacement of the local populous without any measures to accommodate these people. This has impacted and increased the vulnerabilities of the community at large. The narratives that followed showcase the port as a national development icon, but affected the whole community. Keeping this as the baseline, it demands a more scrutinized Environmental Impact Assessment report and adherence to international environmental standards to keep in check the large-scale development projects which disrupt the ecological balance.

Kenya Lamu Coal Plant: A Victory of Environment Activists

The Lamu Coal Plant was a planned 1,050 MW project under the BRI, which was halted in 2019 by Kenya's National Environmental Tribunal due to an inadequate environmental impact assessment. It was being financed by the Industrial and Commercial Bank of China, and the financing was withdrawn subsequently. This withdrawal showcased the victory and dedication of environmental activists of Kenya, which enabled the power of community mobilization in constraining such projects (BBC, 2019).

Social and Cultural Displacement

Hydropower Projects in Myanmar: Displacement and Conflict

The Myitsone Dam, located at the confluence of the Mali and N'Maj river in Kachin state is one of the finest examples of China's BRI funded project, which led to indigenous displacement. The dam was designed to generate over 6,000 megawatts of power, with 90% of the share being exported to China (Ramachandran, 2019). While taking the numerical values, the project has displaced over 12,000 ethnic Kachin people without any incentives or recognition (Ikners, 2016). According to the Kachin Development Networking Group (KDNG), between 2009 and 2011, around 15,000 people from over 60 villages were forcefully migrated to Aung Mya Thar and Mali Yang village. A KDNG spokesperson in 2010 alleged that villagers were forced by the authorities to sign compensation agreements (Business & Human Rights Resource Centre, 2019). The project has also exacerbated armed conflict between the Myanmar military and Kachin Independence Army, with development zones becoming heavily militarized.

Despite being suspended in 2011 due to domestic protests, China continues to pressure for project resumption, citing strategic energy needs and contractual obligations (Harvey, 2011). The project is still framed in BRI literature as an example of clean, renewable energy infrastructure, demonstrating how sustainability narratives are selectively invoked to depoliticize conflict and displacement.

Kenya's Standard Gauge Railway (SGR): Community Protests and Labor Injustice

In East Africa, Kenya's Standard Gauge Railway (SGR), connecting Mombasa to Nairobi, has been celebrated as a model BRI success story. It reduced travel time, improved freight efficiency, and generated thousands of construction jobs. However, these benefits have come at significant social and environmental costs.

A 2020 report by Human Rights Watch documented systemic displacement of landowners, particularly in the Taita-Taveta and Nairobi counties, where compensation was either delayed or never delivered. Many of the communities were forced to move out without any justification, which violated the local constitutional laws and international human rights. Poor working conditions and racial discrimination were also reported by the onsite workers.

During the field interviews, certain reservations and scepticism were also highlighted by the community leaders against the BRI's claim of inclusive development. Although the project was depicted as a positive development, it led to habitat fragmentation and soil erosion in sensitive areas such as the Tsavo Conservation Area and Nairobi National Park. The railway line passing through the latter disrupts wildlife migration and local communities (Nyumba, 2021). In reference to the Tsavo Conservation Area, there has been certain evidence of wildlife displaying behavioural changes, especially elephants, which are displaying aggression and avoidance of railways. The environmental impact assessments were conducted for the project, but problems in these areas prove that the suggested mitigation measures were neglected, which contributed to the deterioration of the ecology of the region (Inter Press Service, 2021).

The evidences provided in the above case studies point that there are contradictions in BRI's sustainability commitment and the ecological havoc it has generated. While China continues to brand the BRI as a vehicle for green growth and mutual prosperity, on-the-ground realities often involve deforestation, biodiversity loss, community displacement, labour exploitation, and weakened governance.

This section affirms the need for a critical, grounded evaluation of large-scale development initiatives, particularly when they operate within asymmetrical power relations and opaque decision-making structures. It also highlights the limitations of technocratic and performative sustainability frameworks, which often fail to account for context-specific, long-term, and community-centered notions of environmental justice.

As the BRI enters its second decade, empirical accountability must become a cornerstone of sustainability assessment. Without it, sustainability will remain what it often already is: a rhetorical promise used to justify unjust practices.

THEORETICAL SYNTHESIS: SUSTAINABILITY AS GOVERNANCE TOOL

The preceding empirical analyses expose the BRI as a development paradigm fraught with contradiction, where sustainability rhetoric is deployed to legitimize projects that frequently engender ecological harm, social displacement, and geopolitical dependency. This section synthesizes those findings through the lens of critical development theory and global governance, advancing the argument that sustainability in the BRI operates as a tool of governance, a strategic apparatus that regulates populations, manages dissent, and consolidates influence under the guise of environmental stewardship.

Drawing on the theoretical contributions of Michel Foucault, James Ferguson, and Antonio Gramsci, this section conceptualizes BRI sustainability as a technocratic, geopolitical, and cultural project. Rather than treating sustainability as an ethical commitment or environmental imperative, it is approached here as a regime of power-knowledge, designed to secure legitimacy, obscure political content, and foster global consent to infrastructural expansion and territorial reordering.

Sustainability as a Technocratic Governance Mechanism

The framing of sustainability in the BRI is deeply embedded in the language of technical rationality, optimization, and scientific management. Through policy documents, project guidelines, and institutional practices, sustainability is rendered measurable, quantifiable, and manageable—reduced to metrics such as carbon offsets, green financing ratios, and ecological impact indices. While such metrics signal accountability, they simultaneously obscure qualitative socio-political concerns such as displacement, consent, and ecological relationality.

This process exemplifies Michel Foucault's concept of governmentality—a mode of governance that operates through the rationalization of social life and the management of populations. Governmentality, in Foucault's terms, is the "conduct of conduct"—a dispersed and capillary form of power that organizes behaviour through norms, procedures, and expert knowledge (Joseph, 2012).

In the BRI context, Green BRI policies, Environmental Impact Assessments (EIAs), and sustainability indices function as techniques of governmentality. They render environmental and social relations into administrable categories, thereby neutralizing their political content. The construction of a railway through a forest is no longer a political act of dispossession or ecological violence; it becomes a problem of mitigation, resettlement logistics, or biodiversity offsets.

Moreover, the BRI's emphasis on "ecological civilization" and "low-carbon growth" masks the extractivist logics embedded in its infrastructure agenda. An argument is always presented to justify the project in place to cover for the ecological disruptions, for instance proposal for dam construction with a promise of providing clean energy in lieu of land space, as was the case of Myanmar's Myitsone Dam. Such contradictions are managed through repeated discussions, negotiating dissent without altering any structural models.

In this way, the projects are implemented and executed under the BRI's sustainability umbrella where environmental critique takes a backseat and rationalization provided prevails over the justice and ethical practices.

Sustainability as a Geopolitical Tool of Legitimation

The sustainability agenda of BRI also serves a geopolitical tool enforcing the key narrative of China's quest for global acceptance and influence. Apart from being an economic initiative, the BRI is a strategic foreign policy through which China is trying to expand its influence, strengthen alliances, and secure long-term free access to global resources and markets. Framing this endeavour as "green" and "sustainable" enables China to distinguish itself from the historically extractive development models of Western imperialism.

Here, James Ferguson's concept of the "anti-politics machine" is illuminating. Ferguson argues that development discourse transforms deeply political processes, such as land use, labour relations, and state control, into technical problems devoid of power dynamics. This depoliticization enables the expansion of state authority and international capital under the guise of neutrality (Ferguson, 1990).

The BRI reproduces this pattern on a global scale. The building of railways, ports, and energy corridors in Africa and Asia is framed not as strategic positioning or resource capture, but as mutual development and South-South solidarity. The narrative of "win-win cooperation" and "community of shared future" conceals the asymmetrical nature of these relationships, where China, as creditor, constructor, and contractor, holds decisive leverage over recipient nations.

Moreover, by positioning itself as a green development partner, China can counter Western narratives of neocolonialism, even as it replicates some of its dynamics. For instance, BRI investments in coal power in Pakistan and Indonesia continue under the justification of energy security, despite being out of step with the Paris Agreement (De Boer et al., 2022). These inconsistencies are overshadowed by high-level diplomatic branding and soft power overtures, such as tree planting campaigns, educational exchanges, and Confucius Institutes.

In this sense, sustainability operates as a geopolitical narrative technology, a way of aligning China's strategic interests with globally accepted environmental norms. Through this sustainability banner, it gathers authorisation for executing projects and practices that may be perceived as exploitative or coercive by other global powers or institutions.

Sustainability as a Cultural Soft Power Device

Apart from projecting BRI as a technological marvel, China is also trying to present it as a sustainable project which is in harmony with nature, thereby projecting itself as an ecologically responsible civilization which believes in sustainable development and green connectivity. The sustainability angle is a way of projecting its soft power in order to change world opinion and bring as many countries to support the BRI.

Antonio Gramsci's theory of cultural hegemony underscores this belief, which states that dominant classes or states maintain their power not just through coercion but also through ideological leadership, whereby their worldview becomes normalized, accepted, and internalized as "common sense" (Cole, 2024). Hegemony, in this framework, is the ability to shape desires and beliefs in ways that stabilize power relations.

China is promoting its sustainability discourse through initiatives like the BRI Environmental Big Data platform, green finance forums, and cooperative agreements with UNEP and other multilateral agencies. This enables it to assimilate the sustainability discourse into the institutional fabric of global environmental governance. Once the sustainability concept is embedded into the BRI project, it becomes easy to sell the project to the recipient countries, which can then justify their participation in the project. The sustainability model becomes especially attractive to countries in the Global South, which are sceptical about Western model of development, thereby creating an opening for China to enter into agreements with these countries on its BRI project.

However, this Chinese push for BRI as a sustainable, ecological and environmental friendly initiative is not without its contradictions. Empirical studies in many countries participating in the BRI project have shown that many of these projects contradict the very ecological values that it espouses. However, the propaganda and hype created by China in international forums through media, education and institutional diplomacy continues to shape perception and public opinion in favour of BRI.

RETHINKING DEVELOPMENT: ALTERNATIVE FRAMEWORKS

The empirical and theoretical critiques of the BRI presented in the preceding sections reveal the urgent need for a paradigmatic shift in the global development agenda. Sustainability, when used as a discursive and technocratic instrument to justify ecologically harmful and socially displacing projects, becomes a hollow signifier—stripped of its transformative potential. This final section proposes a rethinking of development that transcends the extractive, centralized, and capital-intensive models typified by initiatives like the BRI. It outlines alternative frameworks rooted in eco-centrism, community agency, indigenous sovereignty, and environmental justice, while offering policy recommendations for more equitable and ecologically sound global infrastructure development.

Eco-Centric Planning: Centering Nature in Development

At the core of alternative development thinking lies the need to invert anthropocentric and growth-driven logics in favour of eco-centric planning. This approach recognizes that human well-being is inextricably linked to ecological health, and that the economy must be nested within, not above, the environment.

Eco-centric planning challenges the dominant infrastructure paradigm, which treats land, rivers, forests, and oceans as inert spaces awaiting transformation into productive assets. Instead, it emphasizes the intrinsic value of ecosystems, the necessity of maintaining bioregional integrity, and the incorporation of planetary boundaries into development decision-making. It calls for no-go zones for infrastructure development in biodiversity hotspots, river headwaters, and sacred landscapes, where ecological and cultural significance outweigh commercial value (Coskun, 2023).

Examples of eco-centric planning include Masdar City in the United Arab Emirates, a pioneering urban project designed to be a zero-carbon, zero-waste city with a strong emphasis on renewable energy and sustainable infrastructure, and the Küçükçekmece Eco-City in Turkey, which aims to integrate environmental sustainability into urban development through green spaces, energy-efficient buildings, and sustainable water management. These models demonstrate that development need not come at the cost of nature but can instead be guided by principles of ecological harmony and intergenerational justice.

Community-Led Infrastructure Governance

A second pillar of alternative development is community-led governance, which prioritizes participatory decision-making, decentralization, and the recognition of local knowledge systems. Large-scale infrastructure projects are often designed in distant capitals or foreign ministries, with little understanding of or accountability to the people whose lands, waters, and livelihoods are affected.

Community-led governance proposes a reversal of this logic. It advocates for Free, Prior, and Informed Consent (FPIC) processes, local referendum mechanisms, and grassroots planning councils that determine the scope, form, and desirability of infrastructure investments. Crucially, it resituates communities not as passive beneficiaries or "stakeholders," but as rights-holders and planners with decision-making authority (Larsen & Chanthavisouk, 2024).

One illustrative example is Indonesia's adat governance system, where customary land management practices are formally recognized, enabling indigenous communities to govern forests based on traditional law (Simonetti, 2023). In Latin America, territorial planning frameworks in Bolivia and Colombia empower Afro-descendant and indigenous communities to design their own infrastructure and development plans.

These approaches yield more socially cohesive and ecologically grounded outcomes, as they are rooted in intimate knowledge of place, customary land ethics, and long-term communal interests—far removed from the short-termism of state-led or donor-led megaprojects.

Indigenous Sovereignty and Environmental Justice

Indigenous peoples and local communities (IPLCs) manage over a quarter of the Earth's land surface, including some of its most biodiverse and carbon-rich ecosystems. Yet they remain disproportionately exposed to displacement, dispossession, and marginalization under current development regimes.

An alternative model of development must be grounded in indigenous sovereignty, which affirms the right of IPLCs to self-determination, territory, and cultural continuity. It must also foreground environmental justice, which links ecological degradation to histories of colonization, racism, and economic inequality (McGregor et al., 2020).

Policies grounded in these principles must:

- Recognize collective land rights and support legal titling processes.
- Protect sacred natural sites from extractive development.
- Ensure representation of IPLCs in infrastructure governance bodies.
- Support biocultural diversity as an essential component of global sustainability.

A compelling example is the Yasuní-ITT Initiative in Ecuador, which sought to leave oil reserves underground in exchange for international compensation, protecting the territory of uncontacted tribes and one of the world's most biodiverse rainforests. Although eventually shelved due to lack of international support, the initiative remains a paradigmatic case of post-extractive environmental justice thinking (Vallejo et al., 2014).

Learning from Bottom-Up Sustainability Models

There is no shortage of practical, grounded alternatives to top-down, capital-intensive infrastructure. Across the Global South, communities are developing low-impact, high-benefit models of sustainable development:

- Solar Village Projects in Sub-Saharan Africa (e.g., in Tanzania): These initiatives provide decentralized renewable energy using solar microgrids, managed by local cooperatives. They enhance energy access in remote areas without disrupting natural landscapes or requiring foreign debt. In Tanzania, organizations like the Elico Foundation, in collaboration with the government and other stakeholders, have successfully installed solar systems in rural health facilities, ensuring reliable electricity for critical medical services and contributing to the achievement of Sustainable Development Goals (SDGs) (Africa Energy Portal, 2023).

- Green Corridors in India: Initiatives like the Aravalli Biodiversity Park in Gurgaon demonstrate how rewilding and ecological connectivity can be integrated into urban planning and regional development, enhancing both climate resilience and biodiversity (iamgurgaon, n.d.).
- Agroecological zones in Latin America: Community-managed agroforestry systems in Brazil and Peru support food sovereignty, forest conservation, and climate mitigation, demonstrating that alternatives to industrial agriculture and land-use change are viable and scalable (Cossío et al., 2014).

These models emphasize resilience, sufficiency, justice, and local empowerment over profit-maximization, centralization, and technocratic control. They offer living templates for how infrastructure and development can be reimagined in ways that sustain both human and non-human life.

Policy Recommendations for Just Infrastructure Futures

To facilitate the shift toward these alternative paradigms, the following policy recommendations are proposed for future global infrastructure planning:

Binding Social and Environmental Safeguards

All infrastructure projects—especially those with international financing—must be subject to binding environmental and social safeguards that go beyond symbolic compliance. These should include:

- Independent Strategic Environmental Assessments (SEAs) prior to project approval.
- Legally mandated Free, Prior, and Informed Consent (FPIC) processes.
- Clear enforcement mechanisms with sanctions for non-compliance.

Independent Accountability Mechanisms

Multilateral development initiatives should be overseen by independent grievance redressal bodies, composed of civil society, environmental scientists, and local representatives. These bodies should have:

- Investigative powers to assess violations.
- Remedial powers to halt or modify projects.
- Transparency in all monitoring and reporting.

Participatory Planning and Budgeting

Recipient countries should institutionalize participatory development planning frameworks, ensuring infrastructure priorities emerge from bottom-up consultations rather than elite capture or geopolitical pressure. National budgets for infrastructure must be subject to:

- Local development boards.
- Public hearings and comment periods.
- Community-defined success metrics.

The critique of sustainability within initiatives like the BRI is not a call to abandon development but to transform it—from a top-down, extractivist process to a just, regenerative, and participatory practice. Rethinking development means embracing alternatives that honor ecological limits, cultural pluralism, and democratic accountability.

The alternative frameworks outlined in this section are not utopian ideals; they are empirically grounded, ethically defensible, and increasingly necessary in the face of planetary crisis. As climate breakdown, biodiversity collapse, and social inequality converge, the time has come to shift from infrastructure that builds empires to infrastructure that nurtures life.

CONCLUSION: RECLAIMING SUSTAINABILITY THROUGH JUSTICE AND ECOLOGY

This chapter has critically analysed how China has manipulated world opinion on its BRI project by presenting it as a sustainable, environmental friendly, and inclusive project. The project is also an eye-opener on how the concept of sustainability can be instrumentalised as a tool for development to garner legitimacy, deflect dissent and consolidate geopolitical influence. The BRI embodies a model in which sustainability is cleverly and strategically deployed to garner legitimacy, deflect dissent, and consolidate geopolitical and economic legitimacy. On the contrary, BRI functions as a government tool to mask deeply unequal, ecologically destructive, and socially displacing practices.

Through an interdisciplinary framework drawing on political economy, discourse analysis, and critical development theory, the chapter has revealed the diverse roles that sustainability performs in BRI, as a technocratic apparatus that renders political and ecological conflicts into technical problems, as a geopolitical narrative that justifies China's infrastructural expansionism, and as a soft power that projects a gentle image of China as a responsible environment friendly nation. This character of China has been studied and documented in multiple studies conducted in Sri Lanka, Laos, Cambodia, Myanmar, and Kenya, where BRI-linked projects have led to massive deforestation, displacement of people, loss of biodiversity, all while being branded as environment friendly and sustainable.

This analysis leads us to question whether growth-oriented models should be supported or encouraged despite mounting ecological limits and deepening social inequalities. At a time when the world is grappling with its worst environmental and ecological crisis, resource depletion and biodiversity collapse, should large-scale projects like BRI, with their global reach and scale, be encouraged to flourish and expand? If left unchecked, they have the potential to make this planet economically unsustainable for humankind.

What is required, then, is not merely a reformulation of development discourse but a radical shift in development thinking. This requires moving beyond a vision of development that is ecologically grounded, socially equitable, and democratically governed. This requires a reconfiguration of infrastructure planning that begins with ecosystems and communities, not markets or states. It requires consultation with local and indigenous communities, who own and use resources like land and water.

This requires community-led development and infrastructure governance, eco-centric planning, and local ownership. These ideas and practices are not just conjectures and premises, but are already in practice in many countries across the world, be it solar villages in Africa to green corridors in India and agroecological systems in Latin America. These projects are living examples of sustainable development in the real sense.

This chapter has offered policy recommendations to support this shift, including the implementation of binding environmental safeguards, local participation in planning and execution and independent accountability institutions. These are critical steps towards ensuring that future development initiatives, coming from whichever part of the world or whichever country, should be taken into consideration, if we want to do justice to the people of the earth and to move towards a more sustainable development model.

In conclusion, the BRI initiative should not become a discursive battleground for the meaning and future of sustainability. It is an example where competing visions of development, extractive vs regenerative, centralised vs participatory are competing for supremacy. The challenge before scholars and activists is to expose contradictions in different narratives and reimagine development as a process of collective care for people and planet.

REFERENCES

AIIB President says BRI promising. (2019). https://www.globaltimes.cn/page/201905/1149376.shtml

Ashok, D., Paul, J. M., & Menon, V. B. (2023). China's Consensus Hegemony Approach and its Engagement with South Asia. *Deleted Journal*, *2*(1), 1–14. DOI: 10.53989/jcp.v2i1_5_menon

Busbarat, P., Camba, A., Pratiwi, F. I., Po, S., Đ , H., Sengkhamkhoutlavong, B., ... & Thuzar, M. (2023). How Has China's Belt and Road Initiative Impacted Southeast Asian Countries?.

Clark, B., Foster, J. B., & Longo, S. B. (2019). Metabolic Rifts and the Ecological Crisis. In Vidal, M., Smith, T., Rotta, T., & Prew, P. (Eds.), *The Oxford Handbook of Karl Marx* (pp. 651–658). Oxford University Press.

Cole, N. L. (2024, May 18). What is cultural hegemony? *ThoughtCo,* https://www.thoughtco.com/cultural-hegemony-3026121

Coskun, H. (2023). Eco-city planning: Concepts and contemporary models. *Global Journal of Ecology*, *8*(2), 110–119. DOI: 10.17352/gje.000090

Cossío, R., Menton, M., Cronkleton, P., & Larson, A. M. (2014). *Community forest management in the Peruvian Amazon: A literature review*. Bogor: Center for International Forestry Research (CIFOR). Retrieved from https://doi.org/DOI: 10.17528/cifor/004426

Cowen, D. (2017, January 25). Infrastructures of Empire and Resistance. *Verso,* https://www.versobooks.com/en-gb/blogs/news/3067-infrastructures-of-empire-and-resistance?srsltid=AfmBOoqZb6Enr5XWoKiOqZHQ4WlvdgdgVoDKMJjHYODNfHX87Mmj1mvt

Custer, S., Horigoshi, A., & Marshall, K. (2024, March). BRI from the ground up: Leaders from 129 countries evaluate a decade of Beijing's signature initiative. https://docs.aiddata.org/reports/bri-from-the-ground-up/full-report.html

De Boer, D., Nedopil, C., & Danting, F. (2022). Belt and Road must align with Paris Agreement – government guidance. https://dialogue.earth/en/business/belt-and-road-must-align-paris-agreement-government

Demiryol, T. (2019). Political Economy of Connectivity: China's Belt and Road initiative. https://doi.org/DOI: 10.5281/zenodo.3267663

Ferguson, J. (1990). The Anti-Politics Machine. Retrieved from_https://www.supersummary.com/the-anti-politics-machine/summary/

Foster, J. B. (2012). The Planetary Rift and the New Human Exemptionalism: A Political-Economic Critique of Ecological Modernization Theory. *Organization & Environment*, *25*(3), 211–237. https://www.jstor.org/stable/27068852

Gamage, S. (2024). The Illusion of Prosperity: Investigating the Hambantota Port Project. Retrieved from https://www.asisrilanka.lk/post/the-illusion-of-prosperity-investigating-the-hambantota-port-project

Green Finance & Development Center. (n.d.). Retrieved from https://greenfdc.org/countries-of-the-belt-and-road-initiative-bri/

Guidance on Promoting Green Belt and Road. (2017). *SCO Environment Information Sharing Platform.* https://english.mee.gov.cn/Resources/Policies/policies/Frameworkp1/201706/t20170628_416864.shtml

Harvey, R. (2011, September 30). Burma dam: Why Myitsone plan is being halted. *BBC*. https://www.bbc.com/news/world-asia-pacific-15123833

Ikners, N. (2016). Decision Looms on Myitsone Dam. *Institute for Security & Development Policy.* https://www.isdp.eu/decision-looms-myitsone-dam/

Imanche, S. A., Ze, T., Ayom, M. C., & Dalibi, S. G. (2021). An Assessment of Nigerians Perception towards Chinese Foreign Direct Investments and Its Acceptability in Nigeria. *Open Journal of Business and Management*, *09*(03), 1151–1168. DOI: 10.4236/ojbm.2021.93062

Jarvie, M. E. (2016). Brundtland Report. Retrieved from https://www.britannica.com/topic/Brundtland-Report

Jones, A. (2022). Laos' Fast Train to China Brings Connection at a Cost, With Big Promises but Uneven Progress. *Rainforest Journalism Fund.* https://rainforestjournalismfund.org/stories/laos-fast-train-china-brings-connection-cost-big-promises-uneven-progress

Joseph, J. (2012). *Putting governmentality in its place. The Social in the Global: Social Theory, Governmentality and Global Politics*. Cambridge University Press., DOI: 10.1017/CBO9781139149143.003

Kouser, S., Subhan, A., & Abedullah, N. (2020). Uncovering Pakistan's Environmental Risks and Remedies under the China-Pakistan Economic Corridor. *Environmental Science and Pollution Research International*, *27*(5), 4661–4663. DOI: 10.1007/s11356-019-07428-5

Larsen, P. B., & Chanthavisouk, C. (2024). Free, prior, and informed consent, local officials, and changing biodiversity governance in Hin Nam No, Laos. *Conservation biology: the journal of the Society for Conservation Biology, 38*(6), 110–120. https://doi.org/DOI: 10.1111/cobi.14388

McGregor, D., Whitaker, S., & Sritharan, M. (2020). Indigenous environmental justice and sustainability. *Current Opinion in Environmental Sustainability, 43*, 35–40. DOI: 10.1016/j.cosust.2020.01.007

Merdeka Center for Opinion Research. (2022). Social Impact and Community Perception of Belt and Road Initiative Projects in Malaysia. Retrieved from https://asiafoundation.org/wp-content/uploads/2024/08/Social-Impact-and-Community-Perception-of-Belt-and-Road-Initiative-Projects-in-Malaysia.pdf

Myanmar: Myitsone dam project faces widespread opposition due to displacement & environment concerns. (2019). *Business & Human Rights Resource Center.* https://www.business-humanrights.org/en/latest-news/myanmar-myitsone-dam-project-faces-widespread-opposition-due-to-displacement-environment-concerns/

Nyumba, T. (2021, June 29). Kenya's huge railway project is causing environmental damage. Here's how. Down to Earth. https://www.downtoearth.org.in/africa/kenya-s-huge-railway-project-is-causing-environmental-damage-here-s-how-77681

Opaluwah, A. (2016). Participatory Development: A Tool of Pedagogy. *Exchanges the Interdisciplinary Research Journal, 4*(1), 120–139. DOI: 10.31273/eirj.v4i1.151

Ramachandran, S. (2019, April 24). The Standoff Over the Myitsone Dam Project in Myanmar: Advantage China. *The Jamestown Foundation.* https://jamestown.org/program/the-standoff-over-the-myitsone-dam-project-in-myanmar-advantage-china/

Ramírez, C. E. P. (2021). Limits and contradictions of capital in nature. Retrieved from https://www.probdes.iiec.unam.mx/index.php/pde/article/download/69780/62144?inline=1

RECOFTC's strategic plan addresses forestry challenges in Lao PDR. (2023, December 25). Retrieved from https://www.recoftc.org/updates/recoftcs-strategic-plan-addresses-forestry-challenges-lao-pdr

Sachs, W. (2017). The Sustainable Development Goals and *Laudato si'*: Varieties of Post Development? *Third World Quarterly, 38*(12), 2573–2587. DOI: 10.1080/01436597.2017.1350822

Schneider, F., Kallis, G., & Martinez-Alier, J. (2010). Crisis or opportunity? Economic degrowth for social equity and ecological sustainability. Introduction to this special issue. *Journal of Cleaner Production, 18*(6), 511–518. DOI: 10.1016/j.jclepro.2010.01.014

Simonetti, M. (2023). Adat in Indonesian law and society: A tool to build resilience and overcome diversity through cultural and legal pluralism. *The SOAS Journal of Postgraduate Research, 15.* https://doi.org/DOI: 10.25501/SOAS.00040649

Speech by Foreign Minister Wang Yi at the Opening of Symposium on International Developments and China's Diplomacy in 2017. (2017). *Ministry of Foreign Affairs People's Republic of China.* https://www.mfa.gov.cn/eng/wjb/wjbz/jh/202405/t20240527_11312148.html

Tanzania: How Solar Power Improves Health Services in Off-Grid Rural Areas. (2023, April 3). *Africa Energy Portal.* https://africa-energy-portal.org/news/tanzania-how-solar-power-improves-health-services-grid-rural-areas

The Belt and Road Ecological and Environmental Cooperation Plan. (2017). *Ministry of Foreign Affairs People's Republic of China.* https://english.mee.gov.cn/Resources/Policies/policies/Frameworkp1/201706/t20170628_416869.shtml

Vallejo, M. C., Burbano, R., Falconí, F., & Larrea, C. (2014). Leaving oil underground in Ecuador: The Yasuní-ITT initiative from a multi-criteria perspective. *Ecological Economics, 109*, 175–185. DOI: 10.1016/j.ecolecon.2014.11.013

Weatherley, R., & Bauer, V. (2021). A new Chinese modernity? The discourse of Eco civilisation applied to the belt and road initiative. *Third World Quarterly, 42*(9), 2115–2132. DOI: 10.1080/01436597.2021.1905511

Weitzman, A. (2022). Dependency Theory in 21st Century China and Latin America. Retrieved from https://globalpoliticaltheoryproject.pages.wm.edu/2022/08/28/dependency-theory-in-21st-century-china-and-latin-america/

KEY TERMS AND DEFINITIONS

Belt and Road Initiative (BRI): The Belt and Road Initiative (BRI) is an infrastructure and economic initiative started by the People's Republic of China (PRC) in 2013, comprising of two components, i.e., the Silk Road Economic Belt (land component) and the 21st century Maritime Silk Road (maritime component). It aims to connect China with Central Asia, the Middle East and up to Europe with infrastructure, economic and connectivity projects, by resorting to a debt trap diplomacy.

Developmentality: Developmentality is a mode of governance that frames development as a technical and apolitical process, thereby obscuring its power-laden and ecologically destructive dimensions.

Ecological Justice: Ecological Justice is the idea given by thinkers like Peter Singer and Christopher Stone. It recognises the rights of non-human species on this planet as well, along with the rights which they share with the human species. It aims to create such an environment which is liveable, breathable, and healthy for humans as well as all the other species on Earth.

Environmental Degradation: Environmental Degradation is defined as the deterioration/depletion of the resources of the planet for selfish ends. Rampant industrialisation, deforestation, water degradation, and population growth are some of the drivers of environmental degradation, among others.

Geopolitical Ecology: Geopolitical Ecology foregrounds the entanglement of environmental governance with strategic statecraft, capital flows, and territorial influence. A contemporary example of the misuse of this concept is the Belt and Road Initiative (BRI), which operates not only as an economic corridor but also as a geopolitical infrastructure. It enables China to project influence through debt diplomacy, resource access, and infrastructural entanglement, which in turn impacts the environment.

Infrastructural Imperialism: Infrastructural Imperialism is the strategic deployment of infrastructure as a means of securing geopolitical advantage and economic dependency. This process is particularly pronounced in the Global South, where weaker regulatory institutions, socio-political vulnerabilities, and economic precarity render communities disproportionately exposed to the negative externalities of large-scale development.

Infrastructure Development: Infrastructure Development is the creation of physical structures and facilities in a country, city, or area to boost the economy and well-being of people. In the context of the environment, it has a negative connotation. Infrastructure development boosts the economic growth of a nation, but at the same time, it disrupts the environment through air, water and land pollution and depletes the resources of the earth, thereby disturbing the idea of sustainable development.

Sustainability Discourse: Sustainability Discourse derives its name from sustainable development, which means that the utilization of the resources of the planet by the present generation should be such that it does not compromise on the living conditions of future generations. This discourse is arm-twisted by nations like China, which, in the name of development projects like BRI, are disturbing the long-term well-being of Earth.

Chapter 5
Reading Greenwashing Practices From a World–Systems Analysis Perspective

Çagla Vural
https://orcid.org/0000-0001-8474-2316
Akdeniz University, Turkey

Muhammed Onur Çöpoğlu
https://orcid.org/0000-0002-3629-6961
Ordu University, Turkey

ABSTRACT

This chapter examines greenwashing through the lens of World-Systems Analysis, arguing that environmental deception is not a marginal or accidental feature of global capitalism but a structural mechanism that sustains core–periphery inequalities. By connecting concepts such as carbon colonialism and the transboundary waste trade, the chapter shows how sustainability narratives in core countries often mask the outsourcing of environmental harm to semi-peripheral and peripheral zones. Drawing on critical literature, the study contends that greenwashing serves to legitimize ongoing resource extraction, pollution, and ecological injustice. It concludes that meaningful responses require moving beyond superficial reputational fixes and addressing the systemic dynamics that enable the externalization of ecological costs in the world economy.

DOI: 10.4018/979-8-3373-1707-6.ch005

INTRODUCTION

Environmental destruction has become an inseparable feature of global capitalism, yet it is frequently disguised behind the rhetoric of sustainability. Over the last two decades, the term greenwashing has gained prominence to describe the strategic use of misleading environmental claims by corporations and states alike.

This chapter departs from the premise that greenwashing cannot be understood merely as a case of individual deception or regulatory failure. Instead, it argues that such practices are embedded within the broader structural and ideological dynamics of the capitalist world-system. When situated within the framework of World-Systems Analysis (WSA), greenwashing emerges as a mechanism that legitimizes the externalization of environmental costs from core zones to semi-peripheral and peripheral regions—thereby reproducing the ecological inequalities that sustain global accumulation. Drawing on the insights of Immanuel Wallerstein and subsequent scholars, this chapter contends that greenwashing is not simply a matter of public image management but a systemic tool that helps obscure and sustain global environmental injustices.

This study seeks to understand how greenwashing operates as a mechanism within the capitalist world-system and how it connects to wider patterns of environmental exploitation, carbon colonialism, and transboundary waste trade.

By focusing on this question, the chapter challenges mainstream approaches that portray greenwashing as a superficial or isolated problem. Instead, it argues that greenwashing should be analyzed as a discursive technology that supports the reproduction of global inequalities by concealing the real environmental costs of production, consumption, and waste. These costs are not randomly distributed but follow the structural hierarchy of core, semi-peripheral, and peripheral regions, as articulated in World-Systems Analysis (Hornborg, 2006, p. 163; Jorgenson, 2006, pp. 182–184; Wallerstein, 1999, pp. 3–5). Thus, greenwashing should be seen not as a flaw or failure, but as part of how the capitalist world-system reproduces itself.

Methodologically, this chapter adopts a theory-driven, qualitative approach based on a critical literature review. It proceeds through a structured conceptual inquiry that first outlines the key principles of (WSA), emphasizing its relevance for understanding environmental inequality. It then explores how environmental exploitation functions as a structural feature of global capitalism by introducing concepts such as carbon colonialism and transboundary waste trade. The subsequent sections examine how greenwashing operates within these dynamics, not as a set of isolated misrepresentations, but as a systemic strategy that helps preserve core–periphery hierarchies. Drawing on existing literature and illustrative cases, the chapter synthesizes how discursive practices obscure material harm and sustain unequal ecological exchanges in the world economy.

In sum, greenwashing is better understood not as a minor flaw in communication or regulation, but as a structural mechanism embedded in global capitalism. It operates as a built-in feature of the system, one that helps preserve unequal relations between core and peripheral regions while giving the appearance of sustainability. By drawing on the perspective of WSA, the chapter highlights how greenwashing works to protect the legitimacy of growth and accumulation, even as ecological harm deepens. In doing so, it offers a structural explanation for why environmental claims often mask, rather than resolve, global injustice.

MAIN FOCUS OF THE CHAPTER

Theoretical Framework: World-Systems Analysis and Environmental Exploitation

It is necessary to use WSA to comprehend environmental exploitation as a fundamental component of the capitalist world-system. This is not just to repeat Wallerstein's theoretical formulation, but also to show how ecological degradation is structured across global hierarchies of waste, production, and power.

Wallerstein's World-Systems Theory

Wallerstein's World-Systems Theory offers a structural and holistic framework of social analysis that foregrounds how global capitalism has historically generated hierarchical economic and political relationships among nations, thereby shaping patterns of resource use, labor exploitation, and, increasingly, environmental harm (Wallerstein, 2004). From this perspective, the modern world economy, which emerged in the "long sixteenth century," is understood as an interconnected system comprising core, semi-peripheral, and peripheral zones. The core is typified by capital-intensive industries, advanced technology, and strong state mechanisms; the periphery, by contrast, specializes in raw material extraction under weaker governmental structures; the semi-periphery absorbs aspects of both poles, sometimes functioning as a buffer that stabilizes the entire system (Wallerstein, 1982; Babones, 2015, pp. 8-11).

Within this structure, the distribution of economic benefits and environmental burdens is highly uneven. Studies rooted in WSA repeatedly show that core nations enhance their economic power, living standards, and environmental quality domestically by shifting environmentally harmful activities to peripheral zones (Jorgenson, 2006, pp. 182-184; Hornborg, 2006, pp. 163, 171-174). According to Wallerstein (1998, p. 106), the essence of the modern world-system is capital accumulation on a global scale, whereby cores command technology, finance, and legal frameworks that enforce low-cost resource flows from weaker regions. Semi-peripheral nations, such as those with emerging industrial capacities, occupy an intermediate position; they sometimes benefit from investment and technological upgrading, yet they also serve as recipients of pollution-intensive production from the core (Jorgenson, 2006; Hornborg, 2006). Over time, these hierarchies give rise to what Jorgenson (2006, pp. 179-182, 189-190) calls "ecological unequal exchange," in which peripheries endure resource depletion and pollution in exchange for minimal compensation.

To fully grasp Wallerstein's framework, it is essential to situate environmental exploitation within the broader contours of WSA. This perspective offers a macro-sociological framework that clarifies how the global hierarchy of core, semi-periphery, and periphery nations structures not only economic exchange and labor relations but also the distribution of ecological burdens. By foregrounding these relationships, we can better understand why environmental damage is neither accidental nor peripheral to capitalist modernity, but rather a core dynamic that enables continued accumulation in the developed world.

A central feature of Wallerstein's approach is methodological holism, which treats the entire world-economy, rather than the nation-state, as the relevant unit of analysis (Wallerstein, 2004). This standpoint implies that environmental crises cannot be fully understood by focusing on single countries in isolation. Instead, one must examine transnational commodity chains and the ways in which global divisions of labor move primary production and waste processing to peripheral areas where regulation is loose or enforcement is weak (Campling, 2022, pp. 193-195). Semi-peripheral states often import polluting industries in the hope of stimulating growth, only to discover that local labor and ecosystems bear the brunt of environmental harm (Ciccantell 2022, pp. 182-184).

The hierarchical relationships that define the capitalist world-system have given rise to structural asymmetries in environmental footprints. Roberts, Grimes, and Manale (2003, p. 280) demonstrate that high-income core nations maintain relatively strict domestic environmental standards while quietly outsourcing carbon-intensive manufacturing and waste disposal to lower-income countries. The same dynamic holds in the trade of toxic or non-recyclable materials, which flow disproportionately from core to peripheral or semi-peripheral settings (Favarin et al., 2023, p. 220). This outward displacement of ecological costs has led scholars to conceptualize the practice as a continuation of historical patterns of exploitation (Friedman, 2006, p. 74).

Though the early formulations of WSA paid more attention to labor dynamics and commodity flows than to explicit ecological variables, scholars such as Hornborg (2006, pp. 164-173) and Chew (1997, p. 384) have pressed for a deeper integration of ecological processes. They argue that historical capitalism did not simply accumulate capital in the abstract; it also accumulated "low-entropy" resources—land, forests, metals, and water—through conquest, colonization, and unequal trade. The corollary is that the environmental degradation we see today is integral, not accidental, to how the world-system has evolved (Grimes 1999, p. 17). In essence, capitalism's survival has relied upon continually externalizing environmental costs, with pollution sinks, deforestation frontiers, cheap labor, and loose regulations functioning as "pressure release valves" that maintain core affluence (Wallerstein, 1999, pp. 3–5). Environmental injustice thus emerges as a structural outcome of the system's core logic, which maximizes profit by underpricing both labor and nature (Kick & McKinney, 2012, pp. 395–397).

Because peripheral economies face acute needs for foreign currency, jobs, or infrastructural investment, they often accept conditions that facilitate ecological harm, such as disposing of hazardous waste or leasing land for large-scale mining (Kentor & Grimes 2006, pp. 74-76). The result is a feedback loop in which core environmental standards appear to improve, but global ecological harm intensifies—an illusory process of "greening at home" through export of environmental burdens abroad (Sommer & Hargrove, 2020, pp. 271-272, 278-280). Accordingly, Wallerstein's theoretical emphasis on global hierarchies dovetails with contemporary critiques of greenwashing, as wealthy states champion sustainability targets while relocating the actual negative impacts to zones of diminished power.

Moreover, the concept of cyclical rhythms and secular trends within WSA (Wallerstein, 1982, pp. 91-104) suggests that environmental exploitation surges in tandem with periods of economic expansion. Over the course of what some call "long waves" or Kondratieff cycles (multi-decade "long waves" of expansion and stagnation, typically around 40–60 years), each new phase of capitalist growth depends on fresh sites for resource extraction and waste disposal (Grinin & Korotayev, 2022; Chase-Dunn & Grimes, 1995). When these frontiers close or the ecological carrying capacity is exceeded, crises ensue. Thus, it is not an overstatement to say that the longevity of the capitalist world-system has historically hinged on its ability to displace and defer ecological costs. In recent decades, as key frontiers have become saturated and climate change intensifies, these crises are accelerating (Burns, 2012, pp. 400-401).

In the section that follows, we build on these insights to articulate why environmental exploitation can be regarded as not merely a side effect of global capitalism but a fundamental mechanism that sustains the system's profit-oriented logic.

Environmental Exploitation as a Mechanism of the Capitalist World-System

When environmental exploitation is described as a "mechanism," the implication is that it functions systematically to enable capital accumulation, rather than emerging sporadically from poor corporate behavior or loose regulation in isolated locales (Grimes, 1999, p. 15). Capitalism, viewed through the lens of WSA, requires not just labor and markets but also cheap, readily available inputs—wood, coal, oil, minerals, and land—and safe outlets for the waste and pollutants generated by industrial processes (Hornborg, 2006, pp. 161-169). This logic is captured in Wallerstein's contention that modern production patterns rely on continuously externalizing costs, whether those costs appear in the form of underpaid labor, compromised indigenous rights, or polluted river basins (Wallerstein, 1999, pp. 6-7).

Multiple authors have conceptualized this externalization strategy in terms of ecologically unequal exchange or analogous frameworks, thereby underscoring its structural nature (Jorgenson, 2006; Hornborg, 2006; Roberts et al., 2003; Kick & McKinney, 2012). Under this arrangement, peripheral countries deliver raw materials or energy at undervalued prices to the core, while bearing the brunt of soil degradation, deforestation, or toxic by-products. At the same time, peripheral communities receive disproportionately small economic gains from the commodities sold to the world market. Core-based capital finds ways to keep commodity prices artificially low through mechanisms such as corporate lobbying that shapes trade agreements, the exploitation of weak governance by local intermediaries, and, in many cases, political repression that stifles labor and environmental movements demanding fairer conditions (Hornborg, 2006).

In the capitalist production model, environmental exploitation is hardly an afterthought. Instead, it is indispensable for profit maximization. Industries that core nations proclaim as "green" within their own borders—such as electronics, renewable energy components, and consumer goods with sustainability labels—often involve heavily polluting or resource-intensive manufacturing stages outsourced to peripheral or semi-peripheral zones (Lennerfors et al., 2015, pp. 761-768). These zones frequently have insufficient environmental oversight, thus enabling foreign firms to accumulate "green reputations" while dumping real ecological costs on local ecosystems (Roberts & Grimes, 1999, p. 64). The net result is an expansion of production on a planetary scale but with deeply uneven environmental consequences (Frame, 2022, p. 514).

From a historical standpoint, the extraction of resources like sugar, timber, and minerals in the eighteenth and nineteenth centuries anticipated the ecological mechanisms of contemporary capitalism (Moore, 2003, pp. 309-312, 330). European empires drew upon vast colonial territories, using them as sources of primary materials and as waste sinks for industrial by-products. Although the formal colonial era ended, the fundamental pattern of exploiting the periphery's environment persists. What has changed is the sophistication of the legal, financial, and technological systems that facilitate this transfer of environmental burdens (Bunker & Ciccantell, 1999, pp. 120-121). Empirical data on e-waste, for example, confirms that old electronics from Europe and North America end up in informal recycling sites across Africa and Asia, where burning and acid baths expose local workers to toxic substances (Favarin et al., 2023, p. 222).

Equally relevant is the phenomenon of "green growth" strategies in core countries. Such strategies depend on the idea that technology and market mechanisms can decouple economic development from environmental destruction (Burns et al., 2006, p. 34). In reality, much of this so-called decoupling turns out to be an accounting artifact because core economies shift the production of carbon-intensive goods to other regions, thereby appearing to reduce their emissions and ecological footprints (Sommer & Hargrove, 2020, pp. 278–280). Yet the aggregate planetary harm continues to rise, and peripheral communities are the ones experiencing heightened levels of pollution and resource depletion (Eisenmenger & Giljum, 2006, pp. 294-295, 300-302).

Thus, the capitalist drive to expand markets and production systematically incentivizes the underpricing of nature and the shifting of burdens to the global periphery. While much of the managerial and communication-focused literature treats greenwashing as a reputational flaw, an ethical lapse, or a deviation from best practices (Delmas & Burbano, 2011; Walker & Wan, 2012; Torelli et al., 2020), such interpretations obscure the structural role environmental deception plays in sustaining accumulation. Greenwashing and broader environmental exploitation should therefore not be seen as mere anomalies, but as necessary features of a system that externalizes harm to preserve core profitability. Rather, as Wallerstein (1999, p. 10) and Grimes (1999, p. 17) posit, it is integral to the operational logic of capital. If core states were forced to internalize the true environmental costs of manufacturing, energy extraction, and waste disposal, profit margins would drastically shrink, undermining the system's perpetual quest for capital accumulation. While regulatory frameworks like the Basel Convention[1] or various climate agreements attempt to rein in the most egregious forms of exploitation, the structural imperatives of global capitalism continually adapt, finding new ways and new regions in which to relocate negative externalities (Wang et al., 2020, pp. 4-11).

In linking this mechanism to the sections already discussed, we see that the role of the semi-periphery becomes especially salient. Semi-peripheral nations sometimes adopt partial environmental regulations, or they may have industrial capacity advanced enough to handle complex production processes. Yet they often lack sufficient institutional power to bar hazardous imports or to enforce strict environmental protocols against foreign investors (Frame, 2022, p. 514-516). The semi-periphery thus acts as a transitional space where core-like processes of accumulation can coexist with peripheral-like vulnerabilities.

With these considerations in mind, the next section addresses how the world-system's capacity for environmental exploitation has manifested in two particularly visible phenomena: carbon colonialism and the large-scale trade in waste. These processes not only illustrate the mechanisms described here—shifting ecological burdens to less powerful zones—but also expose how greenwashing discourses in the core justify or obscure these exploitative practices. By following the logic of Wallerstein's theoretical framework, we see that carbon colonialism and waste trade stand as prime examples of how environmental degradation is structurally embedded in the capitalist world-system.

Conceptualizing Carbon Colonialism and Waste Trade

Carbon colonialism is a concept that highlights how core nations maintain low domestic emissions—partly by deindustrializing or implementing environmental regulations at home—while relying on imported goods whose production generates significant pollution elsewhere (Lazare, 2020; Roberts et al., 2003, p. 294). This pattern of transferring emission-intensive activities to the periphery imitates earlier colonial logics. Instead of direct political control, core nations wield economic and technological leverage, ensuring that peripheral or semi-peripheral societies take on the ecological cost of resource extraction and manufacturing (Harris, 2015). As a result, the global North can claim leadership in sustainability metrics, even though the net planetary emissions remain high.

In tandem with carbon displacement, waste trade stands out as a stark contemporary practice of externalizing environmental harm. After China's 2018 ban on plastic and e-waste imports (Wang et al., 2020, p. 11), large volumes of waste rerouted to countries such as Türkiye, Malaysia, and Vietnam. This shift revealed a structural reality in which core nations appear to be recycling and reducing waste, yet they actually export significant portions of difficult-to-recycle or hazardous materials to jurisdictions that lack the capacity to process them safely (Greenpeace, 2022). The "green transformation" heralded by developed nations then relies on the ability to send plastic debris, electronic refuse, and toxic by-products to semi-peripheral or peripheral sites, where waste often ends up incinerated or dumped illegally (Favarin & Aziani 2020, p. 356).

Such practices connect with the larger dynamics identified by WSA, showing that the world-system endures by continually identifying and exploiting new "ecological frontiers" able to bear the externalities of advanced industrial growth (Moore, 2003, pp. 323-324). In this regard, carbon colonialism and the waste trade should be seen as interlinked facets of environmental exploitation. They represent two pathways—one centered on emissions, the other on physical refuse—through which the core sustains its economic model. The outward shift of ecological consequences demonstrates precisely how systemic environmental exploitation functions, because the sphere that profits from goods and services is rarely the sphere that confronts the resulting toxic residue. Consequently, a clear link emerges between the theoretical scaffolding of WSA and current manifestations of environmental injustice. By externalizing carbon outputs and offloading material waste onto less advantaged states, the system maintains its center-periphery hierarchies.

While this section has focused on outlining the conceptual basis of carbon colonialism and transboundary waste trade, their practical implications will be revisited in the next section. There, the discussion turns to how these dynamics intersect with greenwashing practices, using literature-based examples to highlight the material and discursive links between environmental exploitation and legitimacy-making in the core. This transition enables a more grounded analysis of how greenwashing operates within the structural hierarchies described above.

Greenwashing as a Systemic Practice

In contemporary discussions on global environmental challenges, the concept of greenwashing has emerged as a powerful lens through which to examine how corporations and other entities cultivate a misleading appearance of ecological responsibility. Far from being a minor marketing ploy, greenwashing has become a systemic phenomenon that permeates multiple industries, political frameworks, and cultural contexts (Delmas & Burbano, 2011, p. 64). Scholars increasingly argue that the practice derives from complex interactions among weak regulatory environments, evolving consumer expectations, and shareholder demands for ever-increasing profits (Aggarwal & Kadyan, 2014, p. 22; Lyon & Montgomery, 2015, pp. 234-235). As highlighted in empirical research, companies often produce sustainability reports or highlight select eco-friendly initiatives while concealing substantial adverse impacts (Adamkiewicz et al., 2022, p. 3; De Freitas Netto et al., 2020, p. 6). At the same time, the expansion of carbon offsetting mechanisms and green certifications, which ostensibly aim to mitigate climate disruption, frequently bolsters deceptive narratives rather than delivering genuine reductions in environmental harm (Kim & Lyon, 2014, pp. 709-710).

Within a broader capitalist world-system, such practices not only mislead stakeholders but also reinforce longstanding patterns of exploitation, wherein core interests enact green policies on paper while outsourcing pollution to less regulated areas. These structural dimensions underscore that greenwashing is bound to ongoing global inequalities and entrenched economic imperatives. Against this background, the following sections examines how greenwashing should be understood as part of a larger systemic matrix of power and profit—a matrix that shapes both corporate strategies and policy formulations worldwide. The discussion begins with an in-depth look at corporate-level strategies, building on the contextual foundations outlined in previous chapters and leading toward the subsequent focus on state-driven greenwashing tactics in later sections.

Corporate Greenwashing

Building on the introductory discussion that situates greenwashing within the wider systemic context of contemporary capitalism, corporate greenwashing emerges as one of the most visible and, arguably, most insidious expressions of deceptive environmental communication. Over time, corporations in diverse industries—from fossil fuel to fashion—have increasingly promoted sustainability initiatives in their public narratives, claiming environmental stewardship that frequently does not align with tangible operational reforms (Aggarwal & Kadyan, 2014, p. 27; Adamkiewicz et al., 2022, p. 5). Evaluating the literature, Lyon & Montgomery argues that scholars examining corporate practices underscore that greenwashing is not merely a rhetorical device or a rare lapse in ethics. Instead, it often constitutes a deliberate strategy shaped by profit motives and enabled by structural shortcomings in both market governance and stakeholder vigilance (Lyon & Montgomery, 2015, pp. 225-226). As a result, despite mounting awareness among consumers and regulators, corporate greenwashing remains widespread, with sophisticated tactics that obscure the disconnect between corporate narratives and actual environmental outcomes (Torelli et al., 2020, p. 408; Li et al., 2022, pp. 18-20).

Recent evidence sheds light on how firm-level strategies translate systemic pressures into practice. In the energy sector, capital flows remain overwhelmingly directed towards hydrocarbons, even as corporate communications highlight commitments to transition. According to the International Energy Agency, oil and gas companies allocated roughly USD 30 billion to clean energy in 2023—less than 4% of total global investment in the sector (International Energy Agency, 2024). Independent analyses of corporate disclosures similarly underscore a persistent gap between rhetorical commitments to transition and the reality of investment priorities (Li, Trencher, & Asuka, 2022).

A related dynamic is the reliance on carbon offsets, which are often deployed as discursive substitutes for immediate decarbonisation. Studies consistently point to structural weaknesses in voluntary offset markets. For example, a multi-country assessment of avoided-deforestation projects concluded that most initiatives failed to deliver significant reductions in deforestation, and where benefits did materialise they were substantially overstated (West et al., 2023). Likewise, an analysis of the 20 largest corporate offset users between 2020 and 2023 found that around 87% of retired credits carried a high risk of failing to generate genuine, additional abatement; moreover, purchases were heavily concentrated in low-cost credit categories (Trencher, Nick, Carlson, & Johnson, 2024). In both instances, offset portfolios appear to serve less as mechanisms of environmental change and more as cost-efficient reputational hedges that defer substantive operational transformation.

Within the corporate sphere, greenwashing operates through multiple channels and communicative strategies, most notably via official sustainability or corporate social responsibility (CSR) reports. These documents are ostensibly designed to enhance transparency about a company's environmental impacts, yet they often function as tools of symbolic compliance or selective disclosure (Kim & Lyon, 2014, p. 705; Yang et al., 2020, p. 1494). Companies tend to highlight minor achievements—such as reducing packaging waste in select product lines or adopting limited eco-friendly materials—while omitting or downplaying larger, systemic harms embedded in their supply chains (Adamkiewicz et al., 2022, p. 3). This discrepancy between declared environmental commitments and underlying operational realities illustrates how corporate sustainability reports risk devolving into curated narratives, appealing to green-conscious investors and consumers without delivering meaningful progress. In many cases, firms also rely on broad, unverified terminology—e.g., "eco-friendly," "carbon neutral," or "low impact"—and support these claims with references to internal guidelines rather than independent audits (Huang et al., 2022, p. 33). By doing so, they exploit knowledge gaps and the absence of robust oversight in environmental labeling.

Another closely related dimension involves the notion of performative or "future-oriented" pledges designed to pre-empt critical scrutiny. Rather than detailing transparent data about present-day ecological footprints, companies emphasize promises such as becoming "net-zero by 2050" or achieving "100% recycled materials" in some distant timeframe (Montgomery et al., 2024, pp. 223-224). As Li et al. (2022) demonstrate through their analysis of major oil firms, future-oriented climate pledges—such as net-zero commitments—often lack alignment with operational and investment behaviour. While companies publicly promote decarbonization roadmaps, they simultaneously expand fossil fuel exploration and production, and continue to invest disproportionately in extractive infrastructure, relying on undeployed technologies to justify these contradictions. This pattern, sometimes referred to as "futurewashing" (Montgomery et al., 2024, p. 224), allows corporations to appropriate the language of environmental transformation without incurring the immediate costs or operational changes that genuine sustainability would demand. The resulting spectacle convinces many external stakeholders that a constructive process is already in motion, blunting the urgency of more robust regulatory or activist challenges.

Empirical research on the automotive sector following the Dieselgate scandal vividly exposes the mechanics of corporate greenwashing in official reporting. Automakers' sustainability documents frequently contained optimistic narratives of innovation, clean engines, and regulatory compliance while masking the manipulation of emissions tests and real-world environmental damage (Boiral et al., 2022, pp. 183-184). In dissecting these disclosures, scholars found strategic omissions and a reliance on vague environmental ambitions that lacked quantitative benchmarks or third-party verification. The mismatch between reports and reality was sustained, in part, by the complexity of vehicle testing procedures and the high reputational stakes involved, as each manufacturer aimed to preserve its green image to reassure both customers and regulators even while systemic cheating continued. Similar discrepancies have been documented in the energy sector, where oil majors such as BP and Shell produce voluminous sustainability statements to portray themselves as harbingers of clean energy transitions while still prioritizing hydrocarbons as their dominant profit engine (Li et al., 2022, p. 19). In many such reports, the textual and visual emphasis on renewable investments far exceeds the firm's actual capital expenditure in new energy ventures, casting doubt on claims of climate leadership.

Beyond formal CSR reports, marketing communications and branding efforts represent an equally critical domain of corporate greenwashing. Studies in the fashion industry, for instance, reveal how brands leverage minimal material changes—such as switching to a small percentage of recycled fabrics—to cultivate an image of comprehensive environmental renewal (Adamkiewicz et al., 2022, p. 3). The promotion of "capsule collections" labeled as "sustainable" can distract both consumers and media outlets from the unaltered mass-production model underlying the remainder of the product lines. By spotlighting one seemingly greener segment, the brand crafts a narrative of corporate responsibility despite no structural transformation. Scholars have coined terms like "helpful hypocrisy" to describe how companies champion green cause marketing to reinforce their CSR reputations, thus leveraging consumer willingness to trust well-advertised environmental claims (Adamkiewicz et al., 2022, p. 6). In practice, corporations invest substantially more resources in polishing the message of sustainability rather than meeting concrete environmental goals.

The success of these tactics partly reflects the psychological and informational dynamics among consumers and investors. Corporate communication frequently resonates because it aligns with rising social awareness of environmental issues. Stakeholders often desire reassurance that the brands they patronize—whether a coffee chain, an automobile manufacturer, or an oil giant—are part of the solution rather than the problem (Torelli et al., 2020). Through carefully orchestrated sustainability campaigns, companies can satisfy this desire, especially if the public lacks the time or expertise to scrutinize supply chains or complex emissions data. Indeed, greenwashing thrives in the presence of information asymmetry, where the institution controlling operational data can selectively frame the narrative (Yang et al., 2020, p. 1499). These dynamics are further amplified by the proliferation of labels and certificates that lack strong verification standards, allowing corporations to sport superficially "green" endorsements on packaging or websites without accountability for their broader ecological footprints (Adamkiewicz et al., 2022, p. 3).

Central to corporate greenwashing are carbon offsetting schemes, which frequently embody what researchers term "the illusion of sustainability." In principle, offsetting is designed to compensate for emissions by funding environmental projects elsewhere, such as reforestation or renewable energy in a different geographic region (Delmas & Burbano, 2011, p. 79). In reality, however, many offset transactions lack transparency and stringent oversight, reducing them to a mechanism by which corporations claim carbon neutrality without actually cutting emissions at source (Kim & Lyon, 2014, p. 709). As Huang et al. (2022, p. 32) observe, firms often publicize environmental commitments—such as forest protection initiatives—through exaggerated sustainability narratives, while their actual operations, including continued hydrocarbon extraction, remain largely unchanged. These practices, facilitated by weak verification and regulatory gaps, allow companies to symbolically address ecological concerns without altering the core drivers of environmental degradation. Others purchase dubious credits in markets where the additionality of projects—defined as the extent to which emission-reducing activities would not have occurred in the absence of the offset mechanism—is at best ambiguous. This pattern, sometimes labeled "carbon colonialism", accentuates the uneven geographic distribution of environmental harms and becomes especially evident within Wallerstein's world-system framework, where corporations and states in the core trumpet offset achievements while outsourcing ecological risks to peripheral zones. From the corporate vantage point, offset claims can powerfully enhance brand image with minimal disruption to profitable business activities (Li et al., 2022, p. 20). Yet from a planetary perspective, these rhetorical moves often forestall the systemic decarbonization urgently needed.

Corporate reliance on offsetting and other green certificates also thrives on the complexity of environmental accounting. Many offset markets operate through multi-layered transactions, indirect trading platforms, and voluntary reporting protocols, creating a fertile space for partial or misleading disclosures. As Comyns et al. (2022, p. 338) explain, stakeholders may hold parent companies accountable for environmental misconduct that originates deeper in the supply chain, even when such violations occur at the facilities of remote or indirect suppliers. This dynamic underscores how lead firms, while operationally distanced from certain practices, remain exposed to reputational risk—particularly when they continue to promote sustainability narratives that contrast with persistent ecological harm embedded in their supplier networks. Through labyrinthine subcontracting and a lack of uniform standards, the firm can highlight token improvements within its direct operations and disregard the bulk of emissions or waste generated upstream. This diffusion of responsibility is often couched in offset language, such as proclaiming a product "carbon neutral from cradle to gate" based on questionable calculations. Though sophisticated in appearance, such practices often amount to environmental smokescreens, drawing attention away from core production activities that remain unchanged.

Critical scholars thus note that corporate greenwashing is integrally tied to a system of incentives rewarding public perceptions of responsibility over genuine ecological performance. In many contexts, corporate executives face pressure to demonstrate immediate returns on sustainability—a phenomenon that fosters symbolic compliance. As long as the market and regulatory environment prize the appearance of green transformation, superficial measures like limited offset purchases or glossy CSR publications can suffice to placate investors, consumers, and some government bodies (Aggarwal & Kadyan, 2014, pp. 23-24; Kim et al., 2017, p. 307). Such conditions explain why numerous corporations repeatedly produce well-designed "green" campaigns even after experiencing public scandals that expose their misrepresentations. In the wake of the Deepwater Horizon spill, for instance, BP continued to highlight images of pristine nature and emphasize technological prowess in its sustainability communications, aiming to visually re-establish legitimacy regardless of ongoing controversies about remediation (Kassinis & Panayiotou, 2018, pp. 36-37). These reflexive corporate strategies underscore that sustainability discourse and branding are crucial elements of corporate risk management, rather than unequivocal commitments to ecological well-being.

Yet the persistence of corporate greenwashing does not mean stakeholders, including consumers, investors, and civil society groups, are powerless. The exposure of large-scale misconduct—such as Dieselgate—demonstrates that even the most polished sustainability communication can collapse under the weight of undeniable empirical evidence (Boiral et al., 2022, p. 191). In some instances, class-action lawsuits and activist pressure have forced corporations to retract misleading environmental claims or pay penalties for false advertising. Over time, heightened activism can instigate modest reforms, such as more rigorous product labeling regulations or mandatory third-party audits. However, even these measures can lead to "arms races" in the intricacy of corporate deception, as companies refine their storytelling to meet evolving oversight (Lyon & Montgomery, 2015, p. 240). Consequently, greenwashing endures as an adaptive phenomenon within the corporate world, capitalizing on any regulatory lag or stakeholder complacency.

Recent legal and regulatory interventions highlight how corporate green claims are increasingly scrutinised against evidence. In aviation, the UK Advertising Standards Authority banned advertisements by Air France-KLM, Lufthansa, and Etihad on 6 December 2023 after finding that they gave a misleading impression of environmental performance, based on AI-assisted monitoring. The rulings reinforced the high evidentiary threshold now required for "carbon neutral" and "net-zero" claims (ASA, 2023a, 2023b, 2023c; Reuters, 2023a). Similarly, on 20 March 2024 the District Court of Amsterdam ruled that parts of KLM Royal Dutch Airlines's

"Fly Responsibly" campaign were misleading and therefore unlawful, making clear that aspirational language and references to offsets cannot be used to suggest climate neutrality in air travel (Rechtbank Amsterdam, 2024; Reuters, 2024). Together, these rulings show how reputational advantage in key markets is often maintained through "green" narratives that mask structural limitations—until regulatory or judicial scrutiny requires them to be substantiated.

Financial services display a similar dynamic. On 25 September 2023, the U.S. Securities and Exchange Commission announced that DWS (Deutsche Bank's asset-management subsidiary) would pay $25 million in penalties in two coordinated actions, including $19 million for misstatements regarding its ESG (environmental, social and governance) investment process (U.S. Securities and Exchange Commission, 2023; Reuters, 2023b). The case illustrates how sustainability claims directed at investors can exceed the capacity of internal controls, highlighting that verification is not simply a disclosure issue but a matter of governance. Viewed through a world-systems perspective, such episodes are less isolated lapses than predictable points of friction—moments when profit-preserving narratives encounter evidentiary scrutiny in core jurisdictions, even as the material impacts of production and supply chains remain spatially displaced.

Viewed within the broader logic of the capitalist world-system, corporate greenwashing is therefore more than a marketing strategy; it is an integral component of how core economic actors manage environmental crises without jeopardizing growth imperatives. As the subsequent section will illustrate, states and international institutions also engage in parallel practices—what might be called state-level or policy-driven greenwashing—that similarly reinforce exploitative structures. By recognizing corporate greenwashing as a systemic norm—rather than an aberration—the conversation can shift to deeper questions of accountability, structural reform, and the possibility of genuine environmental responsibility.

State-Level Greenwashing

State-level greenwashing parallels its corporate counterpart but operates through the formidable capacities of the modern state, including its regulatory monopoly, fiscal power, and diplomatic reach. Core governments—such as those of the European Union, the United States, and other affluent Northern economies—present themselves as stewards of the planet, yet routinely enact policies that improve domestic environmental indicators while shifting ecological degradation to peripheral and semi-peripheral regions (Eberle et al., 2019, pp. 13-14; Lazare 2020). In Wallerstein's terms, a tri-layered world-economy enables states in the core to convert ecological responsibility at home into intensified extraction and pollution in peripheral and semi-peripheral zones (Wallerstein, 2004, p. 28). The result is a carefully curated narrative of sustainability that conceals a deeper continuity of "carbon colonialism" (Foster & Magdoff, 2011, pp. 112-113).

Two recent trends help clarify how policy architectures can improve domestic indicators while shifting risks elsewhere. First, waste-export regimes allow core economies to record progress on recycling or waste reduction while relocating hazards downstream. Official EU figures indicate that the Union exported about 35.1 million tonnes of waste in 2023, with Türkiye the main destination; Eurostat's 2025 update shows Türkiye also remained the top destination for EU exports of recyclable raw materials in 2024 (European Commission 2024; European Commission, 2025a; Eurostat, 2025). UK-specific analyses similarly report an approximately 60% year-on-year increase in UK plastic-waste exports to Türkiye from 2022 to 2023, reaching nearly 141,000 tonnes (Greenpeace UK, 2024). These patterns fit the world-systems claim that core indicators can improve even as aggregate harms are displaced to semi-peripheral sites.

Second, climate-finance and offset accounting can enhance headline metrics without altering core fossil infrastructures. Purchasing credits or financing overseas mitigation may deliver domestic accounting gains, yet without strong additionality rules and supply-chain traceability these tools risk legitimizing externalization rather than reducing total harm. Recent evaluations of forest-conservation offsets and of large corporate offset portfolios underscore these concerns (West et al., 2023; Trencher, Nick, Carlson, & Johnson, 2024). Beyond offsets, the broader politics of climate finance shows the same tension. The long-promised USD 100 billion target was reached in 2022 at USD 115.9 billion, but two years late and with debates over composition (large loan share; mitigation-heavy allocation) (OECD, 2024a, 2024b). At the same time, adaptation needs in developing countries are 10–18 times larger than international public flows, pointing to a widening gap between commitments and lived realities (UNEP, 2023). From a world-systems perspective, totals matter less than whether finance actually reduces outsourced risks and debt burdens in semi-peripheral and peripheral sites.

A related development is the Fund for Responding to Loss and Damage, operationalized at COP28 and moving forward with early pledges and governance steps, including interim hosting arrangements with the World Bank. While institutionally significant, the fund's initial scale remains small relative to estimated needs; effectiveness will hinge on transparent allocation criteria and genuinely new resources that do not displace existing development finance (UNFCCC, 2025; World Bank, 2025; World Bank, 2024). Finance instruments outside the UNFCCC also shape outcomes. The IMF's Resilience and Sustainability Trust provides concessional, loan-based support for climate and resilience, but can add fiscal pressure unless paired with debt relief or grants (IMF, 2025). Meanwhile, the EU's Carbon Border Adjustment Mechanism entered a transitional reporting phase on 1 October 2023, with financial obligations starting 1 January 2026; by pricing embedded carbon at the border, it can align incentives inside the core while shifting compliance costs to exporters unless accompanied by technology transfer and finance (European Commission, 2025b). In short, unless policy is explicitly anti-displacement by design, finance and trade rules can lower reported core emissions while relocating economic and administrative burdens—consistent with the world-systems logic that links state and corporate strategies.

At the same time, the line between state and corporate strategies is porous. Core governments may highlight falling territorial emissions, rising recycling quotas, and generous climate finance, yet the material throughput sustaining their economies continues to rely on peripheral sacrifice zones (Lazare, 2020). The EU's Green Deal exemplifies this contradiction. Domestic targets on renewables and circular-economy reforms coexist with continued flows of plastics, electronic scrap, and embedded carbon to jurisdictions with laxer oversight (Greenpeace, 2022, pp. 6–8; Aktan, 2022).

In the United States, successive administrations have promised clean-energy revolutions at home while licensing new oil and gas projects abroad and underwriting the global reach of American hydrocarbons (Harris, 2015, pp. 21-22; Li et al., 2022, pp. 2-3). These arguments are substantiated by numerous policy analyses and NGO reports, such as those by Eberle et al. (2019), Greenpeace (2022), and Li et al. (2022), which document how governments like those of the United States and the EU enact green energy narratives while outsourcing extractive and polluting activities to the Global South. Tax credits for electric-vehicle buyers or wind farms lower domestic greenhouse-gas inventories, yet the lithium, cobalt, and rare-earth elements on which these technologies depend originate in communities that shoulder the toxic runoff of open-pit extraction (Eberle et al., 2019, p. 13).

Carbon-offsetting schemes further this asymmetry. By financing forestry or energy installations overseas, core polluters obtain accounting reductions without dismantling fossil infrastructures (Foster & Magdoff, 2011, pp. 111-112). Weak additionality checks mean many projects would have occurred anyway, reproducing a global bookkeeping trick whereby peripheral landscapes absorb both the physical pollutants and the statistical burden of mitigation (Lazare, 2020).

Meanwhile, the rhetoric of "clean-tech sovereignty" obscures the extractive violence embedded in supply chains. Turbine magnets, photovoltaic wafers, and battery precursors rely on mining districts in Latin America, Africa, and Central Asia where environmental safeguards are weak and labor protections weaker still. By emphasizing kilowatts installed within their own borders, EU and US officials narrate a low-carbon transition while offshoring its ecological costs. The cumulative outcome is a refined form of carbon colonialism, whereby environmental metrics improve in the core yet the planetary ledger remains in deficit—a dynamic made most visible by the global waste trade.

Waste trade has become a revealing example of how greenwashing strategies operate in a world-economy driven by profit maximization and the displacement of environmental burdens. As established in the preceding paragraphs, the capitalist system tends to externalize its most harmful activities to peripheral and semi-peripheral regions, creating a spatial fix for industrialized countries seeking to minimize ecological costs. This pattern is especially evident following China's 2018 ban on plastic-waste imports, which abruptly disrupted global trade flows and led to Türkiye and several Southeast Asian nations emerging as alternative dumping grounds (Brooks et al., 2018, pp. 2-7). The redirection of waste streams previously destined for China underscores the systemic nature of greenwashing, wherein exporters in the Global North claim environmental responsibility while effectively offloading the hazards to vulnerable destinations.

Prior to 2018, China handled over half of the world's plastic-waste imports, significantly reducing pressure on wealthier nations to develop their own recycling capacities (Wang et al., 2020, pp. 3-7). However, public outcry over pollution and environmental degradation within Chinese borders led authorities to impose a strict ban on post-consumer plastic and other contaminated scraps, prompting a sudden "shock" in established waste networks (Brooks et al., 2018, pp. 2-3). Instead of catalyzing meaningful reductions in plastic production or robust domestic recycling solutions, major exporters in Europe and North America pivoted toward alternative recipients that lacked comparable regulatory frameworks or enforcement capacity. As a consequence, Türkiye, Malaysia, Vietnam, and Thailand quickly witnessed dramatic surges in imported waste volumes (Favarin & Aziani, 2020, pp. 361-362). These rapid shifts illustrate how greenwashing allows states and corporations to laud high recycling rates on paper while disregarding the ultimate fate of the material abroad.

In Türkiye's case, import statistics reveal a marked escalation in plastic-waste arrivals after China exited the market. Official data show that Turkish ports received hundreds of thousands of tons of discarded plastics annually from major European exporters, including the United Kingdom, Germany, and Italy (Tužičková, 2023, pp. 6, 48-49). Although Türkiye nominally endorses the Basel Convention and related amendments, enforcement gaps and insufficient infrastructure create an environment where contaminated waste is often burned, illegally dumped, or processed under conditions hazardous to workers and local communities (Çağlayan & Yüzbaşı, Tobaz 2024, pp. 247-249; Sakowsky & Gündoğdu, 2024, pp. 239-240). Notwithstanding formal compliance with multilateral regulations, the reality on the ground exemplifies waste colonialism, whereby the promise of "green" trade in recyclable material serves mainly to transfer toxic pollution across borders. The illusions of ethical practice remain intact in the exporting countries, which tally these shipments as legitimate recycling—a clear manifestation of greenwashing as systemic practice rather than mere marketing ploy.

A similar dynamic is unfolding in Southeast Asia. Countries such as Malaysia, Vietnam, and Thailand—lacking robust environmental oversight—have become magnets for incoming plastic and e-waste labeled “recyclable” in trade documents (Favarin et al., 2023, p. 217). The legal veneer of compliance rests on paperwork designating these shipments as valuable secondary raw materials. However, field research routinely finds unrecyclable polymers, mixed municipal garbage, or old electronic components concealed under the vague category of “recoverable” plastics (Germani et al., 2015, pp. 377-378). Once landed, waste is off-loaded into poorly managed facilities, open dumps, or informal recycling clusters with minimal controls. This cycle contaminates soil and water, encourages unsafe burning practices, and endangers local laborers exposed to toxins such as heavy metals and brominated flame retardants (Morganti et al., 2018, pp. 106-112). From an environmental-justice perspective, the arrangement intensifies a pattern of neocolonial exchange consistent with broader world-systems hierarchies.

By allowing major economies to claim success in “recycling” or “waste reduction,” waste trade exemplifies greenwashing—the explicit mismatch between purported sustainability commitments and actual ecological outcomes (Kellenberg, 2015, pp. 115-120). Municipalities and corporations in the Global North showcase rising recycling rates while shifting the social and environmental costs to less-regulated settings. Even well-meaning consumer habits—placing plastic in the recycle bin—become complicit when the material is eventually packaged, shipped, and managed under dubious conditions far from public view (Favarin & Aziani 2020, 356, 361-362). Governments in receiving countries may briefly impose import restrictions when backlash grows, yet lobbying from domestic recyclers or foreign investors often triggers swift policy reversals, as when Türkiye rescinded a short-lived polyethylene ban under industry pressure (Sakowsky & Gündoğdu, 2024).

Yet the role of semi-peripheral countries like Türkiye is not merely passive. Despite formal adherence to international frameworks like the Basel Convention, Türkiye exercises considerable agency in shaping its waste import regime. For instance, in 2021, the Turkish government imposed a ban on polyethylene (PE) plastic waste imports, only to reverse it within days following lobbying pressure from domestic recyclers and industrial actors (Human Rights Watch, 2022; Staub, 2021). This policy reversal illustrates how economic incentives and political lobbying can override environmental priorities. Türkiye thus occupies an ambivalent position in the global waste economy—both vulnerable to ecological harm and complicit in facilitating the externalization of environmental costs. Such ambiguity is emblematic of the semi-periphery, where state actors often navigate between dependency and selective autonomy.

Such volatility underscores the strategic interplay between state-level greenwashing and corporate imperatives. Official pronouncements in Türkiye and Southeast Asia often highlight new facilities or regulations, ostensibly to improve local recycling capacity. In practice, this can mask insufficient investment in waste sorting, advanced re-processing plants, or hazardous-materials handling (Favarin et al., 2023, p. 221). The result is a façade of environmental governance, manifested in a patchwork of permits, partial compliance reports, and minimal enforcement that frames these nations as "partners" in a global recycling network while failing to mitigate real contamination on the ground.

A core insight is that China's ban did not eliminate waste streams but merely redirected them to nations with fewer controls—an outcome entirely predictable within a world-systems framework that accentuates the asymmetrical power of core states over peripheral and semi-peripheral regions (Brooks et al., 2018, pp. 3-4). Greenwashing thus benefits exporting countries, which uphold domestic narratives of ecological responsibility, and certain economic actors in recipient states, who profit from the import business. Meanwhile, local populations suffer environmental externalities that have been systematically displaced, revealing the contradiction between official sustainability rhetoric and tangible ecological harm (Favarin & Aziani, 2020, pp. 356, 360-362).

In sum, the post-China reconfiguration of global waste flows illuminates how greenwashing is embedded in the structural logic of capitalist production. By championing "recycling" in policy statements and corporate sustainability reports, core economies sidestep pressure to reduce plastic at its source, effectively shifting both the burden and the blame onto peripheral or semi-peripheral societies. As elaborated above, this practice mirrors broader patterns of carbon colonialism and environmental exploitation in Wallerstein's world-system, where profit and accumulation take precedence over meaningful ecological accountability. Through such strategies, Türkiye and Southeast Asia become the new "global dumps," a status made all the more pernicious by the green veneer cloaking these trades—a veneer that sustains, rather than challenges, the inequitable circulation of waste and its attendant risks.

Discussion

Before turning to the specific analytical subsections, a brief orientation is in order. The preceding chapters established that ecological degradation is woven into the historical fabric of the capitalist world-system and that "green" rhetoric often masks the spatial redistribution of environmental costs. Here we integrate those theoretical insights with contemporary evidence to illuminate three interrelated claims. First, WSA renders greenwashing intelligible as a structural—not incidental—feature of global capitalism. Second, practices of corporate and state-level greenwashing become indispensable whenever accumulation confronts ecological constraint, permitting continued expansion while diffusing opposition. Third, the outward displacement of carbon emissions and toxic wastes—what scholars describe as carbon colonialism and waste colonialism—materialises environmental injustice along enduring core-periphery fault lines. Taken together, the discussion that follows demonstrates how discursive "greening" stabilises the very hierarchies that generate planetary harm, thereby confirming the explanatory power of WSA for contemporary environmental politics.

How World-Systems Analysis Explains Greenwashing

The preceding theoretical discussion demonstrated that WSA views ecological degradation as structurally embedded in the capitalist world-economy (Wallerstein, 1999, pp. 3-5). That insight helps to clarify why practices labelled "greenwashing" seldom represent isolated public-relations abuses but rather reflect the basic territorial organisation of production and legitimation across core, semi-peripheral, and peripheral zones. In WSA terms the core's historical capacity to externalise labour and environmental costs is sustained through what Hornborg calls the conversion of "low-entropy" resources at the periphery into "high-entropy" affluence at the core (Hornborg, 2006, pp. 163, 171-174). Greenwashing extends that logic into the realm of cultural authority by manufacturing an appearance of ecological responsibility that disguises the very flows of energy, waste, and emissions on which core prosperity depends.

WSA's holistic scale of analysis further reveals why greenwashing proliferates at moments when environmental limits become socially visible. Core governments and firms today confront political demands for carbon mitigation and circular-economy reforms that threaten profit margins. Instead of forgoing accumulation, they deploy sustainability rhetoric to preserve legitimacy while continuing to relocate polluting stages of production to jurisdictions with weaker oversight (Roberts et al., 2003, p. 280; Jorgenson, 2006, pp. 182-184). The pattern mirrors earlier cycles in which the geographical displacement of primary extraction and waste disposal enabled renewed rounds of expansion (Wallerstein, 1982, pp. 91-104). Thus, WSA explains greenwashing not as a deviation from capitalism but as a communicative complement to its spatial fix.

Ecologically unequal exchange deepens this explanation. Empirical work shows that peripheries receive little compensation for accepting the toxins and carbon embedded in global commodity chains (Kick & McKinney, 2012, pp. 395-397). Greenwashing makes such asymmetries less politically contentious by framing core consumption as already "greening." Corporate environmental reports that highlight minor packaging changes while omitting upstream emissions (Kim & Lyon, 2014, p. 705) are effective precisely because the wider social structure distances end consumers from degraded landscapes and sacrificed labour, what Jorgenson terms the "distancing" of environmental harm (Jorgenson, 2006, pp. 189-190).

Finally, WSA directs attention to semi-peripheral mediation. Countries such as Türkiye and Malaysia occupy an ambivalent position, simultaneously aspiring to climb global value chains while often acting as intake zones for the core's displaced waste, thereby becoming essential conduits through which greenwashed narratives can be sustained (Frame, 2022, pp. 514-516). Semi-peripheral elites adopt selective environmental reforms to attract foreign investment, while tolerating polluting imports that would undermine green reputations in the core. The dialectic between symbolic environmentalism at the centre and material degradation at the margins, therefore, operates through the hierarchical, historically constituted channels highlighted by WSA. Before turning to the systemic implications, it is useful to contrast WSA with mainstream explanations of greenwashing to clarify the distinct contribution of this perspective.

Contrasting Mainstream Explanations with WSA

Much of the greenwashing literature starts at the firm and field levels. Signaling (highlighting selectively positive facts when outsiders lack information) and agency incentives (pressures on managers to protect their own interests and manage impressions) make disclosure tilt toward good news (Delmas & Burbano, 2011; Lyon & Montgomery, 2015). Work on legitimacy and institutional isomorphism finds that firms often produce decoupling (a gap between talk and action) (Lyon & Montgomery, 2015; de Freitas Netto et al., 2020; Santos et al., 2024). Studies in stakeholder and consumer psychology show how green claims shape beliefs, trust, and purchasing (Torelli et al., 2020). Research linked to ecological modernization and governance argues that policy, disclosure, and technology can support growth with less harm, although many reported "successes" depend on moving production or pollution elsewhere through offshoring and outsourcing.

These approaches clarify important firm- and field-level mechanisms, but they have limits for the questions here. Micro and meso lenses do not fully explain why environmental burdens repeatedly shift to the same regions or why misleading narratives intensify when growth runs into ecological limits. They often treat the wider context as flat and understate core–periphery power and the material flows of energy, waste, and emissions. Claims of decoupling frequently rest on offshoring and outsourcing, which improve indicators in core economies without easing pressure across the whole system (Vogel & Hickel, 2023; Li & Khan, 2024).

WSA adds a structural world-economy view that links these familiar mechanisms to a hierarchical global order. From a WSA perspective, greenwashing is not random or occasional; it helps keep prosperity in the core by legitimizing the export of ecological costs to the semi-periphery and periphery. At the level of discourse, it works with unequal exchange by hiding the displacement of emissions and waste; it normalizes success metrics that face the core (such as territorial emissions or recycling rates) while harms abroad remain off the books; and it positions the semi-periphery as a buffer (Jorgenson, 2006; Hornborg, 2006; Montgomery, Lyon, & Barg, 2024).

Two implications follow for the analysis that comes next. First, the recurrence of greenwashing across sectors can be read as a system requirement when accumulation reaches ecological limits, which helps explain the spread of future-oriented pledges and offset-heavy accounting that postpone substantive change (Lyon & Montgomery, 2015; Montgomery et al., 2024). Second, tools designed to curb greenwashing—disclosure regimes, labels, and audits—need to be assessed at the scale of the world-system; if they improve indicators in the core while leaving cross-border externalization in place, they risk reproducing the very hierarchies they aim to address (Vogel & Hickel, 2023; Li & Khan, 2024).

Greenwashing as a Necessary Element of Capitalist Expansion

While the earlier section documented multiple tactics of corporate and state-level greenwashing, WSA suggests a deeper conclusion, namely that such tactics become indispensable whenever accumulation confronts ecological constraint. Capitalist expansion relies on cheap inputs and externalised wastes (Wallerstein, 1999, pp. 6-7). As regulatory and social pressures rise, the cost of openly disregarding ecological limits increases; greenwashing supplies a comparatively inexpensive solution that safeguards both market demand and investor confidence (Lyon & Montgomery, 2015, pp. 225-226).

At the corporate scale, sustainability disclosure regimes ostensibly discipline firms, yet they often reward symbolic gestures over substantive transformations (Aggarwal & Kadyan, 2014, pp. 23-24). Companies can therefore continue high-throughput production while marketing "net-zero 2050" pledges that defer radical change to a distant horizon (Montgomery et al., 2024, pp. 223-224). From a WSA vantage, these pledges stabilise consumer expectations in core regions during periods of ecological turbulence, facilitating uninterrupted capital flows from periphery to core. The systemic payoff is clear, as profits are maintained, reputational risk is reduced, and pressure for structural reforms that might threaten accumulation is postponed.

State actors engage in analogous manoeuvres. The European Green Deal, for instance, couples stringent domestic targets with expansive supply-chain strategies that deepen resource extraction abroad (Greenpeace, 2022, pp. 7-10). Such policy architectures allow national accounts to record falling territorial emissions while overall material throughput—measured on a world-system scale—continues to climb (Sommer & Hargrove, 2020, pp. 278-280). Greenwashing thus mediates between capitalist expansion's material requisites and the ideological imperative to appear sustainable.

The mechanism is further illustrated by carbon-offset markets. Offsetting allows firms and governments to declare net reductions without altering fossil-fuel infrastructures (Kim & Lyon, 2014, p. 709). In WSA terms, offsets operate as a fictitious commodity, enabling the sale of "negative emissions" produced, in theory, by peripheral sequestration projects. Because additionality and permanence often remain unverifiable, offsetting represents an inexpensive substitute for real decarbonisation—one that replicates unequal exchange by shifting mitigation burdens onto landscapes and communities already paying the cost of extraction (Huang et al., 2022, pp. 32-33).

Importantly, the necessity of greenwashing grows as ecological frontiers shrink. Earlier phases of capitalist development could relocate mines, plantations, or factories to ever-new peripheries (Moore, 2003, pp. 323-324). Today, planetary boundaries and global civil society render straightforward externalisation increasingly visible and politically fraught. Greenwashing, by supplying persuasive narratives of responsibility, becomes the cultural technology that keeps expansion socially acceptable when geographical fixes are less available. Without such discursive work, the legitimacy crisis analysed by Wallerstein would likely accelerate (Friedman, 2006, pp. 74).

In short, capitalist expansion does not merely tolerate greenwashing; it tends to require it. The practice absorbs ideological contradictions, aligns profit with prevailing norms of ecological citizenship, and delays systemic reckonings that might otherwise force fundamental shifts in production and consumption.

Carbon Colonialism and Waste Trade as Environmental Injustice Mechanisms

The displacement logics dissected above reach their most tangible expression in two intertwined phenomena. Carbon colonialism and the contemporary waste trade. Both manifest environmental injustice by allocating the negative externalities of core consumption to peripheral bodies and ecologies, thereby fulfilling the structural imperatives of the world-system.

Carbon colonialism refers to the export of emission-intensive production to regions whose regulatory regimes or socio-political vulnerabilities permit higher pollution thresholds (Lazare, 2020, n.p.). Roberts, Grimes, and Manale's cross-national study showed that semi-peripheral economies exhibit the highest carbon inefficiencies precisely because they accommodate industries fleeing stricter standards in the core (Roberts et al., 2003, p. 294). The result is a global emissions profile in which the territorial carbon budgets of wealthy nations improve, while aggregate planetary emissions rise—a statistical artefact that greenwashing narratives quickly celebrate as progress.

Parallel dynamics govern the waste trade. China's 2018 import ban on post-consumer plastics triggered an abrupt re-routing of millions of tonnes of debris toward Türkiye, Malaysia, Vietnam, and Thailand (Wang et al., 2020, p. 11). Turkish ports alone saw a surge of European plastic shipments that local infrastructure could neither safely recycle nor dispose of, leading to widespread open burning and clandestine dumping (Tužičková, 2023, pp. 48-49; Çağlayan & Yüzbaşı Tobaz, 2024, pp. 247-249). Favarin and Aziani map this relocation as a dense North-to-South illicit network, noting that the fiction of "recyclable" cargo enables European exporters to record high recycling rates while transferring toxic risks abroad (Favarin & Aziani, 2020, p. 356).

These practices reproduce colonial patterns of extraction and sacrifice. Peripheral communities shoulder health hazards—dioxin exposure, contaminated aquifers, devastated agricultural soils—without receiving commensurate economic benefits (Germani et al., 2015, pp. 377-378). The injustice is intensified by informational asymmetry, as documentation accompanying waste cargoes often misclassifies hazardous material as secondary raw input, limiting the legal recourse available to affected populations (Morganti et al., 2018, pp. 106-112). In WSA terms, the periphery continues to function as the global sink for entropy generated by core affluence, while the semi-periphery absorbs fluctuating streams whenever core regulations tighten.

Greenwashing is indispensable to this machinery. Corporate CSR reports highlight waste-reduction targets met "through recycling," omitting the geographic translocation of the residuals. EU policy briefings emphasise circular-economy milestones achieved within European borders, overlooking the plastics exported to Adana or Penang. Such framings re-inscribe the ideological separation between clean centres and dirty margins that has long sustained the capitalist world-system (Eisenmenger & Giljum, 2006, pp. 294-295).

In sum, carbon colonialism and the waste trade embody the broader argument developed throughout this study. They demonstrate how world-system hierarchies materialise through environmental injustice, how greenwashing facilitates these asymmetric transfers, and why any putatively green transition that fails to confront these imbalances risks merely rescaling exploitation rather than ending it. Only by situating ecological harm within the enduring core–periphery architecture can scholarship and policy move beyond superficial indicators toward genuine environmental justice. Taken together, these dynamics show that greenwashing is not a series of isolated misstatements but part of how the world-economy organizes environmental harm. Read through WSA, carbon displacement and cross-border waste flows are not exceptions; they are routine supports for accumulation that rely on core–periphery hierarchies. The conclusion distills this argument and clarifies what it means for how we study environmental claims and power in the contemporary world-system.

CONCLUSION

This chapter argues that greenwashing is not a rare mistake in communication. It is a regular support for how the capitalist world-economy works. Seen through WSA, green narratives help keep prosperity in the core by normalizing the externalization of ecological costs to the semi-periphery and the periphery. The practice expands when growth meets ecological limits, which is why the pattern repeats across sectors and over time. In this sense, deception is patterned, not random.

Mainstream explanations remain useful for understanding firms and fields. Signaling, legitimacy seeking, and consumer-psychology dynamics do shape disclosure and branding. On their own, however, they understate the larger geography of profit and power. A world-systems lens links these micro and meso mechanisms to core–periphery hierarchies. It shows how discursive greening travels with unequal exchange and how success metrics that face the core can hide harms abroad. Carbon displacement and cross-border waste flows make this logic concrete.

Corporate and state practices work together. Companies promote future-oriented pledges and selective achievements while governments adopt rules that improve domestic indicators. Production stages that carry heavy pollution or waste management risks are shifted to jurisdictions with weaker leverage. The semi-periphery matters because it mediates these flows and often absorbs stages that the core no longer hosts. Outcomes vary across places, yet they remain shaped by the same structural pressures.

The contribution of this chapter is conceptual rather than prescriptive. It proposes the world-economy as the right scale of analysis and invites research to follow energy, material, and waste flows across borders. Claims of greening should be read alongside where extraction, emissions, and disposal actually occur. Only then can we separate curated narratives from changes that truly lower harm in the places that bear the costs. This is how World-Systems Analysis clarifies why greenwashing persists and how it stabilizes the current order.

REFERENCES

Adamkiewicz, J., Kochańska, E., Adamkiewicz, I., & Łukasik, R. M. (2022). Greenwashing and sustainable fashion industry. *Current Opinion in Green and Sustainable Chemistry, 38*, 100710. DOI: 10.1016/j.cogsc.2022.100710

Advertising Standards Authority. (2023a, December 6). *ASA ruling on Deutsche Lufthansa AG (A23-1206007).* https://www.asa.org.uk/rulings/deutsche-lufthansa-ag-a23-1206007-deutsche-lufthansa-ag.html

Advertising Standards Authority. (2023b, December 6). *ASA ruling on Air France-KLM (A23-1206006).* https://www.asa.org.uk/rulings/air-france-klm-a23-1206006-air-france-klm.html

Advertising Standards Authority. (2023c, December 6). *ASA ruling on Etihad Airways (A23-1206008).* https://www.asa.org.uk/rulings/etihad-airways-a23-1206008-etihad-airways.html

Aggarwal, P., & Kadyan, A. (2014). Greenwashing: The darker side of CSR. *Indian Journal of Applied Research, 4*(3), 61–66. DOI: 10.15373/2249555X/MAR2014/20

Aktan, İ. (2022, April 2). Nihan Temiz Ataş: Türkiye çöp sömürgesi haline geliyor [Nihan Temiz Ataş: Turkey becomes a waste colony]. *ArtıGerçek.* https://artigercek.com/yazarlar/irfan-aktan/nihan-temiz-atas-turkiye-cop-somurgesi-haline-geliyor

Babones, S. (2015). What is world-systems analysis? Distinguishing theory from perspective. *Thesis Eleven*, 127(1), 3–20. https://doi.org/DOI: 10.1177/0725513615575324

Boiral, O., Brotherton, M. C., Yuriev, A., & Talbot, D. (2022). Through the smokescreen of the Dieselgate disclosure: Neutralizing the impacts of a major sustainability scandal. *Organization & Environment, 35*(2), 175–201. DOI: 10.1177/10860266211043561

Brooks, A. L., Wang, S., & Jambeck, J. R. (2018). The Chinese import ban and its impact on global plastic waste trade. *Science Advances, 4*(6), eaat0131. Advance online publication. DOI: 10.1126/sciadv.aat0131

Bunker, S. G., & Ciccantell, P. S. (1999). Economic ascent and the global environment: World-systems theory and the new historical materialism. In Goldfrank, W. L., Goodman, D., & Szasz, A. (Eds.), *Ecology and the world-system* (pp. 107–122). Praeger.

Burns, T. J. (2012). What is old and what is new? Considering world-systems in the twenty-first century and beyond. In Babones, S. J., & Chase-Dunn, C. (Eds.), *Routledge handbook of world-systems analysis* (pp. 400–401). Routledge.

Burns, T. J., Kick, E. L., & Davis, B. L. (2006). Deforestation in the world-system. In Jorgenson, A., & Kick, E. (Eds.), *Globalization and the environment* (pp. 37–59). Brill.

Çağlayan, S., & Yüzbaşı Tobaz, F. (2024). The waste trade as a tool of colonialism in our age: A sociolegal analysis for Türkiye. In Gündoğdu, S. (Ed.), *Plastic waste trade: A new colonialist means of pollution transfer* (pp. 247–258). Springer Nature., DOI: 10.1007/978-3-031-51358-9_12

Campling, L. (2022). The corporation and resource geography. In M. Himley, E. Havice, & G. Valdivia (Eds.), *The Routledge handbook of critical resource geography* (pp. 188–200). Routledge.

Chase-Dunn, C., & Grimes, P. (1995). World-systems analysis. *Annual Review of Sociology, 21*, 387–417.

Chew, S. C. (1997). For nature: Deep greening world-systems analysis for the 21st century. *Journal of World-systems Research, 3*(3), 381–402.

Ciccantell, P. S. (2022). World-systems theory, nature, and resources. In M. Himley, E. Havice, & G. Valdivia (Eds.), *The Routledge handbook of critical resource geography* (pp. 177–187). Routledge.

Comyns, B., Meschi, P. X., & Norheim-Hansen, A. (2022). Cut them loose? Firms' response strategies to environmental misconduct by supplying firms. *Organization & Environment, 35*(3), 335–364. DOI: 10.1177/10860266211068878

De Freitas Netto, S. V., Sobral, M. F. F., Ribeiro, A. R. B., & Soares, G. R. L. (2020). Concepts and forms of greenwashing: A systematic review. *Environmental Sciences Europe, 32*, 19. DOI: 10.1186/s12302-020-0300-3

Delmas, M. A., & Burbano, V. C. (2011). The drivers of greenwashing. *California Management Review, 54*(1), 64–87. DOI: 10.1525/cmr.2011.54.1.64

Eberle, C., Münstermann, N., & Siebeneck, J. (2019). *Carbon colonialism: A postcolonial assessment of carbon offsetting*. University of Bonn / United Nations University.

Eisenmenger, N., & Giljum, S. (2006). Evidence from societal metabolism studies for ecological unequal trade. In Hornborg, A., & Crumley, C. L. (Eds.), *The world system and the earth system: Global socioenvironmental change and sustainability since the Neolithic* (pp. 289–304). Left Coast Press.

European Commission. (2024, May 20). *New regulation on waste shipments enters into force.* https://environment.ec.europa.eu/news/new-regulation-waste-shipments-enters-force-2024-05-20_en

European Commission. (2025a). *Waste shipments.* https://environment.ec.europa.eu/topics/waste-and-recycling/waste-shipments_en

European Commission. (2025b). *Carbon Border Adjustment Mechanism (CBAM): Transitional phase.* https://taxation-customs.ec.europa.eu/carbon-border-adjustment-mechanism_en

Eurostat. (2025, April 24). *Exports in recyclable raw materials decreased in 2024.* https://ec.europa.eu/eurostat/web/products-eurostat-news/w/ddn-20250424-2

Favarin, S., & Aziani, A. (2020). The global waste trafficking and its correlates. *Journal of Contemporary Criminal Justice*, *36*(3), 351–383.

Favarin, S., Berlusconi, G., Aziani, A., & Corradini, S. (2023). Transnational trafficking networks of end-of-life vehicles and e-waste. *Global Crime*, *24*(3), 215–237.

Foster, J. B., & Magdoff, F. (2011). *What every environmentalist needs to know about capitalism: A citizen's guide to capitalism and the environment.* Monthly Review Press.

Frame, M. L. (2022). Ecological imperialism: A world-systems approach. *American Journal of Economics and Sociology*, *81*(3), 503–527.

Friedman, J. (2006). Sustainable unsustainability: Hegemonic decline in global systems. In Hornborg, A., & Crumley, C. L. (Eds.), *The world system and the earth system: Global socioenvironmental change and sustainability since the Neolithic* (pp. 73–88). Left Coast Press.

Germani, A. R., Pergolizzi, A., & Reganati, F. (2015). Illegal trafficking and unsustainable waste management in Italy: Evidence at the regional level. *Journal of Security and Sustainability Issues*, *4*(4), 369–389.

Greenpeace. (2022). *Atık oyunları geri dönüşümsüz hayatlar: Plastik atıkların çevre ve sağlık etkisi* [Waste games, irreversible lives: The environmental and health impacts of plastic waste]. Greenpeace Mediterranean.

Greenpeace, U. K. (2024, November 5). *"We can no longer bear this load": UK waste exports to Turkey on the rise again*. https://www.greenpeace.org.uk/news/we-can-no-longer-bear-this-load-uk-waste-exports-to-turkey-on-the-rise-again/

Grimes, P. E. (1999). The horsemen and the killing fields: The final contradiction of capitalism. In Goldfrank, W. L., Goodman, D., & Szasz, A. (Eds.), *Ecology and the world-system* (pp. 13–28). Praeger.

Grinin, L., & Korotayev, A. (2022). Introduction: On the forms, patterns and modes of evolutionary development. *History & Mathematics: Historical and Technological Dynamics: Factors, Cycles, and Trends*, 4–24.

Harris, P. (2015). Militarism in environmental disguise: The greenwashing of an overseas military base. *International Political Sociology*, *9*(1), 19–36. DOI: 10.1111/ips.12074

Hornborg, A. (2006). Ecosystems and world-systems: Accumulation as an ecological process. In Chase-Dunn, C., & Babones, S. (Eds.), *Global social change: Historical and comparative perspectives* (pp. 161–175). Johns Hopkins University Press.

Huang, R., Xie, X., & Zhou, H. (2022). 'Isomorphic' behavior of corporate greenwashing. *Zhongguo Renkou Ziyuan Yu Huanjing*, *20*(1), 29–39. DOI: 10.1016/j.cjpre.2022.03.004

Human Rights Watch. (2022). *"It's as if they're poisoning us": The health impacts of plastic recycling in Turkey*. https://www.hrw.org/report/2022/09/21/its-if-theyre-poisoning-us/health-impacts-plastic-recycling-turkey

International Energy Agency. (2024). *World energy investment 2024*. IEA. https://www.iea.org/reports/world-energy-investment-2024

International Monetary Fund. (2025). *Resilience and Sustainability Trust*. https://www.imf.org/en/Topics/Resilience-and-Sustainability-Trust

Jorgenson, A. K. (2006). Global social change, natural resource consumption, and environmental degradation. In Chase-Dunn, C., & Babones, S. (Eds.), *Global social change: Historical and comparative perspectives* (pp. 176–197). Johns Hopkins University Press.

Kassinis, G., & Panayiotou, A. (2018). Visuality as greenwashing: The case of BP and Deepwater Horizon. *Organization & Environment*, *31*(1), 25–47. DOI: 10.1177/1086026616687014

Kellenberg, D. (2015). The economics of the international trade of waste. *Annual Review of Resource Economics, 7,* 109–125. DOI: 10.1146/annurev-resource-100913-012639

Kentor, J., & Grimes, P. (2006). Foreign investment dependence and the environment: A global perspective. In Jorgenson, A., & Kick, E. (Eds.), *Globalization and the environment* (pp. 67–76). Brill.

Kick, E. L., & McKinney, L. A. (2012). World-system structure, natural capital and environmental entropy. In Babones, S. J., & Chase-Dunn, C. (Eds.), *Routledge handbook of world-systems analysis* (pp. 392–399). Routledge.

Kim, E.-H., & Lyon, T. P. (2014, November 1). *Greenwash vs. brownwash: Exaggeration and undue modesty in corporate sustainability disclosure* (Ross School of Business Paper No. 1266). *SSRN.* https://doi.org/DOI: 10.2139/ssrn.2546497

Kim, J., Fairclough, S., & Dibrell, C. (2017). Attention, action, and greenwash in family-influenced firms: Evidence from polluting industries. *Organization & Environment, 30*(4), 304–323. DOI: 10.1177/108602661667341

Lazare, S. (2020, September 14). "Colonizing the atmosphere": How rich, Western nations drive the climate crisis. *In These Times.* https://inthesetimes.com/article/climate-change-wealthy-western-nations-global-north-south-fires-west

Lennerfors, T. T., Fors, P., & van Rooijen, J. (2015). ICT and environmental sustainability in a changing society: The view of ecological world-systems theory. *Information Technology & People, 28*(4), 758–774. DOI: 10.1108/ITP-09-2014-0219

Li, M., Trencher, G., & Asuka, J. (2022). The clean energy claims of BP, Chevron, ExxonMobil and Shell: A mismatch between discourse, actions and investments. *PLoS One, 17*(2), e0263596. DOI: 10.1371/journal.pone.0263596

Li, Y., & Khan, J. (2024). Decoupling with(out) outsourcing? Quantifying emissions embodied in BRI trade with implications for climate policy. *Elementa, 12*(1), 00068. DOI: 10.1525/elementa.2023.00068

Lyon, T. P., & Montgomery, A. W. (2015). The means and end of greenwash. *Organization & Environment, 28*(2), 223–249. DOI: 10.1177/1086026615575332

Montgomery, A. W., Lyon, T. P., & Barg, J. (2024). No end in sight? A greenwash review and research agenda. *Organization & Environment, 37*(2), 221–256. DOI: 10.1177/10860266231168905

Moore, J. W. (2003). The modern world-system as environmental history? Ecology and the rise of capitalism. *Theory and Society*, *32*(3), 307–377. DOI: 10.1023/A:1024404620759

Morganti, M., Favarin, S., & Andreatta, D. (2018). Illicit waste trafficking and loopholes in the European and Italian legislation. *European Journal on Criminal Policy and Research*, *26*, 105–133. DOI: 10.1007/s10610-018-9405-2

OECD. (2024a, May 29). *Climate finance provided and mobilised by developed countries in 2013–2022.* https://www.oecd.org/en/publications/2024/05/climate-finance-provided-and-mobilised-by-developed-countries-in-2013-2022_8031029a.html

OECD. (2024b, May 29). *Developed countries materially surpassed their USD 100 billion climate finance commitment in 2022.* https://www.oecd.org/en/about/news/press-releases/2024/05/developed-countries-materially-surpassed-their-usd-100-billion-climate-finance-commitment-in-2022-oecd.html

Rechtbank Amsterdam. (2024, March 20). *Fossielvrij NL v. KLM (ECLI:NL:RBAMS:2024:1512).* https://www.clientearth.org/media/cx4po41h/klm-judgment-20-march-2024.pdf

Reuters. (2023a, December 6). UK bans airline adverts over "misleading" environmental claims. *Reuters.* https://www.reuters.com/business/aerospace-defense/uk-bans-airline-adverts-over-misleading-environmental-claims-2023-12-06/

Reuters. (2023b, September 25). DWS to pay $25 million to end U.S. probe into ESG misstatements and other violations. *Reuters.* https://www.reuters.com/legal/dws-pay-25-mln-over-us-charges-over-esg-misstatements-other-violations-2023-09-25/

Reuters. (2024, March 20). Dutch court finds KLM ads were misleading in "greenwashing" case. *Reuters.* https://www.reuters.com/business/aerospace-defense/dutch-court-rule-klm-greenwashing-case-2024-03-20/

Roberts, J. T., & Grimes, P. E. (1999). Extending the world-system to the whole system: Toward a political economy of the biosphere. In Goldfrank, W. L., Goodman, D., & Szasz, A. (Eds.), *Ecology and the world-system* (pp. 59–84). Praeger.

Roberts, J. T., Grimes, P. E., & Manale, J. L. (2003). Social roots of global environmental change: A world-systems analysis of carbon dioxide emissions. *Journal of World-systems Research*, *9*(2), 277–315. DOI: 10.5195/jwsr.2003.238

Sakowsky, E. E., & Gündoğdu, S. (2024). An imported problem? Plastic waste effects on Türkiye's environment with specific emphasis on relevant multilateral environmental agreements. In Gündoğdu, S. (Ed.), *Plastic waste trade: A new colonialist means of pollution transfer* (pp. 217–236). Springer Nature., DOI: 10.1007/978-3-031-51358-9_11

Santos, C., Coelho, A., & Marques, A. (2024). A systematic literature review on greenwashing and its relationship to stakeholders: State of art and future research agenda. *Management Review Quarterly, 74*, 1397–1421. DOI: 10.1007/s11301-023-00337-5

Sommer, J. M., & Hargrove, A. (2020). Power and politics in the world-system: A cross-national analysis of environmental governance. *Journal of World-systems Research, 26*(2), 264–284. DOI: 10.5195/jwsr.2020.998

Staub, C. (2021, July 14). *Turkey reverses ban on scrap plastic imports. Resource Recycling.* https://resource-recycling.com/plastics/2021/07/14/turkey-reverses-ban-on-scrap-plastic-imports/

Torelli, R., Balluchi, F., & Lazzini, A. (2020). Greenwashing and environmental communication: Effects on stakeholders' perceptions. *Business Strategy and the Environment, 29*(2), 407–421. DOI: 10.1002/bse.2373

Trencher, G., Nick, S., Carlson, J., & Johnson, M. (2024). Demand for low-quality offsets by major companies undermines climate integrity of the voluntary carbon market. *Nature Communications, 15*(1), 6863. DOI: 10.1038/s41467-024-51151-w

Tužičková, H. (2023). *EU waste management in foreign policy: The case of Turkey* [Bachelor's thesis, Palacký University Olomouc, Department of Political Science and European Studies].

UNEP Copenhagen Climate Centre. (2023, December 13). *Loss and damage at COP28.* https://unepccc.org/wp-content/uploads/2023/12/loss-and-damage-at-cop28-web.pdf

United Nations Environment Programme. (2023). *Adaptation Gap Report 2023.* https://www.unep.org/resources/adaptation-gap-report-2023

United Nations Framework Convention on Climate Change (UNFCCC). (2025). *Fund for responding to loss and damage.* https://unfccc.int/fund-for-responding-to-loss-and-damage

U.S. Securities and Exchange Commission. (2023, September 25). *Deutsche Bank subsidiary DWS to pay $25 million for AML violations and misstatements regarding ESG investments* (Press Release 2023-194). https://www.sec.gov/newsroom/press-releases/2023-194

Vogel, J., & Hickel, J. (2023). Is green growth happening? An empirical analysis of achieved versus Paris-compliant CO_2–GDP decoupling in high-income countries. *The Lancet. Planetary Health, 7*(9), e759–e769. DOI: 10.1016/S2542-5196(23)00174-2

Walker, K., & Wan, F. (2012). The harm of symbolic actions and green-washing: Corporate actions and communications on environmental performance and their financial implications. *Journal of Business Ethics, 109*(2), 227–242. DOI: 10.1007/s10551-011-1122-4

Wallerstein, I. (1982). World-systems analysis: Theoretical and interpretive issues. In Hopkins, T. K., & Wallerstein, I. (Eds.), *World-systems analysis: Theory and methodology* (pp. 91–106). Sage.

Wallerstein, I. (1998). The rise and future demise of world-systems analysis. *Review - Fernand Braudel Center, 21*(1), 103–112. https://www.jstor.org/stable/40241417

Wallerstein, I. (1999). Ecology and capitalist costs of production: No exit. In Goldfrank, W. L., Goodman, D., & Szasz, A. (Eds.), *Ecology and the world-system* (pp. 3–11). Praeger.

Wallerstein, I. (2004). *World-systems analysis: An introduction*. Duke University Press.

Wang, C., Zhao, L., Lim, M. K., Chen, W.-Q., & Sutherland, J. W. (2020). Structure of the global plastic waste trade network and the impact of China's import ban. *Resources, Conservation and Recycling, 153*, 104591. DOI: 10.1016/j.resconrec.2019.104591

West, T. A. P., Wunder, S., Sills, E. O., Börner, J., Rifai, S. W., Neidermeier, A. N., Frey, G. P., & Kontoleon, A. (2023). Action needed to make carbon offsets from forest conservation work for climate change mitigation. *Science, 381*(6660), 873–877. DOI: 10.1126/science.ade3535

World Bank. (2024, June 10). *Board approves World Bank's role as host and trustee for the Fund for Responding to Loss and Damage*. https://www.worldbank.org/en/news/press-release/2024/06/10/board-approves-world-bank-s-role-as-host-and-trustee-for-the-fund-for-responding-to-loss-and-damage

World Bank. (2025). *Funding for loss and damage*. https://www.worldbank.org/en/programs/funding-for-loss-and-damage

Yang, Z., Nguyen, T. T. H., Nguyen, H. N., Nguyen, T. T. N., & Cao, T. T. (2020). Greenwashing behaviours: Causes, taxonomy and consequences based on a systematic literature review. *Journal of Business Economics and Management*, *21*(5), 1486–1507. DOI: 10.3846/jbem.2020.13225

KEY TERMS AND DEFINITIONS

Carbon Offsetting: A mechanism through which companies or countries claim to neutralize their carbon emissions by financing external environmental projects, such as reforestation or renewable energy, is often criticized for failing to reduce emissions at the source and perpetuating "carbon colonialism.

Ecologically Unequal Exchange: A concept describing how core countries externalize environmental costs by importing low-cost natural resources and exporting pollution-intensive processes to semi-peripheral and peripheral regions, creating structural ecological inequalities in the world-system.

Fictitious Commodity: A term coined by Karl Polanyi to refer to entities such as land, labor, and money, which are treated as commodities in capitalist markets despite not being produced for sale.

Semi-Periphery: A category within World-Systems Analysis referring to countries that occupy an intermediate position between core and periphery, often balancing roles as both recipients of environmental harm and enablers of exploitative global trade and production networks.

Spatial Fix: A concept from Marxist geography describing how capitalism overcomes crises by expanding or shifting investment to new geographical regions, thereby deferring economic contradictions.

ENDNOTE

1 Basel Convention on the Control of Transboundary Movements of Hazardous Wastes and Their Disposal, adopted in 1989 and entered into force in 1992, aims to reduce hazardous waste movements between nations, especially from developed to less developed countries. Türkiye became a party in 1994.

Chapter 6
Green, but at What Cost? Ecological and Social Realities of Renewable Energy

Samanvi Narang
https://orcid.org/0000-0001-6053-1928
O.P. Jindal Global University, India

Kavia Ahuja
https://orcid.org/0009-0009-0063-7697
O.P. Jindal Global University, India

ABSTRACT

The ecological and social challenges associated with renewable energy technologies necessitate a critical reassessment of the green transition. Addressing these issues requires stronger policy interventions, ethical supply chain practices, and sustainable material management. A more just and equitable approach to green technology development must incorporate interdisciplinary solutions that balance economic interests with ecological and social well-being.This chapter critically examines the environmental damage and social injustices embedded in the supply chains of rare earth minerals and other critical materials essential for green technology. The analysis extends to trade disputes and waste accumulation, arguing that the current market-driven approach to renewable energy exacerbates global inequalities. The chapter concludes by exploring circular economy models and regulatory frameworks that could mitigate these negative consequences.

DOI: 10.4018/979-8-3373-1707-6.ch006

INTRODUCTION

One of humanity's most ambitious attempts to slow down climate change is the worldwide switch to renewable energy. From solar panels and wind turbines to electric cars and smart grids, digital and renewable energy technologies have been heavily marketed as vital instruments for cutting greenhouse gas emissions while fostering ongoing economic expansion. As governments, businesses, and international organisations unite behind decarbonisation objectives, this sector has seen tremendous growth in recent years, with global investments reaching previously unheard-of heights. According to the International Energy Agency, solar photovoltaics alone will be responsible for more than half of the projected 60% increase in renewable energy capacity between 2020 and 2026 (International Energy Agency [IEA], 2021).

However, there is a complicated reality that calls for critical analysis beneath this optimistic narrative. Even the technologies created to protect our planet from environmental disasters have ecological and social costs that are frequently obscured from public discussion and policy decisions. Human rights violations, environmental damage, and the continuation of historical exploitation patterns are all consequences of the extraction and processing of rare earth minerals and other vital materials needed to manufacture green technologies.

This paradox becomes particularly troubling when viewed through the lens of historical colonialism. Energy resources have been a major component of colonial exploitation since the early 20th century, with extraction of resources from the Global South fueling the growth and development of the Global North. Today's renewable energy transition risks perpetuating these colonial patterns through what scholars increasingly refer to as "green colonialism" or "energy colonialism", the continuation of extractive relationships under the guise of environmental progress (Basak, 2024).

This chapter takes up these paradoxes by examining how the global renewable energy transition is being shaped by trade, law, and governance, and how these frameworks often reproduce rather than resolve existing inequalities. It begins by situating renewable energy within broader debates on sustainability and global economic structures, before turning to the legal and institutional dynamics that govern the transition including WTO jurisprudence, the paralysis of its Appellate Body, and the rise of unilateral and regional initiatives such as the EU Green Deal, CBAM, and the AfCFTA. The discussion then moves to case studies and policy narratives that highlight the tensions between promises of green industrialisation and the persistence of extractivist practices and social injustices. The chapter concludes by outlining a way forward, proposing reforms and strategies that could reorient trade and climate governance toward more equitable, sustainable, and decolonial outcomes.

COLONIAL LEGACIES AND PERSISTENT INEQUALITIES

The advantages of clean energy are geographically separated from the negative social and environmental effects of manufacturing and resource extraction by the intricate worldwide supply chains created by renewable energy technology. The historical patterns of colonialism, in which imperialist nations externalised environmental and social costs to colonised regions, are reflected in this geographical displacement of environmental liabilities.

Colonial policics that turned diverse economies into merely export oriented ones. Imperialist powers used land appropriation, forced labour, export oriented infrastructure like railways and ports and legal frameworks prioritizing foreign investment and the suppression of local industries and manufacturing (Moore, 2015). Most post-colonial states remain locked in their position in this historical exploitative system. This shapes how resources flow globally, including those required for green technologies.

"Green colonialism," as Dunlap describes it, involves replicating colonial patterns of resource appropriation and environmental degradation through clean energy transitions. Large-scale renewable energy projects usually need extensive land areas, displacing communities in the Global South through processes reminiscent of colonial land grabs. Solar projects in Morocco and the supply chains involved in the green energy transition enable and perpetuate historical patterns of inequality, exploitation, and environmental harm. The intense resource extraction involved in the development and manufacture of modern green technology can reinforce colonial legacies and create novel forms of extraction and dispossession when implemented within the existing global power structures (Newell, 2021). Communities in the Global South disproportionately bear the environmental and social costs of green technologies while the benefits primarily accrue to consumers and corporations in wealthy nations. This disconnect enables a form of "green consumption" that remains distant from its grievous material harm, creating a "slow violence" that wreaks havoc on disadvantaged communities (Nixon, 2011). Developing countries predominantly host resource extraction, such as lithium mining for electric vehicle batteries, while the Global North manufactures and consumes these technologies. Critics describe these areas as 'sacrifice zones,' (Sze, 2020), regions where environmental damage provides resources for distant communities' economic activities.

Thc colonial era established these patterns of resource exploitation that shape current trade patterns and relations. The concept of 'extractivism' describes these economic relationships; resource-rich countries specialize in extracting and exporting natural resources with minimal processing, making their economies dependent on this process (Chagnon et al., 2022). This setup was not random; it was deliberately engineered. The wind farms in Mexico, which were started without local consultation, have led to the displacement of indigenous communities and endangered their cultural ties and livelihoods testifies this (Sze, 2020). Critical minerals like lithium, cobalt, nickel and copper are required for the transition to low-carbon technologies. These are often concentrated in regions that were previously colonized. The World Bank estimates that production of minerals like graphite, lithium, and cobalt could increase by nearly 500% by 2050 to meet demand for clean energy technologies (World Bank, 2020). The global lithium demand is projected to rise by 40 times by 2040, primarily for electric vehicle batteries (International Energy Agency [IEA], 2021). Approximately 58% of the world's lithium resources are found in brine deposits beneath salt flats in the "Lithium Triangle" that includes Argentina, Bolivia, and Chile. In areas where water is already scarce, extraction calls for massive amounts of water, up to 2 million litres per tonne of lithium. Water tables are dropping, drinking water is tainted, indigenous communities and traditional livelihoods are in danger_(Barandiarán, 2019).

These supply chains are dominated by multinational corporations headquartered in the Global North. They capture the benefits of extraction while externalizing the social and environmental costs. Just 3 companies control over 60% of the global lithium-ion battery market, weakening transparency and accountability in these trade channels and limiting leverage for communities and workers (Terazono & Sanderson, 2017). This allows powerful nations and corporations to shape regulatory frameworks that work in their interests, like trade agreements that limit environmental and social regulations, investor-state dispute settlement mechanisms, political lobbies against mandatory human rights and environmental due diligence (Gabor, 2021).

During formal colonialism, resource extraction frequently occurred in the same areas that are currently being targeted for green energy minerals. As can be seen in the case of colonial mining that created patterns of labour exploitation and environmental degradation that still exist in Zambia's copper belt, which is currently being revitalised for the green transition (Mususa, 2012). In a similar vein, Belgian colonial rule initially developed the cobalt mines in the Democratic Republic of Congo, establishing governance regimes and extractive infrastructures that still influence modern mining operations. While these examples will be further substantiated in detail in the latter part of the chapter, these historical parallels show how the shift to green energy interacts with colonial processes that are still going on. Green energy transition as a movement is a significant and welcomed step however, it is also imperative to evaluate the environmental and social impacts of these large-scale green energy projects.

LARGE-SCALE RENEWABLE PROJECTS: ENVIRONMENTAL AND SOCIAL IMPACTS

Though the aim of renewable energy is to mitigate climate change and reduce environmental harms associated with fossil fuel extraction and use, the large-scale nature of many projects can cause significant damage to the environment and have adverse effects on the communities living in close vicinity of these projects. These issues persist across the renewable energy sector, from solar and wind to thermal, hydropower and bioenergy, revealing how 'green' technology continues the cycle of environmental and social injustices when implemented within existing power-based structures in the changing political paradigm.

Political ecologists term the appropriation of land for renewable energy development as "green grabbing" (Fairhead et al., 2012). Green initiatives are used to justify this land grabbing, sidelining local impacts and rights. Renewable energy projects require substantial land use, disturbing existing land use patterns and permanently changing landscapes. Solar plants typically require 5-10 acres per megawatt of energy generated (Macknick, 2011). Land for projects is often taken over without consultation with the local communities, displacing them and occupying land they depend on for their subsistence. The International Renewable Energy Agency projects that to achieve net-zero emissions by 2050, solar capacity could grow to 14,000 GW, which is a 1500% increase from 2022. (International Renewable Energy Agency [IRENA], 2021) This implies a massive growth in land use requirements that will further threaten agriculture, green cover, conservation and other traditional land uses. For instance, the Ouarzazate Solar Complex in Morocco is built on 3,000 hectares of land traditionally used by Amazigh agro-pastoralists (Rignall, 2016). The project was installed without consulting the local communities and restricts grazing access and consumes substantial water resources in the water-stressed, arid region. The solar plant generates clean electricity primarily for export to Europe, leaving the locals with few benefits (Rignall, 2016). Mexico's Isthmus of Tehuantepec region hosts several wind energy developments. Multinational energy companies have secured long-term leases on indigenous Zapotec and Huave territories for wind parks, with minimal transparency and inadequate compensation to these communities (Dunlap, 2018). Anthropologist Alexander Dunlap terms this as "counterinsurgency infrastructure", extracting resources for foreign markets while exerting state control over indigenous territories. Renewable energy projects can become instruments in the erasure of indigenous identities and culture when implemented without mutual consultation and following due process.

Deforestation, soil contamination, water and air pollution associated with these energy projects have adverse effects on wildlife. Solar development has fragmented the habitats of the endangered desert tortoise (Gopherus agassizii) in the Mojave

Desert (Lovich & Ennen, 2011). Windmills pose dangers to avian and chiropteran species with specific flight patterns as they are at risk of collision with the turbines. Approximately between 140,000 to 328,000 birds are killed annually at wind parks in the United States (Loss et al., 2013). Hydropower projects involve the construction of large dams, fundamentally altering river hydrology, sediment transport, water temperature and dissolved oxygen levels (Zarfl et al., 2015). These are vital for maintaining the aquatic food web. Migratory fish populations are unable to navigate dams. This occurs despite the installation of fish passage systems (Chen et al., 2023). Hydropower developments contribute to population declines in migratory fish, which in turn affect other wildlife that consume them and any indigenous communities that may depend on them for nutrition. Fragile wildlife whose lives are dependent on the delicate ecosystems decimated for renewable energy infrastructure are perhaps the most overlooked stakeholders. They have no legal right over the land they reside in and are not relocated or compensated; consequently, large-scale renewable energy installations significantly alter ecosystems and can negatively impact biodiversity.

WASTE ACCUMULATION AND END-OF-LIFE CHALLENGES

The collection and disposal of waste has an additional environmental impact, increasing the opportunity cost for these communities. Only a few nations are sufficiently equipped to handle the additional waste streams brought about by the quick adoption of renewable energy technology. With operating lifespans of 25–30 years, solar photovoltaic panels pose a substantial waste management concern as early installations approach end-of-life and replacement rates rise (Wang et al., 2022). The total amount of photovoltaic (PV) waste generated worldwide may reach 78 million tonnes by 2050, generating a sizable new source of waste that may contain potentially dangerous elements like lead, cadmium, selenium, and indium. That, if improperly managed, will cause soil and water pollution (Wang et al., 2022). Nowadays, most decommissioned panels end up in regular waste streams, and there is not much specialised recycling infrastructure available worldwide. Glass and aluminium are the main materials recovered by conventional recycling methods; rare metals and most semiconductor materials are not (Heath et al., 2020). Current procedures, according to environmental engineers, recover less than 15% of the material value embedded in PV panels (Heath et al., 2020). For developing nations that have embraced solar technology at a rapid pace but lack waste processing facilities or PV-specific regulations, this situation poses a significant environmental problem.

Another major waste management challenge is caused by wind turbine blades, which are made of fiberglass-reinforced polymers and are difficult to recycle or repurpose once decommissioned. According to the Electric Power Research Institute, the United States alone will produce over 720,000 tonnes of blade waste by 2040 (Electric Power Research Institute [EPRI], 2020). Now, most decommissioned blades are landfilled or incinerated, with few commercial-scale recycling options available. Waste management is further complicated by battery storage systems, which are necessary for incorporating variable renewable energy into electrical grids. Along with valuable elements like lithium, cobalt, and nickel, lithium-ion batteries also contain hazardous materials that need to be handled carefully when their usage periods are coming to an end (Wesselkämper et al., 2024). Despite the existence of recycling technologies, complex battery designs that prioritise performance over recyclability make economic viability difficult to achieve. Worldwide, less than 5% of lithium-ion batteries are recycled currently; the majority end up in landfills or are kept indefinitely (Thompson et al., 2020).

Inadequate infrastructure and regulations could cause marginalised communities close to disposal sites to be disproportionately impacted by trash from renewable energy projects. Electronic waste, which has many similarities with waste streams from renewable energy, are recycled in places like Guiyu, China, where informal recycling activities are the norm. Similarly, in India, the non-formal sector recycles 95% of e-waste, while formal units handle only 5%. This unregulated recycling can have a negative influence on the environment and human health (Pellow, 2007). Without aggressive legislative interventions and broadened producer responsibility frameworks, waste from renewable energy sources may show similar trends. The waste management issue has a domino effect on communities and societies, especially in indigenous territories.

LIFECYCLE COMPARISON OF RENEWABLE ENERGY SOURCES AND FOSSIL FUELS

The lifecycle environmental implications of fossil fuels and renewable energy sources varies significantly; renewable technologies continuously show reduced greenhouse gas emissions and more favourable energy payback periods. According to Life Cycle Assessment (LCA) studies, fossil fuels like coal and natural gas emit several hundred to more than a thousand grammes of CO_2 per kilowatt-hour, whereas solar photovoltaic systems and wind energy produce between 7.8 and 85 gCO_2 equivalent per kilowatt-hour (NREL, 2025; Smith, Shoaib, & Lal, 2025). Despite not being renewable, nuclear power has low lifespan emissions that are on par with renewables (Earth.org, 2022; World Nuclear Association, 2024). Additionally, compared to fossil fuel facilities' continuous fuel demands, renewable technologies show quick energy payback periods, frequently less than two years (refer to table 1) (NREL, 2005; PMC Biomed Central, 2025).

Although some manufacturing phases of solar and wind technologies present challenges due to the use of hazardous materials and resource extraction, renewables generally outperform fossil fuels in other environmental impact categories like acidification and eutrophication, aside from carbon emissions (Yang et al., 2024; Smith et al., 2025). While wind and photovoltaic solar use less water, making them appropriate for a variety of geographical situations, thermal fossil fuel plants and some concentrating solar power systems consume significantly more water (Montel Energy, 2025; UNESCO, 2024). In contrast to the massive land disturbance brought on by the extraction of fossil fuels, wind allows for multiple uses of land, while nuclear power is the most land-efficient per unit of energy generated (Our World in Data, 2022).

While fossil fuels have inherent limitations because of their carbon content and thermodynamic constraints, technological advancements continue to improve the environmental profiles of renewables, lowering resource intensity and further lowering emissions and payback times (World Nuclear Association, 2024; Yang et al., 2025). These findings, which also take site-specific water and land factors into account, clearly support giving renewable energy expansion top priority within energy policy in order to meet climate targets and minimise wider environmental repercussions (NREL, 2025;, Montel Energy, 2025).

Table 1. Lifecycle Comparison of Renewable Energy and Fossil Fuel Sources

Energy Source	Lifecycle GHG Emissions (gCO_2e/kWh)	Energy Payback Time (years)	Water Consumption	Land Use Efficiency	Environmental Impacts
Solar PV	20 – 85	0.4 – 3.1	Low (mostly cleaning)	Moderate (higher for ground-mounted)	Manufacturing impacts, hazardous materials use
Wind	7.8 – 26	0.4 – 1.7	Negligible	High (dual land use possible)	Steel and rare earth mining impacts
Nuclear	5.1 – 6.4	~1 – 2 (varies)	High (cooling water)	Very high (most land-efficient)	Low emissions but high-water use and radioactive waste concerns
Hydropower	~4 – 14	2 – 5	High (reservoir evaporation)	Moderate to high	Alters water cycles; large land footprint due to reservoirs

continued on following page

Table 1. Continued

Energy Source	Lifecycle GHG Emissions (gCO_2e/kWh)	Energy Payback Time (years)	Water Consumption	Land Use Efficiency	Environmental Impacts
Coal	753 – 1,095	N/A (continuous fuel use)	High (cooling water)	Low (mining land disruption)	High air pollutants, mining impacts
Natural Gas	362 – 891	N/A (continuous fuel use)	High (cooling water)	Low	Methane leaks contribute to GHGs, mining impacts
Oil	547 – 935	N/A (continuous fuel use)	High	Low	Similar to natural gas impacts, Drilling impacts

COMMUNITY DISPLACEMENT AND SOCIAL IMPACTS

Communities that are economically marginalised, rural, and indigenous bear a disproportionate share of the social impacts of renewable energy development because they lack the political clout to affect project design or execution. With the World Commission on Dams estimating that between 40 and 80 million people have been physically displaced by dam construction worldwide, hydropower development has caused especially severe displacement (World Commission on Dams, 2016). When resettlement initiatives are unable to re-establish prior means of subsistence and community structures, these displacements usually lead to poverty and social disarticulation.

One example of the significant social upheavals that might result from significant hydropower development is the Sardar Sarovar Dam on India's Narmada River. 37,000 hectares of land were eventually inundated by the project's reservoir, forcing about 200,000 people to relocate, many of whom were members of Adivasi (indigenous) communities with strong cultural ties to their ancestral lands (Baviskar, 1995). Anthropological research shows how compensation schemes routinely devalued cultural and non-market resources, and resettlement sites lacked access to forest resources and sufficient agricultural land, which were essential for traditional livelihoods (Baviskar, 1995). This led to decades of resistance through the Narmada Bachao Andolan movement which anthropologist Sanjay Sangvai describes as "a struggle not just against a dam but against a development model that systemically excludes the poor from its benefits while imposing its costs" (Sangvai, 2008).

When they alter local economies and power dynamics, even smaller-scale renewable energy technologies can have a big social impact. The agrarian landscapes in Gujarat, India, have been converted into industrial energy zones by solar parks, which have transferred land management from generational farmers to the state and private energy organizations (Stock, 2022). Research shows how these shifts result in fewer, more specialised job options that locals frequently cannot access as they don't have the necessary specialised technical training, while also eliminating agricultural occupations (Baka, 2017). Women, who historically worked in agriculture now face obstacles in employment in the male-dominated energy sectors, are disproportionately disadvantaged by these shifts (Baka, 2017).

In countries in the Global South, renewable energy projects have a significant impact on social dimensions; nevertheless, these effects are very complex when analysed using intersectional and gender-critical frameworks. Due to ingrained social norms, a lack of technical training, and exclusion from decision-making, women continue to face obstacles to receiving equitable benefits from renewable energy initiatives, particularly in rural and marginalised communities (Smith et al., 2024). For instance, women make up less than one-third of the workforce in renewable energy sectors, which have produced thousands of jobs in nations like India and sub-Saharan Africa, but they are frequently restricted to non-technical positions (Smith et al., 2024). By restricting options for earning money and enabling socio-political empowerment through electricity access, this exclusion upholds gender inequality

Renewable energy demands and priorities are shaped by intersecting characteristics like socioeconomic position, ethnicity, and disability, which can increase vulnerability to energy poverty. According to research conducted in Kenya, energy solutions suitable for people with disabilities could not be the same as those suitable for elderly women or low-income households, underscoring the significance of customised interventions (Balint et al., 2023). Over 800 households and health facilities in Rwanda are currently benefited by massive micro-hydropower projects that electrify remote rural areas; however, bureaucratic and financial obstacles frequently restrict local women-led businesses' access to development funds, thereby limiting their potential for empowerment (Imasiku, 2025). Because of this intersectionality, renewable energy projects that disregard several social identities run the danger of making already-existing disparities worse rather than better.

Real-life cases offer evidence of both promise and challenge. In rural India's Sunderbans region, solar energy deployment has improved healthcare and education access, with women actively involved as entrepreneurs in last-mile distribution (Fenice Energy, 2024). Similarly, in Ghana, though renewable energy accounts for a marginal 0.3% of national installed capacity, scaling it up is projected to enhance socio-economic development and health outcomes by reducing household air pollution and related respiratory diseases — burdens disproportionately shouldered by women and children (Imasiku, 2025). However, upfront costs of renewable technologies often restrict poor and female-headed households from benefiting fully, perpetuating energy poverty (Winther et al., 2020; Mohammed et al., 2013).

The mainstreaming of gender-responsive policies is further hindered by women's under-representation in energy governance, leading to energy programs that fail to adequately address affordability, safety, and health issues that are important to women and vulnerable groups (Smith et al., 2024; Feminist Foreign Policy, 2025). Targeted policies must include intersectional frameworks that purposefully involve marginalised people in planning, implementation, and monitoring to fully realise the social potential of renewable energy transitions (Mejia Montero et al., 2023). Enhancing inclusivity and social fairness has been demonstrated to be possible through capacity building via decentralised, community-driven models, financing for women-led businesses, and skills training (Smith et al., 2024; Wang, 2024). Notably, decentralised solar photovoltaic projects in Rwanda and Kenya have empowered women as energy entrepreneurs and enhanced access to healthcare and education (Balint et al., 2023; Fenice Energy, 2024). To promote equitable and sustainable energy futures for communities in the Global South, gender-responsive budgeting must be combined with stringent protections against environmental damage and displacement.

The next part of the chapter discusses the curious case of Cobalt mining in the Democratic Republic of Congo to assess and evaluate the actual environmental and social impacts of the green transition before dealing with global trade inequalities created by these projects and the paradigmatic shift in the global governance in this domain.

CASE STUDY: COBALT MINING IN THE DEMOCRATIC REPUBLIC OF CONGO

The Democratic Republic of the Congo (DRC) has a long and troubled history of mineral extraction, shaped by colonialism and sustained by global demand for its vast natural resources. King Leopold II of Belgium in the late 19th and early 20th centuries, subjected the Congo to intense exploitation (Nzongola-Ntalaja, 2002). Initially focused on rubber and ivory, the colonial economy quickly turned to mining as industrialization progressed. They established the Union Minière du Haut Katanga (UMHK) in 1906, marking the beginning of large-scale mineral extraction in the Katanga region, particularly of copper, tin, and cobalt (Nzongola-Ntalaja, 2002). These operations used forced Congolese labour, enriching Belgian colonial elites while offering no significant benefits to the local population. This system set a precedent for the exploitative nature of mining in the country, which continued even after the DRC gained independence in 1960. Mining was nationalized in 1967, but the sector was plagued by corruption, inefficiency, and continued dependency on foreign corporations, which reaped profits while local communities saw negligible benefits (Nzongola-Ntalaja, 2002).

In the present day, the DRC supplies over 70% of global demand for Cobalt, which is used in lithium-ion batteries powering electric vehicles, smartphones, and renewable energy storage systems (U.S. Geological Survey [USGS], 2023). Mining in the DRC is split between large-scale industrial operations, operated by foreign companies such as Glencore and China Molybdenum, and artisanal and small-scale mining (ASM), which accounts for approximately 30% of the country's cobalt output (Amnesty International, 2016). In the DRC, ASM is extremely informal and frequently hazardous; more than 200,000 Congolese, many of whom are women and children, labor in unlicensed cobalt mines with little safety gears, no labour protections, and are subjected to hazardous dust and frequent workplace accidents (Amnesty International, 2016). The economic benefits of cobalt mining are unevenly distributed. Despite the country's resource wealth, the DRC remains one of the poorest nations in the world, with mining profits disproportionately enriching foreign companies and Congolese elites rather than uplifting the broader population (World Bank, 2024).

The legacy of colonialism is still deeply embedded in Congo's current trade relationships. China has become the dominant actor in the DRC's cobalt trade, refining most of the cobalt extracted from the country and holding major stakes in Congolese mining ventures (Gulley, 2023). Deals such as the 2008 "Sicomines" agreement have secured long-term access to DRC's mineral wealth for Chinese corporations. This ensures that control over strategic resources is once again outsourced to foreign powers under unequal terms, establishing a system of 'neo-colonialism' (Gulley, 2023). Companies use forced evictions and mercenaries to force people out of their homes and farmland and consequently their cultural and social legacy. Mining has consumed the country, creating a system of modern-day slavery where people have no options for alternate employment and are forced to work in this industry (Kara, 2023).

In a significant legal development, in April 2024, the DRC government filed a lawsuit against Apple Inc. in Paris, accusing the company of indirectly profiting from cobalt sourced through exploitative and illegal mining operations in the country. (Ross, 2024) The lawsuit claims that Apple's supply chain sources these minerals from companies linked to human rights violations, particularly in artisanal mining sites where child labour and unsafe conditions are common (Reuters, 2024). The Congolese government alleges that Apple has violated its duty of vigilance under French law, which requires large companies to prevent human rights and environmental violations in their supply chains (Reuters, 2024). Though this case has been closed by the Paris Prosecutor's office, it marks one of the most high-profile attempts by a resource-rich Global South nation to hold a Western tech company legally accountable for its role in perpetuating unethical labour and trade practices in the society (Reuters, 2025).

The conditions of mines in the DRC are reminiscent of the colonial treatment of the people of Congo. The miners work in hazardous conditions, for little to no wages. There are around 150,000 artisanal miners or *creuseurs* in this industry, forced to mine by hand using rudimentary tools and no safety equipment (Amnesty International, 2016). The workers often face significant health problems, prolonged exposure to the dust from the mines results in lung diseases and chronic pain (Amnesty International, 2016). These human rights violations are overlooked by corrupt practices and red tapes in some states. Government initiatives aimed at improving these conditions face challenges in effective execution. Most of the mining activity takes place in unauthorized areas and the governmental agency responsible for regulation and welfare of artisanal miners only operate in authorized artisanal mining areas (ZEAs) implying no safeguard and protection to the majority population engaged in unauthorized mining activities (Amnesty International, 2016).

Cobalt mining in the DRC also causes significant environmental harm, the effects of which are borne by the local communities and not the multinational non-retail consumers of the minerals. Large-scale mining operations involve extreme habitat disruption and felling of millions of trees. Cobalt mining also severally pollutes vital water sources around the mines, a 2024 investigation found that toxic substances like copper, cobalt, arsenic, cadmium, uranium and other heavy metals leak into the surrounding rivers, lakes, streams, groundwater and wetlands (RAID, 2025). Additionally, improper management of the waste containing these heavy metals can leak into the ground. Concentration of heavy metals in the ground can significantly impact soil fertility and agricultural output.

In sharp contrast, Canada, a country that is the member of the Global North, renewable energy makes up approximately 66% of electricity generated. Their renewable installed capacity reached over 200 GW by 2022 (Hemeida et al., 2022), but remote and Indigenous communities still struggle with energy insecurity, these communities, often located off the main grid and reliant on diesel generators, face some of the highest residential electricity rates in Canada, but indigenous communities in Canada play an active role in the renwable energy project on their land. Indigenous Economic Development Corporations (EDCs) have emerged as pivotal vehicles for community ownership and governance of renewable projects, granting First Nations meaningful equity stakes that reinforce self-governance and land stewardship (Savic & Hoicka, 2023). In Saskatchewan, for example, the Peter Ballantyne Cree Nation's partnership in a 2 MW wind farm under the Power Generation Partners program delivered approximately CAD 1.2 million in annual net revenues, which fund community services, and created a cadre of new full-time jobs (Leonhardt et al., 2023). Many Indigenous Nations have pioneered community-led planning models that blend

Traditional Ecological Knowledge (TEK) with technical and economic analyses. The Haíłzaqv Nation's Community Energy Plan embeds Indigenous laws (gvilas) to prioritize solar and micro-hydro over larger dams, establishes youth mentorship in micro-grid maintenance, and allocates 100 percent of project revenues to cultural and language revitalization (Duran et al., 2024).

Thus, while both contexts involve resource extraction and Indigenous or vulnerable peoples, Canadian renewable energy projects prioritize empowerment, partnership, and environmental sustainability rooted in cultural values and treaty rights, whereas cobalt mining in the DRC exemplifies a continuation of colonial extraction marked by environmental devastation, human suffering, and economic disenfranchisement. The Canadian approach demonstrates how Indigenous leadership and governance can mitigate extraction harms and channel resource wealth toward just transitions, while the DRC context exemplifies the risks when global demand for "green" minerals fuels exploitative and environmentally destructive practices disconnected from local rights and wellbeing.

South-South cooperation (SSC) offers the Democratic Republic of the Congo (DRC) opportunities to shift from exploitative mineral extraction toward value-added renewable energy development. Unlike traditional North–South partnerships, SSC emphasizes horizontal exchange of technology, governance models, and financing among developing countries, thereby reducing dependency and promoting shared benefits (Chaturvedi, Fues, & Sidiropoulos, 2012; Pomeroy, 2016). Real-world SSC successes include the International Solar Alliance, which has mobilized over USD 1 billion for solar projects and improved energy access for more than 20 million people through capacity building and technology transfer (Ministry of External Affairs, India, 2023; International Solar Alliance, 2023), and BRICS members' joint deployment of renewable infrastructure—exemplified by China's 100 MW Redstone solar thermal plant in South Africa, which combined foreign investment with local job creation and technical training (State Grid Corporation of China, 2024; BRICS Energy Research Cooperation Platform, 2024). Through SSC, the DRC could develop domestic battery and electric-vehicle manufacturing, leveraging its cobalt and copper resources to capture more value, while learning from Indian and Brazilian policies on local content requirements and green industrial incentives (Sahoo & Ashraf, 2021; United Nations Development Programme [UNDP], 2019).

The DRC must, however, improve governance transparency, uphold contract integrity, and make investments in worker education and skill development if it hopes to guarantee that SSC promotes equitable development rather than reproducing extractive practices (Carmody, 2019). The DRC could export higher-value goods rather than raw resources if SSC frameworks are integrated into the African Continental Free Trade Area, which could further improve regional value chains (African Union, 2022). The DRC can overcome neo-colonial resource dependence and develop a viable, domestic renewable energy sector by putting an emphasis on South-South collaboration, transparent partnerships, and participatory government. The case of the DRC highlight the persisting issues in the green energy industry, the chapter will discuss the mecahnisms that enable this system and posiible policy reforms and governance that that ensure a truly just energy transition.

STRUCTURAL TRADE INEQUALITIES IN THE GREEN ECONOMY

Large-scale renewable projects discussed above, and extractive supply chains draw attention to the injustices that are a part of green transitions, but understanding these issues requires looking at the more fundamental structural disparities that exist within the framework of international trade. Due to systemic barriers created by historical colonial legacies and unequal power dynamics, current trade relations make it difficult for a large portion of the Global South to participate fairly in the green economy.

The primary manifestation of global trade disparities is the persistent reliance of poor nations on the export of raw materials, while remaining consumers of manufactured green technology. Although Africa supplies more than 60% of the world's cobalt and 37% of its manganese, two elements essential to battery technology, the continent only generates 1% of the world's battery manufacturing capacity, according to UNCTAD data (United Nations Conference on Trade and Development, 2022). Developing nations contribute to the clean energy transition while being shut out of value-added manufacturing processes (Gudynas, 2010). The Democratic Republic of Congo produces approximately 70% of the world's cobalt, but it receives less than 5% of the final value of lithium-ion batteries, with most value capture occurring in China, South Korea, and Japan where battery assembly takes place (Amnesty International, 2016).

The social and ecological costs explored in the earlier sections — from mineral extraction in the DRC to the displacement of indigenous communities in Morocco and Mexico — These are symptoms of deeper structural inequities in the global trading system (Bainton & Holcombe, 2018; Temper et al., 2020). These environmental injustices are not isolated externalities but rather are embedded within the historical and institutional fabric of international trade (Gathii, 2011). The green energy transition, while promising a decarbonised future, continues to operate along pathways shaped by colonial extraction, global capitalism and power asymmetries (Eslava, Fakhri & Nesiah, 2017).

At the core of this imbalance lies the division of labour that defines the global economy: resource-rich but industrially underdeveloped countries in the Global

South continue to serve as raw material suppliers, while manufacturing, value addition and consumption are dominated by countries in the Global North (Shiva, 1989; Chang, 2002). These dynamic replicates colonial trade patterns, now enforced through modern supply chains, investment treaties, and trade rules that structurally disadvantage developing economies (Chimni, 2004; Shadlen, 2008).

For instance, while Africa supplies over 60% of the world's cobalt and 37% of its manganesse, critical inputs for battery technology, it contributes less than 1% to global battery manufacturing capacity (UNCTAD, 2022). The Democratic Republic of Congo, which alone provides around 70% of the world's cobalt, receives less than 5% of the final value of lithium-ion batteries (OECD, 2023). The overwhelming majority of processing and technological innovation takes place in China, South Korea, Japan, and the United States (IEA, 2023). The result is a profoundly unequal value chain in which developing countries bear environmental and social harms but capture minimal economic returns (Klinger, 2018).

These trade structures are not coincidental—they are underpinned by a system of global economic governance that restricts the policy space available to poorer nations (Rodrik, 2011). The following sections examine how this inequality is reinforced through legal mechanisms such as intellectual property regimes, financial structures and the institutional crisis within the World Trade Organization.

LEGAL FRAGMENTATION AND STRUCTURAL INEQUTIES

This structural inequity is a legacy of colonial trade relationships, now institutionalized through global supply chains and trade frameworks that externalize environmental and social harms while internalizing economic benefits within the Global North (Bond, 2016; Eslava et al., 2017).

WTO Jurisprudence on Green Measures

The evolution of global trade governance began with the General Agreement on Tariffs and Trade (GATT) in 1947, a post-war effort to promote multilateral cooperation and reduce barriers to trade (Jackson, 1997). While GATT helped institutionalize non-discrimination through principles like Most-Favoured Nation (MFN) and national treatment, it lacked an institutional body with binding enforcement powers. Dispute settlement under GATT was ad hoc and often ineffective (Hoekman & Kostecki, 2009). This changed with the establishment of the World Trade Organization (WTO) in 1995 during the Uruguay Round, which created a structured and binding dispute settlement mechanism, including an Appellate Body (AB), designed to provide consistency and finality in trade rulings (WTO, 1995).

The WTO's Dispute Settlement Body (DSB) and AB were intended to provide predictability and finality in trade adjudication (WTO, 1995). Yet, as environmental concerns entered the trade arena, the limits of this system became apparent. While Article XX of the GATT permits measures "necessary to protect human, animal or plant life or health" or "relating to the conservation of exhaustible natural resources," these exceptions have been narrowly interpreted. Scholars such as Howse (2007) and Marceau (2001) argue that WTO jurisprudence has largely subordinated environmental and developmental objectives to trade liberalisation.

The restrictive approach of the WTO toward green measures is most evident in its case law (refer to table 2 below). In US–Gasoline (1996), the Appellate Body ruled against the United States' clean fuel standards, holding that the environmental exception under Article XX could not justify measures applied in a discriminatory manner. Similarly, in US–Shrimp (1998), the requirement for exporters to use turtle-excluder devices was initially struck down as an illegitimate process and production method (PPM)-based trade restriction. Although compliance was later accepted once the measure was applied multilaterally and with greater flexibility, the case demonstrated the difficulty of reconciling trade rules with environmental objectives. In India–Solar Cells (2016), India's local content requirements for solar energy projects were found to violate national treatment and TRIMS obligations, with the environmental and developmental justification environmental and developmental justifications given little weight. Likewise, in China–Rare Earths (2014), the Appellate Body rejected China's export quotas on rare earth minerals, ruling that environmental exceptions under GATT Article XX could not justify export restrictions unless accompanied by equivalent domestic limitations. Together, these decisions illustrate a structural asymmetry: developed countries' green measures may sometimes be accommodated, whereas similar tools employed by developing countries for industrialisation and climate goals are often struck down.

Table 2. WTO Cases Demonstrating it's Restrictive Approach

Case	Measure Contested	Legal Basis Invoked	WTO Ruling	Implication for Green Transition
US – Gasoline	Clean fuel standards	GATT XX(b), XX(g)	Against US	Limited scope of environmental exceptions
US – Shrimp	Turtle-excluder devices	GATT XX(g)	Against US (initially)	Dispute over PPM-based differentiation
India – Solar Cells	Domestic Content Rules	GATT III:4, TRIMS, XX(j)	Against India	Weak protection for development-linked green goals
China – Rare Earths	Export quotas on minerals	GATT XX(g)	Against China	Export controls must align with domestic restrictions

This jurisprudential tension has been intensified by the paralysis of the WTO Appellate Body since 2019, following the United States' persistent blockage of appointments. With the AB unable to function, panel rulings can now be appealed "into the void," effectively leaving disputes unresolved and depriving the system of authoritative precedent (CSIS, 2024; Shaffer, 2021). The crisis has created profound uncertainty for green trade measures. Were the AB functioning, measures such as the European Union's Carbon Border Adjustment Mechanism (CBAM) would likely face scrutiny under the principles of Most-Favoured Nation (MFN) treatment and national treatment, with the EU forced to justify CBAM under Article XX. In the current vacuum, however, disputes linger unresolved, and major economies face fewer legal constraints in advancing unilateral climate-linked trade policies. In effect, the AB crisis has shifted the governance of trade and climate from law toward power politics, allowing unilateralism and regionalism to fill the void left by multilateral adjudication (Financial Times, 2024; CSIS, 2024).

It is in this institutional vacuum that the European Union has sought to position itself as a global climate regulator through trade. The European Green Deal (2019) and its flagship Carbon Border Adjustment Mechanism (2023) aim to prevent carbon leakage by imposing tariffs on imports of carbon-intensive goods such as cement, steel, aluminium, electricity, fertilizers, and hydrogen (European Commission, 2021). CBAM operates alongside the EU's Emissions Trading System (ETS) and requires foreign producers to purchase carbon certificates equivalent to the price paid by EU firms. Although framed as a climate measure, CBAM has provoked strong reactions from the Global South. Indian trade minister Piyush Goyal has described it as "green protectionism" that will hurt developing countries disproportionately and may even harm EU exporters in the long term (Times of India, 2025). Russia has gone further, filing a WTO complaint against CBAM as discriminatory (Centre for European Reform, 2024). Recent modelling studies suggest that while CBAM could reduce EU import emissions by nearly 5%, it may simultaneously penalise exporters from emerging economies who lack access to green technologies (Arxiv, 2025). With the Appellate Body crisis leaving CBAM's WTO-compatibility unresolved, the EU enjoys a de facto ability to globalise its standards without multilateral oversight.

The African response to this shifting trade–climate landscape has taken a different form. The African Continental Free Trade Area (AfCFTA), operational since 2021, explicitly incorporates sustainable development and industrialisation goals into its framework (UNECA, 2020). African scholars and policymakers argue that CBAM places unfair burdens on African exporters, while offering no corresponding mechanisms for technology transfer or climate finance (Ampofo, 2023). Rather than contest CBAM directly at the WTO, African states are seeking to harness AfCFTA as a vehicle for green industrialisation, focusing on renewable energy corridors, intra-African carbon markets, and climate-linked value chains (ODI, 2024; UNCTAD, 2024). The paralysis of the WTO dispute system paradoxically creates greater space for these regional strategies. With less fear of WTO litigation, African states may experiment with policy tools—such as subsidies or local content requirements—that were previously struck down in cases like India–Solar Cells.

Taken together, WTO jurisprudence, the Appellate Body crisis, and the rise of unilateral and regional frameworks point to a fragmented and asymmetric governance landscape. For developed economies such as the EU, the absence of appellate scrutiny enables them to advance measures like CBAM under the banner of climate ambition. For developing countries, however, the same system that once disciplined their industrial policies now provides no legal recourse to challenge green protectionism. Meanwhile, regional initiatives such as AFCFTA demonstrate a growing determination in the Global South to construct climate-compatible trade frameworks aligned with their developmental needs. The future of trade and energy governance, therefore, appears less tied to multilateral coherence and more to a patchwork of unilateral, bilateral, and regional strategies, where climate justice remains a contested terrain.

Climate Change Treaties and Regional and Bilateral Trade Agreements

The foundational legal tools for climate governance have been established by the Paris Agreement and the United Nations Framework Convention on Climate Change (UNFCCC), which run parallel to trade law. The significance of technology transfer and international cooperation is emphasised by these treaties. To support low-carbon development in the Global South, mechanisms like the Green Climate Fund (GCF) and the Climate Technology Centre and Network (CTCN) were established (UNFCCC, 1992; Paris Agreement, 2015).

These mechanisms are still largely unconnected to trade law. Although climate treaties encourage fair access to technology, they are overshadowed by legally binding

WTO regulations like TRIPS and SCM disciplines, and lack enforceable provisions (WTO, 1994). Article 10 of the Paris Agreement calls for technology transfer and capacity building, and this fragmentation makes it more difficult to operationalise those commitments. Since these agreements are based on mutual consent and trust, and are no binding, they are often overshadowed by WTO agreements, whose provisions are binding and violation of them result in consequences.

Outside of the WTO, Investor-State Dispute Settlement (ISDS) clauses in bilateral investment treaties (BITs) and regional trade agreements (RTAs) frequently give corporations the ability to contest public interest laws. In nations like Spain, Italy, and the Czech Republic, which changed solar feed-in tariffs because of budgetary pressures, these clauses have been used to oppose renewable energy reforms (Energy Charter Secretariat, 2021). A sort of "regulatory chill" has resulted, discouraging states from implementing bold environmental policies out of concern for legal action (Tienhaara, 2018). While modern Regional Trade Agreements increasingly contain environmental chapters, these are frequently aspirational or non-binding. In contrast, investor protection and intellectual property rights are strictly enforceable, reflecting an institutional imbalance that limits environmental policymaking space.

Technology Transfer Barriers and Innovation Divides

The International Renewable Energy Agency (IRENA) estimates that intellectual property protections can raise the cost of renewable energy technologies in developing countries by 25% to 40%.(World Intellectual Property Report, 2024). These elevated costs are compounded by a lack of local manufacturing capacity, limited access to concessional finance, and underdeveloped institutional ecosystems for innovation. As a result, low-income countries often find themselves unable to implement necessary mitigation and adaptation measures, perpetuating a cycle of technological dependency and underdevelopment.

Technology transfer, a key component of sustainable development, remains constrained by proprietary controls and legal regimes that prioritize intellectual property rights over equitable access (Reichman, 2009; Maskus, 2012). The WTO administration of the Agreement on Trade-Related Aspects of Intellectual Property Rights (TRIPS) has placed significant legal and financial obstacles to the distribution of clean technologies. Although it seeks to standardise intellectual property laws around the world, its application has disproportionately benefited developed nations who have robust technology infrastructure and well-established innovation regimes. Although the number of patent applications for renewable energy technology rose by about 13% annually between 2010 and 2020, corporations in developed nations still hold more than 80% of these patents (WIPO, 2023). Because of this concentration of invention in the Global North, countries most at risk from climate change are unable to access technological skills, especially in the areas of sustainable development. This phenomenon is known as the "innovation divide.(Raúl and Bierwirth, 2023)

Small Island Developing States (SIDS) and Least Developed Countries (LDCs) are especially negatively impacted by this dynamic. These countries face some of the most severe climate risks, including rising sea levels, extreme weather events, and ecosystem degradation (UN-OHRLLS, 2021). These countries frequently depend on imports for grid technologies, solar panels, and wind turbines, which are more expensive because of international licensing agreements and intellectual protections.

Legal experts like Keith Maskus and Jerome Reichman argue that the stringent enforcement of intellectual property rights (IPRs) under TRIPS does not consider the needs of developing countries (Maskus & Reichman, 2004; Sumaita, 2021). According to their analysis, robust intellectual property laws that do not include provisions for technology sharing are equivalent to the privatisation of public goods around the world. This means that knowledge necessary to meet global emission targets and facilitate fair energy transitions remains bound by proprietary rights. Because of the intricacy of the law, political pressure, and a lack of institutional capacity, TRIPS's provisions for compulsory licensing, particularly Article 31 (WTO, 1994), are rarely used for environmental technologies. The UNFCCC's principle of "common but differentiated responsibilities" (UNFCCC, 1992) is compromised when IP waivers for green technologies are not taken into consideration.

Financial and Investment Imbalances

Due to disparities in access to funding for clean energy investments, global financial inequality exacerbates technological barriers. According to the Climate Policy Initiative, borrowing costs for renewable energy projects in developing nations are two to three percent higher than in developed nations (Climate Policy Initiative [CPI], 2021). Significant extra costs result from this cost difference, for example, a $1 billion solar project developed in Sub-Saharan Africa as opposed to Europe would incur an additional $200–300 million in financing costs over the course of its lifetime (International Finance Corporation [IFC], 2021).

Despite making up 65% of the world's population and experiencing some of the worst effects of climate change, developing nations only received 15% of global investments in clean energy in 2023, according to the International Energy Agency (IEA, 2024). In international finance, where credit ratings and risk assessments routinely disadvantage developing nations looking to construct green infrastructure, this investment imbalance reflects larger structural disparities.

The underinvestment in the South exacerbates the very extractivist trade patterns discussed in the first half of this chapter, where raw materials are exported under exploitative terms but value addition, innovation, and capital remain concentrated in the North (Bond, 2016; Klinger, 2018). This not only undermines energy sovereignty in poorer countries but perpetuates a form of financial colonization that keeps them structurally dependent.

Without reforms to multilateral development finance—such as the expansion of concessional lending, the deployment of climate risk guarantees, and the restructuring of sovereign debt—it will be impossible to ensure an inclusive green transition. Green finance must be decolonized, just as green trade must be democratized (Ghosh & Mazzucato, 2022).

To fully understand how structural inequalities persist and deepen under the current global trade regime, it is essential to examine the institutional frameworks that govern trade rules and dispute resolution. While financing asymmetries limit the Global South's ability to invest in clean technologies, it is the legal architecture of global trade—particularly the WTO — that restricts policy autonomy, disciplines state intervention, and privileges market liberalization over sustainability. This next section explores how the crisis of the WTO's dispute settlement mechanism, particularly the collapse of its Appellate Body, has undermined efforts to reconcile trade and climate goals, further marginalizing environmentally progressive action in the Global South.

Geopolitical Conflict and Energy Supply Chain Vulnerabilities

The global supply chains necessary for the deployment of renewable energy have been severely disrupted by the conflict between Russia and Ukraine. Russia and Ukraine supply essential raw materials for clean energy technologies. While Russia supplies about 35% of the world's palladium market and 25% of titanium, which is widely used in wind turbines, batteries, and aerospace components, Ukraine supplies about 20% of the neon gas needed for semiconductor etching. (IEA, 2022a).

According to estimates from the International Energy Agency (IEA), the war affected supply chains that accounted for 15–20% of the world's solar photovoltaic (PV) production capacity, which increased prices and disrupted availability. (IEA, 2022b) These interruptions highlight the strategic risks of becoming overly dependent on a small number of suppliers for essential raw materials and highlight how fragile global clean energy supply chains can be.

In addition, the conflict has caused a great deal of volatility in the price of energy. According to Bloomberg NEF, supply chain bottlenecks and rising commodity prices for metals like copper, aluminium, and steel both contributed to an 8–15% increase in the cost of renewable energy projects in 2022. (BloombergNEF, 2023) Due to their smaller financial margins and restricted access to long-term fixed-rate financing or currency hedging, project developers in developing nations have been disproportionately impacted by this volatility, making renewable investments riskier and less alluring. (BloombergNEF, 2023) Such cost shocks have the potential to cause project cancellations or deferrals in areas that are already having difficulty attracting clean energy capital, undermining global decarbonisation efforts and increasing the gap between energy-rich and energy-poor countries.

These developments highlight the increasingly entangled nature of climate, trade, and geopolitical security. In the absence of robust and equitable trade institutions, energy transitions may be shaped less by principles of global cooperation and more by politics and economic self-interest. Developing countries cannot cope with increased prices and uncertainty in supply during times of conflict, especially since they already lack the capabilities and resources to develop robust clean energy infrastructure. For a truly just and effective global green transition, it is imperative to restore and reform multilateral dispute mechanisms while ensuring that security-driven trade responses do not exacerbate existing development disparities.

Green Technology Tariffs and the Weaponization of Trade Policy

The growing politicization of green trade policy illustrates how environmental goals are increasingly subordinated to geostrategic rivalry. Rather than being tools for global cooperation, tariffs and export bans on green technologies are now deployed as weapons in trade wars, particularly between the United States and China.

The cooperative spirit that once underpinned trade liberalisation initiatives in support of climate action has drastically changed with the rise of tariffs on green technologies. As economic nationalism increasingly shapes trade policy in important economies, initiatives like the WTO's Environmental Goods Agreement (EGA), (WTO, 2014) which aimed to lower tariffs on sustainable products, have stalled or failed.

Citing domestic harm, the US imposed Section 201 safeguard tariffs on imported solar panels in 2018, mainly targeting Chinese producers. The tariffs, which were first set at 30%, were raised in 2022 and 2024 (USITC, 2018). The National Renewable Energy Laboratory estimates that between 2018 and 2022, these actions raised project costs by $18–20 billion and decreased solar installations in the United States by 9–11%.[2] Similar actions include European Union anti-dumping duties on Chinese solar modules and U.S. tariffs of up to 58.5% on Chinese wind towers (Bown, 2020).

These protectionist policies introduce a structural contradiction between climate goals and trade policy. Hufbauer and Jung demonstrate that green technology tariffs reduce efficiency and hinder emissions reduction. Their modeling indicates that tariffs in major markets have slowed global solar deployment by 15–20%, potentially delaying global emissions reductions by 2–3 years. (Hufbauer & Jung, 2021) A conflict between trade policy and climate goals is brought about by these protectionist measures. Green technology tariffs can hinder the reduction of emissions and decrease efficiency. Global solar deployment has been slowed by 15–20% due to tariffs in major markets, which could delay global emissions reductions by two to three years (Hufbauer & Jung, 2021).

Additionally, the trade in critical minerals has become more weaponised. China restricted exports of rare earth elements, gallium, and germanium in 2023 in response to U.S. semiconductor sanctions. These materials make up over 80% of the world's supply and are essential for solar cells, electric vehicles, and wind turbines (USGS, 2023). According to the US Geological Survey, such limitations might cause a major delay in the production of clean energy worldwide (USGS, 2023).

In early 2025, U.S. President Donald Trump escalated this by introducing a new round of green technology tariffs. It included a 60% tariff on Chinese electric vehicles (EVs), a 30% tariff on solar inverters and battery cells from Southeast Asia, and broader restrictions on rare earth elements and related clean tech components (The White House, 2025).

The Guardian reports that these actions raised fears of a fresh global economic break down that might sabotage innovation and investment in clean energy. Analysts noted that the United States runs the risk of distancing itself from the global climate movement by making green imports less desirable. (Franklin & Williams, 2025) These policies can hinder the development in the United States and isolate them from the global market. In Southeast Asia, where growing clean energy startups are particularly vulnerable to supply disruptions and capital flight, the effects of these tariff measures. More than half of early-stage clean energy startups had less than six months of operations, according to a 2025 survey conducted by the Indonesian branch of New Energy Nexus (NEX), (Lin, 2025). The majority were in the pilot or prototype stages and mainly relied on inexpensive imports, such as batteries, inverters, and solar panels, which are currently the target of tariff crossfire (Lin, 2025).

As U.S. policy grows more anti-renewable, companies like Indonesian electric motorcycle startup Swap Energi say investor interest has decreased, and clean technology subsidies have been cut in Indonesia due to budget cuts. The closure of USAID and the restructuring of the U.S. International Development Finance Corporation (DFC) have blocked major funding (Lin, 2025). Further, businesses like SmartSolar in Vietnam are looking to expand their alliances. They are looking to Germany and the European Union for financial and technological cooperation because U.S. capital is no longer dependable (Lin, 2025). This change might be a sign of a larger realignment of international clean energy partnerships, which could distance the United States from its previous position of leadership and bring Southeast Asia closer to China and Europe.

In sum, tariff escalation, geopolitical retaliation, and development finance retrenchment poses serious risks to the global green transition. Without a coordinated multilateral response to reintegrate trade and climate governance, fragmented markets and escalating trade wars could significantly delay decarbonization and worsen global inequalities. Powerful countries like the United States and China can alter global trade patterns and supply chains by changing domestic policy and forces less powerful and poorer countries to struggle to adapt.

WAY FORWARD: EQUITABLE APPROACHES TO GREEN TECHNOLOGY DEVELOPMENT

In order to address the ingrained colonial patterns and social injustices that define modern energy systems, the global drive for renewable energy must go beyond decarbonisation. Inclusive governance, structural changes to trade regulations, and policies that acknowledge the historical and current marginalisation of indigenous communities and the Global South are all necessary for a fair and just green transition. In addition to putting climate goals first, these reforms (refer to table 3 below) must aim for equity in participation, resource distribution, and technological advancement.

Table 3. Policy Recommendations for Equitable Renewable Energy Development

Theme	Policy Recommendations (Brief)
Rebalancing Trade Rules with Sustainability Objectives	Reform WTO rules to allow green subsidies; broaden GATT exceptions to include climate change; liberalise environmental goods; make sustainability clauses enforceable; ensure fair market access.
Addressing Power Imbalances in Global Governance	Increase inclusivity in global governance; extend special and differential treatment; integrate environmental harm in dispute settlement; regulate ecological and social impacts of green mining.
Building Just Transitions	Empower local and indigenous communities; ensure free, prior, informed consent; diversify beyond raw material exports; support local manufacturing and research; invest in social protection and education.
Pathways to Implementation	Develop equitable transition strategies; create accountability for green investments; align industrial and trade policy with sustainability.
Decolonizing the Green Transition	Challenge colonial patterns in energy systems; prioritise justice, equity, and indigenous rights; move from extractivist to community-led models.

Rebalancing Trade Rules with Sustainability Objectives

The rigidity of international trade regulations, especially those governed by the World Trade Organisation (WTO), is one of the major obstacles to the development of green technologies. The current regulations are often inadequate to handle the environmental and social aspects of the green transition because they were primarily designed to support liberalised trade. To make sure that trade law promotes sustainability goals rather than impedes them, reforms are required.

Under the WTO's Agreement on Agriculture (WTO, 1994), climate-friendly subsidies which are crucial for promoting the growth of renewable energy, should be given the same ease as agricultural subsidies. Governments would have more policy leeway to encourage sustainable energy innovation without worrying about breaking WTO rules if a special category for green subsidies were established. Additionally, the General Agreement on Tariffs and Trade's (GATT) Article XX environmental exceptions ought to be interpreted more broadly to specifically acknowledge climate change mitigation as a valid policy objective. This would lessen the likelihood that national climate regulations would be overturned as covert trade restrictions.

The way that environmental goods and services are categorised and handled is another significant reform. WTO members have not yet reached a consensus on a list that is widely recognised, despite continuous discussions. Globally, cleaner production would be encouraged by making these definitions clearer and granting them preferential treatment. Finally, rather than being decorative, environmental clauses in trade agreements need to be made enforceable. According to UNEP, trade policy should include legally binding sustainability pledges backed by dispute resolution procedures rather than merely aspirational language or legally ambiguous side agreements (UNEP, 2023).

UNCTAD asserts that for climate policies to be compatible with trade law, developing nations must also have fair access to international markets (UNCTAD, 2022). Climate policy may unintentionally perpetuate current trade structure disparities in the absence of such alignment. This emphasises the necessity of a more comprehensive trade agenda that combines development objectives with environmental integrity.

Addressing Power Imbalances in Global Governance

In addition to legal reform, global governance systems that presently put the interests of rich countries and multinational businesses ahead of those of underprivileged groups need to be changed more broadly. Voices from civil society, especially those from the Global South and indigenous people, are often excluded from decision-making processes in trade and environmental governance. To guarantee that a range of viewpoints are represented in international rulemaking, it is imperative that these agreements be made more transparent and inclusive (Scholte, 2020).

Moreover, rules pertaining to special and differential treatment, which were first created to address the requirements of developing nations, need to be extended and made practical within the framework of environmental legislation. This would give these nations the adaptability and assistance they need to carry out sustainability pledges in line with their unique national conditions. In international dispute resolution, equal treatment is also required. Existing institutions frequently prioritise business interests over environmental harm unless it can be connected to trade discrimination. (Pauwelyn, 2019) A fairer reading of international economic law would be reflected in reforming such institutions to consider environmental issues equally.

These adjustments are particularly urgent given the growing evidence that the mining-based industries fuelling the green economy such as lithium and cobalt mining have significant ecological and social consequences. Although they produce fewer emissions than fossil fuel extraction, they often result in water pollution, biodiversity loss, and displacement of local communities (Earth.Org, 2023). Trade regimes must expand their focus beyond market access and consider the broader sustainability impacts of commodity flows and production chains.

Building Just Transitions: Breaking Colonial Patterns

Extractive, top-down colonial processes cannot be replicated by a just global energy transition. Rather, it must focus on value generation in the Global South, local empowerment, and indigenous knowledge systems. The World Bank asserts that communities and individuals must be at the centre of the shift to a low-carbon economy, acknowledging their right to direct their own destinies (World Bank, 2023). Indigenous assessments, which are based on culturally grounded epistemologies, can be useful substitutes for traditional environmental assessments. These methods lead more fair policy responses and offer context-sensitive methods of quantifying ecological harm (Datta et al., 2024).

To prevent communities from being forced to accept renewable energy projects without their free, prior, and informed consent, it is also necessary to respect indigenous self-determination. Simultaneously, structural economic reforms are required to strengthen resilience against market volatility and lessen reliance on exports of raw materials. Resource-rich nations can advance up the value chain through economic diversification, which is aided by policies that boost indigenous manufacturing, processing, and research capabilities (IEA, 2023). in addition to improving national energy security, a localised strategy for clean energy development creates jobs and boosts wider socioeconomic benefits.

Simultaneously, structural economic reforms are required to strengthen resilience against market volatility and lessen reliance on exports of raw materials. Resource-rich nations can advance up the value chain through economic diversification, which is aided by policies that support local manufacturing, processing, and research capabilities (IEA, 2023). In addition to improving national energy security, a localised strategy for clean energy development creates jobs and promotes wider socioeconomic growth.

This type of diversification must be accompanied by investments in social protection, infrastructure, and education. type of diversification. According to the World Bank, such steps are necessary to reduce the risks involved in moving away from fossil fuels, especially in areas where extractive industries have historically played a significant role in local economies (World Bank, 2023).

Pathways to Implementation

Implementation of equitable green transition strategies requires well-designed policy instruments that account for disparities in access and capacity. Regulatory tools such as feed-in tariffs and renewable portfolio standards must be designed with equity in mind, targeting underrepresented communities. Tax incentives for renewable energy should prioritize low-income households and marginalized regions. Additionally, phasing out polluting technologies must be accompanied by just transition plans that provide financial and occupational support for affected workers.

Simplifying the permitting process for renewable energy projects is another crucial step, particularly in communities that face bureaucratic hurdles to energy access. Policies must be predictable and long-term in scope to attract sustainable investment, and they must integrate social safeguards to ensure that green projects do not exacerbate inequality.

International cooperation is indispensable. Knowledge sharing, harmonization of standards, and South-South cooperation can help scale up renewable energy in developing countries. Mechanisms under the UNFCCC, including the Technology Mechanism, should be strengthened to facilitate technology transfer and local adaptation (UNFCCC, 2025. As UNEP emphasizes, global cooperation must extend beyond trade negotiations to include support for national regulatory capacity and multistakeholder initiatives for sustainable supply chains (UNEP, 2023).

CONCLUSION

It is necessary to rethink the green transition from a decolonisation and justice perspective. Addressing the systemic and historical injustices that influence modern environmental governance is essential to achieving sustainability in its purest form. Models of renewable energy development that put an emphasis on social justice, ecological stewardship, and self-determination must take the place of the extractivist model, which is based on resource exploitation and outside control.

Legal reform, moral supply chain management and inclusive economic policies must all be combined to achieve this goal. A truly sustainable transition must include local manufacturing, fair trade practices, technology transfer, and respect for indigenous sovereignty. The global green economy cannot be made just for everyone unless the colonial legacy is destroyed and interdisciplinary, community-driven approaches are adopted.

REFERENCES

African Union. (2022). *African Continental Free Trade Area: Agreement establishing the AfCFTA*. African Union Commission.

Amnesty International. (2016, January 19). *Democratic Republic of Congo: "This is what we die for": Human rights abuses in the Democratic Republic of the Congo power the global trade in cobalt.* https://www.amnesty.org/en/documents/afr62/3183/2016/en/

Bainton, N., & Holcombe, S. (2018). A critical review of the social aspects of mine closure. *Resources Policy*, *59*, 468–478.

Baka, J. (2017). Making space for energy: Wasteland development, enclosures, and energy dispossessions. *Antipode*, *49*(4), 977–996.

Balint, J.. (2023). Shedding light on vulnerability: Intersectional energy planning for development. *SSRN*. https://papers.ssrn.com/sol3/Delivery.cfm/SSRN_ID4845844_code5044974.pdf

Barandiarán, J. (2019). Lithium and development imaginaries in Chile, Argentina and Bolivia. *World Development*, *113*, 381–391. DOI: 10.1016/j.worlddev.2018.09.019

Basak, O. (2024, September 5). *Green colonialism in the energy transition*. Illuminem. https://illuminem.com/illuminemvoices/about-the-green-colonialism-in-the-energy-transition

Baviskar, A. (1995). *In the belly of the river: Tribal conflicts over development in the Narmada Valley*. Oxford University Press., http://archive.org/details/inbellyofriver tr00bavi

Biomed Central, P. M. C. (2025). Carbon footprint and energy payback time of a micro wind turbine for distributed power generation. https://www.ncbi.nlm.nih.gov/pmc/articles/PMC12255746/

Bloomberg, N. E. F. (2023). *Energy transition investment trends 2023*. Bloomberg New Energy Finance.

Bond, P. (2016). Uneven development and the crisis of climate capitalism. In Panitch, L., & Albo, G. (Eds.), *Socialist Register 2017: Rethinking Revolution* (pp. 86–108). Monthly Review Press.

Bown, C. P. (2020). *How Trump's trade war hit renewable energy*. Peterson Institute for International Economics. https://www.piie.com

Bown, C. P. (2020). Trump's assault on the global trading system: And why decoupling from China will change everything. *Foreign Affairs, 99*(5), 120–130.

BRICS Energy Research Cooperation Platform. (2024). *BRICS energy cooperation roadmap 2025–2030*. New Development Bank.

Carmody, P. (2019). *The scramble for Africa in the 21st century: A view from the South*. Cambridge University Press.

Chagnon, C. W., Durante, F., Gills, B. K., Hagolani-Albov, S. E., Hokkanen, S., Kangasluoma, S. M. J., & Vuola, M. P. S. (2022). From extractivism to global extractivism: The evolution of an organizing concept. *The Journal of Peasant Studies, 49*(4), 760–792. DOI: 10.1080/03066150.2022.2069015

Chang, H. J. (2002). *Kicking away the ladder: Development strategy in historical perspective*. Anthem Press.

Chaturvedi, S., Fues, T., & Sidiropoulos, E. (Eds.). (2012). *Development cooperation and emerging powers: New partners or old patterns?* Zed Books.

Chen, Q., et al. (2023). River damming impacts on fish habitat and associated conservation measures. *Reviews of Geophysics*, 61, e2023RG000819.

Chimni, B. S. (2004). International institutions today: An imperial global state in the making. *European Journal of International Law, 15*(1), 1–37.

Climate Policy Initiative. (2021). *Global landscape of climate finance 2021*. https://www.climatepolicyinitiative.org/publication/global-landscape-of-climate-finance-2021/

Datta, R., Starlight, T., & Mistaken, D. C. (2024). Indigenous elder perspectives on climate change challenges and solutions: Learning reflection from Blackfoot First Nation perspectives, Canada. *AlterNative: An International Journal of Indigenous Peoples*. https://journals.sagepub.com/doi/full/10.1177/11771801241251869

Dunlap, A. (2018). Counterinsurgency for wind energy: The Bíi Hioxo Wind Park in Juchitán, Mexico. *The Journal of Peasant Studies, 45*(3), 630–652.

Duran, S., Hrenyk, J., Sahinyazan, F. G., & Salmon, E. (2024). Re-righting renewable energy research with indigenous communities in Canada. *Journal of Cleaner Production, 445*, 141264.

Earth.org. (2022). Nuclear energy carbon emissions lowest among electricity sources, UN reports. https://earth.org/nuclear-energy-carbon-emissions-lowest-among-electricity-sources-un-reports/

Earth.Org. (2023). *The hidden cost of green technologies.* https://earth.org/environmental-impact-green-mining/

Electric Power Research Institute. (2020). *Preliminary results: Wind turbine blade recycling: Recover, recycle, reuse*. EPRI.

Energy Charter Secretariat. (2021). *Investment arbitration cases under the Energy Charter Treaty.*

Eslava, L., Fakhri, M., & Nesiah, V. (Eds.). (2017). *Bandung, global history, and international law: Critical pasts and pending futures.* Cambridge University Press.

Fairhead, J., Leach, M., & Scoones, I. (2012). Green grabbing: A new appropriation of nature? *The Journal of Peasant Studies, 39*(2), 237–261.

Feminist Foreign Policy. (2025). Challenging entrenched power structures in the energy sector. https://h2diplo.de/wp-content/uploads/2025/02/Study-Report_Energy-Sector-Feminist-Foreign-Policy__final-1.pdf

Fenice Energy. (2024). Renewable energy in remote India: Case studies. Retrieved August 2025, Retrieved from https://feniceenergy.com/renewable-energy-in-remote-communities-case-study/

Franklin, J., & Williams, A. (2025, February 3). Donald Trump faces backlash from business as tariffs ignite inflation fears. *Financial Times.* https://www.ft.com/content/3cc26cc1-57e7-44d0-8c09-6c5dec30cc75

Gabor, D. (2021). The Wall Street consensus. *Development and Change, 52*(3), 429–459.

Gathii, J. T. (2011). *African regional trade agreements as legal regimes.* Cambridge University Press.

Ghosh, J., & Mazzucato, M. (2022). *Reforming development finance for climate goals.* Project Syndicate. https://www.project-syndicate.org

Gudynas, E. (2010). The new extractivism in South America. *The Brown Journal of World Affairs, 17*(2), 37–54.

Gulley, A. L. (2023). China, the Democratic Republic of the Congo, and artisanal cobalt mining from 2000 through 2020. *Proceedings of the National Academy of Sciences of the United States of America, 120*, e2212037120. PMID: 37339197

Heath, G. A.. (2020). Research and development priorities for silicon photovoltaic module recycling to support a circular economy. *Nature Energy, 12*(1), 1–10.

Hemeida, M. G., Hemeida, A. M., Senjyu, T., & Osheba, D. (2022). Renewable energy resources, technologies and life cycle assessment [Review]. *Energies*, *15*, 9417. DOI: 10.3390/en15249417

Hoekman, B. M., & Kostecki, M. M. (2009). *The political economy of the world trading system* (3rd ed.). Oxford University Press.

Howse, R. (2007). WTO dispute settlement and the "green economy". In Sampson, G., & Chambers, W. B. (Eds.), *Trade and environment: A resource book* (pp. 85–97). UNEP/IISD.

Hufbauer, G. C., & Jung, E. (2021, November 11). *Scoring 50 years of US industrial policy, 1970–2020.* Peterson Institute for International Economics. https://www.piie.com/publications/piie-briefings/2021/scoring-50-years-us-industrial-policy-1970-2020

IEA. (2023). *World Energy Investment Report 2023.* International Energy Agency. https://www.iea.org

Imasiku, K. (2025). The social impact of renewable energy on health systems in Kenya, Ghana, and Rwanda: A case study. *Journal of Sustainable Development, 13*(2). https://www.sdewes.org/jsdewes/pid13.0550

NEX Indonesia. (2025). *ASEAN Green Startups and the US-China Trade War: A Market Update.*

International Energy Agency. (2021). *The role of critical minerals in clean energy transitions*. IEA.

International Energy Agency. (2021, December 1). *Renewable electricity growth is accelerating faster than ever worldwide, supporting the emergence of the new global energy economy.* https://www.iea.org/news/renewable-electricity-growth-is-accelerating-faster-than-ever-worldwide-supporting-the-emergence-of-the-new-global-energy-economy

International Energy Agency. (2022). *Solar PV global supply chains*. https://www.iea.org/reports/solar-pv-global-supply-chains

International Energy Agency. (2022). *The role of critical minerals in clean energy transitions*. https://www.iea.org/reports/the-role-of-critical-minerals-in-clean-energy-transitions

International Energy Agency. (2023). *Renewables 2023: Analysis and forecasts*. IEA.

International Energy Agency. (2024). *World energy investment 2024.*

International Finance Corporation. (2021). *The business case for wind power in Africa.*

International Renewable Energy Agency (IRENA). (2021). World Energy Transitions Outlook: Transforming global energy system for a sustainable future. https://www.irena.org/publications/2021/March/World-Energy-Transitions-Outlook-2021

International Solar Alliance. (2023). *Annual report 2022–23: Towards 1000.* ISA Secretariat.

Jackson, J. H. (1997). *The world trading system: Law and policy of international economic relations* (2nd ed.). MIT Press.

Kara, S. (2023). *Cobalt red: How the blood of the Congo powers our lives.* St. Martin's Press.

Klinger, J. M. (2018). *Rare earth frontiers: From terrestrial subsoils to lunar landscapes.* Cornell University Press.

Leonhardt, R., Noble, B., Poelzer, G., Belcher, K., & Fitzpatrick, P. (2023). Government instruments for community renewable energy in northern and Indigenous communities. *Energy Policy*, *177*, 113560. DOI: 10.1016/j.enpol.2023.113560

Lin, B. (2025, April 18). Trump's tariffs threaten growth for Southeast Asia's clean energy startups. *Reccessary.* https://www.reccessary.com/en/news/asean-market/tariffs-disrupt-clean-energy-startups-southeast-asia

Loss, S. R., Will, T., & Marra, P. P. (2013). *Estimates of bird collision mortality at wind facilities in the contiguous United States.* https://repository.si.edu/xmlui/handle/10088/35192

Lovich, J. E., & Ennen, J. R. (2011). Wildlife conservation and solar energy development in the Desert Southwest, United States. *Bioscience*, *61*(12), 982–992.

Macknick, J. (2011). *Review of operational water consumption and withdrawal factors for electricity generating technologies.* National Renewable Energy Laboratory. https://research-hub.nrel.gov/en/publications/review-of-operational-water-consumption-and-withdrawal-factors-fo

Marceau, G. (2001). Conflicts of norms and conflicts of jurisdictions: The relationship between the WTO agreement and MEAs and other treaties. *Journal of World Trade*, *35*(6), 1081–1131.

Maskus, K., & Reichman, J. (2004). The globalization of private knowledge goods and the privatization of global public goods. *Journal of International Economic Law*, *7*(2), 279–320.

Maskus, K. E. (2012). *Private rights and public problems: The global economics of intellectual property in the 21st century.* Peterson Institute for International Economics.

Mejia Montero, L. F., ... (2023). An intersectional approach to energy justice. *Energy Research & Social Science.* https://www.research.ed.ac.uk/files/331400114/Mejia_MonteroEtalERSS2023AnIntersectionalApproachToEnergyJustice.pdf

Ministry of External Affairs. India. (2023). *International Solar Alliance: India's global leadership in renewable energy.* Government of India Press.

Montel Energy. (2025). How does renewable energy impact water use? https://montel.energy/resources/blog/how-does-renewable-energy-impact-water-use

Moore, J. W. (2015). *Capitalism in the web of life: Ecology and the accumulation of capital.* Verso.

Moore, J. W. (2015). *Capitalism in the web of life: Ecology and the accumulation of capital.* Verso.

Mususa, P. (2012). Mining, welfare and urbanisation: The wavering urban character of Zambia's Copperbelt. *Journal of Southern African Studies, 38*(2), 225–244.

National Renewable Energy Laboratory. (2021). *Impacts of Section 201 Tariffs on U.S. Solar Deployment.* https://www.nrel.gov

National Renewable Energy Laboratory (NREL). (2005). What is the energy payback for PV? https://www.nrel.gov/docs/fy05osti/37322.pdf

National Renewable Energy Laboratory (NREL). (2025). Life cycle assessment harmonization: Energy systems analysis. https://www.nrel.gov/analysis/life-cycle-assessment

Nixon, R. (2011). *Slow violence and the environmentalism of the poor.* Harvard University Press.

Nzongola-Ntalaja, G. (2002). *The Congo: From Leopold to Kabila: A people's history.* Zed Books.

OECD. (2023). *Critical Minerals for the Green Transition.* Organisation for Economic Co-operation and Development.

Our World in Data. (2022, June 15). How does the land use of different electricity sources compare? *Our World in Data Environmental Impacts.* https://ourworldindata.org/land-use-per-energy-source

Pauwelyn, J. (2019, July 7). *WTO dispute settlement post 2019: What to expect? What choice to make?* Social Science Research Network. https://papers.ssrn.com/abstract=3415964

Pellow, D. N. (2007). *Resisting global toxics: Transnational movements for environmental justice*. MIT Press.

Pomeroy, M. (2016). South–South cooperation and the changing aid landscape: Implications for development cooperation. *Third World Quarterly*, *37*(4), 579–596.

RAID. (2025). *Beneath the green: A critical look at the cost of industrial cobalt mining in the DRC*. https://raid-uk.org/post-library/report-beneath-the-green/

Reuters. (2024, December 17). *Congo files criminal complaints against Apple in Europe over conflict minerals*. https://www.reuters.com/sustainability/society-equity/congo-files-criminal-complaints-against-apple-europe-over-conflict-minerals-2024-12-17/

Reuters. (2025, February 27). *Paris prosecutor drops case against Apple over Congo minerals, document shows*. https://www.reuters.com/technology/paris-prosecutor-closes-case-against-apple-over-congo-minerals-document-2025-02-27/

Rignall, K. E. (2016). Solar power, state power, and the politics of energy transition in pre-Saharan Morocco. *Environment and Planning A. Economy and Space*, *48*(3), 540–557.

Rodrik, D. (2011). *The globalization paradox: Democracy and the future of the world economy*. W. W. Norton & Company.

Ross, W., & Zane, D. (2024, December 18). Apple accused of using conflict minerals. *BBC News*. https://www.bbc.com/news/

Sahoo, N., & Ashraf, J. (2021). Renewable energy cooperation between India and Brazil: Opportunities and challenges. *Energy Policy*, *158*, 112–125.

Sangvai, S. (2008). People's struggle in the Narmada Valley: Quest for just and sustainable development. In *Water conflicts in India*. Routledge India.

Savic, K., & Hoicka, C. E. (2023). Indigenous legal forms and governance structures in renewable energy: Assessing the role and perspectives of First Nations economic development corporations. *Energy Research & Social Science*, *101*, 103121. DOI: 10.1016/j.erss.2023.103121

Scholte, J. A. (2020). Civil society and global democracy. *Polity*.

Shadlen, K. C. (2008). Globalisation, power and integration: The political economy of regional and bilateral trade agreements in the Americas. *The Journal of Development Studies*, *44*(1), 1–20.

Shaffer, G. (2021). The WTO appellate body crisis and the challenge of multilateralism. In Shaffer, G. (Ed.), *Emerging powers and the world trading system* (pp. 219–240). Cambridge University Press.

Shiva, V. (1989). *Staying alive: Women, ecology and development.* Zed Books.

Smith, M.. (2024). *Empowering women through solar energy: Employment and inclusion in South Asia.* Renewable Energy Journal.

Smith, M., Shoaib, N., & Lal, P. (2025, July 18). Life cycle assessment of New Jersey offshore wind. *Wind Energy Science, 10*, 1389–1402. DOI: 10.5194/wes-10-1389-2025

State Grid Corporation of China. (2024). *BRICS countries join hands to promote green, low-carbon development.* China Three Gorges Corporation.

Stock, R. (2022). Triggering resistance: Contesting the injustices of solar park development in India. *Energy Research & Social Science*, *86*, 102464.

Sumaita, I. (2021). The importance of being earnestly innovative: The increasing role of intellectual property law in the global economy. *The University of Cincinnati Intellectual Property and Computer Law Journal, 6*(1), Article 9.

Sze, J. (2020). *Environmental justice in a moment of danger* (1st ed., Vol. 11). University of California Press., https://www.jstor.org/stable/j.ctvqmp3jn

Temper, L., Del Bene, D., & Martinez-Alier, J. (2020). Mapping the frontiers and front lines of global environmental justice: The EJAtlas. *Journal of Political Ecology*, *27*(1), 819–847.

Terazono, E., & Sanderson, H. (2017, March 5). Electric cars: China's battle for the battery market. *Financial Times.*

The White House. (2025, February 13). *Fact sheet: President Donald J. Trump announces "Fair and Reciprocal Plan" on trade.* https://www.whitehouse.gov/fact-sheets/2025/02/fact-sheet-president-donald-j-trump-announces-fair-and-reciprocal-plan-on-trade/

Thompson, D.. (2020). The importance of design in lithium ion battery recycling – A critical review. *Green Chemistry*, *23*, 2718–2733.

Tienhaara, K. (2018). *Green Keynesianism and the global financial crisis*. Routledge.

UNCTAD. (2022). *The Commodities and Development Report 2022: Harnessing the Potential of Critical Minerals for Sustainable Development.*

UNESCO. (2024, April 23). Water and energy. *UN World Water Development Report 2024.* https://www.unesco.org/reports/wwdr/en/2024/energy

UNFCCC. (2025). *Technology mechanism and climate innovation.* https://unfccc.int/ttclear/

United Nations Conference on Trade and Development. (2022). *Trade and environment review.*

United Nations Environment Programme. (2023). *Greening trade.* https://www.unep.org/resources/report/greening-trade

United Nations Framework Convention on Climate Change. (1992). *UNFCCC*, 1771 UNTS 107. (Entered into force 21 March 1994)

United Nations Office of the High Representative for the Least Developed Countries, Landlocked Developing Countries and Small Island Developing States (UN-OHRLLS). (2021). *Small Island Developing States in numbers: Climate change* (edition 2021). United Nations.

United States International Trade Commission. (2018). *Section 201 global safeguard investigations on crystalline silicon photovoltaic cells* (USITC Pub No. 4739).

U.S. Geological Survey. (2023). *Critical minerals supply chains: A strategy and implementation plan.* https://www.usgs.gov

U.S. Geological Survey. (2023). *Mineral commodity summaries: Cobalt.* USGS.

US Geological Survey. (2023). *Mineral Commodity Summaries 2023.*

Wang, G. (2024). Gender and development: Fuel feminine energy to Africa's clean energy transition. *LSE International Development Blog.* https://blogs.lse.ac.uk/internationaldevelopment/2024/09/04/gender-and-development-fuel-feminine-energy-in-africas-clean-energy-transition/

Wesselkämper, J.. (2024). Towards circular battery supply chains: Strategies to reduce material demand and the impact on mining and recycling. *Resources Policy, 95*, 105160.

Winther, T., ... (2020). Gendered access to solar electricity in rural Kenya: Constraints and opportunities. *Energy Research & Social Science.* https://www.sei.org/wp-content/uploads/2020/04/assessing-the-gender-and-social-equity-dimensions-of-energy-transitions-2020.pdf

World Bank. (2020). *Minerals for climate action: The mineral intensity of the clean energy transition*. World Bank Group.

World Bank. (2024). *Republic of Congo economic update: Designing fiscal instruments for sustainable forestry and economic growth*. https://www.worldbank.org/en/news/press-release/2024/08/13/republic-of-congo-economic-update-designing-fiscal-instruments-for-sustainable-forestry-and-economic-growth

World Commission on Dams. (2016). *Dams and development: A new framework for decision-making*. Routledge.

World Intellectual Property Organization. (2024). *World Intellectual Property Indicators 2024: Patents highlights*. WIPO. Retrieved from https://www.wipo.int/web-publications/world-intellectual-property-indicators-2024-highlights/en/patents-highlights.html

World Nuclear Association. (2024). Comparison of lifecycle greenhouse gas emissions of various electricity generation sources. https://world-nuclear.org/information-library/energy-and-environment/comparison-of-lifecycle-greenhouse-gas-emissions-of-various-electricity-generation-sources.aspx

World Trade Organization. (1994). *Agreement on Trade-Related Aspects of Intellectual Property Rights*, 1869 UNTS 299, art. 31.

World Trade Organization. (1994). *Agreement on Trade-Related Aspects of Intellectual Property Rights (TRIPS)*, 1869 UNTS 299.

World Trade Organization. (1994). *General Agreement on Tariffs and Trade (GATT) 1994*, art. XX.

World Trade Organization. (2014). *Appellate Body Reports, China – Rare Earths*, WT/DS431/AB/R, WT/DS432/AB/R, WT/DS433/AB/R.

WTO. (1995). *The results of the Uruguay Round of multilateral trade negotiations: The legal texts*. World Trade Organization.

WTO. (2014). *China – Measures Related to the Exportation of Rare Earths, Tungsten and Molybdenum: Appellate Body Report, DS431*.

WTO. (2016). *India – Certain Measures Relating to Solar Cells and Solar Modules: Panel and Appellate Body Reports, DS456*.

Yang, H., Zhang, L., Liu, H., Wang, Y., & Hao, C. (2024). A comparative study on the combination of life cycle assessment and ecological footprints: Solar photovoltaic power generation vs. coal power generation in Ningxia. *Frontiers in Energy Research, 12*. Advance online publication. DOI: 10.3389/fenrg.2024.1375820

Zarfl, C., Lumsdon, A. E., Berlekamp, J., Tydecks, L., & Tockner, K. (2015). A global boom in hydropower dam construction. *Aquatic Sciences*, *77*(1), 161–170.

Zolyniak, A. (2021, December 1). An environmentalist case for resurrecting the WTO appellate body. *Council on Foreign Relations*. https://www.cfr.org/blog/environmentalist-case-resurrecting-wto-appellate-body

KEY TERMS AND DEFINITIONS

Carbon Border Adjustment Mechanism (CBAM): An EU trade measure that imposes tariffs on imports based on carbon content.

Circular Economy: An approach to reducing waste and resource extraction through reuse and recycling; in this chapter it is critiqued for reproducing labor exploitation and gender inequities in recycling sectors.

Colonial Legacies: Historical structures of extraction and dispossession established under colonial rule that continue to shape trade, development, and energy systems today.

Displacement: The forced removal or marginalization of communities, especially indigenous and rural populations, due to the siting of large-scale renewable projects.

Energy Transition: The global shift from fossil fuels to low-carbon and renewable energy sources (e.g., solar, wind, hydropower). While often presented as a universal good, the transition also raises questions of justice, governance, and ecological limits when analyzed beyond its technical or economic dimensions.

Extractivism: An economic and political model centered on large-scale removal of natural resources for export, often with minimal local benefit and significant social and ecological harm.

Green Colonialism: The extension of colonial patterns of exploitation under the banner of sustainability, where renewable projects extract resources or occupy land in ways that replicate earlier extractive logics.

Just Energy Transition: A principle emphasizing that the renewable energy shift must avoid reproducing inequalities, ensuring protection and inclusion of vulnerable groups.

Life Cycle Assessment (LCA): A method of evaluating the total environmental impact of a product or technology across its entire lifespan, from raw material extraction and manufacturing to use and disposal.

Renewable Waste: End-of-life materials from solar panels, wind turbines, and batteries, which pose ecological and social challenges that mainstream energy transition narratives understate.

TRIPS (Trade-Related Aspects of Intellectual Property Rights): A WTO agreement on patents and intellectual property.

World Trade Organization (WTO): The global trade body whose dispute settlement rulings show how trade rules often limit the policy space of Global South states seeking to promote domestic renewable energy industries.

Section 3
Justice, Agency, and Social Struggles

Chapter 7
Climate Justice in the Global South

Defne Gönenç
https://orcid.org/0000-0002-5084-2447
Middle East Technical University, Northern Cyprus Campus, Cyprus

ABSTRACT

This chapter explores the concept of climate justice in the context of the Global South, emphasizing the disproportionate impacts of climate change on historically marginalized nations and communities. It first traces the evolution of climate justice from its roots in environmental justice, highlighting how the movement has expanded to address global power imbalances and historical responsibility for carbon emissions. The theoretical framework of climate justice is analyzed through four key dimensions: distributional, procedural, recognitional, and capacity-related justice. The chapter then examines the practical applications of climate justice by assessing global emissions data, coal-related conflicts, and the concept of "climate debt," which holds historically high-emitting countries accountable for financing mitigation and adaptation efforts. Additionally, it discusses within-country inequalities and the role of redistributive policies, such as wealth taxation.

INTRODUCTION

Climate justice has risen as an issue of great importance both in developed countries and especially for those living in the Global South (Coolsaet et al., 2025). In a nutshell, the concept examines how unevenly communities cause and suffer from the impacts of climate change and how differently they contribute to the transition process to renewable economies (Roberts & Parks, 2007, 2009; Okereke, 2010). The Global South, often characterized by colonial exploitation, lower levels of in-

DOI: 10.4018/979-8-3373-1707-6.ch007

dustrialization, and significant poverty and inequality, has been disproportionately suffering from the consequences of climate change, which are mostly caused by the historical carbon emissions from the Global North (Ngcamu 2023; Newell et al., 2021). The uneven distribution of the impacts of climate change is a reflection of the post-colonial world, characterized by persisting structural inequalities and power asymmetries that continue to structure the global political and economic order (Sultana, 2021).

Climate change is already causing natural disasters in the Global South, such as severe hurricanes, droughts, and rising sea levels, destroying hundreds of communities and intensifying existing socio-economic inequalities. These problems were further reinforced when countries struggled to meet the $5 trillion a year financial needs for climate adaptation and mitigation in the Global South at COP29 in Baku, Azerbaijan. The promises of $300 billion, much of which are loans, fall well short of what will be needed to head off the crisis (Guardian, 2024).

The chapter compromises of two parts; namely, climate justice in theory and climate justice in application. The first part starts with a discussion of the evolution from environmental justice to climate justice, examining how the focus has expanded from an initial focus on the local environmental justice issues in the U.S. to encompass global equity issues and problems in the Global South arising out of climate change. A detailed analysis follows of climate justice theory, focusing on its four key dimensions: distributional, procedural, recognitional, and capacity-related justice. The theoretical part finishes by discussing the analytical strength of climate justice concept vis-à-vis other environmental theories.

The chapter then examines the practical application of climate justice through the lens of emissions data, comparing CO_2 emissions from top emitter countries and analyzing historical emissions trends. It also highlights the global distribution of coal-related conflicts, emphasizing their disproportionate concentration in countries of the Global South. The chapter then addresses the climate debt concept, which calls that high-emitting countries, with more of a historical responsibility, bear an obligation to pay for mitigation and adaptation in the Global South (Roberts & Parks, 2009). The chapter also addresses within-country climate injustices, focusing on how socio-economic inequalities exacerbate vulnerability to climate change impacts, both within nations in addition to among nations. Lastly, the chapter calls for redistribution, as a tool of climate justice, with the aim of allowing poor countries and communities access low-carbon pathways.

This chapter concludes that a just, inclusive, and historically informed climate policy is essential for tackling the pressing challenges of today, as well as those we will have to face in the future.

CLIMATE JUSTICE IN THEORY

Tracing the Evolution: From Environmental Justice to Climate Justice

The alteration from environmental justice to climate justice represents a noteworthy move in both scale and scope. While environmental justice movements historically focused on the local impacts of pollution, toxic waste, and industrial hazards, climate justice handles these concerns at global power structures and within systemic inequalities (Schlosberg & Collins, 2014). The climate justice movement critiques the disproportionate burden that climate change places on low-income communities, Indigenous peoples, and Global South nations while also addressing the historical responsibility of high-emitting industrialized countries. In this regard, climate justice is not only concerned with the mitigation and adaptation efforts of different countries but also with the fundamental reorganization of global economic and political structures that have perpetuated environmental harm and exploitation (Tokar, 2014).

The roots of environmental justice can be traced to grassroots movements in the United States during the 1970s and 1980s, where predominantly Black, Indigenous, and low-income communities protested the siting of hazardous waste facilities, toxic dumps, and industrial pollution in their neighborhoods (Bullard, 1990). The landmark 1982 protests in Warren County, North Carolina, against the disposal of PCB-contaminated soil catalyzed the national environmental justice movement. This movement highlighted how environmental degradation was not distributed equally but was deeply intertwined with race, class, and economic marginalization (McGurty, 2009). Similar movements emerged in other parts of the world, as marginalized communities organized against extractive industries, deforestation, and water privatization, all of which disproportionately affected their health and livelihoods (Martinez-Alier, 2002). These battles provided the basis for a more general critique of environmental governance, which favored a corporation-led and state-directed development at the expense of local marginalized communities.

The concept of environmental justice was developed as a critique of traditional environmentalism by its lack of consideration of social inequalities. Mainstream environmental groups have historically focused on conservation and wilderness protection at the expense of how environmental hazards and risks impact low-income communities and communities of color. Environmental justice activists said environmental protection should not be separated from larger fights for civil rights, public health, and economic justice. This argument received additional credibility through the application of social science methods demonstrating that there were racial and economic differences in exposure to related environmental risks (Pellow, 2000).

By reframing environmental issues as social justice concerns, activists successfully challenged dominant environmental discourses and reshaped public narratives on sustainability and equity.

As the global climate crisis mounted, activists, academics, and policymakers understood that concerns with environmental justice cannot be limited to local or national struggles. Global warming intensifies discrimination and disparities, enhancing inequity in existing systems, and disproportionately impacting those least responsible (Roberts & Parks, 2007). As the global climate crisis mounted, activists, academics, and policymakers came to understand that concerns with environmental justice could not be limited to local or national struggles. Global warming compounds discrimination and disparities, enhancing inequity in existing systems, and disproportionately impacting those least responsible (Roberts & Parks, 2007). Climate justice emerged from the roots of environmental justice but broadens the attention from pollution and land-use conflicts to encompass questions of global equity, responsibilities toward future generations, and the historical responsibilities of industrialized countries (Newell, 2022; Shue, 2014). This wider context draws attention to the idea that climate change is inextricably bound up with colonial histories, regimes of resource extraction, and uneven development (Malm & Hornborg, 2014). For example, as a result of colonialism, many Global South countries are economically dependent on extractive industries and are thus more exposed to climate-related disruptions and have a reduced ability to transition towards low-carbon economies (Bassey, 2012).

Despite demands for climate justice delivered by several countries, the UNFCCC failed to provide justice, since power imbalances governed the negotiations by consolidating the unjust status quo (Lefstad & Paavola, 2023; Hurlbert, 2015). In fact, a large portion of citizens in all countries exhibit a lack of trust in international climate agreements too (Schleich et al., 2014). The dominance of powerful developed countries and transnational corporate interests in international climate governance has generally led to responses which favor market-based instruments such as carbon trading and offset regimes over radical overhauls of global energy and economic systems (Bachram, 2004). This failure reflects the broader structural barriers that climate justice advocates seek to dismantle, including the continued prioritization of economic growth over ecological and social well-being. As we move forward, climate justice movements are embracing more transnational activism, legal challenges, and alternative policy frameworks to challenge for more equitable climate action that attends to the rights and needs of those most directly affected (Mohan, 2025; Temper et al., 2018).

The Four Dimensions of Climate Justice

The theory of climate justice is multi-dimensional and captures the inequalities in climate vulnerability and the structural obstacles to addressing it. Aspects like the so-called distributional, procedural, recognitional, and capacity dimensions of climate justice provide a comprehensive framework to understand how climate change impacts disadvantaged people and what can be done to promote justice. Table 1 summarizes these four dimensions and their potential contours for climate justice in the Global South.

Table 1. Multiple Dimensions of Climate Justice

Dimension	Definition	Relevance to the Global South
Distributional Justice	Fair allocation of climate burdens and benefits	The unequal distribution of climate risks and adaptation resources disproportionately affects vulnerable communities
Procedural Justice	Inclusion and participation in decision-making	Many communities in the Global South lack representation in climate governance at national and international levels
Recognitional Justice	Acknowledgment of diverse identities, histories, and vulnerabilities	Indigenous and marginalized groups often face systemic exclusion and discrimination in climate policies
Capacity-Related Justice	Strengthening local adaptive and mitigation capacities	Limited financial, technological, and institutional capacities hinder effective climate responses

Distributional Justice

Distributional justice concerns the equitable allocation of climate-related burdens and benefits across social groups, geographic regions, and generations (Caney, 2009; Page, 2008; Schlosberg, 2007). In the Global South, where climate change amplifies existing socio-economic inequalities, these injustices are multi-layered. First, the wealthiest individuals and countries—historically and presently—are responsible for the majority of greenhouse gas emissions, while low-income populations have contributed the least (Chancel, 2022; Roberts & Parks, 2007). Second, the impacts of climate change, including extreme weather events, rising sea levels, and resource depletion, disproportionately harm the poor, who often lack financial and infrastructural resilience (IPCC, 2022). Third, despite their lower historical responsibility and greater vulnerability, marginalized communities frequently bear a disproportionate share of climate mitigation and adaptation costs (see Table 2). Policies such as regressive carbon taxes and offset programs can place an undue burden on those least responsible while allowing wealthier actors to continue polluting (Bumpus & Liverman, 2008).

Table 2. Layers of Distributional Climate Injustice

Layer of Injustice	Description
1. Unequal Responsibility	The wealthiest individuals and countries have historically contributed to the greenhouse gas emissions more than the poor.
2. Unequal Impacts	The poorest communities and countries suffer the most from climate change, despite their minimal contributions, as they have fewer resources to adapt and recover.
3. Unequal Contributions to Solutions	The poor often bear a disproportionately higher burden in addressing climate change, contributing more relative to their income and resources, while wealthier actors avoid responsibility.

For instance, the Horn of Africa has faced recurrent droughts, disproportionately devastating smallholder farmers and pastoralist communities who contribute minimally to global emissions. Yet, climate finance remains highly skewed, with wealthier developing countries securing a larger share of adaptation funds, leaving least-developed nations struggling to access essential support (Barrett, 2013). Additionally, carbon trading schemes and large-scale renewable energy projects have, in some cases, led to land dispossession rather than equitable climate benefits, exacerbating existing social and economic inequalities (Newell & Mulvaney, 2013).

Addressing these distributional injustices requires a transformative approach to climate finance and governance. This includes scaling up loss and damage funding, ensuring that adaptation resources prioritize the most vulnerable, and restructuring mitigation mechanisms to avoid reinforcing inequalities. Without explicit attention to these disparities, climate policies risk entrenching, rather than alleviating, global climate injustices.

Procedural Justice

Procedural justice concerns the fairness of decision-making processes, emphasizing not only participation but also the meaningful incorporation of diverse voices in climate governance (Young, 2000). While formal mechanisms exist to include Global South actors in climate discussions, participation alone does not guarantee influence. True procedural justice demands that the perspectives of historically marginalized stakeholders are not only acknowledged but also translated into concrete policy outcomes (Schlosberg, 2007).

At the global level, international climate negotiations remain skewed toward high-emitting industrialized nations, with decision-making power concentrated in wealthier states and corporate interests (Okereke, 2008). While platforms such as the United Nations Framework Convention on Climate Change (UNFCCC) provide opportunities for Global South representation, these states often lack the political leverage to shape agreements in ways that reflect their priorities (Roberts & Parks, 2007). Merely having a seat at the table does not equate to influence if dominant actors dismiss or dilute Global South demands, such as calls for climate finance, adaptation support, and technology transfers (Newell, 2005).

At the national level, procedural justice is also compromised by the lack of state capacity and weak institutions, coupled with political instability and limited civil society participation. Marginalized communities – Indigenous peoples, women, rural populations – are often systematically excluded, with their issues overlooked or co-opted by elite interests. However, effective procedural justice needs to contain procedures that can secure not only consultation but also the actual inclusion of different points of view into the policy process (Dryzek, 2000). Such mechanisms would include legally binding protocols for participatory decision-making, transparent governance structures, and strong backing for citizen movements calling for climate justice (Temper et al., 2018). Without them, procedural justice runs the risk of being an empty norm, unmet by genuine opportunities for transformation in climate governance.

Recognitional Justice

Recognition justice is a basic tenet of climate justice, which recognizes that historical and structural inequalities between populations, the plurality of identities, as well as diverse local knowledge systems, must be considered in climate policies (Fraser, 2009). It transcends distributive justice, which involves the fair apportioning of resources, by delving into social and cultural notions of justice—ensuring marginalized communities are not merely invited to be in the decision-making of climate policy but that their knowledge, beliefs, and rights are respected (Schlosberg, 2007).

In the Global South, the failure to acknowledge the distinct vulnerabilities, contributions, and governance systems of Indigenous peoples and other vulnerable groups has led to climate policies that exclude them and do not deliver for them. For example, Indigenous peoples around the world in Latin America, Africa, and Asia have historically been the guardians of biodiversity and traditional ecological knowledge; however, their land and resource rights are often ignored in climate change adaptation and mitigation (Whyte, 2017). These people have traditional knowledge that contributes to sustainable land use, conservation, and disaster resilience, but they are excluded from the climate policy discourse that often favors technocratic and Western science-driven solutions to climate governance (Kashwan, 2020).

One of the primary concerns of recognitional justice is the manner in which projects at the scale of climate projects—such as forestry, carbon offsets, and renewable energy—impact, displace, and dispossess local communities. Indeed, even the United Nations Reduced Emissions from Deforestation and Forest Degradation (UN-REDD+) afforestation initiatives, whose normative, market-supported goals for the conservation of forests would seem to be in line with the rights and needs of forest-dwelling communities, have at times limited the access Indigenous peoples have to their traditional lands and their traditional ways of life (Temper et al., 2018).

To address these injustices, climate policies must integrate diverse epistemologies, respect Indigenous land rights, and ensure that adaptation strategies are co-designed with affected populations. Recognitional justice requires a decolonial approach to climate governance, one that actively challenges the historical marginalization of Indigenous and local knowledge systems in favor of Eurocentric frameworks (Escobar, 2018). This involves fostering participatory decision-making processes that grant marginalized communities full agency in shaping climate action, rather than treating them as passive recipients of externally designed policies (Sultana, 2021). Gender is also a crucial but often neglected dimension of recognitional climate justice. Women in the Global South—particularly those engaged in subsistence agriculture, water collection, and informal care economies—are disproportionately affected by climate shocks. Without a gender perspective, climate governance runs the risk of continuing to reproduce patriarchal structures beneath a veneer of inclusivity.

Hence, incorporating recognitional justice into climate governance is not just an ethical imperative; it is also essential for building effective, equitable, and culturally appropriate climate solutions. Without the meaningful inclusion of Indigenous and marginalized perspectives, climate policies risk perpetuating the very injustices they seek to resolve.

Capacity-Related Justice

Capacity-related aspect of climate justice pays special attention to achieving fair outcomes, not just equal inputs. From this angle, while every community needs support in order to deal with climate change, others—those that are marginalized, like the elderly or from low-income groups—are even more vulnerable and need proportionally larger amounts of help so as not to see comparatively unjust outcomes. Governments thus need to provide different levels of assistance to deal with these disparities. This is particularly so in reconstruction support and adaptation measures (Roberts & Parks, 2007). For instance, people with physical and cognitive disabilities typically see higher mortality rates in climate disasters due to inaccessible evacuation routes, health systems that are not good enough or even fail them completely, and a lack of targeted adaptation measures. Yet disability seldom features in climate finance frameworks or adaptation planning. Disability-inclusive policies, such as accessible infrastructure, early warning systems that take into account sensory needs, and social protection programmes are necessary to ensure that capacity-building efforts can reach all possible vulnerable groups.

To promote capacity-related climate justice, strengthening South-South cooperation in climate technology transfer and enhancing institutional capacities for long-term resilience are essential. Furthermore, capacity-building efforts should recognize and integrate local expertise, empowering communities to lead climate adaptation initiatives in ways that reflect their specific needs and vulnerabilities (Schlosberg, 2012).

To sum, while these four dimensions of justice are useful analytical categories, critics warn that they can become depoliticized if treated descriptively. Without attention to the structural drivers of inequality, they risk serving managerial or Northern-centric agendas rather than advancing transformative justice.

Expanding Justice: From Local Struggles to Global Equity

While early environmental justice movements primarily focused on localized struggles in the U.S., climate justice extends the conversation to global structural inequalities. Climate change is not just an environmental problem; it deeply reflects historic patterns of economic exploitation, imperialism, and global power asymmetries (Okereke 2010).

The transition from environmental justice to climate justice occurred because scholars, activists, and policymakers recognized that people living on the margins are likely to suffer the brunt of climate changes (Roberts, 2007; Pellow et al. 2021). Climate justice has highlighted one important fact: climate change is primarily driven by the developed nations of the Global North, which have historically emitted most greenhouse gases. North America, Canada, and the European Union over centuries built their wealth on carbon-intensive industrialization, leaving the poorer developing countries in Africa, Asia, or Latin America—many of those historic bad boys were subjected to colonial exploitation of one kind or another—to suffer consequences despite being least responsible for creating it. This disparity has become a key issue in the current negotiations on international climate policy.

A turning point in climate justice discourse occurred when the United Nations adopted a principle of common but differentiated responsibilities and respective capacities (CBDR-RC) at its 1992 Earth Summit with signatory countries in Rio de Janeiro. This placed all countries responsible for dealing with climate change while industrialized nations had even greater responsibility because of their past emissions and stronger economies (Roberts, 2007). However, the refusal of developed nations as yet to meet their financial and technological obligations has only deepened tensions between those countries, thus reinforcing the feeling that international climate policy benefits richer nations more than others and leaving people in developing countries—poorer ones—with few resources for adjustment or mitigation (Klein 2014).

The major turning point of climate justice work came at the 2009 Copenhagen Climate Summit (COP15). At the Summit, countries in the Global South—led by the Indian government and its African allies—called for aid and technology from developed countries as they make their transition into countries with lower greenhouse gas emissions. Yet at this time developed countries could not agree on any substantial commitments of climate finance or binding emissions reductions, causing widespread frustration within developing countries and among grassroots activists fighting for climate justice (Kaur & Verma, 2025; Newell & Mulvaney 2013).

Adoption of Climate Justice in the Global South

The term Global South refers to a range of countries, primarily in Africa, Latin America, Asia, and the Pacific, that share historical experiences of colonialism, economic marginalization, and structural inequalities in the global economy. Rather than just a geographical concept, it is a political and economic term that highlights the division of wealth, power, and development level between developed nations and countries historically influenced politically or economically by other states (Dados & Connell, 2012).

The term "Global South" originated in post-colonial and dependency theories, which hold that the world's economic power is unevenly distributed and that much of it was exploited from poorer countries during the period of colonialism (Ghosh, 2015). During the 20th century, many countries in the Global South had political independence while being financially dependent on former colonial powers and related institutions such as the International Monetary Fund (IMF) or World Bank. Consequently, their development paths conformed to this pattern (Amin, 1976).

The concept of the Global South now widely serves as a convenient shorthand for describing the inequalities that structure world politics, development, and environment. The Global South will suffer from environmental catastrophes, climate disruption, and resource scarcity on an unequal scale to the point of total helplessness (Roberts & Parks, 2007). Many of these people depend heavily on agriculture, fishing, or mining for their subsistence. Therefore, they are uniquely vulnerable to climate-related crises of a particularly local kind like drought, desertification, and inundation by sea. As a result, climate justice movements in the Global South focus not only on demanding reparations and financial support from wealthier nations (Gifford & Sauls, 2024) but also on resisting extractivist economic models and advocating for alternative, community-led solutions to climate change (Ogunbode, 2022).

While the climate justice discourse initially gained traction in academic and activist circles in the Global North, it has since been widely embraced in the Global South (Audet, 2013). Southern movements have reframed climate justice beyond legal and financial demands to emphasize issues such as land rights, indigenous sovereignty, food security, and alternative development models that reject neoliberal approaches to climate governance. These movements challenge the dominant paradigm that treats climate change as merely an issue of emissions reduction, instead framing it as a symptom of deeper systemic injustices, including economic dependency, land dispossession, and corporate-driven environmental destruction (Bond, 2012).

One of the earliest and most influential movements to adopt climate justice language in the Global South was La Via Campesina, an international peasant movement advocating for food sovereignty and sustainable agriculture. The organization argues that industrial agriculture—driven by multinational corporations and wealthy nations—contributes significantly to climate change while displacing small farmers and indigenous communities (Martínez-Torres & Rosset, 2010; Hall et al., 2023). La Via Campesina has been a vocal critic of climate policies that prioritize market-based mechanisms such as carbon trading, which it sees as a distraction from real solutions rooted in agroecology, land redistribution, and community-driven adaptation strategies (Taşdemir Yaşın, 2022). More recently, emerging debates critique how AI-driven monitoring and predictive tools, though touted as climate solutions, may amplify existing inequalities if not reoriented through a Global South lens (Mathur & Chamuah, 2025).

Similarly, climate justice has become a key demand of indigenous movements across Latin America, Africa, and Asia. Groups such as the Indigenous Environmental Network (IEN) (Mossett & Caldwell, 2016) and the Pan African Climate Justice Alliance (PACJA) have opposed fossil fuel extraction, deforestation, and carbon market schemes that commodify nature rather than protecting Indigenous and local rights (Allen, 2015; Bond, 2017; Escobar, 2018). Many of these movements emphasize the principle of ecological debt, arguing that the Global North owes reparations to the Global South not only for historical carbon emissions but also for centuries of resource extraction and environmental degradation (Simms, 2009).

In Latin America, climate justice resonates closely with Indigenous and Afro-descendant protests against extractivist industries. Countries such as Ecuador and Bolivia have embedded rights in their constitution for nature, inspired by an Indigenous viewpoint that sees human well-being and environmental health as intertwined (Gudynas, 2011); at the same time, countries such as Ecuador and Bolivia have established laws that protect Mother Earth. In Africa, climate justice has turned into a point of focus for resistance to land grabbing, water privatization, and the expansion of fossil fuel projects backed by multinationals (Bond, 2012). In Asia, climate justice movements have arisen as a response to rapid industrialization, deforestation, and population displacement caused by natural disasters. In India, organizations like the National Alliance of People's Movements (NAPM) and the Centre for Science and Environment (CSE) advocate for climate justice using the argument that environmental degradation is linked to historical injustice and economic inequality (Agarwal & Narain, 1991; Kashwan, 2022). In China, environmental groups such as Friends of Nature (FON) and the China Climate Action Network (CCAN) push for stricter climate policies while highlighting inequalities in burdens from pollution among marginal communities (Shapiro, 2016). In Southeast Asia, groups like Wahana Lingkungan Hidup Indonesia (WALHI) in Indonesia and Kalikasan People's Network for the Environment in the Philippines resist broad-brush forest felling and mining, large-scale deforestation, and oil drilling expansion that impacts severely on Indigenous and low-income communities (Delina, 2021). In these regions, climate justice action increasingly articulates itself as a fight against local and global economic structures beleaguered by environmental injustice that also heightens disparities.

Climate Justice vs. Other Climate Governance Approaches

Approaches to climate governance differ significantly in their underlying assumptions about the relationship between economic systems, environmental sustainability, and social justice. Climate justice, ecological modernization, green growth, and market environmentalism suggest specific approaches to addressing developments in the environment (and emergent issues such as global warming) involving different framings around responsibility, economic structure, and policy instruments. Climate justice, for example, focuses on the historical and structural inequalities at the root of climate change and the disproportionate impacts on marginalized communities and the need for transformative, community-driven solutions (Newell & Mulvaney, 2013).

In contrast, ecological modernization and green growth focus on reform rather than revolution, in which the environmental challenges can be tackled through technological innovation and institutional change within the boundaries of the existing economic system (Mol & Sonnenfeld, 2000; OECD, 2011). Market environmentalism, which is closely associated with green growth, believes that environmental protection can be incorporated into markets by using tools such as carbon pricing and emission trading (Paterson, 2021). Though they are united in their desire to combat climate change, they differ widely in their view on equity, economic transformation, and the place of markets in sustainability.

Environmental modernization and green growth both argue that it is possible for economic growth and environmental sustainability to act as complementary rather than contradictory targets. Ecological modernization, however, emphasizes technological innovation, better institutional frameworks, and corporate conduct to develop a more efficient and less resource-hungry economy (Mol & Sonnenfeld, 2000). Likewise, green growth advocates policies that aim to disentangle economic growth from environmental damages and calls for state-led investments in renewable energy, green infrastructure, and the circular economy (OECD, 2011).

To the extent that they recognize the necessity of systemic change, these approaches still remain trapped within the framework of capitalism, least of all because they also all assume that sustainability can be achieved by making only superficial changes to thc modc of production. Market environmentalism develops this further, thereby situating environmental governance at the heart of economic markets—carbon credits, emissions trading, and monetary incentives drive the move towards sustainable practice (Böhm et al., 2012). The issue critics raise is that these mechanisms work to the advantage of richer states and corporations, permitting them to go on polluting while forwarding the costs to less affluent regions of the world, especially in the Global South (Newell & Mulvaney, 2013).

Market environmentalism becomes aligned with both of these strategies of depoliticization; climate justice, by contrast, is a frontal assault on the depoliticizing aspects of markets and technological hyper-fixes. Many on the market-environmental side will dismiss both of these approaches as less mature, less practical, or less well thought through. Thus, market environmentalism denies the fundamentally economic sources of vulnerability and resilience, paving the path for climate justice, which does not integrate environmental concerns within already historically inequitable institutions and instead proposes their complete overhaul.

Climate Justice in Practice: Emissions and Responsibilities

Climate justice demands a fair and historically informed approach to emissions responsibility. However, prevailing climate governance frameworks often emphasize present-day emissions without adequately accounting for historical contributions or global economic interdependencies. This creates a distorted picture—one that frequently shifts blame onto large emitters in the Global South while downplaying the role of industrialized nations in driving the climate crisis. A just approach to emissions must incorporate multiple perspectives: cumulative emissions, per capita emissions, and consumption-based emissions. This section highlights these dimensions, exposing disparities in responsibility and their implications for global climate policy.

Greenhouse gas emissions are commonly measured by total national output. This method, while straightforward, masks significant inequalities in emissions distribution across populations. As can be seen in Figure 1, as of 2023, the top five CO_2

emitters by total volume were: China, the United States, India, Russia and Japan. (Our World in Data, 2023)

Figure 1. Annual CO2 Emissions, 2023

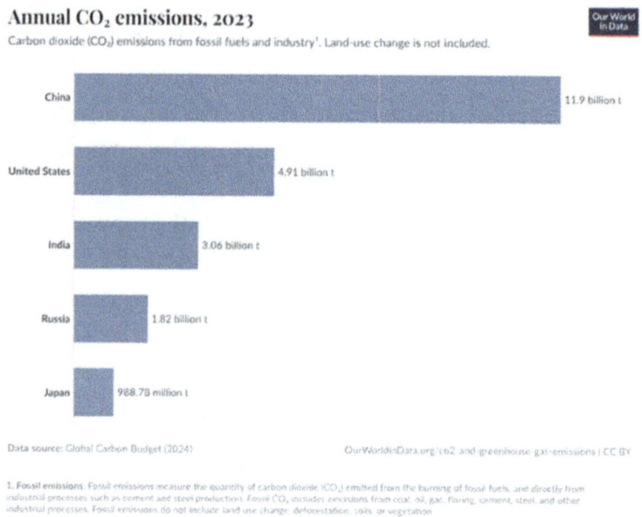

While this ranking suggests that China, India, and other Global South nations are the primary contributors to climate change, it fails to account for population size and energy demands tied to economic development. A more just measure is per capita emissions, which show a starkly different ranking (see Figure 2): Qatar, Brunei, Bahrain, Trinidad and Tobago, and Saudi Arabia.

By contrast, the per capita emissions of much larger developing economies—such as India (2.1 metric tons) or Indonesia (2.6 metric tons)—are significantly lower. This suggests that the nations driving global emissions growth are not necessarily those with the highest individual carbon footprints but rather those with large populations undergoing industrialization (Our World in Data, 2023).

Figure 2. Annual Per Capita CO2 Emissions, 2023

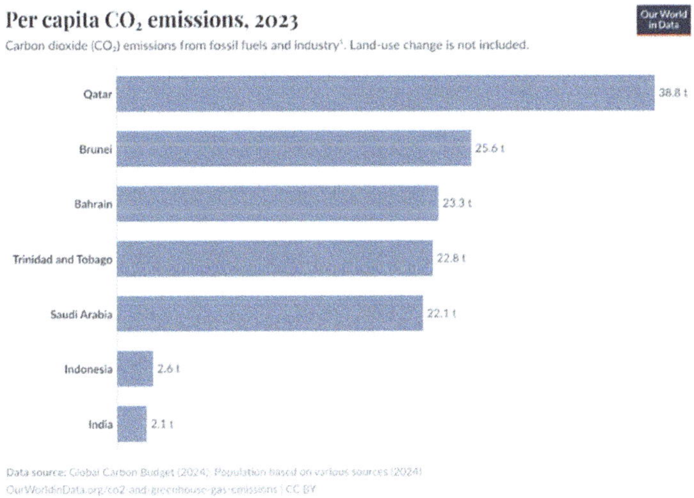

The European Union often presents itself as a global leader in climate action, championing stringent emissions reductions and renewable energy transitions. However, a closer examination of per capita emissions reveals contradictions in this self-image. Many EU states, despite their climate leadership rhetoric, continue to emit disproportionately compared to developing nations. For example: Germany's per capita emissions (7.1 metric tons) are more than three times higher than India's (2.1 metric tons). France (4.1 metric tons) still emits more than double the average for most African nations. This raises a crucial justice question: how can the Global South be expected to commit to deep emissions cuts when the per capita emissions of industrialized countries remain so high? The EU's normative power in climate governance is undermined by the persistence of these inequalities.

Moreover, a fair climate framework must recognize historical responsibility. Industrialized nations accumulated their wealth over centuries of fossil fuel consumption, long before large-scale industrialization began in the Global South. Until the mid-20th century, the vast majority of global CO_2 emissions came from the United States and Europe. The United States remains the largest historical emitter, having released approximately 400 billion tonnes of CO_2 since 1751—accounting for nearly a quarter of total emissions. The European Union, often regarded as a normative power in climate negotiations and green finance, is also a major historical contributor, responsible for nearly one-fifth of all emissions. However, many of today's largest annual emitters, such as India and Brazil, have relatively low historical emissions. Africa's contribution has been minimal, especially when considered in relation to its population size (Our World in Data, 2023). This historical burden is best captured by cumulative emissions (1750–2023), which account for the total carbon emitted by a nation over time (Figure 3).

Figure 3. Cumulative CO2 Emissions

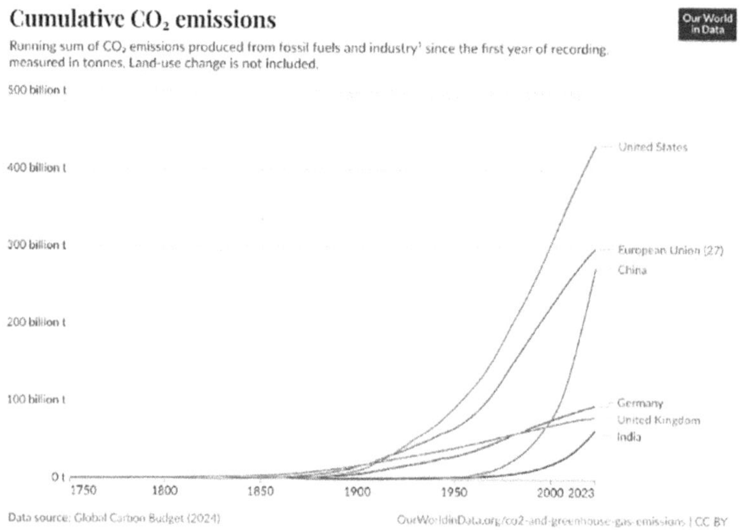

The disparities are striking: while China is now the world's largest annual emitter, its cumulative emissions remain far below that of the United States. The UK and Germany, despite their smaller populations, have historically contributed more CO_2 than entire continents in the Global South. Colonial-era industrialization was fueled by the extraction of raw materials from Africa, Asia, and Latin America, creating economic dependencies that persist today.

Another overlooked aspect of emissions justice is the role of global trade. Conventional carbon accounting attributes emissions to the country where they are produced, rather than where goods and services are consumed. This approach, known as territorial emissions accounting, creates a misleading narrative by making major manufacturing economies—such as China, India, and Indonesia—appear as disproportionately large emitters while downplaying the emissions footprint of wealthier consumer nations. In reality, a significant portion of emissions in these industrial hubs results from the production of goods destined for export markets in North America, Europe, and other high-income regions.

A consumption-based emissions model offers a more just and accurate measure by shifting accountability to the nations that drive demand for carbon-intensive goods. Unlike territorial accounting, which primarily tracks emissions at the site of production, a consumption-based approach reallocates emissions to the country where the final product is consumed. This method reveals that emissions responsibilities are far more intertwined across global supply chains than traditional accounting suggests.

When adjusted for consumption:

- The United States' carbon footprint increases significantly, as it imports vast quantities of manufactured goods, electronics, textiles, and industrial materials from high-emitting countries like China, Vietnam, and Mexico. Studies indicate that if the U.S. accounted for emissions embedded in its imports, its total CO_2 emissions would be nearly 15–20% higher than reported under territorial accounting (Peters et al., 2012).
- The European Union's emissions rise substantially when including the carbon embedded in products imported from the Global South. Countries such as Germany, France, and the United Kingdom rely on outsourced production, which effectively allows them to reduce domestic emissions while shifting industrial pollution to supplier nations. In 2019, roughly 22% of the EU's total emissions were embedded in imported goods, primarily from China, India, and Southeast Asia (Global Carbon Project, 2022).

This shift in perspective suggests that much of the high-emission industrial activity in the Global South is not purely domestic in nature but an extension of consumer demand from the Global North. The prevailing international trade structure reinforces economic inequalities by trapping lower-income nations into resource-intensive production roles while wealthier nations continue to benefit from cleaner industries and service-based economies.

One potential policy solution is the implementation of carbon border adjustment mechanisms (CBAMs)—tariffs on carbon-intensive imports from countries with weaker climate regulations. The EU has already begun introducing such measures, aiming to level the playing field by discouraging the offshoring of emissions. However, CBAMs are controversial, as they risk disproportionately harming Global South economies while failing to address the root issue: the demand-driven nature of carbon emissions.

A more just alternative is for industrialized nations to take responsibility for their consumption-based emissions by financing decarbonization in supplier countries. This could involve direct investment in clean energy infrastructure, technology transfer, and debt relief tied to sustainable development initiatives. Additionally, trade agreements could incorporate climate justice clauses, ensuring that developing nations are not penalized for emissions that ultimately serve wealthier consumers.

In sum, a consumption-based approach to emissions accounting reshapes the debate on climate justice by revealing the hidden dependencies between production and consumption economies. Recognizing these interconnections is essential for crafting equitable policies that do not disproportionately burden the Global South with the costs of a crisis it did not create. While emissions data expose the unequal responsibilities behind the climate crisis, these global disparities also manifest on the ground through resource struggles, most visibly in coal-related conflicts.

Distribution of Coal Conflicts

The distribution of coal-related conflicts worldwide highlights critical issues related to climate justice and the persistent inequalities between the Global North and Global South (Malm, 2016). These conflicts are deeply rooted in the historical patterns of industrialization, economic dependency, and the uneven impacts of climate change. While industrialized nations in the Global North have historically benefited from coal as a primary energy source, many of the burdens associated with coal extraction—such as environmental destruction, displacement of local communities, and health hazards—are disproportionately borne by regions in the Global South.

Over time, coal-related conflicts have escalated significantly, with a particularly sharp increase since the 1990s. This trend reflects the growing tensions surrounding coal extraction, environmental degradation, and socio-economic justice, as illustrated in Figure 4. Figure 4 indicates that coal conflicts have surged dramatically in recent decades, particularly from the 1990s onwards. This period coincides with growing awareness of climate change and international efforts to transition towards renewable energy. However, despite global pledges to reduce fossil fuel reliance, coal continues to be a contentious issue, particularly in the Global South, where economic dependencies on resource extraction often clash with environmental and human rights concerns. The acceleration of these conflicts can be attributed to several factors, including the expansion of coal mining projects driven by rising global energy demands, resistance from affected communities, and the increasing awareness of coal's role in exacerbating climate change.

Figure 4. Initial years of coal conflicts around the world

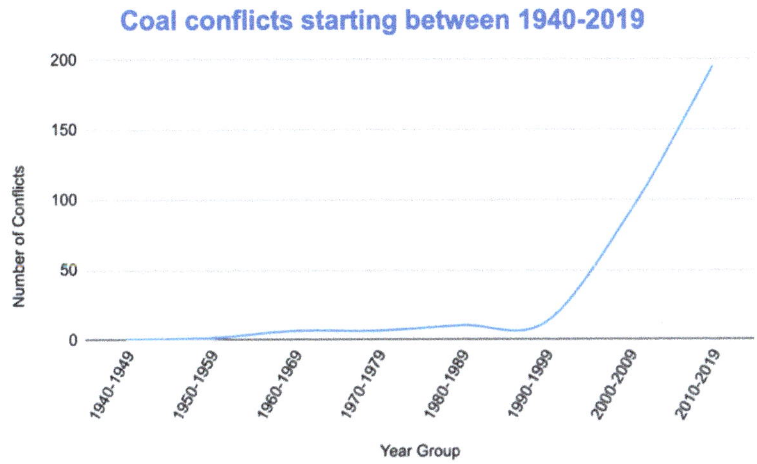

Source: Created by the author with data obtained from Environmental Justice Atlas (2025)

Figure 5 emphasizes the disproportionate burden of coal-related conflicts on the Global South. While coal conflicts exist in both the Global North and Global South, the latter experiences a significantly higher number of disputes (75.2% of total conflicts). Figure 3 further underscores this by showing that the most affected countries—India, China, Indonesia, and South Africa—are all in the Global South.

As climate policies and energy transitions in the Global North lead to the decline of domestic coal industries, multinational corporations have shifted their focus to the Global South, where regulatory frameworks are often weaker, and resistance from local populations is met with state-backed repression. This dynamic exacerbates existing inequalities and raises urgent questions about accountability, historical responsibility, and the need for a just transition away from fossil fuels. The continued reliance on coal not only perpetuates economic and environmental injustices but also undermines global efforts to mitigate climate change and move toward more sustainable energy systems.

Figure 5. Distribution of Coal Conflicts (Global North vs Global South)

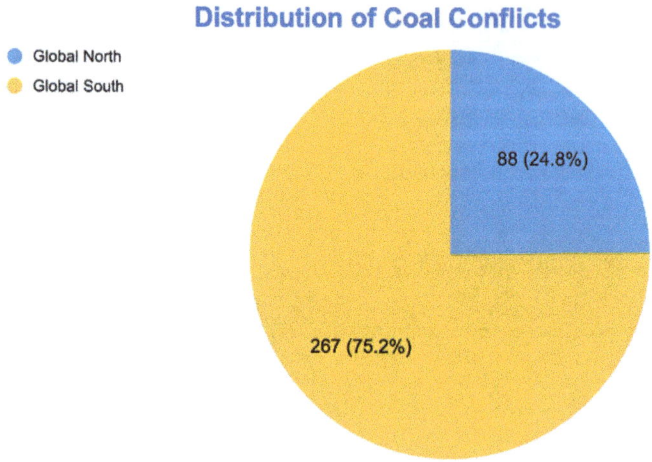

Source: Created by the author with data obtained from Environmental Justice Atlas (2025)

Figure 6. Top Coal Conflict Countries

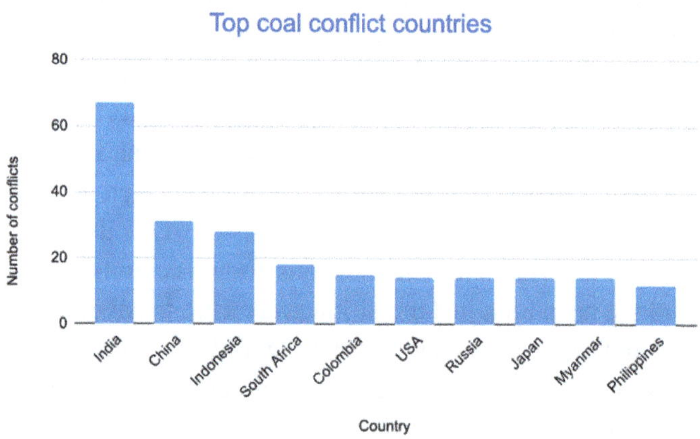

Source: Created by the author with data obtained from Environmental Justice Atlas (2025)

This disparity reflects broader global inequalities: while the Global North historically benefited from industrialization and fossil fuel use without facing the same scale of direct resource conflicts, the Global South now faces intense struggles over land, pollution, displacement, and labor exploitation driven by coal expansion. Additionally, many of these conflicts arise due to extractive projects that serve multinational corporations and markets in the Global North, reinforcing a neocolonial pattern of resource dependency.

The concept of climate justice is central to understanding these conflicts. The top coal conflict countries (such as India and Indonesia) highlight how energy demands, economic pressures, and international investments in coal drive social and environmental tensions. Regional disparities are particularly evident, with 49.3% of coal conflicts located in Asia (Figure 7).

Figure 7. Regional Distribution of Coal Conflicts

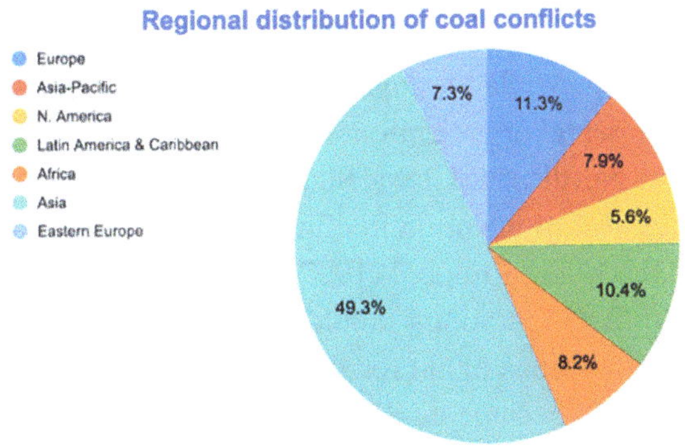

Source: Created by the author with data obtained from Environmental Justice Atlas (2025)

In short, the Figures 4-7 illustrate how coal conflicts are not merely local disputes but are deeply tied to global economic structures, historical injustices, and ongoing climate crises. These disputes are not isolated incidents but symptoms of a broader, systemic issue that reflects longstanding patterns of colonial exploitation, economic dependency, and environmental racism. The rise of these conflicts reveals the interconnected nature of the fossil fuel economy, where decisions made in boardrooms of multinational corporations and policies enacted by governments in the Global North have direct repercussions on communities in the Global South.

Addressing these challenges requires a holistic approach that integrates historical accountability, equitable policy reforms, and meaningful support for communities most affected by coal-driven injustices. Without tackling the root causes embedded in global economic and political systems, the Global South will continue to experience disproportionate harm, exacerbating the existing North-South divide in the face of escalating climate crises. The necessity to tackle the root causes of climate injustices have pushed global climate activists, communities and countries of the Global South to conceptualize and push for climate debt concept, which is explained in detail in the next section.

The Concept of Climate Debt

This is a concept rooted in the idea that richer countries of the industrialized Global North have historically been emitting most greenhouse gases and benefiting economically even as they did so, whereas poorer nations in the Global South bear all the worst effects but are least responsible for it altogether when measured against all contributions to total worldwide emissions divided equally among every nation (Duus-Otterström, 2013; Roberts and Parks, 2007).

Climate debt was first put forward in the early 1990s by environmental and social justice groups, especially during discussions leading up to the 1992 United Nations Conference on Environment and Development (UNCED) in Rio. Organizations considered to be most responsible for popularizing it were likely Acción Ecológica, an Ecuadorian environmental organization, which saw their environmental debt as coming from the Global North to the Global South in ecological terms (Simms, 2005). The concept further gained momentum in climate negotiations, particularly as the preparatory talks for the Kyoto Protocol (1997) took shape. In this context, Global South nations stressed that reparations should reflect their history of development and future financial transactions in aid for sustainable development.

Over time, climate debt became a rallying point for activists and policymakers advocating for climate justice. It was a central theme in the negotiations at the 2009 United Nations Climate Change Conference (COP15) in Copenhagen, where developing nations, particularly the Bolivian delegation, pushed for recognition of historical emissions and compensation mechanisms (Bond, 2012). However, resistance from industrialized nations, particularly the United States and European Union members, led to the sidelining of climate debt in formal climate negotiations, as they opposed it due to concerns over legal liability, potential financial obligations, historical culpability, and the political and economic challenges it could create.

The declining use of the term “climate debt” can be attributed to a number of factors. On the one hand, developed countries have largely resisted framing climate change as a debt issue for fear of legal and financial obligations. Instead, terms like “climate finance” or “loss and damage” have become preferred by international discussions, shifting the narration away from reparations to mere voluntary help at its best (Klein, 2014). Market-based solutions such as carbon trading and offset schemes have also contributed to eclipsing the framework that climate debt implies, namely reparative justice. Also, the fragmented nature of international climate negotiations and the near absence of generally applicable legal mechanisms with which to enforce historical accountability means that political momentum has partly ebbed away from this concept. However, contemporary trade frameworks such as the EU’s Carbon Border Adjustment Mechanism and WTO provisions under GATT

Article XX reproduce climate debt by shifting decarbonization costs onto Global South exporters, underscoring the trade justice dimension of climate inequality.

Though it has become a matter of much lesser interest in official climate talk circles, climate debt is a key tool for analyzing where the international climate policy balance lies between countries. It reminds us of needs for reparation and highlights the unequal nature of politics in global climate governance. An approach to climate debt will need to take into account historical accounting, promote fair policies, and offer practical help to those most affected by climate change, as well as to victims on both ends of climate problems. Just as climate debt highlights inequalities between nations, similar patterns of injustice unfold within states themselves, where wealthier elites often benefit while marginalized communities bear disproportionate climate burdens.

Within-Country Climate Injustices

Within-country climate injustices reveal deep-seated inequalities that mirror the global disparities between the Global North and Global South. While climate change affects entire nations, its impacts are far from evenly distributed within them. Wealthier individuals and corporations contribute disproportionately to emissions, yet it is the poorest and most marginalized communities that suffer the most from environmental degradation, extreme weather events, and inadequate climate adaptation measures. This structural injustice is evident in both developed and developing countries, where class, race, and political power determine who bears the costs of climate change and who benefits from policies that maintain the status quo.

High-consumption lifestyles and investments in fossil-fuel industries are two reasons why the richest people have a far greater carbon footprint than the rest of us. This tendency is questioned by the charity Oxfam, which says that the richest 1% of the world's population produces more carbon than the 50% poorest combined (2020). Shifting from electricity to air conditioning and from a transportation system that fuels remote sprawl transfers real ecological costs to low-income communities. This phenomenon is not merely a matter of individual consumption; the economic and political power of wealthy people means oil companies can still earn money, while any serious climate policy gets resistance.

With the support of billionaire investors, fossil-fuel companies spend billions on lobbying to delay climate action, and weaken environmental regulations. All their policies protect their bottom line rather than people's health. Fossil fuel companies are wasting a lot of money that could be used for public good. In this way, while the most fortunate people go on living high-carbon lives, the poorest and most downtrodden members of society—those who least contribute to climate change—get stuck with its worst consequences, including rising sea levels, intense heat waves, and heavy pollution. Fighting these injustices demands not only curbing emissions but gradually transferring both wealth and power. One of the most straightforward ways is through progressive taxation. The people with the most money and companies polluting world climate are most responsible for change to cleaner technologies and should naturally help pay what costs.

Ultra-high-leverage taxes on extravagant consumption and corporate carbon emissions would yield plenty of revenues to finance climate resilience projects, green energy infrastructure, and welfare programs for the most vulnerable. Climate justice is not just a matter of paying the price; that price should be spread evenly through society. The campaign against climate change is inseparable from the struggle against inequality, and if we fail to address systemic injustices within our own societies, then a just transition will remain difficult to achieve.

Beyond progressive taxation within states, redistributive mechanisms at the international level also form an essential component of climate justice. South-South cooperation initiatives—such as technology sharing, regional renewable energy funds, and cooperative adaptation projects—demonstrate how Global South countries can pool resources and expertise outside of North-dominated institutions. Moreover, climate finance initiatives that are decentralized, but still arrive directly at town governments, producer cooperatives, or grassroots communities, have been better at keeping government officials honest and responsive to local needs. These methods indicate a shift in control over finance and climate governance that is inclusive and decolonized: affected populations are no longer recipients of aid but are actively involved in the transition to a fossil fuel-free future.

Beyond highlighting inequalities, it is also important to note that governments in the Global South are experimenting with institutional reform strategies to integrate justice into climate adaptation. For example, India's state-level climate action plans link adaptation to rural livelihoods, Ecuador and Bolivia have constitutionalized the rights of nature to protect vulnerable communities, and the African Union's African Risk Capacity pools resources to support just disaster responses. These initiatives illustrate diverse regional pathways for embedding justice into adaptation practices, even under conditions of structural inequality.

CONCLUSION

This chapter has demonstrated that climate justice is a fundamental and comprehensive concept, which can help us understand the disproportionate burdens of climate change borne by the Global South. It has traced the evolution of climate justice from its roots in environmental justice, highlighting its expansion from localized struggles against pollution and hazardous waste to a global movement addressing historical responsibility, economic inequality, and systemic power imbalances. By critiquing climate justice through four key dimensions—distribution justice, process justice, recognition justice, and capacity justice—this chapter richly illustrates how structural inequalities in society determine both vulnerability to environmental change as well as responses to it. Additionally, the discussion on emissions responsibilities, coal-related conflicts, and the concept of climate debt has underscored the need for a justice-oriented approach to climate governance, one that prioritizes reparations, historical accountability, and meaningful participation from affected communities.

A key point from this chapter is that climate justice is not simply to be achieved through making cleaner coal or reforestation; it is a matter of changing the socio-economic structures that create and perpetuate environmental injustice in the first place. Furthermore, despite having made the smallest historical contributions to carbon emissions, the Global South suffers the most from climate change impacts—imposed upon it as extreme weather events, rising sea levels, and limited resources for life itself. This situation is not accidental. Rather, it is a consequence of centuries-long unequal exchange, economic dependence, and the systems of global trade currently in place that detriment these nations.

To take one example of these particular disadvantages, while industrialized countries of the Global North have developed their wealth by heavily emitting carbon, many nations in the Global South are still locked into environmentally destructive economic systems. Often this is due to external pressure from multinational corporations, international financial institutions, and market-driven solutions for climate change which fail to deal with root causes of inequality.

One key point discussed in this chapter is that present mechanisms of climate governance, such as the UNFCCC and international climate negotiations, have not essentially delivered climate justice. Though they provide space for discussions about fairness and historic responsibility, because negotiating power in those arenas is unbalanced, the high-emission nations have dominance over weak communities. Successive rounds of negotiations among industrialized nations not only failed to live up to the principle of Common But Differentiated Responsibilities (CBDR), which recognizes uneven capacities and duties among nations, but they also did little in practical terms to provide adequate funding, transfer key know-how for mitigation and adaptation activities, or make significant policy shifts meant for residents in other countries facing climate threats.

Yet, as mentioned earlier in this chapter, the idea of climate debt is an essentially ignored aspect of international climate policy. Though debates on 'climate finance' and 'loss and damage' have gained ground in recent years, the aid proffered by the Global North is seen more in terms of voluntary assistance than as redress for historical emissions causing grievous problems for people living there now. The change in terminology here allows industrialized nations to avoid taking full responsibility for bringing our present predicament upon us. For justice, more immediate measures should involve legally binding commitments to climate finance, large-scale debt cancellation for the developing world, and the direct participation of affected communities in decision-making processes so poor people gain from external funds. Without such measures, the existing financial structures face a very real danger of perpetuating subservience, not empowering countries to generate their own local solutions to sustainability problems.

This chapter has also shown the importance of addressing inequalities in climate suffering within the same country, such as between wealthy elites and less powerful communities—even inside small islands. Even within the South, climate vulnerability is not evenly distributed. Low-income communities, Indigenous peoples, and subsistence farmers are frequently forced to bear the costs while contributing little in emissions. Meanwhile, richer parties within those nations can often be held accountable for a large portion of the greenhouse gas emissions produced. They are also usually major beneficiaries from their carbon-heavy industries and global capitalism that insists that profitability is more important than long-term sustainability. To deal with this state of affairs, we need progressive taxes, a reallocation of wealth, and policies that guarantee climate adaptation and strategies for reducing its impact target the most vulnerable groups. The future of climate justice relies on whether the Global South, grassroots movements, and transnational alliances can push through systemic change or not.

By the emergence of climate justice movements all across Latin America, Africa, and Asia, they are sounding a new note of resistance against exploitative economic practices, clamoring for community-based alternatives to futurology. These movements focus on, besides climate justice—land rights, food sovereignty, indigenous models of governance, and pushing money out. Moreover, for as long as international climate policy negotiations continue to reproduce power imbalances, it will be essential to reinforce South-South cooperation and to erect stand-alone climate finance mechanisms. Future climate policies must not only focus on emissions reductions but also incorporate historical accountability, participatory governance, and mechanisms for wealth redistribution to ensure a just transition for the most affected communities.

Future research on climate justice should explore several key areas to deepen both theoretical and practical understanding. First, scholars increasingly advocate for applying intersectionality to climate justice by highlighting its shared roots in radical theory, focus on marginalized groups, critique of dominant epistemologies, commitment to social justice, and interdisciplinary approach (Mikulewicz, 2023; Terry, 2009; Verlie, 2021). Intersectional perspectives can show us how things like race, class, sex, and colonial history intersect with climate violations in some way or another; they provide a much more detailed grasp of what it means to be vulnerable and fight back. Second, research needs to focus more on alternative economic models that challenge dependence on fossil fuels while still enabling development in the Global South to be equitable. We should study the degrowth movement, post-capitalist economies, and community-led adaptation strategies as viable alternatives to present-day global climate policies. Third, the impact of digital activism and transnational climate justice networks in shaping policy outcomes is an emerging area that receives less scholarly attention than it should. How social movements cross boundaries online for advocacy work, use new media to express their demands, and confront both state and corporate power will dictate the next phase of climate governance. Finally, more empirical research on climate funding mechanisms—especially the effectiveness of and reparatory policies under loss and damage frameworks, for example—is crucial in ensuring that climate justice does not remain merely a rhetorical commitment but becomes factually instantiated in policies and practice.

Climate change is not only a moral imperative; it's also a struggle against unequal power relations on a global scale. Our need for justice-driven responses to problems of global climate change is growing ever stronger as the pace quickens; we cannot stop until we have achieved it. The struggle for climate justice is part and parcel of the larger battles over economic, social, and political rights. Only if we begin to transform our systems in a systemic way can we hope—truly hope—for sustainable as well as just futures.

REFERENCES

Agarwal, A., & Narain, S. (1991). Global Warming. In *An Unequal World: A Case Of Environmental Colonialism*. Centre For Science And Environment.

Allen, F. (2015). The State of the Climate Justice Movement in South Africa. *Capitalism, Nature, Socialism*, *26*(2), 46–57.

Amin, S. (1976). *Unequal Development: An Essay On the Social Formations of Peripheral Capitalism*. Monthly Review Press.

Audet, R. (2013). Climate Justice And Bargaining Coalitions: A Discourse Analysis. *International Environmental Agreement: Politics, Law and Economics*, *13*, 369–386.

Bachram, H. (2004). Climate fraud and carbon colonialism: The new trade in greenhouse gases. *Capitalism, Nature, Socialism*, *15*(4), 5–20.

Barrett, S. (2013). *Environment and statecraft: The strategy of environmental treaty-making*. Oxford University Press.

Bassey, N. (2012). *To cook a continent: Destructive extraction and the climate crisis in Africa*. Pambazuka Press.

Böhm, S., Misoczky, M. C., & Moog, S. (2012). Greening capitalism? A Marxist critique of carbon markets. *Organization Studies*, *33*(11), 1617–1638.

Bond, P. (2012). *Politics Of Climate Justice: Paralysis Above, Movement Below*. University of KwaZulu-Natal Press.

Bond, P. (2017). Climate Justice In, By, And for Africa. In Dietz, M., & Garrelts, H. (Eds.), *Routledge Handbook of the Climate Change Movement*. Routledge.

Bullard, R. D. (1990). Dumping. In *Dixie: Race, Class, And Environmental Quality*. Westview Press.

Bumpus, A. G., & Liverman, D. M. (2008). Accumulation by decarbonization and the governance of carbon offsets. *Economic Geography*, *84*(2), 127–155.

Caney, S. (2009). Justice and the distribution of greenhouse gas emissions. *Journal of Global Ethics*, *5*(2), 125–146.

Chancel, L. (2022). *Unsustainable inequalities: Social justice and the environment*. Harvard University Press.

Coolsaet, B., Agyeman, J., & Kashwan, P.. (2025). Acknowledging The Historic Presence Of Justice In Climate Research. *Nature Climate Change*, *15*(121).

Dados, N., & Connell, R. (2012). The Global South. *Contexts, 11*(1), 12–13.

Delina, L. L. (2021). Climate justice and the Global South: Resistance and Alternatives. In Newell, P., & Roberts, J. T. (Eds.), *The Global Handbook of Environmental Politics* (pp. 245–262). Edward Elgar Publishing.

Dryzek, J. S. (2000). *Deliberative democracy and beyond: Liberals, critics, contestations*. Oxford University Press.

Duus-Otterström, G. (2013). The problem of past emissions and intergenerational debts. *Critical Review of International Social and Political Philosophy, 17*(4), 448–469.

Escobar, A. (2018). *Designs for the Pluriverse: Radical Interdependence, Autonomy, and the Making of Worlds*. Duke University Press.

Fraser, N. (2009). *Scales of justice: Reimagining political space in a globalizing world*. Columbia University Press.

Ghosh, J. (2015). *The Creation of the Next Imperialism. The Institutional Architecture. Monthly Review: An Independent Socialist Magazine, 67 (3)*. July-August.

Gifford, L., & Sauls, L. A. (2024). Defining Climate Finance Justice: Critical Geographies of Justice Amid Financialized Climate Action. *Geography Compass, 18*(11), e70008.

Global Carbon Project. (2022). Global carbon budget 2022. Retrieved from https://www.globalcarbonproject.org/carbonbudget/22/files/GCP_CarbonBudget_2022.pdf 21.03.2025

Guardian. (2024, November 26). Backroom deals and betrayal: how Cop29's late $300bn deal left nobody happy. *Guardian*. https://www.theguardian.com/environment/2024/nov/26/how-late-deal-left-a-sense-of-dissatisfaction-and-betrayal-at-cop29-baku

Gudynas, E. (2011). Buen Vivir: Today's tomorrow. *Development, 54*(4), 441–447.

Hall, R., Grajales, J., Jacobs, R., Sauer, S., Galvin, S. S., & Shattuck, A. (2023). Intertwined histories: JPS at 50, La Via Campesina at 30. *The Journal of Peasant Studies, 50*(2), 447–448.

Hurlbert, M. (2015). Climate Justice: A Call for Leadership. *Environmental Justice, 8*(2). Advance online publication. DOI: 10.1089/env.2014.0035

Intergovernmental Panel on Climate Change (IPCC). (2022). *Climate change 2022: Impacts, adaptation, and vulnerability*. Cambridge University Press.

Kashwan, P. (2020). *Democracy in the woods: Environmental conservation and social justice in India, Tanzania, and Mexico*. Oxford University Press.

Kashwan, P. (2022). *Climate Justice in India*. Cambridge University Press.

Kaur, A., & Verma, S. S. (2025). Understanding India's Role in International Climate Negotiations from a Social Constructivist Perspective. *India Review*, *24*(1), 36–54.

Klein, N. (2014). *This changes everything: Capitalism vs. the Climate*. Simon and Schuster.

Lefstad, A., & Paavola, J. (2023). Climate justice and global governance: The limits of the UNFCCC framework. *Global Environmental Politics*, *23*(1), 75–97.

Lefstad, L., & Paavola, J. (2023). The Evolution of Climate Justice Claims in Global Climate Change Negotiations under the UNFCCC. *Critical Policy Studies*, *18*(3), 363–388.

Malm, A. (2016). *Fossil Capital: The Rise of Steam Power and the Roots of Global Warming*. Verso.

Malm, A., & Hornborg, A. (2014). The geology of mankind? A critique of the Anthropocene narrative. *The Anthropocene Review*, *1*(1), 62–69.

Martinez-Alier, J. (2002). *The environmentalism of the poor: A study of ecological conflicts and valuation*. Edward Elgar.

Martínez-Torres, M. E., & Rosset, P. M. (2010). La Vía Campesina: The birth and evolution of a transnational social movement. *The Journal of Peasant Studies*, *37*(1), 149–175.

Mathur, V., & Chamuah, A. (2025). Navigating AI and climate change in an unequal world. *Climate Policy*, •••, 1–7.

McGurty, E. (2009). *Transforming Environmentalism: Warren County, Pcbs, And The Origins Of Environmental Justice*. Rutgers University Press.

Mikulewicz, M., Caretta, M. A., Sultana, F., & Crawford, J. W., N. (2023). Intersectionality and Climate Justice: A call for synergy in climate change scholarship. *Environmental Politics*, *32*(7), 1275–1286.

Mohan, P. S. (2025). Climate Reparations for a Just Response to Climate Change: A Review of Historical Responsibility and Future Implications. *WIREs Climate Change*, online first. doi: DOI: 10.1002/wcc.70007

Mol, A. P., & Sonnenfeld, D. A. (2000). Ecological modernization around the world: An introduction. *Environmental Politics*, *9*(1), 1–14.

Mossett, K., & Caldwell, R. (2016). "The Inside Is Such a Sterile Place": Organizing with the Indigenous Environmental Network. *Socialism and Democracy, 30*(2), 203–208.

Newell, P. (2005). Race, class and the global politics of environmental inequality. *Global Environmental Politics, 5*(3), 70–94.

Newell, P. (2022). Climate Justice. *The Journal of Peasant Studies, 49*(5), 915–923.

Newell, P. (2022). *Power shift: The global political economy of energy transitions*. Cambridge University Press.

Newell, P., & Mulvaney, D. (2013). The Political Economy Of the Just Transition. *The Geographical Journal, 179*(2), 132–140.

Newell, P., Srivastava, S., & Naess, L. O. (2021). Climate Justice Movements In The Global South: The Politics Of Equity And Inclusion. *Climate Policy, 21*(7), 885–901.

Ngcamu, B. S. (2023). Climate Change Effects on Vulnerable Populations in the Global South: A Systematic Review. *Natural Hazards, 118*, 977–991.

OECD. (2011). *Towards green growth*. OECD Publishing.

Ogunbode, C. A. (2022). Climate Justice Is Social Justice In The Global South. *Nature Human Behaviour, 6*, 1443.

Okereke, C. (2008). *Global justice and neoliberal environmental governance: Ethics, sustainable development and international co-operation*. Routledge.

Okereke, C. (2010). Climate Justice and the International Regime. *Wiley Interdisciplinary Reviews: Climate Change, 1*(3), 462–474.

Our World in Data. (2023). https://ourworldindata.org/ Retrieved on 21.03.2025

Oxfam (2020). *Confronting carbon inequality: Putting climate justice at the heart of the COVID-19 recovery*. Oxfam International.

Page, E. A. (2008). Distributing the burdens of climate change. *Environmental Politics, 17*(4), 556–575.

Paterson, M. (2021). *Climate capitalism: Global warming and the transformation of the global economy*. Cambridge University Press.

Pellow, D. N. (2000). Environmental inequality formation: Toward a theory of environmental injustice. *The American Behavioral Scientist, 43*(4), 581–601.

Pellow, D. N., Williams, E., & Rizo-Centino, A. R. (2021). Collaborative Research and Action for Climate Justice in California. *Capitalism, Nature, Socialism, 33*(2), 85–102.

Peters, G. P., Davis, S. J., & Andrew, R. (2012). A synthesis of carbon in international trade. *Biogeosciences, 9*(8), 3247–3276.

Roberts, J. T., & Parks, B. C. (2007). *A Climate Of Injustice: Global Inequality, North-South Politics, And Climate Policy*. MIT Press.

Roberts, J. T., & Parks, B. C. (2009). Ecologically unequal exchange, ecological debt, and climate justice. *International Journal of Comparative Sociology, 50*(3–4), 385–409.

Schleich, J., Dütschke, E., Schwirplies, C., & Ziegler, A. (2014). Citizens' perceptions of justice in international climate policy: An empirical analysis. *Climate Policy, 16*(1), 50–67.

Schlosberg, D. (2007). *Defining environmental justice: Theories, movements, and nature*. Oxford University Press.

Schlosberg, D. (2012). Climate justice and capabilities: A framework for adaptation policy. *Ethics & International Affairs, 26*(4), 445–461.

Schlosberg, D., & Collins, L. B. (2014). From Environmental to Climate Justice. *Wiley Interdisciplinary Reviews: Climate Change, 5*(3), 359–374.

Shapiro, J. (2016). *China's Environmental Challenges*. Polity Press.

Shue, H. (2014). *Climate Justice: Vulnerability and Protection*. Oxford University Press.

Simms, A. (2009). *Ecological Debt: Global Warming and the Wealth of Nations*. Pluto Press.

Sultana, F. (2021). Decolonizing Climate Justice. *Geoforum, 126*, 23–30.

Sultana, F. (2022). Critical Climate Justice. *The Geographical Journal, 188*(1), 118–124.

Taşdemir Yaşın, Z. (2022). The Environmentalization of the Agrarian Question and the Agrarianization of the Climate Justice Movement. *The Journal of Peasant Studies, 49*(7), 1355–1386.

Temper, L., Bene, D., Martinez-Alier, J., & Demaria, F. (2018). The global environmental justice atlas (EJAtlas): Ecological distribution conflicts as forces for sustainability. *Sustainability Science, 13*(3), 573–584.

Temper, L., Del Bene, D., & Martinez-Alier, J. (2018). Mapping the frontiers and front lines of global environmental justice: The EJAtlas. *Ecological Economics*, *145*, 1–10.

Terry, G. (2009). No Climate Justice without Gender Justice: An Overview of the Issues. *Gender and Development*, *17*(1), 5–18.

Tokar, B. (2014). *Toward climate justice: Perspectives on the climate crisis and social change*. New Compass Press.

Verlie, B. (2021). Climate Justice In More-Than-Human Worlds. *Environmental Politics*, *31*(2), 297–319.

Whyte, K. (2017). Indigenous climate change studies: Indigenizing futures, decolonizing the Anthropocene. *English Language Notes*, *55*(1), 153–162.

Young, I. M. (2000). *Inclusion and democracy*. Oxford University Press.

KEY TERMS AND DEFINITIONS

Climate Debt: The moral and financial responsibility of high-emission countries to compensate poorer nations for climate damages.

Climate Justice: The idea that climate change is not just an environmental issue but also a question of fairness, responsibility, and equity.

Coal Conflicts: Disputes that emerge over coal mining and use, often involving clashes between economic, social, and environmental interests.

Environmental Justice: The principle that all people should have equal access to a healthy environment and should not bear disproportionate ecological harms.

Global North: A term for wealthier, industrialized regions such as Europe, North America, and parts of East Asia.

Global South: A term for regions in Latin America, Africa, Asia, and Oceania that are often less economically developed and more vulnerable to global inequalities.

Progressive Taxation: A tax system in which higher earners pay a greater percentage of their income in taxes than lower earners.

Within-Country Inequality: Economic and social disparities in income, wealth, or opportunities among groups within the same country.

Chapter 8
Beyond Representation: Reclaiming Indigenous Agency in Sustainability Governance – A Case of Indian Tribes

Robin Choudhary
https://orcid.org/0009-0002-9744-0610
Panjab University, Chandigarh, India

Monica Munjial Singh
Panjab University, Chandigarh, India

ABSTRACT

India's tribal communities, particularly the Gond tribe, possess rich cultural traditions and deep-rooted ecological knowledge integral to environmental sustainability. This chapter critically examines the paradox of symbolic representation versus substantive exclusion of the Gond tribe in India's sustainability governance. The study explores how policies like the Forest Rights Act (FRA) 2006, while progressive in intent, have been undermined by bureaucratic inertia, corporate interests, and colonial legacies. Using a postcolonial and environmental justice lens, the chapter highlights how indigenous knowledge is often appropriated without empowering tribal communities. To address this gap, the chapter proposes a participatory governance model emphasizing legal recognition, community-based resource management, and indigenous knowledge co-production. Strengthening traditional institutions like the Gotul and operationalizing Free, Prior, and Informed Consent (FPIC) are identified as key strategies.

DOI: 10.4018/979-8-3373-1707-6.ch008

INTRODUCTION

The earliest known societies in human history are tribal communities. While there is not much explicit information about tribal cultures in antiquity, there are references to certain tribes of people in epics and other ancient literature who are frequently portrayed as the devil Rakshas, demon Ashuras, robber Dashyus, or even monkeys Banors. India is home to the second-largest tribal population in the world, comprising approximately 8 percent of the total Indian population (Census of India, 2011). According to the 2011 census, 109 million people, or 8.6% of India's total population, are classified as belonging to a Tribal Community. A schedule, or list, of the tribal communities that are economically and socially disadvantaged is included in Article 342 of the Indian Constitution. The Gonds comprise the majority of these tribes in Central India (Gondwana). The Raj-Gonds, Khatola-Gonds, Madia-Gonds, Dhur-Gonds, Dadve-Gonds, Mokasi-Gonds, Gaita-Gonds, and Koyas were several subgroups of the Gonds. The Gond tribe is the largest and most culturally significant tribal group in India. It has its own relationship with nature, unique art forms, oral traditions, and community-based resource management (Gupta, 2020). According to Ralph Linton, a tribe is a simple social group whose members cooperate to carry out everyday activities and speak the same dialect. As per Majumdar, "A tribe is a group of families with a common name, who live in the same area, speak the same language, observe certain taboos around marriage, work, or other occupations, and have developed a well-thought-out system of mutual obligation and reciprocity."

Culture and human are seen as two sides of the same coin and are intertwined. The most amazing factor that caused man to create increasingly complicated settings in order to adapt to his new surroundings was cultural creativity. In actuality, culture upholds order, harmony with the natural world, and both supernatural and natural forces through people's attitudes, behaviours, dispositions, and meaningful forms that they bestow upon tangible objects. Cultural heritage, to put it simply, is the collection of cultural resources that humans have produced and preserved, including a variety of activities, beliefs, values, conventions, and cultural traditions that frequently give human life purpose and substance.

The Kuki, Garo, Mizo, Khasi, Naga, and other tribes inhabit the mountain valleys and other parts of northeastern India, which includes States and Union Territories like Assam, Nagaland, Manipur, Meghalaya, Mizoram, Tripura, and Arunachal Pradesh. These tribes are mainly of Mongolian ancestry. In the Himalayan region, the Lepcha, Rabha, and other Mongolian-descendant tribes primarily reside in the sub-Himalayan regions, which include parts of Bengal, Himachal Pradesh, and Uttar Pradesh. In Central India, the older hills and the Chotanagpur Plateau, which separate peninsular India from the Indo-Gangetic basin, are home to numerous tribal peoples, such as the Bhumij, Gond, Ho, Oraon, Munda, and Santal. Gond tribe in central India practices ancestor worship and animism, while the Khasi tribe in northeastern India is primarily Christian. Additionally, the tribes' means of subsistence and occupation vary; some are well-known for their agricultural practices, some for their traditional hunting and gathering practices, and still others for their artistic and craft creations.

The rich cultural legacy of these communities plays a significant role in shaping India's history and identity. We can better appreciate and comprehend the cultural diversity of India if we are aware of the habits, traditions, and practices of different communities (Desgupta, 2018). Significant obstacles and marginalisation, such as poverty, lack of access to healthcare and education, and relocation are frequently experienced by Indian tribal tribes(Xaxa, 2014). Comprehending these concerns is essential for formulating efficacious policies and endeavours to tackle these obstacles. Indian tribal communities have long been guardians of the forest and other natural resources, and they have a special relationship with the environment. Their traditional wisdom may be helpful in maintaining ecological balance and biodiversity.

This chapter talks about the gap between cultural recognition and political inclusion of the Gond tribe. We are critically examining the status of the Gond tribe in terms of sustainability governance. By examining their cultural heritage, ecological practices, and systemic marginalization, the chapter argues for a paradigm shift from tokenistic representation towards genuine indigenous agency..

BACKGROUND

Tribes have a rich and ancient cultural history. Unfortunately, historians and anthropologists find it challenging to document their past because they lack a substantial written heritage. Most of the scholars highlighted the mystery surrounding the tribals' later history up until the Aryan invasion. There is no single race among India's Aborigines. Most of the evidence speaks about their existence from different parts of Asia. There is little information available regarding the beginnings and later histories of the various tribes. Their tale of glories and downfall, however, is rewriteable. The development of scripts and the introduction of written documentation are always beneficial in this context.

Some academics speculate that the indigenous people may have been the architects of the Indus Valley Civilization. There are references to the tribal people in the ancient books of the Vedic era. The Aryans from the North-Western portions of India began to invade during the Vedic period, engaging in combat with the non-Aryans. Throughout the later Vedic era (1000–600 BC), the Aryan and non-Aryan peoples began to blend together. Thus, the tribal people's degrading process persisted. During this assimilation process, the tribes were assigned lower-order tasks, which may have ultimately led to the formation of the inferior caste known as "Sudra." Non-tribal people invaded tribal lands during the feudal era (400–1000 AD). The tribal chiefs were impacted by the Sanskritization process during this time. The governing Brahmin class led the process of Sanskritization, as articulated and popularized by M. N. Srinivas, while Brahmin priests constructed an appropriate genealogy for themselves. In addition to the Moghuls, other tribes that periodically invaded the tribal areas included the Persians, Greeks, Sakas, Huns, and other hordes of nomadic invaders from the Northwest.

In 1911, Census Commissioner E. A. Gait created the first classification to determine the untouchable population. A distinct list of castes and tribes is introduced along with this new census survey collection. Ten distinct criteria were used for separate caste and tribe enumerations. The majority of the requirements have a strong connection to customs and literature from Hindu culture. The word "Depressed class" was used to categorise and tally untouchables. The Depressed Castes were specifically defined as individuals whose touch or contact is considered impure. The Superintendents of Census have not provived a particular definition of Depressed Castes. This led to an unclear picture of the actual population of Untouchables. Although the term "Depressed Classes" had been in use before 1931, was neither conceptualised nor given a precise definition.

CULTURAL CLASSIFICATIONS OF TRIBES

Different scholars have identified various classifications based on region, culture, and economy. Cultural classification is one of the important classifications to understand the diversity in the lifestyles of Indian tribes. For centuries, there was a long-held belief that tribes were related to their Hindu neighbours. Their civilization, economics, religion, and ecology vary from tribe to tribe, region to region. Mazumdar (1947) and Roy Burman (1994) are among the authors who have attempted to determine the degree of integration of tribals with India's mainstream population. Assimilation, the process of regularly exposing one population or group to the culture of another, led to social changes and generated problems due to their isolation and confined existence in relation to the world view. V. Elwin also classified Indigenous Peoples into four classes based on their cultural Development. It is categorised as follows: a) original forest environment; this is based on the assimilation/association of the majority of tribes into their neighbouring groups versus the minority groups that are dispersed over hills and woods. b) Interaction with the plan and any ensuing modifications. c) Tribal people moved into contemporary professions & businesses. d)Minority groups and cross-cultural interactions.

Tribal people in India come into contact with the Hindu community and begin to adopt Hindu customs and practices. This process is known as Hinduization, and some of them convert to Christianity. Different sets of tribes have emerged as a result of this cultural contact on an acculturation level. They were separated into three classes by Ghurye (1963, p. 23): Raj Gonds, or people having a relatively high position in Hindu society, and Hill sections. Partially Hinduized. Bose described this process of tribe integration into the greater Indian civilization as the "Hindu Mode of Absorption." In his 1977 Sanskritization lecture, Srinivasa discussed how members of lower castes are assimilating into upper castes by adopting the lifestyles of those in higher castes. Social mobility is not the same as Sanskritization.

Surajit Sinha (1982) outlined the integration of tribes into the caste-peasant base of Indian civilization. This process involved the tribes adopting agricultural technologies as well as the language and cultural norms of the peasant castes. The quest for political status as an ethnic minority within a constitutional framework inspired by an egalitarian democratic philosophy has superseded the varna Jati model of absorption.

INDIAN TRIBES: DIVERSITY, HISTORY, AND MARGINALIZATION

India is home to over 700 tribal communities, classified as Scheduled Tribes (STs) under Article 342 of the Indian Constitution. These communities, often referred to as Adivasis, have cultural traditions that predate recorded history. From the Bhils of western India to the Khasi of the northeast and the Gonds of central India, these groups exhibit remarkable diversity in language, beliefs, social structures, and livelihoods.

Historically, tribal communities have been marginalized groups faced exclusion and assimilation. The colonial classification of tribes as criminal tribes further entrenched stereotypes, leading to policies of control and surveillance rather than empowerment. Post-independence India continued many of these approaches. However, constitutional safeguards and affirmative action policies were introduced for their lands and livelihoods the classification of tribal groups as ST aimed to address socio-economic disparities through a common identity.

THE GOND TRIBE: CULTURAL HERITAGE AND ECOLOGICAL ETHOS

One of the biggest tribal groups in India is the Gonds, who are distributed throughout the country's eastern and central regions. According to the 2011 Census, there are more than 11.3 million members of the Gond tribe. Gondwana was the region where the Gonds resided. This included Madhya Pradesh, Telangana, Andhra Pradesh, Jharkhand, West Bengal, Odisha, and Vidarbha as they exist now. The Gond tribe primarily inhabits the central and western regions of India, spanning across the states of Madhya Pradesh, Chhattisgarh, Maharashtra, Odisha, Telangana, and Andhra Pradesh.

The inhabitants of the Gondwana region are also called the Gondi people. The most important Gond kingdom was the Chanda kingdom, which was founded in 807 AD. They concentrated on irrigation infrastructure and instituted revenue administration. In Middle India, the Gonds make up the majority (Gondwana). The Raj-Gonds, Khatola-Gonds, Madia-Gonds, Dhur-Gonds, Dadve-Gonds, Mokasi-Gonds, Gaita-Gonds, and Koyas were among the divisions of the Gonds. The Gond people were a large, dispersed group. It was split up into several portions, each with a distinct focus. These groups of clans, which were organised into exogamous phratries within them, were typically endogamous in nature. The smallest social unit was the family. The bulk of people in Middle India are Gonds (Gondwana). Among the divisions composed of Gonds were the Raj-Gonds, Khatola-Gonds, Madia-Gonds, Dhur-Gonds, Dadve-Gonds, Mokasi-Gonds, Gaita-Gonds, and Koyas. The Gonds were a big, widely scattered people. It was divided into multiple sections, each with a different emphasis. Usually endogamous, these clan groups were divided into exogamous phratries within them. The family was the smallest social unit.

Culture plays a pivotal role within the Gond community. They have a strong connection with their natural surroundings, and their lifestyle heavily influences their environment. Agriculture, fishing, hunting, and gathering are their source of livelihood. They hold knowledge about their local ecosystems. The Gond people are renowned for their paintings, characterized by bold lines, intricate patterns, and depictions of nature, animals, and mythical creatures. These paintings were traditionally created on walls and floors. Religion and spirituality are deeply ingrained in the Gond tribe. Rituals, ceremonies, and festivals are organized to honor these deities. Music, dance, and communal gatherings are also part of their culture.

Social structures and community cohesion play a pivotal role in the lives of the Gond tribe. They have a hierarchical social system. Village councils and respected elders make important decisions and resolve disputes. The Gond society places great importance on communal harmony, interdependence, and cooperation.

Marriage Among Gonds

In the Gond tribe, marriage involves a man and a woman entering into a monogamous relationship based on mutual consent, which is approved by the tribal council. The Gonds are rigorous about upholding marriage fidelity even though they have liberal attitudes about premarital sex. Adultery, according to their beliefs, is punished by the spirits of the ancestors and can result in a crop failure or a human or animal pandemic. A Gond wedding is marked by several important rituals. The groom and his bride must go around a wedding post that has been set up in the middle of the wedding booth seven times as part of the traditional wedding ritual.

The only reason polygamy is prohibited is that a man cannot sustain more than one wife. Cross-cousin marriages are common among the Gonds, who much prefer and encourage marriage within their blood family. The *Gotul* system is a common practice among the Gond community. The single young boys and girls in this system live together in independently constructed huts and are free to interact and engage in any activity they choose. They engage in sociocultural activities, such as dancing and singing, during this time to socialize and have fun. They can leave the *Gotul* and get married if everything works out and they are both content.

In traditional Gond society, there were different kinds of marriages such as "Ostasana Marmi" (regular marriage), "Poyse Otttur or Kals Ottur" (by capture marriage), "Lamhade Marmi" (by service marriage), "Kotavalda or Ata sata" (by exchange marriage), "Pat or Tiks Tasana Marmi" (Adult or Widow Marriage), "Yer Dosana Marmi" (Bhul Bihao) (by elopement), "Haiwark wat" (by intrusion), etc. Among the Gonds, it was forbidden for blood relatives to marry. Getting the mother and father's approval is equally crucial. Hindu customs were observed in the marriages of the Raj Gonds, the ruling Gonds, whereas the Baiga performed the marriage rites for the common Gonds (Tiwari, 2002). Marriage for widows was also accepted in Gond society. Additionally, their marriage laws supported women. The procedures for divorce and remarriage are straightforward to understand. The Gonds no longer engage in polygamy. Gonds currently view monogamy as the ideal form and only use polygamy under dire circumstances.

Art and Craft of Gond Tribe

There is a worldwide tie between religion and art. Glimpses of Religious themes can be identified in all forms of tribal art and crafts. In the worship of the god, they are indispensable. Proclaiming one's identity is a key purpose of tribal art and craft, which also holds significant religious meaning. The Community uses artwork, handicrafts, music, dance, and traditional attire to preserve and uphold the rich cultural heritage of their forefathers. The architectural ruins attest to the rich cultural heritage of the ancient Gond Community. Their talent and enthusiasm for artistic creations are evident in the elaborate patterns on the woven fabrics, ornamental mats, and other imaginative handicrafts. Paintings, songs, and dancing are examples of traditional Gond art. Folk songs are used to transmit stories orally. Traditional string instruments, such as the Bana and Kingri, can be used to accompany these. The songs, known as Dhemse, describe the mythology of the Gonds and their sacred past. Folk dancing is another way that stories are shared. They could be done for important occasions, such as weddings and births, as well as other festivals and celebrations. The people dance while imitating peacocks, bees, and other animals; a percussion instrument, such as the dhol, is frequently used to accompany this. Their dancing relies heavily on rhythm. Dancing is frequently accompanied by singing, sometimes with spontaneous lines added to the tunes. Traditionally, Gond paintings have been applied inside homes. Natural materials are used in traditional Gond wall paintings to produce vividly coloured motifs. These patterns, known as Gond Pradhan motifs, are made out of tiny lines, dots, and dashes. Their representation of their spiritual ideas is a significant element in their paintings. Their use of pictures of gods and goddesses, such as Ganesha, reflects this. Hindu rituals and stories of supernatural entities from ancient Hindu texts, as well as a reverence for natural phenomena such as spiritually significant trees or divine beings — including birds and animals that hold spiritual value. These pictures feature numerous cows, which are revered in Hinduism.

Children do a creative ritual at the community temple as a greeting during Bidaripujaas. Instead of using company-made tools and equipment, they carry sacrificial commodities to the objects of their devotion using handcrafted bamboo baskets, gourd pots, and little clay figurines. These are the musical instruments that are required for any traditional dance performance. There are also several traditional Gond dances, which are primarily showcased at the Navakhani festival. It is said that they get divine strength after dancing continuously for an extended period. Singing and dancing are integral parts of the festivities during the socio-religious holidays of the traditional Gond, with Navakhani being the most significant and gayest communal festival. The continuous music of the Karma, Saila, Bhadauni, Biraha, Kaharawa, and Sajani is accompanied by dancing, eating, and drinking. Gond handicrafts have a long history among Indian tribal tribes, and they play a vital role in both their economy and culture. These crafts include Jewellery-making, metalworking, woodworking, textiles, and pottery. The traditional metalwork of the Gujarati tribes is well-known, whereas the textile weaving of the Odisha tribes is well-known.

Certain tribes, including the Toda tribes of Tamil Nadu, are renowned for their traditional woodcarving abilities. They are renowned for their exquisite and detailed wood carvings, which are utilised for both common goods and religious and ceremonial purposes. A significant part of the culture and economy of certain tribes is the jewellery-making tradition that they have long maintained. To create their jewellery, they source materials from within the area, including beads, semi-precious stones, and shells.

Festivals of Gond Tribe

The Gonds observed several religious festivals. These included the festivals of Holi, Phag or Shimga, Dussehra, Akhari, Jiwati, Pola, and Nawo Tindana. A large number of them are related to the farming season. The festivals of the Gond were communal rites. Hareli is the festival of Purification. The Hareli people worship and sacrifice to all the clan and family deities simultaneously during this festival. Farmers in Chhattisgarh take great pride in celebrating the auspicious Hareli Festival, which is closely linked to farming and agriculture. The rural villages are filled with unbounded enthusiasm and unabashed joy during this spectacular event. This event is being observed annually. The purpose of this event is to rid the people and the land of anything that is causing them pain. The purpose of this event is to rid the land and its inhabitants of impurities that make them suffer. It asserts that, although the Gond only witnesses this occurrence, the welfare of all tribes, including non tribes, is the real objective.

Hindu customs influence Gonds fair and festivals. The another major event for the Gonds is Keslapur Jathra. The snake deity Nagoba, whose temple is located in the Keslapur hamlet of the Indervelly mandal of the Adilabad district, is worshipped during this festival. The most well-known dance performed by the Gonds is the Gusadi dance. Wearing headgear embellished with peacock feathers is how it has done. They round their waists with cotton fabric. They cover their bodies with ash, and beards fashioned from animal hair are a significant component of the dance outfits. Another significant event observed by the Gonds is Madai. During this event, Gonds get to meet their relatives who have made their homes across the nation. To please the tribal goddess, people also sacrifice goats beneath the revered village tree during this celebration. They sip alcohol and dance to the sounds of tribal music at night. In addition, they observe the Hindu holiday of Dusshera.

Gotul and Its Significance

Gotul is a crucial social, cultural, and educational institution in the media tribal community. Gotul is a Zuggi-style house that is located both on the village's edge and in the centre. The youth proceed to Gotul after supper and encourage others to participate in different activities. Communities in Gotul engage in singing, dancing, and other activities. particularly a lover's call addressed to her sweetheart as "forest flower." Her lover receives a comb from him, which she puts in her hair as a sign of affection. They put an end to their romance with marriage and refrain from encouraging unrest in their neighbourhood. Gramsadly set up the Gotul position, allowing everyone to join and record their social life training. Since preserving culture is a significant component of gotul, the Madia Gond tribe's views on gotul are constantly evolving. Gotul raises awareness of various facets of tribal society and provides context for them. The Gotul celebrates numerous festivals, religious events, and cultural activities. The younger members of the Gond and Maria tribes are transported to the Gotul—the mixed-sex youth dormitories. The kids living here are required to live in close quarters and participate in sexual practices up to the point of intercourse. There is no group sex allowed in the Gotul.

Privacy during sexual relations is crucial, but not necessary in certain areas, where members are punished for sleeping with the same person for more extended periods of time and are discouraged from developing an emotional relationship with them. Teenagers are, nevertheless, encouraged to engage in monogamous relationships at some Gotul. It is a dwelling entrenched in and treasured by the larger socio-religious site of the Gonds; in Gond tribe society, it is a sacred spot connected to their supreme deity Lingo, where the members can commit no transgressions. In contrast to their counterparts in the Bastar region, the Gotuls of Madia Gond tribes go to their individual homes at night to sleep.

Mahua and Indian Tribes

Native tribes that have lived in and around these forests for a very long time—far before the forest rules that currently govern their relationship—value the mahua tree socially and culturally. It is found throughout most of Central India, mainly in forests and is also being cultivated. The majority of these local populations are members of tribes for whom the Kalpavriksha tree is a symbol of customs, knowledge, and way of life from long ago. The tree remains economically significant today due to the numerous applications of its wood, fruits, seeds, and flowers. We know that Ayurveda has been practiced at least since 200 BCE, as early literature references the mahua tree and its various therapeutic applications, including the seeds and blooms.

The tribe believes that nature is on their side because they have elevated the prestige of plants and animals in their culture to that of their ancestors and have preserved them. This is because the tribe has always tried to understand the wonders of nature. Without them, life is not whole. In this way, as they became wiser, they also learned the significance of and applications for a wide range of natural plants and animals. They have many of these plants and trees, and they are essential to their religious lives. Among these numerous trees, the Mahua tree is considered the most significant. Mahua has a major role in the religious rituals of the Halba and Gond tribes. Their connection to the natural environment and the progenitor of their house is mostly based on mahua. Mahua is used in religious festivals and festivities by the people of Gond and Halba communities to strengthen their ties to the village deity, their ancestors, and the environment. Mahua is essential to performing their many religious rituals. The Madhuca longifolia, or Mahua, tree grows in the wooded plains of central and eastern India. After living in this area for the last 3,000 years, the Santhals, Gonds, Mundas, and Oraons regard to Mahua as their "tree of life" and respect it as such. Mahua's wine was lauded in ancient Hindu texts that reference it. The fourth-century poet Kalidasa wrote about Goddess Parvati garlanded with its blooms. But its culture is much older, and it is most deeply embedded in the tribal interior of India, where a people have refused to convert to Hinduism. Madhya Pradesh, Jharkhand, Chhattisgarh, Odisha, Maharashtra, and Bihar are home to the dry deciduous Mahua tree.

The tree is found in large parts of the tribal states of Jharkhand and Chhattisgarh; in the latter, places such as Bastar are more often associated with the Naxalites. Tribal societies like the Gond and Baiga gather mahua fruits, flowers, seeds, and leaves for their financial value. These tribes generally use mahua flowers, fruits, branches, and leaves for food, firewood, cow feed, art, medicine, and other uses. However, of all the other uses, the beverage "Mahua" is the most well-known. Mahua flowers play a significant role in the local food and commerce. The tribes sell the dried flowers to the nearby breweries. The lack of adequate roads and power supplies usually makes life tough for tribal people. There is a high prevalence of illiteracy and malnutrition. The majority of tribal homes produce rice beer. Almost every adult in the family, including the children, drinks hadiya. Every morning as people wake up, they start working on their daily responsibilities. At eleven in the morning, there is a stoppage due to fatigue, heat, and hunger. During this time, they used to eat very little and finish up the rice from dinner the day before.

Tribal people used the less readily available rice to create and consume gruel. Initially, this liquid had an unpleasant odor. Hadiya was created when people figured out over time how to utilise a special blend of herbs to hasten the rice's fermentation. It has other medicines in addition to alcohol that give a different kind of high. This is because the herbs are added just prior to the start of the brewing process. Once prepared, it must be consumed within a few days. That's when things become nasty. Substance use has detrimental effects on native populations on numerous levels. The health implications include increased vulnerability to infectious diseases, mental health issues, malnutrition, and shorter life spans. Social implications including fractured families, domestic violence, crime, low productivity, and poor school performance all contribute to the poverty cycle. The financial burden encompasses various expenses, including medical costs, lost productivity, reduced earning potential, and reliance on social services.

SYMBOLIC REPRESENTATION VS. SUBSTANTIVE INCLUSION OF INDIGENOUS COMMUNITIES

Debate about indigenous participation in sustainability governance often reveal an apparent contradiction. Traditional cultures and knowledge are often praised in various settings such as speeches, reports, and exhibitions. Tribal Communities themselves remain excluded from decisions that affect their lives. This gap between symbolic recognition and actual inclusion appears both globally and within India. In the case of the Gonds, their art are frequently highlighted as examples of sustainable living. This visibility hardly translates into meaningful decision making. Policies like the FRA were designed to bridge this gap but have own limitations. Policies get delays due to bureaucratic hurdles, and vested interests have kept the agency out of indigenous hands.

Gupta (2020) critiques the superficial engagement with indigenous knowledge systems. He argues that these are often appropriated to lend legitimacy to environmental policies crafted without consultation with indigenous peoples. Baviskar, in 2018, highlights how tribal communities in resource-rich regions like the Narmada Valley are often portrayed as obstacles to development. Their narratives are co-opted to serve state and corporate interests, rather than being incorporated as autonomous agents of sustainability.

Global platforms like the United Nations Framework Convention on Climate Change (UNFCCC) and the Convention on Biological Diversity recognize the role of indigenous knowledge in conservation and climate resilience. However these voices merely translate into actual reality of participation. Indigenous perspectives are filtered through state delegations or non-governmental organizations (NGOs). This dilutes the authenticity and agency of tribal communities. This mediation reinforces existing power asymmetries. This situation severely limits the ability of tribal communities to shape the very policies that have a major impact on their land and their way of life.

Laws like the Forest Rights Act (FRA) of 2006 were created to change the existing conditons by giving tribal communities real power through legal recogniztion of their right. To manage and use the forests they have called home for generations. However, in reality, putting this law into practice has been a huge struggle. The process has been bogged down by long delays, overwhelming red tape, and strong pushback from groups who have a financial interest in keeping things the same. For tribal members, this failed implementation means their daily fight continues. They are still struggling to get official recognition and simply access the lands that have always been theirs.

There's a deep irony at play here. While the government and others often celebrate tribal culture and hold it up as a perfect example of living in balance with nature, this appreciation is usually just for show. This symbolic recognition hardly translates into the actual power or legal rights they need to protect their land and livelihoods. Their culture is admired, but their rights are being ignored.

Indigenous Knowledge as a Pillar of Sustainability

The idea of Traditional Ecological Knowledge, or TEK, is central to understanding how many tribal communities have lived sustainably for generations. It's not just a list of facts; it's a deep and interconnected system of knowledge, practices, and values built up over centuries. This wisdom is based on a holistic view of nature that focuses on balance, giving back, and protecting the world for future generations. The Gond tribe is a perfect example of this. Their entire culture reflects TEK. This is visible in their community led programs i.e., forest management, farming methods. This also reflects in the spiritual rituals they perform to honor and conserve nature. Even their famous art, with its detailed and vibrant paintings of plants and animals, acts as a living record of their environmental philosophy. Despite its proven value, this deep knowledge is almost left out of official government environmental plans. When it is acknowledged, it's often just a token gesture like showcasing the art in a gallery without engaging with the wisdom behind it.

True progress, as experts point out, would come from co-production. This means scientists and indigenous knowledge holders work together to solve environmental problems. This may required the need of a fundamental shift in thinking. Indigenous knowledge must be seen as just as valid and important as Western science, not as some lesser, "unscientific" belief system. Unfortunately, this critical shift has not yet happened where it matters most—in government policy and on-the-ground practice.

Postcolonial theorists argue that the marginalization of indigenous communities is rooted in colonial histories of dispossession and epistemic violence.Spivak's famous question is still extremely relevant today. In simple terms, it asks: Can the oppressed truly be heard? looking at the experience of tribes in India, the answer often seems to be no. Their voices are consistently shut out of the conversations where policies about their land and lives are decided. The legacy of colonial rule still casts a long shadow. British authorities labeled incredibly diverse tribal communities under common identity as primitive. This pattern and way of thinking still influences how governments design policies. Treating these distinct groups as a single problem to be managed, rather than partners to be listened to. This is where environmental justice comes in. It shows that harming the environment and silencing people are two sides of the same coin. The communities with the least power like tribal groups are the ones who suffer the most from pollution, deforestation, and bad policies, even though they did the least to cause these problems. So, excluding indigenous people from governance isn't just an accident or a simple oversight. It is a symptom of much deeper, structural inequalities. The system itself is designed in a way that keeps them from having a real say.

The growing recognition of indigenous rights at international forums, such as the UN Declaration on the Rights of Indigenous Peoples (UNDRIP), has opened avenues for advocacy. Smith (2012) in his stidies noted that participation without power sharing risks becoming performative. For genuine inclusion, governance models must move beyond consultation towards collaboration. Ensuring that indigenous communities have decision making authority over their territories and resources. A good amount of literature is acknowleging the importance of indigenous knowledge but a significant gap in analyzing the structural barriers that prevent substantive indigenous agency in governance. The Gond tribe, despite its rich cultural and ecological heritage, remains underrepresented in academic and policy discourses on sustainability governance. This chapter aims to address this gap by providing a focused case of the Gond community within the broader context of indigenous exclusion in India.

SYSTEMIC EXCLUSION IN GOVERNANCE: THE GAP BETWEEN PRACTICE AND POLICY

Despite their demonstrable contributions to environmental sustainability, the Gond tribe remains systematically excluded from formal governance structures. There are enough instendences to support this argument. This exclusion is both historical and contemporary, rooted in colonial legacies and perpetuated by state and corporate interests.

The Forest Rights Act (FRA) of 2006 was a hope for tribal communities, particularly tribes like the Gonds, whose lives and identities are deeply intertwined with the forests they call home. The law is supposed to recognize the rights of these communities to live on, cultivate, and manage forest lands and resources. It was a bold step to undo the damage of colonial and postcolonial policies. This treated forests as state property, often at the expense of those who depended on them most. However, the gap between the FRA's promise and its reality is stark. For many Gonds and other tribal communities, the dream of secure land rights remains tangled in bureaucracy, resistance, and competing interests.

The FRA, formally known as the Scheduled Tribes and Other Traditional Forest Dwellers (Recognition of Forest Rights) Act, 2006, was a groundbreaking act. It recognized both individual rights such as cultivating land occupied before December 2005 and community rights such as managing forests and protecting traditional knowledge. For the Gonds, whose livelihoods rely on forest resources like bamboo, tendu leaves, and medicinal plants, this was a chance to reclaim ancestral lands. The

Act challenged the colonial mindset that prioritized state control and commercial exploitation over indigenous stewardship, offering a framework to empower communities long marginalized by forest laws.

Implementing the FRA has been a big challenge. Bureaucratic hurdles, uneven progress, and outright resistance make things slower. Many Gonds find their claims for land rights stuck in endless paperwork or rejected on technical grounds such as missing documents or disputes over land boundaries. By 2020, less than half of the claims filed under the FRA had been approved, with states such as Madhya Pradesh and Chhattisgarh, which are home to large Gond populations, showing slow progress. In these regions, claims are often dismissed or left pending for years. A major roadblock is the Forest Department itself. Steeped in a colonial legacy that views forests as state-controlled resources, many officials resist the FRA's push for decentralization. They often see community control as a threat to their authority, clinging to outdated notions of forests as state property rather than shared ecosystems. This resistance is not just bureaucratic it's cultural, rooted in a history that prioritized timber and revenue over people.

Meanwhile, the same system that stalls tribal claims fast-tracks approvals for mining and infrastructure projects. These developments often displace Gond families, severing their cultural and ecological ties to the land. While FRA aims to protect tribal rights, large-scale projects backed by powerful corporate and political interests move forward with little regard for the communities they uproot.

Additionally, many tribal communities lack the resources or awareness to navigate the FRA's complex claim process. Most of the tribal community are first-generation learners. Limited access to legal support and fear of engaging with government systems make it hard for them to protect their rights. Even when claims are filed, they're often bogged down by inconsistent implementation across states, with some regions showing more political will than others.

The FRA's vision was transformative, but its execution has been deeply flawed. For the Gonds and countless others, the Act remains a half-kept promise—a symbol of hope undermined by systemic failures. Until bureaucratic resistance, procedural complexities, and competing interests are addressed, the FRA will fall short of delivering the justice it set out to achieve.

Corporate Interests and Displacement

The Forest Rights Act (FRA) was supposed to protect tribal land, but the government hasn't put it into practice properly. Because of this failure, tribal communities are still being pushed off their land for so-called "development" projects like big mines, factories, and dams. This leads to forced removal from their homes and damage to their environment. The Gond tribe is a perfect example. They live in areas full of valuable minerals, making them a target for these projects. Companies and the government often skip a crucial step: getting the tribe's Free, Prior, and Informed Consent. This means the Gonds aren't properly asked, consulted, or given a real choice before their land is taken. It shows that making money is often seen as more important than protecting tribal rights.

One of the most powerful parts of the FRA is Community Forest Resource (CFR) rights. This would let tribes legally manage and protect their own forests, just as they have for generations. Sadly, this is also the most ignored part of the law. Very few communities have been given these rights. For the Gonds, having CFR rights would mean their traditional knowledge is finally respected and they could legally fight off outsiders trying to take their forests. However, state governments often refuse to give up this control, afraid of losing power and profit.

Even with all these problems, the FRA is still a crucial tool. When tribal communities manage their own forests, they actually do a better job of protecting nature and wildlife than government agencies. Their ancient knowledge is key to conservation. So, for the Gond tribe, this law is more than just a piece of paper—it's a way to have their voice heard and their expertise recognized. But for any of this to happen, there needs to be real political will and a system that holds the government accountable for its promises. The narrative of development in India has often been at odds with the rights of indigenous communities. Gond territories which are rich in mineral resources and biodiversity have been countiously targeted for mining and industrial projects. This has result in forced evictions and ecological degradation. These projects not only disrupt the socio-economic fabric of Gond communities but also erode their cultural connection to the land. The countinous displacement of tribal people has lead to a loss of traditional knowledge and practices. This displacement also undermines community cohesion and create socio-economic vulnerabilities.

DISCUSSION

The Gond tribe, like many indigenous communities in India, is systematically left out of the conversations and decisions about environmental protection and sustainability. Even though the Indian constitution and laws i.e., Forest Rights Act, 2006 are supposed to protect to protect and safeguard their rights. There's a huge gap between what these policies promise and what actually happens on the ground. In reality, their inclusion is often just for show, not meaningful. Using the Gond tribe as an example, we can see how this happens, what stops them from having real power, and how they can reclaim their role in managing their environment. The Gond way of life shows a deep and inherent connection between their culture and living sustainably. Their traditional knowledge isn't just a history lesson; it's a practical guide for how they live every day. This includes their farming techniques, how they manage forests as a community, and a spiritual belief system that sees nature as sacred.

A powerful example of this is Gond art. It's famous for its bright colors and beautiful, intricate patterns of animals, trees, and mythical beings. But this art is much more than just decoration. This is one of the mothod of recording environmental knowledge and expressing their entire worldview. The paintings tell a story about biodiversity and how all living things are connected. For instance, when they paint the Mahua tree, it's not just a pretty picture. That tree represents a whole way of life. It provides food, medicine, fodder for animals, and is central to their culture. So, their art is a direct reflection of their deep ecological wisdom.

The great irony is that this vast knowledge system is almost completely ignored in official government discussions about sustainability. Their art might be put in galleries for people to admire, but the crucial environmental wisdom behind it is rarely acknowledged or used in planning how to protect our natural world. There's a huge and glaring contradiction in how we talk about sustainability: we often celebrate tribal cultures in theory while pushing them to the sidelines in practice. The Gond tribe is a perfect example of this. Their art, which beautifully shows their connection to nature and their myths, is famous worldwide. It's displayed in international galleries and studied by academics as a perfect example of a sustainable worldview. But this cultural recognition almost never turns into real power. The very people who create this art are rarely given a seat at the table when environmental policies are being made.

This is a classic case of a community being spoken *about* but never listened to. Their knowledge of the environment is often borrowed by governments to make their own conservation projects seem more legitimate, but the Gonds themselves are kept out of the decision-making process. Their culture is used to support the government's goals, not to actually empower the tribe itself. This is made worse by so-called "development" projects. The Gonds live in central India, a region rich in minerals, which makes them a target for large mining and infrastructure projects. These projects are frequently approved without getting the community's Free, Prior, and Informed Consent a fundamental right.

The result is that Gond communities are forcibly displaced from their homes. The government's drive for economic growth, combined with outdated stereotypes that label tribal communities as "backward" or "against progress," continues to be used to justify shutting them out of the conversation about their own future.

Epistemic Injustice and the Marginalization of Indigenous Knowledge

Beyond political and economic disenfranchisement, indigenous communities face epistemic injustices that devalue their knowledge systems. Fricker's (2007) notion of epistemic injustice testimonial and hermeneutical aptly describes how Gond ecological knowledge is often dismissed or translated through external actors, thereby losing its authenticity. Agrawal (1995) critiques the artificial divide between scientific and indigenous knowledge, emphasizing that indigenous epistemologies are systematically marginalized in formal governance structures. In the case of the Gonds, traditional practices such as community forest management, sustainable harvesting of non-timber forest products, and conservation rituals are seldom recognized in official policy frameworks (Pathak, 2019). This exclusion not only undermines the efficacy of environmental policies but also perpetuates colonial hierarchies of knowledge.

Non-governmental organizations (NGOs) in India have played a significant role in advocating for tribal rights. However, their interventions often result in a mediated form of participation where tribal communities become passive beneficiaries rather than active decision-makers (Baviskar, 2003). This NGO-State mediation, while well-intentioned, tends to dilute indigenous agency, reinforcing the perception of tribes as recipients of development rather than co-creators of solutions (Gupta, 2020).

The failure to engage directly with Gond governance institutions, such as the Gotul, further alienates communities from the policy-making process. Traditional institutions are sidelined in favor of bureaucratic mechanisms that are ill-equipped to address the nuanced realities of indigenous livelihoods and knowledge systems (Sundar, 2016).

Indigenous Agency and Alternative Governance Models

The concept of indigenous agency necessitates a rethinking of governance frameworks to include tribal communities as partners in sustainability initiatives. Successful models of community-based forest governance, such as the Mendha-Lekha experiment in Maharashtra, demonstrate the potential of indigenous-led conservation (Ramnath, 2021). These models prioritize collective decision-making, equitable benefit-sharing, and the integration of traditional ecological knowledge with contemporary environmental management practices. Knowledge co-production, as advocated by Berkes (2012) and Mauser et al. (2013), offers a pathway for collaborative governance where indigenous and scientific epistemologies are treated as complementary rather than hierarchical.

Reclaiming indigenous agency also entails challenging dominant development paradigms that equate progress with industrialization and resource extraction. The Gond worldview, rooted in reciprocity, ecological balance, and intergenerational equity, offers alternative visions of development that prioritize well-being over economic growth (Gadgil & Guha, 1992). Scholars like Smith (2012) and Xaxa (1999) emphasize the need for decolonizing development discourses by foregrounding indigenous perspectives. This requires not only policy reforms but also a fundamental shift in societal attitudes towards tribal communities—from viewing them as obstacles to recognizing them as knowledge holders and custodians of biodiversity.

Intersectionality and Inclusive Governance

An intersectional approach is crucial for understanding the multiple layers of marginalization faced by Gond communities. Many scholars highlighted that factors such as class, gender, and geographic isolation intersect to shape their experiences of exclusion and discrimination (Rao, 2002). Governance models must be sensitive to these intersections. Special programs with the core focus on capacity building, legal literacy, and leadership development can enhance the participation of tribal groups. Fostering inclusive governance structures that reflect the diversity and complexity of tribal identities (Singh, 2001). Bridging the gap between symbolic recognition and substantive inclusion necessitates a transformative agenda that encompasses legal and political dimensions. Key strategies include:

- Effective implementation of FRA with transparent grievance redressal mechanisms.
- Institutionalizing FPIC to ensure community consent in all development and conservation initiatives.
- Strengthening traditional institutions like Gotul through formal recognition and resource support.
- Promoting indigenous-led research and knowledge documentation.
- Establishing community-based monitoring and accountability frameworks.
- Such measures would not only empower the communities but also enhance the efficacy and resilience of sustainability governance in India.
- The Imperative of Reclaiming Indigenous Agency

The future of sustainability governance in India hinges on the meaningful inclusion of its indigenous communities—not as symbols of cultural diversity, but as active architects of sustainable and just futures.

RETHINKING GOVERNANCE: INDIGENOUS-LED MODELS FOR SUSTAINABILITY

Addressing exclusion requires more than simply proposing new institutions. It always demands confronting the political, legal, and cultural barriers that can shape governance. A more inclusive framework must begin by recognizing indigenous rights in practice. This recognition should be linked to direct representation in decision making bodies and to redistributing resources that tribes like the Gonds depend on. It is essential to build resilience among communties. Integrate traditional knowledge into contemporary sustainability efforts may help in strengthening the communities. Gotul and FPIC are valid entry points, but they must be supported by legal clarity, funding, and safeguards against tokenism.

The first step is Recognition, this means officially acknowledging and valuing three things: their identity as a distinct community, their traditional knowledge about the forest, and their legal rights to the land they have lived on for generations. It's about saying, "Your way of life and your understanding of the natural world are valid and important. Representation: Give them a real seat at the table. It's not enough to just talk about them; they need to be in the room where decisions are made. This means ensuring indigenous community members have direct roles in government committees, forest councils, and any other group that makes policies affecting their lives and land.

The second step is Redistribution: It means actively working to correct historical wrongs by ensuring tribes have secure rights to their ancestral land, a fair share of the benefits from local resources (like forests or water), and access to economic opportunities. It's about leveling the playing field. Resilience is all about support their ability to adapt and thrive. The goal is to strengthen the community's own capacity to handle challenges. The best way to do this is by weaving their traditional knowledge and practices into modern sustainability plans. This approach to governance is built on one simple but powerful idea: the rights of indigenous people to their land, forests, and resources must be truly recognized not just in writing, but in practice. The Forest Rights Act of 2006 was meant to do exactly that. But good laws aren't enough. The problem is a lack of enforcement and accountability. For real change, government institutions must be held responsible for putting these laws into action.

Recognition also means respecting indigenous knowledge as equal to modern science. It's not about one being better than the other, it's about bringing both into the conversation. When policies are made, tribal voices should be heard directly, not filtered or reinterpreted by others. Their wisdom deserves a seat at the table. In Gond society, this is where institutions like the Gotul play a vital role. The Gotul is more than a meeting place for young indidviuals. It is the place where culture is shared, decisions are made, and community life is organized. This model suggests that institutions like the Gotul should be formally included in local governance. Doing so would ensure that policies actually reflect the values and needs of the people they're meant to serve. It would strengthen local leadership and make sustainability efforts more meaningful and effective.

Another essential aspect is Free, Prior, and Informed Consent (FPIC). This means that no project such as mining, dams, conservation zones should be intiated on tribal land without their full agreement. The comunities must be informed early and able to give or refuse consent without pressure. Making FPIC a standard part of development policy would protect tribal rights and ensure that progress doesn't come at the cost of people's lives and livelihoods. This approach is just about including indigenous communities—it's about respecting their knowledge, honoring their governance, and protecting their right to say yes or no to changes that affect their future

Building the capacity of Gond communities to engage in governance processes is a vital enabler of agency. We belive that legal literacy programs can significantlly improve the knowldage level among themseleves. Leadership training for youth and women and skill development initiatives can also enhance the community's ability to articulate their needs, negotiate with external actors, and manage their resources effectively (Xaxa et al., 2014). Such capacity-building measures not only empower individuals but also strengthen the collective resilience of the community. For the governance model to be effective, robust accountability and monitoring mechanisms are essential. Community-based monitoring committees can look at the implementation of policies.(Ramnath, 2021). Social audits and grievance redressal systems anchored in community participation can enhance transparency and trust in governance processes (Sundar, 2016).

CONCLUSION

The exclusion of the Gond tribe from sustainability governance reflects a much broader issue for indigenous peoples in India. Despite the fact that their cultural richness and ecological wisdom, they are too often kept at the margins of decision-making. This chapter has argued that moving beyond tokenism requires a fundamental shift from celebrating tribal culture symbolically to sharing power with tribal communities. Recognition, representation, and redistribution must come together for a better and effective implimentation of policies. This efforts may help strengthen resilience among these communities. None of these is easy or guaranteed, but without them, sustainability will remain incomplete. The Gond experience shows that genuine indigenous agency is not only a matter of justice but also a practical necessity for building sustainable futures in India.

Bridging this gap requires a paradigm change in how indigenous communities are engaged in local governance. Tribal communities should be recognised as a essitial partners as co-creater of solutions not just mere a tokenistic representative. Legal recognition, political representation, and equitable resource redistribution form the pillars of such an approach. The governance model we proposed in this chapter offers a roadmap for operationalizing indigenous agency in sustainability governance. Strengthening community based(local) institutions i.e., Gotul, institutionalizing FPIC and integrating indigenous knowledge through co-production models can be a solution. This approach seeks to democratize environmental governance as well. Furthermore, capacity building, leadership development, and accountability mechanisms are crucial for empowering Gond communities. Ensuring that policies are responsive to the needs and aspirations of tribal individuals. Such an inclusive governance framework will upholds the principles of justice and equity. It also enhances the resilience and effectiveness of sustainability initiatives.

India faces two immense and urgent challenges a rapidly degrading environment and deep-rooted social inequality. To tackle these crises effectively, the active involvement of the country's indigenous communities isn't just beneficial but essential. Taking the example of the Gond tribe, their way of life is built on a profound respect for nature and a powerful sense of responsibility toward future generations. The authorities must move beyond symbolic gestures and build governance models that foster true collaboration. The people who have preserved India's forests and natural heritage for centuries should not be sidelined as passive observers. They must be recognized and supported as the hands-on builders of sustainable development.

REFERENCES

Agrawal, A. (1995). Dismantling the divide between indigenous and scientific knowledge. *Development and Change*, *26*(3), 413–439. DOI: 10.1111/j.1467-7660.1995.tb00560.x

Baviskar, A. (2003). Tribal politics and discourses of environmentalism. *Contributions to Indian Sociology*, *37*(3), 419–444. DOI: 10.1177/006996670303700302

Baviskar, A. (2018). *In the belly of the river: Tribal conflicts over development in the Narmada Valley*. Oxford University Press.

Berkes, F. (2012). *Sacred ecology* (3rd ed.). Routledge.

Fricker, M. (2007). *Epistemic injustice: Power and the ethics of knowing*. Oxford University Press.

Gadgil, M., & Guha, R. (1992). *This fissured land: An ecological history of India*. Oxford University Press.

Gupta, A. (2020). *Indigenous knowledge and environmental sustainability in India*. Routledge.

Mauser, W., Klepper, G., Rice, M., Schmalzbauer, B. S., Hackmann, H., Leemans, R., & Moore, H. (2013). Transdisciplinary global change research: The co-production of knowledge for sustainability. *Current Opinion in Environmental Sustainability*, *5*(3–4), 420–431. DOI: 10.1016/j.cosust.2013.07.001

Pathak, N. (2019). Traditional practices of sustainability in Indian tribes: A study of the Gond community. *Journal of Sustainable Development Studies*, *15*(3), 12–23.

Ramnath, M. (2021). *Decolonizing conservation: Caring for biodiversity in India*. LeftWord Books.

Rao, V. (2002). Symbolic representation and social exclusion: The case of Dalits in India. *Social Research*, *70*(1), 205–218.

Roy Burman, B. K. (1994). Tribal development in India: Myth and reality. *Social Action*, *44*(4), 385–397.

Singh, N. (2001). Indigenous knowledge and its relevance for sustainable development in India. *International Journal of Sustainable Development*, *4*(3), 370–383.

Sinha, S. (1982). State formation and Rajput myth in tribal central India. *Man in India*, *62*(3), 288–310.

Smith, L. T. (2012). *Decolonizing methodologies: Research and indigenous peoples* (2nd ed.). Zed Books.

Spivak, G. C. (1988). Can the subaltern speak? In C. Nelson & L. Grossberg (Eds.), *Marxism and the interpretation of culture* (pp. 271–313). University of Illinois Press.

Sundar, N. (2016). *The burning forest: India's war in Bastar.* Juggernaut Books.

Tiwari, S. K. (2002). *Tribal cultural heritage of central India.* Sarup & Sons.

Xaxa, V. (1999). Tribes as indigenous people of India. *Economic and Political Weekly, 34*(51), 3589–3595.

Xaxa, V.. (2014). *Report of the high-level committee on socio-economic, health and educational status of tribal communities of India.* Ministry of Tribal Affairs, Government of India.

KEY TERMS AND DEFINITIONS

Forest Rights Act (FRA) 2006: A landmark Indian law intended to recognize the rights of forest-dwelling communities over land and resources, but one that has faced challenges in implementation due to bureaucratic resistance, overlapping legal regimes, and political interests.

Free, Prior, and Informed Consent (FPIC): An international standard that requires communities to be meaningfully consulted and give voluntary consent before any project affecting their lands, resources, or rights is undertaken.

Gond Tribe: One of the largest Adivasi (tribal) groups in central India, known for their rich cultural traditions, ecological knowledge, and distinctive social institutions such as the Gotul.

Gotul: A traditional youth dormitory and community institution of the Gond tribe, which functions as a space for learning, cultural transmission, and decision-making, now being reconsidered as a potential model for participatory governance.

Indigenous Agency: The capacity of indigenous communities to actively shape, negotiate, and influence governance and development processes, rather than being passive recipients of policies or symbolic recognition.

Participatory Governance: A governance approach that seeks to involve affected communities—such as indigenous groups—directly in decision-making, resource management, and policy implementation, moving beyond top-down control.

Symbolic Representation: A situation in which indigenous cultures or practices are acknowledged in policy or discourse but without granting actual power or decision-making authority to the communities themselves.

Traditional Ecological Knowledge (TEK): Knowledge systems developed over generations by indigenous and local communities that integrate cultural practices, beliefs, and sustainable interactions with the environment.

Chapter 9
Transformative Discourse vs. Limited Measurement:
The Politics of Gender Data in the SDGs

Şeyda Güdek-Gölçek
https://orcid.org/0000-0001-8753-2998
Niğde Ömer Halisdemir University, Turkey

ABSTRACT

This chapter analyzes how gender equality is represented within the Sustainable Development Goal (SDG) regime and examines the extent to which this representation is reflected in its official indicators, from a feminist critical theory perspective. Gender equality is addressed as both a standalone goal (SDG 5) and a prerequisite for all other goals. Through a comparative analysis of the UN's Gender Snapshot reports (2021–2024), SDG indicators, and the SDG Index, the chapter assesses the alignment between discourse and implementation. Drawing on feminist epistemology and using qualitative content analysis with thematic coding, it identifies key themes and evaluates their translation into measurable outcomes. The findings indicate that although the discourse increasingly reflects intersectional inequalities, the indicator framework lags behind. This gap suggests that gender equality in the SDG agenda is constrained by technical tools. The chapter concludes by urging a revision of global data policies to enable a more inclusive and transformative SDG framework.

INTRODUCTION

The concept of sustainable development presents a normative framework that holistically targets not only the preservation of natural resources but also economic

DOI: 10.4018/979-8-3373-1707-6.ch009

equity, social justice, and institutional inclusivity. Adopted in 2015, the 2030 Agenda for Sustainable Development and its 17 global goals —the Sustainable Development Goals (SDGs)— establish the institutional and political foundation for this multidimensional vision. Within this framework, Gender Equality (SDG 5) is recognized not merely as a standalone objective but as a fundamental prerequisite for the success of all other SDGs (Esquivel & Sweetman, 2016; Yadav, 2023). Indeed, gender inequality poses a structural barrier to sustainable development across numerous domains, from education and health to access to economic resources and political participation (Queisser, 2016).

In this context, gender equality is positioned within the SDGs regime not merely as an ethical objective, but as a strategic and transformative instrument (Leal Filho et al., 2022). Empirical studies of current practices, however, call into question the extent to which this vision is realized through its indicators and monitoring mechanisms (Manzano, 2021). Feminist theory, in particular, posits that although the indicators of the SDGs appear objective and neutral, they often reproduce structural inequalities and can exclude intersectional identities (Mölders, 2019). Moreover, the persistent adherence of data collection and measurement systems to a binary gender model contributes to the invisibilization of LGBTI+ individuals and other marginalized groups (Ababneh et al., 2025).

This chapter conducts an analysis of the discourse-indicator coherence between the Gender Snapshot reports published by UN Women from 2021–2024, and the official SDG indicators and the SDG Index developed by the UN. It is mainly concerned to examine the representation politics that is followed by the regime of SDG for achieving that of gender equality, and to what extent such a discourse is supported by measures that can be counted. Such an interpretation is cognizant of feminist critical theory, and is remarkably based upon the critical interrogation of feminist epistemology of the nature of knowledge, of processes of measure, and of representation.

Here, qualitatively content analysis is conducted on reports of the Gender Snapshot released by UN Women, as also those of the reports mentioned by the researchers are inductively grouped into thematic sets. These themes are then compared against the UN's official indicator set and the SDG Index to analyze the coherence between discourse and action. Fitting into the feminist method of exclusions of data making forefront, analysis pays special attention to those processes of inequality which are not measured or not counted by or under these official reports.

It shows that even as the language of the UN has come to make gender equality increasingly intersectional, multi-layered, contextual forms of late, its discourse developments have not been reflected adequately within its measures. In particular, issues or themes like the effects of COVID-19, climate change, unpaid care, displacement, and classed inequality predominate reports of Gender Snapshot, but these very same urgent concerns are barely represented within accessible indicators (Berik, 2023; Mölders, 2019). This mismatch shows that the SDGs regime's discourse-action gap is no technical fault but an overwhelmingly political, epistemological challenge.

Accordingly, the present chapter is also critical of the ability of the narrative of sustainable development to achieve its vision of achieving gender equality through its measures, ultimately contending that there is a necessity for re-appraisal of data policy that is needed to bridge the gap between rhetoric and reality.

BACKGROUND

Sustainable development is not only the model of economic growth, but an integrated model of environment, human rights, equality, and inclusivity. Hence, the United Nations 2030 Agenda and its corresponding SDGs, agreed upon in 2015, very explicitly stated that only when resource conservation is conservation along with achieving social justice, there is sustainability (Leach et al., 2016). Hence, equality of women to men has transcended from being considered an ethical responsibility to being considered an inevitable determinant of economic, environment, and social sustainability (Leach et al., 2016). What is of interest here is that SDG 5 –the one for gender equality – has an intrinsic sense of interconnectedness to all other goals, due to which its inclusion for all development processes is mandatory (Yadav, 2023).

SDG 5 sets out gender equality as its own separate target but also as its overarching challenge, central to the achievement of all other goals (Leal Filho et al., 2023). It requires of its target that there is an end to all violent and discriminatory practices against women, an end to harmful practices like child marriage and female genital mutilation, and that there is a recognition and equal sharing of unpaid care work. It also sets out to ensure that women have equal access to economic resources, that they have full and effective participation into decision-making, that there is universal access to sexual and reproductive health and rights (Manzano, 2021; UNDP, 2019).

Women's participation in decision-making processes, their inclusion in economic life, and their equal access to essential services like education and health are vital not only for upholding individual rights but also for the holistic welfare of societies (Yadav, 2023; Mondal, 2022). Gender equality is, as such, viewed as an instrument as also an end of sustainable development. Empowerment of women has, as such, been viewed as the condition precedent for realization of human development, realization of economic efficiency, and development of social resilience (Shang et al., 2022).

The empowerment of women has the potential to generate significant spillover effects, spearheading positive transformations in various sectors fundamental to societal development (Manzano, 2021). For example, equal access of women to opportunities of an economic nature has direct benefits for poverty reduction (SDG

1), but indirect benefits for health, nutrition, and even schooling (Beloskar et al., 2024). It is, as such, closely linked to other goals, like SDG 4 (Quality Education), SDG 8 (Decent Work and Economic Growth), SDG 10 (Reduced Inequalities), and SDG 13 (Climate Action) (Jeevanasai et al., 2023). This also holds for environmental sustainability, where representation of women for the purpose of decision-making is of essence (Mondal, 2022; Ababneh et al., 2025). Gender equality is, as such, central for countering climate change, as women's access to resources, women's representation within institutions, as well as environment protective practices, all boost the effectiveness of climate policy (Bilgin Aytaç & Sezgin, 2024).

Inclusion of women's equal representation-enabling policies for political, economic, and public spheres is an absolute stimulant of sustainable development. Facilitating women for productive engagement in decision-making, these policies take the bold change needed for achievement of this goal (Manzano, 2021; Beloskar et al., 2024). Studies of gender equality and women's leadership, including those of leadership- and policy-level leadership, also recognize women's representation of leadership as being instrumental for achievement of these equality outcomes (Beloskar et al., 2024).

The UN's own SDG indicators demonstrate that societies lacking gender equality often face a cascade of multi-layered problems, including the persistence of poverty, limited access to education, poor health outcomes, and increased vulnerability to environmental issues (Queisser, 2016). Gender-based violence, with its severe physical and psychological consequences, not only harms individuals but also fundamentally impedes societal progress (Lima & Guedes, 2024). Indeed, structural barriers such as discrimination, violence, and harmful traditional practices actively undermine the positive nexus between gender equality and sustainable development (UNDP, 2019; Manzano, 2021; Lima & Guedes, 2024). Local-scale studies, for instance in Nepal and India, highlight the decisive role these barriers play in policy implementation (Khanal, 2023; Pokharel, 2024). These challenges are particularly acute in rural settings, where limited access to economic resources and entrenched cultural norms severely hamper the achievement of equality goals (Mustakimah et al., 2023; Bonthala et al., 2023).

The SDGs discourse itself, however, is often framed with limited inclusivity and exhibits significant shortcomings when viewed through a feminist critical lens. Most notable, by conceptualizing gender equality on near-exclusivity along maleness to femaleness axis, the narrative given has chances of excluding those who are of the category of LGBTI+ and non-binaries and reinforcing heteronormative logics (Baumgartinger, 2021; Mölders, 2019). Moreover, the narrative of these within the UN documentation is for large part narrow as well as quantitative. While female representation rate indicators, for instance, take centrality, nuanced consideration of resulting power relations along structural inequalities is under-developed (Ojeda et al., 2025; Lenka, 2023). Such very narrow focus on numerical values has the resultant effect of derailing broader goals of SDG 5, hence extending its general lack of monitorability as well as accountability.

In response to the pressing, multifaceted challenges of realizing gender equality, there is a need for combined, formal mechanisms (Manzano, 2021; Beloskar et al., 2024; Lima & Guedes, 2024). To respond to core challenges like gender violence, for example, innovative, collaborative, creative steps like social design are priceless for creating sustained, productive responses. Finally, even as gender equality plays an indispensable role on the operating as well as the normative levels, realization of its intention is not merely founded upon technical measures, but upon an intense normative dedication to abundance, cultural complexity, and realization of true structural equality.

MAIN FOCUS OF THE CHAPTER

Theoretical Framework

This chapter draws upon feminist critical theory. This theorization of the body identifies gendered unequal treatment as other than the consequence of independent acts of discriminations, but as being inscribed into regimes of normality, social arrangements, regimes of knowledge production, and discourses (Fraser, 1997). From here, even those apparently depoliticizing steps called upon by equality measures and by the international development framework can, unwittingly, re-inscribe and re-perform existing forms of gendered normality.

Critical feminism, in particular, interrogates the ways in which knowledge production is enmeshed with power relations. Consequently, while global policy texts like the SDGs may advocate for noble equality goals, they also necessitate a critical inquiry into how these goals are defined, whose experiences are centered, and who is ultimately excluded. Feminist theory, therefore, seeks to deconstruct the normative assumptions embedded not only in the content of these frameworks but also within the very instruments of their implementation: the indicators, data production methods, and monitoring systems themselves (Bacchi, 2009).

Feminist epistemology reframes data not as a neutral tool for information, but as a political field that demands inquiry into who gets measured, under what conditions, and by which policies. It analyzes gender inequalities not by their visible outcomes alone, but through the very structures, discourses, and modes of knowledge production that generate them (Harding, 1987). This approach, therefore, moves beyond simply advocating for women's visibility; it critically asks for which women, in which contexts, and within which power dynamics this visibility is achieved.

Consequently, this study assesses whether SDGs indicators and their accompanying discourses represent women's multi-layered experiences of inequality, analyzing them not only on a thematic level but also on epistemological and structural grounds.

An intersectional feminist approach is, therefore, central to the analysis presented in this chapter. This approach challenges the treatment of "*women*" as a homogeneous category. Instead, it underscores the necessity of analyzing how multiple identity markers—such as ethnicity, class, age, disability, and migrant status—intertwine and intersect with gender to create unique experiences of inequality (Crenshaw, 1991).

Grounded in this theoretical framework, the central problematic of this chapter is what kind of politics of representation emerges from the interplay between discourse and indicators on the subject of gender equality. Feminist literature asserts that data is not a neutral instrument; rather, it is shaped by political decisions, and choices regarding 'what is measurable, what is monitorable, and what becomes visible' are deeply enmeshed with power relations (D'Ignazio & Klein, 2020). Accordingly, the feminist theory employed in this study aims to expose the normative and structural dynamics that underpin both the discourse and the indicator systems themselves.

Methodology

The data set for this chapter is composed of three primary sources: the annual Gender Snapshot reports, the UN's official SDGs indicator framework, and the indicators used in the SDG Index. Published by UN Women and the UN Statistics Division since 2021, the Gender Snapshot reports are among the most comprehensive documents that evaluate yearly progress on the UN's gender equality goals. Consequently, they provide a critical data source for analyzing the discursive representation of the relationship between gender and the SDGs.

SDG indicators, as part of the 2030 Agenda for Sustainable Development, have 232 measures that supposedly follow 169 targets and 17 goals (UN, 2025). While not an official UN output, the SDG Index is an adjunct monitoring framework of the globe. Authored by command of the United Nations' Sustainable Development Solutions Network (SDSN), the SDG Index is an assessment of the 193 countries' efforts toward the SDGs that is lenient toward the broader narrative of the UN (Sachs et al., 2025). Commentary of official UN measures, amongst other such instruments such as the SDG Index, is an effective academic response, for they shed light on the very tension embedded between institutional rhetoric and operational measurability.

Data, including the Gender Snapshot reports, as also other selected indicators, were content analyzed using qualitative data analysis software MAXQDA. As an efficient qualitative analysis software, MAXQDA codifies thematic coding as also allowing visualizing density of the data. The software's capacity to map inter-code relationships, track discursive shifts over time, and statistically analyze code frequencies provided a robust framework for conducting an in-depth analysis (Kuckartz & Rädiker, 2019).

Coding of the process took place under an inductive process, rather than using pre-defined categories. Adopting upon the feminist methodological framework, reports were examined rigorously for codifying and identifying repeated themes, conceptual patterns, and structural problems of gender. This approach is consistent with feminist research principles, as it facilitates a process of interpretation that emerges organically from the data itself, rather than being imposed upon it (Bryman, 2016).

Inductive coding process produced an initial list of themes that also were condensed into a main code framework and its sub-codes. As illustrated in Table 1, this process consolidated the data into six primary themes: Vulnerability, Intersectionality, Access to Basic Services, Women's Economic Inclusion, Agency and Representation, and Gender Mainstreaming. Each primary theme encompasses a set of sub-codes representing specific concepts or problem areas frequently identified in the reports, such as Gender-based Violence, Displacement, Unpaid Care Work, the STEM Gap, and Gender-Responsive Budgeting.

Table 1. Code Book

Themes	Codes	
Vulnerability	→ Covid-19	
	→ Gender-based Violence	
	Climate Change	→ Food Insecurity
		→ Water Stress
	→ Poverty	
	→ Conflict	
	→ Displacement	
Intersectionality	→ Socioeconomic Identities	→ Displaced Girls and Women
		→ Class-based Background (Poorest and Rural)
		→ Age
		→ Marital Status
	→ Structural Vulnerabilities	→ Disabilities
		→ Ethnic Identities
		→ Indigenous Women
		→ Religion
		→ Gender Identities

continued on following page

Table 1. Continued

<table>
<tr><th>Themes</th><th colspan="3">Codes</th></tr>
<tr><td rowspan="5">Access to Basic Services</td><td rowspan="2">→ Education</td><td colspan="2">→ Women's Education</td></tr>
<tr><td colspan="2">→ Girls in Schooling</td></tr>
<tr><td rowspan="3">→ Health</td><td colspan="2">→ Health and Well-being</td></tr>
<tr><td colspan="2">→ Sexual and Reproductive Health</td></tr>
<tr><td colspan="2">→ Access to Health Services</td></tr>
<tr><td rowspan="10">Women's Economic Inclusion</td><td rowspan="5">→ Labor Market Inequalities</td><td colspan="2">→ Unpaid Care Work</td></tr>
<tr><td colspan="2">→ Employment</td></tr>
<tr><td colspan="2">→ Poor Labor Standards</td></tr>
<tr><td colspan="2">→ Pay Gap</td></tr>
<tr><td colspan="2">→ Women's Access and Control of Economic Resources</td></tr>
<tr><td rowspan="5">→ Women in Exclusive Sectors</td><td rowspan="2">→ Digitalization</td><td>→ Gender Gap in STEM</td></tr>
<tr><td>→ Digital Divide</td></tr>
<tr><td colspan="2">→ Food Production</td></tr>
<tr><td colspan="2">→ Management of Water Resources</td></tr>
<tr><td colspan="2">→ Energy</td></tr>
<tr><td rowspan="3">Agency and Representation</td><td colspan="3">→ Women in Positions of Power and Decision-making</td></tr>
<tr><td colspan="3">→ Social Participation</td></tr>
<tr><td colspan="3">→ Women's Transformative Role</td></tr>
<tr><td rowspan="5">Gender Mainstreaming</td><td colspan="3">→ Gender Responsive Law and Policy</td></tr>
<tr><td colspan="3">→ Funding</td></tr>
<tr><td colspan="3">→ Gender Responsive Social Protection</td></tr>
<tr><td colspan="3">→ Gender Responsive Budget</td></tr>
<tr><td colspan="3">→ Gender Data Gap and Monitoring</td></tr>
</table>

Then, these resultant data of the codifying process were stringently assessed through the official SDG indicators as well as the SDG Index. This type of comparison analysis had its main assignment of ascertaining if indeed there are measurable indicators that follow influential themes of the discourse, so as to draw out the representation between technical means of measure and the world of discursive practice. This type of approach method goes into the very core of feminist critical theory, i.e., its self-prescribed mission of problematizing coherence between practice and discourse as well as making structural exclusions vocal (Bacchi, 2009).

The resulting code book was then systematically compared against the official SDG indicators and the SDG Index. This comparative analysis was framed by key concepts from feminist literature, particularly the concepts of gender data gaps and the politics of representation (Zimmermann & Binswanger, 2021). Moreover, incorporating critiques of multidimensional measurement deficiencies (Berik, 2023), the study went beyond the mere presence or absence of data to investigate how data is produced and, crucially, what —or who— it excludes.

FINDINGS

Thematic Analysis of the UN's SDG Discourse

Vulnerability: Multi-layered Risks within Structural Inequalities

The codes categorized under the theme of Vulnerability illuminate the multidimensional vulnerabilities that women encounter as a direct consequence of structural inequalities. In the context of the SDGs, these codes represent the intersectional problem areas that fundamentally reshape women's living conditions. Figure 1 provides a visual breakdown of the distribution of these codes within this theme.

Figure 1. Frequency of Codes within the Vulnerability Theme

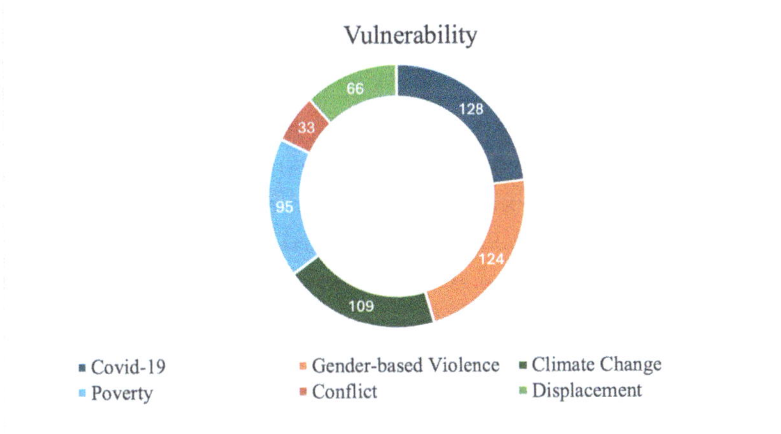

As illustrated in Figure 1, the impacts of the COVID-19 pandemic emerge as a dominant code. The pandemic's ramifications for women extended far beyond health, exacerbating pre-existing structural inequalities, including an increased burden of care labor, widespread job losses, and gaps in social protection. According to one Snapshot report, 54 million women lost their jobs in 2020, while another 45 million left the workforce entirely (UN Women, 2021). The pandemic also diminished access to health services, leading to severe disruptions in prenatal care, family planning, and psychosocial support (UN Women, 2021). While the pandemic's impact might appear conjunctural, it in fact serves as a stark example of women's heightened vulnerability to the negative consequences of any crisis.

Gender-based violence —encompassing early marriage, sexual and physical violence, and digital violence— is a pervasive issue for women that is known to intensify during periods of crisis, such as pandemics and conflicts. A 2024 report highlights the scale of the problem: globally, one in eight women experienced intimate partner violence in the past year, a rate that climbs to as high as one in three in some nations. The same report projects that, at the current pace, child marriage will not be fully eliminated until 2092 (UN Women, 2024). These statistics reveal that gender-based violence is not a fleeting issue but a deeply entrenched domain of vulnerability, resistant to slow-paced change.

The Climate Change code underscores the disproportionate burden the climate crisis places on women. They are more exposed to its adverse effects, such as food insecurity and difficulties in accessing water, particularly in the wake of climate-related disasters. A 2023 report projects that the direct impacts of climate change could drive an additional 158 million women and girls into extreme poverty by 2050 — a figure 16 million higher than for their male counterparts (UN Women, 2023). Moreover, the burden of unpaid labor—including tasks like collecting water and other forms of domestic work— falls predominantly on women, which in turn increases their workload and curtails educational opportunities for girls (UN Women, 2024).

Armed conflicts, environmental degradation, and other crises continue to drive female displacement, establishing Displacement as a key gendered vulnerability. Women in these regions, whether displaced or remaining in their communities, face heightened exposure to forced migration and its cascading consequences of poverty, violence, and health crises. Closely related, the Conflict code highlights a distinct yet intertwined domain of vulnerability. In such settings, women are often deprived not only of physical safety but also of essential services, including access to healthcare, safe childbirth facilities, and psychological support. For instance, the 2024 report indicates that women in conflict zones such as Gaza, Sudan, Afghanistan, and Ukraine are under extraordinary duress, with severe impacts on their physical and mental health (UN Women, 2024).

The final vulnerability code highlighted in Figure 2 is Poverty. Certain groups of women —particularly mothers, the elderly, and single women— are structurally more susceptible to poverty. Data from 2024 indicates that 9.8% of women live in extreme poverty (on less than $2.15 a day), a rate higher than that for men (UN Women, 2024). This situation is exacerbated by gender-based gaps in social protection systems, which in turn serve to perpetuate female poverty.

In summary, the codes within the Vulnerability theme collectively illustrate the multidimensional disadvantages that arise from gender inequality. The thematic analysis reveals that the vulnerabilities facing women and girls are not isolated events but are deeply intersectional in nature. Consequently, structural shocks —such as the COVID-19 pandemic, the climate crisis, conflict, displacement, and poverty—yield far more severe consequences for women when layered upon a pre-existing foundation of gender-based discrimination.

Intersectionality: The Interplay of Identity and Inequality

The theme of "*Intersectionality*" demonstrates how various identities intersect with structural inequalities to compound and intensify vulnerability. Within this theme, the analysis reveals two primary axes of identity: i) socioeconomic identities and ii) structural identities.

Socioeconomic Identities

The theme of Socioeconomic Identities encompasses the various class-based, demographic, and familial positions that shape the experiences of women and girls. As the UN Women Gender Snapshot documents frequently emphasize, variables such as poverty, age, migration, and marital status are key determinants of their access to equal opportunities.

Figure 2 illustrates the distribution of these identity codes, with Displaced Girls and Women being a prominent example. This sub-code refers to those forced to migrate due to conflict, disaster, climate change, or political instability. According to a 2024 report, 612 million women and girls currently live in conflict zones, and those who are displaced face heightened risks of human trafficking, sexual abuse, and an inability to access healthcare services (UN Women, 2024).

The Class-based Background sub-code identifies the distinct vulnerabilities faced by the poorest women and those residing in rural areas. The poorest women often encounter significant disadvantages in accessing social protection and essential services. Similarly, women in rural areas face severe barriers, particularly in relation to education, healthcare, and digital technology. The educational gap is particularly stark: a 2022 report indicates that the secondary school completion rate for the poorest rural women is up to 70% lower than that of their wealthiest urban counterparts (UN Women, 2022).

Figure 2. Frequency of Sub-codes within the Socioeconomic Identities Code

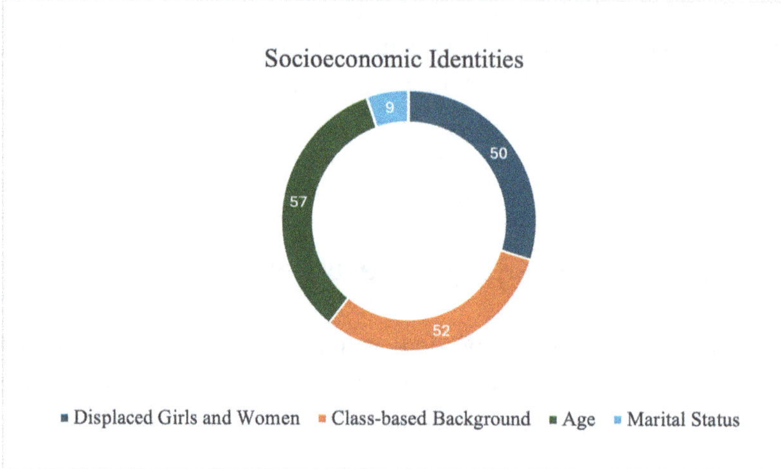

The Age code addresses the distinct sets of vulnerabilities faced by two key demographic groups: i) older women and ii) girls and young women. Older women are often confronted with risks such as social isolation, inadequate pension rights, and both physical and psychological violence. Furthermore, their longer life expectancy means they typically require access to healthcare, social support, and secure housing for a more extended period. In contrast, the defining challenges for girls and young women primarily revolve around unequal access to education, the threat of child marriage, and vulnerability to sexual abuse.

The Marital Status code highlights the specific challenges confronting divorced women and female-headed households. The analysis indicates that female-headed households, particularly those led by single mothers, are significantly more exposed to poverty. This vulnerability is compounded by inadequate social protections. For instance, 2024 data reveals that over 50% of women lack direct access to social protection systems, with divorced women often having diminished pension rights (UN Women, 2024).

Structural Identities

The Structural Identities code pertains to inequalities that stem from women's fixed or immutable characteristics — those attributes that cannot be easily changed. While these particular domains of vulnerability have often been underrepresented in broader international documents, they receive growing emphasis in the 2021–2024 Snapshot reports. Figure 3 provides a breakdown of the sub-codes classified under this code.

Figure 3. Frequency of Sub-codes within the Structural Identities Code

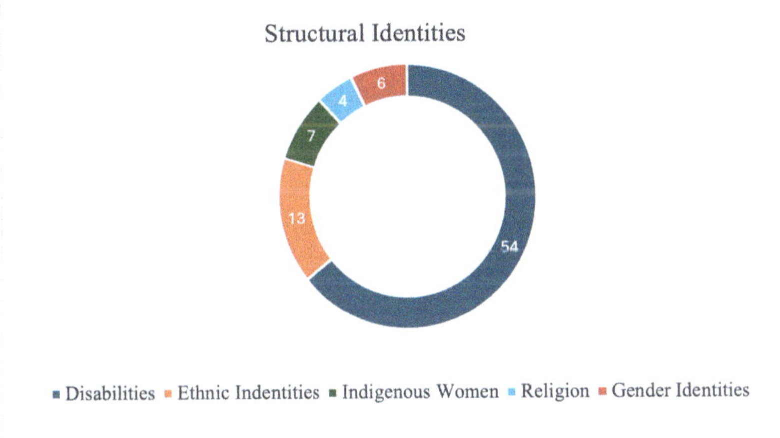

The Disabilities code represents a prominently featured intersectional disadvantage within the analyzed documents. Women with disabilities confront formidable structural barriers, particularly in accessing healthcare, education, and employment. Their rates of educational attainment, for example, are significantly lower than those of women without disabilities. Moreover, this group faces a heightened risk of experiencing both violence and discrimination (UN Women, 2023).

Women from ethnic minorities —particularly migrants, refugees, and members of indigenous communities— often face intense discrimination, which can lead to their exclusion from fundamental areas like healthcare, education, and citizenship rights. Ethnic Identities are also linked to significant inequalities in accessing health and social services. The Indigenous women sub-code specifically points to those who lose their habitats due to environmental degradation from mining and energy projects, while also being subjected to violence and economic exclusion. The lack of political representation is stark: 2024 data shows that only 19 countries have policies in place to ensure the participation of indigenous women in decision-making processes related to water and environmental management (UN Women, 2024).

Discrimination on the basis of religious identity can also constrain women's participation in public life and their access to social services, particularly for those belonging to minority faiths. This issue, however, is addressed more obliquely in the 2023 and 2024 reports compared to other identity markers.

Finally, individuals who identify outside of binary gender norms face a dual threat of societal violence and systematic discrimination. The 2022 and 2023 reports specifically highlight this vulnerability in relation to digital violence, social exclusion, and barriers to accessing healthcare.

Access to Basic Services: Gender Gaps in Education and Healthcare

While education and health are enshrined as core objectives in SDG 4 and SDG 3 respectively, women continue to face multi-layered inequalities in both domains. Figure 4 presents the distribution of the codes identified within these two areas.

Figure 4. Frequency of Codes and Sub-codes within the Access to Basic Services Theme

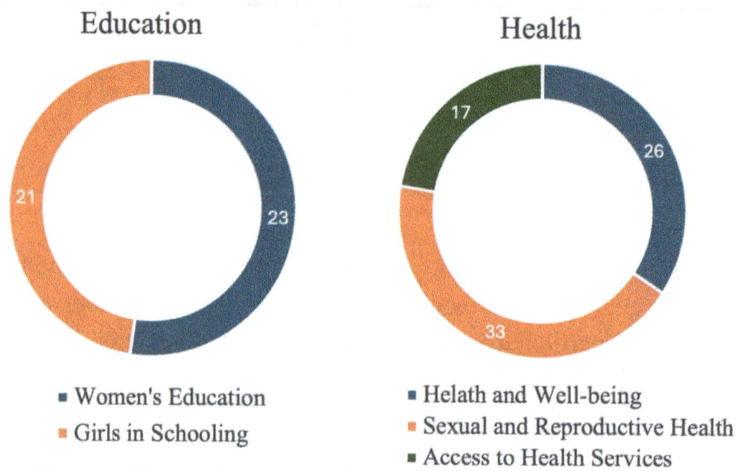

Women's access to lifelong learning, including professional and vocational training, is often severely constrained by gender norms, caregiving responsibilities, and economic barriers. For girls, the risk of being excluded from education is exacerbated by factors such as early marriage, poverty, the burden of unpaid care work, and a lack of school safety. The scale of this issue is immense: 2024 data shows that 119.3 million girls globally remain out of school, with enrollment rates being dramatically low in the poorest rural areas (UN Women, 2024). It is therefore evident that the right to education is not merely a matter of access, but is fundamentally intertwined with gender-based structural injustices.

Similarly, women's access to healthcare is adversely affected by a range of factors tied to gender inequality, with their physical and mental health being directly impacted by external crises like climate change, conflict, and economic instability. The Snapshot reports from 2021 and 2024 emphasize these disparities, particularly in the realm of Sexual and Reproductive Health, a key target of SDG 3.7. Inequalities are highlighted in access to prenatal care, family planning services, and skilled attendance at birth. For instance, in Sub-Saharan Africa, 40% of women lack access to a skilled health professional during childbirth (UN Women, 2022). Moreover, 2024 data indicates that 800 million women lack access to modern contraceptive methods — a gap that is fundamentally linked to the issue of women's bodily autonomy (UN Women, 2024).

Women's inability to fully access and benefit from health systems stems from both structural and societal barriers. Structural barriers include a lack of insurance, geographical remoteness, and inadequate infrastructure, while societal barriers encompass issues like intra-family control, stigmatization, and low health literacy. Underscoring the scale of this problem, a 2023 report states that over 50% of women lack direct access to healthcare services. These challenges are often most acute for women in rural areas and among migrant populations.

Women's Economic Empowerment

The Women's Economic Empowerment theme offers a lens through which to analyze women's unequal position in economic life, considering both labor market dynamics and issues of sectoral representation. The sub-codes within this theme are particularly significant, as they reveal how the UN constructs its gender equality perspective in relation to SDG 5 (Gender Equality), SDG 8 (Decent Work and Economic Growth), and SDG 9 (Industry, Innovation, and Infrastructure). The two primary codes explored here illuminate a dual challenge: the persistent structural inequalities in traditional labor markets, and women's exclusion from emerging sectors shaped by digitalization and the green transition.

Labor Market Inequalities: The Structural Exclusion of Women

The Labor Market Inequalities theme examines the multi-layered inequalities and structural barriers that women confront in their economic participation. The various sub-codes representing these challenges, and their distribution within the data, are illustrated in Figure 5.

Figure 5. Frequency of Sub-codes within the Labor Market Inequalities Code

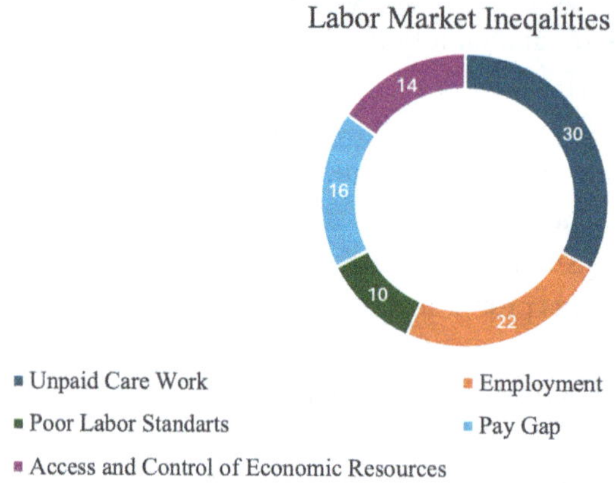

The Unpaid Care Work sub-code represents a primary driver of both time poverty and income inequality among women. The Gender Snapshot reports from 2022 and 2023 consistently highlight this disparity, revealing that women perform, on average, 2.8 hours more of unpaid domestic and care work per day than men. This invisible labor not only restricts women's ability to participate in the formal paid economy but also severely impedes their access to social protection.

Barriers stemming from gender inequality, particularly the burden of unpaid work, mean that women continue to have lower employment rates and face a higher risk of unemployment than men. For instance, a 2024 report indicates that in the post-COVID-19 recovery, women have returned to the workforce at a slower rate than their male counterparts. Furthermore, women are often concentrated in low-wage, precarious, and informal jobs, which lays the groundwork for the Poor Labor Standards sub-code — another significant barrier to economic empowerment. This sub-code encompasses conditions such as informal employment, poor safety standards, excessive work hours, and a lack of social security, all of which contribute to the exploitation of female labor. Indeed, a 2022 report confirms that informal employment remains highly prevalent among women globally.

The Pay Gap sub-code addresses not just the disparity in wages, but the broader gap in total earnings, which encompasses elements like bonuses and social benefits. A 2021 report quantifies this disparity, indicating that women earn, on average, 20% less than men. Furthermore, this gap is not static; it widens significantly depending on factors such as age, motherhood, and economic sector.

The Access and Control of Economic Resources sub-code highlights the persistent barriers women face in accessing and controlling key assets, including land, finance, credit, and technology. This exclusion from the formal financial system is striking:

2023 data indicates that only 29% of women have a bank account. Similarly, in the agricultural sector, women constitute just 15% of all landowners (UN Women, 2023).

Women in Exclusive Sectors

The Women in Exclusionary Sectors code and its sub-codes focus on the underrepresentation of women in male-dominated fields, highlighting the challenges this poses to both gender equality and broader sustainability objectives. Figure 6 illustrates these sectors and the distribution of their corresponding codes.

Figure 6. Frequency of Sub-codes within the Women in Exclusionary Sectors Code

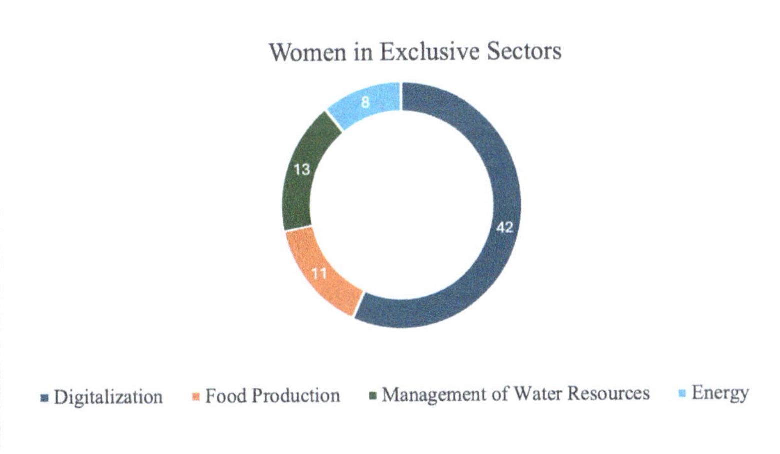

The Digitalization code reveals the persistence of gender inequality in a defining sector of our age and is composed of two key sub-codes: i) Gender Gap in STEM and ii) Digital Divide. Women remain significantly underrepresented in STEM fields; a 2024 report, for example, indicates that they constitute less than 25% of the workforce in engineering and information technology. Similarly, a stark Digital Divide persists, with women lagging behind men in accessing digital technologies. Data from 2023 illustrates this gap: 327 million fewer women than men have access to the internet globally, and only 28% of women worldwide possess digital skills (UN Women, 2023). This digital disparity severely limits women's ability to participate in the ongoing digital transformation and obstructs their path to economic empowerment.

The Food Production code stems from a central paradox: women are key actors in ensuring food security, especially as small-scale agricultural producers, yet they often remain invisible within the sector. For example, while a 2023 report indicates that women are active in 70% of food production, their access to agricultural tools and credit remains severely limited. This reality also makes women's role in combating climate change strategically vital.

Similarly, the Management of Water Resources code points to another sector where women's contributions are essential yet overlooked. Although women are the primary users and managers of water at the household level, they remain significantly underrepresented in decision-making processes. A 2024 report underscores this gap, noting that only 19 countries have implemented measures to promote the effective participation of women in water management.

In the Energy sector, the representation of women in technical, managerial, and engineering roles also remains critically low. This underrepresentation has a dual negative impact: it not only curtails women's economic opportunities within the sector but also diminishes the influence of their perspectives in vital climate-related decision-making processes.

Agency and Representation: Women's Voice and Transformative Influence in Decision-Making

The codes within the Agency and Representation theme reveal that the UN discourse frames gender equality not merely as a right to be protected, but as a process of cultivating active agency and political participation. This perspective underscores the need to recognize women not just as rights-holders, but as vital political, social, and environmental actors. Figure 7 provides a visual breakdown of these codes.

Figure 7. Frequency of Codes within the Agency and Representation Theme

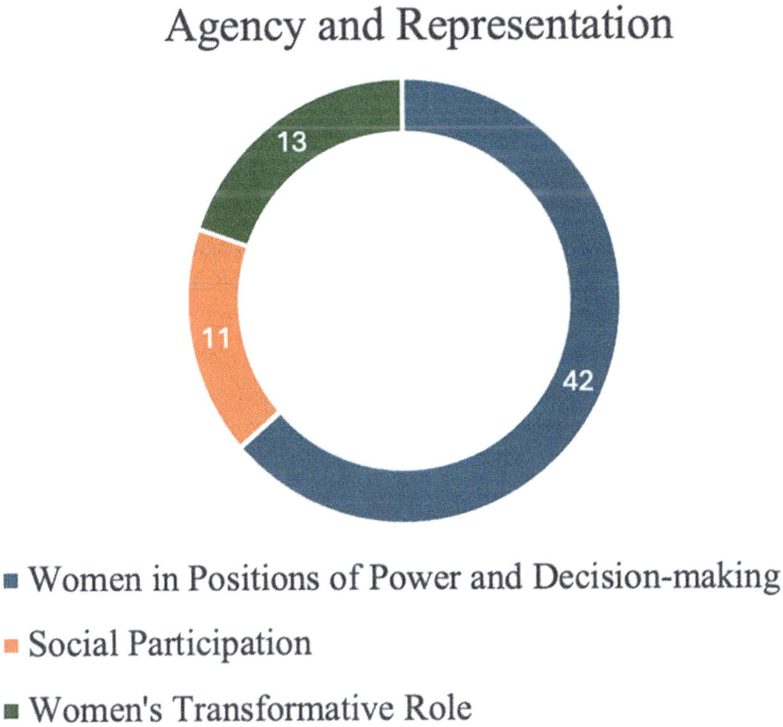

The code Women in positions of power and decision-making refers to women's presence in areas such as political representation, institutional leadership, and policymaking processes. According to the 2024 Gender Snapshot report, women's representation in parliaments globally stands at 26.7%, while in local governments, this figure is 36%. However, the core issue is not merely numerical representation but the power inherent in that representation. Women are often placed in "*low politics*" areas such as health and education, while being excluded from "*high politics*" domains like economy, security, and energy. The Gender Snapshot documents explicitly address this disparity, highlighting the symbolic equality that arises when women are merely "*represented*" rather than truly "*decision-makers*."

The emergence of the Transformative Role code signifies a discursive shift towards a more constructive approach, framing gender equality not as a passive right, but as an active instrument of transformation. This code positions women not merely as vulnerable or disadvantaged groups, but as transformative actors — a role that is particularly prominent in the context of climate action. The 2022 and 2023 Gender Snapshot reports, for instance, highlight the foundational roles women play in food production, water resource management, and community-based environmental initiatives. Furthermore, the reports note that women's participation in areas like peace processes, crisis response, and social reconstruction demonstrably yields more sustainable and inclusive outcomes, creating a direct link to SDG 16 (Peace, Justice, and Strong Institutions).

The Social Participation code addresses the conditions that impede women's full and equal engagement in public area. Women's capacity for visibility and active participation is often constrained by a combination of gender norms, safety concerns, and inadequate infrastructure. The 2023 and 2024 reports highlight these issues, pointing specifically to public transportation, street safety, and the need for woman-friendly public services (e.g., adequate lighting, hygienic toilets, and child-care facilities). The code's scope extends beyond mere physical presence to include equal representation in digital arenas, access to cultural activities, and participation in sports. Ultimately, it draws attention to the barriers that prevent the realization of women's fundamental right to engage with society on equal terms.

Gender Mainstreaming: The Dimensions of Policy, Finance, and Data

The theme of Gender Mainstreaming refers to the integration of a gender equality perspective as a horizontal principle across all policy domains. Within the context of the SDGs, its objective is to establish an egalitarian governance model for their implementation. Figure 8 illustrates both the key strategies employed for gender mainstreaming and the areas where significant gaps and challenges persist.

Figure 8. Frequency of Codes within the Gender Mainstreaming Theme

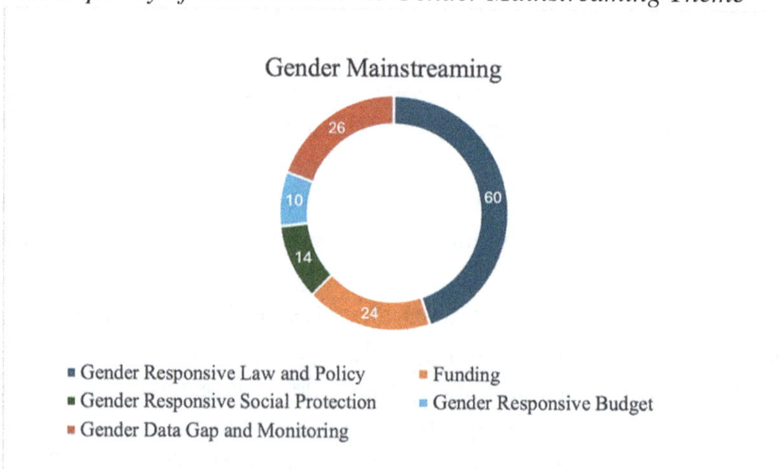

The high frequency of the Gender-Responsive Law and Policy code signifies the discursive importance placed on creating gender-sensitive legislation and policy frameworks. The 2023 and 2024 reports repeatedly stress that when policies in key areas —such as climate, disaster management, energy, and digital transformation— fail to incorporate a gender perspective, they produce exclusionary outcomes for women. For example, the 2024 Snapshot report reveals that only 16 countries treat gender equality as a central theme in their national climate action plans. This statistic underscores a critical reality: Significant deficiencies in legal and strategic frameworks remain a pervasive challenge at the global level.

Lack of adequate financing represents one of the most fundamental structural barriers to the implementation of gender equality policies. A 2021 report, for example, highlighted this disparity, revealing that a mere 0.1% of funds in post-COVID-19 recovery plans were earmarked for gender equality initiatives. Furthermore, the heavy reliance of women-focused projects in developing nations on donor financing often jeopardizes their long-term sustainability. This trend is also evident in climate finance, where a 2024 report indicates that the share of funding addressing women's specific needs remains critically low. Consequently, the Funding code identifies a crucial impediment to the successful mainstreaming of gender equality.

Gender-responsive budgeting is an approach that places egalitarian principles at the center of public resource allocation. However, its adoption remains limited; a 2022 report noted that only 26 countries currently integrate gender analysis into their national budgeting processes. Without such an analysis, even seemingly "*neutral*" expenditures can inadvertently reproduce or deepen existing inequalities. Therefore, expanding this practice to key sectors like education, health, infrastructure, and employment is essential for maximizing their contribution to gender equality.

Gender-responsive social protection systems are vital for alleviating women's unpaid care burden, reducing precarious employment, and breaking cycles of poverty. Yet, access remains severely limited: a 2023 report indicates that only 26% of women can directly benefit from comprehensive social protection systems. Certain groups —notably female-headed households, migrant women, and those in the informal sector— are often excluded from these social safety nets. Compounding this issue, a 2024 report finds that the number of countries with targeted policies designed to support these specific groups remains exceedingly small.

Overall, the analysis indicates a strong discursive focus on the level of law and policy, while the practical dimensions of implementation —namely budgeting, funding, and data— are comparatively underrepresented. This imbalance suggests that the gap between political rhetoric and concrete action persists. Within the financial context, gender equality is frequently framed as an issue requiring additional resources, an approach that causes its integration to be treated as optional and temporary, rather than as a fundamental component of all policy.

Data-driven policymaking is another critical dimension for increasing the impact of gender equality initiatives. The Gender Data Gap and Monitoring code is therefore highlighted as a vital mechanism for both tracking progress and ensuring accountability in gender mainstreaming. A recurring critique in the 2022 and 2023 reports is that data pertaining to women is often limited, incomplete, and outdated. Underscoring this point, a 2024 report reveals that only 15 countries currently collect gender-responsive data for the SDG indicators. This systemic lack of gender-sensitive data makes it exceedingly difficult to monitor progress, particularly on SDG 5, and severely undermines accountability.

Comparative Analysis: Gender Representation in SDG Discourse vs. Indicators

Dominant Codes in the SDG Discourse

To identify the dominant narratives in the Gender Snapshot reports, it is essential to first determine the primary areas of discursive concentration. Figure 9 presents the frequency distribution of the top ten most-coded themes identified in the analysis. This quantitative breakdown allows for a clear examination of the discourse's main priorities and, by extension, its potential gaps or areas of lesser focus.

The prominence of the COVID-19 code, as illustrated in Figure 9, indicates that the pandemic rapidly became a top-priority issue within the discourse on gender equality. This focus was driven by the pandemic's potential to reverse hard-won gains and exacerbate existing inequalities. The 2021 and 2022 reports, for instance, centered on the pandemic's impact on women's job losses, the increased burden of care work, disruptions in healthcare access, and the surge in gender-based violence. Consequently, the pandemic served to foreground gender equality, positioning it as a critical component of emergency management, social protection, and human rights responses.

Figure 9. Frequency Distribution of the Top Ten Codes in the Gender Snapshot Reports

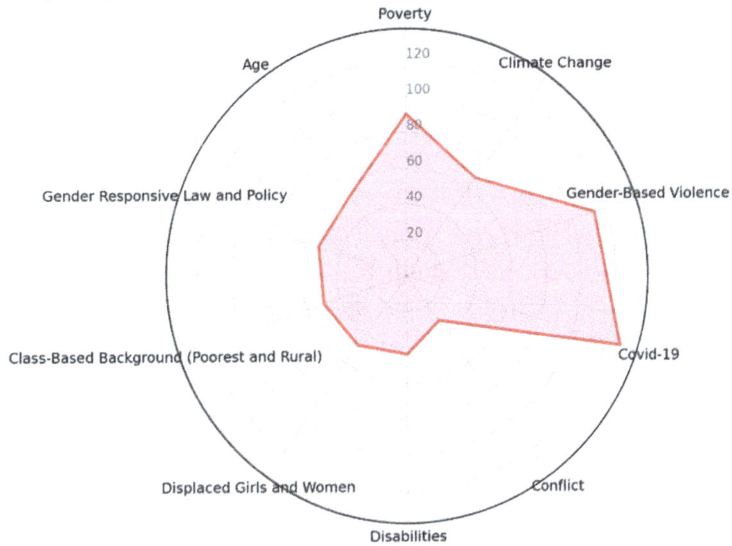

Gender-Based Violence is the second most frequent code in the analysis, closely following COVID-19. This finding highlights a key distinction: while the pandemic represents a conjunctural crisis, GBV is presented as a persistent and structural problem. Indeed, across all the analyzed reports, various forms of GBV —notably child marriage, intimate partner violence, and digital violence— are consistently framed as a fundamental crisis. The code's high frequency thus demonstrates that securing women's safety holds a powerful and central place within the official UN discourse.

The Poverty code consistently highlighted women's greater vulnerability concerning social protection, property rights, and income inequality. Similarly, the Climate Change code was prominent in the 2023 and 2024 reports, often framed through the narrative of the feminization of climate vulnerability, which defines women as the group most affected by and least protected from the crisis. The Age code was also notably disaggregated, addressing the distinct challenges of girls and young women (e.g., education, child marriage) and older women (e.g., access to care, social isolation). This differentiation points to an increasingly layered analysis of gender within the UN documents, one that considers its impacts across the entire life cycle. Collectively, the high frequency of these three codes —Poverty, Climate Change, and Age— demonstrates a growing recognition of intersectional inequalities within the official discourse.

The Gender-Responsive Law and Policy code appears with a relatively low, yet noteworthy, frequency. This suggests that while the institutionalization of gender equality is acknowledged as important, it is treated as a secondary-tier priority within the discourse. In other words, while the integration of gender is present at the policy level, its impact is less pronounced in codes related to practical implementation, such as budgeting, funding, and data.

Similarly, the moderate frequency of the Class-Based Background code reflects a general recognition of women's class positions, especially for those in rural and impoverished contexts. This recognition, however, is largely framed through a lens of vulnerability and aid, rather than one of agency and empowerment.

While the Displaced Girls and Women code is frequently invoked, particularly in the context of conflict and crisis, holistic policy solutions that address their structural needs are seldom presented in the documents. Similarly, despite the severe inequalities they face in accessing services and their heightened risk of violence, the discursive representation of women with disabilities remains notably limited. Finally, the Conflict code is represented in the documents in two primary ways: first, as a general acknowledgment of the vulnerabilities created by conflict, and second, as a geographically limited reflection on the acute crises facing women in specific regions like Gaza, Sudan, and Afghanistan.

Overall, the analysis of the most frequent codes (Figure 9) indicates that the discourse on the SDG-gender nexus is predominantly crisis-driven and oriented toward intersectional inequalities. While acute crisis areas like COVID-19, climate change, and violence were the most emphasized themes, awareness of structural issues such as poverty and age was also high. In stark contrast, the strategic tools required for implementation —such as closing data gaps, institutional monitoring, and concrete policy integration through budgeting and funding— were significantly underrepresented and thus absent from the top-coded themes. This discrepancy suggests that the documents adopt an equality approach that prioritizes discourse over action, ultimately offering a narrative that is strong in representation but limited in its transformative potential.

The Alignment of Discourse Themes and SDG Indicators

An analysis of the thematic distribution in the Gender Snapshot reports over time reveals a significant expansion of the discourse on gender equality, both in its thematic diversity and its intersectional depth. The high frequency of codes related to gender-based violence, poverty, COVID-19, care work, reproductive health, women's decision-making, climate change, and socioeconomic inequalities is particularly telling. This concentration of themes demonstrates that the official discourse is predominantly crisis-driven and sharply focused on structural inequalities.

However, a stark discrepancy emerges when this discursive richness is contrasted with the official indicator sets monitored by the UN and those used in the SDG Index. As the comparative diagram and code matrix in Figure 10 illustrate, a clear misalignment exists between the two realms. While a few codes are strongly represented in both the discourse and the measurement systems, many prominent themes are confined to the discursive realm, lacking corresponding quantitative indicators.

Figure 10. Intensity of Association between Thematic Codes and SDG Indicator Sets

Figure 10 reveals that a specific subset of thematic codes has strong linkages to multiple indicators, demonstrating their visibility not only within the discourse but also at the level of measurability. Chief among these well-aligned codes is Gender-Based Violence. As the line thickness in the diagram indicates, this theme is robustly represented in both the official SDG targets (particularly SDG 5.2) and the various index indicators, with data regularly collected on issues like femicide and intimate partner violence. Consequently, Gender-Based Violence, along with Sexual and Reproductive Health, Employment, and Political Representation, are codes that achieve high visibility precisely because they are tied to established, measurable indicators.

While many intersectional identities —such as Displaced Girls and Women and Indigenous Women— are prominent in the discourse as vulnerable groups, they are largely absent from the indicator map in Figure 10. This absence is primarily due to a lack of specific, gender-disaggregated data for these groups. The notable exceptions are Disabilities and Class-based Background, which find limited representation in the indicators through variables like disability status and the urban-rural divide. Consequently, a major gap is evident: A wide range of crucial, intersectional vulnerabilities, despite being increasingly detailed in the discourse, remain largely invisible at the level of practical measurement.

Sexual and Reproductive Health is another theme with strong indicator alignment, being directly addressed under SDG Target 3.7 and included in the SDG Index. It is measured through concrete indicators such as access to contraceptive methods and the presence of skilled health personnel at birth.

Following this, Gender-Responsive Law and Policy also demonstrates a relatively strong connection to the indicators, appearing within the sub-indicators of SDG 5, SDG 4, and SDG 8. Similarly, Women in Positions of Power and Decision-Making is tracked through indicators in both SDG 5 and SDG 16. The SDG Index, for instance, explicitly uses the metric 'seats held by women in national parliaments' to measure this dimension

A key finding is that while strategic tools within the Gender Mainstreaming theme —such as Gender-responsive Law and Policy, Gender-responsive Budgeting, and Gender Data Gap Monitoring— have been coded with increasing frequency in recent years, their measurable counterparts are limited. This suggests a significant gap: although policy integration and institutional monitoring mechanisms are well-defined in the discourse, the instruments for their practical implementation remain underdeveloped.

Comparative Analysis: The Tension Between Discursive Ambition and Measurable Reality

The UN' Gender Snapshot reports from 2021-2024 frame gender equality within a multi-layered and intersectional context. The discourse consistently links the issue not only to a human rights foundation but also to broader structural development goals, including economic sustainability, poverty reduction, and climate action. Prominent areas of discursive focus include the social impacts of the COVID-19 pandemic, gender-based violence, the climate crisis, age and class-based inequalities, and the specific vulnerabilities of groups such as displaced, disabled, and rural women. This overarching narrative demonstrates that the UN positions gender equality as both a normative objective and an instrument for structural transformation.

However, when this discursive framework is examined against the measurable indicators used in the official SDG framework and the SDG Index, a stark misalignment comes into view. The comparative analysis (Figures 9 & 10) reveals that the indicators establish only weak links with the broader discourse; indeed, many of the most prominent discursive themes are entirely absent from the measurement frameworks.

While a select few codes —notably gender-based violence (SDG 5.2), poverty, and reproductive health— find clear representation at the indicator level, a vast number of other critical issues cannot be tracked. For instance, the gendered impacts of the COVID-19 pandemic, the intersection of gender and climate change, the plight of displaced women, and class-based inequalities are all powerful themes in the discourse, yet their substantiation through concrete indicators remains largely absent.

This limitation within the indicator sets severely constrains the SDG regime's capacity for practical implementation and accountability. Ultimately, it renders many vulnerable groups structurally invisible, creating a clear paradox: despite their significant discursive emphasis, these critical issues are not defined in a way that makes them measurable, and therefore, actionable.

A primary reason for this misalignment is that the SDG regime is largely constructed upon pre-existing national data sets and indicators. Deficiencies in the capacity for data disaggregation diminish the visibility of groups with intersectional identities, thereby hindering the translation of discursively prominent vulnerabilities into measurable metrics. This should be understood not merely as a technical inadequacy, but as a structural limitation shaped by the institutional and political choices that determine which indicators are prioritized and which are ultimately excluded. As a result, the SDG regime, constrained by its narrow data boundaries, is often incapable of fully tracking the complex structural inequalities that its own discourse highlights.

In conclusion, while the Gender Snapshot reports present a remarkably comprehensive, critical, and multidimensional vision of gender equality, the SDG regime's capacity to translate this vision into a measurable and monitorable framework through its indicators and indices remains severely limited. This reveals a fundamental disconnect: The discourse-action inconsistency is not merely an issue of symbolic representation, but a significant structural problem that undermines the core principles of accountability and monitorability.

DISCUSSION & CONCLUSION

The discourse presented in the Gender Snapshot reports frames gender equality not merely as a human rights issue, but as an indispensable dimension of structural development, economic sustainability, and social justice. The analysis of coded themes reveals a primary focus on intersectional inequalities, governance mechanisms, and crisis-driven forms of inequality. However, this transformative discourse finds markedly limited representation within the monitoring architecture of the SDG indicators and indices. This analysis, therefore, points to a significant discourse-indicator misalignment, arguing that it is shaped by both technical limitations and political choices (Mariano & Molari, 2022).

This chapter highlights three primary areas of misalignment between the discourse in the Gender Snapshot reports and the official SDG indicators. First, a significant portion of the most prominent themes in the discourse —notably displacement, disabilities, class-based background, and age— find no direct counterparts in the indicator frameworks. The limited capacity of data-driven monitoring systems severely constrains the measurability of such intersectional inequalities (Leal Filho et al., 2023). This corresponds directly to what feminist literature identifies as the problem of data blindness — where what is not measured is not seen (Zimmermann & Binswanger, 2021).

Second, key elements of governance remain largely unmeasured. Although institutional and structural governance tools —such as gender-responsive lawmaking, budgeting, and social protection— feature prominently in the discourse, these concepts are not systematically translated into the indicator frameworks. As a result, the measurement of gender equality becomes heavily skewed towards tracking outcomes (e.g., rates of violence, female employment), rather than monitoring the implementation and effectiveness of the structural policy interventions designed to produce those outcomes (Connell et al., 2020).

Third and finally, the indicators tend to rely on a homogenized representation of woman, effectively erasing diverse experiences. While the indicators often treat women as a single, monolithic category, they fail to capture the unique experiences of groups with intersectional identities, such as women with disabilities, displaced women, and those in rural areas. The result is a critical paradox: the very groups that are increasingly included in the discourse are the ones rendered invisible by the data, thereby hindering targeted and effective policy interventions (Mölders, 2019).

Themes that feature with high frequency in the discourse —such as displacement, aging, disability, class inequality, and care labor— often lack adequate representation within the current system of indicators. This reveals that the resulting data gap is not merely a technical failing but also a political choice, reflecting decisions about what, and who, is deemed important enough to measure (Odera & Mulusa, 2020). Consequently, this asymmetry challenges not only the regime's monitoring capacity but also raises fundamental questions about who is rendered visible and who remains excluded in the international policymaking arena.

In this context, the production of inclusive data and the comprehensiveness of indicators are critically important for advancing gender equality. Most existing gender inequality indicators fail to capture the multidimensionality of women's lived experiences. When these complex inequalities go unmeasured, policy interventions designed to address them risk being incomplete or, worse, misdirected (Berik, 2022). Consequently, the lack of disaggregated and inclusive data on critical issues —such as women's economic participation, access to social protection, the burden of care work, and coping mechanisms for violence— severely constrains policymakers' capacity to design and implement effective interventions.

To truly understand women's poverty and gender inequality, data-driven, multidimensional analyses are critically important. Women's experiences cannot be captured by singular indicators like income or education alone; they are deeply intertwined with dynamic factors such as care burdens, exposure to violence, access to resources, decision-making power, and social exclusion. These factors often create a cyclical pattern of disadvantage. For instance, violence can impede a woman's ability to work, while a lack of economic independence can, in turn, exclude her from decision-making processes (Güdek-Gölçek, 2022; 2025). Therefore, effective gender-based indicators must measure not only outcomes but also the underlying causes and structural linkages that perpetuate inequality.

Despite this necessity, the current SDG indicator system largely fails to capture these complex interrelations. This inadequacy resonates with feminist data critiques, which treat data not as a neutral tool, but as a political instrument with the power to both represent reality and produce real-world impacts. This void, termed the gender data gap in the literature, therefore points to a measurement system that systematically renders women and their diverse experiences invisible (Zimmermann & Binswanger, 2021).

Furthermore, this lack of representation at the indicator level renders key institutional governance codes —such as gender-responsive budgeting, laws, and monitoring mechanisms— effectively unmonitorable, despite their prominence in the Gender Snapshot reports. This, in turn, leads to a narrow, outcome-based monitoring of SDG 5, where the structural interventions capable of producing equality are themselves left unevaluated (Connell et al., 2020).

In conclusion, while the Gender Snapshot reports articulate a remarkably inclusive, intersectional, and transformative vision for gender equality, the capacity of the SDG indicator framework to translate this vision into a measurable and monitorable reality remains severely limited. The resulting gap between discourse and data is therefore not merely a technical issue of monitoring capacity. Rather, it opens up a crucial epistemological and political debate about whose experiences are rendered visible, and whether the multidimensional realities of women's lives are truly being integrated into the global policymaking process.

REFERENCES

Ababneh, A., Lok, K., Abdeyazdan, H., Opoku, A., & Chen, C. (2025). Gender equality in smart sustainable cities: Literature review. *Frontiers in Sustainable Cities*, *7*, 1535561. DOI: 10.3389/frsc.2025.1535561

Bacchi, C. (2009). *Analysing Policy: What's the problem represented to be?* Pearson Education.

Baumgartinger, P. (2021). Transitioning Gender Equality to the Equality of Sex-gender Diversity. In Binswanger, C., & Zimmermann, A. (Eds.), *Transitioning to Gender Equality* (pp. 85–94). MPDI., DOI: 10.3390/books978-3-03897-867-1-7

Beloskar, V. D., Haldar, A., & Gupta, A. (2024). Gender equality and women's empowerment: A bibliometric review of the literature on SDG 5 through the management lens. *Journal of Business Research, 172*, 114442. DOI: 10.1016/j.jbusres.2023.114442

Berik, G. (2022). Towards improved measures of gender inequality. Discussion Paper. UN Women. https://www.unwomen.org/en/digital-library/publications/2022/11/discussion-paper-towards-improved-measures-of-gender-inequality

Bilgin Aytaç, G., & Sezgin, A. (2024). Gender Equality as a Sustainable Development Goal: Women's Participation in Decision-Making Mechanisms in Türkiye. In Garan, Ö., Karagöz Özenç, F., Mumcu Akan, H. D., & Engin Balın, B. (Eds.), *Pursuing Sustainable Development Goals: The Performance of Türkiye in the Centennial of the Republic* (pp. 221–239). İstanbul University Press.

Bonthala, S., Shirota, Y., & Chakraborty, B. (2023). SDGs Gender Equality Analysis in India by using SHAP Interpretation. 2023 1st International Conference on Optimization Techniques for Learning (ICOTL), 1-6. https://doi.org/DOI: 10.1109/ICOTL59758.2023.10435062

Bryman, A. (2016). *Social Research Methods* (5th ed.). Oxford University Press.

Connell, A., Holder, A., & Kearney, H. (2020). Equal Measures 2030: A new approach for advocacy and influencing beyond Beijing +25. *Gender and Development*, *28*(2), 405–423. DOI: 10.1080/13552074.2020.1750218

Crenshaw, K. (1991). Mapping the Margins: Intersectionality, Identity Politics, and Violence against Women of Color. *Stanford Law Review*, *43*(6), 1241–1299. DOI: 10.2307/1229039

D'Ignazio, C., & Klein, L. F. (2020). *Data Feminism*. MIT Press.

Esquivel, V., & Sweetman, C. (2016). Gender and the Sustainable Development Goals. *Gender and Development, 24*(1), 1–8. DOI: 10.1080/13552074.2016.1153318

Fraser, N. (1997). *Justice Interruptus: Critical Reflections on the "Postsocialist" Condition*. Routledge.

Güdek-Gölçek, Ş. (2022). *Neoliberal ekonomide kadın yoksulluğu: Alternatif bir ölçüm modeli*. Unpublished doctoral thesis. Ege University.

Güdek-Gölçek, Ş. (2025). Beyond economic measures: Exploring social deprivation among women in Türkiye. *Women's Studies International Forum, 109*(March-April), 103053. DOI: 10.1016/j.wsif.2025.103053

Harding, S. (1987). *Feminism and Methodology: Social Science Issues*. Indiana University Press.

Jeevanasai, A., Saole, P., Rath, A., Singh, S., Rai, S., & Kumar, M. (2023). Shades & shines of gender equality with respect to sustainable development goals (SDGs): The environmental performance perspectives. *Total Environment Research Themes, 8*. Advance online publication. DOI: 10.1016/j.totert.2023.100082

Khanal, S. (2023). Gender Equality in Sustainable Development Goals: Some Reflections from Nepal. *Journey for Sustainable Development and Peace Journal., 1*(02), 147–161. DOI: 10.3126/jsdpj.v1i02.58267

Kuckartz, U., & Rädiker, S. (2019). *Analyzing qualitative data with MAXQDA: Text, audio, and video*. Springer.

Leach, M., Mehta, L., & Prabhakaran, P. (2016). Gender equality and sustainable development: A pathways approach. Discussion Paper, UN Women. https://www.unwomen.org/sites/default/files/Headquarters/Attachments/Sections/Library/Publications/2016/DPS-Gender-equality-sustainable-development.pdf

Leal Filho, W., Kovaleva, M., Tsani, S., îrcă, D., Shiel, C., Dinis, M. A. P., Nicolau, M., Sima, M., Fritzen, B., Salvia, A. L., Minhas, A., Kozlova, V., Doni, F., Spiteri, J., Gupta, T., Wakunuma, K., Sharma, M., Barbir, J., Shulla, K., & Tripathi, S. (2023). Promoting gender equality across the sustainable development goals. *Environment, Development and Sustainability, 25*, 14177–14198. DOI: 10.1007/s10668-022-02656-1 PMID: 36124160

Lenka, P. (2023). Philosophy of Sustainable Development: Understanding the Significance of Gender Equality in Business Organisations. *Problems of Sustainable Development, 18*(2), 121–127. DOI: 10.35784/preko.3950

Lima, R., & Guedes, G. (2024). Sustainable Development Goals and Gender Equality: A Social Design Approach on Gender-Based Violence. *Sustainability, 16*(2), 914. DOI: 10.3390/su16020914

Manzano, I. R. (2021). Gender Equality And Women's Leadership For Sustainable Development. In A. G. Shirin, M. V. Zvyaglova, O. A. Fikhtner, E. Y. Ignateva, & N. A. Shaydorova (Eds.), *Education in a Changing World: Global Challenges and National Priorities,* vol 114. European Proceedings of Social and Behavioural Sciences (pp. 51-58). European Publisher. https://doi.org/DOI: 10.15405/epsbs.2021.07.02.7

Mariano, S., & Molari, B. (2022). Gender equality from the MDGs to the SDGs: a feminist analysis. Revista de Administração Pública. https://doi.org/DOI: 10.1590/0034-761220220124x

Mölders, T. (2019). Rethinking gender: feminist perspectives on Sustainable Development Goals in the light of (re)productivity. *GAIA - Ecological Perspectives for Science and Society, 28(2)*, 95-99. https://doi.org/DOI: 10.14512/gaia.28.2.6

Mondal, J. (2022). Sustainable Development and Gender Mainstreaming in Present Contemporary Society. International Journal of Modern Engineering Research, 11(1), ss. 54-57. http://ijmer.in.doi./2022/11.01.89

Mustakimah, L., Huriani, Y., & Zulaeha, E. (2023). Tantangan Mewujudkan Sustainable Development Goals (SDGs) Tentang Kesetaraan Gender pada Masyarakat Desa. *Az-Zahra: Journal of Gender and Family Studies*, *4*(1), 12–29. DOI: 10.15575/azzahra.v4i1.25462

Odera, J. A., & Mulusa, J. (2020). SDGs, Gender Equality and Women's Empowerment: What Prospects for Delivery? In Kaltenborn, M., Krajewski, M., & Kuhn, H. (Eds.), *Sustainable Development Goals and Human Rights. Interdisciplinary Studies in Human Rights* (Vol. 5). Springer., DOI: 10.1007/978-3-030-30469-0_6

Ojeda, L., Ginieis, M., & Papaoikonomou, E. (2025). Gender Equality in Sustainability Reporting: A Systematic Literature Review. *Corporate Social Responsibility and Environmental Management*, *32*(2), 2710–2727. DOI: 10.1002/csr.3089

Pokharel, B. (2024). Gender equality in Nepal: How is it going as a goal of SDG? *Journey for Sustainable Development and Peace Journal*, *2*(1), 112–127. DOI: 10.3126/jsdpj.v2i1.63260

Queisser, M. (2016). Gender equality and the Sustainable Development Goals. In Love, P. (Ed.), *Debate the Issues: New Approaches to Economic Challenges* (pp. 87–90). OECD Publishing., DOI: 10.1787/9789264264687-16-

Sachs, J. D., Lafortune, G., Fuller, G., & Iablonovski, G. (2025). *Financing Sustainable Development to 2030 and Mid-Century. Sustainable Development Report 2025. Paris: SDSN.* Dublin University Press.

Shang, Y., Sivertsen, G., Cao, Z., & Zhang, L. (2022). Gender differences among first authors in research focused on the Sustainable Development Goal of Gender Equality. *Scientometricsi*, *127*, 4769–4796. DOI: 10.1007/s11192-022-04430-6

UN. (2025). The 17 Goals. https://sdgs.un.org/goals

UNDP. (2019). Human Development Report 2019 – Beyond income, beyond averages, beyond today: Inequalities in human development in the 21st century. https://hdr.undp.org/content/human-development-report-2019

Women, U. N. (2021). Progress on the Sustainable Development Goals: Gender Snapshot 2021. https://www.unwomen.org/en/digital-library/publications/2021/09/progress-on-the-sustainable-development-goals-the-gender-snapshot-2021

Women, U. N. (2022). Progress on the Sustainable Development Goals: Gender Snapshot 2022. https://unstats.un.org/sdgs/gender-snapshot/2022/#:~:text=Home%20The%20Gender%20Snapshot%202022&text=The%20report%20shows%20that%20the,the%20outlook%20for%20gender%20equality

Women, U. N. (2023). Progress on the Sustainable Development Goals: Gender Snapshot 2023. https://www.unwomen.org/sites/default/files/2023-09/progress-on-the-sustainable-development-goals-the-gender-snapshot-2023-en.pdf

Women, U. N. (2024). Progress on the Sustainable Development Goals: Gender Snapshot 2024. https://www.unwomen.org/en/resources/gender-snapshot

Yadav, S. (2023). Gender Equality as a Tool for Sustainable Development. International Journal of Teaching [IJTLE]. *Learning and Education*, *2*(2), 1–3. DOI: 10.22161/ijtle.2.2.1

Zimmermann, A., & Binswanger, C. (2021). Transitioning to gender equality-Introduction. In Binswanger, C., & Zimmermann, A. (Eds.), *Transitioning to gender Equality* (pp. 1–13). MDPI.

KEY TERMS AND DEFINITIONS

Data Gap: A data gap refers to the lack of sufficient, reliable, and regularly collected data on specific social groups or phenomena. This absence of data can render the groups in question invisible within policy processes, leading to their exclusion. In the context of gender and intersectional identities, such data gaps are particularly damaging, as they often serve to reinforce and deepen existing inequalities

Discourse: Discourse refers to the entire system of linguistic and cultural practices that shape the ways a particular topic is understood and discussed. In the realm of policy, discourses determine how problems are framed, which actors are recognized as legitimate, and what solutions are considered viable. Discourses do not simply reflect reality; they actively construct social realities and, in doing so, produce and reproduce power relations.

Indicator: An indicator is an instrument that provides measurable information about a specific social or environmental phenomenon. In the context of development policy, indicators play a crucial role in monitoring and evaluating progress toward established goals. However, indicators are not value-free or neutral tools; they are embedded with normative choices that determine which information becomes visible and which is ultimately excluded.

Intersectionality: Intersectionality is an analytical framework arguing that various social and political identities —such as gender, race, class, age, and sexual orientation— do not exist in isolation but intersect to create unique, multi-layered experiences of both discrimination and privilege. This framework provides a lens for analyzing inequalities not through singular categories, but through their complex and interactive structures. The concept is therefore essential for developing truly inclusive social policies that address the multifaceted realities of people's lives.

Vulnerability: Vulnerability is the condition in which individuals or groups are disproportionately exposed or susceptible to harm from social, economic, and environmental shocks and stresses. This condition is often exacerbated by a lack of access to resources, inadequate institutional protections, and processes of structural exclusion. Identifying and understanding these vulnerabilities is therefore a critical first step in developing just and inclusive development policies.

Section 4
Law, Governance, and International Contradictions

Chapter 10
Analyzing the Impact of International Law and Sanctions Mechanisms Towards Sustainable Outcomes

Vidisha Shekhawat
https://orcid.org/0009-0009-7816-3591
Manipal University Jaipur, India

Pranjal Khare
https://orcid.org/0000-0002-9937-9588
Jindal Global Law School, O.P. Jindal Global University, India

ABSTRACT

This chapter examines how international law, along with sanctions regimes, can interfere with the quest for sustainability by surprisingly stopping progress on global development goals. While the Sustainable Development Goals and the Paris Agreement now make sustainability a main goal, international sanctions are seen as conflicting tools in that field. Using research and case studies from Iran, Russia, North Korea and Venezuela, it focuses on how sanctions prevent effective action in climate, health, energy transition and environmental protection. It looks at how sanctions have evolved, from covering all groups to just specific targets and asks whether these actions still follow basic rules of international law. The chapter ultimately calls for more sustainable thinking about sanctions and suggests innovations including impact assessments, special carve-outs for humanitarian action and ESG

DOI: 10.4018/979-8-3373-1707-6.ch010

standards mechanism. Because we are facing climate, conflict and weakening institutions all at once, the chapter suggests supporting both peace and sustainable development more thoroughly.

INTRODUCTION

In the current decade, the emergence of geopolitical conflict and global deterioration of the environment has increased the complexity of achieving sustainable development outcomes. International law has worked, through treaties, rules of custom, and bodies' mandates to ascend the enshrining sustainability as a fundamental goal, especially from the adoption of United Nations Sustainable Development Goals (SDGs) in 2015. At the same time, sanctions have come to the surface as the tool of international relations par excellence, supposedly to impose compliance with international norms. However, the imposition of sanctions usually leads to a result that stretches far beyond their political or even security objectives. Sanctions regimes, be they multilateral or single-sided, regularly undermine the economic structures, and the public services, and that restrict access to vital technologies, of which these are inherently part of any nation's ability to move towards long-term sustainability. The incongruence between the juridical ideal of sustainability embedded in international legal orders and the material facts of coercive economic arrangements cast the issue of coherence and legitimacy of contemporary international law into doubt. These strains are no longer marginal, they are located at the epicentre of global governance, influencing everything from climate remediation to social equality and institutional survival. This chapter seeks to conduct a systematic inquiry into such tensions that asks how international law enables, and even limits sustainable development, especially through the political filter of sanctions (Suleiman et al., 2024).

The chapter overcomes these problems by combining doctrinal law analysis with case studies and some elements of studying policies in different countries. The doctrinal part deals with the framework and rules of international sanctions as described in the United Nations Charter and Security Council resolutions, as well as in EU regional bodies' resolutions. This analysis sits within the framework consisting of the 2030 Agenda for Sustainability, the Paris Agreement and different human rights treaties that relate to socioeconomic matters. To understand what a state must do and what its institution is for, you need legal interpretation, but it does not fully cover judging actual outcomes. Therefore, in this chapter, case studies of selected states that were touched by international sanctions and have made promises toward global sustainability are considered. Information from these case studies relates to sanctions' effects on the strength of public institutions, access to new technology, decision-making in renewable energy, environment protection and public health.

By integrating different methods, the approach helps to check points of agreement between legal, political and welfare outcomes, leading to a stronger and context-related analysis of the link between international law, sustainability and constraint (Zuhra & Sabirin, 2024).

The study takes place where international law, global governance and development studies meet by applying both theory and practise. The theory looks at whether international law for promoting peace and security can be coherent when the tools for sanctions are also used in conjunction with rules for sustainable development. This study also helps create a wider stream of research that highlights the importance of bringing legal and institutional thinking together. Practically, the chapter explains what policymakers, legal advisors and global organisations do to set up or support sanctions regimes. Based on the findings, departments should reconsider pitching exemptions, include humanitarian considerations and press for changes that remove sustainability-related fields from the reach of coercive measures. Also, using actual case studies and policy reviews, this chapter suggests practical ways to strengthen and legitimise international sanctions and sustainability regimes. The plan is to reform international law, so it addresses global concerns together, mainly because threats to security, climate change and fading institutions are now so interconnected (Kim & Bosselmann, 2015).

The chapter then discusses the main principles of international sanctions such as their legal authority; how many kinds exist and how they are put into effect. Your main concern in this unit is to understand how sustainability is supported by law worldwide, with a focus on the Sustainable Development Goals and environmental agreements and their interaction with human rights law. In the next section, the authors analyse at the main legal and policy disagreements arising at the point where sustainability demands conflict with existing guidelines. In this section, case studies are introduced to show how sanctions have negatively affected efforts to make farms and economies environmentally sustainable around the world. The fifth section, afterward, studies these cases side by side to highlight what helps or hinders the legal system in its support for sustainable development. In the final section, the authors survey how audience legal states and institutions face the issues of sanctions and climate change goals. Overall, in this paper, we highlight the main points regarding sanctions and sustainability and make some recommendations for what can be done going ahead (Bantekas & Akestoridi, 2023).

The research question behind this chapter is, then, whether international sanctions are fundamentally inconsistent with the values of sustainability or whether international sanctions can be modified so that they can contribute to global development and environmental conservation. Putting the question this way frames the analysis as a critical evaluation rather than a descriptive one, and this aspect of the chapter enables it to go beyond case-specific observations to theorising the structural tensions between coercion, sovereignty and sustainability in international law.

BACKGROUND

Achieving sustainability is now a key goal that countries work towards together around the world. The idea which started with ethics, has grown to become a major rule and policy in worldwide governance. At present, using international sanctions as a way to keep others in line, discourage aggression and demonstrate displeasure with actions not accepted by international standards is very common for states. However, when we look at these frameworks, suitability and sanctions, neither measures up as a true reflection of global concern, since they do not support each other and instead present contradictions in international law. In the latter part of the 20th century, environmental treaties started to recognize sustainability; later, the issue grew to take into account general development concerns. A key achievement of Our Common Future, released by the Brundtland Commission in 1987, was helping to define sustainability as a way to meet the requirements of the present and the future. In 1992, the Rio Declaration was created and followed in 2015 by the Paris Agreement, all supported by the UN Sustainable Development Goals. Such treaties intend to give states ideas for how to tackle climate change, lower poverty and achieve equal development. Even though international law counts on countries sharing duties, not every state can respond on the same scale because institutions and resources differ among nations (Rochat & Tsouloufas, 2024).

Today's debates about sustainability strongly depend on the progress of international law and the strength of global sanctions. As the problems of environmental damage, loss of resources and climate change grow, many nations are beginning to turn to legislation and regulations for sustainable change. Multilateral environmental agreements under international law help states to act together by creating guidelines for how to behave. But whether the policy is applied or not depends on what states prefer and how well the related sanctions are established.

Over the years, sanctions using economic, trade or diplomatic methods have been used to influence events. Still, they become more complicated when applied to take care of nature. They can also encourage countries to obey international rules about the environment, but they might also damage efforts at cooperation if they look like a firm punishment instead of an encouragement. Also, because sanctions disproportionately affect developing countries, people worry about equal and just efforts toward global sustainability. This chapter explores how international regulations impact the way sanctions create sustainability effects. It studies these issues to learn how they either benefit or hinder efforts to be sustainable globally, given the dynamics and disproportion of global power and conflicts.

LITERATURE REVIEW

A desire for better sustainable development and the practical challenges faced are clear in the growing conversations about this subject in international law, most especially after the inclusion of sanctions. The reason many researchers study this issue is largely due to the SDGs. According to Hak, Janoušková and Moldan (2016), even though the needed indicators appear in global agreements, their usage varies greatly based on how nations and groups cooperate. Poorhashemi (2024) argues that, although there are improved rules for protecting the environment today, countries often apply sanctions which hinder the enforcement of such rules in practice. It is demonstrated in national research that sanctions impact a country's long-term sustainability goals. The authors (Noorollahi et al., 2021) point out that sanctions on Iran have delayed its move toward clean energy by limiting access to new technologies and loans. In much the same way, Gorodkov (2024) points out that because of post-2014 sanctions, Russia had to switch from promoting sustainability to adopting environmental policies centred on security and the state. Several researchers examine these issues from a legal coherence point of view. Rajamani and colleagues argue that "fair shares" principles are needed in international climate law, warning that the combination of various roles and responsibilities in different jurisdictions can harm efforts to reduce global emissions. The topic becomes more serious with Rowhani (2023) pointing out that UN sanctions regimes lack proper defences for human rights and the responsibilities related to sustainable development.

Butt (2021) explains that the structures in place to achieve the SDGs are not well coordinated and that many sanctions are at variance with them. Bantekas (2022) and Akestoridi (2023) discuss these subjects and provide proof that some soft law measures are successfully printed into international law, even though they result in very little in the way of sanctions. According to Biglari, Beiglary and Arthanari (2022), sanctions tend to postpone or alter how closely related economies reach their SDGs. They show, using economic information, that the negative impacts of sanctions can harm the organisations needed to support progress toward SDGs in health, education and energy. Reforms under discussion are now designed to resolve these contradictions. Jessen (2021) advises that integrated sanctions schemes should comply with important obligations worldwide and this includes humanitarian and environmental exemptions. They show that sanctions do not just affect tourism's economy but also make it harder for the sector to plan. Many of these studies point out that while sustainability is popular internationally, its importance in laws and policies often fades when policies are challenged by politics. We need legal reforms, better use of sanctions and improvements to institutions that protect development and the environment from being excluded by strategic priorities.

What is conspicuously lacking in most of the sanctions and sustainability literature is an engagement with the basic scholarship. Joy Gordon Invisible War explains how sanctions regimes, especially against Iraq, led to systematic humanitarian disasters, and Erika de Wet offers a critique on the legality of sanctions by the UN in international law. TWAIL scholars like Antony Anghie and Makau Mutua have also demonstrated that sanctions can be neo-colonial tools of dependency and inequality in the Global South. Combining these views makes the analysis more robust as it places the discussion of sustainability in the context of the issues of legitimacy, justice, and power imbalance in global governance.

THEORETICAL FRAMEWORK

International Law and the Global Sustainability Framework

The idea of sustainability was first introduced at international forums in the last decades of the last century, and environmental law was its first application. The following years gradually expanded it to apply to social and economic aspects of life. In 1987, the report of the Brundtland Commission, Our Common Future, showed that until then, sustainable development had only been supported by a few, but was now accepted worldwide as a general goal. Seeing environmental stewardship as distinct from both economic equity and social justice indicated a big departure from the past. The three-fold approach was institutionalized at the United Nations Conference on Environment and Development (Rio de Janeiro, 1992). Rio Declaration and Agenda 21 formed the first important steps to bring about sustainability in all legal and policy aspects. Over the years, sustainability was no longer only seen as a goal, as it was included in international agreements, national governments' constitutions and began being mentioned in court decisions. It shows up in the way states now agree in treaties to align their policies with both environmental and social targets. At present, states, trade, finance and the environment are legally obliged to comply with sustainable development (Poorhashemi, 2024).

The main tools that encourage sustainability are the Rio Declaration on Environment and Development in 1992, the Paris Agreement in 2015 and the UN Sustainable Development Goals that year. It may have 27 basic principles, but the Rio Declaration still made sustainability the primary legal basis for the first time. Usually, people act on the environment by following community participation, estimating environmental effects and setting environment protection measures.

Things are now at a new level with sustainability governance because of the Paris Agreement. Rather than the Kyoto Protocol's requirement for states to hit certain emissions levels, the Paris Agreement asks countries to send in their own targets (NDCs). While they are legally required, these targets may not be very ambitious. Using this method, which is both flexible and strong, legal changes help each nation continue to contribute, while helping reach worldwide climate goals. Even so, while SDGs are not considered a treaty, they rely on strict legal and normative regulations. Because the UN adopted the 17 SDGs worldwide with open arms, these goals made sustainability real through announcing clear aims in education, energy, health and climate. From all these points, it appears that, in the writers' opinion, development and security have sustainability as a basic ingredient, as it shapes new international law (Bantekas & Akestoridi, 2022).

Sustainability is overseen by many different soft laws like declarations, guidelines and voluntary commitments, alongside firm treaties and resolutions. Because of this hybridity, international law sometimes fails to support sustainability. Though soft, non-binding laws such as the Rio Declaration and Agenda 21 affect expectations, help build customary international law and arrive first before any binding rules don't appear. Their greatest advantage is that they provide flexibility, are recognized by governments and can be adjusted when regular treaties cannot be made. As an alternative, the Paris Agreement (in terms of its rules for operating), the CBD and several human rights treaties are examples of hard law instruments that enforce sustainability. As a result, the government's efforts include protecting nature, improving healthcare and reducing discrimination when developing different regions. As a result of the combination of soft and hard law, the hybrid arrangement is reliable and based on norms. Still, because of these two aspects, the system can allow for ambiguity and breakup of goals, usually occurring when sanctions stand in the way of states reaching their goals for the environment or society. Looking at the dual nature is necessary in understanding how sustainability can be increased and reduced by related laws that often work together (Adanma & Ogunbiyi, 2024).

There are several important global groups that take on the role of sustainability guardians, bringing cares about sustainability into international statutes. The United Nations Environment Programme (UNEP) guides environmental administration participates in drafting agreements and assists in helping countries apply multilateral environmental agreements (MEAs) at home. The Montevideo Programme and the Global Environmental Outlook report are UNEP contributions to encouraging agreement on sustainable actions and science-based confidence. From that moment, the UNFCCC and the Conference of Parties (COP) take lead in setting the rules for climate change action. Through this agreement, nations pledge to cut emissions, give funds to climate initiatives and actively put efforts towards preparing for climate change, all given their required duty to build stronger climate resilience. Although the World Trade Organisation (WTO) is not usually considered a sustainability actor, it works through trade rules to influence sustainability in economics. More and more often, WTO panels assess whether environmental laws affecting trade are justified, as they did in the Shrimp-Turtle and EU-Seals cases. Together, these groups make up a multi-institutional setting where sustainability norms are debated, judged and set. However, applying trade liberalisation may be inconsistent with environmental or social policy which highlights the issue of institutional contradictions discussed in the book chapter later, specifically regarding sanctions (Rajamani et al., 2021).

Some essential rules of law support how sustainability law is interpreted and implemented across nations. Three concepts are equity, precautionary principle and common but differentiated responsibilities (Khare et al., 2025). When equity is present, development can be just and welcomed by the people now and by people to come. The ICJ Gabcikovo – Nagymaros judgment is just one of many cases where the principle is frequently applied to see that environmental concerns do not hinder development. If uncertainty exists in the scientific facts, this uncertainty should not hold up the taking of steps to prevent damage to the environment. Many MEAs now include this principle which helps reduce climate change and protect biodiversity. CBDR stands out here because it started in the Rio Declaration and demands that countries share in caring for the environment with their commitments different based on their past emissions, development and ability to act. It reinforces the Paris Agreement's rules by making it possible to clarify which countries must do more under the agreement. If used together, these rules help us decide if national sovereignty can be reconciled with collective action and they help us disentangle whether sanctions regimes build or conflict with sustainability goals. (Heyl et al., 2021).

The further insight into the issue of sanctions and sustainability also implies the involvement of critical theories of international law. Third World Approaches to International Law (TWAIL) contend that sanctions tend to reify structural inequalities because more powerful states that implement sanctions can impose their will on less powerful states in the name of legality. On the same note, feminist legal critiques also point out how coercive economic actions affect women and marginalized groups disproportionately through healthcare and education interruptions, and social services. In this regard, legal coherence does not only refer to the alignment of the sanctions law with sustainability norms but also to the aspect of normative legitimacy i.e. whose interests are being catered to and whose voices are not being heard.

Sanctions in International Law: Legal Bases, Mechanisms, and Controversies

Sanctions are used by governments and international bodies to steer others' behaviour; hit out against acts they disagree with and express disapproval of violations of international laws. Basically, sanctions use pressure that doesn't involve warfare to try and meet foreign policy or security goals. How sanctions work is very useful: economic sanctions involve commerce, financial actions and investments; diplomatic sanctions cut down or eliminate contact with other countries; military sanctions involve banning the sale of arms and travel bans and asset freezes target certain individuals or organizations. Most often, conflict is justified by mentioning that international law has been broken through breaches of peace, aggressive acts, violation of human rights and spreading of nuclear weapons. Sanctions are commonly applied to send signals about disapproval to countries that do not comply, but their effectiveness in implementing those sanctions is usually quite limited. By law, military operations must follow the UN Charter and agree with common rules of international law, especially proportionality, due process and non-intervention. There is no common agreement that sanctions are governed by an acceptable or constant law. The incomplete system gives way to incoherent and generally ambiguous laws, as authority and rule overspill into every area of regulation. The way different sanctions work and why they were designed is very important for understanding how they influence a country's ability to achieve sustainability (Jessen, 2021).

Chapter VII of the United Nations Charter is the main reason for the UNSC to have the power to impose sanctions to secure or reinforce peace and security worldwide. The UNSC can mandate economic sanctions, ban weapons shipments and other measures against all UN member states as soon as a threat to peace is confirmed by Article 41. As sanctions from the Security Council come first, according to international law, they form a major part of the world's legal structure. Even so, sanctions have parted ways with WTO law through the twentieth century; DSB rulings have seen states establish trade retaliation upon getting affirmation. Though they serve the same function as sanctions, technically they are what is known as countermeasures and must follow WTO regulations. For example, the EU and AU have developed their independent methods of sanctioning countries. Mainly, it sets up and commonly implements sanctions given by the UN or on its own initiative, by using its CFSP. Such regional restrictions should be implemented respecting international law and the treaties' rights. The rising appeal of these agencies, however, is leading people to ask about fragmentation, overlap and uncertain laws. If a country finds itself under different and sometimes opposite, sets of sanctions, there is no way to know which rules apply and this can make it hard to uphold other international duties, most importantly those supporting sustainable development (Butt, 2021).

During the last two decades, the types of sanctions used have shifted from broad embargoes against Iraq in the 1990s, to more targeted options such as smart sanctions. Instead of banning all products or services from a country, they are aimed at members of the business sector who have behaved in a way that can't be corrected. The government uses actions such as travel bans, locking up funds and embargoing sectors to ensure the accuracy and trustworthiness of its actions. Often, it is hard to tell if something is smart or harmful. Even so such economic burdens can lead to declining international trade and dissuade other countries from working with the United States on health or energy matters. Hitting others that do business with sanctioned parties is considered a controversial type of secondary sanctions. Measures such as these which are popular with nations such as the United States, are enabling domestic laws to impact other nations in ways that challenge sovereignty, non-intervention and what an authority can claim to judge under its laws. Some argue that sanctions help fill gaps in enforcement, while others say they result in people and groups doing more than they should and favouring caution over activity which aggravates long-term development problems for people and organizations. As a result, even though smart sanctions are both politically supported and lawful, their real effects tend to be overlooked in studying how sustainability issues are handled by governance. It is the difference between what people want and what results that causes the main conflicts studied in this research (Zuhra & Sabirin, 2024).

METHODOLOGY

The information in this chapter was gathered using doctrinal law, case studies and comparison of various policies. How the rules of international organisations shape the possibilities for sustainable development in a country is something we want to know. Since the law and economy are closely related, this study looks at how legal tools are put into practice in specific areas. The research aims to review how international sanctions are structured and what behaviour is required from Sanctioned countries. We include in our study part of the UN Charter, key judgments from the UN Security Council and the EU's Common Foreign and Security Policy (CFSP). In addition, the Rio Declaration, the Paris Agreement and the SDGs are investigated by research. Here, the team analyses how international law affects consistency and what economic sanctions might oppose advancements in environmental, social and economic areas. Real-life examples of countries subject to international sanctions that are still working on green issues are presented in the chapter to compensate for the gaps in a legal approach. The named states are Iran, Russia, Venezuela, North Korea, Myanmar, Sudan and South Africa. The research question and the presence of information about outcomes and the environment led us to use these cases. The case studies investigate sustainable technologies, public health, energy transition, caring for the environment and the strength of institutions (Bantekas & Akestoridi, 2023).

The choice of Iran, Russia, Venezuela, North Korea, Myanmar, Sudan and South Africa as case studies was informed by three factors: (i) they have all been subjected to long-lasting sanctions imposed by key international actors, (ii) they are all also signatories of global sustainability programs such as the SDGs and Paris Agreement and (iii) their policy and institutional data is available. The study is based on a mixed methodology: doctrinal legal research of UN and regional sanction regimes; structured comparison of national sustainability responses; and secondary data research of SDG indicators, access to climate finance, and institutional resilience. This triangulation technique increases validity in that it matches normative statements with empirical results.

Moreover, the study examines variations and similarities between the cases. It looks at institutional responses, policy adjustments and progress across the chosen nations to uncover main insights related to sanctions and sustainability. Emphasis is given to how policies are spread across many levels, resulting in generated legal conflicts and the strategies states develop when their choices are constrained. In addition, the analysis makes use of information from treaty documents, UN reports, academic works and documents on policies. Using these three methods together improves the validity of any findings by comparing interpretations of the law, with what was seen and what is written by others. The use of a mix of legal, political and social sciences lets the study recognize how international law supports or hinders policies in various countries. In general, the design of this process combines both normative and empirical aspects which allows for detailed examination of how currently applied and interpreted international law impacts sustainability in situations where nations are under sanctions. The point of the method is to bring insights useful to scholars, decision-makers and world organizations wanting to align peace, development and environmental goals (Ershov, 2023).

FINDINGS

The Impact of Sanctions on Sustainability Outcomes

Sanctions may look different from sustainability from a brief view. The most common ways to use sanctions are by banning trade, freezing someone's money or banks or isolating a nation economically. Nonetheless, sustainability is concerned with long-lasting strongpoints, ensuring fairness and billing the environment, economy and society to the next generation. Even though their objectives are different, these two forces usually influence each other in ways that create important legal and policy problems. Sustainable Development Goals, the Paris Agreement and many human rights treaties require countries to act on climate, health and inclusive development. On the other hand, if a country is hit by sanctions that block its trading or access to other countries' money, it finds it hard to meet all its duties. Experts in law and policy encourage countries to bring their laws together instead of allowing them to cause conflicting results. That is the situation we face right now. Although sanctions are meant to promote international standards, they regularly damage public bodies, economic systems and national control over rulemaking. This overlap must be understood. Sanctions should not be studied just as foreign policy tools since their effects often extend within countries and can harm vital parts of their governments (Nikolaev et al., 2024).

Sanctions may weaken a country's ability to comply with environmental responsibilities included in multilateral environmental agreements. The inability of a sanctioned country to use green technologies, clean energy or gather international climate finance may stop them from fulfilling both Paris Agreement and national biodiversity targets. By putting limitations on the oil and gas industry, it's possible to slow down a country's shift to renewable energy, leading to harder-to-use and costlier renewable systems. A similar effect results from technology export bans, preventing access to vital technology needed for monitoring pollution, environmental reporting or preparing for disasters. When a country's economy relies on resources, sanctions often lead it to put economic survival in the near term over protecting the environment from harm caused by more resource extraction. Sometimes, to save money lost because of the sanctions, the environment's safety rules may be switched off or forgotten, hurting international conservation. If such a country finds itself on the losing side in global environmental talks, as has happened during important climate meetings, it also struggles to meet world standards and is less able to access help. They demonstrate an understudied challenge: sanction regimes never look at alternatives with environmentally friendly controls, even if their impacts are against global sustainability (Biglari et al., 2022).

Sanctions in the past two decades shifted from very restrictive total bans, as seen in the Iraq sanction regime of the 1990s, to methods that affect only certain individuals or groups. They target specific people's companies or fields connected to improper behaviour, rather than punishing everyone at once. U.S. sanctions for travel, money and some industries such as oil should lead to a better focus on what the sanctions are meant to do. The edge between what is smart and what is unhealthy sometimes is not clear. While the measures affect only a small part of the economy, they keep critical products out and discourage other countries from cooperating on vital subjects like health and energy. These sanctions are problematic when they punish totally unconnected third parties for doing business with sanctioned parties. With systems like these, main countries like the United States apply their domestic rules outside their own borders, often testing things related to sovereignty, non-intervention and lawful jurisdiction. For many, it is a positive side factor since it fills in gaps in enforcement, while others argue it can pressure people so much that those who help with sustainability shut down their operations, resulting in problems for civil bodies and development. As a result, because smart sanctions are both politically acceptable and lawful, their non-explicit impacts in sustainability governance have not yet been explored. This gap between what was intended, and the actual results is at the heart of the disputes looked at in the study (Galloro & Guida, 2024).

When sanctions improve over time, they raise doubts about whether they are reasonable and helpful, mainly because they may not align with the bigger legal rules around the world. The inconsistency in deciding which violations are punished through sanctions, since it depends on world politics, is damaging to the status of sanctions systems. The critics repeatedly use a different standard for countries with alike human rights challenges which makes people question if these actions are motivated by politics. Secondary sanctions add strain because they make third states and businesses obey legal rules that are set by the United States and not in their own countries. Practices involving the use of force often run into rules of international law and could, therefore, contradict the UN Charter. The biggest problem for most, considering how sanctions hurt people, is the humanitarian side. Several UN studies and reports document how sanctions lead to a scarcity of needed medicine, food and sustainable energy, especially in areas with poor critical infrastructure. It is not clear if these consequences are rightly legalized by the doctrine of proportionality. In addition, providing humanitarian aid and making exceptions in sanctions is often discouraging, since it is bureaucratic or executed incorrectly. As a result, legal innovation and systemic changes are needed – they are especially important when the actions meant to support peace and security lead to higher sustainability risks (Jessen, 2021).

Case Studies of Sanctions and Sustainability in Practice

Iran: Impact on Energy Transition and Climate Commitments

There are strong tensions between challenging international sanctions and trying to be environmentally responsible in Iran. Many sanctions actions, unilateral and from various countries, have been directed at Iran because of its nuclear goals over several decades. With these sanctions in place, the nation is unable to access climate finance worldwide, bring in new and sustainable energy systems, or renew its dilapidated infrastructure. Even though Iran has promised to follow the Paris Agreement and produce energy and emission plans, its slow adoption is mainly caused by difficulties in obtaining needed external funds and technology. Punitive measures have made acquiring modern solar panels, installing wind farms, or joining international environmental collaborations tough. It's important to mention that adversity has sometimes resulted in new solutions. Since imports have been limited, Iran has invested in creating and manufacturing renewable technology, although only on a limited scale. The government has increased its work with partners outside the Western world, such as China and India, on energy efficiency matters. Despite being problematic, these adjustments explain the complicated way sanctions work. They prevent development but on occasion, stimulate strengths inside the country and new approaches to governance. Yet, because Iran has such limited capacity to reach sustainability targets, sanctions measures should be made flexible to handle these issues (Noorollahi et al., 2021).

Russia: Post-2014 and 2022 Sanctions and Sustainability Challenges

The moves taken against Russia after 2014 and 2022 proved that very severe isolation in the international arena can change a country's sustainability course over time. The European Union and the United States directed most of the sanctions at banking, oil and gas, and high technology sectors. They put limits on Russia's chances to benefit from clean energy investments in the West and pushed the country to create new businesses in fossil fuels abroad. At the same time, some progress has occurred. In several places, the sanctions prompted officials to look closely at their heavy dependence on oil and technology from other countries. For this reason, Russia has both raised its domestic wind energy production and started to focus more on hydrogen technology, wanting to avoid any unpredictable issues in fossil fuels and still matter in the shift towards clean energy. Even in Russia, certain local administrations in St. Petersburg and Kazan, as well as elsewhere, have worked on green municipal policies despite federal rules. But, as these cases show, these improvements generally have constraints given the outside political and economic conditions. Russia shows that sanctions push local development in sustainability, but sometimes this comes at the price of larger, national achievements (Gorodkov, 2024).

North Korea and Venezuela: Sanctions and Humanitarian/Environmental Degradation

North Korea and Venezuela are clear examples of how powerful economic sanctions can cause major environmental and social damage. Not only have sanctions made the government in North Korea politically isolated, but they have also blocked basic infrastructure progress. The lack of fuel and poor technology means the country depends mainly on deforestation and burning coal for energy, which drives continual soil and air pollution. Trying to plan for sustainability is almost impossible without support from other countries or access to their environmental information. Sanctions aimed at oil in Venezuela have only added to the country's economic collapse, which began when its leaders managed the country poorly. Both neglected areas used for oil and trouble with wastewater treatment led to pollution all over the country, and a broken healthcare system no longer keeps up with diseases linked to climate change. Despite all that, such severe situations sometimes bring about some useful responses. Organizations in Venezuela have started urban farming and permaculture to increase how much food is available while preserving the environment. Informal bartering has become common in North Korea, as well as ways to use less energy. Even though these are not enough, they point out that communities facing severe hurdles can still work on their kind of sustainability projects. They make us think about how sanctions could be revised to encourage, instead of limiting, examples of grassroots innovation (Lim, 2021).

Besides, the effect of sanctions cannot be explained without referring to cross-cutting themes, including gender and climate finance. In Venezuela, sanctions impacted women access to healthcare, which was already unequal, disastrously. Similarly, intellectual property restrictions and sanctions have denied access to Green Climate Fund resources or renewable energy technologies to some of the sanctioned countries, which harms their ability to aim at a just transition. These cases illustrate how sanctions do not only hinder technological progress but also increase social vulnerability posing new questions on the distributive justice in the field of sustainability governance.

Positive Sanctions Outcomes: South Africa, Myanmar (Partial), and Sudan (Environment-Specific Carve-Outs)

Although negative outcomes are frequently mentioned, sometimes sanctions have helped support sustainability. A case in point is when apartheid-controlled South Africa. In 1985, the people established democracy and the country's leaders chose to focus on social equality, defence of the environment and sustainable development. The situation in Myanmar also mirrors what I've described. As sanctions were placed on some individuals beginning in the early 2010s, they brought more attention to how critical democratisation is. As a result, Myanmar introduced new environmental legislation, and many nations got involved in protecting forests and biodiversity. But most of this changed after the 2021 military takeover. Sudan also teaches us valuable things. Apart from other kinds of sanctions, special permission for food and environmental reasons allowed several international groups to promote climate resilience in drought-stricken areas. These exceptions show that including sustainability in the creation of sanctions makes a big difference. So, sanctions are used for punishment, but they can help create important benefits, too. Development of real improvements can be triggered by significant countries, set objectives and careful exception clauses directly supporting the vulnerable. What happens next typically depends on the area's rules and if solid structures exist after the sanctions are lifted, even so (Majid, 2024).

A cross-case comparison of the case studies shows shared patterns and differences. Iran and Russia demonstrate the slackening impact of sanctions on energy transition due to the restricted access to climate finance and technology, and Venezuela and North Korea demonstrate the humanitarian and environmental disaster of decades-long isolation. South Africa and Sudan, in contrast, demonstrate that sanctions do have the potential to facilitate reforms or carve-outs that can help in achieving sustainability under conditions. These cases together suggest that the effect of sanctions on sustainability is not only dependent on legal design, but also on local institutional capacity and global political will.

RECOMMENDATIONS & SUGESSTIONS

At present, the international sanctions regime is shaped mainly to achieve security and political aims, with less attention given to the consequences of sanctions on development. Case studies have shown that frequently, sanctions influence basic areas such as health, environment, and education termed critical to sustainable development. This shows that we need to reform current methods. Using sanctions does not, on its own, go against sustainability. Still, the methods used to create and enforce them often result in major harm people did not mean to cause. Since sanctions policy doesn't focus enough on sustainability, there are problems with efficiency and legitimacy. Any updated framework will acknowledge that sanctions have effects far beyond the world of diplomacy among countries. In other words, these principles of the environment and human rights should be incorporated into the making of sanctions. It is both essential morally and practically wise to reform sanctions. Repeat offences in design mean sanctions hardly reach their expected results and lead to resentment among affected people. Now is when we should reconsider sanctions as ways of accountable action, not just as punishments for wrongdoing (Sjåfjell et al., 2019).

A better sanctions regime depends on more cooperative systems designed to check and expect accountability from nations. The system of applying sanctions currently consists of multiple, scattered measures, usually determined by states or groups such as the EU and the US on their own. Because countries do not apply sanctions equally, they seem less fair to many people. For multilateral accountability, we would enhance the part that global organizations play in making and policing sanctions (Fu et al., 2023). Although the United Nations Security Council is vital, it looks mainly at justifying and controlling its own decisions and rarely assesses how sustainable its sanctions are. It can also be that an independent panel called the

Sanctions Impact Review Panel and managed by the UN or by the WTO, WHO, and UNEP, is established. The panel would have access to Sanctions Hub data and could report on how the intervention affects both people and the environment in real time. Also, current Special Rapporteurs on human rights and the environment at the UN could be asked to help oversee sanctions. If we make these processes open and rely on clear evidence, results will be better and there will be less suspicion that dominant states are coercing others with sanctions (Rapsikevičius et al., 2022).

People are starting to use ESG principles as a method for making sanctions more sustainable. ESG-informed sanctions are designed to reward companies that follow environmental and social standards, in contrast with the usual style of sanctions that target their income or social image. Narrow sanctions could be forced on those harming nature or people, but at the same time, encouragement could be offered to firms showing strong environmental commitment. In return, the system could provide rewards for good outcomes as well as for bad ones (Khare et al., 2025). Great ways to implement this approach rely on legal innovation. ESG compliance clauses can be added to both trade deals and environmental treaties by international organizations or treaty bodies, ensuring provably good or bad behaviour wins or loses specific benefits. Sustainability standards might be respected when reviewing disputes related to sanctions by giving regional human rights courts and investment arbitration tribunals a role. Even in their earliest form, ESG sanctions may be designed to guide toward improved, long-term friendships and better systems rather than just push away the countries they target (Brus, 2018).

To make reforms operational, sanctions regimes must: (i) incorporate sustainability impact assessments as a prerequisite to adoption, (ii) incorporate humanitarian and climate-related exemptions, (iii) create monitoring mechanisms, such as a Sanctions Impact Review Panel, within the UN system, and (iv) be more about incentivizing ESG-aligned corporate behaviour than punishment. The ability to frame sanctions as positive instruments of positive international governance, as opposed to coercive measures, provides a means of reconciling the goals of peace, security, and sustainability. (Skjærseth et.al., 2006).

CONCLUSION

The chapter has examined situations where international sanctions can either help or not help meet the goals for global sustainability. While sanctions have long protected peace and security, there has not been enough attention paid to how they affect sustainable development. Surprisingly, using sanctions can delay improvements in public health, protection of the environment, use of green technology and a steady economy, all needed to achieve the SDGs. According to the research, tough legal policies do not match the teamwork needed for sustainability. While sanctions mostly promote sustainability, their actual enforcement fails to ensure proper planning, complete legal backing or responsibility. Strict and unforgiving international sanctions make it hard for the very people the law is meant to support. It is also a weakness in the international system that no meaningful efforts deal with security, human rights and environmental protection. Enforcing sanctions on Iran and on Venezuela and North Korea has many times prevented those nations from switching to greener energy (Lim, 2021).

The researchers also pointed out certain good possibilities for reforming the system. Evidence from the UN in West Africa, the FATF's teamwork and post-Kadi judgments in the EU suggest that it is now common practise for sanctions programmes to be consultative and agency focused. Studying uses of ESG-based sanctions, assessing their negative or positive effect on nature and devising plans for international bodies to cheque their effects. This research extends the library of academic studies that argue for improvements in making and shaping international laws. The research suggests that reforming sanctions could make them greener, more humanitarian and stronger evidence-driven for the use of policymakers and international groups. We need to put sustainability principles in sanctions policies, keep review processes simple and correct and make sure vital economic areas such as health, food and clean energy are not endangered (Rowhani, 2023).

Going forward, we need new research to focus on two primary fields. It's important to first study what sanctions mean for sustainable development when applied to various sectors. In addition, experts in law and regulation should aim to position sustainable practises as central to the laws they produce. It is obvious that international law should contribute to lasting security, peaceful relations and the thriving of both people and the environment. Our intention here and throughout the book is to support projects aimed at unifying and simplifying laws for everyone.

REFERENCES

Adanma, U. M., & Ogunbiyi, E. O. (2024). A comparative review of global environmental policies for promoting sustainable development and economic growth. *International Journal of Applied Research in Social Sciences*, *6*(5), 954–977. DOI: 10.51594/ijarss.v6i5.1147Fepbl+1ResearchGate+1

Bantekas, I., & Akestoridi, K. (2022). Sustainable development goals, between politics and soft law: The emergence of "political normativity" in international law. *Emory International Law Review*, *37*, 499. https://scholarlycommons.law.emory .edu/eilr/vol37/iss4/1

Biglari, S., Beiglary, S., & Arthanari, T. (2022). Achieving sustainable development goals: Fact or fiction? *Journal of Cleaner Production*, *332*, 130032. DOI: 10.1016/j. jclepro.2021.130032

Brus, M. M. (2018). Soft law in public international law: A pragmatic or a principled choice? Comparing the Sustainable Development Goals and the Paris Agreement. *Springer*, 243–266. https://doi.org/DOI: 10.1007/978-3-319-77522-7_13

Butt, M. J. (2021). The role of international law in shaping the governance for sustainable development goals. *Journal of Law and Political Sciences*, *28*(3), 87–164. DOI: 10.5281/zenodo.4904817

Ershov, D. N. (2023). Legal framework for sustainable development and current global challenges. *Sustainable Social Development*, *1*(1). Advance online publication. DOI: 10.54517/ssd.v1i1.2196

Fu, Q., Gong, Q., Zhao, X. X., & Chang, C. P. (2023). The effects of international sanctions on green innovations. *Technological and Economic Development of Economy*, *29*(1), 141–164. DOI: 10.3846/tede.2022.18034

Galloro, L., & Guida, M. (2024). The limits of UN Security Council action in imposing economic sanctions under UN Charter and international law: The subtle balance between international security and human rights compliance. *Charles University in Prague Faculty of Law Research Paper No. 2024/III/4*. https://doi.org/ DOI: 10.2139/ssrn.5026499

Gorodkov, V. (2024). *Securitization of Russian polity: Russia's discursive, legislative and institutional response to international sanctions in 2014–2021*. Carlcton University., DOI: 10.22215/etd/2024-16312

Hák, T., Janoušková, S., & Moldan, B. (2016). Sustainable Development Goals: A need for relevant indicators. *Ecological Indicators*, *60*, 565–573. DOI: 10.1016/j.ecolind.2015.08.003

Heyl, K., Döring, T., Garske, B., Stubenrauch, J., & Ekardt, F. (2021). The Common Agricultural Policy beyond 2020: A critical review in light of global environmental goals. *Review of European, Comparative & International Environmental Law*, *30*(1), 95–106. DOI: 10.1111/reel.12351

Jessen, H. (2021). Multilateral and unilateral sanctions: Compliance and challenges. *Springer International Publishing*, 570–580. https://doi.org/DOI: 10.1007/978-3-319-95960-3_51

Khare, P., Raghuwanshi, V., & Sharma, P. (2025). Impact of Israel-Palestine Conflict on Global Economic Relations. *IGI Global Scientific Publishing*, 163-186. https://doi.org/DOI: 10.4018/979-8-3693-8674-3.ch007

Kim, R. E., & Bosselmann, K. (2015). Operationalizing sustainable development: Ecological integrity as a grundnorm of international law. *Review of European, Comparative & International Environmental Law*, *24*(2), 194–208. DOI: 10.1111/reel.12109

Lim, S. (2021). The paradox of unsustainability in UN Sustainable Development Goals (SDGs): The North Korean case in the context of accountability and fragile states under sanctions. *Journal of Peace and Unification*, *11*(1), 55–78. DOI: 10.31780/jpu.2021.11.1.55

Majid, S. H. (2024). Implications of sanctions on local populations in Africa: A case study of United States of America's sanctions against Sudan. *University of Nairobi*. https://erepository.uonbi.ac.ke/handle/11295/166852

Nikolaev, P. P., Vaseltsova, I. A., Gryaznov, S. A., & Levchenko, A. V. (2024, April). Crises, sanctions, and conflicts on the way to achieving sustainable development goals. *Springer Nature Switzerland*, 442–450. https://doi.org/DOI: 10.1007/978-3-031-67372-6

Noorollahi, Y., Lund, H., Nielsen, S., & Thellufsen, J. Z. (2021). Energy transition in petroleum rich nations: Case study of Iran. *Smart Energy*, *3*, 100026. DOI: 10.1016/j.segy.2021.100026

Poorhashemi, A. (2024). International environmental law. *Routledge*, 453–466. https://doi.org/DOI: 10.4324/9781003451327-19

Rajamani, L., Jeffery, L., Höhne, N., Hans, F., Glass, A., Ganti, G., & Geiges, A. (2021). National 'fair shares' in reducing greenhouse gas emissions within the principled framework of international environmental law. *Climate Policy*, *21*(8), 983–1004. DOI: 10.1080/14693062.2021.1970504

Rapsikevičius, J., Bruneckienė, J., Krušinskas, R., & Lukauskas, M. (2022). The impact of structural reforms on sustainable development performance: Evidence from European Union countries. *Sustainability*, *14*(19), 12583. DOI: 10.3390/su141912583

Rochat, M., & Tsouloufas, G. (2024). The effectiveness of smart sanctions: Examining divergent outcomes in Myanmar and Zimbabwe. *Journal of Asian and African Studies*, *59*(1), 55–78. DOI: 10.1177/00219096241300448

Rowhani, M. (2023). Rights-based boundaries of the United Nations sanctions. *University of Bologna Law Review*, *8*(1), 129–148. https://doi.org/DOI: 10.6092/issn.2531-6133/17799

Sjåfjell, B., Mähönen, J., Taylor, M. B., Maitre-Ekern, E., van der Velden, M., Novitz, T., Gammage, C., Cullen, J., Andhov, M., & Caranta, R. (2019). *University of Oslo*. https://ssrn.com/abstract=3503310

Skjærseth, J. B., Stokke, O. S., & Wettestad, J. (2006). Soft law, hard law, and effective implementation of international environmental norms. *Global Environmental Politics*, *6*(3), 104–120. DOI: 10.1162/glep.2006.6.3.104

Suleiman, N. M., Ahmed, S. S., Zuhair, M., Dahash, Z. M., & Chornomordenko, I. (2024). A socioeconomic analysis of the effects of international sanctions on targeted nations. *Journal of Ecohumanism*, *3*(5), 833–850. DOI: 10.5281/zenodo.10802166

Zuhra, A., & Sabirin, A. (2024). How do international economic laws impact sustainable development goals? *ADLIYA: Jurnal Hukum Dan Kemanusiaan*, *18*(2), 127–152. DOI: 10.15575/adliya.v18i2.35985

KEY TERMS AND DEFINITIONS

Case Study Methodology: An approach to research where experts look deeply into specific places to find out how laws or policies affect reality. In this chapter, the authors discuss how sanctions influence sustainability in Iran, Russia, Venezuela and similar countries.

Environmental Governance: How countries organise laws and institutions to deal with environmental matters and resources. There are different actors at all three levels of government and both types of agreements are included.

International Sanctions: Steps taken by states or organizations to penalize or force those who violate widely accepted international rules. There are economic, diplomatic and military types of sanctions and they are most often allowed by international law to help maintain peace and security.

Law that is based on principles: A way of carrying out legal research by analysing laws, treaties and legal judgments to make clear what is required, allowed and established in a country's legal system.

Legal Coherence: How the international environmental law, human rights law and sanctions law exist independently of each other and do not contradict one another's goals.

SDGs (Sustainable Development Goals): A group of 17 important worldwide objectives set up by the United Nations in 2015 to help solve urgent environmental, economic and social issues by 2030. They act as a basic system for planning development policies all over the world.

Smart Sanctions: Those sanctions that minimise harm to others by being used against people or businesses of significance, rather than through general economic approaches. They are meant to make sanctions more powerful and less destructive for people not involved.

Sustainable Development: A way of developing nations that addresses the requirements of today while safeguarding the ability of tomorrow's people to do the same. Included in this are actions for the environment, financial equality and social fairness as established in major international documents such as the SDGs and the Brundtland Report

Chapter 11
Sustainability as Strategic Narrative:
The Canadian Aporetic Condition and Global Environmental Governance

John Bessai
https://orcid.org/0009-0003-2755-6623
Independent Researcher, Canada

ABSTRACT

The research examines how sustainability functions as a strategic narrative framework for global environmental management, using Canada as a case study. The research establishes the Canadian aporetic condition through the analysis of climate targets and ongoing resource extraction activities, studying three specific areas to demonstrate how narrative coherence enables people to accept conflicting material outcomes. The chapter employs discourse analysis and critical political ecology to evaluate Canadian policy statements by comparing them with Indigenous land governance and just-transition planning, and degrowth frameworks. This chapter presents two counterarguments regarding incremental reform and establishes fundamental definitions for readers unfamiliar with this subject area. The final section outlines specific steps organizations should take to achieve their targets through structural adjustments and enhanced monitoring systems.

DOI: 10.4018/979-8-3373-1707-6.ch011

INTRODUCTION

Sustainability functions as the fundamental principle which guides public sector policy development and corporate strategic planning within market systems and public sectors. Leaders promote sustainable development as an approach which unites economic achievement with environmental stewardship. The discussion continues to be marked by active conflicts because organizations pursue growth while also working to protect ecological boundaries. Strategic narratives transform these conflicts into believable stories that people accept and follow, enabling coordinated action. The analysis in this chapter examines sustainability as a storytelling practice to evaluate its impact on extraction activities, infrastructure development, and regulatory choices. The Canadian aporetic condition refers to Canada's ongoing pattern of establishing broad climate targets, reconciliation goals, and market protection measures, while supporting the development of high-emission infrastructure (Bessai, 2024). The three indicators I use to identify aporetic moments include (1) international climate ambition alongside domestic growth of extractive industries; (2) legitimating narratives of "ethical oil," "clean growth," and "climate leadership" that bridge the contradiction; and (3) the results of projects, subsidies, and regulatory frameworks that generate lasting emissions. In this chapter, "aporia" means a structured impasse: institutions hold aims that pull in different directions without a ready resolution. "The Canadian aporetic condition" is my diagnostic frame for Canada's sustainability politics, where three concurrent aims—decarbonization, Indigenous reconciliation, and global competitiveness—coexist and generate contradictory choices and narrative workarounds. I flag "aporetic moments" using the three markers below.

The chapter follows a three-step progression. The document begins by presenting definitions and research findings on strategic narratives, environmental discourse, and settler-colonial political economy. Second, it describes the methodology, corpus, and coding scheme used to identify aporetic moments. The research begins by analyzing Canada's climate position and extractive systems, as well as its green policy tools, before moving on to discuss governance approaches for implementing policy commitments through structural changes. The research examines how Canada employs sustainability narratives in its domestic and international operations to assess their impact on policy development and extraction activities, as well as their influence on Indigenous governance systems.

STRATEGIC NARRATIVES AND THE MARKETIZATION OF SUSTAINABILITY

The research examines sustainability as a strategic framework which operates within global environmental governance systems. States, international organizations, and corporations employ strategic narrative as a method to create public understanding of environmental problems through purposeful storytelling, which guides people toward their institutional objectives (Roselle, Miskimmon, & O'Loughlin, 2013). The twenty-first century has made sustainability its primary focus, uniting environmental protection with financial success in the business world. The United Nations Sustainable Development Goals (SDGs) serve as a policy framework that integrates environmental protection with poverty reduction, inclusive growth, and governance reforms (United Nations, 2015). Critical scholarship reveals that mainstream uptake frequently channels sustainability through growth-oriented models and managerial practices (Demaria et al.,2013; Hickel & Kallis, 2020). The institutional speakers establish credibility through their presentations, which connect sustainability to smart growth, a clean economy, and sustainable finance, and present a clear development trajectory (Tienhaara & Walker, 2021; Ofori-Parku & Koomson, 2023). The system uses symbolic capital to establish its reputation and maintain its authority and stability through sustainability initiatives.

I keep the Canadian aporetic condition at the centre of the analysis. The condition exists as a long-term policy framework that maintains three incompatible elements: decarbonization, Indigenous reconciliation, and global competitiveness, which produce contradictory choices and funding decisions. Canada leads climate change efforts by participating in international climate meetings while working to achieve its carbon reduction goals and expand oil and gas exports through large-scale infrastructure projects (Natural Resources Canada, 2021; Government of Canada, 2021). The identification of aporetic moments occurs through three distinct markers: international climate ambition, domestic extractive growth, and legitimating narratives that connect these opposing elements. These narratives are further supported by material results that produce higher emissions through projects, subsidies, and regulatory frameworks. The lens keeps the chapter focused on evidence and consequences.

The chapter studies three planes of marketization. Leaders utilize narrative production to create sustainable branding, which enables them to gain public consensus. Policy instrumentation serves as the second stage in developing market-ready programs from goals by implementing carbon pricing and financial tools, as well as offset mechanisms. The third performance element of institutions involves reputational performance, which enables them to establish trust with the public and gain investor confidence. The structure follows the aporetic condition through its analysis of how narrative elements, instrumental aspects, and performance elements maintain a sense of extractive continuity.

SUSTAINABILITY DISCOURSE AND HEGEMONY

Sustainability discourse emerges from the intersection of language systems, institutional power structures, and representation methods. Work in environmental discourse analysis and Gramscian theory details how meaning emerges from struggles among states, firms, civil society, and transnational bodies (Dryzek, 2013; Hajer, 1995; Gramsci, 1971/2000). The way public audiences accept discourse as common sense and its support of powerful decision-making interests results in its establishment as hegemonic (Bäckstrand & Lövbrand, 2006). The vocabulary of sustainable development employs market-based solutions to present a positive view of technology and quantitative growth indicators (Adams, 2009; Escobar, 1995). The orientation system employs alternative concepts within a single framework, allowing the term to have multiple possible meanings. The dominant usage of "green growth" and "sustainable innovation" serves as indicators that show both responsibility and credibility. The research by Tienhaara and Walker (2021) suggests that these statements coincide with increasing Canadian fossil fuel development investments, which are driven by pipeline politics. Strategic narratives shape perception, channel critique, and project moral authority (Miskimmon et al.,2013). They also establish boundaries on what constitutes a feasible action and on which knowledge gains standing (Demaria et al.). The study of biodiversity has become a critical field of research since the 1990s, according to Shiva (2005) and Demaria et al. (2013).

Environmental political theory provides a map of the main currents of thought. Ecological modernization and liberal environmentalism integrate market-driven innovation into policy solutions (Dryzek, 2013). The critical environmental frameworks of Deep ecology and eco-socialism require value changes and institutional reforms, and demand reduction according to Dobson (2007). The Brundtland Commission established the global development standard through its definition, which states that development requires meeting present needs and preserving the ability of future generations to meet their own needs (WCED, 1987, p. 43). The definition's adaptable nature makes it suitable for various applications; however, it leads to imprecise analysis, as noted by Adams (2009). The theory of Strategic narrative explains how political and corporate leaders link organizational goals with meaning systems (Miskimmon, O'Loughlin, & Roselle, 2013). The institutional position of discourse stems from role claims, which include "climate leader," "green innovator," and "inclusive growth champion." However, these claims conceal the extractive characteristics of policy development (Tienhaara & Walker, 2021).

Public interpretation throughout different sectors relies on the use of narratives. The government sets future goals through net-zero targets, yet the same governments allow extractive operations to proceed. Corporate sustainability organizations release reports that showcase their community involvement and carbon reduction plans, while continuing their fundamental manufacturing activities (Ofori-Parku & Koomson, 2023). International organizations, such as the United Nations, promote the SDGs as universal goals; however, researchers have shown that these goals lack representation of historical accountability, power dynamics, and social inequalities (Dehm, 2016). Gramsci explains that social forces establish cultural hegemony through the process of turning particular beliefs into dominant social standards. Organizations that use sustainability as symbolic capital gain both moral and political power, which restricts the opportunity for intense criticism (Bourdieu, 1991). The pattern requires making minor modifications but prohibits discussing fundamental system changes.

Urban development demonstrates this concept. Growth coalitions use sustainability branding to attract capital, consolidate legitimacy, and dampen ecological dissent (Ofori-Parku & Koomson, 2023). Neoliberal governance requires sustainability as a fundamental necessity for development, which hinders the achievement of fair distribution and equitable solutions. The formal policy forums do not support alternative models which unite Indigenous research with community activism to build responsible and mutually beneficial connections between different age groups (Dehm, 2016; Hickel, 2020b). The following analysis employs the aporetic condition to identify which stories emerge and which tools convey them, as well as the physical outcomes that result from these processes.

DISSENT, MARGINALIZATION, AND THE DEPOLITICIZATION OF SUSTAINABILITY

Sustainability remains a central theme in institutional storytelling, yet people continue to express opposition to it. The current policy-making system lacks integration of Indigenous knowledge systems and environmental justice frameworks, which are based on relational accountability, land-based ethics, and intergenerational well-being (Shiva, 2005; Escobar, 2012; Whyte, 2020). The research methods focus on environmental destruction production by social systems through historical development pattern analysis. The initial discussions about sustainability focused on criticizing developmentalism due to its adverse effects on society and the environment (Dehm, 2016). Subsequent acceptance of sustainability by mainstream society transformed this energy into corporate management terminology. The current powerful actors link sustainability with smart growth, green finance, and clean innovation to establish legitimacy while controlling risks and demonstrating ethical commitment (Ofori-Parku & Koomson, 2023; Tienhaara & Walker, 2021). Social media serves as a tool to protect corporate image, yet it hinders organizations from undergoing fundamental changes.

Depoliticization enables this outcome. The widespread adoption of net-zero and green transition commitments creates an illusion of advancement, diverting public attention from issues of equity, consumption, and structural violence (Hajer, 1995; Hickel, 2020b). Technocracy employs its own set of terms, which serve as replacements for traditional political evaluation systems and ethical assessment frameworks. Agencies frequently draw from marginalized historical viewpoints, but they do not provide these perspectives with decision-making power. Post-development scholars have established worldwide sustainability frameworks that establish common development criteria, thereby removing political distinctions between countries (Escobar, 2012). Analysts of the SDGs document gaps on power and responsibility even as the goals proclaim inclusion (Dehm, 2016). Justice-oriented models determine which future scenarios to safeguard, which knowledge systems will inform decisions, and which groups will benefit from sustainability frameworks, employing pluralistic and accountable methods. The assessment of these questions occurs through the aporetic condition, which reveals how international ambition aligns with domestic expansion but legitimizes narratives to resolve disputes, and policy choices create physical borders that block future options. This research examines how sustainability operates as a dominant discourse that hinders the development of new systems, as institutional support from elite members maintains its position. This focus invites close attention to definition and implementation, which the next subsections provide through narrative and marketization analysis.

MARKETIZATION MECHANISMS: NARRATIVES, INSTRUMENTS, AND PERFORMANCE

Green growth and sustainable development narratives serve as communication tools that political organizations and corporate entities use to convey their messages. The stories depict environmental targets and economic development as interconnected forces, showing how collaboration leads to shared success. The United Nations established SDGs as global standards in 2015, which unite economic growth with environmental stewardship and social cohesion. The essential research indicates that the vision retains its permanent structural elements, which include control by the extractive industry and unbalanced trade systems, as well as colonial patterns of wealth distribution (Hickel & Kallis, 2020). Organizations utilize strategic narratives to establish their reputation and secure policy support and market access through intentional storytelling (Roselle, Miskimmon, & O'Loughlin, 2014).

Through sustainability targets, governments can create partnerships to attract green investment while integrating environmental goals into their economic development plans. The corporate world releases sustainability reports that showcase its chosen environmental projects, yet continues to maintain its fundamental carbon-emitting business activities (Tienhaara & Walker, 2021; Ofori-Parku & Koomson, 2023). The terms become familiar to people through their proper environments, which function as reputation-building tools that showcase both innovative approaches and corporate social responsibility. The Trans Mountain Pipeline research indicates that sustainability and public benefit claims from officials supported pipeline expansion, which in turn strengthened extractive practices and limited available policy choices (Tienhaara & Walker, 2021). The narrative structures demonstrate that sustainability operates as a shared concept, integrating into current governance frameworks and market frameworks. The market for sustainability branding is evolving through green finance, carbon trading, clean technology, and eco-tourism products, which present themselves as ethical investments. The discursive economy utilizes sustainability as symbolic capital to demonstrate modernity, accountability, and leadership.

Instrumentalization structures practice. Organizations use sustainability language to establish legitimacy, mitigate reputational risk, and lower regulatory exposure. The programs generate local benefits, while other initiatives help businesses achieve stability and foster a positive public perception of their social commitment. The authors, Ofori-Parku and Koomson (2023), demonstrate how Tullow Oil in Ghana utilizes its development partner role to create a benevolent image for itself, while portraying communities as beneficiaries of corporate charity, thereby maintaining social order and shifting attention away from environmental and social problems. The communication methods serve to protect authority positions while dealing with important feedback. Green innovation strategic narratives create unified narratives that conceal the extraction activities required to maintain profit levels. These stories establish the rules of interaction while deciding which statements will spread throughout the community. Leaders create a situation through their actions that enables them to raise climate ambition, while using legitimating narratives to support investments that result in longer-lasting emissions.

The theoretical framework demonstrates that sustainability functions as a leading discourse, implementing a system of concepts and operational methods that operate through uneven power dynamics. Universal claims conceal gaps between image and infrastructure, as well as between symbols and outcomes. Buen vivir (Gudynas, 2011), degrowth economics (Hickel, 2020a), and Escobar's pluriverse (2018) present new governance frameworks that adopt pluralistic methods to achieve community well-being and site-based management. Research on environmental justice reveals that areas that have historically lacked environmental responsibility now experience the most severe environmental damage, while facing difficulties in obtaining fair compensation (Agyeman et al., 2016). The evaluation criteria for sustainability narratives and practice-based aporetic moments are established through the provided perspectives.

METHODOLOGY

I employed a qualitative critical design approach, which integrated discourse analysis with an in-depth examination of Canada as my case study. The research aims to understand how political entities, corporate bodies, and institutional organizations present sustainability concepts while establishing links between storytelling activities and actual results in extraction operations, infrastructure development, and regulatory frameworks. The research draws on four main sources, including UNFCCC submissions, Canadian leadership speeches, sustainability reports from major resource companies, and UN documents such as the 2030 Agenda (United Nations, 2015). The research draws on environmental politics, development studies, and sustainability science to examine how sustainability operates as an ideological framework (Adams, 2009; Escobar, 2018; Hickel & Kallis, 2020). I monitor recurring patterns in the text, which include win-win solutions and technological solutions, and I apply postcolonial analysis to study power imbalances in governance and knowledge systems (Shiva, 2005; Dehm, 2016).

The research is based on the principles of Critical Discourse Analysis (CDA). I code for metaphors—such as climate leadership and bridges to the future—selective inclusion and exclusion, and alignment with institutional interests. The government produces documents that describe Canadian oil as ethical and sustainable; however, these texts use language to establish extraction practices as normal while presenting environmental benefits (Ofori-Parku & Koomson, 2023). The research employs three interconnected case studies to analyze Canadian climate agreements under the Kyoto and Paris frameworks, as well as domestic extractive activities through oil sands development and the Trans Mountain project, and national policy instruments, including carbon pricing, clean energy funding, and federal sustainability plans. I verify the information by combining official statements, corporate communications, policy texts, academic research, NGO reports, and investigative journalism.

I focus on achieving deep comprehension by using exact analytical methods. I demonstrate how narrative claims shape greenhouse gas pathways and regulatory systems, which subsequently influence the effects on local communities. I combine political theory, economic sociology, and environmental science to create a comprehensive understanding of sustainability through narrative practices. Canada demonstrates this point through its example, and I use comparative examples to show how other jurisdictions follow similar patterns. The Canadian political system combines Indigenous self-governance structures with federal-provincial ties, which provide valuable lessons for resource-based areas that have experienced colonial rule and multiple governing bodies. An ethics note: I prioritize respectful citation, especially of Indigenous scholarship, and I assess policy texts in light of consent and land governance. The design system examines how actors employ sustainability to build legitimacy while controlling opposition and creating public discourse. The case study structure grounds the analysis and links the aporetic condition to traceable decisions and investments.

SUSTAINABILITY AS STRATEGIC NARRATIVE IN GLOBAL ENVIRONMENTAL GOVERNANCE

Sustainability serves as a strategic framework that directs worldwide environmental management frameworks. Global institutions promote sustainability through a unified approach, presenting it as a single initiative. All 193 United Nations member states accepted the Sustainable Development Goals (SDGs), which established wide-ranging targets for climate action, poverty reduction, biodiversity protection, and economic development (United Nations, 2015). The SDGs employ inclusive terminology, which fosters a shared narrative of global engagement and facilitates diplomatic consensus across diverse political systems. The core vocabulary of the field encompasses institutional barriers and political compromises that must exist for actual change to become possible (Adams, 2009). The central plot of this story establishes a link between economic development and environmental conservation. Concepts such as "green growth" and "low-carbon prosperity" claim that technological innovation and market mechanisms can decouple development from ecological harm. The World Bank and World Economic Forum work to support renewable energy and clean technology investments because they offer economic benefits while solving climate problems (Tienhaara & Walker, 2021; Hickel & Kallis, 2020). The presentation demonstrates investor and executive confidence through its explanation of how capitalism serves as a method to achieve sustainability targets. Empirical research questions the growth-compatibility storyline. Research indicates that certain industries have successfully decoupled their growth from environmental impact; however, absolute reductions in ecological impact remain rare during periods of economic development (Hickel & Kallis, 2020). Academic experts recommend two structural changes: reducing consumption in wealthy economies and redistributing resources (Hickel, 2020a). Research and activism are showing an increasing interest in these methods, but official bodies remain uninterested in implementing them.

The SDGs face internal conflicts, highlighting the limitations of achieving a universal agreement. The eighth goal focuses on economic development and fair employment, but the thirteenth goal requires an immediate response to climate change. Each government allocates its resources based on the strategic objectives that it has set. States that produce fossil fuels build new infrastructure while working to meet their GDP targets and present themselves as environmentally friendly. Balanced-transition rhetoric maintains extractive reliance and sustains reputational credibility (Dehm, 2016). The concept of universal obligation fails to recognize that countries have produced different levels of historical greenhouse gas emissions. Yet, it is developing nations that face the majority of the climate change impacts. Climate justice frameworks establish their approach through three core principles, which include historical responsibility, equitable finance, and differentiated obligations (Shiva, 2005; Demaria et al., 2013). The research methods of postcolonial and Indigenous studies demand scholars to acknowledge how colonial systems have used their power to exploit and suppress knowledge since colonial times (Escobar, 2018).

International agreements serve as evidence that these narrative shifts have occurred. The 1997 Kyoto Protocol set binding targets for wealthy nations. The 2015 Paris Agreement requires each nation to develop its own nationally determined contributions, while countries must collaborate to enhance their climate targets. Paris extended its participation while reducing the effectiveness of its mechanisms that promote equity. States can establish their own ambition targets through the nationally determined contribution model, which replaces mandatory rules with peer pressure for implementation (Roselle, Miskimmon, & O'Loughlin, 2014). Powerful states benefit from the flexibility. The adoption of "nature-based solutions" and "net-zero" targets demonstrates how sustainability discourse exercises power through its symbolic environmental promises. Poorly regulated offset markets and speculative carbon-removal technologies enable high-emissions trajectories while projecting environmental virtue (Ofori-Parku & Koomson, 2023). I studied these trends through the analysis of leaders who set higher climate targets, developed supporting narratives and funded projects that resulted in increased emissions.

Corporate narratives mirror this pattern. The reports demonstrate how businesses operate as development partners, enabling them to create responsible innovation through their efforts to mitigate social and environmental impacts. The strategic language of corporations establishes their moral authority while portraying affected communities as entities that need consultation or assistance. The research identifies this structure as soft domination because it sets development terms while concealing the existing power imbalances between nations (Ciplet & Roberts, 2017). The global sustainability dialogue presents environmental protection as something that can be achieved within current systems of governance and economic growth. The framework unites different perspectives, but it blocks thorough examinations of power systems, natural boundaries, and entrenched discriminatory systems. The following section examines how these factors are reflected in Canadian climate policy and national identity, as well as their impact on the outcomes of extractive development.

The main entities that use "Sustainability" as a strategic concept are states, international organizations, and corporations. States use sustainability narratives to achieve their strategic objectives. The two countries of India and China demonstrate how emerging economies can present themselves as modern through their commitment to renewable energy while continuing to operate coal facilities to draw green investments. China shows its commitment to the Paris Agreement by rapidly expanding its renewable energy systems, thereby enhancing its international influence. Developed countries employ sustainability framing to maintain moral authority. The European Union utilizes the European Green Deal and climate diplomacy as indicators of shared identity; however, member states continue to fund foreign fossil fuel projects, while domestic resistance prevents them from implementing stringent environmental regulations. Some governments worldwide employ sustainability as a tool to support specific business sectors. The Norwegian government presents itself as a sustainable offshore petroleum producer through its renewable energy-based extraction operations and funding for rainforest conservation, which establishes the state as a responsible oil producer. The Saudi government supports a circular carbon economy and extensive afforestation programs to enhance its reputation while continuing to develop its hydrocarbon resources.

International organizations achieve sustainability promotion through their work of creating industry standards and gathering successful practices. United Nations agencies release reports that highlight corporate commitments, national plans, and international cooperation for achieving climate goals. Students can evaluate their performance through the stories, which also serve to spread new policies and build institutional trust. Institutional optimism often outweighs attention to delivery gaps and implementation risk, which reinforces program coherence more than structural diagnosis. Corporations operationalize sustainability through branding and governance. Companies utilize Corporate Social Responsibility (CSR) and Environmental, Social, and Governance (ESG) reporting to meet the expectations of their consumers, investors, and regulatory bodies. The oil industry operates its traditional fossil fuel activities while using renewable energy terminology and visual elements. Fashion brands launch "conscious" lines, and technology companies announce renewable-powered data centres. The established frameworks operate as usual while their reputation value continues to grow.

A Canadian case study illustrates this method. The Pathways Alliance, which represents an oil sands coalition, supports a 2050 net-zero commitment through investments in carbon capture technology. Advertising emphasizes future reductions and omits rising current emissions and dependence on public funding. The Narwhal conducted independent research in 2024, discovering that public communications often spread false information while omitting crucial details (The Narwhal, 2024). The net-zero narrative enabled businesses to grow in the short term by allowing them to make forward-looking promises, which maintained public backing while preventing immediate, strict regulatory enforcement (The Narwhal, 2024). The majority of fossil fuel corporations operate with comparable business models. The Paris Agreement receives support from executives who set ambitious carbon reduction targets; however, they allocate minimal funds to renewable energy development and utilize their resources to influence policy through political power, while also extracting additional benefits. Businesses utilize sustainability language to establish a connection between their corporate identity and global targets through environmental protection practices. The outcome leads to reputational resilience instead of operational transformation. The stories create confusion between climate action and reputation management, which makes it challenging to identify the responsible party.

Sustainability narratives serve to improve the existing governance systems which currently govern our world. The creation of global frameworks stems from meetings between representatives of states and corporate interests. The preferred solutions implement investment-driven methods and public-private partnerships which operate under neoliberal economic frameworks. Redistributive policies, along with Indigenous land governance systems, remain underexamined, despite research demonstrating their ability to produce lasting results. Alternative solutions operate independently of official dialogues, yet they achieve exceptional results when implemented in local settings. The grassroots movement presents an alternative perspective. The climate-justice movement advocates for a just transition that safeguards workers and vulnerable communities during the transition to carbon-neutral operations. The agenda finds support through scientific research and indigenous wisdom, which proves that social inequality hinders effective cooperation and resilience (Hickel, 2020b; Shiva, 2005). The system comprises organizations that utilize language to promote both fairness and equality. Countries have endorsed climate finance for developing nations and have underdelivered on pledges. The patterns demonstrate that sustainability functions as a shared communication method which produces better group comprehension than actual accountability. The results show both positive language elements and ongoing narratives and material choices, which maintain high emission levels in accordance with the aporetic condition. The section shows how sustainability functions as a discursive resource which maintains the existing dominant power structure. The system retains its value through its ethical integrity, its ability to handle new situations, and its flexible meaning structure. The system enables various groups of people to collaborate toward achieving global objectives. The following section analyzes Canada to understand how leaders apply these narratives when addressing resource dependence, international obligations, and environmental stewardship.

The Canadian Aporetic Condition shows how Canada maintains conflicting environmental sustainability goals through its ongoing practice of resource extraction. Canada serves as a significant research subject for analyzing sustainability discourse due to its national structure, which incorporates various opposing elements. The nation possesses high human development standards, along with extensive renewable energy resources and successful conservation efforts, while maintaining its ties to resource-intensive sectors. Federal officials showcase Canada as a climate leader through evidence-based policy and multilateral cooperation; yet, the economy relies heavily on oil, gas, mining, and forestry. The "Canadian aporetic condition" refers to a long-standing policy structure that maintains three incompatible elements: climate change reduction goals, Indigenous reconciliation efforts, and international market competitiveness. The condition occurs when three elements match: (a) International climate ambition grows while domestic extractive industries expand; (b) The legitimating narratives of "ethical oil," "clean growth," and "climate leadership" create a connection between the two opposing elements; and (c) The actual results establish permanent high-emissions infrastructure and regulatory systems. The three domains of international climate commitments, domestic extractive regimes, and green policy initiatives serve as the foundation for both analysis and diagnostic criteria of aporetic moments.

At COP21, Prime Minister Justin Trudeau announced that Canada had returned as a global environmental leader, having withdrawn from the Kyoto Protocol under the Harper government in 2011 (The Guardian, 2015). The former Environment Minister Peter Kent used compliance penalties and targets he considered unworkable to justify the growth of oil sands (The Guardian, 2011). These episodes show the core disagreement which runs through all federal climate policy systems. The federal government established national carbon pricing and supported the development of clean technology while setting Paris Agreement-compliant targets. Ministers also approved and financed major fossil-fuel infrastructure. The Environment and Climate Change Canada (2024) reports that oil and gas emissions continue to grow at the highest rate in Canada. The cabinet approved the Trans Mountain Pipeline expansion in 2019, despite Parliament declaring a climate emergency and Prime Minister Trudeau stating that Canadians wanted both economic growth and environmental protection (The Guardian, 2024). The sequence demonstrates an aporetic situation because leaders express climate ambition through their policies, yet they continue to increase production capacity during the same period. Green-growth language presents Canadian oil as a moral replacement because the world needs to obtain its oil supply from countries with robust regulatory systems. The process of extracting oil from oil sands generates high levels of carbon emissions, making it challenging to achieve decarbonization goals, as noted by Nikiforuk (2012) and Jaccard (2020).

The terms "clean Canadian oil" and "the world's most ethical energy" operate as rhetorical devices which link the process of oil extraction to environmental conservation. The production of oil sands continues because supporters use regulatory standards to demonstrate that Canadian supply is better than unregulated sources (The Guardian, 2024). The substitution logic supports extraction operations while showing proper resource management. The researchers, along with activists, present evidence on carbon intensity and policy misalignment, as per Jaccard (2020) and Nikiforuk (2012). The aporetic condition serves as an analytical tool, manifesting through three specific signs: official policy documents that continue to make promises of transition while engaging in extraction activities, and the general population and investment community accepting these conflicting practices through established storytelling patterns. The official messages present both an urgent crisis atmosphere and a controlled transformation approach, utilizing sequential expert-led solutions. The pattern serves as part of a larger method that employs narrative techniques to counter criticism by transforming opposing viewpoints into evidence that upholds dominant systems (Miskimmon et al., 2013). The administrative system of sustainability operates as a control mechanism for extractive activities, while providing symbolic support for small-scale policy improvements through carbon pricing and backing for clean technology. However, it prevents essential changes to remove high-emission assets and their revenue sources. Canada's climate architecture includes meaningful reforms, as well as approvals and investments that extend high-emissions infrastructure. The extractive nature of institutions persists through transition language, as outlined in the concept of "aporia" in this chapter. The combination demonstrates a key element of Canadian environmental governance, while illustrating how the dominant sustainability discourse operates within a liberal democratic system.

RESOURCE EXTRACTION REGIMES: OIL SANDS, PIPELINES, AND SUSTAINABILITY CLAIMS

Canada's political economy relies on natural resource extraction. The fur and timber industries created initial patterns which mining and petroleum development later used to construct modern-day infrastructure, labour systems and regional priorities (Adkin, 2016). The Alberta oil sands, which had operated as a primary driver of economic growth, became a major source of disagreement in worldwide climate policy during the twenty-first century. The manufacturing of bitumen needs substantial energy and water resources to produce synthetic crude through its production process. The combination of technological progress and rising oil prices after 2000 enabled Canada to reach the position of one of the world's leading oil producers, according to Nikiforuk (2010). The revenue growth of Canada and its increasing national greenhouse gas (GHG) emissions made it hard for the country to maintain its position in climate negotiations (Harrison, 2007). Federal and provincial officials present oil-sands development as an operation which they consider both sustainable and responsible. The companies demonstrate environmental responsibility through the implementation of regulatory systems and technological solutions, which include tailings reclamation, reforestation, and carbon capture (Natural Resources Canada, 2021; Pembina Institute, 2022). Industry reports indicate that emissions intensity has reduced by 20–30% per barrel since the 1990s (CAPP, n.d.). Absolute emissions rose by more than 450% during the period from 1990 to 2020, according to Environment and Climate Change Canada (ECCC, 2025). The growth of the economy did not lead to increased productivity. Reclamation remains limited. Research indicates that certified reclamation exists on less than 1% of lands that have been disturbed, according to Nikiforuk (2010) and Teelucksingh & Poland (2011).

The project has resulted in documented environmental impacts, including forest destruction, biodiversity decline, and water pollution of the watershed. The complete extraction and combustion of oil reserves containing carbon will create a climate risk. Research on energy systems recommends preserving a substantial portion of fossil fuel reserves, as this helps achieve the 1.5 °C climate target, according to McGlade and Ekins (2015). The Canadian energy planning system continues to support long-term extraction activities through its implementation of technical mitigation methods. The planning process focuses on pipeline expansion as its core element. Projects such as Trans Mountain and Keystone XL have drawn national and international scrutiny as contested infrastructure projects. The federal government supports pipeline expansion for three main reasons: to enhance regulatory quality, demonstrate that pipelines transport oil more safely than rail, and foster national unity and support Indigenous economic growth (Natural Resources Canada, 2021). Climate scientists, in collaboration with Indigenous leaders, confirm that constructing new pipelines will maintain active fossil fuel usage, thereby undermining the climate goals of the Paris Agreement (Carter & Zalik, 2016; Waldron, 2022). The core conflicts become evident through Indigenous reactions to extraction activities. Multiple nations have refused to sign benefit-sharing agreements due to environmental risks, government corruption, and land seizure activities (Whyte, 2020). The Coastal GasLink pipeline project through Wet'suwet'en land became a major national issue in 2020 because it exposed the traditional governance system of hereditary leaders and Indigenous land ownership rights and Canadian obligations to follow UNDRIP. The United Nations Declaration on the Rights of Indigenous Peoples requires indigenous peoples to obtain free, prior and informed consent.

The Canadian government prioritizes economic stability, according to Borrows & Tully (2018). The term "ethical oil" serves as a marketing strategy that Canadian state and industry communicators use to distinguish their oil production from other supplies that do not meet labour and environmental protection standards. The authors link narrative extraction to liberal-democratic values through their argument that Canadian oil represents the most ethical choice (Le Menestrel & Van Wassenhove, 2009). According to critics, the frame functions to divert public focus away from environmental consequences while maintaining colonial control over land and resources (Eisenstein, 2009; Teelucksingh & Poland, 2011). The communication process in mining operations operates through the same sequence. Canada supports "responsible mining" operations, which focus on extracting critical minerals needed for clean-energy supply chains. The 2022 federal Critical Minerals Strategy includes oversight systems and transparency protocols and establishes Indigenous participation according to the Pembina Institute (2022).

The new technological requirements have resulted in weak enforcement and ongoing environmental damage, according to Environmental and Indigenous organizations (Zalik, 2018). The continued business activities in unconsulted regions raise questions about the actual commitment of these organizations to their justice pledges. Forestry and fisheries produce both beneficial and detrimental effects in their operations. The certification systems, along with community fisheries, continue to operate while old-growth logging persists and biodiversity continues to decline. The federal government has not achieved its biodiversity targets, according to Boyd (2010). The policy frameworks of different sectors work to enhance extraction operations without changing the fundamental development approach. The financial dependence on royalties creates limited choices, as Alberta and Saskatchewan rely on fossil fuel income to build alliances that fight against carbon pricing, transition investments, and stricter regulatory measures (Harrison, 2012). The Canadian Centre for Policy Alternatives (2023) reports that Federal "Just Transition" planning lacks specific information about when changes will occur and what support systems will be in place for workers. Future climate reduction targets are outlined in national climate plans, which also enable ongoing infrastructure development. National Climate Planning: Targets, Instruments, and Current Expansion. The following section demonstrates how the aporetic condition manifests in real-world situations. The government supports environmental protection through its approval of extractive activities. The institutions promote technological optimism by implementing step-by-step reforms and inclusion policies which maintain existing authority structures to enable emission-reducing technological advancements. Higher output levels produce more emissions; yet, sustainability operates as a management system that deals with ongoing conflicts through narrative development.

NATIONAL CLIMATE PLANNING: TARGETS, INSTRUMENTS, AND CURRENT EXPANSION

The following section demonstrates how the aporetic condition manifests in real-world situations. The primary mechanism for implementing carbon pricing is in place as the main instrument. The federal backstop system, which began at $20 per tonne in 2019, is expected to reach $170 per tonne by 2030. The design sends revenue back to the households located in the provinces that have implemented the charge. This feature supports equity and public legitimacy, aligning with the Prime Minister's "price on pollution" message (Harrison, 2023). The policy remained in place through electoral cycles, and the Supreme Court of Canada upheld its constitutionality in 2021 (Supreme Court of Canada, 2021). Provinces with fossil-dependent economies continue to contest the policy. Environment and Climate Change Canada predicts major decreases will occur by 2030 (Environment and Climate Change Canada, 2024). Exemptions for trade-exposed sectors and political restrictions on price levels reduce the transformative impact of the policy. The government provides funding through both federal and provincial programs for the development of clean technology, the construction of electric vehicle infrastructure, and energy-efficient housing initiatives. British Columbia implemented its first carbon tax, while Quebec utilized hydropower and electric vehicle policies, and Ontario abandoned its renewable energy program, as noted by Jaccard (2020).

Clean-energy gains create a new national leadership framework. By 2025, non-emitting sources will generate more than 80% of Canada's electricity, led by hydro and nuclear. The eastern provinces have nearly eliminated coal, and the federal government has set a target to phase out coal by 2030. Incentives for electric vehicles lifted sales. The government demonstrates these results through the terms "clean growth" and "clean economy," which establish connections between environmental programs, job development, and business success (Clean Energy Canada, 2022). The oil and gas industry remains the primary driver of production levels and job creation in the region. The government uses fossil fuel revenue to fund clean energy initiatives and existing programs which work to decrease our present reliance on fossil fuels. Analysts question whether an incremental approach meets climate obligations as cumulative emissions rise and stranded-asset risks grow (Hickel & Kallis, 2020). The Net-Zero Emissions Accountability Act (2021) established a 2050 target date and multiple five-year checkpoints, which help monitor progress and support necessary changes (Government of Canada, 2021). The country of Canada faces ongoing difficulties in its pursuit of economic growth through sustainable environmental practices.

The policy roadmaps track the development of carbon-intensive sectors while utilizing technological solutions to achieve reductions in emissions. The plans focus on carbon capture and hydrogen technology platforms while keeping production targets on an upward trajectory (Jaccard, 2020). The Environment Minister suggested that peak demand would lead to reduced production, but provincial leaders dismissed this idea, revealing the political aspects of controlled decline. People in the public sector demonstrate high levels of concern about climate change; however, their support for carbon pricing systems that provide financial benefits to families varies based on their geographic location and professional position, while their views on the speed and policy tools also vary. The federal government supports carbon capture projects in producer provinces while continuing to develop renewable energy systems and working with public supporters of climate change action. The adoption of biofuels and small modular reactors (SMRs) generates specific trade-offs, as ethanol production requirements compromise food security and land resources. At the same time, SMR development encounters obstacles related to high costs, safety concerns, and waste disposal issues (Winfield et al., 2006). "All options" messaging keeps multiple tools in play and leaves the retirement of high-emissions assets without a fixed schedule.

Urban policy operates with a standard organizational framework. Federal programs support transit systems, smart-city pilot projects, and retrofitting initiatives, but the problems of car dependency and urban sprawl persist. Local governance systems, real estate markets, and voter preferences all play a role in determining election results, as they influence small-scale political development. The public discussion about sustainability establishes mandatory guidelines, which market-based systems often prioritize financial gains over environmental defence and social justice (Demaria et al., 2013). Canada has experienced various positive developments despite ongoing conflicts, according to its historical data. The case illustrates how strategic narratives maintain existing arrangements and offer symbols of transition. The analysis leads to the final section, which evaluates global discussions about ethical principles and their capacity to bring about actual governance changes.

TRANSFORMATIVE PATHWAYS: INDIGENOUS GOVERNANCE AND DEGROWTH

The research reveals the methods through which the company uses narrative management to expand its business operations. The research evidence serves as a foundation for this chapter, which develops policy approaches that support Indigenous self-governance while promoting public health and well-being. The pathways link specific commitments to particular, dated instruments and public indicators, allowing for the monitoring of actual material changes. The foundation of consent-based development starts with the governance systems which Indigenous peoples employ to oversee their territories. The recording process for Free, Prior, and Informed Consent (FPIC) involves Indigenous land and water projects through agreements, meeting minutes, and independent verification steps. The establishment of Indigenous Protected and Conserved Areas and co-governance arrangements between governments and nations requires defined roles for land-use decisions, monitoring and enforcement and benefit-sharing. Public finance provides backing for land-back agreements and guardianship programs, as well as the implementation of Indigenous law, to protect water, salmon, and caribou resources (Borrows & Tully, 2018; Whyte, 2020). The current measures work to prevent conflicts while creating sustainable systems for environmental protection. The production and demand levels are set through a managed decline and sufficiency approach. The production schedule follows a declining pattern which matches the targets of Canada's carbon budget and its five-year milestones. Legislatures establish specific timeframes to eliminate fossil-fuel subsidies, redirecting the funds toward building retrofitting, public transit development, grid modernization, and community-based energy systems. The planning authorities use sufficiency standards to manage building and vehicle development, while banning high-carbon advertisements and supporting dense neighbourhoods with a range of services. The instruments reduce energy consumption, redirecting funds toward the construction of low-emission infrastructure (Demaria et al., 2013; Hickel & Kallis, 2020; Jaccard, 2020).

The architecture of just transition ensures job preservation during industrial transformation processes. The government offers wage protection programs, portable benefits, and paid training that result in certified positions in construction work, ecosystem restoration, and public power operations. The establishment of regional transition agencies by provinces includes Indigenous representatives and members from labour groups, municipalities, and industry sectors to oversee procurement processes, supply chain management, local hiring, and timeline coordination. Project approvals include community-benefit agreements and worker-voice provisions, which enhance transition planning to improve job quality alongside emissions outcomes (Government of Canada, 2021; Canadian Centre for Policy Alternatives, 2023; Pembina Institute, 2023). The financial and accountability systems operate as a system which links market activities to transition plans. The government has established a system which selects low-carbon materials and services for all ministries through climate-aligned procurement. The windfall-profit levy system generates revenue that supports investments in grid resilience projects, Indigenous stewardship programs, and transition initiatives. The disclosure of securities must include specific time-based targets, spending plans, and restrictions on offsetting practices within regulatory compliance systems. The review process of independent audits verifies system alignment between infrastructure and financial systems before releasing results to Parliament and the public (Jaccard, 2020; Pembina Institute, 2023). The implementation process depends on clear indicators that show progress and specific triggers which help make adjustments. The public dashboards display emissions data alongside biodiversity results, employment metrics, training achievements, consent verification, and revenue distribution. The aporia check functions at all decision points because it allows corrective measures through these instruments to address the combination of international ambition and domestic growth, as well as a legitimating narrative, until performance indicators verify that promises match actual outcomes.

CONCLUSION

Canada develops its sustainability narrative in response to the primary issues that global environmental governance faces. The chapter shows how sustainability operates as an organizational system for consent through its presentation as an ethical framework for decision-making. The Canadian aporetic condition is characterized by its promising environmental goals alongside its ongoing practice of resource extraction, which remains a core issue. I use this tool to track how leaders advance climate ambition and to assess the ways stories confirm their choices and funding enables ongoing emission levels (Miskimmon, O'Loughlin, & Roselle, 2013; Hickel & Kallis, 2020).

1. Sustainability as an instrument and ideology. Sustainability language serves as a tool that helps organizations build trust with their audience while handling criticism from the public and maintaining market control. Federal officials present fossil expansion and climate leadership as compatible and address both environmental and industrial audiences. The oil-sands industry operates extraction as its primary business function, while employing "net-zero" marketing approaches to build favourable public opinion (Ciplet & Roberts, 2017; Tienhaara & Walker, 2021). This pattern lifts incremental steps to the status of transformation. The SDGs promote both inclusive methods and technological optimism; however, they do not address core structural imbalances and environmental depletion within their core framework (United Nations, 2015; Escobar, 2018; ENCATC, 2020).
2. Trade-offs and political will. The technical solutions which can be implemented depend on the choices made through policy decisions. Canada's exit from the Kyoto Protocol illustrates how leaders prioritize "jobs and growth" when climate rules take effect (The Guardian, 2011). The data indicate that worldwide emissions have continued to rise across every treaty period (Friedlingstein et al. 2023). The narrative approach to progress shows improvement, but it does not

recognize that Earth has reached its maximum sustainable capacity. Sustainability risks serve as a communication system rather than a governance system within that particular context.

3. Power, inequity, and carbon colonialism. The primary social discussion portrays all actors as equal but overlooks their varying levels of power. Canada serves as a climate advocate while exporting fossil fuels, which demonstrates carbon colonialism because wealthy states shift their environmental expenses to other nations while maintaining control over policy decisions (Bond, 2012; Ofori-Parku & Koomson, 2023). The TWAIL scholarship supports emission distribution through a system which considers both past emission records and present production capabilities (Gathii, 2011). The Canadian Indigenous communities experience two main destructive impacts and restricted decision-making power (Whyte, 2020). A just sustainability framework requires three essential elements: redress, resource redistribution, and shared control.
4. Contested meanings and critical alternatives, the main duty of institutional actors requires them to execute managerial reforms and innovations by working within current organizational systems. The sustainability framework, which incorporates degrowth, pluriverse, and buen vivir principles, requires both the definition of limits and the fair distribution of resources, as outlined by Demaria et al. (2013), Escobar (2018), and Gudynas (2011). The IPCC directs its efforts toward demand-side mitigation and equity, which aligns with this shift in perspective. Canada demonstrates this approach through its support for equitable transition measures. The execution of policies yields different results, but actual opportunities for transformation persist.
5. Reflexivity and institutional accountability. Organizations need to establish procedures which connect their objectives to performance outcomes in order to generate lasting results. The Net-Zero Emissions Accountability Act of Canada and the Paris Global Stocktake create review cycles which allow for adjustments to be made (Government of Canada, 2021). The Pembina Institute (2023) explains that independent oversight which conducts climate alignment audits on infrastructure and finance systems leads to better cycle performance. Organizations can achieve this by making learning experiences visible to the public and establishing particular triggers that lead to corrective actions.
6. Transforming the dominant storytelling power structure. The implementation of effective transition work creates new investment opportunities that transform the entire business narrative. Environmental protection policies, together with fair distribution initiatives, establish new social standards that follow the same patterns as previous human rights and public health movements. Canadian institutions have begun to change due to youth climate activism, divestment campaigns, and court rulings that support Indigenous rights. A new narrative

structure based on sufficiency and care for well-being emerges as an alternative to the current growth-oriented framework. Leaders face the aporetic condition when they must decide between preserving fossil assets and advancing alternative energy solutions, as well as supporting Indigenous governance and just transition initiatives.

The data from Canada suggests that sustainability needs to transition from its current flexible state to a more stringent moral framework. Our current small adjustments will produce long-lasting effects because they change our operational frameworks. The solution to this problem requires three fundamental components: declining fossil fuel investment schedules, new infrastructure standards that prevent additional lock-ins, and financial resources that support climate targets. The worsening climate emergency, characterized by wildfires, floods, and population migration, has made physical resources more valuable than non-physical protective systems. The foundation of sustainable practices depends on responsible actions and collective accountability. The Canadian situation presents a direct opportunity to determine whether strategic narratives can drive actual change by influencing decisions or if they will continue to serve as tools for perception management, despite the persistence of extractive operations. The aporetic condition establishes the measurement criteria, which require ambition to meet narrative goals and produce material results that achieve rapid decarbonization and justice.

REFERENCES

Adams, W. M. (2009). *Green development: Environment and sustainability in a developing world* (3rd ed.). Routledge.

Adkin, L. E. (Ed.). (2016). *First world petro-politics: The political ecology and governance of Alberta*. University of Toronto Press.

Agyeman, J., Schlosberg, D., Craven, L., & Matthews, C. (2016). Trends and directions in environmental justice: From inequity to everyday life, community, and just sustainabilities. *Annual Review of Environment and Resources*, *41*, 321–340. DOI: 10.1146/annurev-environ-110615-090052

Bäckstrand, K., & Lövbrand, E. (2006). Planting trees to mitigate climate change: Contested discourses of ecological modernization, green governmentality and civic environmentalism. *Global Environmental Politics*, *6*(1), 50–75.

Bessai, J. W. (2024). *Art as a public service: The National Film Board of Canada's role in shaping democratic dialogues and societal transformation* (Doctoral dissertation). Trent University, Peterborough, Ontario, Canada.

Bond, P. (2012). *Politics of climate justice: Paralysis above, movement below*. University of KwaZulu-Natal Press.

Borrows, J., & Tully, J. (2018). *Resurgence and reconciliation: Indigenous-settler relations and Earth teachings*. University of Toronto Press.

Bourdieu, P. (1991). *Language and symbolic power (J. B. Thompson* (Raymond, G., & Adamson, M. Eds. & Trans.). Harvard University Press.

Boyd, D. R. (2010). *The environmental rights revolution: Constitutions, human rights, and the environment* (Doctoral dissertation, University of British Columbia, Vancouver, Canada).

Canadian Association of Petroleum Producers. (n.d.). *CAPP stats handbook*.

Canadian Centre for Policy Alternatives. (2023). *Don't wait for the state* [Report]. Author.

Carter, A., & Zalik, A. (2016). Fossil capitalism and the rentier state: Towards a political ecology of Alberta's oil economy. In Adkin, L. E. (Ed.), *First world petro-politics: The political ecology and governance of Alberta* (pp. 51–77). University of Toronto Press., DOI: 10.3138/9781442699410-007

Ciplet, D., & Roberts, J. T. (2017). Climate change and the transition to neoliberal environmental governance. *Global Environmental Change, 46*, 148–156. DOI: 10.1016/j.gloenvcha.2017.09.003

Clean Energy Canada. (2022). *The state of clean energy in Canada*. Author.

Dehm, J. (2016). Carbon colonialism or climate justice? Interrogating the international climate regime from a TWAIL perspective. *Windsor Yearbook of Access to Justice, 33*(3), 65–95. DOI: 10.22329/wyaj.v33i3.4893

Demaria, F., Schneider, F., Sekulova, F., & Martinez-Alier, J. (2013). What is degrowth? From an activist slogan to a social movement. *Environmental Values, 22*(2), 191–215.

Dobson, A. (2007). *Green political thought* (4th ed.). Routledge.

Dryzek, J. S. (2013). *The politics of the Earth: Environmental discourses* (3rd ed.). Oxford University Press.

Eisenstein, H. (2009). *Feminism seduced: How global elites use women's labour and ideas to exploit the world*. Routledge.

Environment and Climate Change Canada. (2024). *Canada's greenhouse gas emissions projections 2024*. Ottawa, ON: Government of Canada. Retrieved from Environment and Climate Change Canada. (2025, March 21). *Greenhouse gas emissions*.

ENCATC. (2020). Cultural management and policy in a post-digital world – navigating uncertainty: Proceedings of the 11th Annual ENCATC Education and Research Session (Online, Nov 9–10, 2020). Brussels, Belgium: ENCATC. (ISBN 978-92-990088-2-9)

Escobar, A. (1995). *Encountering development: The making and unmaking of the Third World*. Princeton University Press.

Escobar, A. (2012). *Encountering development: The making and unmaking of the Third World* (New ed.). Princeton, NJ: Princeton University Press.

Escobar, A. (2018). *Designs for the pluriverse: Radical interdependence, autonomy, and the making of worlds*. Duke University Press.

Friedlingstein, P., (2023). Global Carbon Budget 2023. *Earth System Science Data, 15*, 5301–5369. DOI: 10.5194/essd-15-5301-2023

Gathii, J. T. (2011). TWAIL: A brief history of its origins, its decentralized network, and a tentative bibliography. *Trade, Law and Development, 3*(1), 26–64.

Government of Canada. (2021). *Canadian Net-Zero Emissions Accountability Act*. Government of Canada.

Gramsci, A. (1971). Selections from the prison notebooks. In (Hoare, Q., & Nowell Smith, G., Eds. & Trans.). International Publishers.

Gudynas, E. (2011). Buen vivir: Today's tomorrow. *Development*, *54*(4), 441–447.

Hajer, M. A. (1995). *The politics of environmental discourse: Ecological modernization and the policy process*. Oxford University Press.

Harrison, K. (2007). The road not taken: Climate change policy in Canada and the United States. *Global Environmental Politics*, *7*(4), 92–117.

Harrison, K. (2012). A tale of two taxes: The fate of environmental tax reform in Canada. *The Review of Policy Research*, *29*(3), 383–407.

Harrison, K. (2023). *The challenge of federalism for Canadian climate policy* (Climate Governance Policy Paper). Ottawa, ON: Forum of Federations.

Hickel, J. (2020a). *Less is more: How degrowth will save the world*. Penguin Random House.

Hickel, J. (2020b). What does degrowth mean? A few points of clarification. *Globalizations*, *18*(7), 1105–1111. DOI: 10.1080/14747731.2020.1812222

Hickel, J., & Kallis, G. (2020). Is green growth possible? *New Political Economy*, *25*(4), 469–486. DOI: 10.1080/13563467.2019.1598964

Jaccard, M. (2020). *The citizen's guide to climate success: Overcoming myths that hinder progress*. Cambridge University Press.

Le Menestrel, M., & Van Wassenhove, L. N. (2009). Ethics outside, companies inside: Lessons from the Enron debacle. *Omega*, *37*(1), 1–10.

McGlade, C., & Ekins, P. (2015). The geographical distribution of fossil fuels that can be used without exceeding a 2 °C limit on global warming. *Nature*, *517*(7533), 187–190. DOI: 10.1038/nature14016 PMID: 25567285

Miskimmon, A., O'Loughlin, B., & Roselle, L. (2013). *Strategic narratives: Communication power and the new world order*. Routledge.

Natural Resources Canada. (2021). *Trans Mountain Pipeline Expansion Project*. Government of Canada.

Nikiforuk, A. (2010). *Tar sands: Dirty oil and the future of a continent* (Rev. & updated ed.). Vancouver, BC: Greystone Books.

Nikiforuk, A. (2012). *The energy of slaves: Oil and the new servitude*. Greystone Books.

Ofori-Parku, S. S., & Koomson, P. (2023). Corporate sustainability as a hegemonic discourse of globalization: The discourse-historical approach as a critical issues and stakeholder analysis tool. *Public Relations Review*, *49*(1), 102275.

Pembina Institute. (2022). *Canada's critical minerals strategy: A sustainability perspective*. Pembina Institute.

Pembina Institute. (2023). *Evaluating climate alignment in infrastructure investment*. Pembina Institute.

Shiva, V. (2005). *Earth democracy: Justice, sustainability and peace*. South End Press.

Supreme Court of Canada. (2021). *Reference re Greenhouse Gas Pollution Pricing Act, 2021 SCC 11*.

Teelucksingh, C., & Poland, B. (2011). Energy solutions, neo-liberalism, and social diversity in Toronto, Canada. *International Journal of Environmental Research and Public Health*, *8*(1), 185–202. DOI: 10.3390/ijerph8010185 PMID: 21318023

The Guardian. (2011, December 13). Canada pulls out of the Kyoto Protocol.

The Guardian. (2015, December 3). Trudeau's climate rhetoric is riveting. So what about the reality? The Guardian. (2019, June 19). Canada declares climate emergency – and then approves oil pipeline.

The Guardian. (2024, May 2). Canada is proposing to lead on climate, but it's doubling down on oil.

The Narwhal. (2024, April 4). 'Detached from reality': Researchers say Pathways Alliance misleading public with greenwashing.

Tienhaara, K., & Walker, J. (2021). Fossil capital, "unquantifiable risk" and neoliberal nationalizations: The case of the Trans Mountain Pipeline in Canada. *Geoforum*, *124*, 120–131.

United Nations. (2015). *Transforming our world: The 2030 Agenda for Sustainable Development*. United Nations.

Waldron, I. R. G. (2022, July 5). Pipelines and protests: Legacies of struggle and resistance in the fight against environmental racism in Canada. *The Brown Journal of World Affairs*, *28*(2).

Whyte, K. (2020). Indigenous environmental justice: Anti-colonial action through kinship. In Adamson, J., Davis, M., & Huang, H. (Eds.), *The Routledge handbook of ecocriticism and environmental communication* (pp. 127–138). Routledge.

Winfield, M., Jamison, A., Wong, R., & Czajkowski, P. (2006). *Nuclear power in Canada: An examination of risks, impacts and sustainability*. Pembina Institute.

World Commission on Environment and Development. (1987). *Our common future*. Oxford University Press.

Zalik, A. (2018). Mining the seabed, enclosing the Area: Ocean grabbing, proprietary knowledge and the geopolitics of the extractive frontier beyond national jurisdiction. *International Social Science Journal*, *68*(229–230), 343–358. DOI: 10.1111/issj.12159

KEY TERMS AND DEFINITIONS

Aporia (Aporetic Condition): A structured impasse that keeps two incompatible commitments in play (here: climate ambition and extractive continuity).

Carbon Lock-in: Self-reinforcing dependence on high-emissions infrastructure, technologies, and institutions.

Degrowth: A program that prioritizes ecological limits and social well-being over aggregate GDP expansion.

Free, Prior, and Informed Consent (FPIC): Standard under UNDRIP that requires Indigenous consent before activities affecting lands and resources.

Green Growth: A policy frame that promises economic growth alongside environmental protection through innovation and efficiency.

Just Transition: Policy package that links decarbonization with decent work, regional planning, and social protection.

Net-Zero Target: A balance of emissions and removals by a specified year, requiring steep absolute reductions and limited offsets.

Strategic Narrative: Deliberate storytelling by institutions to shape perceptions and normalize preferred policies.

Section 5
Security, Militarization, and Planetary Frontiers

Chapter 12
Natural Resources as Strategic Liabilities:
Extractivism and Conflict Persistence in Divided Societies

Fadıl Ersözer
https://orcid.org/0000-0001-8348-321X
European University of Lefke, Cyprus

ABSTRACT

This chapter examines how natural resource governance affects peacebuilding in divided societies. While extractive wealth is often viewed as a catalyst for cooperation, in practice it frequently reinforces exclusion, entrenches geopolitical divisions, and marginalizes civic and environmental voices. Drawing on political ecology, critical peacebuilding, and international political economy, the chapter frames extractivism as a political project tied to contested authority and unequal recognition. It identifies four recurring dynamics: exclusionary control over resources, militarization of extractive zones, suppression of community perspectives, and the shifting status of hydrocarbons from assets to liabilities. Rather than offering technical fixes, the chapter advocates for justice-based, post-extractivist approaches centered on sustainability, inclusion, and democratic participation. Examples from Cyprus, Palestine, Western Sahara, and Northern Iraq show how extractive regimes deepen conflict, and how alternative governance models may open pathways toward more sustainable peace.

DOI: 10.4018/979-8-3373-1707-6.ch012

INTRODUCTION

Natural resources, particularly oil, gas, and valuable minerals have often been described in both academic and policy circles as potential foundations for peace and prosperity in post-conflict situations and divided societies. In policy discourse and mainstream peacebuilding literature, there is a prevailing assumption that resource wealth, if properly managed, can serve as a vehicle for rebuilding war-torn economies, financing reconciliation processes, and fostering inter-group cooperation. International institutions such as the World Bank and the United Nations have promoted frameworks for "resource-led development" and "shared dividends," wherein revenue-sharing mechanisms, joint management bodies, and transparent governance systems are expected to transform natural endowments into instruments of stabilization.

However, these assumptions have not always held up in practice—particularly in societies marked by deep ethno-political divisions, contested sovereignties, and unresolved status conflicts. This chapter questions the optimistic narrative that portrays natural resource extraction as an inherently stabilizing force. Drawing on insights from critical peacebuilding (Mac Ginty, 2011), political ecology (Watts, 2015), and resource governance studies (Ross, 2012), it argues that in divided or unrecognized polities, such as Western Sahara, Northern Iraq, Sudan, Cyprus and Palestine, natural resource development has more often exacerbated conflict dynamics than mitigated them. This is often compounded by resource nationalism, where the assertion of state control over natural resources becomes a tool for consolidating power and legitimizing unilateral claims, further marginalizing other groups and intensifying disputes over sovereignty. In such settings, extractive governance tends to mirror and amplify the existing asymmetries in recognition, legitimacy, and power. Far from generating trust or incentivizing compromise, the politics of extraction frequently reflect broader patterns of exclusion, power asymmetry, and institutional weakness that can escalate tensions—especially when international actors fail to address the governance roots of resource-related conflicts (Le Billon, 2007).

At the heart of this analysis lies the concept of "extractivism", understood not only as a material process of resource exploitation but also as a political and institutional logic. Extractivism, in this sense, denotes a development model premised on the large-scale removal of natural resources for external markets, often governed by elite bargains, foreign investment contracts, and state-centered sovereignty claims (Burchardt & Dietz, 2014). In divided societies or de facto partitions, such practices do not resolve disputes but frequently reproduce them. Energy or mineral sectors then become new sites of zero-sum rivalry, even when framed by external actors as opportunities for growth and cooperation.

This dynamic is especially pronounced in cases where unresolved sovereignty disputes shape who is recognized as the legitimate custodian of resources. Resource licensing, exploration rights, and revenue management are often monopolized by internationally recognized governments, leaving other communities excluded from both decision-making and material benefits. Such practices amount to a form of resource nationalism, where dominant actors assert a sovereign right to control resources in ways that strengthen their own legitimacy while simultaneously delegitimizing rivals. What emerges is a pattern of governance asymmetry that undermines trust and, in practice, entrenches the very political divides that peacebuilding initiatives are meant to overcome (Cox & Sisk, 2017).

The role of external actors deepens these asymmetries. Multinational corporations, donor agencies, and regional powers rarely act as neutral brokers. Instead, they tend to pursue contracts and partnerships only with recognized governments, thereby sidelining unrecognized authorities and marginalized communities. This selective recognition produces what I refer to as a form of "extractive diplomacy," in which strategic and economic interests are prioritized over inclusivity or conflict transformation. International deals with Baghdad against the Kurdistan Regional Government, or with Morocco in occupied Western Sahara, illustrate how energy contracts can reinforce political exclusion and embolden militarized responses from weaker parties (Boukhars & Roussellier, 2014).

Environmental and social concerns tend to be pushed aside in many extractive regimes. Although impact assessments are often produced, they frequently operate as box-ticking exercises and rarely capture the lived experiences or anxieties of affected communities. Where sovereignty itself is disputed, environmental groups and grassroots organizations typically encounter institutional hurdles to participation; in some cases they are denied any recognition as legitimate actors. The consequences are visible: ecological degradation goes largely unchecked, and at the same time communities perceive a deeper deficit of procedural justice. Political ecologists have pointed to this pattern repeatedly, showing how the language of sustainability is used less to protect the environment than to consolidate territorial claims (Temper et al., 2015).

These exclusions become more troubling in light of broader global shifts. The economic case for large-scale fossil fuel development is weakening. Volatile prices, commitments under international climate agreements such as the Paris Accord, and rapid advances in renewable technologies have undermined earlier assumptions that oil and gas can guarantee prosperity. Projects that seemed bankable a decade ago now carry the risk of becoming stranded assets—financially fragile, politically disputed, and environmentally costly. For divided or fragile societies, this raises a difficult question: is extractivism still a credible development pathway, or has it turned into a strategic liability that ties states to outdated and conflict-prone models?

In this chapter, I take the view that resource politics must be understood less as a technical matter of economic management and more as a question of power and recognition. Extractivism should be seen not only as an economic practice but also, and more importantly, as a political project that reflects competing claims to sovereignty and legitimacy. Understanding why resource-driven peacebuilding so often disappoints requires us to look at these asymmetries. Drawing on the literatures of political ecology (Watts, 2015), critical peacebuilding (Mac Ginty, 2011), and resource governance (Ross, 2012), I suggest that natural resources belong at the center of conflict dynamics in divided societies, not at the margins.

The chapter proceeds thematically rather than through a single case study. I use examples from Cyprus, Western Sahara, Palestine, and Sudan to illustrate recurring patterns of exclusion, securitization, and institutional fragmentation. These cases are not methodologically comparable in a narrow sense, but they serve as empirical entry points to highlight how extractivism intersects with contested governance and unresolved sovereignty. The analysis is organized around four interrelated themes: exclusionary sovereignty claims in resource governance, the militarization of extractive zones, the sidelining of environmental and community voices, and the shifting perception of hydrocarbons from valuable assets to potential liabilities.

By synthesizing these themes, I aim to contribute to a growing research agenda that views natural resource governance not as an ancillary concern but as constitutive of peacebuilding itself. The discussion that follows develops this claim further. My argument is that extractivism in such contexts does not usually foster reconciliation; it more often reproduces exclusion and political contestation. If this is the case, then the challenge is to imagine alternatives. I argue that post-extractivist and justice-oriented approaches, which emphasize ecological sustainability, inclusion, and democratic participation, offer more credible routes toward durable peace.

BACKGROUND

The expectation that natural resources could be harnessed for peacebuilding gained significant traction in both policy circles and academic discussions during the early 2000s. Within the broader agenda of "post-conflict recovery," the regulation and distribution of resource wealth were frequently identified as central to preventing renewed violence and consolidating fragile states. This idea was particularly influenced by the experiences of Sierra Leone, Angola, and Liberia, where diamonds and oil revenues had prolonged civil wars but where subsequent peace agreements placed resource management at the heart of reconstruction strategies. In these cases, governments, often with donor support, introduced reforms such as new legal frameworks, externally supervised reconstruction programs, and revenue oversight systems designed to reduce the risk of conflict relapse.

International organizations also promoted this linkage between extractive governance and peacebuilding. The UNDP, World Bank, and African Union advanced initiatives that framed resources as potential "dividends" for stability, encouraging strategies of inclusive development and equitable benefit-sharing. Alongside these narratives, global instruments such as the Extractive Industries Transparency Initiative (EITI) and the Natural Resource Charter were launched to establish benchmarks for accountability and transparency in resource management (World Bank, 2011; UNEP, 2009).

Together with these developments, academic literature also started to move beyond from the "resource curse" arguments. The researchers increasingly examined the conditions under which natural wealth could be used toward development and peace rather than violence. This body of work emphasized the importance of institutional capacity, the incentives that shape elite decision-making, and the role of external actors in influencing outcomes. Rather than treating resources as inherently destabilizing, scholars investigated how governance arrangements, revenue-sharing mechanisms, and monitoring systems might alter conflict trajectories in more constructive directions (Le Billon, 2005; Lujala, 2009). Post-conflict and divided societies thus came to be seen as important arenas in which resource-based approaches to peacebuilding and state-building could be tested and refined.

Despite the appeal of these policy and scholarly initiatives, they often rested on technocratic expectations that proved difficult to meet. It was assumed, for instance, that internationally recognized governments would act as neutral managers of collective wealth, that institutional reforms would gain legitimacy across social and political divides, and that greater transparency could neutralize disputes over ownership. In practice, these assumptions were rarely borne out in situations where sovereignty itself was contested. In Iraq, Sudan, Western Sahara, or Palestine, struggles over resources have consistently been linked not only to fiscal management but also to the more fundamental question of who has the right to represent the state. There are a few cases in which stronger institutions, fairer revenue-sharing formulas, and active involvement of civil society have enabled resources to play a stabilizing role. Such experiences, however, remain exceptional. In most deeply divided societies, extractive economies have reinforced existing inequalities rather than reducing them.

The Sudanese case illustrates this point clearly. Oil revenues played a decisive role in the South's secessionist movement, yet the creation of two states did not end disputes over production and transit. Tensions simply reappeared in new forms. In Iraq, hydrocarbons continue to drive contention between Baghdad and the Kurdistan Regional Government, with repeated breakdowns in negotiations reflecting broader struggles over recognition and autonomy (Alkış, 2022). A parallel can be observed in Western Sahara, where Morocco's offshore oil exploration in disputed waters—conducted with the support of international companies and the tacit acceptance of outside powers—has reinforced occupation and made prospects for negotiated governance even more remote.

Efforts led by donors and international organizations have often struggled to adapt to these realities. Initiatives on transparency or revenue management have frequently been introduced without sufficient regard for the institutional and social contexts in which they were expected to operate. As a result, local actors, particularly in unrecognized or peripheral regions, have had little opportunity to influence the frameworks imposed upon them. This disconnect has generated a persistent legitimacy gap: reforms appear externally driven and are rarely responsive to the grievances of ~communities most directly affected by extraction (Hilson & Maconachie, 2009).

Complicating matters further, the global energy landscape has shifted in ways that reduce the appeal of fossil-fuel-based growth. The urgency of the climate crisis, coupled with international agreements such as the Paris Accord and regional initiatives like the EU Green Deal, has placed pressure on governments to reconsider reliance on hydrocarbons. At the same time, campaigns for a "just transition" have reframed extraction as a liability rather than a guaranteed pathway to development (Aggestam *et. al.*, 2019). In this environment, large-scale fossil fuel projects in divided or politically fragile territories are increasingly seen as risky, both economically and politically.

The prospect of stranded assets, frequent swings in global commodity prices, and tighter regulatory oversight have made new extraction projects look far less secure than they once did. At the same time, resistance from environmental justice movements, Indigenous organizations, and transnational advocacy networks has gained visibility, challenging the dominant narrative that extraction equals progress. These movements often highlight the disproportionate environmental and social costs borne by marginalized communities, reflecting what Martinez-Alier (2002) terms "the environmentalism of the poor"—a form of resistance that emerges from the lived experiences of those most affected by ecological degradation and argue for alternative models of development centered on ecological sustainability, land rights, and democratic participation, often drawing on place-based struggles and alternative ontologies of development (Escobar, 2008). Human rights organizations, such as Amnesty International (2016), have extensively documented the adverse impacts of extractive industries on local communities, including forced displacement, loss of livelihoods, and environmental damage.

Within this evolving global context, critical scholarship has turned toward the structural and political dimensions of extractivism. Rather than focusing on corruption or weak governance alone, scholars now interrogate how extractive regimes are embedded in broader hierarchies of power—both within states and at the international level. The lens of political ecology has illuminated how extraction produces not just economic value but also environmental violence and socio-political dispossession. Similarly, scholars of critical peacebuilding argue that peace cannot be built on exclusionary or asymmetrical foundations—especially when the beneficiaries of resource exploitation are closely tied to state elites or foreign interests.

This reorientation has generated a set of deeper questions: What kinds of peace do extractive interventions actually produce? Who benefits and who is excluded from resource governance? How do resource projects reinforce or reshape existing political orders in contested settings? And what would it mean to pursue post-extractivist peacebuilding models that prioritize justice, sustainability, and recognition over growth or efficiency?

The background outlined here emphasizes the need to reassess the promises and limitations of resource-based peacebuilding. While the allure of natural wealth remains strong, the historical and comparative evidence suggests that without deliberate attention to power, justice, and inclusion, extractivism is more likely to reproduce conflict than resolve it. This chapter enters that debate by building a framework for understanding extractive politics in divided societies—not as a deviation from the norm, but as a revealing expression of global political and economic structures. Building on this foundation, the following section critically reviews the academic literature that has shaped current understandings of the linkages between natural resources, conflict, and peacebuilding. It traces the evolution from early "resource curse" theories toward more nuanced analyses of governance, legitimacy, and global political economy, highlighting the conceptual gaps this chapter seeks to address.

LITERATURE REVIEW

Building upon the background context, this section addresses the academic debates surrounding natural resources and conflict in order to clarify how the field has evolved. For many years, the topic has attracted the attention of political economists, peacebuilding specialists, and environmental analysts. During the 1990s and 2000s, a significant body of academic literature focused on what is called the "resource curse." Writers such as Auty (1993) and Ross (2004) argued that countries which are rich in oil or other natural resources often experienced negative outcomes in political and developmental outcomes. Their academic work suggested that heavy reliance on primary commodities was connected with rentier forms of politics, weak institutions, and higher risks of authoritarianism, underdevelopment, and civil war. These points were also further confirmed through quantitative studies by linking resource dependence with corruption and a reduced likelihood of democratic consolidation, stressing the potential of resource wealth to destabilize fragile states.

As debates on resources and conflict progressed, some of the earlier generalizations came under closer scrutiny. Scholars such as Le Billon (2005) and Collier, Hoeffler, and Söderbom (2008) argued that abundance in itself could not explain divergent outcomes. What mattered, they suggested, was the way resources were managed and embedded in political institutions. This line of work introduced distinctions that remain influential: lootable versus non-lootable resources, point-source versus diffuse commodities, and the contrast between settings with strong or fragile state capacity. These categories illustrated why resource wealth sometimes produced war economies and in other situations did not destabilize the state to the same degree. The emphasis of the field thus shifted away from deterministic claims toward a closer focus on governance practices and the choices of political actors.

By the late 2000s, a more optimistic perspective entered policy debates and scholarly writing. International organizations such as the UN, the World Bank, and the African Union began framing natural resources as potential assets for post-conflict recovery. Programming documents spoke of "peace dividends" or "shared benefits," underpinned by reforms designed to improve transparency, encourage participation, and channel revenues toward reconstruction. Normative instruments such as the Extractive Industries Transparency Initiative (EITI) and the Natural Resource Charter codified these ideas in the form of "best practices" for contract disclosure, revenue-sharing, and oversight (UNEP, 2009; World Bank, 2011). Academic analyses often echoed this view, exploring whether carefully designed resource governance could stabilize fragile states and even support reconciliation (Pugh, Cooper, & Goodhand, 2004).

Yet this optimism was quickly tempered by critical perspectives. Scholars of peacebuilding began to highlight the limitations of liberal governance reforms and questioned whether transparency and capacity-building could really address the deeper drivers of conflict (Mac Ginty, 2010; Richmond, 2011). The liberal peace paradigm was criticized for exporting technocratic models that were not rooted in local political economies and often lacked legitimacy in divided or postcolonial contexts. Critics emphasized that institutional reforms could disguise, rather than resolve, underlying asymmetries of power. In practice, such reforms often consolidated the authority of the elites, while pushing the actors from unrecognized or disenfranchised communities to the margins and marginalizing them.

Empirical studies have reinforced and deepened these critiques. Lujala (2009), for instance, showed that the durability of peace was shaped not only by the presence of natural resources but by where those resources were located and who controlled them. Contexts with a framework incorporating a wider group of actors into governance and greater decentralization of authority to the local level were more likely to sustain peace, while concentrated control tended to fuel renewed contestation. On the same line, Le Billon and Nicholls (2007) demonstrated how struggles over resource governance often became entangled by bigger projects of nation-building, generating competing narratives of legitimacy and belonging. Together, these contributions highlights the limitations of relying on transparency mechanisms on their own, since formal oversight could not address structural inequalities on how political power is distributed.

Political ecology introduces an additional dimension to these debates by treating extractive governance as an inherently political practice. Authors such as Robbins (2012) and Bridge and Le Billon (2017) emphasized how extraction is linked to territorial control, the displacement of communities, and the privileging of particular interests, regardless if these are the interests of domestic elites, multinational investors, or state authorities. Even the language surrounding resource governance, including terms such as "sustainability" or "energy security," was shown to operate less as neutral descriptors and more as discursive tools that legitimized extraction while this practice ignores concerns over equity and justice.

From a different point of view, post-extractivist academic works take the critique further. Scholars such as Gudynas (2013) and Acosta (2013) argued that development strategies centred on extraction were not compatible with ecological sustainability and social justice. They highlight that even governments with progressive agendas often maintained extractive dependence, centralising power in the state and excluding local communities from participating in the political processes. Post-extractivism thus emerged not only as a critique but also as a set of proposals for alternative models of development. This is frequently framed in terms of buen vivir (living well), which emphasize environmental care and community autonomy. Although initially tied to Latin American contexts, this approach has increasingly guided debates in other contexts that are dependent on resources, such as the Middle East and North Africa.

Bringing these strands of academic literature together (critical peacebuilding, political ecology, and post-extractivism) has made a significant impact on how scholars approach the question of natural resources in divided and conflict-affected environments. Rather than treating resources as neutral factors that can either cause or resolve wars, extraction is now more often seen as a political project that shapes, and is shaped by, struggles over sovereignty, recognition, and legitimacy. In cases such as Cyprus, Iraq, Palestine, and Western Sahara, disputes over oil, gas, or minerals are less about how to divide revenues efficiently than about whose authority and identity claims are recognized.

This body of work also highlights the influence of external actors. Ferguson's (2006) account of "selective sovereignty" shows how extractive partnerships often operate by privileging internationally recognized governments, while sidelining unrecognized authorities and marginalized groups. The result is what some scholars have described as "extractive diplomacy," in which international engagement reproduces inequalities and weakens incentives for inclusive peacebuilding.

More recently, the literature has engaged with the implications of global energy transitions. Fluctuations in fossil fuel markets, the growing political weight of climate imperatives, and the rise of renewable alternatives have cast doubt on the viability of resource-led peacebuilding. Analysts warn of the risks of stranded assets and stress that extractive projects are increasingly contested on economic, political, and environmental grounds (Hagen & Kollenbach, 2024). These debates call for closer attention to renewable energy strategies and community-driven initiatives that could provide more sustainable forms of peace support.

MAIN FOCUS OF THE CHAPTER

Theoretical Framework

This section brings together insights from political ecology, critical peacebuilding, and international political economy (IPE) to highlight the complex ways extractivism interacts with divided societies. These perspectives complicate the assumption that resource wealth is simply a matter of technical management or an economic input for growth. Instead, they emphasize how extractive governance is shaped by wider political struggles, uneven structures of power, and patterns of exclusion that reach beyond the resource sector itself (Le Billon, 2001; Fairhead et al., 2012). From this angle, extractivism is better understood not only as an economic process but as a political project, embedded in questions of legitimacy, recognition, and authority.

Political Ecology and the Politics of Resource Governance

Political ecology provides a powerful lens for understanding environmental and resource-related issues as sites of political struggle, rather than as technical challenges. It shifts focus from how resources are managed to how authority over them is constructed, exercised, and contested. In deeply divided or post-conflict settings, access to land, water, energy, or minerals is rarely just about allocation—it is fundamentally tied to competing narratives of legitimacy and belonging (Robbins, 2012; Fairhead et al., 2012; Le Billon, 2001; Bridge et al., 2018). This perspective helps unpack how environmental governance frequently serves to consolidate power, formalize asymmetries, and marginalize alternative claims, particularly in contexts marked by historical grievance and political exclusion.

State and quasi-state actors often use environmental discourses strategically to justify decisions about resource allocation. Invocations of "energy independence," "sustainability," or "national development" tend to be framed as universal objectives, detached from political context. Yet, these narratives frequently serve to legitimize the priorities of dominant groups while sidelining dissenting perspectives. Political ecology encourages a critical reading of these claims by asking: Who constructs these narratives? Whose knowledge is recognized as authoritative? And who is left out of decision-making processes? In disputed territories, where political recognition is already fragmented, these questions become especially urgent.

Scholarship within this tradition has long warned that managerial or technocratic language can obscure the underlying power dynamics of resource control. Bakker (2010) and Swyngedouw (2009), for instance, highlight how technical language around infrastructure or environmental regulation can depoliticize struggles over access and ownership. Similarly, Bridge and Le Billon (2017) show how extractive regimes often rely on legal infrastructures, policing, and at times militarization to establish what they call "environments of enclosure"—landscapes where state or elite control is enforced under the guise of order and progress. These enclosures not only secure access to the resource itself but also institutionalize the marginalization of communities deemed peripheral to the national project.

Geography is not incidental in this process. Resource extraction tends to be spatially selective, concentrated in peripheral, ecologically sensitive, or geopolitically ambiguous areas. As Watts (2015) observes, this spatial distribution often maps onto regions already marked by economic neglect or political instability. When extraction is introduced under these conditions, it frequently intensifies local grievances rather than alleviating them. Resource development becomes a way to extend state authority, not necessarily to meet development needs. In such cases, material extraction is accompanied by symbolic territorialization—a process that redefines the physical landscape in service of political control.

The concept of "resource territorialization" (Peluso & Lund, 2011) captures this well. It describes how control over natural resources becomes a vehicle for asserting political authority and reshaping contested space. In practice, licensing regimes, land demarcations, and security operations turn natural landscapes into instruments of governance. In divided societies, where competing sovereignty claims often coexist, these practices enable internationally recognized authorities to expand their de facto control, even when political negotiations remain stalled. Rival actors, meanwhile, are denied access to resource governance and often criminalized when they attempt to assert their own claims.

These patterns are evident in territories such as Northern Cyprus, Western Sahara, and Palestine, where questions of natural resource control are deeply intertwined with contested claims to statehood. Extraction in these contexts is not merely an economic act; it is a statement of political dominance. Multinational corporations and international donors typically engage only with recognized governments, thereby reinforcing international hierarchies. Unrecognized or de facto authorities are excluded not only from economic benefits but also from the legitimacy conferred by participation in transnational environmental governance.

Political ecology thus reframes resource extraction as a process saturated with political meaning—one that both reflects and shapes broader geopolitical hierarchies. Discourses such as "green growth," "resilience," or "climate adaptation" may appear benign or progressive, but in practice they often serve to reinforce asymmetries and shut down alternatives. By scrutinizing these narratives and the institutional arrangements they support, political ecology helps expose how exclusion is normalized and dissent is delegitimized in the name of progress. It also invites us to consider what an alternative, more inclusive environmental politics might look like in contested and divided societies.

Critical Peacebuilding and Governance Asymmetries

Critical peacebuilding provides an alternative to mainstream approaches by focusing on the issues of power, exclusion, and justice. These issues are often overlooked in traditional peacebuilding perspectives. While the liberal peace model emphasizes the significance of institutional capacity, market liberalization, and technical reform; critical peacebuilding perspectives highlight the structural asymmetries that prevent such reforms from translating into genuine peace (Mac Ginty, 2011; Richmond, 2014; Pugh, 2005). In environments affected by contested sovereignty or unresolved statehood, the limitations of traditional liberal approaches become particularly visible.

For most of the 1990s and 2000s, international actors increasingly tried to incorporate natural resource governance into peacebuilding strategies. Revenue-sharing mechanisms, anti-corruption initiatives, and transparency tools were advanced as ways to stabilize fragile states (UNEP, 2009; World Bank, 2011). Yet, this approach often framed resource exploitation as a technical problem of oversight rather than a political struggle. By treating resource conflicts as issues of legal design, donors frequently sidelined the perspectives of communities excluded from formal recognition, such as in Palestine, Northern Iraq, or Western Sahara.

A central insight of the critical peacebuilding literature is its challenge to technocratic fixes. Resource contracts signed by internationally recognized governments may be legally sound, but in divided societies they often lack legitimacy in the eyes of those excluded from decision-making. Such arrangements risk institutionalizing exclusion, reinforcing unilateralism, and entrenching elite control. Transparency mechanisms, while useful, can mask the reality that extractive revenues frequently serve ruling coalitions while bypassing communities most affected by extraction.

For this reason, critical scholars argue for a shift away from elite-centric and top-down strategies toward more participatory and locally grounded practices (Mac Ginty, 2010). In this view, peace is not only the functioning of institutions or the absence of violence; it also involves inclusive processes, recognition of competing claims, and the redistribution of power. Community-led protests, Indigenous resistance, and grassroots environmental justice campaigns are therefore not marginal to peacebuilding but essential components of it.

Equally important are the procedural dimensions of peace: who is allowed to participate, whose voices carry weight, and which governance arrangements gain legitimacy. Where non-recognized groups are excluded, post-conflict reforms can reproduce the same grievances they aim to resolve. Research by Le Billon (2005) and Lujala et al. (2005) suggests that durable peace emerges only when extractive governance rests on inclusive political settlements rather than on narrow bargains that privilege established elites.

External actors have a decisive influence on these dynamics, although not always in ways that encourage inclusivity. Donors, international financial institutions, and development agencies often focus on strengthening central authority and ensuring conditions favorable to investment. This approach, while understandable from their perspective, tends to sideline the question of whether governance structures are inclusive or responsive to marginalized groups. As Mac Ginty and Richmond (2013) argue, this produces a form of "liberal conflict management," where the goal is stability and predictability rather than transformation. In practice, growth targets, institutional performance indicators, and the language of "good governance" can create the appearance of order, yet they do little to address the exclusions that lie at the heart of many conflicts.

These critiques highlight one of the central contributions of critical peacebuilding: the reminder that peace cannot be sustained through transparency rules or technical reforms alone. What matters are deeper issues of recognition, participation, and justice. In the extractive sector this means asking difficult questions about distribution—who gains from resource wealth, who is left out, and what forms of governance might allow for more pluralistic and equitable arrangements. Too often, however, the outcome is what Mac Ginty (2010) terms "hybrid peace." Liberal reforms and institutional frameworks may be introduced, but they coexist with entrenched local power structures and practices of exclusion. This hybridity may bring a degree of stability, yet it tends to reproduce the same injustices and asymmetries that caused tensions in the first place.

International Political Economy and Extractivism

The concept of post-extractivism emerged from Latin American critiques of development strategies that prioritized large-scale oil, gas, and mineral extraction. Even governments with progressive or redistributive agendas often relied on revenues from extractive sectors to fund welfare programs and infrastructure. Yet, critics pointed out that such models reproduced existing inequalities, centralized political authority, and imposed significant environmental costs (Gudynas, 2013; Acosta, 2013). Rather than viewing extraction as an inevitable or necessary foundation for development, post-extractivist thinkers questioned its long-term sustainability and social legitimacy. They proposed alternatives built around ecological balance, social justice, and participatory governance.

In conflict-affected or politically divided societies, resource extraction rarely functions as a neutral economic activity. It often becomes a mechanism for asserting state authority and consolidating power, particularly in fragile or contested regions. Political elites tend to present extractive projects as pragmatic responses to economic stagnation or reconstruction needs. However, these strategies carry considerable risks. They can entrench dependence on volatile commodity markets, deepen ecological harm, and further marginalize communities that are already excluded from political representation or economic decision-making. In such settings, extraction is not merely about growth. It becomes part of a broader struggle over recognition, legitimacy, and territorial control.

This is where post-extractivism intersects with both political ecology and critical peacebuilding. All three approaches emphasize that natural resource governance is deeply political. They highlight the ways in which extractive development reinforces entrenched hierarchies, excludes alternative perspectives, and legitimizes elite control. The concept of buen vivir (living well) captures the normative core of post-extractivist thinking. It prioritizes harmony with nature, community well-being, and intergenerational responsibility over GDP growth or investor confidence. Although rooted in Latin American experience, this framework resonates in other contested contexts such as Western Sahara, Palestine, and Cyprus, where resource governance is inseparable from struggles over identity, autonomy, and justice.

Critical perspectives from international political economy add another layer to this analysis. They direct attention to the global dimensions of extractivism and to the structures that link local projects with international systems of capital, law, and recognition. From this point of view, extractive regimes are not simply shaped by domestic institutions. They are embedded in transnational configurations involving multinational corporations, donor agencies, international legal frameworks, and foreign governments (Burchardt & Dietz, 2014; Bridge & Le Billon, 2017). These actors play decisive roles in determining which authorities are treated as legitimate, which territories receive investment, and what governance standards are enforced.

In divided societies, such external engagements often reinforce existing asymmetries. International oil and gas firms typically sign contracts only with internationally recognized governments, excluding rival or unrecognized authorities from participation in resource governance. Similarly, development banks and donor institutions usually provide financing and technical assistance to those actors with formal statehood or diplomatic recognition. This practice results in what Ferguson (2006) terms "selective sovereignty." Access to the benefits of extraction depends less on local legitimacy and more on standing within international legal and political hierarchies. In effect, international recognition becomes a gatekeeping mechanism for resource access and political authority.

The political implications of this dynamic are far-reaching. By privileging one actor in a contested setting, external actors risk entrenching unilateral control over disputed territories. This marginalizes competing claims, reduces the incentives for compromise, and may even escalate political tensions. Where natural resources are closely tied to national narratives or claims to self-determination, the stakes of exclusion become even higher. In such contexts, resource control is not just about economics; it becomes a tool of political consolidation and geopolitical signaling.

Security concerns further complicate the picture. As natural resource zones become increasingly securitized, militarization often accompanies extraction. Offshore gas platforms, pipeline routes, and mining corridors are frequently protected by state or paramilitary forces. These security arrangements are rarely neutral. They are often embedded in regional security architectures and interstate alliances. In the Eastern Mediterranean, for example, the development of gas fields is closely tied to military deployments, naval exercises, and bloc formations such as the East Mediterranean Gas Forum. This illustrates how extraction can be woven into wider geopolitical rivalries and strategic calculations.

Together, the lenses of post-extractivism and international political economy challenge any assumption that resource wealth can be harnessed for peace and development through technical reform alone. They reveal how extractive governance is structured by layers of inequality, recognition politics, and global economic interests. While transparency initiatives and institutional strengthening are often presented as solutions, these tools have limited transformative capacity when the underlying power structures remain intact. The central question becomes not only how resources are managed, but also whose interests are prioritized, whose claims are legitimized, and whose risks and losses are externalized in the name of growth.

Moving beyond extractive dependence therefore requires more than reforming institutions. It involves rethinking development models, redistributing power, and centering ecological and social justice in governance debates. These principles are not abstract ideals. In divided and conflict-affected societies, they are essential if peacebuilding is to be inclusive, equitable, and sustainable.

Toward an Integrated Framework

Political ecology, critical peacebuilding, and post-extractivism each bring distinct but complementary insights into the limits of resource-centred peacebuilding in divided and conflict-affected societies. Political ecology emphasizes that environmental governance is inseparable from power struggles and territorial claims. Critical peacebuilding directs attention to legitimacy and inclusion, especially in contexts where statehood is contested and governance lacks broad participation. International political economy expands the scope by locating extractive regimes within transnational hierarchies of capital, legal recognition, and geopolitical influence.

Bringing these approaches into conversation helps explain why natural resources often generate friction rather than fostering stability. The liberal peace model tends to assume that resource wealth can be transformed into a shared dividend through institutional reform and legal mechanisms. However, this vision often fails to consider monopolized control, elite capture, and the systematic exclusion of unrecognized actors. When these political asymmetries are combined with environmental harm and procedural injustice, trust in governance is further undermined.

This framework does not deny the possibility that natural resources could support peace. Instead, it shifts the discussion to the conditions under which this might be possible. Durable peace in divided societies requires more than transparency mechanisms or revenue-sharing arrangements. It depends on deeper structural changes, including the recognition of rival claims, the inclusion of historically marginalized populations, and an emphasis on both procedural and distributive justice.

Post-extractivist peacebuilding provides a particularly compelling alternative. It questions the assumption that economic growth through extraction is either inevitable or inherently beneficial. It promotes pluralistic governance, ecological sustainability, and community agency. It also brings to the surface the limitations imposed by global commodity markets, investor interests, and geopolitical alliances, all of which shape what is considered viable or legitimate in post-conflict settings.

Together, these perspectives encourage a shift in how extractivism is understood. Rather than treating it as a neutral development strategy, they reveal it as a contested field shaped by power, sovereignty, and competing claims to justice. In societies where natural resource control is deeply entangled with unresolved struggles over recognition and statehood, such an analytical lens is not only useful but essential. The next section outlines the methodological approach used in this study.

Methodology

This chapter employs a qualitative, conceptually oriented methodology, drawing on interpretive and critical approaches in international political economy, peace and conflict studies, and environmental politics. The analysis combines theoretical insights with a close reading of academic literature, policy reports, and normative frameworks in order to explore how extractivism and peacebuilding intersect in societies marked by division.

The approach is rooted in critical theory, which allows attention to the underlying assumptions and power relations that shape dominant narratives of post-conflict development and natural resource governance. By engaging with political ecology, critical peacebuilding, and post-extractivist scholarship, the chapter questions the widespread idea that natural resources necessarily stabilize fragile contexts or support development.

Instead of conducting a set of full case studies, the chapter draws on selected examples from places such as Cyprus, Western Sahara, Palestine, Northern Iraq, and Sudan. These are presented not for systematic comparison but to illustrate recurring dynamics: governance asymmetries, unilateral control of extraction, environmental marginalization, and the securitization of resources. This choice anchors theoretical discussion in concrete realities, while avoiding overly general claims that a comparative study might imply.

This approach has limits. It cannot provide causal inference or detailed country-specific analysis. Its strength lies elsewhere: in developing a conceptual framework that can explain patterns of extractive governance across different settings. The assumption guiding this choice is that many of the logics shaping extractive politics—questions of sovereignty, recognition, and the global political economy—are structural and transnational. They reappear in different contexts, even though their expression is historically and locally specific.

Methodologically, the chapter engages in theory-building through synthesis. It integrates distinct strands of critical scholarship to construct an analytical lens that emphasizes power, justice, recognition, and sustainability in the governance of resources. The aim is not to measure causal variables, but to develop a vocabulary that can explain why extractive interventions often reproduce exclusion and instability rather than produce peace.

This methodology also carries a normative commitment. By questioning depoliticized or technocratic accounts of resource management, it emphasizes the importance of perspectives from marginalized communities, the ecological limits of extraction, and the need for more justice-oriented visions of peacebuilding in the twenty-first century.

Building on this conceptual approach, the chapter draws on five illustrative cases: Cyprus, Palestine, Western Sahara, Northern Iraq, and Sudan. These cases are selected for their diversity in political status, conflict dynamics, and extractive governance models. Together, they represent a spectrum of recognition and control: from partially recognized administrations and unresolved sovereignties to internationally recognized but deeply divided states. This variation enables a comparative lens on how natural resource governance intersects with contested authority, securitization, and civic exclusion across different contexts. These cases are not intended as exhaustive case studies, but as focused vignettes that reflect recurring patterns in extractive governance under conditions of political division. The analysis draws from existing academic and policy literature. The aim is to identify thematic parallels rather than to provide comprehensive empirical coverage. This approach allows the chapter to foreground conceptual insights while anchoring them in real-world cases.

FINDINGS

The experience of extractivism in conflict-affected and divided societies shows that natural resource governance often entrenches division rather than encouraging cooperation or reconciliation. Instead of acting as drivers of peace, hydrocarbons and other strategic assets frequently deepen inequalities of recognition, strengthen exclusionary governance, and heighten geopolitical rivalries. This chapter highlights five recurring dynamics visible across diverse cases, including Cyprus, Western Sahara, Northern Iraq, Palestine, and Sudan that illustrate how extractive practices become intertwined with contested legitimacy, unresolved conflicts, and persistent structural asymmetries.

Governance Asymmetries and Institutionalized Exclusion

In many divided or contested settings, natural resource governance not only reflects but also magnifies pre-existing inequalities in recognition and institutional access. Internationally recognized states usually monopolize licensing rights, revenue collection, and contractual authority with multinational companies and financial institutions. This practice effectively excludes rival administrations, unrecognized entities, and marginalized communities from meaningful participation in decisions about extraction or benefit-sharing. The resulting asymmetries institutionalize exclusion and reduce the scope for trust-building.

Cyprus illustrates this dynamic clearly: the Republic of Cyprus negotiated hydrocarbon exploration agreements with international firms and regional partners without bi-communal frameworks, sidelining Turkish Cypriot claims and reinforcing the political status quo. Similar tensions are visible in Iraq, where disputes between Baghdad and the Kurdistan Regional Government over oil production, export routes, and revenue allocation embody larger struggles over autonomy and legitimacy. In Western Sahara and Palestine, resource projects carried out by Morocco and Israel proceed without consultation or equitable benefit-sharing for occupied populations, often drawing criticism from human rights bodies and international observers.

These examples underline a wider pattern: extractive regimes embedded in asymmetric recognition frameworks serve to entrench unilateral authority while delegitimizing alternative claims. This produces governance structures that appear functional externally but lack local legitimacy, thereby foreclosing opportunities for cooperation. In the long run, such asymmetries perpetuate mistrust and hinder peacebuilding, since resources become tools of exclusion rather than shared assets that might support reconciliation or institutional compromise.

Contested authority and uneven recognition frequently result in extractive governance regimes that systematically exclude marginalized actors from decision-making. In Western Sahara, the Moroccan government has unilaterally issued licenses for phosphate mining and offshore oil exploration in a territory whose legal status remains unresolved under international law. Despite the 1975 Advisory Opinion of the International Court of Justice and repeated UN resolutions affirming the Sahrawi people's right to self-determination, resource deals have proceeded without their consent. The EU Court of Justice has ruled that trade and fisheries agreements involving Western Sahara require the explicit consent of the Sahrawi population, yet enforcement remains inconsistent. Organizations such as Western Sahara Resource Watch have documented continued extraction, while a recent Transnational Institute report argues that even renewable energy initiatives in the region serve to entrench Moroccan control rather than advance a just transition, amounting to a form of "greenwashing" (Western Sahara Resource Watch, 2010; Transnational Institute, 2021). These practices exemplify how recognition asymmetries can institutionalize exclusion in resource governance.

A parallel dynamic is visible in Palestine, particularly in Gaza's maritime zone and the West Bank's Area C. Israeli authorities maintain full control over access to natural resources, including water, minerals, and potential offshore gas fields. In Gaza, the development of the Gaza Marine gas field has been repeatedly obstructed by Israeli security restrictions and the absence of internationally recognized Palestinian sovereign rights over territorial waters. In the West Bank, the Palestinian Authority has limited jurisdiction, while Israeli settlement expansion increasingly encroaches on resource-rich areas. Licenses and development rights are granted by Israeli authorities, effectively sidelining Palestinian institutions. However, legal and diplomatic momentum may be shifting. According to Michael Barron, a US-based energy consultant, formal recognition of Palestinian statehood could unlock stalled gas projects, potentially worth up to $4 billion and reduce aid dependency (Anadolu Agency, 2025; Wintour, 2025). Recent ICJ deliberations have further affirmed Palestinian maritime rights, reinforcing the legitimacy of sovereign claims and highlighting how extractive governance in contested territories remains deeply entangled with recognition and self-determination struggles (Rettig et. al., 2025).

These cases underscore how extractive governance in divided societies frequently reinforces political exclusion rather than fostering shared benefit. Institutional asymmetries are not merely technical problems but are embedded in deeper structures of sovereignty, legal ambiguity, and external alignment. Where resource governance is monopolized by recognized actors, rival claims are often delegitimized, and sustainable, inclusive development remains out of reach.

Geopolitical Securitization and External Alignment

In divided societies, extractive frontiers often evolve into geopolitical battlegrounds rather than neutral spaces of economic activity. Hydrocarbon discoveries in the Eastern Mediterranean illustrate this dynamic well: exploration has been accompanied not only by technical surveys but also by naval deployments, defense procurement, and the consolidation of regional blocs. Energy politics in this context becomes inseparable from questions of deterrence, alliance-building, and strategic signaling. Comparable patterns are visible elsewhere. In Iraq, for example, offshore and onshore hydrocarbon facilities require constant military protection, tying resource extraction to wider questions of internal security and regional stability. Similarly, in the Gulf of Guinea, offshore oil has attracted both state militarization and private security arrangements, embedding extraction within broader security economies.

External actors amplify these dynamics. Multinational energy corporations, foreign governments, and international institutions frequently conclude agreements with internationally recognized authorities, thereby consolidating their legitimacy while sidelining rival claimants. Such practices reflect what may be termed "extractive diplomacy": the use of contracts, aid, and security cooperation to bind resource governance into larger geopolitical alignments. While this approach may satisfy investors' demands for stability and states' desire for recognition, it often sharpens existing divides by treating contested territories as strategic assets rather than shared spaces.

The consequences are rarely limited to the energy sector. Exclusive alignments can provoke a range of countermeasures, from unilateral drilling and legal disputes to armed resistance and diplomatic estrangement. Rather than reducing tensions, securitization frequently transforms resource projects into flashpoints that both reflect and reproduce broader conflicts. In this way, extraction becomes not only an economic venture but also a mechanism through which international hierarchies and regional rivalries are reinforced.

These dynamics are obvious in the case of Cyprus, where offshore gas discoveries have turned resource governance into a source of intensified geopolitical conflict. One of the most illustrative cases of resource securitization and geopolitical alignment in a divided society is Cyprus. Following the discovery of offshore hydrocarbons in the Eastern Mediterranean in the late 2000s, the Republic of Cyprus (RoC) proceeded to delineate its Exclusive Economic Zone (EEZ) and issue exploration licenses to international energy companies such as ENI, Total, and ExxonMobil. These actions were taken unilaterally, without consultation with Turkish Cypriots, whose claims to resource co-ownership remain unrecognized by the RoC. The Turkish Cypriot administration and Turkey have both rejected the legitimacy of these arrangements, framing them as exclusionary and provocative (see International Crisis Group 2023a). In response, Turkey deployed its own drilling vessels and naval escorts into contested zones, escalating tensions in the region and transforming what began as an economic opportunity into a security flashpoint (Denizeau 2021, p. 5).

This securitization dynamic has been further entrenched through emerging regional alliances. The formation of the East Mediterranean Gas Forum (EMGF) in 2019 institutionalized a network of cooperation between Egypt, Greece, Israel, Cyprus, and others, explicitly excluding Turkey and Turkish Cypriots (İpek & Gür, 2021). The EMGF functions not only as an energy consortium but as a geopolitical alignment tool, reinforcing existing divisions. As multiple states increased naval presence in disputed maritime zones, Cyprus became a focal point for strategic posturing involving NATO, the EU, and regional actors. What might have been a shared development project became instead a driver of strategic confrontation and militarized deterrence.

This case illustrates how extractive governance in contested contexts is rarely a neutral economic endeavor. It often reflects broader questions of sovereignty, recognition, and alliance-building. Rather than incentivizing cooperation, the hydrocarbons discoveries in Cyprus have deepened political cleavages and created disincentives for compromise. The securitization of energy has not only reinforced the island's division but has also complicated the space for inclusive governance or shared benefit.

Environmental Governance and Civic Exclusion

In many conflict-affected and divided societies, environmental governance around extractive industries systematically marginalizes communities that are already politically excluded. Populations in unrecognized, occupied, or peripheral territories often find themselves outside the formal structures of consultation and decision-making.

Environmental impact assessments, when conducted, are frequently produced by external contractors or aligned institutions, with little or no engagement with local knowledge systems. As a result, the lived realities of affected groups—ranging from displacement and loss of livelihoods to degraded water and soil quality—rarely feature in official evaluations. Cases from Northern Iraq, Gaza, and Western Sahara highlight how this exclusion is not accidental but deeply embedded in contested sovereignty and unequal institutional access.

Civil society organizations have attempted to contest these dynamics, whether by documenting ecological damage, advocating for alternative development pathways, or mobilizing international legal frameworks. Yet such initiatives face formidable obstacles: limited resources, restricted political space, and, in some cases, outright repression. These constraints create what can be described as an "environmental governance deficit," where extractive activity continues without meaningful accountability or redress for those most affected. The burdens—ecological, social, and intergenerational—are externalized onto groups that lack political voice, thereby reinforcing cycles of disenfranchisement.

In Sudan, extractive projects have frequently advanced without environmental safeguards or meaningful consultation with affected communities. During the oil boom of the late 1990s and early 2000s, the government prioritized rapid petroleum development in the southern and western regions of the country. These areas, already marked by conflict and marginalization, experienced widespread environmental degradation, including oil spills, deforestation, and water contamination. Investigations by NGOs such as Human Rights Watch and the Sudanese Organisation Against Torture documented that local populations were rarely informed of development plans and widespread displacement and human rights violations (Human Rights Watch, 2003). Oil infrastructure was often built under military protection, turning extraction into a vector of dispossession and fear.

Large-scale infrastructure projects, such as the Merowe and Kajbar dams in Northern Sudan, have followed a similar pattern. These projects led to the forced displacement of Nubian and other communities, without adherence to international standards of prior informed consent or adequate resettlement. Local resistance was met with repression, while environmental assessments were either bypassed or conducted with minimal transparency (Dirar et. al., 2015). As a result, Sudan's resource governance model became emblematic of how extractivism can erode environmental rights and civic participation.

These dynamics did not change significantly after South Sudan's secession in 2011. In both Sudan and the new Republic of South Sudan, oil extraction continues to be dominated by government and military elites, often in partnership with foreign firms. Civil society remains weak, environmental accountability is minimal, and local communities bear the brunt of pollution and displacement (Askouri, 2005).

The Sudan case thus highlights how environmental governance in conflict-affected states can reinforce civic exclusion, with natural resources becoming tools for authoritarian consolidation rather than sustainable development.

This dynamic illustrates a broader critique advanced by political ecology: environmental management framed as a technocratic exercise often masks the profoundly political nature of resource governance. By sidelining grassroots actors and privileging elite or external decision-makers, extractive governance entrenches civic exclusion while simultaneously eroding the democratic legitimacy of peacebuilding and development agendas.

Hydrocarbons As Strategic Liabilities

Hydrocarbons have traditionally been regarded as strategic assets, symbols of prosperity and leverage in international politics. Yet in the current global context they increasingly resemble liabilities—economically, environmentally, and politically. The accelerating shift toward decarbonization, driven by international climate agreements and the rapid growth of renewable alternatives, has cast doubt on the long-term viability of fossil- fuel-based strategies. For societies already marked by fragility or division, the risks are particularly acute. Investment in hydrocarbons often ties political elites and institutions to volatile global markets, creating cycles of dependency that are difficult to escape.

This dynamic is clearly visible in divided contexts. In Cyprus, proposals such as the EastMed pipeline were initially framed as opportunities for regional cooperation and energy security, but they have become mired in criticism over environmental impact, questionable financial feasibility, and their potential to entrench rather than resolve political divisions (Ellinas, 2022). In Sudan and Iraq, fluctuating oil revenues have produced fiscal instability, deepened elite rivalries, and undermined long-term economic planning (International Crisis Group, 2023b; Ali, 2023). Instead of delivering development, hydrocarbons frequently lock states into unstable political bargains and unsustainable fiscal structures.

At the geopolitical level, hydrocarbons can also entrench rival alignments, drawing in external actors whose strategic interests may overshadow local concerns. Projects pursued under conditions of unresolved conflict risk becoming flashpoints of contestation rather than foundations for peace. In this sense, hydrocarbons illustrate how once-celebrated "strategic resources" can generate more liabilities than benefits, reinforcing the urgency of exploring post-extractivist approaches centered on sustainability, resilience, and inclusive governance.

In Northern Iraq, the Kurdistan Regional Government (KRG) has pursued a strategy of resource-based autonomy in the aftermath of protracted conflict and displacement. Oil has become the linchpin of its economic model, underpinning both internal governance and foreign relations, but also reinforcing patterns of dependency characteristic of a quasi-state. Since 2007, the KRG has signed independent contracts with international oil companies, built its own pipeline to Turkey, and directly exported crude—moves that Baghdad has repeatedly contested. These unilateral actions have intensified tensions over sovereignty and resource control, often resulting in legal disputes and fiscal blockades from the federal government (International Crisis Group, 2023b).

This extractive strategy has allowed the KRG to finance public services and maintain a degree of stability, yet it has also entrenched structural vulnerabilities. The region remains highly dependent on volatile oil revenues and politically fragile arrangements with Ankara and Baghdad. Moreover, oil-based development has not translated into widespread prosperity. Public sector salaries dominate the economy, while infrastructure and service delivery remain uneven. Periodic salary delays, budget disputes, and elite capture have provoked public protests, revealing the limits of extraction as a post-conflict recovery model (Wahab, 2023). Legal disputes remain active. In 2022, Iraq's Federal Supreme Court ruled the KRG's oil law unconstitutional. Tensions have further escalated in 2025 as Baghdad officially accused the KRG of ongoing oil smuggling and declared it legally responsible, reinforcing the fragility of unilateral resource governance in contested federal arrangements (Reuters, 2025).

This case illustrates the paradox of post-conflict extractivism. While natural resources can provide short-term stability and political leverage, they rarely deliver durable peace or inclusive development in contexts marked by contested authority and fragmented sovereignty. In the KRG, oil has served as both a tool of empowerment and a source of dependency, demonstrating the ambivalent role of extractive governance in divided societies.

Post-Conflict Extractivism and the Politics of Stability

In many divided or post-conflict societies, natural resource extraction is framed not only as an economic pathway but also as a means of political normalization. Particularly in frozen conflicts, extractivism is woven into state-building narratives that emphasize the authority of internationally recognized governments. By granting licenses, advancing sovereign claims, and securing external partnerships, these governments consolidate territorial control while simultaneously signaling legitimacy to international actors.

This practice reflects a form of institutional stabilization—where outwardly functional governance structures allow post-conflict regimes to appear legitimate, even though fundamental political divides remain unaddressed (Schneckener, 2016). Energy projects in Cyprus, Western Sahara, or Northern Iraq illustrate this tendency: multinational firms and donor agencies frequently engage with recognized authorities, bypassing rival administrations or communities. Such arrangements often translate into de facto recognition of unilateral control, reinforcing the asymmetries that lie at the heart of contested sovereignty.

The consequences extend beyond political symbolism. Post-conflict extractivism can actively reshape the trajectory of peace processes by privileging economic functionality over justice or reconciliation. International companies and donors, focused on investment security, tend to pursue contracts that entrench exclusion rather than promote compromise. For affected communities, this creates a paradox: resource development projects that promise modernization simultaneously deepen their political marginalization. Moreover, technocratic reforms, such as transparency initiatives, compliance frameworks, or fiscal oversight, rarely address deeper grievances of recognition, participation, and equality. By reducing extractive governance to a technical exercise, underlying disputes are depoliticized rather than resolved. Extraction thus becomes a tool of normalization, managing inequality without redressing it, and stabilizing fragile regimes without transforming them.

This dynamic reinforces the central argument of the chapter: that resource development in divided societies is unlikely to deliver durable peace unless it is reimagined through pluralistic governance and inclusive participation. The case of the Kurdistan Regional Government (KRG) in Northern Iraq exemplifies these dynamics. In the aftermath of conflict and displacement, the KRG relied on oil exports to build an autonomous fiscal and political infrastructure. While this strategy enabled a degree of institutional consolidation and international engagement, it also created structural dependencies on volatile oil prices and bilateral deals with Baghdad and Ankara. Public sector salaries dominate the economy, infrastructure remains patchy, and periodic fiscal crises have triggered mass protests (International Crisis Group, 2023b). This case highlights how resource wealth can enable short-term stability in post-conflict settings while simultaneously entrenching elite-driven governance, external dependencies, and long-term fragility.

Table 1. Comparative Overview of Extractive Governance in Divided and Conflict-Affected Societies

Case	Recognition Status	Lead Institutions	Form of Securitization	Civic Inclusion Level	Environmental Safeguards	Revenue Disposition	Project Risk
Cyprus	Partial (RoC recognized, TRNC unrecognized)	RoC government, EMGF partners	Naval deployments, alliances	Low (Turkish Cypriots excluded)	Minimal (no bicommunal EIA)	Controlled by RoC	High (disputes, tensions)
Western Sahara	Disputed (Moroccan control not recognized by UN)	Moroccan agencies	Military presence, resource militarization	None (Sahrawis excluded)	Poor (greenwashing critiques)	Centralized to Rabat	High
Palestine	Partial (PA limited recognition)	Israeli ministries, some donor input	Blockade, permit restrictions	Very Low (PA excluded in Gaza)	Limited	Israeli oversight, potential for PA	Moderate
Northern Iraq	KRG (semi-recognized region)	KRG Ministry of Natural Resources	Internal disputes, Baghdad–Erbil standoffs	Medium (local governance active)	Some	Revenue-sharing conflicts	High
Sudan	Recognized but unstable	Military-led government, foreign firms	Coup-led militarization	Very Low (civic space shrinking)	Weak (conflict zones unmonitored)	Opaque, elite-controlled	Very High

SOLUTIONS AND RECOMMENDATIONS: RETHINKING RESOURCE GOVERNANCE IN DIVIDED SOCIETIES

The analysis above shows that extractive governance in divided and conflict-affected societies rarely functions as a neutral instrument of development. Instead, it frequently magnifies political asymmetries, strengthens exclusionary institutions, sidelines environmental and civic voices, and heightens geopolitical rivalries. Natural resources that are often framed as peace dividends thus become tools for consolidation by dominant actors, rather than platforms for reconciliation or inclusion. Addressing these challenges requires moving beyond technocratic fixes and rethinking the underlying logic of extractive governance itself. Building on the integrated insights of political ecology, critical peacebuilding, and post-extractivism, this section outlines six interrelated directions for reform.

Rethink Development through Post-Extractivist Alternatives

A first step is to challenge the assumption that resource extraction is the unavoidable basis of development. In fragile or contested polities, the social, environmental, and political costs of extractivism routinely exceed its economic returns. Overdependence on hydrocarbons or minerals exposes states to volatile global markets, while at the same time entrenching elite capture, environmental degradation, and the militarization of politics.

Post-extractivist approaches, first articulated in Latin America but increasingly relevant elsewhere, call for investment in renewable energy, diversified economies, and locally embedded sectors that do not inflame territorial disputes. This does not amount to rejecting development; rather, it reframes development in terms of ecological sustainability, resilience, and community empowerment. For divided societies, such a reorientation also changes the terms of peacebuilding. Stability should not be equated with distributing resource rents more fairly, but with questioning whether large-scale extraction should remain the cornerstone of economic strategy at all.

As a concrete mechanism, international donors and financial institutions should prioritize transition funds that incentivize non-extractive economic alternatives. These funds could be linked to inclusive development benchmarks, such as gender equity in project leadership, local ownership thresholds, and ecological safeguards, to ensure that resource transitions benefit marginalized communities and reduce conflict incentives.

Institutionalize Inclusive and Shared Sovereignty over Resources

Resource governance cannot support peace if it rests on exclusion. More inclusive arrangements are needed at all stages of decision-making: licensing, oversight, regulation, and revenue distribution. This requires creating shared spaces of authority that move beyond a narrow reliance on international recognition.

Examples exist, though often partial or flawed. The Joint Water Committee under the Oslo Accords, despite deep political shortcomings, at least attempted to institutionalize cooperative management across conflict lines. In Cyprus, proposals to share gas revenues through internationally supervised mechanisms highlight the possibility of frameworks that involve both communities, even if broader negotiations remain stalled. Elsewhere, the African Union has experimented with joint resource management in disputed borderlands.

Such initiatives suggest that shared sovereignty need not await a comprehensive political settlement. Informal, transitional, or hybrid mechanisms can still provide a degree of recognition and trust-building. Where rival authorities are deeply entrenched, international organizations—whether the UN, EU, or regional bodies—can play a facilitative role, creating mechanisms that acknowledge plural claims while reducing incentives for unilateralism.

As a concrete mechanism, escrow arrangements offer a practical way to distribute resource revenues in contested contexts. Revenue generated from extraction can be held in internationally supervised accounts, with disbursement linked to agreed benchmarks, such as participation in joint governance bodies, community consultation requirements, or environmental standards. These mechanisms can help build trust, reduce fiscal capture by dominant actors, and align extraction with broader peacebuilding goals.

Embed Environmental Justice and Civic Participation

The ecological dimension of extractivism is often treated as secondary, yet in divided societies it is central to questions of justice and legitimacy. Communities that live closest to extractive sites, especially in unrecognized or marginalized regions, usually bear the heaviest environmental burdens while being excluded from governance structures. These dynamic fuels alienation, weakens social cohesion, and undermines prospects for peace.

Peacebuilding frameworks therefore, need to adopt an environmental justice perspective. This means moving beyond procedural consultations toward mechanisms that give affected groups real influence over decisions that shape their lives. Environmental governance must be reoriented from a technocratic exercise into a democratic process grounded in inclusion, accountability, and ecological integrity.

As a concrete mechanism, governments and international actors should establish Community-Based Environmental Monitoring Committees (CBEMCs) with statutory authority in extraction zones. These committees should include local community representatives, independent experts, and civil society groups, and be empowered to (1) review environmental impact assessments, (2) monitor ongoing compliance with ecological standards, and (3) initiate grievance procedures. Funding for CBEMCs should be integrated into licensing fees or corporate social responsibility contributions, ensuring sustainability and independence.

These participatory mechanisms not only improve environmental outcomes but also introduce plural perspectives, hold powerful actors accountable, and help rebuild civic trust in governance. In practice, such reforms are not easy; many civic groups in conflict zones face repression, limited resources, or donor dependency. Yet without their meaningful involvement, environmental reforms risk being cosmetic and extractive governance will continue to reproduce the exclusions it claims to address.

Hold External Actors Accountable to Conflict-Sensitive Standards

External actors, multinational firms, donors, and international institutions, shape extractive governance in decisive ways. Their tendency to prioritize recognized authorities and contractual security often reinforces asymmetries and undermines prospects for peace. Shifting this pattern requires embedding conflict sensitivity into international norms and corporate practices.

This entails more than generic transparency initiatives. Firms and donors should be required to engage with a wider range of stakeholders, including marginalized communities and rival authorities, when operating in contested settings. Investment agreements could be restructured to include safeguards for inclusivity, while donor funding could be tied to demonstrable efforts at conflict-sensitive governance.

International frameworks already exist that could serve as reference points. The UN Guiding Principles on Business and Human Rights, as well as the OECD Guidelines for Multinational Enterprises, provide standards for responsible engagement in fragile contexts. Yet these remain underused in practice. Conditioning contracts, loans, and aid on compliance with such standards would help shift incentives, encouraging companies and donors to see inclusive governance not as optional but as integral to political stability.

Design Hybrid Institutions for Contested Settings

Standard governance templates borrowed from liberal peacebuilding—focused on transparency, rule of law, and anti-corruption—are important but insufficient where sovereignty and recognition are themselves contested. In such settings, institutional innovation is essential.

Hybrid institutions are particularly suited to these environments. Flexible and adaptive, they combine elements of formal and informal governance and can accommodate overlapping claims of legitimacy. Practical designs might include joint licensing bodies co-chaired by rival parties, environmental committees with multi-level representation, or escrow accounts for revenues tied to political benchmarks. These mechanisms do not resolve the underlying conflict, but they create interim spaces of cooperation and reduce the zero-sum logic that often surrounds resource politics.

Importantly, hybrid institutions also help manage expectations. By acknowledging plural realities rather than insisting on a singular legal authority, they make governance more reflective of the actual conditions on the ground. While they may be temporary or partial, such institutions can provide a crucial bridge between conflict management and longer-term transformation.

Anchor Peacebuilding in Justice and Recognition

Finally, peacebuilding efforts in extractive contexts must resist the temptation to equate stability with justice. Too often, international interventions focus on maintaining order, supporting recognized governments, and avoiding "politicization." This risks constructing frameworks that ignore the grievances of marginalized groups and legitimize exclusionary governance.

A justice-oriented approach requires putting recognition, participation, and redistribution at the center of reform. Rather than bypassing sovereignty disputes, resource governance needs to acknowledge and engage with them. Institutions that emerge in such contexts must reflect contested realities, not paper over them with idealized templates.

Justice also requires a rethinking of the purpose of peacebuilding itself. If resource governance is used only to manage inequality rather than transform it, then extraction risks becoming another mechanism of conflict consolidation. Sustainable peace depends on embedding inclusion and recognition into the very foundations of governance, not treating them as add-ons once stability is achieved.

The challenge is not only to improve the efficiency of governance frameworks, but to fundamentally reimagine how peacebuilding intersects with extractivism. This involves moving from extractive peace to post-extractivist peace; from procedural inclusion to substantive justice; and from narrowly technocratic reforms to transformative structural change. Only by reframing natural resources as political, social, and ecological issues, rather than as purely economic commodities, can divided societies hope to turn extractivism from a driver of conflict into a potential platform for cooperation.

Figure 1. Integrated Framework for Extractive Governance in Divided Societies

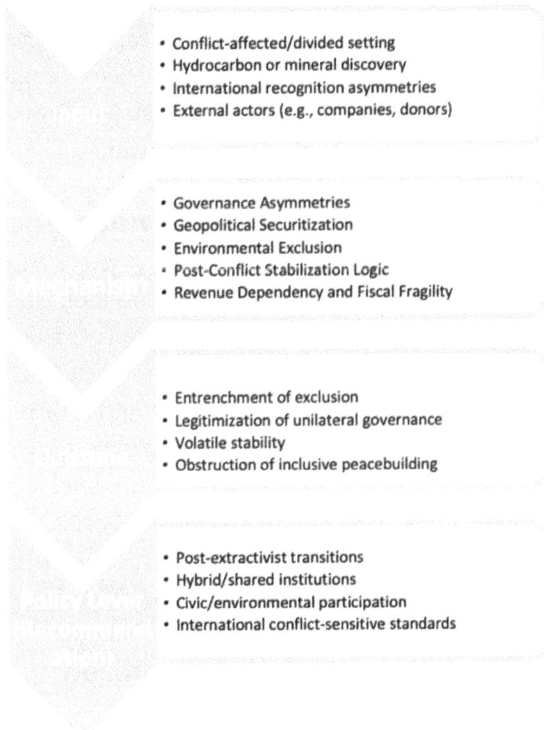

FUTURE RESEARCH DIRECTIONS

This chapter has argued that extractive governance in divided societies is not merely a symptom of weak institutions or mismanagement, but a structural feature embedded in political asymmetries, contested sovereignty, and international recognition regimes. While the analysis draws on interdisciplinary literatures, particularly political ecology, critical peacebuilding, post-extractivism, and international political economy, there remains significant scope for further research to deepen and extend these insights. This final section outlines five key avenues for future inquiry that can help advance a more grounded, pluralistic, and justice-oriented research agenda.

Ethnographic and Micro-Level Studies of Extractivism

Much of the literature on resource governance in conflict settings remains focused on macro-level institutions, state actors, or geopolitical alignments. Future research should incorporate micro-level and ethnographic perspectives that foreground the experiences of communities directly affected by extractive projects. This includes populations in unrecognized territories, peripheral regions, and environmentally degraded zones. Such studies could explore how local actors engage with, resist, or adapt to extractive regimes, thereby enriching our understanding of agency, everyday governance, and alternative imaginaries of development.

Operationalizing Post-Extractivism in Divided Societies

While post-extractivism has gained normative traction as an alternative to fossil-fuel dependency and extractive capitalism, there is limited research on how such transitions could unfold in divided or post-conflict contexts. Empirical studies are needed to assess the feasibility, risks, and opportunities of implementing post-extractivist policies in contested territories. For instance: Can renewable energy projects support inclusive governance and intercommunal cooperation? What institutional forms might support non-extractive, justice-oriented economies under conditions of limited sovereignty? How can post-extractivist strategies be tailored to fragmented authority and legal ambiguity?

Environmental Peacebuilding in Unrecognized and Contested Territories

Environmental peacebuilding has primarily focused on transboundary resource cooperation among recognized states. Yet in many conflict zones—such as Palestine, Western Sahara, or Northern Cyprus—environmental governance itself is entangled in disputes over recognition and legitimacy. Future research should examine how environmental initiatives operate in spaces where governance is fragmented, sovereignty is disputed, and civic engagement is constrained. What forms of environmental cooperation are possible in such contexts? Under what conditions can environmental projects contribute to shared governance or reconciliation?

Comparative Research Across Sovereignty-Contested Regions

There is a growing need for comparative frameworks that go beyond traditional cases in Sub-Saharan Africa or Latin America. Many divided societies—such as Cyprus, Kosovo, Somaliland, Palestine, and Northern Iraq—share features of contested sovereignty, international legal ambiguity, and exclusion from global governance regimes. Systematic comparative research could help identify common patterns of extractive exclusion, variations in institutional innovation, and pathways toward inclusive governance. Comparative work would also help situate the Cyprus case within broader global trends, contributing to theory-building across regions.

The Role of International Law and Recognition in Shaping Resource Politics

Extractive governance in contested regions is deeply shaped by the dynamics of international law, recognition, and legitimacy. Multinational corporations, donor agencies, and legal regimes often treat recognized governments as sole interlocutors, sidelining rival claims. This raises critical questions: How do legal doctrines around sovereignty and investment shape extractive alliances? In what ways do international legal ambiguities reinforce exclusionary governance? How can international legal and regulatory frameworks be made more inclusive of marginalized or unrecognized actors?

CONCLUSION

This chapter has sought to challenge the assumption that natural resource extraction, particularly in the form of large-scale hydrocarbons and minerals, can be harnessed as a straightforward engine of peacebuilding in societies divided by conflict. The claim that resources can be transformed into peace dividends has often rested on liberal and technocratic views that if contracts are signed, revenues shared, and transparency mechanisms introduced, then political cooperation will supposedly develop. Drawing on a theoretical perspective informed by political ecology, critical peacebuilding, and international political economy, the discussion here has shown that this assumption does not frequently manifest as expected. Rather than providing a foundation for reconciliation, extractive governance in contested and post-conflict contexts more often entrenches the very divisions it is expected to resolve. Instead of easing tensions, it deepens asymmetries of power, recognition, and participation, and frequently introduces new environmental and geopolitical pressures that complicate fragile political settlements.

The discussion identified five recurring dynamics across different cases. First, governance asymmetries show how internationally recognized authorities consolidate power by monopolizing contracts, licenses, and diplomatic partnerships, sidelining rival administrations and marginalized groups. Examples such as Cyprus's unilateral offshore licensing, Baghdad's disputes with the Kurdistan Regional Government, and Morocco's control of Western Sahara illustrate how recognition hierarchies are reproduced. Second, hydrocarbons frequently become securitized and politicized. Discoveries in the Eastern Mediterranean have triggered naval deployments, arms buildups, and shifting diplomatic blocs, mirroring patterns seen in Iraq and the Gulf of Guinea. Energy zones thus become sites of confrontation rather than cooperation.

Third, environmental and civic voices remain marginalized. Assessments, where conducted, often exclude those most affected, while civil society organizations face repression or institutional neglect. Such dynamics perpetuate what political ecologists describe as "technocratic environmentalism," which obscures deeper questions of justice. Fourth, hydrocarbons are increasingly seen as liabilities. Market volatility and the accelerating global energy transition render projects like the EastMed pipeline economically uncertain and environmentally problematic. In Iraq and Sudan, reliance on oil revenues has intensified fiscal crises and elite rivalries, contributing to instability.

Finally, post-conflict extractivism often consolidates the status quo. Resource projects are framed as proof of sovereignty and normality, even in unresolved conflicts, while international firms and donors reinforce these arrangements by working with recognized governments alone. This "status quo governance" allows extraction to proceed as if disputes were settled, narrowing the space for inclusive political solutions. Taken together, these dynamics demonstrate that the failures of resource-based peacebuilding are not anomalies but structural features of an extractive order. This order privileges recognized authority, capital accumulation, and international alignment over justice, inclusion, and sustainability. When governance is monopolized, marginalized actors are denied not only material benefits but also the political recognition essential to participation in reconstruction and reconciliation. Under such conditions, natural resources rarely generate peace dividends; instead, they entrench fragmented sovereignty and deepen societal cleavages.

In response to these limitations, the chapter has outlined a vision for what might be termed post-extractivist peacebuilding. This vision emphasizes ecological sustainability, pluralistic governance, and inclusive participation as foundational to just resource politics. It rejects the presumption that extraction is the inevitable or desirable path to development, particularly in divided societies where resources are closely tied to sovereignty and identity. Instead, it asks under what conditions resources can be governed in ways that build trust, enhance legitimacy, and promote justice, rather than exacerbate exclusion and rivalry.

Such a vision requires several shifts. It demands institutional innovation that moves beyond the liberal peacebuilding template of legal reform and transparency initiatives. While those reforms are important, they cannot substitute for deeper questions of recognition and participation. It also calls for external engagement that avoids reinforcing unilateralism. Donors, corporations, and international organizations must adopt conflict-sensitive standards that recognize the risks of exclusionary extractivism. And it necessitates frameworks that acknowledge the legitimacy of marginalized and non-recognized actors, rather than treating internationally recognized governments as the sole gatekeepers of sovereignty.

Importantly, this is not only an analytical but also a normative intervention. The analysis presented here reframes extractivism as a political and moral question, not simply a developmental one. Peacebuilding cannot succeed if it rests on the exclusion of entire communities, the militarization of resource frontiers, or the silencing of environmental and civic voices. Durable peace requires more than revenue-sharing or procedural reforms; it requires transformation in how power, territory, and development are conceptualized and negotiated.

This perspective also responds to the global context of ecological crisis and energy transition. As the world moves toward decarbonization, the rationale for new hydrocarbon projects in fragile and divided societies becomes increasingly untenable. Resource politics in such settings must be rethought not only as part of conflict resolution, but also as part of a broader shift toward sustainable and just economies. The question is not simply how to manage extraction more effectively, but whether reliance on extraction remains viable at all in a world facing climate breakdown.

Ultimately, the chapter contributes to a growing body of scholarship that treats extractive governance as central to the study of peace and conflict. It argues that the logic of extractivism, far from being a neutral or technical matter, is deeply implicated in the reproduction of political inequalities and geopolitical rivalries. Yet it also suggests that resource politics, if reimagined, can offer opportunities for building more just and sustainable futures. By embedding peacebuilding in post-extractivist frameworks that foreground justice, recognition, and ecological responsibility, societies may begin to move beyond the paradox of resources as both promise and peril.

In conclusion, extractivism in divided societies cannot be understood simply as a question of economic growth or state capacity. It is a political terrain where sovereignty, legitimacy, and justice are contested, and where choices about governance reverberate across domestic, regional, and global scales. The task ahead is not to perfect technocratic fixes for resource governance, but to reimagine peacebuilding itself: from extractive peace to post-extractivist peace, from procedural inclusion to substantive justice, and from narrow institutional reform to transformative structural change. In an era defined by ecological crisis and geopolitical flux, the urgency of developing such alternatives has never been greater.

REFERENCES

Acosta, A. (2013). Extractivism and neoextractivism: Two sides of the same curse. In Lang, M., & Mokrani, D. (Eds.), *Beyond Development: Alternative Visions from Latin America* (pp. 61–86). Rosa Luxemburg Foundation.

Aggestam, K., Leonardsson, H., & Persson, A. (2019). Environmental peacebuilding: The genesis, evolution and future of a field. *Environmental Politics*, *28*(1), 1–19.

Alkış, M. (2022). How oil resources affect the foreign relations of the Kurdistan Regional Government (KRG). *Energy Research & Social Science*, *91*, 102758. DOI: 10.1016/j.exis.2022.101146

Amnesty International. (2016). *When land is lost, where do we go? Coal mining and human rights in India.* Amnesty International Publications. https://www.amnesty.org/en/documents/asa20/4391/2016/en/

Anadolu Agency. (2025, August 29). *Recognition of Palestine could unlock Gaza Marine gas resources: Experts.* https://www.aa.com.tr/en/energy/energy-diplomacy/recognition-of-palestine-could-unlock-gaza-marine-gas-resources-experts/51424

Askouri. (2005). The Merowe Dam: Controversy and displacement in Sudan. *Forced Migration Review.*

Auty, R. M. (1993). *Sustaining development in mineral economies: The resource curse thesis.* Routledge. https://doi.org/DOI: 10.4324/9780203422595

Bakker, K. (2010). *Privatizing water: Governance failure and the world's urban water crisis.* Cornell University Press. http://www.jstor.org/stable/10.7591/j.ctt7z9jv

Boukhars, A., & Roussellier, J. (Eds.). (2014). *Perspectives on Western Sahara: Myths, nationalisms and geopolitics.* Rowman & Littlefield., https://www.bloomsbury.com/us/perspectives-on-western-sahara-9781442226852/

Bridge, G., & Le Billon, P. (2017). *Oil.* Polity Press.

Bridge, G., Özkaynak, B., & Turhan, E. (2018). Energy infrastructure and the fate of the nation: Introduction to special issue. *Energy Research & Social Science*, *46*(1), 1–11. DOI: 10.1016/j.erss.2018.04.029

Collier, P., Hoeffler, A., & Söderbom, M. (2008). Post-conflict risks. *Journal of Peace Research*, *45*(4), 461–478. DOI: 10.1177/0022343308091356

Cox, F. D., & Sisk, T. D. (2017). *Peacebuilding in Deeply Divided Societies: Toward Social Cohesion?* Springer Nature., DOI: 10.1007/978-3-319-50715-6

Denizeau, A. 2021. "Mavi Vatan, the 'Blue Homeland': The Origins, Influences and Limits of an Ambitious Doctrine for Turkey." *Études de l'Ifri*, Ifri. https://www.ifri.org/en/studies/mavi-vatan-blue-homeland-origins-influences-and-limits-ambitious-doctrine-turkey

Dirar, A., el Moghraby, A., Jalal Hashim, M., & Zeitoun, M. (2015). Displacement and resistance induced by the Merowe Dam: The influence of international norms and justice (DEV Reports and Policy Paper Series). School of International Development, University of East Anglia. Retrieved from https://devresearch.uea.ac.uk/wp-content/uploads/2022/04/DEV-RPP-17.pdf

Ellinas, C. (2022). Energy and geopolitics in the Eastern Mediterranean. Atlantic Council. https://www.atlanticcouncil.org/wp-content/uploads/2022/02/AC_EastMediterranean.pdf?utm_source=chatgpt.com

Escobar, A. (2008). *Territories of difference: Place, movements, life, redes.* Duke University Press., DOI: 10.2307/j.ctv1198wg2

Fairhead, J., Leach, M., & Scoones, I. (2012). Green grabbing: A new appropriation of nature? *The Journal of Peasant Studies, 39*(2), 237–261. DOI: 10.1080/03066150.2012.671770

Ferguson, J. (2006). *Global shadows: Africa in the neoliberal world order.* Duke University Press., DOI: 10.1215/9780822387640

Gudynas, E. (2013). Debates on development and its alternatives in Latin America. A brief heterodox guide. In M. Lang & D. Mokrani (Eds.), *Beyond Development: Alternative Visions from Latin America.* Rosa Luxemburg Foundation. https://www.tni.org/files/download/beyonddevelopment_complete.pdf

Hagen, A & Kollenbach, G. (2024). *The Political Economy of Stranded Assets: Climate Policies, Investments and the Role of Elections.* Berlin School of Economics Discussion Papers, No. 0033, Berlin School of Economics. DOI: DOI: 10.48462/opus4-5348

Hilson, G., & Maconachie, R. (2009). "Good governance" and the extractive industries in sub-Saharan Africa. *Mineral Processing and Extractive Metallurgy Review, 30*(1), 52–100.

Human Rights Watch. (2003). Sudan, Oil, and Human Rights. https://www.hrw.org/report/2003/11/24/sudan-oil-and-human-rights

International Crisis Group. (2023a). An Island Divided: Next Steps for Troubled Cyprus. Report No 268. https://www.crisisgroup.org/europe-central-asia/western-europemediterranean/cyprus/268-island-divided-next-steps-troubled-cyprus

International Crisis Group. (2023b). *Iraq: Staving off instability in the near and distant futures. Middle East Report No. 227.* https://www.crisisgroup.org/middle-east-north-africa/gulf-and-arabian-peninsula/iraq/iraq-staving-instability-near-and-distant-futures

İpek, P., & Gür, V. T. (2021). Turkey's Isolation from the Eastern Mediterranean Gas Forum: Ideational mechanisms and material interests in Energy Politics. *Turkish Studies, 23*(1), 1–30. DOI: 10.1080/14683849.2021.1925884

Le Billon, P. (2001). The political ecology of war: Natural resources and armed conflicts. *Political Geography, 20*(5), 561–584. DOI: 10.1016/S0962-6298(01)00015-4

Le Billon, P. (2005). *Fuelling war: Natural resources and armed conflict.* Routledge., DOI: 10.4324/9781315019529

Le Billon, P. (2007). Natural resources, armed conflicts, and the UN Security Council (Working Paper UNSC07-001). Liu Institute for Global Issues, University of British Columbia. https://sppga.ubc.ca/wp-content/uploads/sites/5/2016/03/30May2007_Natural_Resources_Armed_Conflicts_UNSC07-001.pdf

Le Billon, P., & Nicholls, E. (2007). Ending 'Resource Wars': Revenue Sharing, Economic Sanction or Military Intervention? *International Peacekeeping, 14*(5), 613–632. DOI: 10.1080/13533310701753941

Lujala, P. (2009). Deadly combat over natural resources: Gems, petroleum, drugs, and the severity of armed civil conflict. *The Journal of Conflict Resolution, 53*(1), 50–71. DOI: 10.1177/0022002708327644

Mac Ginty, R. (2010). Hybrid peace: The interaction between top-down and bottom-up peace. *Security Dialogue, 41*(4), 391–412. DOI: 10.1177/0967010610374312

Mac Ginty, R. (2011). *International peacebuilding and local resistance: Hybrid forms of peace*. Palgrave Macmillan., DOI: 10.1057/9780230307032

Mac Ginty, R., & Richmond, O. (2013). The local turn in peace building: A critical agenda for peace. *Third World Quarterly, 34*(5), 763–783. DOI: 10.1080/01436597.2013.800750

Martinez-Alier, J. (2002). *The environmentalism of the poor: A study of ecological conflicts and valuation*. Edward Elgar., DOI: 10.4337/9781843765486

Peluso, N. L., & Lund, C. (2011). New frontiers of land control: Introduction. *The Journal of Peasant Studies, 38*(4), 667–681. DOI: 10.1080/03066150.2011.607692

Pugh, M. (2005). The political economy of peacebuilding: A critical theory perspective. *International Journal of Peace Studies, 10*(2), 23–42. https://www.jstor.org/stable/41852928

Pugh, M., Cooper, N., & Goodhand, J. (2004). *War economies in a regional context: Challenges of transformation*. Lynne Rienner Publishers., DOI: 10.1515/9781685855284

Rettig, E., Friedman, S., & Spanier, B. (2025). Reflections on our article 'Postwar development of offshore energy resources: Legal and political models for developing the Gaza Marine gas field'. *Leiden Journal of International Law, 38*(1), 30–39. DOI: 10.1017/S092215652510040X

Reuters. (2025). Iraq holds Kurdish government legally responsible for continued oil smuggling. June 5. https://www.reuters.com/world/middle-east/iraq-holds-kurdish-government-legally-responsible-continued-oil-smuggling-2025-06-05/

Richmond, O. P. (2011). *A post-liberal peace*. Routledge., DOI: 10.4324/9780203810262

Robbins, P. (2012). *Political ecology: A critical introduction* (2nd ed.). Wiley-Blackwell.

Ross, M. L. (2004). What do we know about natural resources and civil war? *Journal of Peace Research, 41*(3), 337–356. DOI: 10.1177/0022343304043773

Ross, M. L. (2012). *The oil curse: How petroleum wealth shapes the development of nations*. Princeton University Press., DOI: 10.1515/9781400841929

Schneckener, U. (2016). Peacebuilding in crisis? Debating peacebuilding paradigms and practices. In Debiel, T., Held, T., & Schneckener, U. (Eds.), *Peacebuilding in Crisis: Rethinking Paradigms and Practices of Transnational Cooperation*. Routledge.

Swyngedouw, E. (2009). The political economy and political ecology of the hydro-social cycle. *Journal of Contemporary Water Research & Education, 142*(1), 56–60. DOI: 10.1111/j.1936-704X.2009.00054.x

Temper, L., del Bene, D., & Martinez-Alier, J. (2015). Mapping the frontiers and front lines of global environmental justice: The EJAtlas. *Journal of Political Ecology, 22*(1), 255–278. DOI: 10.2458/v22i1.21108

UNEP (United Nations Environment Programme). (2009). *From conflict to peacebuilding: The role of natural resources and the environment*. UNEP. https://www.iisd.org/system/files/publications/conflict_peacebuilding.pdf

Wahab, B. (2023). Two Decades of Uneven Federalism in Iraq. Middle East Report, MERIP https://merip.org/2023/04/the-rise-and-fall-of-kurdish-power-in-iraq/

Watts, M. (2015). Now and then: The origins of political ecology and the rebirth of adaptation as a form of thought. In Perreault, T., Bridge, G., & McCarthy, J. (Eds.), *The Routledge handbook of political ecology* (pp. 19–50). Routledge., DOI: 10.4324/9781315759289

Western Sahara Resource Watch. (2010). *UN Human Rights Council discusses illegal resource exploitation in Western Sahara*. Western Sahara Resource Watch. https://wsrw.org/en/archive/1089

Wintour, P. (2025). Recognised Palestinian state could develop disputed gas resources, expert says. 20 July, The Guardian. https://www.theguardian.com/world/2025/jul/20/recognised-palestinian-state-could-develop-disputed-gas-resources-expert-says

World Bank. (2011). *World development report 2011: Conflict, security, and development*. World Bank Publications. https://openknowledge.worldbank.org/entities/publication/25f2300c-f9d4-54de-8a56-30566e72003a

KEY TERMS AND DEFINITIONS

Critical Peacebuilding: An alternative to liberal peacebuilding frameworks that focuses on structural causes of conflict, including inequality, exclusion, and contested sovereignty. Critical peacebuilding emphasizes justice, recognition, and meaningful participation, arguing that peace requires more than institutional reform. It calls for transformative approaches that address asymmetries of power and include marginalized voices in post-conflict governance.

Extractive Diplomacy: The use of resource governance as a tool of international alignment and strategic recognition. Through contracts, partnerships, and diplomatic engagement, states and companies reinforce the legitimacy of recognized governments. In divided societies, extractive diplomacy often excludes unrecognized authorities, embedding resource politics within broader geopolitical and legal hierarchies.

Extractivism: A development strategy focused on the large-scale removal of natural resources for export, often reinforcing centralized authority and international investment. It prioritizes short-term economic gains over ecological and social well-being and tends to marginalize local communities. Extractivism is associated with global market dependency and governance models that concentrate power and reduce public participation in decision-making.

Political Ecology: An interdisciplinary approach that examines environmental issues through power relations, historical context, and inequality. Political ecology rejects the idea that environmental problems are purely technical, instead analyzing how governance structures, discourses, and institutions shape access to resources. It also explores how terms like "sustainability" or "development" can legitimize exclusion and reinforce dominant interests.

Post-Extractivism: A critique of extractivist development models, emphasizing sustainability, social justice, and democratic governance. Post-extractivism challenges the assumption that growth requires resource exploitation and promotes alternatives grounded in local agency, renewable energy, and community-driven economies. It seeks to redefine prosperity through ecological balance and inclusive participation rather than export-oriented extraction.

Resource Nationalism: A state-led assertion of control over natural resources, framed as protecting sovereignty and promoting national benefit. While it can support redistribution, in divided or contested societies it often legitimizes unilateral authority and excludes rival claims. Resource nationalism can escalate tensions where ownership and sovereignty are politically disputed.

Resource Territorialization: The process by which actors, including states and corporations, assert control over land and resources by regulating access, ownership, and use. It often involves licensing regimes, boundary-making, and security enforcement. In contested areas, this process consolidates authority for dominant actors while sidelining alternative claims, reinforcing exclusionary political and spatial orders.

Chapter 13

The Sustainability Discourse of Mega Satellite Constellations:

Contradictions With the SDGs and a Critical Review

Aybüke İnan-Şimşek
https://orcid.org/0000-0002-4684-380X
Niğde Ömer Halisdemir University, Turkey

ABSTRACT

This paper critically analyzes the sustainability narratives of mega-satellite constellations like Starlink, OneWeb, and Amazon Kuiper. While promising digital inclusion and global internet access, these projects reveal structural contradictions that exacerbate environmental neglect, transparency issues, and social inequalities. Using a Marxist political economy approach and Critical Discourse Analysis, it demonstrates that these initiatives serve as ideological justifications for capital accumulation rather than technical solutions. The findings indicate that they cause both direct and indirect conflicts with sustainable development goals. The study also advocates for binding international regulations, environmental impact assessments, and transparent partnership mechanisms to monitor the social and environmental effects of these projects. Consequently, the sustainability discourse often functions as a marketing tool, acting as a form of ideological dominance that sustains global inequalities.

DOI: 10.4018/979-8-3373-1707-6.ch013

INTRODUCTION

Today, mega-satellite constellations in Low Earth Orbit (LEO) are quickly expanding alongside discussions about universal digital infrastructure and democratizing internet access. Initiatives like Starlink (SpaceX), OneWeb (Bharti-Eutelsat), and Project Kuiper (Amazon) are crucial to the sustainability conversation, asserting their role in achieving global digital equity, innovation, and development objectives scale. However, these projects serve not only as instruments of digital inclusion but also as vehicles for new forms of domination, including data exploitation, surveillance capitalism, and digital colonization.

This study intends to critically analyze the hegemonic framework of these initiatives, which revolve around discourses like "internet for all", "global digital inclusion", and "technological equality". While primarily conducted in the context of SDG 9 (infrastructure and innovation), SDG 13 (climate action), SDG 16 (peace, justice and strong institutions) and SDG 17 (partnerships for the goals), the study will also assess the contradictions associated with other goals such as SDG 4 (quality education), SDG 10 (reducing inequalities), SDG 12 (responsible production and consumption) and SDG 15 (life on land). Indeed, Losch, Galli and Schildknecht (2024) argue that the existing 17 goals are insufficient to address the unique sustainability challenges of space activities, and that a space-specific 18th SDG should be proposed. This shows how mega-satellite constellations pose a critical challenge to global governance and sustainability.

The research's theoretical foundation is rooted in the Marxist tradition of political economy. This framework examines the ideas of Karl Marx, David Harvey, Antonio Gramsci, Louis Althusser, and Christian Fuchs together. Concepts like commodity fetishism, spatial fixation, hegemony, ideological apparatuses, and surveillance capitalism are employed to examine both the technical and the ideological and political aspects of projects. This theoretical framework facilitates a multi-layered understanding of how digital infrastructures reproduce global inequalities. Thus, the study extends beyond a technical analysis and aims to provide a multi-layered understanding of how digital infrastructures legitimize global inequalities.

The study employs Norman Fairclough's three-dimensional Critical Discourse Analysis (CDA) methodology. The primary reason for selecting this method lies in its ability to analyze the construction of sustainability discourses surrounding mega-satellite constellations across not only textual dimensions but also social, institutional, and ideological levels. By connecting textual elements to social practices, CDA uncovers both the contextual and ideological structural dimensions of discourses. This method analyzes how corporate discourses relate to the SDG framework and global development goals, which structural interests they legitimize, and how they create discourse-action contradictions.

The discourses examined in this study include primary sources like the corporate websites of Starlink, OneWeb, and Kuiper, as well as press releases, company reports, and statements from prominent individuals such as Elon Musk and Jeff Bezos. These discourses are analyzed concerning concepts such as data exploitation, infrastructure dependency, and hegemonic reproduction within the framework of digital capitalism. Furthermore, media content, UN SDG documents, and sectoral assessment reports were comparatively evaluated to identify potential contradictions between discourse and action. This CDA analysis aligns with Marxist theories such as ideology (Althusser), hegemony (Gramsci), spatial fixation (Harvey), and digital domination (Fuchs) to uncover the structural workings behind discourses.

This method is considered a holistic tool to analyze the ideological apparatuses through which corporate discourses circulate, the function of these discourses in the production of social consent, and how they are positioned in contradiction to the SDGs. This research aims to demonstrate how technology companies establish ideological hegemony through sustainability discourses, reveal this hegemony through discourse-action contradictions, and reproduce global inequalities. Thus, the development of sustainability discourse as a legitimizing tool for capital accumulation strategies is critically questioned.

THEORETICAL AND METHODOLOGICAL FRAMEWORK

The theoretical and methodological framework selected for this study offers a comprehensive structure that facilitates the analysis of not only the technical aspects but also the social, economic, and ideological dimensions of high-tech initiatives like mega-satellite constellations. In this context, the concepts of theorists such as Karl Marx, David Harvey, Antonio Gramsci, Louis Althusser, and Christian Fuchs are utilized. The common characteristic of these theorists is their contributions to analyzing the relationships between technology, ideology, and capital within the Marxist tradition of thought. Therefore, the theoretical structure favored in this study is not only the sum of individual conceptual frameworks but also an extension of a critical Marxist body of analysis.

These names were selected because they provide a thorough examination of technology's function within capitalist production relations, the types of hegemony that arise from this process, and the societal implications of digital infrastructures. Marx and Harvey were selected to analyze economic structures, while Gramsci and Althusser were chosen to explain ideological modes of production. Fuchs was included to examine how these processes are reproduced in the context of digital capitalism. This theoretical framework upholds the study's integrity while enhancing both critical discourse analysis and structural analysis. This theoretical diversity allows for the examination of mega-satellite projects as both technical entities and as expressions of discursive and structural power relations.

The Marxist approach evaluates technological developments not as neutral and universal means of progress but as products of social relations embedded in class interests (Eagleton, 2011, pp. 38-40; Ollman, 2003, p. 109). Marx's concept of 'the fetishism of commodities' refers to the fact that in capitalist relations of production, commodities are presented as if they have an independent value in their own right, thereby rendering invisible the role of labor in their production (Marx, 1976, pp. 163-177). This leads to viewing technological products and services as natural and inevitable tools, separate from production processes and class relations. In this sense, the technological services marketed by Starlink with discourses such as 'global internet access' should be evaluated not only as a technical solution, but also as an ideological re-presentation that renders invisible the processes of capital accumulation, the use of labor, and global competition behind them.

David Harvey's theory of 'spatial fixation' reveals that capital tends to constantly create new spaces and investment areas in order to overcome its crises and maintain profit rates (Harvey, 2003, p. 88). This concept involves the extension of capital into new geographical regions to address the accumulation crisis in areas where capital growth becomes saturated or profitability begins to wane. This expansion process extends beyond physical spaces; it encompasses legal, economic, and ideological restructuring (Harvey, 2003, pp. 110-112). Harvey (2003, p. 88) states that spatial fixation enables investments to be tied to specific locations, thereby allowing capital to delay a crisis temporarily. Space, particularly Low Earth Orbits (LEO), has emerged as a new zone for capital accumulation in this context. The competition for satellite orbits, in the race for slots through the ITU (International Telecommunication Union), can be seen as a concrete example of sharing space according to market logic and spatial fixation. This example positions the orbits as a natural resource and places them under private ownership, thereby enabling the integration of space into capitalist circulation.

The commercialization of satellite orbits is similar to privatizing public spaces and aligns with Marx's idea of 'primitive accumulation'. Primitive accumulation refers to the process of transferring natural resources and means of production from public or common ownership to private ownership during the period before the capitalist mode of production began (Marx, 1976, pp. 873-904). Today, the commercialization of space can be regarded as a contemporary form of this historical process. Historically, primitive accumulation was initially shaped by the enclosure of agricultural lands that accompanied the dissolution of feudal property, followed by the detachment of the labor force from their lands during the process of industrialization (Marx, 1976, pp. 877-895). Throughout the 20th century, as colonies integrated into central capitalist economies, this process expanded into new geographical regions. Today, these accumulation dynamics have evolved to reflect the usage of space by transnational corporations within a private property regime. The distribution of orbital positions, the privatization of spectrum rights, and the predominance of private launch companies in infrastructure demonstrate that capital accumulation in space persists through 'new enclosure' processes.

Gramsci's concept of 'hegemony' describes the process by which ruling classes establish ideological leadership by presenting their own interests as the general interest of society, without resorting to physical coercion (Gramsci, 1971, p. 12). Hegemony is established not only through political or economic pressure but also by transforming the values, norms, and worldviews of individuals. In this context, media, education, and technology serve a crucial role in spreading hegemonic discourses (Cox, 1983, p. 51). Discourses such as 'global inclusion', 'digital equality' and 'internet for all' create the impression that these technological projects are not only technical but also ethically and socially beneficial, thus making the interests of the ruling classes acceptable to large segments of society. Through these discourses, mega-satellite projects often reproduce global inequalities instead of diminishing them, while simultaneously reinforcing the legitimacy of these inequalities. Gramsci's theory of hegemony helps us understand how these discourses are framed as natural and universal values, shielding them from critical examination.

In this context, Althusser's concept of 'ideological apparatuses' holds significance; he posits that ideology facilitates the system's reproduction by positioning individuals within specific roles of the social structure. In addition to the direct repressive apparatuses of the state, structures such as the media, education, law, religion, and technology function indirectly, making individuals the subjects of the system while simultaneously rendering this situation seem natural and inevitable (Althusser, 1971, pp. 130-133). According to Althusser, these apparatuses operate not only through external rules but also by appealing to the desires and identifications of individuals. Thus, ideology not only represses individuals but also fosters their participation, consent, and sense of belonging (Althusser, 1971, pp. 167-168). This study examines how technological narratives redefine individuals as roles like users, citizens, or entrepreneurs, thereby integrating them voluntarily into this digital infrastructure. In this context, the concept of 'surveillance capitalism'[1] is emphasized in the text. The services provided by large satellite constellations are marketed to individuals with assurances of digital engagement, accessibility, and growth. This is crucial for understanding how this system maintains its ideological consistency and influences personal identities.

Christian Fuchs' concepts of 'technology fetishism'[2] and 'digital capitalism'[3] provide a critical perspective against the legitimization of digital technologies as ideologically neutral by presenting them as independent of social relations and production processes (Fuchs, 2022). Technology fetishism hides the labor and social inequalities involved in digital products and services, portraying technology as a self-evident and progressive force. Fuchs (2022, p. 110) argues that in digital capitalism, the commodification of data allows users to engage with platforms not just as consumers but also as prosumers, actively participating in capital accumulation. This process also sets the stage for digital colonialism: digital infrastructures in the Global South transform these areas into centers for data production, while simultaneously excluding them from decision-making and governance processes. In the digital landscape, where companies oversee satellite infrastructures and data flow, a framework is developing that facilitates data exploitation, centralizes information, and expands social surveillance mechanisms, overshadowing the initial promises of digital accessibility. Fuchs' perspective shows that these technologies function not just as technical instruments, but also as ideological tools that perpetuate capitalist domination. In particular, the concept of 'platform capitalism'[4] is useful for understanding how Western technology giants establish a new form of digital colonialism by controlling the installation of digital infrastructure on a global scale (Fuchs, 2022, p. 58). In this context, initiatives like Kuiper and Starlink not only offer connectivity but also centralize the management of information flow.

Thus, the study's theoretical framework enables an analysis of both the surface-level representations of dominant technological discourses and the underlying class, economic, and ideological structures associated with them. The theoretical background provides critical depth that directly informs the discourse analysis method of the study. The methodological approach outlined below directly relates to the theoretical foundations and integrates discursive analysis with structural analysis in a holistic manner.

The methodological approach based on these theoretical foundations focuses on discourse analysis and seeks to reveal how the 'sustainability' discourse of mega satellite constellations is structured, which interest groups it serves, and what kind of inequalities it renders invisible. This method enables us to question not only textual structures but also the social relations that shape these structures. Therefore, CDA is especially effective in demonstrating how dominant ideologies are legitimized through seemingly natural and inevitable discourses. To achieve this, the CDA method developed by Norman Fairclough (2010) was employed. In accordance with Fairclough's three-dimensional discourse model, the analyzed discourses were assessed in terms of: (1) the concepts, metaphors, and rhetorical strategies employed at the textual level; (2) the contexts of production and circulation of the discourse; (3) the social structures and ideologies on which the discourse is founded and reproduced (Fairclough, 2010, pp. 10-11). For example, while analyzing the concepts with which expressions such as "global connectivity" are textually associated (e.g., development, inclusiveness), it was also evaluated how these discourses are produced in the context of the neoliberal economy and how they are re-functionalized in global data markets. Nonetheless, because this approach focuses solely on textual data, it does not facilitate direct observation of how discourses translate into practice. Although this enhances the study's interpretative capacity, it necessitates thoughtful consideration of the results' implications on practice.

The dataset consists of corporate texts (company reports, press releases, websites, leader statements), United Nations SDG documents, international treaties, media reports, as well as recent scientific books and peer-reviewed articles on the Starlink, OneWeb and Kuiper projects. This diversity made it possible to conduct a multi-layered assessment not only at the discourse level, but also from technical, legal and social perspectives. These projects were selected not only for their technological scale, but also for their strong public visibility, sustainability claims and the central role they play in global digital infrastructure discourses.

Within the framework of Fairclough's three-dimensional Critical Discourse Analysis model, discourses from these sources were coded under thematic categories such as "inclusion", "environmental responsibility", "technological equity" and "partnerships". However, there are differences in data access across projects. For example, since the Kuiper project has not yet reached a large-scale satellite capacity, it has received limited coverage in academic and technical sources. In contrast, the fact that Starlink is already the mega-constellation with the largest number of satellites has created a more intense area of analysis in both institutional documents and academic literature. OneWeb, on the other hand, is particularly prominent in sources on public-private partnerships and regional collaborations. These differences were taken into account in balancing the dataset and each project was evaluated in its own context.

This study incorporates Fuchs' (2022) analysis of digital capitalism to enhance the theoretical framework of CDA. In particular, concepts such as data exploitation, digital colonialism, and technology fetishism enrich the analysis of ideological content. The CDA method can effectively tackle both the linguistic strategies and the political economy involved in digital capitalist discourses. This framework enables the study to clarify the formal analysis of discourse and its structural outcomes. Nonetheless, the limitations of discourse analysis were acknowledged, particularly its inability to directly observe extra-discursive practices and the focus on the representation level within the study. A primary aim of this research is to examine the discourse surrounding the sustainability claims of mega-satellite constellations, along with the impacts of these narratives on economic, ecological, and social dimensions.

CONTRADICTIONS IN RHETORIC AND DIVERGENCES WITH THE SDG

The Sustainable Development Goals (SDGs), adopted by the United Nations in 2015, are structured to align with the universal aims of eradicating poverty, protecting the planet, and enhancing prosperity for all by 2030. This study specifically focuses on four key goals: SDG 9 (Industry, Innovation and Infrastructure), SDG 13 (Climate Action), SDG 16 (Peace, Justice and Strong Institutions), and SDG 17 (Partnerships for the Goals). SDG 9 emphasizes the equitable and inclusive development of infrastructure, while SDG 13 prioritizes reducing environmental impacts and addressing the climate crisis. SDG 16 promotes the establishment of transparent and accountable institutions, whereas SDG 17 advocates for global partnerships grounded in fair and responsible cooperation, including public-private partnerships (United Nations, 2015).

These goals are directly related to the discursive structure and implementation practices of mega-satellite constellations. The four SDGs question whether digital infrastructures serve as a public service or a commercialized tool; how their environmental impacts become invisible; to what extent governance processes are transparent and inclusive; and which power relations these projects reproduce. Therefore, the projects in question are evaluated not only in technical but also in social, environmental, and political terms.

In light of the concepts presented in the theoretical and methodological framework, the contradictions between the discursive structure of the sustainability claims of mega-satellite constellations and the SDGs become increasingly apparent. The SDGs are structured around goals such as poverty reduction, eliminating inequalities, quality education, combating climate change, and inclusive governance. However, the discourse that associates projects like Starlink, OneWeb, and Kuiper with these goals is underpinned by a serious ideological framework. In accordance with the concepts developed in the theoretical and methodological framework, the sustainability claims of these projects systematically contradict the SDGs. The rhetoric surrounding projects like Starlink, OneWeb, and Kuiper, which asserts alignment with the UN goals, is often framed ideologically and strategically, while in practice, they generate serious structural tensions and inequalities.

Starlink

Starlink is a satellite internet network developed by SpaceX, a company owned by Elon Musk. Musk promotes Starlink as a global inclusion tool that provides 'internet access for all', emphasizing themes of digital equality, economic development, and technological freedom (Shaengchar & Kraiwanit, 2023, p. 2). While this discourse has found support, especially in the global South, it has faced serious criticism regarding the privatization of basic services and the commercialization of digital infrastructure. Starlink's 'internet for all' rhetoric has been significantly questioned due to its holding of more than 50% of the satellites in LEO and its efforts to eliminate competitors through loss-leader pricing (Open Markets Institute, 2022, pp. 1-2). The inconsistencies between Starlink's rhetoric of 'global access' and its actual practices expose the ideological functions of this technology.

Starlink's expansion strategy has specifically targeted Latin America. Offering services to 28 countries and territories as of November 2024, the company has nearly monopolized the Brazilian Amazon region, leading to conflicts of interest with local infrastructure providers (Leins, 2024). This example demonstrates that digital infrastructure is organized in a way that encourages monopolization instead of promoting competition, thus contradicting SDG 16's principles of transparency, fair governance, and equal participation. It also undermines the goal of inclusive and sustainable infrastructure emphasized in SDG 9, as Starlink's infrastructure investments are influenced by centralized control and increased external dependence rather than local capacity building.

In the same period, the close relations between the far-right government in Argentina and Elon Musk revealed that digital infrastructure functions as a geopolitical bargaining tool. Following Musk's statements on lithium resources and his support for the regime, the fact that Starlink operated in the country without facing regulatory hurdles sparked public debate (Evans-Pritchard, 2024). Conversely, documents submitted to the Federal Communications Commission (FCC) indicated that in order to receive approximately 1 billion dollars in rural infrastructure funds, Starlink claimed to have coverage in areas where it could not provide service, leading to the cancellation of its funding application (Open Markets Institute, 2022, p. 4). Additionally, allegations suggested that Starlink swiftly entered some markets due to trade negotiations during the first term of US President Donald Trump, which continued into his second term, accompanied by claims that lawsuits against Elon Musk were dropped (Ingram, 2025). All this demonstrates that digital infrastructure has evolved into not only a technological asset but also a diplomatic and strategic tool of negotiation.

In terms of environmental impacts, Starlink faces serious criticism. Scientific findings indicate that aluminum oxide emissions from Starlink satellites during their entry into the atmosphere may threaten the ozone layer, suggesting that this system poses long-term risks in light of the climate crisis (Pultarova, 2024). Boley and Byers (2021, p. 4) state that Starlink's five-year renewal cycle will lead to a daily accumulation of about 2 tons of aluminum-based material in the atmosphere, which could significantly exceed the amount of aluminum coming in naturally (meteroids, etc.). This accumulation could increase the Earth's reflectivity, leading to an uncontrolled climate crisis that could result in further damage to the ozone layer.

During rocket launches for the transportation of satellites, harmful particles such as black carbon (BC) and alumina are released into the atmosphere. These substances accumulate in the upper atmosphere (stratosphere) and absorb sunlight, causing both warming of the atmosphere and ozone depletion (Maloney et al., 2022). Recent modeling by Maloney et al. (2022, p. 14) has shown that even just 10 Gg/year of black carbon emissions create a "warming umbrella" in the stratosphere, affecting air circulation systems and increasing ozone loss, especially around the Arctic. Over time, these effects upset the global temperature balance and affect climate systems.

The effects of satellite launches on the atmosphere are not only a technical issue. It also has serious implications for environmental ethics. Although the SpaceX rockets that carry Starlink are designed to be reusable, systems such as the Soyuz rockets used by OneWeb and the Long March rockets used by China are not (Boley & Byers, 2021, p. 4). The second stages of these rockets enter the atmosphere uncontrolled, increasing the environmental burden. These rocket fragments occasionally fall into sensitive ecosystems. For example, Inuit communities in the Arctic have reported that their way of life and food sources are threatened by falling toxic debris (Byers & Byers, 2017; Weber, 2018). In this context, it can be concluded that the impact of Falcon 9 rockets on environmental pollution on the planet as a result of their reusability is relatively less compared to other companies; however, it should not be forgotten that the excessive number of Starlink satellites and launches poses a structural threat to the global climate balance by causing enough damage to the atmosphere and space.

These regions are critical ecosystems not only locally but also globally; North Water Polynya in particular is central to Inuit hunting and fishing activities, thanks to its high biological productivity. Unsymmetrical dimethylhydrazine (UDMH) left over from rocket stages is a carcinogenic and persistent pollutant that, when released into the atmosphere, breaks down into even more toxic compounds such as formaldehyde and nitrosamines, and UDMH is not an immediate pollutant but leaves a long-term toxic legacy (Byers & Byers, 2017, pp. 5-6). This poses an existential threat to Inuit food security and cultural identity. There are also strong arguments that the 'obligation to do no harm' in Article IX of the Outer Space Treaty of 1967 and the 'right to be consulted' (Article 19) of the UN Declaration on the Rights of the Indigenous Peoples have been violated.

These results show that current rocket technologies can lead to long-term global atmospheric changes, not just temporary pollution. Thus, the development of these technologies becomes imperative not only from an environmental ethical point of view, but also in line with the principles of climate justice and intergenerational responsibility. Particularly in the context of SDG 3 (Health and Quality of Life), increased UV exposure due to stratospheric ozone loss threatens human health, while in the context of SDGs 14 and 15, falling rocket fragments disrupt fragile marine and terrestrial ecosystems. Maloney et al. (2022) show that the radiative effects of these particle emissions can lead to atmospheric changes that last not just a few months but years.

Moreover, the increasing number of satellites contributes to space debris and hinders astronomical observations. Starlink is the company with the largest number of satellites in the mega satellite constellations, with 12000 satellites planned to be launched by 2027 (Jing-shi, et.al, 2024, p. 162). It has been reported that approximately 5% of Starlink satellites operating in low Earth orbit have failed, which poses a serious long-term threat to orbital traffic (Open Markets Institute, 2022, p. 4). Additionally, if these companies that provide internet by launching thousands of satellites into the sky plan to create satellite constellations, light pollution will occur, making it impossible for scientists to observe space (Ferreira, 2020).

Indeed, empirical studies reveal the tangible impact of Starlink satellites on astronomical observations. According to an analysis of data from the Zwicky Transient Facility, at the end of 2019, the signatures of the satellites affected only 0.5% of observations, while by August 2021, this had increased to 18%; if the number of Starlink satellites reaches 10,000, all twilight observations are expected to be affected (Mróz et al., 2022, p. 1). Moreover, although new satellite designs with visors have been found to reduce brightness by a factor of 4.6, 67% of these satellites are still above the brightness limit accepted by astronomers (Mróz et al., 2022, p. 11). In large projects such as the Rubin Observatory, it is predicted that most observations will be interrupted by the signatures of these satellites (Lawrence et.al, 2022, p. 10). These data show that Starlink's negative impacts on astronomy are not just a theoretical risk, but a numerically observable problem already.

The right to observe the sky and stars at dusk has been recognized as a cultural, scientific, and environmental common heritage of humanity (Marin, 2011, p. 449). For this reason, these activities of private companies are viewed as a security threat to humanity from outer space, raising concerns about potential disasters caused by obstacles to sky observation. SpaceX has developed some technical adaptations at its own cost in response to the growing criticism: DarkSat, painted black to reduce brightness; VisorSat, equipped with a canopy to reduce reflectivity; and new initiatives such as dielectric film coating, ultra-black paint, and changing the orientation of satellites are examples of these efforts (Koplow, 2024, p. 275). However, these technical adjustments had limited effects, showing that the company's claims of environmental responsibility did not fully correspond to practice when compared to the "greener connection" rhetoric promoted in marketing materials. This is considered a typical example of greenwashing strategies[5].

The use of Starlink in war and crisis zones raises important debates about the neutrality of digital infrastructure. Thanks to Starlink, the people of Ukraine were heard by the world from the first days of the war, which helped mobilize international public opinion. After the Russian invasion of Ukraine in 2022, Starlink terminals sent at the request of the Ukrainian government were used to support civilian and military communications. In this process, the security of the network, the risk of dual use, and operational control mechanisms have been the subject of serious debate. In particular, the active use of Starlink by the Ukrainian military has faced criticism for the risks of integrating a private infrastructure into military operations concerning international law and space security (Yanyun & Huang, 2023).

However, Starlink's military transformation is not limited to the Ukrainian war. Since 2019, test programs conducted in collaboration with the US Air Force and Space Force demonstrate that this transformation is part of a long-term strategy (Peiwen, 2024, pp. 3-4). This transformation is not only technological but also represents a symbolic production of hegemony. Announced in 2022 by SpaceX, the StarShield project is viewed as a militarized version of Starlink. StarShield was developed for military missions such as remote sensing, sensitive communications, and data encryption, and it is integrated with Starlink's civilian infrastructure. This structure clearly demonstrates the 'dual-use' characteristic of digital infrastructures, illustrating how civilian-looking technologies can simultaneously enhance military capabilities. There are serious warnings that Starlink could use user data for commercial purposes and sell it to third parties due to the weak data protection regime in the US (Open Markets Institute, 2022, p. 7).

In particular, the global connectivity provided by Starlink has become critical infrastructure not only for communication but also for military applications such as target detection, imaging, and instant data flow. This system, developed for the US military, is considered by some experts to provide a new control capacity in nuclear deterrence strategies and has the potential to change global strategic balances (Peiwen, 2024, p. 3). In this respect, Starlink exhibits a deeper incompatibility with SDG 16's principles of peace, neutrality, and democratic governance. Moreover, this military capacity has been controversially used not only in interstate conflicts but also in humanitarian crises.

On the other hand, during the humanitarian crisis in Palestine in 2023, it was reported that UN-supported aid teams' attempts to establish communication infrastructure were blocked by Starlink, severely disrupting aid coordination (Al Jazeera, 2023). This example demonstrates that digital infrastructures are moving away from the principle of neutrality and pursuing strategic advantage in humanitarian processes, which is in even deeper conflict with SDG 16. Additionally, Starlink's lack of sustainable partnerships with the UN and humanitarian organizations at the corporate level is incompatible with the goal of multi-stakeholder partnerships highlighted in SDG 17.

On the other hand, Shaengchart and Kraiwanit's (2023) quantitative research in Thailand details the effects of the Starlink satellite project on internet provider services in emerging economies concerning user behavior and demographic variables. In particular, the study finds that male users, individuals with higher levels of education, and heavy users of social media platforms (especially Twitter) are more likely to utilize Starlink. Additionally, the duration of internet use and home internet connection are reported to be among the determinants of this effect. These findings suggest that Starlink is not only a technical solution but also a socially and culturally shaped form of digital infrastructure. However, these effects are not homogeneous; due to intersecting social factors such as gender, education, class and access to digital equipment, the effects of infrastructure are distributed unequally among different groups. Therefore, despite its claim of equality, Starlink can produce new digital divides and inequalities for marginalized groups when evaluated from an intersectionality perspective (Shaengchart & Kraiwanit, 2023, pp. 3-5).

Starlink's engineering model is considered in the literature as a positive innovation compared to conventional satellite designs. Jing-shi et al. (2024, pp. 162-164) emphasize that unlike traditional Walker-based[6] approaches, Starlink's multi-shell, synchronized and ground track configuration provides flexibility and feasibility in terms of both global coverage and in-orbit coordination. From this perspective, Starlink is an example of a successful design that can provide dense coverage and an orderly architecture for satellite links while staying within regulatory constraints. However, this positive technical assessment focuses only on the engineering aspects of the system, leaving out issues such as environmental sustainability, astronomical impacts and global justice. Thus, while it is acknowledged that Starlink presents a technically innovative model, the risk that this success masks the sustainability and equity issues it raises at the global level should not be ignored.

It is evident that Elon Musk constructs technology as an ideological tool, transforming digital access into political influence through symbolic actions such as the Tesla Roadster he sent into space and projects like Starlink. Thus, Starlink presents a multidimensional bundle of contradictions that do not align with the sustainability discourse; it conflicts with several fundamental principles of the SDGs, both through its individual leadership figure and its institutional practices.

OneWeb

In 2020, the UK government poured $500 million into OneWeb to prevent its bankruptcy, acquiring about 18% ownership. The principal stakeholder is India's Bharti Global, which holds a 30% share. Eutelsat's largest investor is France's state-owned investment bank, Bpifrance, owning 20% (ESPI Brief no. 60, 2022). However, after the merger in 2023, the company was restructured under the name "Eutelsat Group". This investment serves not only as a financial opportunity but also aligns with the UK's space strategy to create an alternative to global navigation systems and uphold national security (Goulding, 2020).

In July 2024, the first flight of ESA's Ariane 6 took place, a critical step towards restoring Europe's independent reach. This development shows that companies like OneWeb should not rely solely on outsourced launch systems (Orbital Today, 2024). After OneWeb's crisis with Russian Soyuz rockets (36 satellites were stranded at Baikonur in 2022) and the need to turn to SpaceX and India's LVM3 system (Roulette, 2023), the strategic importance of Ariane 6 for Europe has increased. While Ariane 6 offers the capacity to reduce the dependence of OneWeb-like networks on third countries in the future, for now OneWeb continues to rely on SpaceX and LVM3. This is directly related to SDG 9's goal of infrastructure development and SDG 17's principles of regional resilience and equitable partnership, but as dependency persists, multi-stakeholder cooperation and technology sovereignty cannot be fully achieved.

OneWeb's approach to its relationship with local providers, which focuses solely on the use of infrastructure while avoiding direct access to the end user, can be seen as a model that risks commercial dominance rather than supports local capacity building (Froehlich, 2019, p. 71). This partnership model is being realized not only at the level of government-to-government relations but also between the private sector and local connectivity providers. For example, in 2024, Eutelsat OneWeb signed an agreement with South Africa-based Paratus to integrate the company's GEO/LEO satellite capacity into Paratus' 20,000-kilometer fiber infrastructure to provide high-bandwidth internet services to businesses in remote areas (Eutelsat Group, 2024). This approach contradicts the principles of local capacity building and equitable infrastructure distribution envisioned by SDG 9, as it reinforces an externally dependent network model instead of technology transfer and local engineering capacity.

Infrastructure projects, particularly in former colonial regions such as Africa and South Asia, are executed without sufficient consultation with local communities, raising concerns about digital colonialism. For example, in the regulatory processes undertaken in Nigeria, OneWeb's non-transparent attitude towards 'landing rights' practices and limited feedback to public consultation documents indicate that a healthy balance with local authorities has not been established (Froehlich, 2019, p. 73). Critics argue that OneWeb, while providing access to these regions with investments from partners such as India, prioritizes the interests of the company and its shareholders over the local needs of these infrastructures. The impact of geopolitical tensions on digital infrastructure investments is evident in the India-

Pakistan case (Biswas, 2025). This contradicts SDG 16's principles of transparency and accountability, which severely limit the participation of local authorities and communities in decision-making processes.

In this context, OneWeb's special agreements with African Union countries have increased the company's authority over regional data flows. The exclusion of local operators from projects in Nigeria, Ghana, and Kenya has been criticized for fostering a one-sided development of digital infrastructure and the externalization of data management. Moreover, Eutelsat OneWeb's satellite earth stations in South Africa and Mauritius, along with planned additional earth stations in Ghana and Angola, demonstrate that the company is constructing a polycentric network structure where it can directly control the flow of data (Eutelsat Group, 2024). This situation reinforces criticisms that data sovereignty may shift from local governments to transnational corporations and is considered a reflection of digital colonialism at the infrastructure level. This directly contradicts SDG 9's digital sovereignty and SDG 17's inclusive partnership goals, as data control is delegated to a transnational actor while local capacity and oversight mechanisms are excluded. Froehlich (2019, p. 71) argues that OneWeb initiatives in Africa do not adequately address structural challenges such as the lack of basic infrastructure (e.g., electricity, transportation), which can create long-term incompatibilities. This directly contradicts the content of SDG 9, which emphasizes not only physical infrastructure but also digital sovereignty and local capacity building.

OneWeb's public-private partnership structure directly challenges the principle of fair and accountable partnership as defined in SDG 17. The lack of consultation processes with local stakeholders in the company's infrastructure projects creates serious weaknesses in the production of social consent, indicating that decision-making processes are far from participatory. For example, in these projects, technical experts are often consulted, but the everyday needs and recommendations of local communities are not included in decision-making processes. These deficiencies correspond to symbolic forms of participation that occupy the lowest levels of Arnstein's ‘ladder of citizen participation’[7] model (Arnstein, 1969). In countries such as Nigeria and Bangladesh, international media and NGOs have criticized the local governments' lack of involvement and their reliance on technical opinions (ICTWorks, 2024).

In addition to these shortcomings in strategic restructuring, OneWeb's commercial priorities also tend to deviate from the principle of public interest. The Analysys Mason (2024) report reveals that OneWeb has made high bandwidth connectivity services for the aviation sector via satellites in low earth orbit a strategic priority. This demonstrates that the company prioritizes sectors with high revenue potential rather than the goal of social digital inclusion. However, SDG 9 and SDG 17 call for a fair and inclusive distribution of technological infrastructure. This is in direct contradiction with SDG 16's goal of inclusive decision-making and SDG 17's concept of transparent partnership.

In addition to these strategic restructuring shortcomings, OneWeb's commercial priorities also tend to deviate from the public interest principle. The Analysys Mason (2024) report reveals that OneWeb has made high bandwidth connectivity services for the aviation sector via satellites in low earth orbit a strategic priority. This shows that the company is prioritizing sectors with high revenue potential rather than the societal digital inclusion goal. This orientation is therefore in conflict with SDG 9's equitable infrastructure distribution and SDG 17's public interest-based partnership principles.

The integration of Eutelsat's 36 GEO satellites and OneWeb's 648 LEO satellites aims to meet the growing demand for connectivity in areas such as air and maritime transportation, fixed data, and government services. This combination, along with the development of 5G and cloud technologies, seeks to deliver low latency and high bandwidth services (ESPI Brief no. 60, 2022). Technically, the software-induced 48-hour service outage in 2024 (SatNews, 2025a) illustrates how fragile digital infrastructure can be during times of crisis. The inadequacy of OneWeb's crisis communication and emergency response during this outage undermined the infrastructure's reliability. Additionally, leaving failed satellites in orbit creates the risk of collisions, which increases the danger of space debris (Rainbow, 2021), directly contradicting the responsible production-consumption goals of SDG 12 and the climate action goals of SDG 13. For example, the first stages of the Soyuz rockets used by OneWeb were not reusable and the re-entry of the second stages could not be controlled. This increased the environmental burden and led to unpredictable impacts of rocket parts on sensitive ecosystems (Boley & Byers, 2021, p. 4). Therefore, this example shows how critical it is to require environmental impact assessments for space technologies not only under SDG 13 (Climate Action) but also under SDG 12 (Responsible Production and Consumption), which envisages resource efficiency in the production and use cycle.

UNICEF, particularly through initiatives like Project Connect, aims to digitally map schools worldwide that lack internet access and provide connectivity to these areas. Driven by the rhetoric of 'internet for every child', these efforts seek to reduce the digital divide and eliminate inequalities in education. However, achieving this goal requires not only well-intentioned policies but also strong and sustainable technical infrastructures. While companies like OneWeb seem to support these goals rhetorically, concrete progress remains limited as infrastructure is still inadequate in many regions. UNICEF's Project Connect map visualizing its vision for digital inclusion clearly shows that a significant proportion of schools globally are still offline (Project Connect, 2024). This picture is directly linked to the equitable cooperation goals of SDG 4 (Quality Education), SDG 10 (Reducing Inequalities) and SDG 17 (Partnerships for the Goals), and illustrates the gap between OneWeb's promises and the reality on the ground.

OneWeb's 'children's right to the internet' discourse can be considered a strategic form of discourse used to cover up practices that contradict the principles of environmental sustainability and social equality. The example of Rwanda illustrates how this discourse works in practice. OneWeb's partnership with the Rwandan government aims to equip schools in rural areas with satellite internet connections (Martin, 2020, pp. 66-67). However, the fact that such initiatives are not sustained in practice, and that internet service in many regions cannot be maintained due to systemic infrastructure deficiencies, indicates that these discourses serve the purpose of producing more symbolic policies. This picture is directly linked to SDG 4 (Quality Education) and SDG 10 (Reducing Inequalities), because while equal opportunities in education are emphasized in discourse, in practice inequalities are reproduced. Moreover, this contradicts SDG 17's concept of functional and sustainable partnership, where the gap between corporate rhetoric and practice can be explained by "greenwashing" tactics.

All these elements make OneWeb's rhetoric, such as 'every child's right to access the internet', questionable and demonstrate that it produces contradictions rather than contributions to the SDG targets regarding infrastructure inequalities, governance issues, and environmental impacts. Although Eutelsat Group's expansion plan in Africa is based on the rhetoric of 'inclusive development', the fact that ownership of infrastructure and control over data flow remains entirely with Eutelsat OneWeb (Eutelsat Group, 2024) is in direct contradiction with SDG 9's goal of building local capacity and SDG 16's principle of transparency. Moreover, the company's lack of a clear policy on data ownership paves the way for local data to be controlled by external actors, which contradicts SDG 16's accountability goal.

The environmental issues discussed in the Starlink case are similarly applicable to OneWeb. Since both projects operate with thousands of satellites in low Earth orbit, space debris, chemical residues from satellites entering the atmosphere and obstacles to astronomical observations are common risk areas. OneWeb's smaller-scale constellation structure does not eliminate these impacts; on the contrary, the acceleration of new launches in a globally competitive environment leads to an exponential increase in the environmental burden. Thus, OneWeb, like Starlink, generates environmental costs that conflict with SDG 12 (Responsible Production and Consumption), SDG 13 (Climate Action) and SDG 15 (Life on Land).

Amazon Kuiper

The Kuiper project, developed by Amazon under the leadership of Jeff Bezos, is not only an 'accessible internet' but also a strategic initiative that further deepens

Amazon's global data infrastructure. Amazon's cloud computing platform AWS (Amazon Web Services) already serves the Pentagon, the CIA, and 17 other US intelligence agencies on an exclusive basis, increasing the company's influence on government-sponsored digital infrastructures. In particular, AWS established a private cloud infrastructure for the US intelligence community under a $600 million contract signed with the CIA in 2013 (Konkel, 2014). In this context, Kuiper can be considered not only as an internet infrastructure but also as a new phase that carries this existing surveillance system into orbit. The increased capacity for instant decision-making on the battlefield, thanks to the combination of satellite data with artificial intelligence algorithms, shows that these technologies constitute a prototype for future military operations. This represents a new form of surveillance capitalism, as conceptualized by Zuboff (2019), expanding into space, directly contradicting the transparency and accountability goals of SDG 16 (Peace, Justice and Strong Institutions).

Kuiper's effort to build a satellite-based data stream by moving Amazon's existing data infrastructure into orbit can be seen as part of a strategy of global digital dominance that goes beyond the discourse of digital access. The integration of satellite systems with artificial intelligence algorithms increases not only civilian communication but also military targeting and surveillance capacity. The direct integration of this technological infrastructure through contracts between AWS and the US Department of Defense and intelligence agencies reveals that Kuiper is part of not only commercial but also strategic and military communication networks. The direct integration of data traffic through Kuiper with security agencies represents a new phase of surveillance capitalism expanding into space. Therefore, the integration of Kuiper data traffic with security agencies constitutes an example that excludes democratic oversight and contradicts peace-based governance in the context of SDG 16.

Kuiper's deployment strategies are also hindered by technical and operational limitations. According to Amazon's official statements, Project Kuiper aims to bridge the digital divide in South America and collaborates with local organizations. This initiative, announced by the company with the rhetoric of 'global broadband access', promises to improve internet access, especially in rural and low-income areas (Amazon Website, 2024). However, independent industry sources report that there have been serious delays in Kuiper's planned satellite launches and that Amazon is struggling to fulfill its obligations to the project on time (O'Grady, 2024). The delayed launch schedule raises questions about the credibility of Amazon's commitments, particularly in regions seeking time-sensitive solutions to address digital inequality. Thus, a disconnect appears to exist between Amazon's promotional rhetoric and the on-the-ground realities. This clearly contradicts the goals of SDG 9 (Industry,

Innovation and Infrastructure) on reliable and sustainable infrastructure and SDG 17 (Partnerships for the Goals) on inclusive cooperation.

Amazon's Kuiper project has only launched a small fraction of the planned 3,236 LEO satellites and has not yet achieved the basic network infrastructure needed to launch the service. By the end of 2023, only two prototype satellites had been sent into space, suggesting that a limited beta version of the service would be available by the end of 2025 (Christiansen, 2025). The service launch, originally announced for the end of 2024, was postponed due to disruptions in both the production and launch processes. Furthermore, according to FCC regulations, Amazon is required to put at least half of its 3,236 satellites into orbit by 2026, but only two prototypes have been launched as of March 2025 (SatNews, 2025). This demonstrates a lack of both technical capacity and regulatory harmonization, directly contradicting SDG 9's goal of reliable infrastructure and SDG 12's (Responsible Production and Consumption) principles of resource efficiency.

Furthermore, Project Kuiper argues that governments should be encouraged to develop regulatory measures or best practices to ensure that satellites above a certain altitude are maneuverable (Rainbow, 2023). This approach could provide a technical and political solution to growing concerns about space debris and collision risks, while also contributing to the principles of transparent and responsible governance under SDG 16 (Peace, Justice and Strong Institutions).

The carbon footprint of LEO satellite megastars could be 31 to 91 times higher than that of terrestrial mobile broadband infrastructures used in rural and remote areas. In the analysis, emissions of 3.02 tons CO_2 equivalent per subscriber for Kuiper, 1.70 tons for OneWeb, and 1.04 tons CO_2 equivalent for Starlink were calculated in the worst-case scenario (Osoro et al., 2023, p. 1). In addition to carbon emissions, the rocket fuels used in launch processes produce toxic compounds, posing additional risks to environmental sustainability. This picture contradicts not only SDG 13 (Climate Action), but also the ecosystem conservation targets of SDG 15 (Life on Land). Amazon has prioritized discourses such as 'global access' and 'connectivity across the planet' in its public marketing strategies, pushing these environmental impacts to the background. This can be considered a typical example of a corporate greenwashing strategy as defined by Bowen (2014). The company's campaigns with phrases such as 'infrastructure for future generations' render environmental damages invisible and create the perception of green development.

As a result, the Kuiper project is not only a technical attempt at digital inclusion but also creates a space of structural contradiction that instrumentalizes the discourse of sustainability as a component of data capitalism, governance weaknesses, and environmental neglect. In this context, Amazon owner Jeff Bezos' approach, which turns the space industry into a prestige project, is also open to criticism. Tourist flights for celebrities and billionaire entrepreneurs through the Bezos-owned Blue

Origin company (Chao-Fong and Ambrose, 2025) represent both the commercialization of space technology and the birth of a space tourism industry that deepens social inequalities. This clearly contradicts the principles of SDG 10 (Reducing Inequalities) and SDG 13 (Climate Action). The Kuiper project should therefore be seen within a framework where space is instrumentalized not only for digital inclusion but also for global visibility, brand prestige and capital accumulation. The implicit synchronization between Kuiper and Blue Origin projects can be read as part of Amazon's strategy to expand its presence in space not only through digital infrastructure but also on an ideological plane through popular culture and media.

However, the environmental and scientific concerns raised by Amazon Kuiper are not limited to technical or commercial uncertainties. As in the case of Starlink, Kuiper sends thousands of satellites into low Earth orbit, increasing the risk of space debris and creating light pollution that hinders astronomical observations (Mroz et al., 2022). This contradicts scientific and cultural approaches that consider the sky as a shared heritage of humanity, and poses an indirect threat to goals such as climate action (SDG 13) and quality education (SDG 4). It is clear that the large-scale satelliteization of Kuiper has the potential to replicate the problems seen in Starlink, especially given the functions of astronomy that generate global benefits such as monitoring climate change and asteroid impact risks. In this context, Kuiper's rhetoric to render invisible the environmental impacts and pressures on astronomical observation makes the coherence of the sustainability discourse even more questionable.

The three major satellite projects analyzed in this chapter refer to sustainability in their rhetoric, but in practice, they structurally and systematically contradict the SDGs. Starlink, OneWeb, and Kuiper demonstrate the instrumentalization of the discourse of sustainable development and its reproduction of global inequalities in dimensions such as data sovereignty, environmental neglect, lack of transparency in governance, and political manipulation.

A comparison of these three examples illustrates that sustainability discourse is utilized in various ways across each project. Starlink, driven by Elon Musk's personal brand power and political engagements, transforms digital access into a geopolitical tool, while OneWeb replicates postcolonial relations through its public-private partnership model and overlooks governance transparency. Amazon Kuiper, conversely, reinforces data capitalism with space infrastructure, expanding surveillance mechanisms and embodying a more technical yet profound aspect of digital colonization.

All three examples are in direct conflict with SDG 9 (infrastructure, industry, innovation), SDG 13 (climate action), SDG 16 (peace, justice and strong institutions) and SDG 17 (partnerships for the goals). In addition, the discourse on digital inclusion in the context of SDG 4 (quality education) and SDG 10 (reducing inequalities) creates new gaps rather than ensuring equality in education and access. SDG 12 (responsible production and consumption) is being violated with failed satellites left in orbit and uncontrolled decline of rocket stages. SDG 15 (terrestrial life) is ignored due to the impact of toxic fuels and rocket parts on ecosystems. Thus, mega-satellite constellations should be considered not only as technical projects, but also as instruments of economic, environmental and ideological hegemony.

THEORETICAL DISCUSSION AND CRITICAL EVALUATION

The sustainability discourses surrounding mega-satellite constellations not only express technical innovations and digital inclusiveness but also facilitate the establishment of a new ideological hegemony on a global scale. In this context, the Marxist approaches discussed in the study's theoretical framework play a critical role in making these hegemonic relations visible. While Marx's concept of commodity fetishism aids in understanding how these companies idealize digital technologies and present the process of capital accumulation as a natural and inevitable advancement, Harvey's concept of spatial fixation illustrates how these technologies are reorganized globally to create new markets and absorb surplus capital. For instance, although Starlink's access services are framed as a technical solution, the fact that this service is available only to certain groups highlights the digital form of commodity fetishism. The commodification of the service transforms communication, a public right, into a subject of private property.

In this regard, Althusser's concept of ideological apparatuses is also significant. Shaped through the ideological apparatuses of the state and the private sector, these projects are not only infrastructural investments but also a means of producing meaning. Education, media, corporate discourses, and international institutions present these technological initiatives as a natural part of sustainable development, which facilitates the reproduction of consent at the discursive level. For example, OneWeb's collaboration with UNICEF is a concrete manifestation of this ideological production. Discourses such as 'children's right to the internet' become strategic tools to soften criticism by rendering the company's infrastructure deficiencies invisible.

Within the framework of Gramsci's hegemony theory, the sustainability claims of Starlink, OneWeb, and Kuiper can be viewed as part of the production of social consent. Phrases such as 'internet for all', 'digital inclusion', or 'digital equality' serve as ideological tools employed to secure social acceptance of technological projects. For the Kuiper project, phrases such as 'infrastructure for future generations' and 'global access' promote a dominant narrative that increases social acceptance while downplaying the shortcomings of the technical infrastructure and environmental impacts. However, this production of consent often overlooks fundamental principles such as governance, environmental justice, and economic independence. At this point, the technical 'dual-use' nature of these projects is also important. These systems, which carry both civilian and military functions at the same time, further strengthen hegemonic strategies. This is because companies use the ambiguity of the dual-use and dual-purpose distinction[8] to render the military potential invisible, so that the public perceives these projects as innocent civilian infrastructures (Ortega, 2023). This shows that technical uncertainties play a functional role in the production of social consent as much as discursive strategies.

The concept of primitive accumulation is particularly striking in this context. The space environmentalism approach developed by Lawrence et al. (2022) is important. The authors argue that space should be considered not only as a technical domain but also as an ecosystem, just like the oceans or the atmosphere. This perspective puts forward the argument that space is a finite environment with a "carrying capacity" and emphasizes that the overuse of orbits can cause irreversible damage. Thus, the dynamics of capitalist accumulation positioning space as an unlimited resource space directly contradicts the perspective of environmental sustainability.

The process of transferring natural resources and public assets to private ownership, as described by Marx, is today reappearing in the commercialization of space. Commercial priorities in the regulation of space orbits, spectrum bands, and even the sky are examples of the allocation of public commons to private corporate interests. At this point, Starlink's early allocation rights through the FCC, OneWeb's station plans in Africa, and Kuiper's penetration of regulatory processes despite its delayed fulfillment of its FCC obligations reflect digital versions of this primitive accumulation process. This process is deepening not only at the economic but also at the legal level. In particular, the dual-use character of constellations, that is, their potential to serve both civilian and military purposes, facilitates the use of public spaces by private interests (Ortega, 2023) and reinforces the logic of primitive accumulation by making the military dimension of this use invisible.

This context became more visible during the war in Ukraine. Starlink terminals were initially sent to Ukraine to provide internet to civilians, but soon turned into a critical infrastructure for military communication and operational coordination. Thus, the commodification of the public sphere through primitive accumulation acquired a military function through the ambiguity of dual-use, clearly revealing how capital and security interests are intertwined behind the civil discourse.

In this context, the critical discourse analysis method employed in this study has been effective in revealing the discursive construction of these projects and the contradictions between discourse and action. Inspired by Fairclough's (2010) approach, discourse is understood not only as a linguistic structure but also as a form of action that reconstructs social relations. This method enabled us to uncover the discursive strategies through which companies construct their sustainability claims, how these discourses operate ideologically, and what structural contradictions they align with in practice. For example, Starlink's claim of 'green connectivity' is directly contradicted by the chemical waste generated by satellites entering the atmosphere; Kuiper's 'future of the planet' discourse is directly contradicted by its high carbon footprint; and OneWeb's UNICEF partnerships are directly contradicted by connectivity inefficiencies.

These discursive and structural contradictions are particularly evident in SDG 9 (industry, innovation and infrastructure), SDG 13 (climate action), SDG 16 (peace, justice and strong institutions), and SDG 17 (partnerships for the goals). Starlink's regulatory bypasses, OneWeb's lack of consultation mechanisms, and Kuiper's data sovereignty strategies all run counter to the SDGs' vision of inclusive, equitable, and sustainable development. Organizations such as the International Telecommunication Union (ITU) and the United Nations are key actors in coordinating these mega-projects. However, their regulatory powers are very limited in relation to private companies. The ITU's orbit allocation processes lack transparency, leaving developing countries out of the race. This contradicts the principle of equitable partnership envisioned by SDG 17.

Moreover, the environmental impacts of these projects extend beyond just the carbon footprint. Factors such as space debris, atmospheric chemical residues, and interference with astronomical observations directly pressure scientific sustainability. However, astronomy is not only the science of observing the sky, but also a common heritage deeply connected to social life. Throughout history, it has directly contributed to society with functions such as measuring time, tracking the seasons, navigation and understanding natural disasters; today, it has become a critical field of knowledge in solving global problems such as climate change and meteorite threats (Audouze, 2009). The interruption of astronomical observations by mega-satellite constellations threatens the sustainability of this public knowledge, causing not only scientific but also cultural and social loss.

In particular, Kuiper generates 31 to 91 times more carbon emissions than rural mobile broadband infrastructure, threatening environmental sustainability significantly. In line with Fuchs' critique of digital capitalism, these projects often aim to monopolize data and expand surveillance systems, thereby creating new relations of dependency instead of promoting social equality.

Finally, within the concept of technology fetishism, projects are evaluated not only as technological advancements but also as symbolic displays of power. Elon Musk's sending the Tesla Roadster into space is linked not just to technical prowess but also to the creation of personal brand iconography. Similarly, Blue Origin's activities synchronized with Kuiper demonstrate that technological progress is transformed into a public relations tool. Actions such as Jeff Bezos' Blue Origin carrying celebrities into orbit serve as demonstrations that possess cultural and ideological meanings beyond mere technological capacity. These demonstrations reveal that the capitalist system utilizes technology not only instrumentally but also as a means of aesthetic and political representation.

However, it should be noted that hegemonic discourses are not unidirectional and absolute. Schmidt and Ditrych (2022) emphasize that epistemic communities in space can form an alternative line of resistance to these corporate-centered hegemonic discourses by developing cosmopolitan norms and values. According to them, scientists, international organizations and civil society networks play a critical role in norm-making processes that question the sustainability claims of mega-satellite constellations and reassert the idea of humanity's common heritage. This perspective complements the structural critiques offered by Marxist political economy and makes it possible to analyze not only hegemonic domination but also counter-hegemonic norm construction.

In conclusion, mega-satellite constellations are legitimized through the sustainability discourse. However, when this legitimacy is questioned through theoretical analysis, it reveals contradictions such as ideological domination, environmental destruction, and a governance crisis. This confirms that the sustainability discourse operates not only as a technical rhetoric of development but also as a tool of economic and ideological hegemony. In this context, it is evident that these structures require not only technical but also political and economic critique.

CONCLUSION AND POLICY RECOMMENDATIONS

This study demonstrates that the sustainability discourse surrounding mega-satellite constellations like Starlink, OneWeb, and Project Kuiper is not only a narrative of technological advancement but also a means to legitimize economic interests, environmental infractions, and ideological control. While the projects analyzed rhetorically align with the UN SDGs 9, 13, 16, and 17, they reveal significant structural contradictions with these goals in practice.

Rather than addressing digital infrastructure inequalities, these projects establish new data sovereignties and environmental costs while disregarding principles of transparency and local participation in governance. In light of this analysis, it is essential to develop more inclusive, transparent, and socially beneficial policy approaches to counter the ideological instrumentalization of sustainability discourse. First and foremost, a binding international space governance framework should be created to align private sector activities in space with the SDGs under the auspices of the United Nations.

This need is all the more urgent given that no binding space treaty has been concluded since 1979. This framework should consider not only technological standards but also social, environmental, and ethical dimensions. In particular, the impacts of LEO satellites, such as carbon emissions, atmospheric debris, and space junk generation, must undergo standardized and internationally recognized environmental impact assessment processes. Moreover, the inadequacy of existing international legal norms is particularly evident in the "due regard obligation". As demonstrated by Zha and Su (2024), this principle is not sufficient to address the environmental and social risks posed by mega-constellations. Article IX of the OST therefore needs to be redefined to make environmental impact assessment and consultation mechanisms binding.

Nozawa et al. (2023, p. 4) show that the economic costs of space debris can reach trillions of dollars, making regulation not only an ethical and environmental but also an economic imperative. At this point, as Lawrence et al. (2022, pp. 9-10) suggest, binding Environmental Impact Assessment processes should be mandated for all satellite projects. Furthermore, the development of a Space Traffic Footprint, similar to the carbon footprint, to track the use of orbits would make the responsibilities of companies measurable and transparent. Such an approach would enable mega-constellations to be audited not only for technical efficiency but also for ecosystem sustainability.

However, it is important that investments in digital infrastructure are not only based on technical efficiency but also on the consent of local communities, data ownership, and public interest. Therefore, ethical regulations requiring local participation in infrastructure projects should be implemented. Companies' sustainability claims should be verified by independent auditing mechanisms, and legal sanctions should be enforced against greenwashing practices. Furthermore, in order to protect the rights of the astronomical community, the OST's principles of "due regard" and "cooperation" should be redefined in a binding manner, and mandatory consultation mechanisms between companies and scientific institutions should be put in place (Koplow, 2024, p. 289). Finally, an independent international monitoring mechanism should be established to assess the social impact of such technological projects and evaluate them based on digital inclusion, data justice, and environmental responsibility. These recommendations are crucial for transforming the sustainability discourse from a mere corporate communication tool into a vision for transformation that prioritizes social equality and environmental justice.

REFERENCES

Althusser, L. (1971). *Lenin and philosophy and other essays*. Monthly Review Press.

Arnstein, S. R. (1969). A ladder of citizen participation. *Journal of the American Institute of Planners*, *35*(4), 216–224. DOI: 10.1080/01944366908977225

Audouze, J. (2009). Is astronomy useful for societies? *The Role of Astronomy in Society and CultureProceedings IAU Symposium*, No. 260, doi:DOI: 10.1017/S1743921311002559

Biswas, S. (2025, May 15). How India and Pakistan share one of the world's most dangerous borders. *BBC News*. https://www.bbc.com/news/articles/cgmj7l0lne3o

Boley, A. C., & Byers, M. (2021). Satellite mega-constellations create risks in Low Earth Orbit, the atmosphere and on Earth. *Scientific Reports*, *11*, 1–8. PMID: 34017017

Bowen, F. (2014). *After greenwashing: Symbolic corporate environmentalism and society*. Cambridge University Press.

Byers, M., & Byers, C. (2017). Toxic splash: Russian rocket stages dropped in Arctic waters raise health, environmental and legal concerns. *The Polar Record*, •••, 1–12. DOI: 10.1017/S0032247417000547

Chao-Fung, L., & Ambrose, T. (2025, April 14). Katy Perry, Jeff Bezos' fiancee Lauren Sanchez and four others arrive back on Earth after space flight – as it happened. *The Guardian*. https://www.theguardian.com/science/live/2025/apr/14/katy-perry-lauren-sanchez-jeff-bezos-blue-origin-gayle-king-live-updates-news

Christiansen, P. (2025, May 1). When Will Amazon's Project Kuiper Be Available? *HighSpeedInternet.com*. https://www.highspeedinternet.com/resources/when-will-project-kuiper-be-available

Cox, R. W. (1983). Gramsci, hegemony and international relations: An essay in method. *Millennium*, *12*(2), 162–175. DOI: 10.1177/03058298830120020701

Eagleton, T. (2011). *Why Marx was right*. Yale University Press.

European Space Policy Institute (ESPI). (2022). Brief No. 60: Rising opportunities in the Satellite Connectivity market: Eutelsat and OneWeb combination. https://www.espi.or.at/wp-content/uploads/2022/12/ESPI-Brief-NO-60-Eutelsat-OneWeb-Combination__Final.pdf

Eutelsat Group. (2024, January 19). Eutelsat OneWeb supports Paratus South Africa for the launch of its South Africa Connectivity Services. https://docs.publicnow.com/viewDoc?filename=39428%5CEXT%5CD8BA737FD8F4444742369916525392E0E1337AF7_815F141E328A353A744A6BAC18BB93B123812E6C.PDF

Eutelsat OneWeb. (2023). Our Story. *Eutelsat Group Web Site*. https://oneweb.net/about-us/our-story

Evans-Pritchard, A. (2024, May 9). Why a Cold War is breaking out over Milei's lithium 'gold rush'. *The Telegraph.* https://www.telegraph.co.uk/business/2024/05/09/argentina-lithium-triangle-china-milei-trump-card/?ICID=continue_without_subscribing_reg_first

Fairclough, N. (2010). *Critical discourse analysis: The critical study of language* (2nd ed.). Routledge.

Ferreira, B. (2020). Amazon Satellites Add to Astronomers' Worries About the Night Sky, The *New York Times*, https://www.nytimes.com/2020/08/10/science/amazon-project-kuiper.html

Froehlich, A. (2019). *Legal aspects around satellite constellations*. Springer., DOI: 10.1007/978-3-030-06028-2

Fuchs, C. (2022). *Digital capitalism: Media, communication and society* (2nd ed.). Routledge.

Goulding, T. (2020). Untangling the OneWeb web. London Economics: *Space In Focus*, Issue 3, August 2020.

Gramsci, A. (1971). Selections from the prison notebooks. In (Hoare, Q., & Nowell Smith, G., Eds. & Trans.). International Publishers.

Harvey, D. (2003). *The new imperialism*. Oxford University Press.

ICTWorks. (2024). Nigeria: News and Practical Insights on Deploying ICT4D Solutions. *ICTWorks.* https://www.ictworks.org/tag/nigeria/

Ingram, D. (2025, May 11). Elon Musk's regulatory troubles have begun to melt away in Trump's second term. *NBC News.* https://www.nbcnews.com/tech/elon-musk/elon-musks-regulatory-issues-begun-melt-away-trumps-second-term-rcna202848

Jazeera, A. (2023, November 1). Gaza suffers another communications blackout amid Israeli bombardment. *Al Jazeera.* https://www.aljazeera.com/news/2023/11/1/israel-imposes-communication-blackout-on-gaza-second-time-in-five-days

Jing-shi, T., Ying-ying, Q., & Qi, W. (2024). Analysis and Design of Starlink-like Satellite Constellation. *Chinese Astronomy and Astrophysics, 48*(1), 161–189.

Konkel, F. (2014, July 14). The Details About the CIA's Deal With Amazon. *The Atlantic*. https://www.theatlantic.com/technology/archive/2014/07/the-details-about-the-cias-deal-with-amazon/374632/

Koplow, D. A. (2024). Large Constellations of Small Satellites: The Good, the Bad, the Ugly, and the Illegal. *Harvard National Security Journal, 15*(2), 257–292.

Lawrence, A., Rawls, M. L., Jah, M., Boley, A., & Vruno, F. D. (2022). *Case for Space Environmentalism. Astronomy: Faculty Publications*. Smith College., https://scholarworks.smith.edu/ast_facpubs/85

Leins, T. (2024, November 12). Reach for the Stars: How Starlink Conquered Latin America. *TeleGeography WebSite,* https://blog.telegeography.com/reach-for-the-stars-how-starlink-conquered-latin-america

Losch, A., Galli, A., & Schildknecht, T. (2024). History, concepts and challenges of proposing an 18th UN Sustainable Development Goal related to Space. *Space Policy Journal, 68*, 1–4. DOI: 10.1016/j.spacepol.2024.101631

Maloney, C. M., Portmann, R. W., Ross, M. N., & Rosenlof, K. H. (2022). The Climate and Ozone Impacts of Black Carbon Emissions From Global Rocket Launches. *Journal of Geophysical Research, D, Atmospheres, 127*, 1–17. DOI: 10.1029/2021JD036373

Marin, C. (2011). Starlight: A Common Heritage, The Role of Astronomy in Society and Culture. *Proceedings IAU Symposium*, 260: 449-456.

Marx, K. (1976). *Capital: A critique of political economy* (Vol. 1; Fowkes, B., Trans.). Penguin Books. (Original work published 1867)

Mason, A. (2024, July). Inflight connectivity: Exploring the potential of LEO satellites. Retrieved from https://www.analysysmason.com/contentassets/e39ab885a1d8489590e6e5c020e47dc6/analysys_mason_inflight_connectivity_leo_jul2024_nsi042.pdf

Mróz, P., Otarola, A., Prince, T. A., Prince, T. A., Dekany, R., Duev, D. A., Graham, M. J., Groom, S. L., Masci, F. J., & Medford, M. S. (2022). Impact of the SpaceX Starlink Satellites on the Zwicky Transient Facility Survey Observations. *The Astrophysical Journal. Letters, 924*(2), 1–13.

Nozawa, W., Kurita, K., Tamaki, T., & Managi, S. (2023). To What Extent Will Space Debris Impact the Economy? *Space Policy Journal*, *66*, 1–24. DOI: 10.1016/j.spacepol.2023.101580

O'Grady, V. (2024, July 1). Amazon's plans for Project Kuiper satellite launch are delayed. Developing *Telecoms.* https://developingtelecoms.com/telecom-technology/satellite-communications-networks/16936-amazon-s-plans-for-project-kuiper-satellite-launch-are-delayed.html

Ollman, B. (2003). *Dance of the Dialectic: Steps in Marx's Method.* University of Illinois Press.

Open Markets Institute. (2022). The monopolization of the satellite broadband market: How Elon Musk's Starlink is raising prices, reducing innovation, and harming consumers. *Center for Journalism & Liberty.* https://www.journalismliberty.org/publications/policy-brief-monopolization-of-the-satellite-broadband-market

Ortega, A. A. (2023, June 5). Not a Rose by Any Other Name: Dual-Use and Dual-Purpose Space Systems. *Lawfare.* https://www.lawfaremedia.org/article/not-a-rose-by-any-other-name-dual-use-and-dual-purpose-space-systems

Osoro, O. B., Oughton, E. J., Wilson, A. R., & Rao, A. (2023). Sustainability assessment of Low Earth Orbit (LEO) satellite broadband mega-constellations. *Research Square*, DOI:DOI: 10.21203/rs.3.rs-3325730/v1

Peiwen, W. (2024). Starlink Militarization: Challenges and Responses to Space Intelligence and Information Security, Interpret: China. https://interpret.csis.org/translations/starlink-militarization-challenges-and-responses-to-space-intelligence-and-information-security/

Project Connect. (2024). *UNICEF & ITU Giga initiative - live school connectivity map*. https://maps.giga.global/map.

Pultarova, T. (2024, October 17). How much do SpaceX's reentering Starlink satellites pollute Earth's atmosphere? *Space.com News*, https://www.space.com/spacex-starlink-reentry-pollution-damage-earth-atmosphere

Rainbow, J. (2021, November 24). OneWeb mulls debris-removal service for failed satellite. *SpaceNews*. https://spacenews.com/oneweb-mulls-debris-removal-service-for-failed-satellite/

Rainbow, J. (2023, June 15). Project Kuiper urges regulators to focus on satellite maneuverability rules. *SpaceNews.* https://spacenews.com/project-kuiper-urges-regulators-to-focus-on-satellite-maneuverability-rules/

Roulette, J. (2023, March 15). OneWeb 'moves on' from Soyuz-stranded satellites as its network nears completion. *Reuters.* https://www.reuters.com/lifestyle/science/oneweb-moves-on-soyuz-stranded-satellites-its-network-nears-completion-2023-03-15/

SatNews. (2025a, January 6). Eutelsat suffers flak over OneWeb outage. *SatNews.* https://news.satnews.com/2025/01/06/more-about-eutelsat-suffers-flak-over-oneweb-outage/

SatNews. (2025b, March 19). Project Kuiper facing regulatory deadline. *SatNews.* https://news.satnews.com/2025/03/19/project-kuiper-facing-regulatory-deadline/

Today, O. (2024, October 18). Ariane 6 vs Starship: Is There a Competition? https://orbitaltoday.com/2024/10/18/ariane-6-vs-starship-is-there-a-competition/

1967Treaty, O. S. Treaty on Principles Governing the Activities of States in the Exploration and Use of Outer Space, including the Moon and Other Celestial Bodies. https://www.unoosa.org/oosa/en/ourwork/spacelaw/treaties/introouterspacetreaty.html

UN Declaration on the Rights of Indigenous Peoples. (2007). https://www.ohchr.org/en/indigenous-peoples/un-declaration-rights-indigenous-peoples

United Nations. (2015). Transforming our world: The 2030 Agenda for Sustainable Development. https://sdgs.un.org/goals

Weber, B. (2018, April 24). Inuit Group Angered Over Toxic Russian Headed for Baffin Bay. *The Weather Channel.* https://weather.com/en-CA/canada/science/news/2018-04-24-inuit-russian-rocket-canada

Website, A. (2024, June 12). 4 ways Project Kuiper can help bridge the digital divide in South America. https://www.aboutamazon.com/news/innovation-at-amazon/amazon-project-kuiper-in-south-america

Yanyun, D., & Huang, Z. (2023). Starlink Militarization and Its Impact on Global Strategic Stability. Interpret: China. https://interpret.csis.org/translations/starlink-militarization-and-its-impact-on-global-strategic-stability/

Zha, H. & Su, J. (2024). The "due regard" obligation in the deployment and operation of satellite mega-constellations. *Space Policy Journal*, 1-14. https://doi.org/DOI: 10.1016/j.spacepol.2024.101674

Zuboff, S. (2019). *The age of surveillance capitalism: The fight for a human future at the new frontier of power.* PublicAffairs.

KEY TERMS AND DEFINITIONS

Commodity Fetishism (Karl Marx): The abstraction of goods (commodities) from social relations of production presents them as natural and inevitable entities. In this study, it refers to the detachment of technological products from the political context.

Critical Discourse Analysis (CDA): The discourse analysis method developed by Norman Fairclough goes beyond the textual level to examine the relationship between discourse and social structures.

Digital Capitalism (Christian Fuchs): It is a modern form of capitalist order in which digital infrastructures play a central role in capital accumulation processes based on data exploitation.

Digital Colonialism: The economic and governance relations of dependency established by transnational corporations through digital infrastructure, particularly in Global South countries.

Dual-use Technologies: They are technologies that can serve both civilian and military purposes. The use of Starlink in war zones is explored in this context.

Greenwashing: Companies mask their environmental obligations by claiming to be eco-friendly. Initiatives like Starlink and Kuiper have faced backlash for employing these tactics.

Hegemony (Antonio Gramsci): The ruling class generates social consent by portraying its own interests as universal. Discourses such as "internet for all" exemplify this mechanism.

Ideological Devices (Louis Althusser): In addition to direct repression, the state binds individuals to the social order through media, education, and technology. Corporate discourses are regarded as part of these apparatuses.

Mega-Satellite Constellations (LEO Mega-Constellations): They consist of thousands of small satellites working together in Low Earth Orbit (LEO) to provide high-speed internet access around the world. Starlink, OneWeb, and Kuiper are examples of these systems.

Primitive Accumulation: The genesis of capital accumulation arises from the transfer of common property to private ownership. The commercialization of space today serves as a contemporary example of this process.

SDG (Sustainable Development Goals): It refers to the 17 global goals established by the United Nations as part of the 2030 agenda. In this study, SDGs 9, 13, 16, and 17 are specifically evaluated.

Spatial Fixation (David Harvey): The process of capital expansion into new geographical areas to overcome its crises. In this context, satellite systems transform space into a new field of accumulation.

Sustainability Discourse: It is a linguistic and strategic tool that companies use to legitimize their projects by presenting them as offering environmental, social, and economic benefits. This often results in a contradiction between discourse and action.

ENDNOTES

1 Surveillance capitalism presents a new economic order in which human experiences are converted into free raw materials for data extraction, behavior prediction and commercial sales. In this order, the production of goods and services is subordinated to a global digital architecture designed to direct the individuals' behavior. According to Zuboff, this structure is a 'coup from above' that systematically usurps human rights as a form of power, threatening social sovereignty and undermining market democracy (Zuboff, 2019, pp. 8-9).

2 Technological fetishism is an ideological perspective that views technology as a force separate from social and class relations, functioning independently and inevitably changing society. In this understanding, technology becomes a subject rather than a human being; its social effects are either depicted solely positively (technological optimism) or misrepresented as exclusively negative (technological pessimism). Structural relations such as class exploitation, digital labor, algorithmic domination, and data capital are made invisible. In this context, technological fetishism plays a crucial ideological role in legitimizing digital capitalism (Fuchs, 2022, pp. 94-95).

3 According to Fuchs (2022, p. 28), digital capitalism refers to the aspect of capitalist society in which processes such as capital accumulation, decision-making power, and reputation are carried out and organized through digital technologies. Fuchs argues that economic, political, and cultural processes are determined by digital products and structures.

4 Platform capitalism is a dimension of digital capitalism, recognized as a system that advances highly precarious labor. Although digital platforms, such as Uber, were established with the promise of workers becoming their own bosses, the profit that the platform makes from each piece of work workers receive causes them to work longer to survive, creating a new order of exploitation (Fuchs, 2022, p. 58).

5 According to Frances Bowen (2014, p. 17), greenwashing is when companies produce symbolic discourses to appear environmentally conscious, but these discourses are not structurally reflected in corporate practices. This approach

leads companies to neutralize public scrutiny by using environmental discourses as a strategic legitimacy tool.

6 The Walker constellation consists of one or more planes, each containing several satellites placed at different locations. Classical Walker-based systems have been criticized for their lack of flexibility and inability to provide dense coverage and secure coordination (Jing-shi, et.al, 2024, pp. 162-164).

7 The 'ladder of citizen participation' is an eight-step model developed by Sherry R. Arnstein (1969) that categorizes the levels of citizen participation in decision-making processes hierarchically. In this model, participation is presented in a progressive structure, ranging from token levels such as information, consultation, and appeasement to more effective forms of participation like joint decision-making and citizen control. Specifically, situations where local stakeholders are kept only at the informational level are categorized as "tokenism," as defined by Arnstein (Arnstein, 1969, pp. 217-219).

8 Dual-use refers to the ability of a space system to be used for both civilian/commercial and military purposes at the same time, while dual-purpose refers to systems that are ostensibly developed for civilian purposes but, due to their technical characteristics, may also serve military purposes in the future. The blurring of the boundary between these two categories creates serious legal and security issues as to whether space infrastructures are legitimate civilian tools or potential military targets (Ortega, 2023).

Compilation of References

1967Treaty, O. S. Treaty on Principles Governing the Activities of States in the Exploration and Use of Outer Space, including the Moon and Other Celestial Bodies. https://www.unoosa.org/oosa/en/ourwork/spacelaw/treaties/introouterspacetreaty.html

Ababneh, A., Lok, K., Abdeyazdan, H., Opoku, A., & Chen, C. (2025). Gender equality in smart sustainable cities: Literature review. *Frontiers in Sustainable Cities*, *7*, 1535561. DOI: 10.3389/frsc.2025.1535561

Acosta, A. (2013). Extractivism and neoextractivism: Two sides of the same curse. In Lang, M., & Mokrani, D. (Eds.), *Beyond Development: Alternative Visions from Latin America* (pp. 61–86). Rosa Luxemburg Foundation.

Adamkiewicz, J., Kochańska, E., Adamkiewicz, I., & Łukasik, R. M. (2022). Greenwashing and sustainable fashion industry. *Current Opinion in Green and Sustainable Chemistry*, *38*, 100710. DOI: 10.1016/j.cogsc.2022.100710

Adams, C. E., Charles, C., Green, J., & Swan, M. (1985). New Designs in Conservation/Ecology Education. *The American Biology Teacher*, *47*(8), 463–469.

Adams, W. M. (2009). *Green development: Environment and sustainability in a developing world* (3rd ed.). Routledge.

Adanma, U. M., & Ogunbiyi, E. O. (2024). A comparative review of global environmental policies for promoting sustainable development and economic growth. *International Journal of Applied Research in Social Sciences*, *6*(5), 954–977. DOI: 10.51594/ijarss.v6i5.1147Fepbl+1ResearchGate+1

Adkin, L. E. (Ed.). (2016). *First world petro-politics: The political ecology and governance of Alberta*. University of Toronto Press.

Advertising Standards Authority. (2023a, December 6). *ASA ruling on Deutsche Lufthansa AG (A23-1206007).* https://www.asa.org.uk/rulings/deutsche-lufthansa-ag-a23-1206007-deutsche-lufthansa-ag.html

Advertising Standards Authority. (2023b, December 6). *ASA ruling on Air France-KLM (A23-1206006).* https://www.asa.org.uk/rulings/air-france-klm-a23-1206006-air-france-klm.html

Advertising Standards Authority. (2023c, December 6). *ASA ruling on Etihad Airways (A23-1206008).* https://www.asa.org.uk/rulings/etihad-airways-a23-1206008-etihad-airways.html

African Union. (2022). *African Continental Free Trade Area: Agreement establishing the AfCFTA.* African Union Commission.

Agarwal, A., & Narain, S. (1991). Global Warming. In *An Unequal World: A Case Of Environmental Colonialism.* Centre For Science And Environment.

Aggarwal, P., & Kadyan, A. (2014). Greenwashing: The darker side of CSR. *Indian Journal of Applied Research, 4*(3), 61–66. DOI: 10.15373/2249555X/MAR2014/20

Aggestam, K., Leonardsson, H., & Persson, A. (2019). Environmental peacebuilding: The genesis, evolution and future of a field. *Environmental Politics, 28*(1), 1–19.

Agrawal, A. (1995). Dismantling the divide between indigenous and scientific knowledge. *Development and Change, 26*(3), 413–439. DOI: 10.1111/j.1467-7660.1995.tb00560.x

Agyeman, J., Schlosberg, D., Craven, L., & Matthews, C. (2016). Trends and directions in environmental justice: From inequity to everyday life, community, and just sustainabilities. *Annual Review of Environment and Resources, 41*, 321–340. DOI: 10.1146/annurev-environ-110615-090052

AIIB President says BRI promising. (2019). https://www.globaltimes.cn/page/201905/1149376.shtml

Akman, B., & Kozok, F. (2022, October 14). Erdogan welcomes Putin's idea to make Turkey a gas hub. *Bloomberg.* https://www.bloomberg.com/news/articles/2022-10-14/erdogan-welcomes-putin-s-idea-to-make-turkey-a-natural-gas-hub

Aktan, İ. (2022, April 2). Nihan Temiz Ataş: Türkiye çöp sömürgesi haline geliyor [Nihan Temiz Ataş: Turkey becomes a waste colony]. *ArtıGerçek.* https://artigercek.com/yazarlar/irfan-aktan/nihan-temiz-atas-turkiye-cop-somurgesi-haline-geliyor

Alaimo, S., & Hekman, S. (Eds.). (2008). *Material feminisms.* Indiana University Press.

Alcidi, C., Corti, F., Gros, D., & Liscai, A. (2022). Towards a Socially Just Green Transition: The Role of Welfare States and Public Finances. In Cerniglia, F., & Saraceno, F. (Eds.), *Greening Europe: 2022 European Public Investment Outlook.* Open Books.

Alkış, M. (2022). How oil resources affect the foreign relations of the Kurdistan Regional Government (KRG). *Energy Research & Social Science, 91*, 102758. DOI: 10.1016/j.exis.2022.101146

Allen, F. (2015). The State of the Climate Justice Movement in South Africa. *Capitalism, Nature, Socialism, 26*(2), 46–57.

Althusser, L. (1971). *Lenin and philosophy and other essays.* Monthly Review Press.

Amin, S. (1976). *Unequal Development: An Essay On the Social Formations of Peripheral Capitalism.* Monthly Review Press.

Amnesty International. (2016). *When land is lost, where do we go? Coal mining and human rights in India.* Amnesty International Publications. https://www.amnesty.org/en/documents/asa20/4391/2016/en/

Amnesty International. (2016, January 19). *Democratic Republic of Congo: "This is what we die for": Human rights abuses in the Democratic Republic of the Congo power the global trade in cobalt.* https://www.amnesty.org/en/documents/afr62/3183/2016/en/

Anadolu Agency. (2025, August 29). *Recognition of Palestine could unlock Gaza Marine gas resources: Experts.* https://www.aa.com.tr/en/energy/energy-diplomacy/recognition-of-palestine-could-unlock-gaza-marine-gas-resources-experts/51424

Arnstein, S. R. (1969). A ladder of citizen participation. *Journal of the American Institute of Planners, 35*(4), 216–224. DOI: 10.1080/01944366908977225

Ashok, D., Paul, J. M., & Menon, V. B. (2023). China's Consensus Hegemony Approach and its Engagement with South Asia. *Deleted Journal, 2*(1), 1–14. DOI: 10.53989/jcp.v2i1_5_menon

Askouri. (2005). The Merowe Dam: Controversy and displacement in Sudan. *Forced Migration Review.*

Audet, R. (2013). Climate Justice And Bargaining Coalitions: A Discourse Analysis. *International Environmental Agreement: Politics, Law and Economics, 13*, 369–386.

Audouze, J. (2009). Is astronomy useful for societies? *The Role of Astronomy in Society and CultureProceedings IAU Symposium*, No. 260, doi:DOI: 10.1017/S1743921311002559

Auty, R. M. (1993). *Sustaining development in mineral economies: The resource curse thesis*. Routledge. https://doi.org/DOI: 10.4324/9780203422595

Ayers, A. J. (2008). *Gramsci, political economy, and international relations theory: Modern princes and naked emperors*. Palgrave Macmillan.

Aykut, S. C., Pavenstädt, C. N., Datchoua-Tirvaudey, A., D'Amico, E., Braun, M., Hinks, E. K., . . . Rödder, S. (2022b). *Circles of global climate governance* (CSSR Working Paper No. 2). University of Hamburg, Center for Sustainable Science Research. https://www.cen.uni-hamburg.de/en/cen-forschung/working-papers/working-paper-2.pdf

Aykut, S. C., & Dahan, A. (2022). Geopolitical boomerang: Can we still hope to meet the climate challenge? *GREEN*, *2*(1), 31–38. DOI: 10.1016/j.green.2022.100031

Aykut, S. C., & Maertens, L. (2022). The climatization of global politics: Introduction to the special issue. In Aykut, S. C., Morena, E., & Foyer, J. (Eds.), *The climatization of global politics* (pp. 1–18). Springer., DOI: 10.1007/978-3-030-88551-9_1

Babones, S. (2015). What is world-systems analysis? Distinguishing theory from perspective. *Thesis Eleven*, 127(1), 3–20. https://doi.org/DOI: 10.1177/0725513615575324

Bacchi, C. (2009). *Analysing Policy: What's the problem represented to be?* Pearson Education.

Bachram, H. (2004). Climate fraud and carbon colonialism: The new trade in greenhouse gases. *Capitalism, Nature, Socialism*, *15*(4), 5–20.

Bäckstrand, K., & Lövbrand, E. (2006). Planting trees to mitigate climate change: Contested discourses of ecological modernization, green governmentality and civic environmentalism. *Global Environmental Politics*, *6*(1), 50–75.

Bainton, N., & Holcombe, S. (2018). A critical review of the social aspects of mine closure. *Resources Policy*, *59*, 468–478.

Baka, J. (2017). Making space for energy: Wasteland development, enclosures, and energy dispossessions. *Antipode*, *49*(4), 977–996.

Bakker, K. (2010). *Privatizing water: Governance failure and the world's urban water crisis*. Cornell University Press. http://www.jstor.org/stable/10.7591/j.ctt7z9jv

Balint, J.. (2023). Shedding light on vulnerability: Intersectional energy planning for development. *SSRN*. https://papers.ssrn.com/sol3/Delivery.cfm/SSRN_ID4845844_code5044974.pdf

Bantekas, I., & Akestoridi, K. (2022). Sustainable development goals, between politics and soft law: The emergence of "political normativity" in international law. *Emory International Law Review*, *37*, 499. https://scholarlycommons.law.emory.edu/eilr/vol37/iss4/1

Barad, K. (2006). *Meeting the Universe Halfway: Quantum Physics and the Entanglement of Matter and Meaning*. Duke University Press.

Barandiarán, J. (2019). Lithium and development imaginaries in Chile, Argentina and Bolivia. *World Development*, *113*, 381–391. DOI: 10.1016/j.worlddev.2018.09.019

Barlow, N., Hepp, C., Herbert, J., Rilović, A., Saey-Volckrick, J., Smessaert, J., & von Andrian, N. (2020). A degrowth perspective on the coronavirus crisis. *Visions for Sustainability*, 14. https://doi.org/DOI: 10.13135/2384-8677/5280

Bärnthaler, R. (2023). Towards eco-social politics: A case study of transformative strategies to overcome forms-of-life crises. *Environmental Politics*. Advance online publication. DOI: 10.1080/09644016.2023.2180910

Barrett, S. (2013). *Environment and statecraft: The strategy of environmental treaty-making*. Oxford University Press.

Basak, O. (2024, September 5). *Green colonialism in the energy transition*. Illuminem. https://illuminem.com/illuminemvoices/about-the-green-colonialism-in-the-energy-transition

Bassey, N. (2012). *To cook a continent: Destructive extraction and the climate crisis in Africa*. Pambazuka Press.

Baumgartinger, P. (2021). Transitioning Gender Equality to the Equality of Sex-gender Diversity. In Binswanger, C., & Zimmermann, A. (Eds.), *Transitioning to Gender Equality* (pp. 85–94). MPDI., DOI: 10.3390/books978-3-03897-867-1-7

Baum, L. M. (2012). It's not easy being green. Or is it? A content analysis of environmental claims in magazine advertisements from the United States and United Kingdom. *Environmental Communication*, *6*(4), 423–440. DOI: 10.1080/17524032.2012.724022

Baviskar, A. (1995). *In the belly of the river: Tribal conflicts over development in the Narmada Valley*. Oxford University Press., http://archive.org/details/inbellyofrivertr00bavi

Baviskar, A. (2003). Tribal politics and discourses of environmentalism. *Contributions to Indian Sociology*, *37*(3), 419–444. DOI: 10.1177/006996670303700302

Bayer, L., & Tamma, P. (2020, July 9). EU countries scrap for cash from new green scheme. *Politico*. https://www.politico.eu/article/eu-countries-scrap-for-just-transition-cash/

Beck, U., Giddens, A., & Lash, S. (1994). *Reflexive Modernization: Politics, Tradition and Aesthetics in the Modern Social Order*. Stanford University Press.

Bee, J. (2025 forthcoming). Klimarassismus, Umweltgewalt und Extraktivismus – Medienklimagerechtigkeit aus rassismuskritischer Perspektive. In Alkin, Ö., Amirpur, D., Ha, K. N., & Mustafa, I. (Eds.), *Rassismus. Ein transdisziplinäres Kompendium*. Springer.

Bell, K. (2016). Green Economy or Living Well? Assessing divergent paradigms for equitable eco-social transition in South Korea and Bolivia. *Journal of Political Ecology*, *23*, 71–92.

Beloskar, V. D., Haldar, A., & Gupta, A. (2024). Gender equality and women's empowerment: A bibliometric review of the literature on SDG 5 through the management lens. *Journal of Business Research*, *172*, 114442. DOI: 10.1016/j.jbusres.2023.114442

Berik, G. (2022). Towards improved measures of gender inequality. Discussion Paper. UN Women. https://www.unwomen.org/en/digital-library/publications/2022/11/discussion-paper-towards-improved-measures-of-gender-inequality

Berkes, F. (2012). *Sacred ecology* (3rd ed.). Routledge.

Bernstein, S. (2001). *The compromise of liberal environmentalism*. Columbia University Press.

Bessai, J. W. (2024). *Art as a public service: The National Film Board of Canada's role in shaping democratic dialogues and societal transformation* (Doctoral dissertation). Trent University, Peterborough, Ontario, Canada.

Bieler, A., & Morton, A. D. (2003). Globalisation, the state and class struggle: A 'Critical Economy' engagement with Open Marxism. *British Journal of Politics and International Relations*, *5*(4), 467–499. DOI: 10.1111/1467-856X.00114

Bieler, A., & Morton, A. D. (2004). A critical theory route to hegemony, world order and historical change: Neo-Gramscian perspectives in international relations. *Capital and Class*, *28*(1), 85–113. DOI: 10.1177/030981680408200106

Biermann, F., & Pattberg, P. (2008). Global environmental governance: Taking stock, moving forward. *Annual Review of Environment and Resources*, *33*, 277–294. DOI: 10.1146/annurev.environ.33.050707.085733

Biglari, S., Beiglary, S., & Arthanari, T. (2022). Achieving sustainable development goals: Fact or fiction? *Journal of Cleaner Production, 332*, 130032. DOI: 10.1016/j.jclepro.2021.130032

Bilgin Aytaç, G., & Sezgin, A. (2024). Gender Equality as a Sustainable Development Goal: Women's Participation in Decision-Making Mechanisms in Türkiye. In Garan, Ö., Karagöz Özenç, F., Mumcu Akan, H. D., & Engin Balın, B. (Eds.), *Pursuing Sustainable Development Goals: The Performance of Türkiye in the Centennial of the Republic* (pp. 221–239). İstanbul University Press.

Biomed Central, P. M. C. (2025). Carbon footprint and energy payback time of a micro wind turbine for distributed power generation. https://www.ncbi.nlm.nih.gov/pmc/articles/PMC12255746/

Biswas, S. (2025, May 15). How India and Pakistan share one of the world's most dangerous borders. *BBC News.* https://www.bbc.com/news/articles/cgmj7l0lne3o

Blättel-Mink, B. (Ed.). (2021). *Nachhaltige Entwicklung in einer Gesellschaft des Umbruchs.* Springer VS.

Bloomberg, N. E. F. (2023). *Energy transition investment trends 2023.* Bloomberg New Energy Finance.

Blühdorn, I. (2009). *Reinventing green politics: Environmentalism and the pursuit of sustainability.* Routledge.

BMZ. Bundeszentrale für wirtschaftliche Zusammenarbeit und Entwicklung (2025). Nachhaltigkeit aus dem Lexikon für Entwicklungspolitik. Online: https://www.bmz.de/de/service/lexikon/nachhaltigkeit-nachhaltige-entwicklung-14700 (12.04.2025).

Bodansky, D. (2016). The Paris climate change agreement: A new hope? *The American Journal of International Law, 110*(2), 288–319. DOI: 10.5305/amerjintelaw.110.2.0288

Böhm, S., Misoczky, M. C., & Moog, S. (2012). Greening capitalism? A Marxist critique of carbon markets. *Organization Studies, 33*(11), 1617–1638. DOI: 10.1177/0170840612463326

Bohnenberger, K. (2020). Money, Vouchers, Public Infrastructures? A Framework for Sustainable Welfare Benefits. *Sustainability, 12*(2), 596. DOI: 10.3390/su12020596

Boiral, O., Brotherton, M. C., Yuriev, A., & Talbot, D. (2022). Through the smokescreen of the Dieselgate disclosure: Neutralizing the impacts of a major sustainability scandal. *Organization & Environment, 35*(2), 175–201. DOI: 10.1177/10860266211043561

Boley, A. C., & Byers, M. (2021). Satellite mega-constellations create risks in Low Earth Orbit, the atmosphere and on Earth. *Scientific Reports*, *11*, 1–8. PMID: 34017017

Bond, P. (2010, January 19). The carbon market ship is sinking fast, *ZNet*. https://ccs.ukzn.ac.za/files/bond%20climate%20justice%20articles%20Sept%2009%20through%20may%2010.pdf

Bond, P. (2012). *Politics of climate justice: Paralysis above, movement below*. University of KwaZulu-Natal Press.

Bond, P. (2012). *Politics Of Climate Justice: Paralysis Above, Movement Below*. University of KwaZulu-Natal Press.

Bond, P. (2016). Uneven development and the crisis of climate capitalism. In Panitch, L., & Albo, G. (Eds.), *Socialist Register 2017: Rethinking Revolution* (pp. 86–108). Monthly Review Press.

Bond, P. (2017). Climate Justice In, By, And for Africa. In Dietz, M., & Garrelts, H. (Eds.), *Routledge Handbook of the Climate Change Movement*. Routledge.

Bonthala, S., Shirota, Y., & Chakraborty, B. (2023). SDGs Gender Equality Analysis in India by using SHAP Interpretation. 2023 1st International Conference on Optimization Techniques for Learning (ICOTL), 1-6. https://doi.org/DOI: 10.1109/ICOTL59758.2023.10435062

Bookchin, M. (1971[1986]). *Post-Scarcity Anarchism*, Oakland: AK Press.

Bookchin, M. (1989). The Meaning of Confederalism, *Green Perspectives* 20. http://dwardmac.pitzer.edu/anarchist_archives/bookchin/gp/perspectives20.html

Borrows, J., & Tully, J. (2018). *Resurgence and reconciliation: Indigenous-settler relations and Earth teachings*. University of Toronto Press.

Boukhars, A., & Roussellier, J. (Eds.). (2014). *Perspectives on Western Sahara: Myths, nationalisms and geopolitics*. Rowman & Littlefield., https://www.bloomsbury.com/us/perspectives-on-western-sahara-9781442226852/

Bourdieu, P. (1991). *Language and symbolic power (J. B. Thompson* (Raymond, G., & Adamson, M. Eds. & Trans.). Harvard University Press.

Bowen, F. (2014). *After greenwashing: Symbolic corporate environmentalism and society*. Cambridge University Press.

Bown, C. P. (2020). *How Trump's trade war hit renewable energy*. Peterson Institute for International Economics. https://www.piie.com

Bown, C. P. (2020). Trump's assault on the global trading system: And why decoupling from China will change everything. *Foreign Affairs*, *99*(5), 120–130.

Boyd, D. R. (2010). *The environmental rights revolution: Constitutions, human rights, and the environment* (Doctoral dissertation, University of British Columbia, Vancouver, Canada).

Braidotti, R. (2013). *The posthuman*. Polity Press.

Brand, B., & Missaoui, R. (2014). Multi-criteria analysis of electricity generation mix scenarios in Tunisia. *Renewable & Sustainable Energy Reviews*, *39*, 251–261. DOI: 10.1016/j.rser.2014.07.069

Brandl, J., & Zielinska, I. (2020). Reviewing the Smart City Vienna Framework Strategy's Potential as an Eco-Social Policy in the Context of Quality of Work and Socio-Ecological Transformation. *Sustainability*, *12*, 859.

Brand, U., & Wissen, M. (2021). *The imperial mode of living: Everyday life and the ecological crisis of capitalism*. Verso.

Bremmer, I. (2010). The end of the free market: Who wins the war between states and corporations? *European View*, *9*(2), 249–252. DOI: 10.1007/s12290-010-0124-y

BRICS Energy Research Cooperation Platform. (2024). *BRICS energy cooperation roadmap 2025–2030*. New Development Bank.

Bridge, G., & Le Billon, P. (2017). *Oil*. Polity Press.

Bridge, G., Özkaynak, B., & Turhan, E. (2018). Energy infrastructure and the fate of the nation: Introduction to special issue. *Energy Research & Social Science*, *46*(1), 1–11. DOI: 10.1016/j.erss.2018.04.029

Brooks, A. L., Wang, S., & Jambeck, J. R. (2018). The Chinese import ban and its impact on global plastic waste trade. *Science Advances*, *4*(6), eaat0131. Advance online publication. DOI: 10.1126/sciadv.aat0131

Brüggemann, M., Elgesem, D., Bienzeisler, N., Gertz, H. D., & Walter, S. (2020). Mutual group polarization in the blogosphere: Tracking the hoax discourse on climate change. *International Journal of Communication*, *14*, 1026–1052.

Brundtland, G. H., & WCED. (1987). Report of the world commission on environment and development: "Our common future." United Nations.

Brus, M. M. (2018). Soft law in public international law: A pragmatic or a principled choice? Comparing the Sustainable Development Goals and the Paris Agreement. *Springer*, 243–266. https://doi.org/DOI: 10.1007/978-3-319-77522-7_13

Bryant, L. (1995). Book reviews: THE ENVIRONMENTAL IMPERATIVE: ECO-SOCIAL CONCERNS FOR AUSTRALIAN AGRICULTURE Frank Vanclay and Geoffrey Lawrence. *Journal of Sociology (Melbourne, Vic.)*, *34*(1), 96–97.

Bryman, A. (2016). *Social Research Methods* (5th ed.). Oxford University Press.

Buch-Hansen, H. & Koch, M. (2019). Degrowth through income and wealth caps? *Ecological Economics*, *160*, 264–271.

Buch-Hansen, H., & Nesterova, I. (2023). Less and more: Conceptualising degrowth transformations. *Ecological Economics*, *205*. Advance online publication. DOI: 10.1016/j.ecolecon.2022.107731

Buci-Glucksmann, C. (1980). *Gramsci and the state*. Lawrence & Wishart.

Bullard, R. D. (1990). Dumping. In *Dixie: Race, Class, And Environmental Quality*. Westview Press.

Bumpus, A. G., & Liverman, D. M. (2008). Accumulation by decarbonization and the governance of carbon offsets. *Economic Geography*, *84*(2), 127–155.

Bunker, S. G., & Ciccantell, P. S. (1999). Economic ascent and the global environment: World-systems theory and the new historical materialism. In Goldfrank, W. L., Goodman, D., & Szasz, A. (Eds.), *Ecology and the world-system* (pp. 107–122). Praeger.

Burchell, J. (2002). *The evolution of green politics*. Earthscan.

Burns, T. J. (2012). What is old and what is new? Considering world-systems in the twenty-first century and beyond. In Babones, S. J., & Chase-Dunn, C. (Eds.), *Routledge handbook of world-systems analysis* (pp. 400–401). Routledge.

Burns, T. J., Kick, E. L., & Davis, B. L. (2006). Deforestation in the world-system. In Jorgenson, A., & Kick, E. (Eds.), *Globalization and the environment* (pp. 37–59). Brill.

Busbarat, P., Camba, A., Pratiwi, F. I., Po, S., Đ , H., Sengkhamkhoutlavong, B., ... & Thuzar, M. (2023). How Has China's Belt and Road Initiative Impacted Southeast Asian Countries?.

Butt, M. J. (2021). The role of international law in shaping the governance for sustainable development goals. *Journal of Law and Political Sciences*, *28*(3), 87–164. DOI: 10.5281/zenodo.4904817

Byers, M., & Byers, C. (2017). Toxic splash: Russian rocket stages dropped in Arctic waters raise health, environmental and legal concerns. *The Polar Record*, •••, 1–12. DOI: 10.1017/S0032247417000547

Çağlayan, S., & Yüzbaşı Tobaz, F. (2024). The waste trade as a tool of colonialism in our age: A sociolegal analysis for Türkiye. In Gündoğdu, S. (Ed.), *Plastic waste trade: A new colonialist means of pollution transfer* (pp. 247–258). Springer Nature., DOI: 10.1007/978-3-031-51358-9_12

Campbell-Culver, M. (2006). *A Passion For Trees: The Legacy Of John Evelyn.* Transworld Publishers.

Campling, L. (2022). The corporation and resource geography. In M. Himley, E. Havice, & G. Valdivia (Eds.), *The Routledge handbook of critical resource geography* (pp. 188–200). Routledge.

Canadian Association of Petroleum Producers. (n.d.). *CAPP stats handbook.*

Canadian Centre for Policy Alternatives. (2023). *Don't wait for the state* [Report]. Author.

Caney, S. (2009). Justice and the distribution of greenhouse gas emissions. *Journal of Global Ethics*, *5*(2), 125–146.

Carmi, D. (2016). Implementing eco-social policies: Barriers and opportunities. A preliminary comparative analysis, UNRISD Working Paper, No. 2016-12, United Nations Research Institute for Social Development (UNRISD), Geneva

Carmody, P. (2019). *The scramble for Africa in the 21st century: A view from the South.* Cambridge University Press.

Carrington, D. (2013, October 16). David Attenborough: Anyone who thinks you can have infinite growth on a finite planet is either a madman or an economist. *The Guardian.* https://www.theguardian.com/environment/2013/oct/16/attenborough-poorer-countries-concerned-environment

Carter, N. (2001). *The Politics of the Environment: Ideas, Activism, Policy.* Cambridge University Press.

Cattaneo, C., & Engel-Di Mauro, S. (2015). Urban Squats as Eco-Social Resistance to and Resilience in the Face of Capitalist Relations. *PArtecipazione e COnflitto, 8*(2), 343–366.

CCICED (China Council for International Cooperation on Environment and Development). (2011). *Development mechanism and policy innovation of China's green economy*. CCICED.

Chagnon, C. W., Durante, F., Gills, B. K., Hagolani-Albov, S. E., Hokkanen, S., Kangasluoma, S. M. J., & Vuola, M. P. S. (2022). From extractivism to global extractivism: The evolution of an organizing concept. *The Journal of Peasant Studies, 49*(4), 760–792. DOI: 10.1080/03066150.2022.2069015

Chancel, L. (2022). *Unsustainable inequalities: Social justice and the environment.* Harvard University Press.

Chang, H. J. (2002). *Kicking away the ladder: Development strategy in historical perspective.* Anthem Press.

Chao-Fung, L., & Ambrose, T. (2025, April 14). Katy Perry, Jeff Bezos' fiancee Lauren Sanchez and four others arrive back on Earth after space flight – as it happened. *The Guardian.* https://www.theguardian.com/science/live/2025/apr/14/katy-perry-lauren-sanchez-jeff-bezos-blue-origin-gayle-king-live-updates-news

Chase-Dunn, C., & Grimes, P. (1995). World-systems analysis. *Annual Review of Sociology, 21*, 387–417.

Chaturvedi, S., Fues, T., & Sidiropoulos, E. (Eds.). (2012). *Development cooperation and emerging powers: New partners or old patterns?* Zed Books.

Chen, Q., et al. (2023). River damming impacts on fish habitat and associated conservation measures. *Reviews of Geophysics*, 61, e2023RG000819.

Chew, S. C. (1997). For nature: Deep greening world-systems analysis for the 21st century. *Journal of World-systems Research, 3*(3), 381–402.

Chimni, B. S. (2004). International institutions today: An imperial global state in the making. *European Journal of International Law, 15*(1), 1–37.

Christiansen, P. (2025, May 1). When Will Amazon's Project Kuiper Be Available? *HighSpeedInternet.com.* https://www.highspeedinternet.com/resources/when-will-project-kuiper-be-available

Chung, F. (2019, September 24). Nearly 30 years before Greta Thunberg, a 12-year-old girl shamed world leaders at the United Nations. *News.com.au.* https://www.news.com.au/technology/environment/climate-change/nearly-30-years-before-greta-thunberg-a-12yearold-girl-shamed-world-leaders-at-the-united-nations/news-story/7ccf24544d7f47e4d6cb0da1ea8a0f51

Ciccantell, P. S. (2022). World-systems theory, nature, and resources. In M. Himley, E. Havice, & G. Valdivia (Eds.), *The Routledge handbook of critical resource geography* (pp. 177–187). Routledge.

Ciplet, D., & Roberts, J. T. (2017). Climate change and the transition to neoliberal environmental governance. *Global Environmental Change, 46*, 148–156. DOI: 10.1016/j.gloenvcha.2017.09.003

Clark, B., Foster, J. B., & Longo, S. B. (2019). Metabolic Rifts and the Ecological Crisis. In Vidal, M., Smith, T., Rotta, T., & Prew, P. (Eds.), *The Oxford Handbook of Karl Marx* (pp. 651–658). Oxford University Press.

Clarke, B. J., Ellis, J., Bullard, R., Chen, D., Epstein, P., Gelobter, M., Pastor, M., Pastor, P., Talberth, J., & Wolf, L. (2006). Equity and the Environment: Rebuilding Green—Rebuilding Black. *Race, Poverty & the Environment*, 13(1), 27–32. http://www.jstor.org/stable/41495681

Clean Energy Canada. (2022). *The state of clean energy in Canada*. Author.

Climate Policy Initiative. (2021). *Global landscape of climate finance 2021*. https://www.climatepolicyinitiative.org/publication/global-landscape-of-climate-finance-2021/

Cole, N. L. (2024, May 18). What is cultural hegemony? *ThoughtCo*, https://www.thoughtco.com/cultural-hegemony-3026121

Collier, D., & Mahon, J. E.Jr. (1993). Conceptual "Stretching" Revisited: Adapting Categories in Comparative Analysis. *The American Political Science Review, 67*(4), 845–855.

Collier, P., Hoeffler, A., & Söderbom, M. (2008). Post-conflict risks. *Journal of Peace Research, 45*(4), 461–478. DOI: 10.1177/0022343308091356

Comyns, B., Meschi, P. X., & Norheim-Hansen, A. (2022). Cut them loose? Firms' response strategies to environmental misconduct by supplying firms. *Organization & Environment, 35*(3), 335–364. DOI: 10.1177/10860266211068878

Connell, A., Holder, A., & Kearney, H. (2020). Equal Measures 2030: A new approach for advocacy and influencing beyond Beijing +25. *Gender and Development, 28*(2), 405–423. DOI: 10.1080/13552074.2020.1750218

Cook, S., Smith, K., & Utting, P. (2012). Green economy or green society? Contestation and policies for a fair transition, UNRISD Occasional Paper: Social Dimensions of Green Economy and Sustainable Development, No. 10, ISBN 978-92-9085-091-5, United Nations Research Institute for Social Development (UNRISD), Geneva

Cook, E. A. (1969). Some Recent Anthropological Research Trends in Melanesia. *Anthropologica, 11*(1), 117–150.

Coole, D. H., & Frost, S. (2010). *New materialisms: Ontology, agency, and politics*. Duke University Press.

Coolsaet, B., Agyeman, J., & Kashwan, P.. (2025). Acknowledging The Historic Presence Of Justice In Climate Research. *Nature Climate Change*, *15*(121).

Coote, A. (2015). People, Planet, Power: Toward a New Social Settlement. *International Journal of Social Quality*, *5*(1), 8–34.

Coskun, H. (2023). Eco-city planning: Concepts and contemporary models. *Global Journal of Ecology*, *8*(2), 110–119. DOI: 10.17352/gje.000090

Cossío, R., Menton, M., Cronkleton, P., & Larson, A. M. (2014). *Community forest management in the Peruvian Amazon: A literature review*. Bogor: Center for International Forestry Research (CIFOR). Retrieved from https://doi.org/DOI: 10.17528/cifor/004426

Cotta, B. (2024). Unpacking the eco-social perspective in European policy, politics, and polity dimensions. *European Political Science*, *23*(1), 1–13.

Cowen, D. (2017, January 25). Infrastructures of Empire and Resistance. *Verso*, https://www.versobooks.com/en-gb/blogs/news/3067-infrastructures-of-empire-and-resistance?srsltid=AfmBOoqZb6Enr5XWoKiOqZHQ4WlvdgdgVoDKMJjHYODNfHX87Mmj1mvt

Cox, F. D., & Sisk, T. D. (2017). *Peacebuilding in Deeply Divided Societies: Toward Social Cohesion?* Springer Nature., DOI: 10.1007/978-3-319-50715-6

Cox, R. W. (1981). Social forces, states and world orders: Beyond international relations theory. *Millennium*, *10*(2), 126–155. DOI: 10.1177/03058298810100020501

Cox, R. W. (1983). Gramsci, hegemony and international relations: An essay in method. *Millennium*, *12*(2), 162–175. DOI: 10.1177/03058298830120020701

Cox, R. W. (1987). *Production, power and world order: Social forces in the making of history*. Columbia University Press.

Craig, M. P. A. (2017). *Ecological Political Economy and the Socio-Ecological Crisis*. Palgrave Macmillan.

Crehan, K. (2016). *Gramsci's common sense: Inequality and its narratives*. Duke University Press.

Crenshaw, K. (1991). Mapping the Margins: Intersectionality, Identity Politics, and Violence against Women of Color. *Stanford Law Review*, *43*(6), 1241–1299. DOI: 10.2307/1229039

Custer, S., Horigoshi, A., & Marshall, K. (2024, March). BRI from the ground up: Leaders from 129 countries evaluate a decade of Beijing's signature initiative. https://docs.aiddata.org/reports/bri-from-the-ground-up/full-report.html

D'Alisa, G., & Kallis, G. (2016). A political ecology of maladaptation: Insights from a Gramscian theory of the state. *Global Environmental Change*, *38*, 230–242. DOI: 10.1016/j.gloenvcha.2016.03.006

D'Ignazio, C., & Klein, L. F. (2020). *Data Feminism*. MIT Press.

Dabis, A. (2014). The South Tyrolean Party System. *Minority Research*, *17*, 33–52.

Dados, N., & Connell, R. (2012). The Global South. *Contexts*, *11*(1), 12–13.

Dalby, S. (2013). Biopolitics and the Anthropocene. *Geoforum*, *48*, 14–19.

Datta, R., Starlight, T., & Mistaken, D. C. (2024). Indigenous elder perspectives on climate change challenges and solutions: Learning reflection from Blackfoot First Nation perspectives, Canada. *AlterNative: An International Journal of Indigenous Peoples*. https://journals.sagepub.com/doi/full/10.1177/11771801241251869

De Boer, D., Nedopil, C., & Danting, F. (2022). Belt and Road must align with Paris Agreement – government guidance. https://dialogue.earth/en/business/belt-and-road-must-align-paris-agreement-government

de Freitas Netto, S. V., Sobral, M. F. F., Ribeiro, A. R. B., & da Luz Soares, G. (2020). Concepts and forms of greenwashing: A systematic review. *Environmental Sciences Europe*, *32*(19). Advance online publication. DOI: 10.1186/s12302-020-0300-3

Dean, H. (2012). *Social Policy*. Polity Press.

Dehm, J. (2016). Carbon colonialism or climate justice? Interrogating the international climate regime from a TWAIL perspective. *Windsor Yearbook of Access to Justice*, *33*(3), 65–95. DOI: 10.22329/wyaj.v33i3.4893

Delina, L. L. (2021). Climate justice and the Global South: Resistance and Alternatives. In Newell, P., & Roberts, J. T. (Eds.), *The Global Handbook of Environmental Politics* (pp. 245–262). Edward Elgar Publishing.

Delmas, M. A., & Burbano, V. C. (2011). The drivers of greenwashing. *California Management Review*, *54*(1), 64–87. DOI: 10.1525/cmr.2011.54.1.64

Demaria, F., Schneider, F., Sekulova, F., & Martinez-Alier, J. (2013). What is degrowth? From an activist slogan to a social movement. *Environmental Values*, *22*(2), 191–215.

Demirel, P., Li, Q. C., Rentocchini, F., & Tamvada, J. P. (2019). Born to be green: New insights into the economics and management of green entrepreneurship. *Small Business Economics*, *52*(4), 759–771. DOI: 10.1007/s11187-017-9933-z

Demiryol, T. (2019). Political Economy of Connectivity: China's Belt and Road initiative. https://doi.org/DOI: 10.5281/zenodo.3267663

Deng, G. (1997). Chinese Maritime Activities and Socioeconomic Development, c. 2100 B.C. – 1900 A.D., Westport: Greenwood Press.

Denizeau, A. 2021. "Mavi Vatan, the 'Blue Homeland': The Origins, Influences and Limits of an Ambitious Doctrine for Turkey." *Études de l'Ifri*, Ifri. https://www.ifri.org/en/studies/mavi-vatan-blue-homeland-origins-influences-and-limits-ambitious-doctrine-turkey

Despret, V., Haraway, D., Harrasser, K., & Solhdju, K. (2011). Stay where the trouble is. *Zeitschrift für Medienwissenschaft*, *3*(1), 92–102.

Dirar, A., el Moghraby, A., Jalal Hashim, M., & Zeitoun, M. (2015). Displacement and resistance induced by the Merowe Dam: The influence of international norms and justice (DEV Reports and Policy Paper Series). School of International Development, University of East Anglia. Retrieved from https://devresearch.uea.ac.uk/wp-content/uploads/2022/04/DEV-RPP-17.pdf

Dobson, A. (2007). *Green political thought* (4th ed.). Routledge.

Dolphijn, R., & van der Tuin, I. (2012). *New materialism: Interviews & cartographies*. Open humanities press.

Dourish, P., & Bell, G. (2011). *Divining a Digital Future: Mess and Mythology in Ubiquitous Computing*. MIT Press.

Doyal, L., & Gough, I. (1984). A theory of human needs. *Critical Social Policy*, *4*(10), 6–38. DOI: 10.1177/026101838400401002

Doyal, L., & Gough, I. (1986). Human Need and Strategies for Social Change. In Ekins, P. (Ed.), *The Living Economy: A New Economics in the Making* (pp. 68–79). Routledge.

Doyal, L., & Gough, I. (1991). *A Theory of Human Need*. Macmillan Press.

Drolet, J. (2016). Introduction. In Drolet, J. (Ed.), *Social Development and Social Work Perspectives on Social Protection* (pp. 1–16). Routledge.

Dryzek, J. S. (2000). *Deliberative democracy and beyond: Liberals, critics, contestations*. Oxford University Press.

Dryzek, J. S. (2013). *The politics of the Earth: Environmental discourses* (3rd ed.). Oxford University Press.

Dukelow, F. (2022). What Role for Activation in Eco-Social Policy? *Social Policy and Society*, *21*(3), 496–507.

Du, M. M. (2016). China's "One Belt, One Road" initiative: Context, focus, institutions, and implications. *The Chinese Journal of Global Governance*, *2*(1), 30–43. DOI: 10.1163/23525207-12340009

Dunlap, A. (2018). Counterinsurgency for wind energy: The Bíi Hioxo Wind Park in Juchitán, Mexico. *The Journal of Peasant Studies*, *45*(3), 630–652.

Duran, S., Hrenyk, J., Sahinyazan, F. G., & Salmon, E. (2024). Re-righting renewable energy research with indigenous communities in Canada. *Journal of Cleaner Production*, *445*, 141264.

Durmaz, G. (2024). *European Green Deal from a Neo-Gramscian perspective: A case of green trasformismo* (Doctoral dissertation, Middle East Technical University). Middle East Technical University Open Access Repository. https://open.metu.edu.tr/handle/11511/109116

Duus-Otterström, G. (2013). The problem of past emissions and intergenerational debts. *Critical Review of International Social and Political Philosophy*, *17*(4), 448–469.

Eagleton, T. (2011). *Why Marx was right.* Yale University Press.

Earth.org. (2022). Nuclear energy carbon emissions lowest among electricity sources, UN reports. https://earth.org/nuclear-energy-carbon-emissions-lowest-among-electricity-sources-un-reports/

Earth.Org. (2023). *The hidden cost of green technologies.* https://earth.org/environmental-impact-green-mining/

Eberle, C., Münstermann, N., & Siebeneck, J. (2019). *Carbon colonialism: A postcolonial assessment of carbon offsetting*. University of Bonn / United Nations University.

Eisenmenger, N., & Giljum, S. (2006). Evidence from societal metabolism studies for ecological unequal trade. In Hornborg, A., & Crumley, C. L. (Eds.), *The world system and the earth system: Global socioenvironmental change and sustainability since the Neolithic* (pp. 289–304). Left Coast Press.

Eisenstein, H. (2009). *Feminism seduced: How global elites use women's labour and ideas to exploit the world.* Routledge.

Electric Power Research Institute. (2020). *Preliminary results: Wind turbine blade recycling: Recover, recycle, reuse*. EPRI.

Elkerbout, M., Egenhofer, C., Núñez Ferrer, J., Catuti, M., Kustova, I., & Rizos, V. (2020). *The European Green Deal after Corona: Implications for EU climate policy* (CEPS Policy Insights 2020-06). CEPS. https://www.ceps.eu/ceps-publications/the-european-green-deal-after-corona/ ESCAP/ADB/UNEP. (2012). *Green growth, resources and resilience: Environmental sustainability in Asia and the Pacific*. United Nations ESCAP & Asian Development Bank.

Ellinas, C. (2022). Energy and geopolitics in the Eastern Mediterranean. Atlantic Council. https://www.atlanticcouncil.org/wp-content/uploads/2022/02/AC_EastMediterranean.pdf?utm_source=chatgpt.com

Ely, J. (1991). Review essay. *Capitalism, Nature, Socialism*, *2*(3), 111–126. DOI: 10.1080/10455759109358464

Ely, J. (1993). Post-Fordist restructuring in Germany: What role for the new social movements? *New Political Science*, *12*(1-2), 145–173. DOI: 10.1080/07393149308429682

ENCATC. (2020). Cultural management and policy in a post-digital world – navigating uncertainty: Proceedings of the 11th Annual ENCATC Education and Research Session (Online, Nov 9–10, 2020). Brussels, Belgium: ENCATC. (ISBN 978-92-990088-2-9)

Energy Charter Secretariat. (2021). *Investment arbitration cases under the Energy Charter Treaty*.

Environment and Climate Change Canada. (2024). *Canada's greenhouse gas emissions projections 2024*. Ottawa, ON: Government of Canada. Retrieved from Environment and Climate Change Canada. (2025, March 21). *Greenhouse gas emissions*.

Erjavec, E., & Turk, J. (1998). Agricultural reform, markets and prices in Slovenia. In Mergos, G. (Ed.), *Agricultural price reform under transition in Bulgaria, Romania, and Slovenia* (pp. 19–35). CIHEAM.

Ershov, D. N. (2023). Legal framework for sustainable development and current global challenges. *Sustainable Social Development*, *1*(1). Advance online publication. DOI: 10.54517/ssd.v1i1.2196

ESCAP/ADB/UNEP. (2021). *Green growth, resources and resilience: Environmental sustainability in Asia and the Pacific*. United Nations ESCAP & Asian Development Bank. https://www.unescap.org/sites/default/files/Full-report.pdf

Escobar, A. (2012). *Encountering development: The making and unmaking of the Third World* (New ed.). Princeton, NJ: Princeton University Press.

Escobar, A. (1995). *Encountering development: The making and unmaking of the Third World.* Princeton University Press.

Escobar, A. (2008). *Territories of difference: Place, movements, life, redes.* Duke University Press., DOI: 10.2307/j.ctv1198wg2

Escobar, A. (2018). *Designs for the pluriverse: Radical interdependence, autonomy, and the making of worlds.* Duke University Press.

Escobar, A. (2018). *Designs for the Pluriverse: Radical Interdependence, Autonomy, and the Making of Worlds.* Duke University Press.

Eslava, L., Fakhri, M., & Nesiah, V. (Eds.). (2017). *Bandung, global history, and international law: Critical pasts and pending futures.* Cambridge University Press.

Esquivel, V., & Sweetman, C. (2016). Gender and the Sustainable Development Goals. *Gender and Development, 24*(1), 1–8. DOI: 10.1080/13552074.2016.1153318

European Commission. (2006). *Green paper: A European strategy for sustainable, competitive and secure energy* (COM(2006) 105 final). Author. https://europa.eu/documents/comm/green_papers/pdf/com2006_105_en.pdf

European Commission. (2010). *Europe 2020: A strategy for smart, sustainable and inclusive growth* (COM(2010) 2020). Author.

European Commission. (2019a). *The European Green Deal* (COM/2019/640 final). Author.

European Commission. (2019b). Press remarks by President von der Leyen on the occasion of the adoption of the European Green Deal Communication. *Press corner.* European Commission. https://ec.europa.eu/commission/presscorner/detail/en/speech_19_6749

European Commission. (2019c). Turning challenge into opportunity on the course to becoming the first climate-neutral continent [Press remarks]. *Press corner.* European Commission. https://ec.europa.eu/commission/presscorner/detail/en/ac_19_6778

European Commission. (2019d). *Industry and the Green Deal.* Author. https://commission.europa.eu/strategy-and-policy/priorities-2019-2024/european-green-deal/industry-and-green-deal_en

European Commission. (2024, May 20). *New regulation on waste shipments enters into force*. https://environment.ec.europa.eu/news/new-regulation-waste-shipments-enters-force-2024-05-20_en

European Commission. (2025). *Just transition funding sources*. Author. https://commission.europa.eu/strategy-and-policy/priorities-2019-2024/european-green-deal/finance-and-green-deal/just-transition-mechanism/just-transition-funding-sources_en

European Commission. (2025a). *Waste shipments*. https://environment.ec.europa.eu/topics/waste-and-recycling/waste-shipments_en

European Commission. (2025b). *Carbon Border Adjustment Mechanism (CBAM): Transitional phase*. https://taxation-customs.ec.europa.eu/carbon-border-adjustment-mechanism_en

European Council. (2025). *EU sanctions against Russia explained*. https://www.consilium.europa.eu/en/policies/sanctions/restrictive-measures-against-russia-over-ukraine/sanctions-against-russia-explained/#sanctions

European Space Policy Institute (ESPI). (2022). Brief No. 60: Rising opportunities in the Satellite Connectivity market: Eutelsat and OneWeb combination. https://www.espi.or.at/wp-content/uploads/2022/12/ESPI-Brief-NO-60-Eutelsat-OneWeb-Combination__Final.pdf

Eurostat. (2025, April 24). *Exports in recyclable raw materials decreased in 2024*. https://ec.europa.eu/eurostat/web/products-eurostat-news/w/ddn-20250424-2

Eutelsat Group. (2024, January 19). Eutelsat OneWeb supports Paratus South Africa for the launch of its South Africa Connectivity Services. https://docs.publicnow.com/viewDoc?filename=39428%5CEXT%5CD8BA737FD8F4444742369916525392E0E1337AF7_815F141E328A353A744A6BAC18BB93B123812E6C.PDF

Eutelsat OneWeb. (2023). Our Story. *Eutelsat Group Web Site*. https://oneweb.net/about-us/our-story

Evans-Pritchard, A. (2024, May 9). Why a Cold War is breaking out over Milei's lithium 'gold rush'. *The Telegraph*. https://www.telegraph.co.uk/business/2024/05/09/argentina-lithium-triangle-china-milei-trump-card/?ICID=continue_without_subscribing_reg_first

Eyer do Valle, C. (2009). Innovative Actions That contributed Toward Protecting the Environment in Brazil. In *Science Without Borders: Transactions of the International Academy of Science H&E, 2007/2008*, 3, 209-2016.

Eyerman, R., & Jamison, A. (1991). *Social Movements: A Cognitive Approach.* The Pennsylvania State University Press.

Fairclough, N. (2010). *Critical discourse analysis: The critical study of language* (2nd ed.). Routledge.

Fairhead, J., Leach, M., & Scoones, I. (2012). Green grabbing: A new appropriation of nature? *The Journal of Peasant Studies*, *39*(2), 237–261.

Falkner, R. (2012). Global environmentalism and the greening of international society. *International Affairs*, *88*(3), 503–522. DOI: 10.1111/j.1468-2346.2012.01085.x

Falkner, R. (2016). The Paris Agreement and the new logic of international climate politics. *International Affairs*, *92*(5), 1107–1125. DOI: 10.1111/1468-2346.12708

Fathi, K. (2022). *Multi-Resilience - Development – Sustainability: Requirements for securing the future of societies in the 21st century*. Springer.

Faul, M. V. (2016). *Multi-Sectoral Partnerships and Power: Background paper prepared for the UNRISD Flagship Report 2016 Policy Innovations for Transformative Change*. UNRISD.

Favarin, S., & Aziani, A. (2020). The global waste trafficking and its correlates. *Journal of Contemporary Criminal Justice*, *36*(3), 351–383.

Favarin, S., Berlusconi, G., Aziani, A., & Corradini, S. (2023). Transnational trafficking networks of end-of-life vehicles and e-waste. *Global Crime*, *24*(3), 215–237.

Feminist Foreign Policy. (2025). Challenging entrenched power structures in the energy sector. https://h2diplo.de/wp-content/uploads/2025/02/Study-Report_Energy-Sector-Feminist-Foreign-Policy__final-1.pdf

Fenice Energy. (2024). Renewable energy in remote India: Case studies. Retrieved August 2025, Retrieved from https://feniceenergy.com/renewable-energy-in-remote-communities-case-study/

Ferguson, J. (1990). The Anti-Politics Machine. Retrieved from_https://www.supersummary.com/the-anti-politics-machine/summary/

Ferguson, J. (2006). *Global shadows: Africa in the neoliberal world order*. Duke University Press., DOI: 10.1215/9780822387640

Ferreira, B. (2020). Amazon Satellites Add to Astronomers' Worries About the Night Sky, The *New York Times*, https://www.nytimes.com/2020/08/10/science/amazon-project-kuiper.html

Fink-Hafner, D., & Knep, M. (2015). Factors affecting green party development: Explaining the decline of green parties in Slovenia. *Romanian Journal of Political Science, 15*(1), 129–158.

Fink-Hafner, D., Knep, M., & Novak, M. (2015). *The Slovenian Greens: From Early Success to Long-Term Failure*. FDV.

Fitzpatrick, T. (2011a). Introduction. In Fitzpatrick, T. (Ed.), *Understanding the Environment and Social Policy* (pp. 1–16). The Policy Press.

Forgacs, D. (Ed.). (1988). *A Gramsci reader*. Lawrence & Wishart.

Foster, J. B. (2012). The Planetary Rift and the New Human Exemptionalism: A Political-Economic Critique of Ecological Modernization Theory. *Organization & Environment, 25*(3), 211–237. https://www.jstor.org/stable/27068852

Foster, J. B., & Magdoff, F. (2011). *What every environmentalist needs to know about capitalism: A citizen's guide to capitalism and the environment*. Monthly Review Press.

Frame, M. L. (2022). Ecological imperialism: A world-systems approach. *American Journal of Economics and Sociology, 81*(3), 503–527.

Frankel, B. (2001). *When the Boat Comes in: Transforming Australia in the Age of Globalisation*. Pluto Press.

Franklin, J., & Williams, A. (2025, February 3). Donald Trump faces backlash from business as tariffs ignite inflation fears. *Financial Times*. https://www.ft.com/content/3cc26cc1-57e7-44d0-8c09-6c5dec30cc75

Fraser, N. (1997). *Justice Interruptus: Critical Reflections on the "Postsocialist" Condition*. Routledge.

Fraser, N. (2009). *Scales of justice: Reimagining political space in a globalizing world*. Columbia University Press.

Fricker, M. (2007). *Epistemic injustice: Power and the ethics of knowing*. Oxford University Press.

Friedlingstein, P., (2023). Global Carbon Budget 2023. *Earth System Science Data, 15*, 5301–5369. DOI: 10.5194/essd-15-5301-2023

Friess, P. (2022). *Internet of Things*. CRC Press.

Froehlich, A. (2019). *Legal aspects around satellite constellations*. Springer., DOI: 10.1007/978-3-030-06028-2

Froggatt, A., & Quiggin, D. (2021). *China, EU and US cooperation on climate and energy*. Chatham House. https://www.chathamhouse.org/sites/default/files/2021-03/2021-03-26-china-eu-uscooperation-froggatt.pdf

Fuchs, C. (2022). *Digital capitalism: Media, communication and society* (2nd ed.). Routledge.

Fu, Q., Gong, Q., Zhao, X. X., & Chang, C. P. (2023). The effects of international sanctions on green innovations. *Technological and Economic Development of Economy*, *29*(1), 141–164. DOI: 10.3846/tede.2022.18034

Gabor, D. (2021). The Wall Street consensus. *Development and Change*, *52*(3), 429–459.

Gadgil, M., & Guha, R. (1992). *This fissured land: An ecological history of India*. Oxford University Press.

Galloro, L., & Guida, M. (2024). The limits of UN Security Council action in imposing economic sanctions under UN Charter and international law: The subtle balance between international security and human rights compliance. *Charles University in Prague Faculty of Law Research Paper No. 2024/III/4*. https://doi.org/ DOI: 10.2139/ssrn.5026499

Gamage, S. (2024). The Illusion of Prosperity: Investigating the Hambantota Port Project. Retrieved from https://www.asisrilanka.lk/post/the-illusion-of-prosperity-investigating-the-hambantota-port-project

Gathii, J. T. (2011). *African regional trade agreements as legal regimes*. Cambridge University Press.

Gathii, J. T. (2011). TWAIL: A brief history of its origins, its decentralized network, and a tentative bibliography. *Trade, Law and Development*, *3*(1), 26–64.

Geiser, K., & Waneck, G. (1983). PCBs and Warren County. *Science for the People*, (July), 13–17.

Germani, A. R., Pergolizzi, A., & Reganati, F. (2015). Illegal trafficking and unsustainable waste management in Italy: Evidence at the regional level. *Journal of Security and Sustainability Issues*, *4*(4), 369–389.

Ghosh, J., & Mazzucato, M. (2022). *Reforming development finance for climate goals*. Project Syndicate. https://www.project-syndicate.org

Ghosh, J. (2015). *The Creation of the Next Imperialism. The Institutional Architecture. Monthly Review: An Independent Socialist Magazine, 67 (3)*. July-August.

Gifford, L., & Sauls, L. A. (2024). Defining Climate Finance Justice: Critical Geographies of Justice Amid Financialized Climate Action. *Geography Compass, 18*(11), e70008.

Gill, S. (1993). Epistemology, ontology and the 'Italian School. In Gill, S. (Ed.), *Gramsci, historical materialism and international relations* (pp. 21–48). Cambridge University Press.

Gill, S. (1995). Globalisation, market civilisation, and disciplinary neoliberalism. *Millennium, 24*(3), 399–423. DOI: 10.1177/03058298950240030801

Global Carbon Project. (2022). Global carbon budget 2022. Retrieved from https://www.globalcarbonproject.org/carbonbudget/22/files/GCP_CarbonBudget_2022.pdf 21.03.2025

Gorodkov, V. (2024). *Securitization of Russian polity: Russia's discursive, legislative and institutional response to international sanctions in 2014–2021.* Carleton University., DOI: 10.22215/etd/2024-16312

Gorz, A. (1993). Political ecology: Expertocracy versus self-limitation. *New Left Review*, •••, 55–55.

Gorz, A. (2012). *Capitalism, Socialism, Ecology*. Verso. (Original work published 1991)

Gotev, G. (2020a, March 17). Czech PM urges EU to ditch Green Deal amid virus. *Euractiv*. https://www.euractiv.com/section/energy-environment/news/czech-pm-urges-eu-to-ditch-green-deal-amid-virus/

Gotev, G. (2020b, March 17). EU should scrap emissions trading scheme, Polish official says. *Euractiv*. https://www.euractiv.com/section/emissions-trading-scheme/news/eu-should-scrap-emissions-trading-scheme-polish-official-says/

Gough, I. (2011). Climate change, double injustice and social policy: A case study of the United Kingdom, UNRISD Occasional Paper: Social Dimensions of Green Economy and Sustainable Development, No. 1, ISBN 978-92-9085-083-0, United Nations Research Institute for Social Development (UNRISD), Geneva

Gough, I. (2013a). Climate change, social policy, and global governance. *Journal of International and Comparative Social Policy*, 29(3), 185-203. ISSN 2169-9763 DOI: DOI: 10.1080/21699763.2013.852128

Gough, I. (2015). Macroeconomics, climate change and 'recomposition' of consumption. *PRIME*, 1-17.

Gough, I. (2021a). Climate change: the key challenge the key challenge A framework for an eco-social A framework for an eco-social contract contract', ETUI – Conference Report.

Gough, I. (2021b). Two scenarios for sustainable welfare: New Ideas for an eco-social contract, *etui*, working paper.

Gough, I. (2012). *New policies are needed to reconcile climate mitigation and social equity in the UK. Debating Environmental Policy*. British Politics and Policy Blog. August.

Gough, I. (2013b). Carbon Mitigation Policies, Distributional Dilemmas and Social Policies. *Journal of Social Policy*, *42*(2), 191–213.

Gough, I. (2013c). The challenge of climate change for social policy. In *Social Policy Association Annual Conference*,8-10 July, 2013, Sheffield, UK.

Gough, I. (2017a). *Heat, Greed and Human Need: Climate Change, Capitalism and Sustainable Wellbeing*. Edward Elgar.

Gough, I. (2017b). Recomposing consumption: Defining necessities for sustainable and equitable well-being. *Phil. Trans. R. Soc. A.*, *37520160379 20160379*. Advance online publication. DOI: 10.1098/rsta.2016.0379

Gough, I. (2022). Two scenarios for sustainable welfare: A framework for an eco-social contract. *Social Policy and Society*, *21*(3), 460–472.

Gough, I., Abdallah, S., Johnson, V., Ryan-Collins, J., & Smith, C. (2012). The distribution of total greenhouse gas emissions by households in the UK, and some implications for social policy. *Centre for Analysis of Social Exclusion. CASE (Philadelphia, Pa.)*, •••, 152.

Gough, I., & Doyal, L. (1986). Human Needs and Socialist Welfare. *PRAXIS International*, *1*, 43–69.

Goulding, T. (2020). Untangling the OneWeb web. London Economics: *Space In Focus*, Issue 3, August 2020.

Government of Canada. (2021). *Canadian Net-Zero Emissions Accountability Act*. Government of Canada.

Gramlich, N. (2021). *Mediengeologisches Sorgen*. Mit Otobong Nkanga gegen Ökolonialität.

Gramsci, A. (1985). *Selections from cultural writings* (D. Forgacs & G. Nowell-Smith, Eds.; W. Boelhower, Trans.). Lawrence & Wishart.

Gramsci, A. (1971). *Selections from the prison notebooks* (Hoare, Q., & Smith, G. N., Eds. & Trans.). International Publishers.

Gramsci, A. (1971). Selections from the prison notebooks. In (Hoare, Q., & Nowell Smith, G., Eds. & Trans.). International Publishers.

Gramsci, A. (1977). *Selections from political writings, 1910–1920 (Q. Hoare* (Matthews, J. Ed. & Trans.). Lawrence & Wishart.

Gramsci, A. (1995). *Further selections from the prison notebooks* (Boothman, D., Ed. & Trans.). Lawrence & Wishart.

Gramsci, A. (1996). *Prison notebooks* (Vol. 2; Buttigieg, J. A., Ed. & Trans.). Columbia University Press.

Gramsci, A., Hoare, Q., & Nowell-Smith, G. (1971). *Selections from the Prison Notebooks of Antonio Gramsci*. International Publishers.

Green Finance & Development Center. (n.d.). Retrieved from https://greenfdc.org/countries-of-the-belt-and-road-initiative-bri/

Greenpeace, U. K. (2024, November 5*). "We can no longer bear this load": UK waste exports to Turkey on the rise again*. https://www.greenpeace.org.uk/news/we-can-no-longer-bear-this-load-uk-waste-exports-to-turkey-on-the-rise-again/

Greenpeace. (2022). *Atık oyunları geri dönüşümsüz hayatlar: Plastik atıkların çevre ve sağlık etkisi* [Waste games, irreversible lives: The environmental and health impacts of plastic waste]. Greenpeace Mediterranean.

Grinin, L., & Korotayev, A. (2022). Introduction: On the forms, patterns and modes of evolutionary development. *History & Mathematics: Historical and Technological Dynamics: Factors, Cycles, and Trends*, 4–24.

Grober, U. (2007). *Deep roots - a conceptual history of 'sustainable development'* (Nachhaltigkeit). (Discussion Papers / Wissenschaftszentrum Berlin für Sozialforschung, 2007-002). Berlin: Wissenschaftszentrum Berlin für Sozialforschung gGmbH. https://nbn-resolving.org/urn:nbn:de:0168-ssoar-110771

Grove, R. H. (1995). *Green imperialism: Colonial expansion, tropical island Edens and the origins of environmentalism, 1600-1860*. Cambridge University Press.

Guardian. (2024, November 26). Backroom deals and betrayal: how Cop29's late $300bn deal left nobody happy. *Guardian*. https://www.theguardian.com/environment/2024/nov/26/how-late-deal-left-a-sense-of-dissatisfaction-and-betrayal-at-cop29-baku

Güdek-Gölçek, Ş. (2022). *Neoliberal ekonomide kadın yoksulluğu: Alternatif bir ölçüm modeli.* Unpublished doctoral thesis. Ege University.

Güdek-Gölçek, Ş. (2025). Beyond economic measures: Exploring social deprivation among women in Türkiye. *Women's Studies International Forum, 109*(March-April), 103053. DOI: 10.1016/j.wsif.2025.103053

Gudynas, E. (2013). Debates on development and its alternatives in Latin America. A brief heterodox guide. In M. Lang & D. Mokrani (Eds.), *Beyond Development: Alternative Visions from Latin America.* Rosa Luxemburg Foundation. https://www.tni.org/files/download/beyonddevelopment_complete.pdf

Gudynas, E. (2010). The new extractivism in South America. *The Brown Journal of World Affairs, 17*(2), 37–54.

Gudynas, E. (2011). Buen vivir: Today's tomorrow. *Development, 54*(4), 441–447.

Gudynas, E. (2011). Buen Vivir: Today's tomorrow. *Development, 54*(4), 441–447.

Gugushvili, D., & Otto, A. (2023). Determinants of Public Support for Eco-Social Policies: A Comparative Theoretical Framework. *Social Policy and Society, 22*(1), 1–15.

Guidance on Promoting Green Belt and Road. (2017). *SCO Environment Information Sharing Platform.* https://english.mee.gov.cn/Resources/Policies/policies/Frameworkp1/201706/t20170628_416864.shtml

Gulley, A. L. (2023). China, the Democratic Republic of the Congo, and artisanal cobalt mining from 2000 through 2020. *Proceedings of the National Academy of Sciences of the United States of America, 120*, e2212037120. PMID: 37339197

Gunn, E. L., Rica, M., Zorrilla-Miras, P., Vay, L., Mayor, B., Pagano, A., Altamirano, M., & Giordano, R. (2021). The natural assurance value of nature-based solutions: A layered institutional analysis of socio ecological systems for long term climate resilient transformation. *Ecological Economics, 186*, 107053.

Gupta, A. (2020). *Indigenous knowledge and environmental sustainability in India.* Routledge.

Hadden, J. (2015). *Networks in contention: The divisive politics of climate change.* Cambridge University Press.

Hagen, A & Kollenbach, G. (2024). *The Political Economy of Stranded Assets: Climate Policies, Investments and the Role of Elections.* Berlin School of Economics Discussion Papers, No. 0033, Berlin School of Economics. DOI: DOI: 10.48462/opus4-5348

Hajer, M. A. (1995). *The politics of environmental discourse: Ecological modernization and the policy process*. Oxford University Press.

Hák, T., Janoušková, S., & Moldan, B. (2016). Sustainable Development Goals: A need for relevant indicators. *Ecological Indicators*, *60*, 565–573. DOI: 10.1016/j.ecolind.2015.08.003

Hall, R., Grajales, J., Jacobs, R., Sauer, S., Galvin, S. S., & Shattuck, A. (2023). Intertwined histories: JPS at 50, La Via Campesina at 30. *The Journal of Peasant Studies*, *50*(2), 447–448.

Hall, S. (1986). Gramsci's relevance for the study of race and ethnicity. *The Journal of Communication Inquiry*, *10*(2), 5–27. DOI: 10.1177/019685998601000202

Hancock, T. (2015). Population health promotion 2.0: An eco-social approach to public health in the Anthropocene, *Canadian. Public Health*, *106*(4), e252–e255.

Han, H., & Ahn, S. W. (2020). Youth mobilization to stop global climate change: Narratives and impact. *Sustainability*, *12*(10), 4127. DOI: 10.3390/su12104127

Haraway, D. (2012a). Species Matters, Humane Advocacy. In M. DeKoven & M. Lundblad (Eds.), *Species Matters* (pp. 17–26). Columbia University Press; JSTOR.

Haraway, D. (2010). When Species Meet: Staying with the Trouble. *Environment and Planning. D, Society & Space*, *28*(1), 53–55.

Haraway, D. (2011). Speculative fabulations for technoculture's generations: Taking care of unexpected country. *Australian Humanities Review*, *50*, 95–118.

Haraway, D. (2012b). *The companion species manifesto: Dogs, people, and significant otherness (6th print)*. Prickly Paradigm Press.

Haraway, D. (2016). *Staying with the trouble: Making kin in the Chthulucene*. Duke University Press.

Harding, S. (1987). *Feminism and Methodology: Social Science Issues*. Indiana University Press.

Harrison, K. (2023). *The challenge of federalism for Canadian climate policy* (Climate Governance Policy Paper). Ottawa, ON: Forum of Federations.

Harrison, K. (2007). The road not taken: Climate change policy in Canada and the United States. *Global Environmental Politics*, *7*(4), 92–117.

Harrison, K. (2012). A tale of two taxes: The fate of environmental tax reform in Canada. *The Review of Policy Research*, *29*(3), 383–407.

Harris, P. (2015). Militarism in environmental disguise: The greenwashing of an overseas military base. *International Political Sociology*, *9*(1), 19–36. DOI: 10.1111/ips.12074

Harvey, R. (2011, September 30). Burma dam: Why Myitsone plan is being halted. *BBC*. https://www.bbc.com/news/world-asia-pacific-15123833

Harvey, D. (2003). *The new imperialism*. Oxford University Press.

Hasanaj, V. (2023). The shift towards an eco-welfare state: Growing stronger together. *Journal of International and Comparative Social Policy*, •••, 1–22. DOI: 10.1017/ics.2023.2

Hayward, T. (1990). Ecosocialism – Utopian and Scientific. *Radical Philosophy*, *56*, 2–14.

Heath, G. A.. (2020). Research and development priorities for silicon photovoltaic module recycling to support a circular economy. *Nature Energy*, *12*(1), 1–10.

Helne, T., & Hirvilammi, T. (2017). The relational conception of wellbeing as a catalyst for the ecosocial transition. In Matthies, A.-L., & Närhi, K. (Eds.), *The Ecosocial Transition of Societies: The contribution of social work and social policy* (pp. 36–53). Routledge.

Hemeida, M. G., Hemeida, A. M., Senjyu, T., & Osheba, D. (2022). Renewable energy resources, technologies and life cycle assessment [Review]. *Energies*, *15*, 9417. DOI: 10.3390/en15249417

Hermwille, L. (2022). The 2021 Glasgow Climate Pact—A fragile victory for multilateralism. *Climate Policy*, *22*(2), 147–152. DOI: 10.1080/14693062.2022.2036952

Heryford, R. (2020). "The Mold-life": Dickinson's Poetics of Decay. *The Emily Dickinson Journal*, *29*(1), 27–47.

Hesketh, C., & Morton, A. D. (2014). Spaces of uneven development and class struggle in Bolivia: Transformation or trasformismo? *Antipode*, *46*(1), 149–169. DOI: 10.1111/anti.12033

Heyl, K., Döring, T., Garske, B., Stubenrauch, J., & Ekardt, F. (2021). The Common Agricultural Policy beyond 2020: A critical review in light of global environmental goals. *Review of European, Comparative & International Environmental Law*, *30*(1), 95–106. DOI: 10.1111/reel.12351

Hickel, J. (2019). Degrowth: A theory of radical abundance. *Real-World Economics Review*, *87*(19), 54–68.

Hickel, J. (2020a). *Less is more: How degrowth will save the world.* Penguin Random House.

Hickel, J. (2020b). What does degrowth mean? A few points of clarification. *Globalizations, 18*(7), 1105–1111. DOI: 10.1080/14747731.2020.1812222

Hickel, J., & Kallis, G. (2020). Is green growth possible? *New Political Economy, 25*(4), 469–486. DOI: 10.1080/13563467.2019.1598964

Hildingsson, R., & Koch, M. (2016). Market solutions to climate change: examples of personal carbon-trading and carbon-rationing. In Koch, M., & Mont, O. (Eds.), *Sustainability and the Political Economy of Welfare* (pp. 109–124). Routledge.

Hilson, G., & Maconachie, R. (2009). "Good governance" and the extractive industries in sub-Saharan Africa. *Mineral Processing and Extractive Metallurgy Review, 30*(1), 52–100.

Hirvilammi, T., Häikiö, L., Johansson, H., Koch, M., & Perkiö, J. (2023). Social Policy in a Climate Emergency Context: Towards an Ecosocial Research Agenda. *Journal of Social Policy, 52*(1), 1–23. DOI: 10.1017/S0047279422000721

Hirvilammi, T., & Koch, M. (2020). Sustainable Welfare beyond Growth. *Sustainability, 12*(5), 1824. DOI: 10.3390/su12051824

Hoekman, B. M., & Kostecki, M. M. (2009). *The political economy of the world trading system* (3rd ed.). Oxford University Press.

Hoffmann, C., & Ergenc, C. (2022). A greening dragon in the desert? China's role in the geopolitical ecology of decarbonisation in the Eastern Mediterranean. *Journal of Balkan & Near Eastern Studies, 24*(5), 1–20. DOI: 10.1080/19448953.2022.2067424

Hofmeister, S. (2002). Intermediate 'Time-spaces': The Rediscovery of Transition in Spatial Planning and Environmental Planning. *Time & Society, 11*(1), 105–130. DOI: 10.1177/0961463X02011001007

Hoppe, K. (2021). *Die Kraft der Revision: Epistemologie, Politik und Ethik bei Donna Haraway*. Campus Verlag.

Hörl, E. (2013). Tausend Ökologien. Der Prozeß der Kybernetisierung und die allgemeine Ökologie. In D. Diederichsen, A. Franke, & Haus der Kulturen der Welt Berlin (Eds.), *The Whole Earth: Kalifornien und das Verschwinden des Außen (Dritte Auflage)*. Sternberg Press.

Hörl, E. (Ed.). (2011). *Die technologische Bedingung: Beiträge zur Beschreibung der technischen Welt* (1. Aufl). Suhrkamp.

Hornborg, A. (2006). Ecosystems and world-systems: Accumulation as an ecological process. In Chase-Dunn, C., & Babones, S. (Eds.), *Global social change: Historical and comparative perspectives* (pp. 161–175). Johns Hopkins University Press.

Howse, R. (2007). WTO dispute settlement and the "green economy". In Sampson, G., & Chambers, W. B. (Eds.), *Trade and environment: A resource book* (pp. 85–97). UNEP/IISD.

Huang, R., Xie, X., & Zhou, H. (2022). 'Isomorphic' behavior of corporate greenwashing. *Zhongguo Renkou Ziyuan Yu Huanjing*, *20*(1), 29–39. DOI: 10.1016/j.cjpre.2022.03.004

Hufbauer, G. C., & Jung, E. (2021, November 11). *Scoring 50 years of US industrial policy, 1970–2020*. Peterson Institute for International Economics. https://www.piie.com/publications/piie-briefings/2021/scoring-50-years-us-industrial-policy-1970-2020

Hujo, K., & Carter, M. (2019). *Transformative Change for Children and Youth in the Context of the 2030 Agenda for Sustainable Development.* UNRISD, Innocenti Working Paper WP-2019-02.

Human Rights Watch. (2003). Sudan, Oil, and Human Rights. https://www.hrw.org/report/2003/11/24/sudan-oil-and-human-rights

Human Rights Watch. (2022). *"It's as if they're poisoning us": The health impacts of plastic recycling in Turkey*. https://www.hrw.org/report/2022/09/21/its-if-theyre-poisoning-us/health-impacts-plastic-recycling-turkey

Hurlbert, M. (2015). Climate Justice: A Call for Leadership. *Environmental Justice*, *8*(2). Advance online publication. DOI: 10.1089/env.2014.0035

ICTWorks. (2024). Nigeria: News and Practical Insights on Deploying ICT4D Solutions. *ICTWorks*. https://www.ictworks.org/tag/nigeria/

IEA. (2023). *World Energy Investment Report 2023*. International Energy Agency. https://www.iea.org

Ikners, N. (2016). Decision Looms on Myitsone Dam. *Institute for Security & Development Policy*. https://www.isdp.eu/decision-looms-myitsone-dam/

ILO (International Labour Organization). (2020). *Green entrepreneurship: Creating green jobs through sustainable enterprise development*. ILO. https://www.ilo.org/wcmsp5/groups/public/---ed_emp/---emp_ent/documents/publication/wcms_250688.pdf

Imanche, S. A., Ze, T., Ayom, M. C., & Dalibi, S. G. (2021). An Assessment of Nigerians Perception towards Chinese Foreign Direct Investments and Its Acceptability in Nigeria. *Open Journal of Business and Management, 09*(03), 1151–1168. DOI: 10.4236/ojbm.2021.93062

Imasiku, K. (2025). The social impact of renewable energy on health systems in Kenya, Ghana, and Rwanda: A case study. *Journal of Sustainable Development, 13*(2). https://www.sdewes.org/jsdewes/pid13.0550

Ingram, D. (2025, May 11). Elon Musk's regulatory troubles have begun to melt away in Trump's second term. *NBC News*. https://www.nbcnews.com/tech/elon-musk/elon-musks-regulatory-issues-begun-melt-away-trumps-second-term-rcna202848

Inhofe, J. (2012). *The greatest hoax: How the global warming conspiracy threatens your future*. WND Books.

Intergovernmental Panel on Climate Change (IPCC). (2022). *Climate change 2022: Impacts, adaptation, and vulnerability*. Cambridge University Press.

International Crisis Group. (2023a). An Island Divided: Next Steps for Troubled Cyprus. Report No 268. https://www.crisisgroup.org/europe-central-asia/western-europemediterranean/cyprus/268-island-divided-next-steps-troubled-cyprus

International Crisis Group. (2023b). *Iraq: Staving off instability in the near and distant futures. Middle East Report No. 227*. https://www.crisisgroup.org/middle-east-north-africa/gulf-and-arabian-peninsula/iraq/iraq-staving-instability-near-and-distant-futures

International Energy Agency. (2021). *The role of critical minerals in clean energy transitions*. IEA.

International Energy Agency. (2021, December 1). *Renewable electricity growth is accelerating faster than ever worldwide, supporting the emergence of the new global energy economy*. https://www.iea.org/news/renewable-electricity-growth-is-accelerating-faster-than-ever-worldwide-supporting-the-emergence-of-the-new-global-energy-economy

International Energy Agency. (2022). *Solar PV global supply chains*. https://www.iea.org/reports/solar-pv-global-supply-chains

International Energy Agency. (2022). *The role of critical minerals in clean energy transitions*. https://www.iea.org/reports/the-role-of-critical-minerals-in-clean-energy-transitions

International Energy Agency. (2023). *Renewables 2023: Analysis and forecasts*. IEA.

International Energy Agency. (2024). *World energy investment 2024.*

International Energy Agency. (2024). *World energy investment 2024.* IEA. https://www.iea.org/reports/world-energy-investment-2024

International Finance Corporation. (2021). *The business case for wind power in Africa.*

International Monetary Fund. (2025). *Resilience and Sustainability Trust.* https://www.imf.org/en/Topics/Resilience-and-Sustainability-Trust

International Renewable Energy Agency (IRENA). (2021). World Energy Transitions Outlook: Transforming global energy system for a sustainable future. https://www.irena.org/publications/2021/March/World-Energy-Transitions-Outlook-2021

International Solar Alliance. (2023). *Annual report 2022–23: Towards 1000.* ISA Secretariat.

İpek, P., & Gür, V. T. (2021). Turkey's Isolation from the Eastern Mediterranean Gas Forum: Ideational mechanisms and material interests in Energy Politics. *Turkish Studies*, *23*(1), 1–30. DOI: 10.1080/14683849.2021.1925884

Isah, H. M., Sawyerr, H. O., Raimi, M. O., Bashir, B. G., Haladu, S., & Odipe, O. E. (2020). Assessment of Commonly Used Pesticides and Frequency of Self-Reported Symptoms on Farmers Health in Kura, Kano State, Nigeria. *Journal of Education and Learning Management*, *1*(1), 31–54.

Jaccard, M. (2020). *The citizen's guide to climate success: Overcoming myths that hinder progress.* Cambridge University Press.

Jackson, J. H. (1997). *The world trading system: Law and policy of international economic relations* (2nd ed.). MIT Press.

Jakobsson, N., Muttarak, R., & Schoyen, M. A. (2018). Dividing the pie in the eco-social state: Exploring the relationship between public support for environmental and welfare policies. *Environment and Planning C. Politics and Space*, *36*(2), 313–339.

Jänicke, M. (2012). "Green growth": From a growing eco-industry to economic sustainability. *Energy Policy*, *48*, 13–21. DOI: 10.1016/j.enpol.2012.04.045

Jarvie, M. E. (2016). Brundtland Report. Retrieved from https://www.britannica.com/topic/Brundtland-Report

Jazeera, A. (2023, November 1). Gaza suffers another communications blackout amid Israeli bombardment. *Al Jazeera.* https://www.aljazeera.com/news/2023/11/1/israel-imposes-communication-blackout-on-gaza-second-time-in-five-days

Jeevanasai, A., Saole, P., Rath, A., Singh, S., Rai, S., & Kumar, M. (2023). Shades & shines of gender equality with respect to sustainable development goals (SDGs): The environmental performance perspectives. *Total Environment Research Themes, 8*. Advance online publication. DOI: 10.1016/j.totert.2023.100082

Jeffery, R. D., Krogh, C., & Horner, B. (2013). Adverse health effects of industrial wind turbines. *Canadian Family Physician Médecin de Famille Canadien, 59*(5), 473–475.

Jessen, H. (2021). Multilateral and unilateral sanctions: Compliance and challenges. *Springer International Publishing*, 570–580. https://doi.org/DOI: 10.1007/978-3-319-95960-3_51

Jessoula, M., & Mandelli, M. (2019). *The Right to Energy for All Europeans Coalition: A Case of Green-Red Mobilization?* Laboratorio di Politica Comparata e filosofia Pubblica, working paper. Torino: LEPF Centro Einaudi.

Jing-shi, T., Ying-ying, Q., & Qi, W. (2024). Analysis and Design of Starlink-like Satellite Constellation. *Chinese Astronomy and Astrophysics, 48*(1), 161–189.

Jones, A. (2022). Laos' Fast Train to China Brings Connection at a Cost, With Big Promises but Uneven Progress. *Rainforest Journalism Fund.* https://rainforestjournalismfund.org/stories/laos-fast-train-china-brings-connection-cost-big-promises-uneven-progress

Jones, P., Miles, D., Francis, A., & Rajeev, S. P. (2011). Preface. In Jones, P., Miles, D., Francis, A., & Rajeev, S. P. (Eds.), *Eco-social Justice: Issues, Challenges and Ways Forward, Voices from De Novo'11*. Books for Change.

Joseph, J. (2012). *Putting governmentality in its place. The Social in the Global: Social Theory, Governmentality and Global Politics*. Cambridge University Press., DOI: 10.1017/CBO9781139149143.003

Kaasch, A., Koch, M., & Martens, K. (2019). Exploring theoretical approaches to global social policy research: Learning from international relations and inter-organisational theory. *Global Social Policy, 19*(1-2), 87–104.

Kannengießer, S. (2022). *Digitale Medien und Nachhaltigkeit: Medienpraktiken für ein gutes Leben*. Springer Fachmedien Wiesbaden.

Kannengießer, S. (2023). From Millennium Development Goals to Sustainable Development Goals: Transforming development communication to sustainability communication. *Studies in Communication Sciences, 23*(1).

Kant, I. (2017). *The metaphysics of morals*. Cambridge University Press.

Kara, S. (2023). *Cobalt red: How the blood of the Congo powers our lives.* St. Martin's Press.

Kashwan, P. (2020). *Democracy in the woods: Environmental conservation and social justice in India, Tanzania, and Mexico*. Oxford University Press.

Kashwan, P. (2022). *Climate Justice in India*. Cambridge University Press.

Kassinis, G., & Panayiotou, A. (2018). Visuality as greenwashing: The case of BP and Deepwater Horizon. *Organization & Environment, 31*(1), 25–47. DOI: 10.1177/1086026616687014

Kaur, A., & Verma, S. S. (2025). Understanding India's Role in International Climate Negotiations from a Social Constructivist Perspective. *India Review*, *24*(1), 36–54.

Kellenberg, D. (2015). The economics of the international trade of waste. *Annual Review of Resource Economics*, *7*, 109–125. DOI: 10.1146/annurev-resource-100913-012639

Keohane, R. O., & Raustiala, K. (2010). Toward a post-Kyoto climate change architecture: A political analysis. In Dryzek, J. S., Norgaard, R. B., & Schlosberg, D. (Eds.), *The Oxford handbook of climate change and society* (pp. 103–122). Oxford University Press.

Khanal, S. (2023). Gender Equality in Sustainable Development Goals: Some Reflections from Nepal. *Journey for Sustainable Development and Peace Journal.*, *1*(02), 147–161. DOI: 10.3126/jsdpj.v1i02.58267

Khan, J., Emilsson, K., & Fritz, M.. (2022). Ecological ceiling and social floor: Public support for eco-social policies in Sweden. *Sustainability Science*. Advance online publication. DOI: 10.1007/s11625-022-01221-z

Khare, P., Raghuwanshi, V., & Sharma, P. (2025). Impact of Israel-Palestine Conflict on Global Economic Relations. *IGI Global Scientific Publishing*, 163-186. https://doi.org/DOI: 10.4018/979-8-3693-8674-3.ch007

Kim, E.-H., & Lyon, T. P. (2014, November 1). *Greenwash vs. brownwash: Exaggeration and undue modesty in corporate sustainability disclosure* (Ross School of Business Paper No. 1266). *SSRN*. https://doi.org/DOI: 10.2139/ssrn.2546497

Kim, J., Fairclough, S., & Dibrell, C. (2017). Attention, action, and greenwash in family-influenced firms: Evidence from polluting industries. *Organization & Environment*, *30*(4), 304–323. DOI: 10.1177/108602661667341

Kim, R. E., & Bosselmann, K. (2015). Operationalizing sustainable development: Ecological integrity as a grundnorm of international law. *Review of European, Comparative & International Environmental Law*, *24*(2), 194–208. DOI: 10.1111/reel.12109

Klein, N. (2014). *This changes everything: Capitalism vs. the Climate*. Simon and Schuster.

Klinger, J. M. (2018). *Rare earth frontiers: From terrestrial subsoils to lunar landscapes*. Cornell University Press.

Knox, P. L. (1981). Convergence and Divergence in Regional Patterns of Infant Mortality in the United Kingdom from 1949-51 to 1970-72. *Social Science & Medicine*, *5*(4), 537–539.

Koch, M. (2019). Elements of a political economy of the postgrowth era, *Real-world economics review*, 87.

Koch, M. (2018). Sustainable welfare, degrowth and eco-social policies in Europe. In Banhercke, B., Ghailani, D., & Sabato, S. (Eds.), *Social policy in the European Union: state of play 2018* (pp. 35–50). ETUI.

Koch, M. (2020). The state in the transformation to a sustainable postgrowth economy. *Environmental Politics*, *29*(1), 115–133. DOI: 10.1080/09644016.2019.1684738

Koch, M. (2022). State of the Art Social Policy Without Growth: Moving Towards Sustainable Welfare States. *Social Policy and Society*, *21*(3), 447–459.

Koch, M., & Buch-Hansen, H. (2020). The IPE of degrowth and sustainable welfare. In Vivares, E. (Ed.), *The Routledge Handbook to Global Political Economy: Conversations and Inquiries* (pp. 375–390). Routledge.

Koch, M., & Fritz, M. (2014). Building the Eco-social State: Do Welfare Regimes Matter?'. *Journal of Social Policy*, *43*(4), 679–703.

Köhler, G. (2018). *Creative Coalitions in a Fractured World An Opportunity for Transformative Change?* Draft paper prepared for the UNRISD Conference Overcoming Inequalities in a Fractured World: Between Elite Power and Social Mobilization 8–9 November 2018, Geneva, Switzerland.

Köhler, G. (2016). Tapping the Sustainable Development Goals for progressive gender equity and equality policy? *Gender and Development*. Advance online publication. DOI: 10.1080/13552074.2016.1142217

Konkel, F. (2014, July 14). The Details About the CIA's Deal With Amazon. *The Atlantic*. https://www.theatlantic.com/technology/archive/2014/07/the-details-about-the-cias-deal-with-amazon/374632/

Koplow, D. A. (2024). Large Constellations of Small Satellites: The Good, the Bad, the Ugly, and the Illegal. *Harvard National Security Journal*, *15*(2), 257–292.

Kouser, S., Subhan, A., & Abedullah, N. (2020). Uncovering Pakistan's Environmental Risks and Remedies under the China-Pakistan Economic Corridor. *Environmental Science and Pollution Research International*, *27*(5), 4661–4663. DOI: 10.1007/s11356-019-07428-5

Krause, D. (2021). Uncovering different degrees of eco-social policy. *Global Social Policy*, *21*(2), 332–334.

Krausman, P., & Mahoney, S. P. (2015). How the Boone and Crockett Club (B&C) shaped North American conservation. *The International Journal of Environmental Studies*, *72*(5), 746–755. DOI: 10.1080/00207233.2015.1073474

Kronberger, A. (2024). Respons-Able Trees. On Permaculture Ethics of Responsibility in the Films of the Exhibition „Cambio" (2020). Ecozon@: European Journal of Literature. *Culture and Environment*, *15*(2), 126–140.

Kuckartz, U., & Rädiker, S. (2019). *Analyzing qualitative data with MAXQDA: Text, audio, and video*. Springer.

Laffitte, T. (2021, November 29). Europe's energy transition: Ukraine's salvation? *Green European Journal*. https://www.greeneuropeanjournal.eu/europes-energy-transition-ukraines-salvation/

Lakeman, S. (2021). IOs and Climate Change: Toward Global Eco-Social Policy. In Martens, K., Niemann, D., & Kaasch, A. (Eds.), *International Organizations in Global Social Governance* (pp. 255–273). Palgrave Macmillan.

Lan, Q., Tang, W., & Hu, Q. (2022). Estimation of China's green investment efficiency in Belt and Road countries based on SBM-Undesirable Model and Malmquist Index Model. *Frontiers in Energy Research*, *9*, 907. DOI: 10.3389/fenrg.2021.778907

Larsen, P. B., & Chanthavisouk, C. (2024). Free, prior, and informed consent, local officials, and changing biodiversity governance in Hin Nam No, Laos. *Conservation biology: the journal of the Society for Conservation Biology*, *38*(6), 110–120. https://doi.org/DOI: 10.1111/cobi.14388

Laruffa, F. (2022). The dilemma of "sustainable welfare" and the problem of the future in capacitating social policy. *Sustainability: Science. Practice and Policy, 18*(1), 822–836. DOI: 10.1080/15487733.2022.2143206

Laruffa, F., McGann, M., & Murphy, M. P. (2022). Enabling Participation Income for an Eco-Social State. *Social Policy and Society, 21*(3), 508–519.

Latour, B. (2004). Why Has Critique Run out of Steam? From Matters of Fact to Matters of Concern. *Critical Inquiry, 30*(2), 225–248.

Latour, B. (2022). *Wir sind nie modern gewesen: Versuch einer symmetrischen Anthropologie* (8th ed.). (Roßler, G., Trans.). Suhrkamp.

Lawrence, A., Rawls, M. L., Jah, M., Boley, A., & Vruno, F. D. (2022). *Case for Space Environmentalism. Astronomy: Faculty Publications.* Smith College., https://scholarworks.smith.edu/ast_facpubs/85

Lazare, S. (2020, September 14). "Colonizing the atmosphere": How rich, Western nations drive the climate crisis. *In These Times.* https://inthesetimes.com/article/climate-change-wealthy-western-nations-global-north-south-fires-west

Le Billon, P. (2007). Natural resources, armed conflicts, and the UN Security Council (Working Paper UNSC07-001). Liu Institute for Global Issues, University of British Columbia. https://sppga.ubc.ca/wp-content/uploads/sites/5/2016/03/30May2007_Natural_Resources_Armed_Conflicts_UNSC07-001.pdf

Le Billon, P. (2001). The political ecology of war: Natural resources and armed conflicts. *Political Geography, 20*(5), 561–584. DOI: 10.1016/S0962-6298(01)00015-4

Le Billon, P. (2005). *Fuelling war: Natural resources and armed conflict.* Routledge., DOI: 10.4324/9781315019529

Le Billon, P., & Nicholls, E. (2007). Ending 'Resource Wars': Revenue Sharing, Economic Sanction or Military Intervention? *International Peacekeeping, 14*(5), 613–632. DOI: 10.1080/13533310701753941

Le Menestrel, M., & Van Wassenhove, L. N. (2009). Ethics outside, companies inside: Lessons from the Enron debacle. *Omega, 37*(1), 1–10.

Leach, M., Mehta, L., & Prabhakaran, P. (2016). Gender equality and sustainable development: A pathways approach. Discussion Paper, UN Women. https://www.unwomen.org/sites/default/files/Headquarters/Attachments/Sections/Library/Publications/2016/DPS-Gender-equality-sustainable-development.pdf

Leal Filho, W., Kovaleva, M., Tsani, S., îrcă, D., Shiel, C., Dinis, M. A. P., Nicolau, M., Sima, M., Fritzen, B., Salvia, A. L., Minhas, A., Kozlova, V., Doni, F., Spiteri, J., Gupta, T., Wakunuma, K., Sharma, M., Barbir, J., Shulla, K., & Tripathi, S. (2023). Promoting gender equality across the sustainable development goals. *Environment, Development and Sustainability*, *25*, 14177–14198. DOI: 10.1007/s10668-022-02656-1 PMID: 36124160

Lefstad, A., & Paavola, J. (2023). Climate justice and global governance: The limits of the UNFCCC framework. *Global Environmental Politics*, *23*(1), 75–97.

Lefstad, L., & Paavola, J. (2023). The Evolution of Climate Justice Claims in Global Climate Change Negotiations under the UNFCCC. *Critical Policy Studies*, *18*(3), 363–388.

Legge, M. (1999). Wild geese and solidarity: Conjunctural praxis for a spirit-filled ethics. *Union Seminary Quarterly Review*, *53*(3/4), 165–185.

Leibowitz, L. (1975). Changing views of women in society, 1975. *Revista de Antropologia*, *2*(4), 532–538. DOI: 10.1080/00988157.1975.9977205

Leins, T. (2024, November 12). Reach for the Stars: How Starlink Conquered Latin America. *TeleGeography WebSite,* https://blog.telegeography.com/reach-for-the-stars-how-starlink-conquered-latin-america

Lenka, P. (2023). Philosophy of Sustainable Development: Understanding the Significance of Gender Equality in Business Organisations. *Problems of Sustainable Development*, *18*(2), 121–127. DOI: 10.35784/preko.3950

Lennerfors, T. T., Fors, P., & van Rooijen, J. (2015). ICT and environmental sustainability in a changing society: The view of ecological world-systems theory. *Information Technology & People*, *28*(4), 758–774. DOI: 10.1108/ITP-09-2014-0219

Leonhardt, R., Noble, B., Poelzer, G., Belcher, K., & Fitzpatrick, P. (2023). Government instruments for community renewable energy in northern and Indigenous communities. *Energy Policy*, *177*, 113560. DOI: 10.1016/j.enpol.2023.113560

Li, M., Trencher, G., & Asuka, J. (2022). The clean energy claims of BP, Chevron, ExxonMobil and Shell: A mismatch between discourse, actions and investments. *PLoS One*, *17*(2), e0263596. DOI: 10.1371/journal.pone.0263596

Lima, R., & Guedes, G. (2024). Sustainable Development Goals and Gender Equality: A Social Design Approach on Gender-Based Violence. *Sustainability*, *16*(2), 914. DOI: 10.3390/su16020914

Lim, S. (2021). The paradox of unsustainability in UN Sustainable Development Goals (SDGs): The North Korean case in the context of accountability and fragile states under sanctions. *Journal of Peace and Unification, 11*(1), 55–78. DOI: 10.31780/jpu.2021.11.1.55

Lin, B. (2025, April 18). Trump's tariffs threaten growth for Southeast Asia's clean energy startups. *Reccessary*. https://www.reccessary.com/en/news/asean-market/tariffs-disrupt-clean-energy-startups-southeast-asia

Li, Y., & Khan, J. (2024). Decoupling with(out) outsourcing? Quantifying emissions embodied in BRI trade with implications for climate policy. *Elementa, 12*(1), 00068. DOI: 10.1525/elementa.2023.00068

Loh, J. (2022). Posthumanism and Ethics. In Herbrechter, S., Callus, I., Rossini, M., Grech, M., de Bruin-Molé, M., & Müller, C. J. (Eds.), *Palgrave handbook of critical posthumanism*. Palgrave Macmillan.

López, D., Callén, B., Tirado, F., & Domènech, M. (2010). How to become a guardian angel Providing safety in a home telecare service. In A. Mol, I. Moser, & J. Pols (Eds.*), Care in Practice* (pp. 73–92). transcript Verlag.

Losch, A., Galli, A., & Schildknecht, T. (2024). History, concepts and challenges of proposing an 18th UN Sustainable Development Goal related to Space. *Space Policy Journal, 68*, 1–4. DOI: 10.1016/j.spacepol.2024.101631

Loss, S. R., Will, T., & Marra, P. P. (2013). *Estimates of bird collision mortality at wind facilities in the contiguous United States*. https://repository.si.edu/xmlui/handle/10088/35192

Lovich, J. E., & Ennen, J. R. (2011). Wildlife conservation and solar energy development in the Desert Southwest, United States. *Bioscience, 61*(12), 982–992.

Lujala, P. (2009). Deadly combat over natural resources: Gems, petroleum, drugs, and the severity of armed civil conflict. *The Journal of Conflict Resolution, 53*(1), 50–71. DOI: 10.1177/0022002708327644

Lyon, T. P., & Montgomery, A. W. (2015). The means and end of greenwash. *Organization & Environment, 28*(2), 223–249. DOI: 10.1177/1086026615575332

Mac Ginty, R. (2010). Hybrid peace: The interaction between top-down and bottom-up peace. *Security Dialogue, 41*(4), 391–412. DOI: 10.1177/0967010610374312

Mac Ginty, R. (2011). *International peacebuilding and local resistance: Hybrid forms of peace*. Palgrave Macmillan., DOI: 10.1057/9780230307032

Mac Ginty, R., & Richmond, O. (2013). The local turn in peace building: A critical agenda for peace. *Third World Quarterly, 34*(5), 763–783. DOI: 10.1080/01436597.2013.800750

Macknick, J. (2011). *Review of operational water consumption and withdrawal factors for electricity generating technologies*. National Renewable Energy Laboratory. https://research-hub.nrel.gov/en/publications/review-of-operational-water-consumption-and-withdrawal-factors-fo

Majid, S. H. (2024). Implications of sanctions on local populations in Africa: A case study of United States of America's sanctions against Sudan. *University of Nairobi*. https://erepository.uonbi.ac.ke/handle/11295/166852

Malm, A. (2016). *Fossil Capital: The Rise of Steam Power and the Roots of Global Warming*. Verso.

Malm, A., & Hornborg, A. (2014). The geology of mankind? A critique of the Anthropocene narrative. *The Anthropocene Review, 1*(1), 62–69.

Maloney, C. M., Portmann, R. W., Ross, M. N., & Rosenlof, K. H. (2022). The Climate and Ozone Impacts of Black Carbon Emissions From Global Rocket Launches. *Journal of Geophysical Research, D, Atmospheres, 127*, 1–17. DOI: 10.1029/2021JD036373

Mandelli, M. (2022b). *Mapping eco-social policy mixes for a just transition in Europe*. ETUI, working paper.

Mandelli, M. (2022a). Understanding eco-social policies: A proposed definition and typology. *Transfer: European Review of Labour and Research, 28*(3), 333–348.

Manning, R. E. (1984). Men and Mountains Meet: Journal of the Appalachian Mountain Club, 1876-1984. *Journal of Forest History, 28*(1), 24–33.

Manzano, I. R. (2021). Gender Equality And Women's Leadership For Sustainable Development. In A. G. Shirin, M. V. Zvyaglova, O. A. Fikhtner, E. Y. Ignateva, & N. A. Shaydorova (Eds.), *Education in a Changing World: Global Challenges and National Priorities,* vol 114. European Proceedings of Social and Behavioural Sciences (pp. 51-58). European Publisher. https://doi.org/DOI: 10.15405/epsbs.2021.07.02.7

Marceau, G. (2001). Conflicts of norms and conflicts of jurisdictions: The relationship between the WTO agreement and MEAs and other treaties. *Journal of World Trade, 35*(6), 1081–1131.

Marden, S., & Gough, I. (2011). Fiscal costs of climate mitigation programmes in the UK: A challenge for social policy? Centre for Analysis of Social Exclusion. *CASE (Philadelphia, Pa.)*, •••, 145.

Mareis, C., & Held, M. (2023). Preface. In L. Perraudin, C. Winkler, C. Mareis, & M. Held (Eds.), *Material Trajectories: Designing With Care*? meson press.

Mariano, S., & Molari, B. (2022). Gender equality from the MDGs to the SDGs: a feminist analysis. Revista de Administração Pública. https://doi.org/DOI: 10.1590/0034-761220220124x

Marin, C. (2011). Starlight: A Common Heritage, The Role of Astronomy in Society and Culture. *Proceedings IAU Symposium*, 260: 449-456.

Marlon, J. R., Howe, P. D., Mildenberger, M., Leiserowitz, A., & Wang, X. (2018). Yale Climate Opinion Maps 2018. *Yale Program on Climate Change Communication*. https://climatecommunication.yale.edu/visualizations-data/ycom-us-2018/

Marston, G. (2019). Basic Income in Australia: Implementation Challenges. In Klein, E., Mays, J., & Dunlop, T. (Eds.), *Implementing a Basic Income in Australia: Pathways Forward*. Palgrave Macmillan.

Martinez-Alier, J. (1991). Ecology and the Poor: A Neglected Dimension of Latin American History. *Journal of Latin American Studies*, *23*(3), 621–639.

Martinez-Alier, J. (1993). Distributional Obstacles to International Environmental Policy: The Failures at Rio and Prospects after Rio. *Environmental Values*, *2*(2), 97–124.

Martinez-Alier, J. (2002). *The environmentalism of the poor: A study of ecological conflicts and valuation*. Edward Elgar.

Martínez-Torres, M. E., & Rosset, P. M. (2010). La Vía Campesina: The birth and evolution of a transnational social movement. *The Journal of Peasant Studies*, *37*(1), 149–175.

Martin, M., & Islar, M. (2020). The "end of the world" vs. the "end of the month": Understanding social resistance to sustainability transition agendas, a lesson from the Yellow Vests in France. *Sustainability Science*, *16*(3), 601–614. DOI: 10.1007/s11625-020-00844-0

Marx, K. (1976). *Capital: A critique of political economy* (Vol. 1; Fowkes, B., Trans.). Penguin Books. (Original work published 1867)

Maskus, K. E. (2012). *Private rights and public problems: The global economics of intellectual property in the 21st century*. Peterson Institute for International Economics.

Maskus, K., & Reichman, J. (2004). The globalization of private knowledge goods and the privatization of global public goods. *Journal of International Economic Law*, *7*(2), 279–320.

Mason, A. (2024, July). Inflight connectivity: Exploring the potential of LEO satellites. Retrieved from https://www.analysysmason.com/contentassets/e39ab885a1d8489590e6e5c020e47dc6/analysys_mason_inflight_connectivity_leo_jul2024_nsi042.pdf

Mathur, V., & Chamuah, A. (2025). Navigating AI and climate change in an unequal world. *Climate Policy*, •••, 1–7.

Matthies, A.-L., Turunen, P., Albers, S., Boeck, T., & Närhi, K. (2000). An eco-social approach to tackling social exclusion in European cities: A new comparative research project in progress. *European Journal of Social Work*, *3*(1), 43–52. DOI: 10.1080/714052811

Mauser, W., Klepper, G., Rice, M., Schmalzbauer, B. S., Hackmann, H., Leemans, R., & Moore, H. (2013). Transdisciplinary global change research: The co-production of knowledge for sustainability. *Current Opinion in Environmental Sustainability*, *5*(3–4), 420–431. DOI: 10.1016/j.cosust.2013.07.001

McDonald, M., & Mitchell, A. (2017). *Posthuman International Relations*. Cambridge University Press.

McGann, M., & Murphy, M. P. (2023). Income Support in an Eco-Social State: The Case for Participation Income. *Social Policy and Society*, *22*(1), 16–30.

McGlade, C., & Ekins, P. (2015). The geographical distribution of fossil fuels that can be used without exceeding a 2 °C limit on global warming. *Nature*, *517*(7533), 187–190. DOI: 10.1038/nature14016 PMID: 25567285

McGregor, D., Whitaker, S., & Sritharan, M. (2020). Indigenous environmental justice and sustainability. *Current Opinion in Environmental Sustainability*, *43*, 35–40. DOI: 10.1016/j.cosust.2020.01.007

McGurty, E. (2009). *Transforming Environmentalism: Warren County, Pcbs, And The Origins Of Environmental Justice*. Rutgers University Press.

McKinsey & Company. (2020). *Carbon-neutral Poland 2050: Turning a challenge into an opportunity.* McKinsey & Company. https://www.mckinsey.com/~/media/McKinsey/Industries/Electric%20Power%20and%20Natural%20Gas/Our%20Insights/Carbon%20neutral%20Poland%202050%20Turning%20a%20challenge%20into%20an%20opportunity/Carbon-neutral-Poland-2050.pdf

McLuhan, M., Fiore, Q., & Agel, J. (1996). *The medium is the massage: An inventory of effects.* HardWired.

McNally, C. A. (2012). Sino-capitalism: China's reemergence and the international political economy. *World Politics, 64*(4), 741–776. DOI: 10.1017/S0043887112000146

Mehra, P., Babita, K., & Gangandeep, B. (2021). The Degrowth Alternative: Need Of The Hour. In Thakur, D. J., Verma, P., & Sharma, D. (Eds.), *Management Practices Amidst COVID-19.* Weser Books.

Mejia Montero, L. F., ... (2023). An intersectional approach to energy justice. *Energy Research & Social Science.* https://www.research.ed.ac.uk/files/331400114/Mejia_MonteroEtalERSS2023AnIntersectionalApproachToEnergyJustice.pdf

Merdeka Center for Opinion Research. (2022). Social Impact and Community Perception of Belt and Road Initiative Projects in Malaysia. Retrieved from https://asiafoundation.org/wp-content/uploads/2024/08/Social-Impact-and-Community-Perception-of-Belt-and-Road-Initiative-Projects-in-Malaysia.pdf

Merz, S., Jaehn, P., Mena, E., Pöge, K., Strasser, S., & Saß, A.-C. Rommel, A., Bolte, G. & Holmberg, C. (2021). Intersectionality and eco-social theory: A review of potentials for public health knowledge and social justice. *Critical Public Health.* Advance online publication. DOI: 10.1080/09581596.2021.1951668

Meyer-Renschhausen, E. (2014). Community gardening in Berlin and New York: A new eco-social movement. In A. Viljoen & K. Bohn (Eds.) *Second Nature Urban Agriculture: Designing Productive Cities* (pp. 146-153), London: Routledge. 146-153.

Migendt, M., Polzin, F., Schock, F., Täube, F. A., & von Flotow, P. (2017). Beyond venture capital: The finance-innovation-policy nexus in cleantech. *Industrial and Corporate Change, 26*(6), 973–996. DOI: 10.1093/icc/dtx018

Mikulewicz, M., Caretta, M. A., Sultana, F., & Crawford, J. W., N. (2023). Intersectionality and Climate Justice: A call for synergy in climate change scholarship. *Environmental Politics, 32*(7), 1275–1286.

Milman, O. (2019, September 23). Greta Thunberg condemns world leaders in emotional speech at UN. *The Guardian.* https://www.theguardian.com/environment/2019/sep/23/greta-thunberg-speech-un-2019-address

Ministry of External Affairs. India. (2023). *International Solar Alliance: India's global leadership in renewable energy*. Government of India Press.

Miskimmon, A., O'Loughlin, B., & Roselle, L. (2013). *Strategic narratives: Communication power and the new world order*. Routledge.

Mohan, P. S. (2025). Climate Reparations for a Just Response to Climate Change: A Review of Historical Responsibility and Future Implications. *WIREs Climate Change*, online first. doi: DOI: 10.1002/wcc.70007

Mol, A. (2011). *The logic of care: Health and the problem of patient choice* (Transferred to digital printing 2010). Routledge.

Mol, A. P., & Sonnenfeld, D. A. (2000). Ecological modernization around the world: An introduction. *Environmental Politics*, *9*(1), 1–14.

Mol, A., Moser, I., & Pols, J. (Eds.). (2010). *Care in Practice: On Tinkering in Clinics, Homes and Farms*. transcript.

Mölders, T. (2019). Rethinking gender: feminist perspectives on Sustainable Development Goals in the light of (re)productivity. *GAIA - Ecological Perspectives for Science and Society, 28(2)*, 95-99. https://doi.org/DOI: 10.14512/gaia.28.2.6

Mondal, J. (2022). Sustainable Development and Gender Mainstreaming in Present Contemporary Society. International Journal of Modern Engineering Research, 11(1), ss. 54-57. http://ijmer.in.doi./2022/11.01.89

Montel Energy. (2025). How does renewable energy impact water use? https://montel.energy/resources/blog/how-does-renewable-energy-impact-water-use

Montgomery, A. W., Lyon, T. P., & Barg, J. (2024). No end in sight? A greenwash review and research agenda. *Organization & Environment*, *37*(2), 221–256. DOI: 10.1177/10860266231168905

Moore, J. (2009). *A Primitivist Primer*, Library.Anarhija.Net.

Moore, B. (1952). Review: *Bernhard Eduard Fernow* by Andrew Denny Rodgers. *Empire Forestry Review*, *31*(1), 57–59.

Moore, J. W. (2003). The modern world-system as environmental history? Ecology and the rise of capitalism. *Theory and Society*, *32*(3), 307–377. DOI: 10.1023/A:1024404620759

Moore, J. W. (2015). *Capitalism in the web of life: Ecology and the accumulation of capital*. Verso.

Moore, P. (2007). *Globalisation and labour struggle in Asia: A neo-Gramscian critique of South Korea's political economy*. Bloomsbury.

Moreno, C., Allam, Z., Chabaud, D., Gall, C., & Pratlong, F. (2021). Introducing the "15-Minute City": Sustainability, Resilience and Place Identity in Future Post-Pandemic Cities. *Smart Cities, 4*, 93–111.

Morganti, M., Favarin, S., & Andreatta, D. (2018). Illicit waste trafficking and loopholes in the European and Italian legislation. *European Journal on Criminal Policy and Research, 26*, 105–133. DOI: 10.1007/s10610-018-9405-2

Morton, A. D. (2007). *Unravelling Gramsci: Hegemony and passive revolution in the global economy*. Pluto Press.

Morton, A. D. (2010). The continuum of passive revolution. *Capital and Class, 34*(3), 315–342. DOI: 10.1177/0309816810378294

Mossett, K., & Caldwell, R. (2016). "The Inside Is Such a Sterile Place": Organizing with the Indigenous Environmental Network. *Socialism and Democracy, 30*(2), 203–208.

Mouffe, C. (1979). Hegemony and ideology in Gramsci. In Mouffe, C. (Ed.), *Gramsci and Marxist theory* (pp. 168–204). Routledge & Kegan Paul.

Mróz, P., Otarola, A., Prince, T. A., Prince, T. A., Dekany, R., Duev, D. A., Graham, M. J., Groom, S. L., Masci, F. J., & Medford, M. S. (2022). Impact of the SpaceX Starlink Satellites on the Zwicky Transient Facility Survey Observations. *The Astrophysical Journal. Letters, 924*(2), 1–13.

Müller-Rommel, F. (2022). The "lifespan" of Green parties in Western Europe: An evaluation. In *Parties, institutions and preferences: The shape and impact of partisan politics* (pp. 123–148). Springer Fachmedien Wiesbaden., DOI: 10.1007/978-3-658-34553-8_7

Muller, W. C., & Steininger, B. (1996). Christian Democracy in Austria: The Austrian People's Party. In Hanley, D. (Ed.), *Christian Democracy in Europe: A Comparative Perspective* (pp. 87–100). Pinter.

Murphy, M. P. (2013). Translating degrowth into contemporary policy challenges: A symbiotic social transformation strategy. *Irish Journal of Sociology, 21*(2), 76–89.

Mustakimah, L., Huriani, Y., & Zulaeha, E. (2023). Tantangan Mewujudkan Sustainable Development Goals (SDGs) Tentang Kesetaraan Gender pada Masyarakat Desa. *Az-Zahra: Journal of Gender and Family Studies, 4*(1), 12–29. DOI: 10.15575/azzahra.v4i1.25462

Mususa, P. (2012). Mining, welfare and urbanisation: The wavering urban character of Zambia's Copperbelt. *Journal of Southern African Studies, 38*(2), 225–244.

Myanmar: Myitsone dam project faces widespread opposition due to displacement & environment concerns. (2019). *Business & Human Rights Resource Center.* https://www.business-humanrights.org/en/latest-news/myanmar-myitsone-dam-project-faces-widespread-opposition-due-to-displacement-environment-concerns/

Naess, A. (1973). The shallow and the deep, long-range ecology movement: A summary. *Inquiry: An Interdisciplinary Journal of Philosophy, 16*(1–4), 95–100. DOI: 10.1080/00201747308601682

NASA. (2025). *What is climate change?* NASA. https://climate.nasa.gov/global-warming-vs-climate-change/

National Renewable Energy Laboratory (NREL). (2005). What is the energy payback for PV? https://www.nrel.gov/docs/fy05osti/37322.pdf

National Renewable Energy Laboratory (NREL). (2025). Life cycle assessment harmonization: Energy systems analysis. https://www.nrel.gov/analysis/life-cycle-assessment

National Renewable Energy Laboratory. (2021). *Impacts of Section 201 Tariffs on U.S. Solar Deployment.* https://www.nrel.gov

Natural Resources Canada. (2021). *Trans Mountain Pipeline Expansion Project.* Government of Canada.

Nedopil, C., De Boer, D., Danting, F., & Tang, Y. (2021, August 18). What China's new guidelines on "green development" mean for the Belt and Road. *China Dialogue.* https://chinadialogue.net/en/business/what-chinas-new-guidelines-on-green-development-mean-for-the-belt-and-road/

Newell, F. H. (1895). The American Forestry Association. *Science, 2*(39), 385–390.

Newell, P. (2005). Race, class and the global politics of environmental inequality. *Global Environmental Politics, 5*(3), 70–94.

Newell, P. (2019). Trasformismo or transformation? The global political economy of energy transitions. *Review of International Political Economy, 26*(1), 25–48. DOI: 10.1080/09692290.2018.1511448

Newell, P. (2022). Climate Justice. *The Journal of Peasant Studies, 49*(5), 915–923.

Newell, P. (2022). *Power shift: The global political economy of energy transitions.* Cambridge University Press.

Newell, P., & Mulvaney, D. (2013). The Political Economy Of the Just Transition. *The Geographical Journal, 179*(2), 132–140.

Newell, P., Srivastava, S., & Naess, L. O. (2021). Climate Justice Movements In The Global South: The Politics Of Equity And Inclusion. *Climate Policy, 21*(7), 885–901.

NEX Indonesia. (2025). *ASEAN Green Startups and the US-China Trade War: A Market Update*.

Ngcamu, B. S. (2023). Climate Change Effects on Vulnerable Populations in the Global South: A Systematic Review. *Natural Hazards, 118*, 977–991.

Nikiforuk, A. (2010). *Tar sands: Dirty oil and the future of a continent* (Rev. & updated ed.). Vancouver, BC: Greystone Books.

Nikiforuk, A. (2012). *The energy of slaves: Oil and the new servitude*. Greystone Books.

Nikolaev, P. P., Vaseltsova, I. A., Gryaznov, S. A., & Levchenko, A. V. (2024, April). Crises, sanctions, and conflicts on the way to achieving sustainable development goals. *Springer Nature Switzerland*, 442–450. https://doi.org/DOI: 10.1007/978-3-031-67372-6

Nixon, R. (2011). *Slow violence and the environmentalism of the poor*. Harvard University Press.

Noorollahi, Y., Lund, H., Nielsen, S., & Thellufsen, J. Z. (2021). Energy transition in petroleum rich nations: Case study of Iran. *Smart Energy, 3*, 100026. DOI: 10.1016/j.segy.2021.100026

Novais, P., ... (2023). *Ambient Intelligence – Software and Applications* – 14th International Symposium on Ambient Intelligence. 1st ed. 2023. Cham: Springer Nature Switzerland.

Nozawa, W., Kurita, K., Tamaki, T., & Managi, S. (2023). To What Extent Will Space Debris Impact the Economy? *Space Policy Journal, 66*, 1–24. DOI: 10.1016/j.spacepol.2023.101580

Nulman, E. (2015). *Climate change and social movements: Civil society and the development of national climate change policy*. Palgrave Macmillan.

Nyumba, T. (2021, June 29). Kenya's huge railway project is causing environmental damage. Here's how. Down to Earth. https://www.downtoearth.org.in/africa/kenya-s-huge-railway-project-is-causing-environmental-damage-here-s-how-77681

Nzongola-Ntalaja, G. (2002). *The Congo: From Leopold to Kabila: A people's history*. Zed Books.

O'Grady, V. (2024, July 1). Amazon's plans for Project Kuiper satellite launch are delayed. Developing *Telecoms*. https://developingtelecoms.com/telecom-technology/satellite-communications-networks/16936-amazon-s-plans-for-project-kuiper-satellite-launch-are-delayed.html

Obama, B. H. (2009, June 27). Weekly presidential address [Video]. *C-SPAN*. https://www.c-span.org/video/?287322-101/weekly-presidential-address

Odera, J. A., & Mulusa, J. (2020). SDGs, Gender Equality and Women's Empowerment: What Prospects for Delivery? In Kaltenborn, M., Krajewski, M., & Kuhn, H. (Eds.), *Sustainable Development Goals and Human Rights. Interdisciplinary Studies in Human Rights* (Vol. 5). Springer., DOI: 10.1007/978-3-030-30469-0_6

OECD. (2011). *Towards green growth*. OECD Publishing.

OECD. (2011a). *Towards green growth: A summary for policymakers*. OECD.

OECD. (2011b). *Towards green growth: Monitoring progress—OECD indicators*. OECD.

OECD. (2023). *Critical Minerals for the Green Transition*. Organisation for Economic Co-operation and Development.

OECD. (2024a, May 29). *Climate finance provided and mobilised by developed countries in 2013–2022*. https://www.oecd.org/en/publications/2024/05/climate-finance-provided-and-mobilised-by-developed-countries-in-2013-2022_8031029a.html

OECD. (2024b, May 29). *Developed countries materially surpassed their USD 100 billion climate finance commitment in 2022*. https://www.oecd.org/en/about/news/press-releases/2024/05/developed-countries-materially-surpassed-their-usd-100-billion-climate-finance-commitment-in-2022-oecd.html

Ofori-Parku, S. S., & Koomson, P. (2023). Corporate sustainability as a hegemonic discourse of globalization: The discourse-historical approach as a critical issues and stakeholder analysis tool. *Public Relations Review*, *49*(1), 102275.

Ogilvie, M., & Rootes, C. (2015). The impact of local campaigns against wind energy developments. *Environmental Politics*, *24*(6), 874–893.

Ogunbode, C. A. (2022). Climate Justice Is Social Justice In The Global South. *Nature Human Behaviour*, *6*, 1443.

Ojeda, L., Ginieis, M., & Papaoikonomou, E. (2025). Gender Equality in Sustainability Reporting: A Systematic Literature Review. *Corporate Social Responsibility and Environmental Management*, *32*(2), 2710–2727. DOI: 10.1002/csr.3089

Okereke, C. (2008). *Global justice and neoliberal environmental governance: Ethics, sustainable development and international co-operation*. Routledge.

Okereke, C. (2010). Climate Justice and the International Regime. *Wiley Interdisciplinary Reviews: Climate Change*, *1*(3), 462–474.

Ollman, B. (2003). *Dance of the Dialectic: Steps in Marx's Method*. University of Illinois Press.

Opaluwah, A. (2016). Participatory Development: A Tool of Pedagogy. *Exchanges the Interdisciplinary Research Journal*, *4*(1), 120–139. DOI: 10.31273/eirj.v4i1.151

Open Markets Institute. (2022). The monopolization of the satellite broadband market: How Elon Musk's Starlink is raising prices, reducing innovation, and harming consumers. *Center for Journalism & Liberty*. https://www.journalismliberty.org/publications/policy-brief-monopolization-of-the-satellite-broadband-market

Ortega, A. A. (2023, June 5). Not a Rose by Any Other Name: Dual-Use and Dual-Purpose Space Systems. *Lawfare*. https://www.lawfaremedia.org/article/not-a-rose-by-any-other-name-dual-use-and-dual-purpose-space-systems

Osoro, O. B., Oughton, E. J., Wilson, A. R., & Rao, A. (2023). Sustainability assessment of Low Earth Orbit (LEO) satellite broadband mega-constellations. *Research Square*, DOI:DOI: 10.21203/rs.3.rs-3325730/v1

Ossewaarde, M., & Ossewaarde-Lowtoo, R. (2020). The EU's Green Deal: A third alternative to green growth and degrowth? *Sustainability*, *12*(23), 9825. DOI: 10.3390/su12239825

Otto, A., & Gugushvili, D. (2020). Eco-Social Divides in Europe: Public Attitudes towards Welfare and Climate Change Policies. *Sustainability*, *12*, 404. DOI: 10.3390/su12010404

Otto, F. (2023). *Klimaungerechtigkeit: Was die Klimakatastrophe mit Kapitalismus, Rassismus und Sexismus zu tun hat*. Ullstein Taschenbuch Verlag.

Our World in Data. (2022, June 15). How does the land use of different electricity sources compare? *Our World in Data Environmental Impacts*. https://ourworldindata.org/land-use-per-energy-source

Our World in Data. (2023). https://ourworldindata.org/ Retrieved on 21.03.2025

Oxfam (2020). *Confronting carbon inequality: Putting climate justice at the heart of the COVID-19 recovery*. Oxfam International.

Page, E. A. (2008). Distributing the burdens of climate change. *Environmental Politics, 17*(4), 556–575.

Parikka, J. (2015). *A geology of media*. University of Minnesota Press.

Parks, L., & Tsioumani, E. (2023). Transforming biodiversity governance? Indigenous peoples' contributions to the Convention on Biological Diversity. *Biological Conservation, 280*, 109933.

Parsons, J. J. (1981). Human Influences on the Pine and Laurel Forests of the Canary Islands. *Geographical Review, 71*(3), 253–271.

Patel, R., & Moore, J. W. (2018). *A history of the world in seven cheap things: A guide to capitalism, nature, and the future of the planet*. University of California Press.

Paterson, B. (2009). Trasformismo at the World Trade Organization. In Bieler, A., & Morton, A. D. (Eds.), *Gramsci and global politics* (pp. 56–71). Routledge.

Paterson, M. (2021). *Climate capitalism: Global warming and the transformation of the global economy*. Cambridge University Press.

Pathak, N. (2019). Traditional practices of sustainability in Indian tribes: A study of the Gond community. *Journal of Sustainable Development Studies, 15*(3), 12–23.

Pauwelyn, J. (2019, July 7). *WTO dispute settlement post 2019: What to expect? What choice to make?* Social Science Research Network. https://papers.ssrn.com/abstract=3415964

Peiwen, W. (2024). Starlink Militarization: Challenges and Responses to Space Intelligence and Information Security, Interpret: China. https://interpret.csis.org/translations/starlink-militarization-challenges-and-responses-to-space-intelligence-and-information-security/

Pellow, D. N. (2000). Environmental inequality formation: Toward a theory of environmental injustice. *The American Behavioral Scientist, 43*(4), 581–601.

Pellow, D. N. (2007). *Resisting global toxics: Transnational movements for environmental justice*. MIT Prcss.

Pellow, D. N., Williams, E., & Rizo-Centino, A. R. (2021). Collaborative Research and Action for Climate Justice in California. *Capitalism, Nature, Socialism, 33*(2), 85–102.

Peluso, N. L., & Lund, C. (2011). New frontiers of land control: Introduction. *The Journal of Peasant Studies*, *38*(4), 667–681. DOI: 10.1080/03066150.2011.607692

Pembina Institute. (2022). *Canada's critical minerals strategy: A sustainability perspective*. Pembina Institute.

Pembina Institute. (2023). *Evaluating climate alignment in infrastructure investment*. Pembina Institute.

Peters, G. P., Davis, S. J., & Andrew, R. (2012). A synthesis of carbon in international trade. *Biogeosciences*, *9*(8), 3247–3276.

Peters, M. A. (2017). Oil geopolitics and eco-nightmares. *Educational Philosophy and Theory*, *49*(5), 435–438. DOI: 10.1080/00131857.2017.1286135

Plagerson, S. (2012). *'Human Well-Being and Capabilities', From Science to Practice: Research and Knowledge to Achieve the SDGs*. Consultation Document.

Plumhans, L.-A. (2021). *Operationalizing eco-social policies: a mapping of energy poverty measures in EU member states*. Working Paper Reihe der AK Wien - Materialien zu Wirtschaft und Gesellschaft 212, Kammer für Arbeiter und Angestellte für Wien, Abteilung Wirtschaftswissenschaft und Statistik.

Poguntke, T. (2002). Green parties in national governments: From protest to acquiescence? *Environmental Politics*, *11*(1), 133–145. DOI: 10.1080/714000579

Pokharel, B. (2024). Gender equality in Nepal: How is it going as a goal of SDG? *Journey for Sustainable Development and Peace Journal*, *2*(1), 112–127. DOI: 10.3126/jsdpj.v2i1.63260

Pomeroy, M. (2016). South–South cooperation and the changing aid landscape: Implications for development cooperation. *Third World Quarterly*, *37*(4), 579–596.

Poorhashemi, A. (2024). International environmental law. *Routledge*, 453–466. https://doi.org/DOI: 10.4324/9781003451327-19

Postman, N. (2006). Media Ecology Education. *Explorations in Media Ecology*, *5*(1), 5–14.

Poulantzas, N. (1978). *State, power, socialism* (Camiller, P., Trans.). Verso.

Project Connect. (2024). *UNICEF & ITU Giga initiative - live school connectivity map*. https://maps.giga.global/map.

Pugh, M. (2005). The political economy of peacebuilding: A critical theory perspective. *International Journal of Peace Studies*, *10*(2), 23–42. https://www.jstor.org/stable/41852928

Pugh, M., Cooper, N., & Goodhand, J. (2004). *War economies in a regional context: Challenges of transformation.* Lynne Rienner Publishers., DOI: 10.1515/9781685855284

Puig de La Bellacasa, M. (2017). *Matters of care: Speculative ethics in more than human worlds.* University of Minnesota press.

Pultarova, T. (2024, October 17). How much do SpaceX's reentering Starlink satellites pollute Earth's atmosphere? *Space.com News*, https://www.space.com/spacex-starlink-reentry-pollution-damage-earth-atmosphere

Queisser, M. (2016). Gender equality and the Sustainable Development Goals. In Love, P. (Ed.), *Debate the Issues: New Approaches to Economic Challenges* (pp. 87–90). OECD Publishing., DOI: 10.1787/9789264264687-16-

RAID. (2025). *Beneath the green: A critical look at the cost of industrial cobalt mining in the DRC.* https://raid-uk.org/post-library/report-beneath-the-green/

Raimi, M. O., Vivien, O. T., Alima, O., Akpojubaro, E. H., & Williams, E. A. (2021). Articulating the Effect of Pesticides Use and Sustainable Development Goals (SDGs): The Science of Improving Lives through Decision Impacts. https://ssrn.com/abstract=3838210

Rainbow, J. (2021, November 24). OneWeb mulls debris-removal service for failed satellite. *SpaceNews.* https://spacenews.com/oneweb-mulls-debris-removal-service-for-failed-satellite/

Rainbow, J. (2023, June 15). Project Kuiper urges regulators to focus on satellite maneuverability rules. *SpaceNews.* https://spacenews.com/project-kuiper-urges-regulators-to-focus-on-satellite-maneuverability-rules/

Rajamani, L., Jeffery, L., Höhne, N., Hans, F., Glass, A., Ganti, G., & Geiges, A. (2021). National 'fair shares' in reducing greenhouse gas emissions within the principled framework of international environmental law. *Climate Policy*, *21*(8), 983–1004. DOI: 10.1080/14693062.2021.1970504

Ramachandran, S. (2019, April 24). The Standoff Over the Myitsone Dam Project in Myanmar: Advantage China. *The Jamestown Foundation.* https://jamestown.org/program/the-standoff-over-the-myitsone-dam-project-in-myanmar-advantage-china/

Ramírez, C. E. P. (2021). Limits and contradictions of capital in nature. Retrieved from_https://www.probdes.iiec.unam.mx/index.php/pde/article/download/69780/62144?inline=1

Ramnath, M. (2021). *Decolonizing conservation: Caring for biodiversity in India.* LeftWord Books.

Rao, V. (2002). Symbolic representation and social exclusion: The case of Dalits in India. *Social Research, 70*(1), 205–218.

Rapsikevičius, J., Bruneckienė, J., Krušinskas, R., & Lukauskas, M. (2022). The impact of structural reforms on sustainable development performance: Evidence from European Union countries. *Sustainability, 14*(19), 12583. DOI: 10.3390/su141912583

Raworth, K., Wykes, S. & Bass, S. (2014). *Securing social justice in green economies: A review and ten considerations for policymakers.* International Institute for Environment and Development, Issue Paper, October.

Rechtbank Amsterdam. (2024, March 20). *Fossielvrij NL v. KLM (ECLI:NL:RBAMS:2024:1512).* https://www.clientearth.org/media/cx4po41h/klm-judgment-20-march-2024.pdf

RECOFTC's strategic plan addresses forestry challenges in Lao PDR. (2023, December 25). Retrieved from https://www.recoftc.org/updates/recoftcs-strategic-plan-addresses-forestry-challenges-lao-pdr

Rettig, E., Friedman, S., & Spanier, B. (2025). Reflections on our article 'Postwar development of offshore energy resources: Legal and political models for developing the Gaza Marine gas field'. *Leiden Journal of International Law, 38*(1), 30–39. DOI: 10.1017/S092215652510040X

Reuters. (2022, September 29). Kremlin says Nord Stream incidents look like state-sponsored "terrorism." *Reuters.* https://www.reuters.com/business/energy/kremlin-says-nord-stream-gas-leaks-look-like-act-terrorism-2022-09-29/

Reuters. (2023a, December 6). UK bans airline adverts over "misleading" environmental claims. *Reuters.* https://www.reuters.com/business/aerospace-defense/uk-bans-airline-adverts-over-misleading-environmental-claims-2023-12-06/

Reuters. (2023b, September 25). DWS to pay $25 million to end U.S. probe into ESG misstatements and other violations. *Reuters.* https://www.reuters.com/legal/dws-pay-25-mln-over-us-charges-over-esg-misstatements-other-violations-2023-09-25/

Reuters. (2024, December 17). *Congo files criminal complaints against Apple in Europe over conflict minerals.* https://www.reuters.com/sustainability/society-equity/congo-files-criminal-complaints-against-apple-europe-over-conflict-minerals-2024-12-17/

Reuters. (2024, March 20). Dutch court finds KLM ads were misleading in "greenwashing" case. *Reuters.* https://www.reuters.com/business/aerospace-defense/dutch-court-rule-klm-greenwashing-case-2024-03-20/

Reuters. (2025). Iraq holds Kurdish government legally responsible for continued oil smuggling. June 5. https://www.reuters.com/world/middle-east/iraq-holds-kurdish-government-legally-responsible-continued-oil-smuggling-2025-06-05/

Reuters. (2025, February 27). *Paris prosecutor drops case against Apple over Congo minerals, document shows.* https://www.reuters.com/technology/paris-prosecutor-closes-case-against-apple-over-congo-minerals-document-2025-02-27/

Richmond, O. P. (2011). *A post-liberal peace.* Routledge., DOI: 10.4324/9780203810262

Rieger, S. (2025). Bio(techno)logie und Medientheorie. In Ernst, C., Krtilova, K., Schröter, J., & Sudmann, A. (Eds.), *Handbuch Medientheorien im 21. Jahrhundert* (pp. 1–15). Springer Fachmedien Wiesbaden.

Rignall, K. E. (2016). Solar power, state power, and the politics of energy transition in pre-Saharan Morocco. *Environment and Planning A. Economy and Space, 48*(3), 540–557.

Robbins, P. (2012). *Political ecology: A critical introduction* (2nd ed.). Wiley-Blackwell.

Roberts, J. T., Grimes, P. E., & Manale, J. L. (2003). Social roots of global environmental change: A world-systems analysis of carbon dioxide emissions. *Journal of World-systems Research, 9*(2), 277–315. DOI: 10.5195/jwsr.2003.238

Roberts, J. T., & Parks, B. C. (2007). *A Climate Of Injustice: Global Inequality, North-South Politics, And Climate Policy.* MIT Press.

Roberts, J. T., & Parks, B. C. (2009). Ecologically unequal exchange, ecological debt, and climate justice. *International Journal of Comparative Sociology, 50*(3–4), 385–409.

Rochat, M., & Tsouloufas, G. (2024). The effectiveness of smart sanctions: Examining divergent outcomes in Myanmar and Zimbabwe. *Journal of Asian and African Studies, 59*(1), 55–78. DOI: 10.1177/00219096241300448

Rodrik, D. (2011). *The globalization paradox: Democracy and the future of the world economy.* W. W. Norton & Company.

Rootes, C. (2004). Environmental Movements. In Snow, D., Sarah, A. S., & Hanspeter, K. (Eds.), *The Blackwell Companion to Social Movements* (pp. 608–640). Blackwell.

Rosenstone, S. J., Behr, R. L., & Lazarus, E. H. (2018). *Third parties in America: Citizen response to major party failure* (2nd ed.). Princeton University Press.

Ross, W., & Zane, D. (2024, December 18). Apple accused of using conflict minerals. *BBC News*. https://www.bbc.com/news/

Ross, M. L. (2004). What do we know about natural resources and civil war? *Journal of Peace Research, 41*(3), 337–356. DOI: 10.1177/0022343304043773

Ross, M. L. (2012). *The oil curse: How petroleum wealth shapes the development of nations*. Princeton University Press., DOI: 10.1515/9781400841929

Rothe, K. (2016). Medienökologie – Zu einer Ethik des Mediengebrauchs.

Roulette, J. (2023, March 15). OneWeb 'moves on' from Soyuz-stranded satellites as its network nears completion. *Reuters*. https://www.reuters.com/lifestyle/science/oneweb-moves-on-soyuz-stranded-satellites-its-network-nears-completion-2023-03-15/

Rousell, D., & Cutter-Mackenzie-Knowles, A. (2020). A systematic review of climate change education: Giving children and young people a 'voice' and a 'hand' in redressing climate change. *Children's Geographies, 18*(2), 191–208. DOI: 10.1080/14733285.2019.1705010

Rowhani, M. (2023). Rights-based boundaries of the United Nations sanctions. *University of Bologna Law Review, 8*(1), 129–148. https://doi.org/DOI: 10.6092/issn.2531-6133/17799

Roy Burman, B. K. (1994). Tribal development in India: Myth and reality. *Social Action, 44*(4), 385–397.

Sabato, S., & Mandelli, M. (2018). The EU's potential for promoting an ecosocial agenda. Report prepared for the project "Sustainable welfare societies: Assessing linkages between social and environmental policies", NOVA Norwegian Social Research. Brussels: European Social Observatory, December, 35p.

Sabato, S., Mandelli, M., & Jessoula, M. (2022). Towards an EU eco-social agenda? From Europe 2020 to the European Green Deal. In M. A. Schoen, B. Hvinden & M. D. Leiren (Eds.), *Towards Sustainable Welfare States in Europe: Social Policy and Climate Change* (pp. 199-219), Cheltham, Edward Elgar.

Sacchi, G. (2019). Social innovation matters: The adoption of participatory guarantee systems within Italian alternative agri-food networks. *Strategic Change, 28*, 241–248.

Sachs, J. D., Lafortune, G., Fuller, G., & Iablonovski, G. (2025). *Financing Sustainable Development to 2030 and Mid-Century. Sustainable Development Report 2025. Paris: SDSN*. Dublin University Press.

Sachs, W. (2017). The Sustainable Development Goals and *Laudato si'*: Varieties of Post Development? *Third World Quarterly*, *38*(12), 2573–2587. DOI: 10.1080/01436597.2017.1350822

Sahoo, N., & Ashraf, J. (2021). Renewable energy cooperation between India and Brazil: Opportunities and challenges. *Energy Policy*, *158*, 112–125.

Sangvai, S. (2008). People's struggle in the Narmada Valley: Quest for just and sustainable development. In *Water conflicts in India*. Routledge India.

Sanne, C. (2002). Willing costumers – or locked-in? Policies for a sustainable consumption. *Ecological Economics*, *42*(1-2), 273–287.

Santos, C., Coelho, A., & Marques, A. (2024). A systematic literature review on greenwashing and its relationship to stakeholders: State of art and future research agenda. *Management Review Quarterly*, *74*, 1397–1421. DOI: 10.1007/s11301-023-00337-5

Sartori, G. (1970). Concept Misformation in Comparative Politics. *The American Political Science Review*, *64*(4), 1033–1053.

Sartori, G. (1991). Comparing and Miscomparing. *Journal of Theoretical Politics*, *3*. Advance online publication. DOI: 10.1177/0951692891003003001

SatNews. (2025a, January 6). Eutelsat suffers flak over OneWeb outage. *SatNews*. https://news.satnews.com/2025/01/06/more-about-eutelsat-suffers-flak-over-oneweb-outage/

SatNews. (2025b, March 19). Project Kuiper facing regulatory deadline. *SatNews*. https://news.satnews.com/2025/03/19/project-kuiper-facing-regulatory-deadline/

Savic, K., & Hoicka, C. E. (2023). Indigenous legal forms and governance structures in renewable energy: Assessing the role and perspectives of First Nations economic development corporations. *Energy Research & Social Science*, *101*, 103121. DOI: 10.1016/j.erss.2023.103121

Schleich, J., Dütschke, E., Schwirplies, C., & Ziegler, A. (2014). Citizens' perceptions of justice in international climate policy: An empirical analysis. *Climate Policy*, *16*(1), 50–67.

Schlosberg, D. (2007). *Defining environmental justice: Theories, movements, and nature*. Oxford University Press.

Schlosberg, D. (2012). Climate justice and capabilities: A framework for adaptation policy. *Ethics & International Affairs, 26*(4), 445–461.

Schlosberg, D., & Collins, L. B. (2014). From Environmental to Climate Justice. *Wiley Interdisciplinary Reviews: Climate Change, 5*(3), 359–374.

Schneckener, U. (2016). Peacebuilding in crisis? Debating peacebuilding paradigms and practices. In Debiel, T., Held, T., & Schneckener, U. (Eds.), *Peacebuilding in Crisis: Rethinking Paradigms and Practices of Transnational Cooperation*. Routledge.

Schneider, F., Kallis, G., & Martinez-Alier, J. (2010). Crisis or opportunity? Economic degrowth for social equity and ecological sustainability. Introduction to this special issue. *Journal of Cleaner Production, 18*(6), 511–518. DOI: 10.1016/j.jclepro.2010.01.014

Scholte, J. A. (2020). Civil society and global democracy. *Polity.*

Schoyen, M. A., Hvinden, B., & Leiren, M. D. (2022). Welfare state sustainability in the 21st century. In M. A. Schoen, B. Hvinden & M. D. Leiren (Eds.), *Towards Sustainable Welfare States in Europe: Social Policy and Climate Change* (pp. 2-27), Cheltham, Edward Elgar.

Schoyen, M. A., & Hvinden, B. (2017). Climate change as a challenge for European welfare states. In Kennett, P., & Lendvai-Bainton, N. (Eds.), *Handbook of European Social Policy* (pp. 371–385). Edward Elgar.

Schrader, A. (2015). Abyssal intimacies and temporalities of care: How (not) to care about deformed leaf bugs in the aftermath of Chernobyl. *Social Studies of Science, 45*(5), 665–690. PMID: 26630816

Shadlen, K. C. (2008). Globalisation, power and integration: The political economy of regional and bilateral trade agreements in the Americas. *The Journal of Development Studies, 44*(1), 1–20.

Shaffer, G. (2021). The WTO appellate body crisis and the challenge of multilateralism. In Shaffer, G. (Ed.), *Emerging powers and the world trading system* (pp. 219–240). Cambridge University Press.

Shang, Y., Sivertsen, G., Cao, Z., & Zhang, L. (2022). Gender differences among first authors in research focused on the Sustainable Development Goal of Gender Equality. *Scientometricsi, 127*, 4769–4796. DOI: 10.1007/s11192-022-04430-6

Shapiro, J. (2016). *China's Environmental Challenges*. Polity Press.

Shiva, V. (1989). *Staying alive: Women, ecology and development*. Zed Books.

Shiva, V. (2005). *Earth democracy: Justice, sustainability and peace*. South End Press.

Shue, H. (2014). *Climate Justice: Vulnerability and Protection*. Oxford University Press.

Simms, A. (2009). *Ecological Debt: Global Warming and the Wealth of Nations*. Pluto Press.

Simon, F. (2020, March 17). Basescu: European Green Deal risks pushing "two or three countries" towards EU exit. *Euractiv*. https://www.euractiv.com/section/energy-environment/interview/basescu-european-green-deal-risks-pushing-two-or-three-countries-towards-eu-exit/

Simonetti, M. (2023). Adat in Indonesian law and society: A tool to build resilience and overcome diversity through cultural and legal pluralism. *The SOAS Journal of Postgraduate Research, 15*. https://doi.org/DOI: 10.25501/SOAS.00040649

Simon, R. (1982). *Gramsci's political thought: An introduction*. Lawrence & Wishart.

Singh, S. (2021). Socio-Economic Dimensions of Sustainable Development. In D. K. Singh & P. S. Khare (Eds.), *Earth-II [Environmental Sustainability and Conservation]*. Prayagraj: Krishna Computer Sansthan.

Singh, N. (2001). Indigenous knowledge and its relevance for sustainable development in India. *International Journal of Sustainable Development*, *4*(3), 370–383.

Sinha, S. (1982). State formation and Rajput myth in tribal central India. *Man in India*, *62*(3), 288–310.

Sjåfjell, B., Mähönen, J., Taylor, M. B., Maitre-Ekern, E., van der Velden, M., Novitz, T., Gammage, C., Cullen, J., Andhov, M., & Caranta, R. (2019). *University of Oslo*. https://ssrn.com/abstract=3503310

Skjærseth, J. B., Stokke, O. S., & Wettestad, J. (2006). Soft law, hard law, and effective implementation of international environmental norms. *Global Environmental Politics*, *6*(3), 104–120. DOI: 10.1162/glep.2006.6.3.104

Smith, L. T. (2012). *Decolonizing methodologies: Research and indigenous peoples* (2nd ed.). Zed Books.

Smith, M.. (2024). *Empowering women through solar energy: Employment and inclusion in South Asia*. Renewable Energy Journal.

Smith, M., Shoaib, N., & Lal, P. (2025, July 18). Life cycle assessment of New Jersey offshore wind. *Wind Energy Science*, *10*, 1389–1402. DOI: 10.5194/wes-10-1389-2025

Soldatkin, V., & Kobzeva, O. (2022, October 12). Putin moots gas hub in Turkey with Nord Stream supplies. *Reuters*. https://www.reuters.com/world/europe/putin-moots-major-gas-hub-turkey-with-nord-stream-supplies-2022-10-12/

Sommer, J. M., & Hargrove, A. (2020). Power and politics in the world-system: A cross-national analysis of environmental governance. *Journal of World-systems Research, 26*(2), 264–284. DOI: 10.5195/jwsr.2020.998

Sparhawk, W. N. (1949). The History of Forestry in America. In Stefferud, A. (Ed.), *Trees: the yearbook of agriculture, 1949*. D.C., US Government Printing Office.

Speech by Foreign Minister Wang Yi at the Opening of Symposium on International Developments and China's Diplomacy in 2017. (2017). *Ministry of Foreign Affairs People's Republic of China*. https://www.mfa.gov.cn/eng/wjb/wjbz/jh/202405/t20240527_11312148.html

Spivak, G. C. (1988). Can the subaltern speak? In C. Nelson & L. Grossberg (Eds.), *Marxism and the interpretation of culture* (pp. 271–313). University of Illinois Press.

Spivak, G. C. (1988). Can the Subaltern Speak? In C. Nelson & L. Grossberg (Eds.), *Marxism and the Interpretation of Culture* (pp. 271–313). University of Illinois Press.

Sposato, G. (2021). Italy: Approval and EIA process for RE power plants simplified. Rödl & Partner, 17 November. https://www.roedl.com/insights/renewable-energy/2021/november/italien-approval-eia-process-simplified

Sprenger, F. (2019). Epistemologien des Umgebens: Zur Geschichte, Ökologie und Biopolitik künstlicher environments.

Spretnak, C. (1994). A Living Memorial. In Kelly, P. K. (Ed.), *Thinking Green! Essays on Environmentalism, Feminism, and Nonviolence* (pp. 151–154). Parallax Press.

Stamm, I. (2023). Ecosocial work and services for unemployed people: The challenge to integrate environmental and social sustainability. *Nordic Social Work Research, 13*(1), 134–147. DOI: 10.1080/2156857X.2021.1975154

State Grid Corporation of China. (2024). *BRICS countries join hands to promote green, low-carbon development*. China Three Gorges Corporation.

Staub, C. (2021, July 14). *Turkey reverses ban on scrap plastic imports. Resource Recycling*. https://resource-recycling.com/plastics/2021/07/14/turkey-reverses-ban-on-scrap-plastic-imports/

Steele, W. (2022). Wild infrastructure. *Current Opinion in Environmental Sustainability, 55*, 101171.

Steinfeld, E. S. (2010). *Playing our game: Why China's rise doesn't threaten the West*. Oxford University Press.

Stephen, M. (2011). Globalisation and resistance: Struggles over commonsense in the global political economy. *Review of International Studies*, *37*(1), 209–228. DOI: 10.1017/S0260210510000530

Stern, N. (2007). *The economics of climate change: The Stern review*. Cambridge University Press.

Stevenson, K., & Peterson, N. (2015). Motivating action through fostering climate change hope and concern and avoiding despair among adolescents. *Sustainability*, *8*(1), 6. DOI: 10.3390/su8010006

Stock, R. (2022). Triggering resistance: Contesting the injustices of solar park development in India. *Energy Research & Social Science*, *86*, 102464.

Suleiman, N. M., Ahmed, S. S., Zuhair, M., Dahash, Z. M., & Chornomordenko, I. (2024). A socioeconomic analysis of the effects of international sanctions on targeted nations. *Journal of Ecohumanism*, *3*(5), 833–850. DOI: 10.5281/zenodo.10802166

Sultana, F. (2021). Decolonizing Climate Justice. *Geoforum*, *126*, 23–30.

Sultana, F. (2022). Critical Climate Justice. *The Geographical Journal*, *188*(1), 118–124.

Sumaita, I. (2021). The importance of being earnestly innovative: The increasing role of intellectual property law in the global economy. *The University of Cincinnati Intellectual Property and Computer Law Journal*, *6*(1), Article 9.

Sundar, N. (2016). *The burning forest: India's war in Bastar*. Juggernaut Books.

Supreme Court of Canada. (2021). *Reference re Greenhouse Gas Pollution Pricing Act, 2021 SCC 11*.

Svensson, A., & Wahlström, M. (2023). Climate change or what? Prognostic framing by Fridays for Future protesters. *Social Movement Studies*, *22*(1), 1–22. DOI: 10.1080/14742837.2022.2107954

Swyngedouw, E. (2009). The political economy and political ecology of the hydro-social cycle. *Journal of Contemporary Water Research & Education*, *142*(1), 56–60. DOI: 10.1111/j.1936-704X.2009.00054.x

Swyngedouw, E. (2010). Apocalypse forever? Post-political populism and the spectre of climate change. *Theory, Culture & Society*, *27*(2–3), 213–232. DOI: 10.1177/0263276409358728

Sze, J. (2020). *Environmental justice in a moment of danger* (1st ed., Vol. 11). University of California Press., https://www.jstor.org/stable/j.ctvqmp3jn

Tanzania: How Solar Power Improves Health Services in Off-Grid Rural Areas. (2023, April 3). *Africa Energy Portal.* https://africa-energy-portal.org/news/tanzania-how-solar-power-improves-health-services-grid-rural-areas

Taşdemir Yaşın, Z. (2022). The Environmentalization of the Agrarian Question and the Agrarianization of the Climate Justice Movement. *The Journal of Peasant Studies*, *49*(7), 1355–1386.

Teelucksingh, C., & Poland, B. (2011). Energy solutions, neo-liberalism, and social diversity in Toronto, Canada. *International Journal of Environmental Research and Public Health*, *8*(1), 185–202. DOI: 10.3390/ijerph8010185 PMID: 21318023

Temper, L., Bene, D., Martinez-Alier, J., & Demaria, F. (2018). The global environmental justice atlas (EJAtlas): Ecological distribution conflicts as forces for sustainability. *Sustainability Science*, *13*(3), 573–584.

Temper, L., Del Bene, D., & Martinez-Alier, J. (2018). Mapping the frontiers and front lines of global environmental justice: The EJAtlas. *Ecological Economics*, *145*, 1–10.

Temper, L., Del Bene, D., & Martinez-Alier, J. (2020). Mapping the frontiers and front lines of global environmental justice: The EJAtlas. *Journal of Political Ecology*, *27*(1), 819–847.

Terazono, E., & Sanderson, H. (2017, March 5). Electric cars: China's battle for the battery market. *Financial Times*.

Terry, G. (2009). No Climate Justice without Gender Justice: An Overview of the Issues. *Gender and Development*, *17*(1), 5–18.

The Belt and Road Ecological and Environmental Cooperation Plan. (2017). *Ministry of Foreign Affairs People's Republic of China.* https://english.mee.gov.cn/Resources/Policies/policies/Frameworkp1/201706/t20170628_416869.shtml

The Guardian. (2011, December 13). Canada pulls out of the Kyoto Protocol.

The Guardian. (2015, December 3). Trudeau's climate rhetoric is riveting. So what about the reality? The Guardian. (2019, June 19). Canada declares climate emergency – and then approves oil pipeline.

The Guardian. (2024, May 2). Canada is proposing to lead on climate, but it's doubling down on oil.

The Narwhal. (2024, April 4). 'Detached from reality': Researchers say Pathways Alliance misleading public with greenwashing.

The White House. (2025, February 13). *Fact sheet: President Donald J. Trump announces "Fair and Reciprocal Plan" on trade.* https://www.whitehouse.gov/fact-sheets/2025/02/fact-sheet-president-donald-j-trump-announces-fair-and-reciprocal-plan-on-trade/

Thomas, P. (2009). *The Gramscian moment: Philosophy, hegemony and Marxism.* Brill.

Thompson, D.. (2020). The importance of design in lithium ion battery recycling – A critical review. *Green Chemistry, 23*, 2718–2733.

Tienhaara, K. (2018). *Green Keynesianism and the global financial crisis.* Routledge.

Tienhaara, K., & Walker, J. (2021). Fossil capital, "unquantifiable risk" and neoliberal nationalizations: The case of the Trans Mountain Pipeline in Canada. *Geoforum, 124*, 120–131.

Tiwari, S. K. (2002). *Tribal cultural heritage of central India.* Sarup & Sons.

Today, O. (2024, October 18). Ariane 6 vs Starship: Is There a Competition? https://orbitaltoday.com/2024/10/18/ariane-6-vs-starship-is-there-a-competition/

Tokar, B. (2014). *Toward climate justice: Perspectives on the climate crisis and social change.* New Compass Press.

Torelli, R., Balluchi, F., & Lazzini, A. (2020). Greenwashing and environmental communication: Effects on stakeholders' perceptions. *Business Strategy and the Environment, 29*(2), 407–421. DOI: 10.1002/bse.2373

Trencher, G., Nick, S., Carlson, J., & Johnson, M. (2024). Demand for low-quality offsets by major companies undermines climate integrity of the voluntary carbon market. *Nature Communications, 15*(1), 6863. DOI: 10.1038/s41467-024-51151-w

Trihartono, A., Viartasiwi, N., & Nisya, C. (2020). The giant step of tiny toes: Youth impact on the securitization of climate change. *IOP Conference Series: Earth and Environmental Science, 485*(1), 012007. IOP Publishing. https://doi.org/DOI: 10.1088/1755-1315/485/1/012007

Trinkaus, S. (2020). The Green Sticky Spawn of the Stars' – Trump, Affekt, Fernsehen im Chthulucene. In Maeder, D. (Ed.), *Trump und das Fernsehen: Medien, Realität, Affekt, Politik.* Herbert von Halem Verlag.

Tronto, J. C. (2020). *Moral boundaries: A political argument for an ethic of care* (1st ed.). Routledge.

Tsing, A. L., Bubandt, N., Gran, E., & Swanson, H. A. (Eds.). (2017). *Arts of Living on a Damaged Planet*. University of Minnesota Press.

Turnock, D. (1995). The Rural Transition in Eastern Europe. *GeoJournal, 36*(4), 420–426.

Tužičková, H. (2023). *EU waste management in foreign policy: The case of Turkey* [Bachelor's thesis, Palacký University Olomouc, Department of Political Science and European Studies].

Tyrrell, I. (2002). Modern Environmentalism. In Agnew, J.-C., & Rosenzweig, R. (Eds.), *A Companion to Post-1945 America* (pp. 328–342). Blackwell Publishing.

U.S. Geological Survey. (2023). *Critical minerals supply chains: A strategy and implementation plan*. https://www.usgs.gov

U.S. Geological Survey. (2023). *Mineral commodity summaries: Cobalt*. USGS.

U.S. Securities and Exchange Commission. (2023, September 25). *Deutsche Bank subsidiary DWS to pay $25 million for AML violations and misstatements regarding ESG investments* (Press Release 2023-194). https://www.sec.gov/newsroom/press-releases/2023-194

UN Declaration on the Rights of Indigenous Peoples. (2007). https://www.ohchr.org/en/indigenous-peoples/un-declaration-rights-indigenous-peoples

UN. (2025). The 17 Goals. https://sdgs.un.org/goals

UNCTAD. (2022). *The Commodities and Development Report 2022: Harnessing the Potential of Critical Minerals for Sustainable Development*.

UNDP. (2019). Human Development Report 2019 – Beyond income, beyond averages, beyond today: Inequalities in human development in the 21st century. https://hdr.undp.org/content/human-development-report-2019

UNEP (United Nations Environment Programme). (2009). *From conflict to peacebuilding: The role of natural resources and the environment*. UNEP. https://www.iisd.org/system/files/publications/conflict_peacebuilding.pdf

UNEP (United Nations Environment Programme). (2011). *Towards a green economy: Pathways to sustainable development and poverty eradication*. UNEP.

UNEP Copenhagen Climate Centre. (2023, December 13). *Loss and damage at COP28*. https://unepccc.org/wp-content/uploads/2023/12/loss-and-damage-at-cop28-web.pdf

UNESCO. (2024, April 23). Water and energy. *UN World Water Development Report 2024*. https://www.unesco.org/reports/wwdr/en/2024/energy

UNFCCC. (1992). *United Nations Framework Convention on Climate Change*. United Nations.

UNFCCC. (1997). *Kyoto Protocol to the United Nations Framework Convention on Climate Change*. United Nations.

UNFCCC. (2015). *Paris Agreement*. United Nations. https://unfccc.int/sites/default/files/english_paris_agreement.pdf

UNFCCC. (2025). *Technology mechanism and climate innovation*. https://unfccc.int/ttclear/

United Nations Conference on Trade and Development. (2022). *Trade and environment review*.

United Nations Development Programme. (2022). What are carbon markets and why are they important? *UNDP Climate Promise*. https://climatepromise.undp.org/news-and-stories/what-are-carbon-markets-and-why-are-they-important

United Nations Development Programme. (2025). *Carbon justice for all: How carbon markets can advance equitable climate action globally*. UNDP Climate Promise. https://climatepromise.undp.org/news-and-stories/carbon-justice-all-how-carbon-markets-can-advance-equitable-climate-action

United Nations Environment Programme. (2023). *Adaptation Gap Report 2023*. https://www.unep.org/resources/adaptation-gap-report-2023

United Nations Environment Programme. (2023). *Greening trade*. https://www.unep.org/resources/report/greening-trade

United Nations Framework Convention on Climate Change (UNFCCC). (2025). *Fund for responding to loss and damage*. https://unfccc.int/fund-for-responding-to-loss-and-damage

United Nations Framework Convention on Climate Change. (1992). *UNFCCC*, 1771 UNTS 107. (Entered into force 21 March 1994)

United Nations Office of the High Representative for the Least Developed Countries, Landlocked Developing Countries and Small Island Developing States (UN-OHRLLS). (2021). *Small Island Developing States in numbers: Climate change* (edition 2021). United Nations.

United Nations. (2015). Transforming our world: The 2030 Agenda for Sustainable Development. https://sdgs.un.org/goals

United Nations. (2015). *Transforming our world: The 2030 Agenda for Sustainable Development*. United Nations.

United Nations. Climate Change. (2025). *Emissions trading*. https://unfccc.int/process/the-kyoto-protocol/mechanisms/emissions-trading

United States International Trade Commission. (2018). *Section 201 global safeguard investigations on crystalline silicon photovoltaic cells* (USITC Pub No. 4739).

UNRISD. (2016). *Policy Innovations for Transformative Change: Implementing the 2030 Agenda for Sustainable Development*. United Nations Research Institute for Social Development.

US Geological Survey. (2023). *Mineral Commodity Summaries 2023*.

Utting, P. (2013). Pathways to sustainability in a crisis-ridden world. In Genevey, R., Pachauri, R., & Tubiana, L. (Eds.), *Reducing inequalities: A Sustainable Development Challenge* (pp. 175–190). TERI Press.

Vallejo, M. C., Burbano, R., Falconí, F., & Larrea, C. (2014). Leaving oil underground in Ecuador: The Yasuní-ITT initiative from a multi-criteria perspective. *Ecological Economics*, *109*, 175–185. DOI: 10.1016/j.ecolecon.2014.11.013

van Apeldoorn, B. (2002). *Transnational capitalism and the struggle over European integration*. Routledge.

van Apeldoorn, B., & Horn, L. (2018). *Critical political economy*. Freie Universität Berlin.

van den Bergh, J. C. J. M., & Kallis, G. (2012). Growth, A-Growth or Degrowth to Stay within Planetary Boundaries? *Journal of Economic Issues*, *46*(4), 909–919.

van Haute, E. (2016). Green parties in Europe. In van Haute, E. (Ed.), *Green parties in Europe* (pp. 1–14). Routledge.

Vanhercke, B., Sabato, S., & Ghailani, D. (2018). Conclusions: The European Pillar of Social Rights as a game changer. In Vanhercke, B., Ghailani, D., & Sabato, S. (Eds.), *Social Policy in the European Union: state of play 2018*. ETUI.

Vastola, A., Cozzi, M., Viccaro, M., Grippo, V., Romano, S., Kawakami, J., & Shimpo, N. (2020). Exploring Urban Gardening Experiences in Europe and Asia: Rome vs. Tokyo. In *Green Metamorphoses: Agriculture, Food, Ecology, Proceedings of the LV Conference of SIDEA Studies* (pp. 289-294), Wageningen Academic Publishers: Wageningen, The Netherlands.

Verlie, B. (2021). Climate Justice In More-Than-Human Worlds. *Environmental Politics*, *31*(2), 297–319.

Vogel, J., & Hickel, J. (2023). Is green growth happening? An empirical analysis of achieved versus Paris-compliant CO_2–GDP decoupling in high-income countries. *The Lancet. Planetary Health*, *7*(9), e759–e769. DOI: 10.1016/S2542-5196(23)00174-2

Wahab, B. (2023). Two Decades of Uneven Federalism in Iraq. Middle East Report, MERIP https://merip.org/2023/04/the-rise-and-fall-of-kurdish-power-in-iraq/

Waldron, I. R. G. (2022, July 5). Pipelines and protests: Legacies of struggle and resistance in the fight against environmental racism in Canada. *The Brown Journal of World Affairs*, *28*(2).

Walker, K., & Wan, F. (2012). The harm of symbolic actions and green-washing: Corporate actions and communications on environmental performance and their financial implications. *Journal of Business Ethics*, *109*(2), 227–242. DOI: 10.1007/s10551-011-1122-4

Wallerstein, I. (1982). World-systems analysis: Theoretical and interpretive issues. In Hopkins, T. K., & Wallerstein, I. (Eds.), *World-systems analysis: Theory and methodology* (pp. 91–106). Sage.

Wallerstein, I. (1998). The rise and future demise of world-systems analysis. *Review - Fernand Braudel Center*, *21*(1), 103–112. https://www.jstor.org/stable/40241417

Wallerstein, I. (2004). *World-systems analysis: An introduction*. Duke University Press.

Wang, G. (2024). Gender and development: Fuel feminine energy to Africa's clean energy transition. *LSE International Development Blog*. https://blogs.lse.ac.uk/internationaldevelopment/2024/09/04/gender-and-development-fuel-feminine-energy-in-africas-clean-energy-transition/

Wang, C., Zhao, L., Lim, M. K., Chen, W.-Q., & Sutherland, J. W. (2020). Structure of the global plastic waste trade network and the impact of China's import ban. *Resources, Conservation and Recycling*, *153*, 104591. DOI: 10.1016/j.resconrec.2019.104591

Watts, J. (2019, April 23). The Greta Thunberg effect: At last, MPs focus on climate change. *The Guardian*. https://www.theguardian.com/environment/2019/apr/23/greta-thunberg

Watts, M. (2015). Now and then: The origins of political ecology and the rebirth of adaptation as a form of thought. In Perreault, T., Bridge, G., & McCarthy, J. (Eds.), *The Routledge handbook of political ecology* (pp. 19–50). Routledge., DOI: 10.4324/9781315759289

Weatherley, R., & Bauer, V. (2021). A new Chinese modernity? The discourse of Eco civilisation applied to the belt and road initiative. *Third World Quarterly*, *42*(9), 2115–2132. DOI: 10.1080/01436597.2021.1905511

Weber, B. (2018, April 24). Inuit Group Angered Over Toxic Russian Headed for Baffin Bay. *The Weather Channel*. https://weather.com/en-CA/canada/science/news/2018-04-24-inuit-russian-rocket-canada

Website, A. (2024, June 12). 4 ways Project Kuiper can help bridge the digital divide in South America. https://www.aboutamazon.com/news/innovation-at-amazon/amazon-project-kuiper-in-south-america

Weidner, H. (1993). Mediation as a policy instrument for resolving environmental disputes: With special reference to Germany, WZB Discussion Paper, No. FS II 93-301, Wissenschaftszentrum Berlin für Sozialforschung (WZB), Berlin.

Weitzman, A. (2022). Dependency Theory in 21st Century China and Latin America. Retrieved from https://globalpoliticaltheoryproject.pages.wm.edu/2022/08/28/dependency-theory-in-21st-century-china-and-latin-america/

Wesselkämper, J.. (2024). Towards circular battery supply chains: Strategies to reduce material demand and the impact on mining and recycling. *Resources Policy*, *95*, 105160.

Western Sahara Resource Watch. (2010). *UN Human Rights Council discusses illegal resource exploitation in Western Sahara*. Western Sahara Resource Watch. https://wsrw.org/en/archive/1089

West, T. A. P., Wunder, S., Sills, E. O., Börner, J., Rifai, S. W., Neidermeier, A. N., Frey, G. P., & Kontoleon, A. (2023). Action needed to make carbon offsets from forest conservation work for climate change mitigation. *Science*, *381*(6660), 873–877. DOI: 10.1126/science.ade3535

Whyte, K. (2017). Indigenous climate change studies: Indigenizing futures, decolonizing the Anthropocene. *English Language Notes*, *55*(1), 153–162.

Whyte, K. (2020). Indigenous environmental justice: Anti-colonial action through kinship. In Adamson, J., Davis, M., & Huang, H. (Eds.), *The Routledge handbook of ecocriticism and environmental communication* (pp. 127–138). Routledge.

Winfield, M., Jamison, A., Wong, R., & Czajkowski, P. (2006). *Nuclear power in Canada: An examination of risks, impacts and sustainability*. Pembina Institute.

Winther, T., ... (2020). Gendered access to solar electricity in rural Kenya: Constraints and opportunities. *Energy Research & Social Science*. https://www.sei.org/wp-content/uploads/2020/04/assessing-the-gender-and-social-equity-dimensions-of-energy-transitions-2020.pdf

Wintour, P. (2025). Recognised Palestinian state could develop disputed gas resources, expert says. 20 July, The Guardian. https://www.theguardian.com/world/2025/jul/20/recognised-palestinian-state-could-develop-disputed-gas-resources-expert-says

Women, U. N. (2021). Progress on the Sustainable Development Goals: Gender Snapshot 2021. https://www.unwomen.org/en/digital-library/publications/2021/09/progress-on-the-sustainable-development-goals-the-gender-snapshot-2021

Women, U. N. (2022). Progress on the Sustainable Development Goals: Gender Snapshot 2022. https://unstats.un.org/sdgs/gender-snapshot/2022/#:~:text=Home%20The%20Gender%20Snapshot%202022&text=The%20report%20shows%20that%20the,the%20outlook%20for%20gender%20equality

Women, U. N. (2023). Progress on the Sustainable Development Goals: Gender Snapshot 2023. https://www.unwomen.org/sites/default/files/2023-09/progress-on-the-sustainable-development-goals-the-gender-snapshot-2023-en.pdf

Women, U. N. (2024). Progress on the Sustainable Development Goals: Gender Snapshot 2024. https://www.unwomen.org/en/resources/gender-snapshot

World Bank. (2011). *World development report 2011: Conflict, security, and development*. World Bank Publications. https://openknowledge.worldbank.org/entities/publication/25f2300c-f9d4-54de-8a56-30566e72003a

World Bank. (2018, May 9). *Green growth for sustainable development* [Video]. World Bank. https://www.worldbank.org/en/news/video/2018/05/09/green-growth-for-sustainable-development

World Bank. (2020). *Minerals for climate action: The mineral intensity of the clean energy transition*. World Bank Group.

World Bank. (2023a, April 20). *China: Overview – Context*. World Bank. https://www.worldbank.org/en/country/china/overview

World Bank. (2023b, April 20). *China: Overview – Strategy*. World Bank. https://www.worldbank.org/en/country/china/overview#2

World Bank. (2024). *Republic of Congo economic update: Designing fiscal instruments for sustainable forestry and economic growth*. https://www.worldbank.org/en/news/press-release/2024/08/13/republic-of-congo-economic-update-designing-fiscal-instruments-for-sustainable-forestry-and-economic-growth

World Bank. (2024, June 10). *Board approves World Bank's role as host and trustee for the Fund for Responding to Loss and Damage*. https://www.worldbank.org/en/news/press-release/2024/06/10/board-approves-world-bank-s-role-as-host-and-trustee-for-the-fund-for-responding-to-loss-and-damage

World Bank. (2025). *Funding for loss and damage*. https://www.worldbank.org/en/programs/funding-for-loss-and-damage

World Commission on Dams. (2016). *Dams and development: A new framework for decision-making*. Routledge.

World Commission on Environment and Development. (1987). *Our common future*. Oxford University Press.

World Intellectual Property Organization. (2024). *World Intellectual Property Indicators 2024: Patents highlights*. WIPO. Retrieved from https://www.wipo.int/web-publications/world-intellectual-property-indicators-2024-highlights/en/patents-highlights.html

World Nuclear Association. (2024). Comparison of lifecycle greenhouse gas emissions of various electricity generation sources. https://world-nuclear.org/information-library/energy-and-environment/comparison-of-lifecycle-greenhouse-gas-emissions-of-various-electricity-generation-sources.aspx

World Trade Organization. (1994). *Agreement on Trade-Related Aspects of Intellectual Property Rights (TRIPS)*, 1869 UNTS 299.

World Trade Organization. (1994). *Agreement on Trade-Related Aspects of Intellectual Property Rights*, 1869 UNTS 299, art. 31.

World Trade Organization. (1994). *General Agreement on Tariffs and Trade (GATT) 1994*, art. XX.

World Trade Organization. (2014). *Appellate Body Reports, China – Rare Earths*, WT/DS431/AB/R, WT/DS432/AB/R, WT/DS433/AB/R.

WTO. (1995). *The results of the Uruguay Round of multilateral trade negotiations: The legal texts*. World Trade Organization.

WTO. (2014). *China – Measures Related to the Exportation of Rare Earths, Tungsten and Molybdenum: Appellate Body Report, DS431.*

WTO. (2016). *India – Certain Measures Relating to Solar Cells and Solar Modules: Panel and Appellate Body Reports, DS456.*

Wullweber, J. (2019). Constructing hegemony in global politics: A discourse-theoretical approach to policy analysis. *Administrative Theory & Praxis, 41*(2), 148–167. DOI: 10.1080/10841806.2019.1593544

Xaxa, V. (1999). Tribes as indigenous people of India. *Economic and Political Weekly, 34*(51), 3589–3595.

Xaxa, V.. (2014). *Report of the high-level committee on socio-economic, health and educational status of tribal communities of India.* Ministry of Tribal Affairs, Government of India.

Xi's. "new normal" theory. (2014, November 10). *China.org.cn.* http://www.china.org.cn/world/2014-11/10/content_34012582.htm

Xi-Ji. (1986). Pricing System Reform for Agricultural Products and Price Policy Adjustment in China (1979-1984). In A. Maunder & U. Renborg (Eds.), *Agriculture in a Turbulent World Economy: Proceedings of the Nineteenth International Conference of Agricultural Economists* (pp. 449-465), Gower.

Yadav, S. (2023). Gender Equality as a Tool for Sustainable Development. International Journal of Teaching [IJTLE]. *Learning and Education, 2*(2), 1–3. DOI: 10.22161/ijtle.2.2.1

Yang, H., Zhang, L., Liu, H., Wang, Y., & Hao, C. (2024). A comparative study on the combination of life cycle assessment and ecological footprints: Solar photovoltaic power generation vs. coal power generation in Ningxia. *Frontiers in Energy Research, 12.* Advance online publication. DOI: 10.3389/fenrg.2024.1375820

Yang, Z., Nguyen, T. T. H., Nguyen, H. N., Nguyen, T. T. N., & Cao, T. T. (2020). Greenwashing behaviours: Causes, taxonomy and consequences based on a systematic literature review. *Journal of Business Economics and Management, 21*(5), 1486–1507. DOI: 10.3846/jbem.2020.13225

Yanyun, D., & Huang, Z. (2023). Starlink Militarization and Its Impact on Global Strategic Stability. Interpret: China. https://interpret.csis.org/translations/starlink-militarization-and-its-impact-on-global-strategic-stability/

Young, I. M. (2000). *Inclusion and democracy.* Oxford University Press.

Yusoff, K. (2018). *A billion black Anthropocenes or none*. University of Minnesota Press.

Zalik, A. (2018). Mining the seabed, enclosing the Area: Ocean grabbing, proprietary knowledge and the geopolitics of the extractive frontier beyond national jurisdiction. *International Social Science Journal, 68*(229–230), 343–358. DOI: 10.1111/issj.12159

Zaniewicz, M., & Bieliszczuk, B. (2021). *Implications of Nord Stream 2's completion for Ukraine*. Polish Institute of International Affairs. https://pism.pl/publications/implications-of-nord-stream-2s-completion-for-ukraine

Zarfl, C., Lumsdon, A. E., Berlekamp, J., Tydecks, L., & Tockner, K. (2015). A global boom in hydropower dam construction. *Aquatic Sciences, 77*(1), 161–170.

Zemanek, E. (2019). Medienwissenschaft. In Kluwick, U., & Zemanek, E. (Eds.), *Nachhaltigkeit interdisziplinär: Konzepte, Diskurse, Praktiken: ein Kompendium*. Böhlau Verlag.

Zha, H. & Su, J. (2024). The "due regard" obligation in the deployment and operation of satellite mega-constellations. *Space Policy Journal*, 1-14. https://doi.org/DOI: 10.1016/j.spacepol.2024.101674

Zimmermann, A., & Binswanger, C. (2021). Transitioning to gender equality-Introduction. In Binswanger, C., & Zimmermann, A. (Eds.), *Transitioning to gender Equality* (pp. 1–13). MDPI.

Zolyniak, A. (2021, December 1). An environmentalist case for resurrecting the WTO appellate body. *Council on Foreign Relations*. https://www.cfr.org/blog/environmentalist-case-resurrecting-wto-appellate-body

Zuboff, S. (2019). *The age of surveillance capitalism: The fight for a human future at the new frontier of power*. PublicAffairs.

Zuhra, A., & Sabirin, A. (2024). How do international economic laws impact sustainable development goals? *ADLIYA: Jurnal Hukum Dan Kemanusiaan, 18*(2), 127–152. DOI: 10.15575/adliya.v18i2.35985

About the Contributors

Şeyda Güdek-Gölçek, Ph.D., is currently an Assistant Professor in the Department of Political Science and International Relations at Niğde Ömer Halisdemir University, Türkiye. She completed her Ph.D. on women's poverty in neoliberal economies, focusing on Türkiye. Her research interests include IR theories, gender in IR, women's studies, gender inequality, poverty and IPE. She can be reached at seydagudek@ohu.edu.tr.

Günseli Durmaz, Ph.D., is currently a Dr. Research Assistant in the Department of Political Science and International Relations at Niğde Ömer Halisdemir University, Türkiye. She completed her Ph.D. at Middle East Technical University on the European Green Deal from a Neo-Gramscian perspective. She was a recipient of the Jean Monnet Scholarship and conducted research on food activism at Scuola Normale Superiore, Italy. Her research interests include international political economy, green transformation politics, and contemporary environmental and food movements. She can be reached at gunseli.durmaz@ohu.edu.tr.

Aybüke İnan-Şimşeks, Ph.D., is currently serves as a Research Assistant at the Department of Political Science and International Relations at Niğde Ömer Halisdemir University. Her research focuses on international space governance, polar studies, international law, and global governance, with a particular interest in the principles of the common heritage of humankind. She has published articles and book chapters on outer space security, Arctic governance, and international organizations. Her recent work explores the role of epistemic space communities in shaping global governance frameworks.

***

Kavia Ahuja is a final-year law student at Jindal Global Law School with a keen interest in environmental law and policy.

Judith Anne Lal is an Assistant Professor from the Department of Political Science and International Studies at Christ (Deemed to be University), Delhi NCR.

John W. Bessai is an independent scholar and media producer whose work bridges media studies, environmental politics, and public policy. He develops the concept of the Canadian aporetic condition to analyze how sustainability narratives shape extraction, infrastructure, and governance. His doctoral dissertation at Trent University, Art as a Public Service: The National Film Board of Canada's Role in Shaping Democratic Dialogues and Societal Transformation, investigates public storytelling infrastructures across film and interactive media. Current projects trace civic media and narrative infrastructures in Canada and across transnational contexts.

Muhammed Onur Çöpoğlu completed his undergraduate studies at Gazi University, his master's degree at Karadeniz Technical University, and his PhD in International Relations at Middle East Technical University (METU). He completed his doctoral dissertation in 2025, analyzing the security narratives surrounding the 2021 forest fires in Turkey through the lens of Vernacular Security theory. His main areas of research include Critical Security Studies, environmental security, and qualitative research methods. He is currently working as a research assistant in the Department of Political Science and Public Administration at the Faculty of Economics and Administrative Sciences, Ordu University.

Fadıl Ersözer is an Assistant Professor in International Relations at the European University of Lefke, Cyprus, and previously held a lectureship at the University of Manchester. His research focuses on EU Politics, conflict resolution, natural resources in conflict contexts, and the Cyprus conflict, with a current emphasis on the EU's post-accession involvement in Cyprus. He holds a PhD from the University of Manchester and an MSc from the London School of Economics and Political Science.

Defne Gönenç is an Associate Professor and program coordinator at the Department of Political Science and International Relations at the Middle East Technical University, Northern Cyprus Campus. Her academic research interests include global environmental politics, climate justice, critical theory, and the political economy of developing countries. (particularly Türkiye, Greece, and India). She obtained her Ph.D. from the Geneva Graduate Institute and her M. Phil. from the University of Cambridge (Wolfson College). Her articles appeared in various journals, including Environmental Politics, International Environmental Agreements: Politics, Law and Economics, VOLUNTAS, Southeast European and Black Sea Studies, Journal of Balkan and Near Eastern Studies, and Cambridge Review of International Affairs.

Pranjal Khare is a distinguished corporate lawyer and is currently working as a law faculty at O.P. Jindal Global University, India. He has UGC-NET certification and is also a registered advocate under Bar Council of India. He is also pursuing his PhD from Rajiv Gandhi National University of Law, Patiala, India. He specializes in Property Law, Corporate laws, Intellectual Property Rights, and International law. Mr. Pranjal is a highly regarded scholar and has published on numerous issues related to international affairs, economy, politics, data & privacy, artificial intelligence and IP disputes. He is also a frequent speaker at legal conferences and has served as a consultant to numerous law firms and corporations.

Alisa Kronberger, Ph.D., is a research associate (PostDoc) at the Institute for Media Studies at Ruhr University Bochum and an associate member of the CRC 1567 Virtual Lifeworlds. During the 2025 summer semester, she was a substitute professor for Media Theory & Communication Studies at RUB, and beginning in the 2025/26 winter semester, she will be a substitute professor for Media Theory at HfG Offenbach am Main, Germany. Her research interests in media, art, and cultural studies lie in (eco-)feminist (media) theories, media ecology and philosophy, and the discursive field of New Materialism. In her habilitation project, she is currently focusing on trust ecologies in and for digital worlds from a media-philosophical and new-materialist perspective.

Eugene Nulman is Associate Professor in Sociology at the University of Florence. He was previously Assistant Professor in Political Science at the Scuola Normale Superiore, Florence, Italy and Senior Lecturer in Sociology at Birmingham City University, Birmingham, UK. He received his PhD in Sociology from the University of Kent and his undergraduate degree in Political Science from the University of California, Berkeley. He also holds an MA in Political Sociology from the University of Kent. Professor Nulman is a researcher in the areas of social movements, political sociology, and popular culture. He is the author of the books Climate Change and Social Movements: Civil Society and the Development of National Climate Change Policy (2015), Coronavirus Capitalism Goes to the Cinema (2021), How Popular Culture Destroys Our Political Imagination: Capitalism and Its Alternatives in Film and Television (2025), and Social Movements and Social Change: An Applied Introduction (forthcoming). He has published academic work in journals such as Third World Quarterly; Media, Culture and Society; Journal of Youth Studies; and Environmental Politics. He has also co-authored and directed the documentary film The Psychosis of Whiteness.

Shruti Rathore is a research scholar from the Department of International Studies at Christ (Deemed to be University), Delhi NCR, specializing in the Indo-Pacific region.

Vidisha Shekawat is a highly motivated and passionate law educator, dedicated to fostering practical legal skills and empowering students. She has cleared UGC-NET and is also a registered advocate under Bar Council of India. She is also enrolled as a PhD student in Manipal University Jaipur, India. Known for being a quick learner and committed to continuous professional growth. Experienced in organizing moot court training, workshops, and developing resources like handbooks to enhance advocacy skills. Focused on creating engaging and impactful learning experiences by simplifying complex legal principles and integrating technology into teaching. Enthusiastic about guiding students in both academic and professional excellence. Deeply passionate about research and committed to contributing to legal scholarship through interdisciplinary studies, publications, and policy development, while mentoring aspiring legal professionals.

Cagla Vural is currently a Postdoctoral Fellow at Akdeniz University, where she is conducting a research project on the impacts of marine invasive alien species in the Eastern Mediterranean on Turkey's economic, ecological, and human security. Her research areas include international relations theories, environmental security, climate change policies, environmental issues, and waste trafficking. Dr. Vural's work particularly focuses on the security implications of environmental challenges and their connections to global dynamics. She has published numerous articles and book chapters on national and international platforms and presented her findings at scientific conferences. Her research adopts a solution-oriented perspective on complex global issues, offering in-depth analyses of environmental and security policies. In addition to her academic endeavors, Dr. Vural has participated as a researcher in various projects. Through her interdisciplinary approach, she continues to contribute significantly to the fields of international relations and environmental security.

Index

A

C

D

E

R

S

T

W

www.ingramcontent.com/pod-product-compliance
Lightning Source LLC
LaVergne TN
LVHW062341300926
849161LV00007B/1773